Current Psychotherapies
Third Edition

Current Psychotherapies

Raymond J. Corsini
With the Assistance of Danny Wedding

Third Edition

F.E. PEACOCK PUBLISHERS, INC.
ITASCA, ILLINOIS 60143

To My Teachers

Rudolf Dreikurs
J. L. Moreno
Carl Rogers

Contributors

JACOB A. ARLOW, M.D., Clinical Professor of Psychiatry, State University of New York, New York, N.Y.

RAYMOND J. CORSINI, Ph.D., Affiliate Graduate Faculty, University of Hawaii, Honolulu, Hawaii.

JOHN M. DUSAY, M. D., Psychiatrist, Private Practice, San Francisco; Assistant Clinical Professor, University of California Medical School, San Francisco, California

KATHERINE MULHOLLAND DUSAY, M.A., California Licensed Marriage, Family and Child Counselor, Private Practice, San Francisco, California

ALBERT ELLIS, Ph.D., Executive Director, Institute for Advanced Study in Rational Psychotherapy, New York, N.Y.

VINCENT D. FOLEY, Ph.D., Department of Counselor Education, St. John's University, Jamaica, N.Y.

WILLIAM GLASSER, M.D., President, Institute for Reality Therapy and Educator Training Center, Los Angeles, California

YORAM KAUFMANN, Ph.D., Private Practice, Psychotherapy, New York, N.Y.

ARNOLD A. LAZARUS, Ph.D., Clinical Psychologist, Princeton, N.J.; Distinguished Professor, Rutgers University, Piscataway, N.J.

ROLLO MAY, Ph.D., Private Practice, Tiburon, California

BETTY D. MEADOR, Ph.D., Director, Center for Studies of the Person, La Jolla, California

HAROLD H. MOSAK, Ph.D., Private Practice, Psychotherapy, Chicago, Illinois

CARL R. ROGERS, Ph.D., Resident Fellow, Center for Studies of the Person, La Jolla, California

JAMES S. SIMKIN, Ph.D., Director, Simkin Training Center in Gestalt Therapy, Big Sur, California

G. TERENCE WILSON, Ph.D., Distinguished Professor, Graduate School of Applied and Professional Psychology, Rutgers University, Piscataway, N.J.

GARY M. YONTEF, Ph.D., Gestalt Associates, Santa Monica, California

IRVIN YALOM, M.D., The Department of Psychiatry and Behavioral Sciences, Stanford University School of Medicine, Stanford, Connecticut

Contents

Acknowledgments

Dr. Danny Wedding, my collaborator on *Great Cases in Psychotherapy,* has read the entire manuscript and has made numerous suggestions, most of which I have accepted. He wrote the glossary and has been helpful in other ways. Dr. Nancy Haynie wrote the section on "Neuro-linguistic Psychotherapy" in Chapter 14, which I revised with her approval. Bonnie Ozaki, my assistant editor for the *Encyclopedia of Psychology*, has read parts of this manuscript and has contributed ideas. The galley proofs were read for errors by Lynette Tanaka and Rosemary Terem. My wife, Dr. Kleona Rigney, supported my editing efforts by her good humor and common sense.

Naturally, the authors of the chapters deserve the greatest appreciation. They were asked to do what is unnatural for most authors: to write on their systems in accordance to the constraints of space and in terms of the requirements of a pre-established outline.

It is my hope that *Current Psychotherapies* will serve a more important purpose than merely explaining some two dozen systems of psychotherapy. From the very beginning my aim has been to help advance and improve psychotherapy. My view is that eventually a final psychotherapy will result from all the special systems uniting, in the same manner that small rivers unite to become the Mississippi.

Possibly some day some reader of this book will do just that.

Raymond J. Corsini
Honolulu, Hawaii

Preface

The continuing favorable reception of *Current Psychotherapies* is due to three factors:

1. Judicious selections of the more important current psychotherapies.
2. Chapters written by authorities, in some cases, by their originators.
3. Its unique format which permits point-by-point comparisons between the various systems.

In this third edition there are four new chapters: "Introduction," "Existential Psychotherapy," "Multi-Modal Therapy", and "Innovative Psychotherapy," as well as a "Glossary."

"Behavior Therapy" has a new author. "Reality Therapy" has been completely rewritten. "Gestalt Therapy" has a co-author and has been extensively revised. In addition, the "old" chapters have been revised and updated.

The various chapters in this book are written by partisans. This leads not only to authoritative accounts but also to exciting reading since each author believes in the superiority of the system that he or she is writing on.

To control such passionate enthusiasms there is the double constraint of the common outline which requires authors to stay within narrow page limits writing on specified topics and the close scrutiny with which I, as editor, have examined each chapter. No chapter was accepted on its first writing. In one case four revisions were required. My role as editor is to act as mediator between the strong partisanships of the authors, and the need for readers to get complete, accurate, basic information.

A major reason for periodic revisions of this book is simply that the field of psychotherapy is in constant ferment and change. "Minor" systems begin to become more popular. "Major" systems begin to fade. Some systems begin to change. Splitting occurs with contending groups heading rival viewpoints. New ideas, new concepts, new views which amount to complete new systems, arise. In illustration of this, there are currently at least 250 innovative systems of psychotherapy in existence.

Every five years the publisher sends out a questionnaire to professors who use *Current Psychotherapies* as a text, asking them for desired changes. More than 300 professors replied to the questionnaire relative to the second edition. Dr. Danny Wedding and I each read half of these replies and we independently came to the conclusions for needed revisions.

Changes depend upon my decision of what is most useful for students who want to understand the current psychotherapies, taking into consideration many factors including publisher's page limitations, what professors state they want, the opinions of various advisers, and my own perception of what is most important to include and exclude.

Outline of Book

Chapter 14. INNOVATIVE PSYCHOTHERAPIES: Body Therapies, p. 532; Ego-State Therapy; p. 533; Impasse/Priority Therapy, p. 534; Morita Psychotherapy, p. 536; Neurolinguistic Psychotherapy, p. 537; Primal Therapy, p. 538; Provocative Psychotherapy, p. 539; Psychoimagination Therapy, p. 541; Psychodrama, p. 542; Strategic Therapy, p. 543; Twenty-Four Hour Therapy, p. 545; Z-Process Attachment Therapy, p. 547.

1

Introduction

Psychotherapy cannot be defined with any precision. A dictionary definition might go as follows:

Psychotherapy is a formal process of interaction between two parties, each party usually consisting of one person but with the possibility that there may be two or more people in each party, for the purpose of amelioration of one of the two parties relative to any of the following areas of disability or malfunction or any combination thereof: cognitive functions (disorders of thinking), affective functions (suffering or emotional discomforts), or behavioral functions (inadequacy of behavior) with the treatment party having some theory of personality's origins, development, maintenance and change and some modality of treatment logically related to the theory, with the treatment party generally having professional and legal approval to act as a therapist.

This definition may appear rather comprehensive but as will soon be evident, some modes of therapy will not fit this definition.

Would the system of psychotherapy that Sigmund Freud underwent, about which Karen Horney (1942) wrote a book, and which Theodore Reik (1948) claimed to be the best of all therapies, fit this definition? The system is *self-therapy*. In self-therapy there is only one party; there is no formality, no professional or legal approval, and so forth, and yet it certainly is therapy.

If we examine various theories and procedures in psychotherapy we find a truly bewildering set of ideas and behaviors, some of which will appear quite bizarre. There have been systems of therapy that

had no therapist (Schmidhoffer, 1952); systems in which the therapist says and does nothing (Bion, 1948); systems in which patients are symbolically rebirthed (Bindrim, 1981; Orr & Ray, 1977); systems in which patients are asked to scream or to strike out in violent manners (Bach & Goldberg, 1975; Janov, 1970) and in contrast methods which call for meditation or imagining (Ahnsen, 1965; Cautela, 1981; Shorr, 1972; Wolpe, 1958); methods in which the therapist makes fun of the patient, treating him with apparent disrespect (Farrelly & Brasma, 1974) and in contrast methods which treat the patient or client with utmost respect, attempting to encourage through kindness (Losoncy, 1977); methods in which patients are treated as children (Painter & Vernon, 1981); methods which stress religion (Lair & Lair, 1973; Van Kaam, 1976); and methods which are composites or conglomerates of a wide variety of procedures (Gazda, 1981; Shostrom & Montgomery, 1978).

All these and many other strange and wonderful concepts and procedures have been employed in that which is called psychotherapy. It is important to note that what some authority considers to be psychotherapy may be completely different from how another person sees the process. There is no way at present to settle any differences; so even though A and B may be doing completely different and contradictory things, both are doing psychotherapy. We come to the same conclusion as Lewis Carroll in his *Through the Looking Glass* that a word means what you want it to mean.

A comment about counseling and psychotherapy: they are the same qualitatively; they differ only quantitatively. Based on an analysis published some years ago (Corsini, 1968), I came to the conclusion that there was nothing that a psychotherapist did that a counselor did not do. Table 1.1 illustrates this basic point:

TABLE 1.1
Estimation of Percent of Time Spent by "Counselors" and "Psychotherapists" in Professional Activities*

Process	Counseling	Psychotherapy
Listening	20	60
Questioning	15	10
Evaluating	5	5
Interpreting	1	3
Supporting	5	10
Explaining	15	5
Informing	20	3
Advising	10	3
Ordering	9	1

*Based on "Counseling and Psychotherapy" in E. F. Borgatta and W. W. Lambert (Eds.), *Handbook of Personality Theory and Research* (Chicago, Rand McNally, 1968).

From Table 1.1, which attempts to generalize about all counseling methods and all verbal psychotherapeutic procedures, it can be seen that differences are only quantitative rather than qualitative and that there is really no fundamental difference between counseling and psychotherapy.

This position will be strongly resisted by many on various grounds, but I submit that no definition can be made which will include all psychotherapies and exclude all counseling methods. The various at-tempts to separate the psychotherapies and exclude all counseling methods have failed. The concept that psychotherapy goes into depth while counseling does not is gainsaid by such procedures as behavior modification which explicitly does not go into depth, sticking mostly at the level of symptom removal. Behavior modifiers could hardly be called counselors, since they do not counsel. And when we have a term such as *nondirective counseling* we have a semantic absurdity if one thinks about it long enough.

All modes of trying to help people improve themselves via symbolic methods can be called psychotherapy just as all methods to help improve psychological functioning through medications, surgery, electric shock, and other somatic procedures may be called psychiatry. Consequently, the interview, hypnosis, roleplaying, projective techniques, and the like which we shall take up in this book can be considered procedures in counseling/psychotherapy, but it is best, in my judgment, to call them all processes of psychotherapy. Therefore, when Carl Rogers repeats what you have said, using his own terminology (as he did with me when I was in therapy with him), *this is psychotherapy;* and when Rudolph Dreikurs, an Adlerian, informs someone of his basic life-style errors (as he did for me when I was in therapy with him), *this is psychotherapy;* and when Albert Ellis contradicts your point of view (as he has done with me when I have interacted with him), *this is psychotherapy;* and when J. L. Moreno had people play different roles in front of a group (as I did many times when working with him) then *that is psychotherapy.*

A number of years ago, in Paris, at an outdoor cafe, I met with a French colleague, and during the course of our conversation I mentioned psychotherapy.

"Ah," she said, "Psychotherapie comme ça—ou comme ça?" (Psychotherapy like this—or like this?). At the first *ça* she put the palms of her hands about an inch apart and at the second *ça,* she moved her hands out as far as she could, with the palms still facing each other. By that she was asking me whether I had a narrow conception of psychotherapy or a wide one. We can do the same thing with the hands vertically and ask about the depth of psychotherapy. Essentially, depth is a function of time spent rather than a matter of technique, and the same person with the same theory and technique will vary with respect to depth depending on many factors, but primarily with the time spent with the client. (Incidentally, I prefer to call the subjects of psychotherapy *clients* if one sees them in a private office, and *patients* if they are in a hospital or institution.)

An Unusual Example of Psychotherapy

About 40 years ago when I was working as a psychologist at Auburn Prison in New York, I participated in what I believe was the most successful and most elegant psychotherapy I have ever done. This is the story.

One day an inmate who had made an appointment to see me, came into my office. He was a fairly attractive man in his early 30s. I pointed to a chair and he sat down, and I waited to find out what he wanted. The conversation went somewhat as follows:

Prisoner: I am leaving on parole Thursday.

Corsini: Yes?

P: I did not want to leave until I thanked you for what you had done for me.

C· What was that?

P: When I left your office about two years ago, I felt like I was walking on air. When I went into the prison yard everything looked different, even the air smelled different. I was like a new person. Instead of going over to the group I usually hung out with—they were a bunch of thieves—I went over to another group of square Johns [prison talk for noncriminal types]. I changed from a cushy job in the kitchen to the machine shop where I could learn a trade. I started going to the prison high school and I now have a high school diploma. I took a correspondence course in drafting and I have a drafting job when I leave Thursday. I started back to church even though I had given up my religion many years ago. I started writing to my parents and to my family again, and they have come up to see me, and they remember you in their prayers. I now have hope. I know who and what I am. I know I will succeed in life. I plan to go to college. You have freed me. I used to think you bug doctors [prison slang for psychologists and psychiatrists] were for the birds, but now I know better. I thank you for changing my life.

I listened to this tale in wonderment, since to the best of my knowledge I had never spoken with him. I looked at his folder and the only notation there was that I had given him an IQ test about two years before.

"Are you sure it was me?" I finally said. "I am not a psychotherapist, and I have no memory of ever having spoken to you. What you are reporting is the sort of personality and behavior change that takes many years to accomplish—and I certainly have not done anything of the kind."

"It was you alright," he replied with great conviction, "and I will never forget what you said to me which changed my life."

"What was that?" I asked in wonderment.

"You told me I had a high IQ," he replied.

By this one sentence of five words I had (inadvertently) changed this person's life.

Let us try to understand this event. If the reader at this point is clever enough to understand why this man changed so drastically as a result of hearing these five words, my guess is that you have the capacity to be a good therapist.

Intrigued by his reaction to these words (which before and subsequently I have said to many people, and never gotten any unusual reactions) I asked him why this sentence about his IQ had such a profound effect.

As a result of a talk we then engaged in, I learned that up to the time that he heard these five words he had always thought of himself as "stupid" and "crazy"—terms that had been applied to him many times—by his family, his teachers, and his friends. In school, he had always gotten poor grades which confirmed his belief of his mental subnormality. His friends did not approve of the way he thought and they called him crazy. And so he was convinced that he was an ament (low intelligence) and a dement (insane)—but when I said "You have a high IQ" he had an AHA experience which explained *everything*. In a flash he understood why he could solve crossword puzzles better than any of his friends. He now knew why he read Sinclair Lewis rather than Edgar Rice Burroughs. Why he preferred to play chess rather than checkers. Why he liked symphonies rather than jazz. With great and sudden intensity he realized through my five words that he was really normal and bright and not crazy or stupid. No wonder he felt like he was walking on air

when he left my office two years before!

His interpretation of my five words generated a complete change of self-concept—and consequently a change in behavior and a change in his feelings about himself and others.

In short, I had performed psychotherapy in a completely innocent and informal way. Even though what happened in no way accords to the definition given above, even though there was no agreement between us, no theory was involved, no intention of changing him—the five word comment had a most pronounced effect, and so it *was* psychotherapy, even though there was no intention on my part or his to achieve the profound personality changes that did occur.

And to balance the score, I have had two long-term clients—seeing each for over 10 years, and in neither case did I do much for them as far as I can tell.

MODES OF PSYCHOTHERAPY

This incident leads to a theoretical discussion about modes of psychotherapy. In this book you will be reading about 12 major systems of psychotherapy, and later you will read about a dozen unusual systems selected to be as different from one another as possible, to give you a full scope of understanding of the different philosophies, different theories, and different procedures in what some people call psychotherapy.

What all psychotherapies have in common is that they are methods of learning. All psychotherapies are intended to change people: to make them think differently (cognition), to make them feel differently (affection), and to make them act differently (behavior). Psychotherapy is learning: one may be learning something new, or relearning something one has forgotten, it may be learning how to learn, it may be unlearning, and paradoxically, it may even be learning what one already knows.

Cognition

There are two general ways we learn: directly by experience, or indirectly by symbols.

To give a simple example: a family buys a toaster and a child of about three years of age sees the toast shooting up, and he goes for the shiny gadget to touch it. The child has no idea that the toaster is hot. Now, how can the child learn that a toaster can be hot and can hurt? One way would be for the child to touch the toaster thus learning by direct experience. Another way is by symbols (words) by being told: "When we use the toaster, it gets hot, and if you touch it you will be burned."

In both cases, the child learns, in one case actively (through experience) and in another case passively (through information).

Some therapists tend to use "active" methods so that their clients essentially learn on their own, while some therapists tend to make their clients passive learners. In this book two strongly contrasting learning styles are represented by Carl Rogers's and Albert Ellis's methodologies. In psychoanalysis, both modes occur. For example, while free associating the patient may be said to be learning actively. Let us show this by a hypothetical example.

Patient: ". . . and I really think my mother liked my brother more than she liked me. l really cannot understand why. I tried so hard to win her affection but somehow I never was able to make her really like me. But recently when I spoke about this with my brother he told me he always thought that I was mother's

favorite. How could this be? Could I have misinterpreted my mother? He thought I was the favorite and I thought he was. Who was? Maybe no one was? Maybe we both are pessimists and think that no one can like us? Maybe mama liked us both equally, or as equally as possible. How did we come to have opposite conclusions? I think we are just both pessimists, that's what it is! I am sure of it, both of us misinterpreted mother. . . ."

This is an example of someone talking to himself, doing a kind of self-analysis, engaged in active learning.

An example of passive learning follows. A female client is telling a dream:

P: I had the funniest dream. I was being chased by a rooster, and I was running for my life, and I knew if I got to Lokonner Bay that I would be safe.

T: How do you spell that?

P: I don't know. It is pronounced LOKONNER BAY.

T: And you don't know any such place?

P: No.

T: Can you figure out what Lokonner means?

P: I have been thinking all day about it. It makes no sense to me.

T: Should I tell you what I think it means?

P: Please. I have absolutely no idea.

T: Well, dreams are all symbols. The rooster that is chasing you is a symbol of the male sexual organ, so you are running away from sex. But you believe you will be safe if you can get to Lokonner Bay.

P: But what does Lokonner Bay mean? l have never heard of such a place.

T: Lokonner is probably a contraction for "Love, honor, and obey." What you are saying to yourself in your dream is this: some man is pressuring you to have sex and you want him to marry you. You are afraid to have sex but if you can get him to marry you (love, honor, and obey) you will be safe.

We have now seen two general ways of learning in psychotherapy: more or less actively on one's own through the exâmple of self-analysis of the patient talking about his mother and his brother; and passively through being helped to understand the meaning of a dream by being given an interpretation.

Behavior

Learning can occur not only by self-talking and by other talking, but also by action. Below is an early example of psychotherapy through action.

During World War I, Ernst Simmel (1949), a German army psychiatrist, concerned with curing severely neurotic German solders who were suffering from what was then called shell shock, believing that their condition was caused by repressed hatred of their officers, gave these men bayoneted rifles and had them attack straw-filled dummies dressed as German officers.

If we had looked on during this psychotherapeutic treatment, we would have seen solders repeatedly stabbing mannequins. The modality of treatment therefore was physical action. Plain physical exercise is believed to be psychotherapeutic by some people. Action modality is used in a number of psychotherapies, especially those which call for body work.

One argument for body therapies is that there is no mind. If we can affect the body that is all that is needed: the body learns, the body is real, all else is an illusion. A contrary argument for body therapies is that the mind does exist; and conditions of the body affect the mind, and if we work from the outside in, by changing the body we can change the mind. An example might be plastic surgery. Changing a person's looks can affect how a person views himself or herself.

Other examples of physical behavior as psychotherapy would include complex physical activities, such as roleplaying, or doing therapeutic "homework," that is, doing under direction things one would not ordinarily do, such as asking someone for a date or looking for a job. As in the case of cognitive therapies, behavioral work in therapy can range from mostly active to mostly passive. In examining the various systems in this book, the reader may want to consider how much physical behavior is called for in the particular therapy.

Affection

A third modality in psychotherapy is "affection," known more popularly as emotions or feelings. The therapist may believe that this modality will be most effective with a particular client or patient, and so will do things to stir up the person: to raise the individual's emotional state through attempts to make the person fearful, anxious, angry, hopeful, and so on. We cannot really work directly with the emotions and must reach them indirectly through the intellect or the body.

The issue is somewhat complicated here. Emotions are an important part of human psychology. However, they are reachable by both the therapist and the client only indirectly, consequently we cannot manipulate emotions in the sense we can manipulate thinking or behaving. Some systems of psychotherapy are intended to reduce or negate emotions, seeing them as hindering the therapeutic process. Adlerian psychotherapy, for example, is essentially a cognitive therapy, and

Adlerians see emotions usually as sabotaging efforts in the therapeutic process. However, in psychodrama, for example, both the words that the therapist will employ and the behavior directed by the other actors are intended to generate strong emotions.

Some people see emotions as an epiphenomenon accompanying but not affecting therapeutic change, while others see emotions as a powerful agent leading to change; and still others will see emotions as evidence of a change occurring. The whole issue of the relationship of emotions to psychotherapy is unsettled. The reader would do well to attempt to see the place of emotions in the various systems described. Perhaps the single most clear-cut example of the use of emotions is in the very unusual method of Z-process psychotherapy in which the therapist attempts to generate rage in the client as a necessary part of the therapy (Zaslow & Menta, 1977).

All therapies are essentially combinations of all three of these modalities. While some are rather pure in that an attempt is made to deal only with the body, the intellect or the emotions, elements of each apply in most cases. Thus, for example, in Rational-Emotive Therapy even though the therapist utilizes rational thinking for the most part in dealing with the patient, he may give the client direct orders to do certain things (homework) and thus there will be a strong behavioral component. And in a cognitive therapy such as Transactional Analysis, emotionally upsetting situations will develop.

A theoretician or a therapist may think that improvement is a function of one thing but the curative process may actually be something else. It may not be a massage that generates a change, but rather the interpretation that the client gives to being handled. Were exactly the same treatment to be done by a robot, it might not have any beneficial psychological effect: Change may well result from the interpretation "someone cares for me enough to do this to me."

One final common pathway for all therapies is a new way of seeing life, a reevaluation of self and others. If so, then all therapies are essentially cognitive. Still another way of considering psychotherapy is to see it as a process of "selling"—trying to help a person to accept a new view of self and of others. From this point of view the psychotherapist is a persuader or a facilitator in attempting to change opinions.

A clear-cut example of persuasion would be attempting to do psychotherapy with someone with a fixed paranoid delusion. A more common example is dealing with a person with incapacitating feelings of inferiority by trying "to sell him" on the notion that he is really OK. Another common example would be dealing with someone with mistaken ideas of marriage or of parenting. In all these cases, the therapist is, in a real sense, a sales-person attempting to sell new ideas, new concepts, and new behaviors.

THE CURRENT SITUATION IN PSYCHOTHERAPY

In another book (Corsini, 1981) a list of 250 different systems of psychotherapy is to be found. Just as there are some religions that are well known and well accepted, so too, some psychotherapies are well known and well accepted. And just as there are splinter religions viewed as unorthodox and absurd, there are systems of psychotherapy that exist on the fringe of traditional approaches.

I was originally trained as a Rogerian therapist (which I believe is probably the best way for a would-be therapist to start training—and for some people the best way to remain). After having had some 10 years experience in this mode of therapy, I applied for a job at a prestigious institute and while being interviewed I was asked how I dealt with the problem of transference. I think I could not have shocked my learned colleagues more had I slapped them on the face, when I replied, "To the best of my knowledge, none of my clients ever formed a transference relationship with me." They held their mouths open, staring first at me and then at each other, unable to believe what they had heard me say. For this particular group, transference was a necessary factor in psychotherapy, and for someone who claimed to be a psychotherapist to deny transference was unthinkable.

In psychotherapy, ideological enclaves are found. Some enclaves consist of people who believe that they have the right, the final, the complete, and the only answer—and that all other systems are incomplete, tentative, weak, or simply mistaken. These enclaves are little islands of belief.

People within these enclaves (better known as schools of therapy) tend to communicate mostly with others they meet at conventions; they read each other's writings, and they tend over time to develop specialized vocabularies. They reinforce one another by recounting their successes with the clients of people of different persuasions, and in general "proving" to one another the superiority of their way of thinking and acting. As time goes on, within any particular method of psychotherapy, alternative positions tend to develop, and schismatic groups begin to form, and then these groups are either expelled from the original enclave or take off on their own. In the history of psychotherapy, as will be evident by reading the various chapters that follow,

we will see that this has happened many times in the case of people who were originally trained as Freudian psychoanalysts.

Correction of a Historical Error

In many historical accounts found in textbooks, an essentially incorrect view of the early years of psychotherapy is recounted. The story given generally goes as follows: in the beginning Sigmund Freud started a brand new concept of psychotherapy called psychoanalysis. A number of other people learned about it and became his students. In later years, for a variety of reasons they decided to separate from him and went on to start their own systems of thought.

In reality, in the late 1800s and early 1900s there was a considerable amount of interest in personality theory and in the treatment of personality problems. Numerous people preceded Freud by doing psychotherapy in a variety of ways. We may start with the Swiss physician, Paul Dubois, one of the first psychotherapists in the modern sense of the term since his method of treating psychotics was to talk with them in a reasonable manner. Dubois, however, was accused by Hippolyte Bernheim of having "annexed" his discovery. Bernheim declared himself to be the true founder of psychotherapy. Still another person to be considered is Pierre Janet, who had been a pupil of the most renowned neurologist of his time, Jean-Martin Charcot. Janet is referred to by Ellenberger (1970) as "the first person to found a new system of dynamic psychiatry aimed at replacing those of the nineteenth century" (p. 331). Janet, at about the time that Sigmund Freud began his work, was the best known and most respected psychotherapist of his time.

As can be seen, there was a great deal of interest and activity in psychotherapy prior to Freud and there were already the conflicts, schisms, claims, and jealousies which were also to be found later. The whole history of psychotherapy is replete with such incidents, personality clashes and other signs of struggles for superiority.

In 1902, Sigmund Freud, who had studied with Charcot in Paris, invited several colleagues to meet with him to discuss personality theory. The group was later to be called the Wednesday Psychological Society. Some of the members were independent thinkers, each with his own position relative to psychology such as differential behavior, the nature of the human mind, causation, explanation of the neuroses, methods of treatment—topics which they shared with one another. Freud, the oldest, the best known and the most published, was the host. It is important to understand that some of the members of this group were *psycho-analysts* and not *psychoanalysts.* Spelled with two words it meant that these people were interested in the analysis of the psyche; spelled as one word it meant that they were followers of Sigmund Freud.

Of the members of this Wednesday night group, three stand out and are the subject of the next three chapters: Sigmund Freud, Alfred Adler, and Carl Jung. From the beginning these three moved in quite different directions. Freud was a mechanistic deterministic thinker who developed a system of psychology with essentially biological and hydraulic elements: a system of stresses and strains, conflicts, tensions, with a dynamic interaction between biological instinctive drives and social demands. Adler was essentially a commonsense thinker with a shrewd understanding of people's motivations. Jung was an internalized person, mystical, religious, creative. Freud was the ideal German scientist, a keen student of minutiae, a pedant; Adler was a man of the people, socially oriented and concerned; Jung was an introverted, distant but friendly person. Their theories of personality and their psychotherapeutic systems can be seen as direct extensions of their manifest personalities.

Since the deaths of Freud in 1939, Adler in 1937, and Jung in 1961, the theories of the latter two have remained more or less constant. On the other hand the theory of Freud has divided into a number of different approaches, some quite different from Freud's original thinking. There are now a variety of psychoanalytic groups with varying orientations. To make a religious analogy, psychoanalysis may be likened to Protestantism with various groups using the same ultimate authority (writings of Freud—the Bible) but having different interpretations of these basic writings.

During the period from about 1910 to about 1940, these big three dominated psychotherapy in Europe and the United States. However, there were a number of other points of view in existence at that time, most of which have either disappeared or have been incorporated into eclectic thinking, including the theories of such people as Pierre Janet, Jules Déjèrine, Trigant Burrow, Albert Korzybski, Otto Rank, and Wilhelm Reich. However, a number of theories and methodologies which are considered to be deviations from pure Freudian psychoanalysis, such as the therapies of Harry Stack Sullivan, Karen Horney, and Theodore Reik, are still very much alive.

Since 1940 when Carl Rogers gave his historic Psi Chi paper in Minnesota, a considerable number of alternative systems of psychotherapy have begun It is difficult to establish dates of their beginnings since there is generally a considerable lapse of time between when a system started and when evidence about it was published, due to a relatively long incubation period between the conceptualization and results. But it might not be too far off to say that from about 1900 to 1940 there were three major points of view and about a dozen minor ones in psychotherapy and that during the next 40 years from 1940 to 1980 there were a dozen major points of view (including the original three) and perhaps a dozen other ones of consequence.

A thought about this situation leads to the speculation that as time goes on there may continue to be a kind of expanding universe of major and minor systems of psychotherapy. If psychotherapy is essentially a matter of philosophy, then ultimately there will be an infinity of systems; if it be essentially a matter of science, then ultimately there will be one eclectic system.

PSYCHOTHERAPY AND PSYCHOTHERAPIST

In this book the reader will find detailed accounts of twelve major systems of psychotherapy and condensed statements of another twelve innovative systems. Selections of the first group essentially depended on estimates of their popularity as well as historical importance. The second group was selected in terms of a variety of considerations including popularity, the uniqueness of their theories and/or therapeutic procedures, and their apparent differences from one another.

One of the reasons for this melange of theories and methodologies is to help the reader understand psychotherapy in greater depth, should the reader be interested in going into the field of psychotherapy.

This leads to a major point: there appears to be a concordance between the personality of a psychotherapy innovator and the system he or she has developed. In 1956 I wrote an article called "Freud, Rogers and Moreno" in which I made a comparison between the manifest personalities of these three men and their systems of psychotherapy. I never met Freud, but there is a good deal of biographical information about him, and there seems to be no question that his personality and his method of psychoanalysis were in congruence. Freud was a rather shy person, uncomfortable with people, a pedantic bookish type, an intellectual. His methodology, having people lie down with him sitting behind them out of sight with his feet pointed towards the client's head while he listened intently to what they said, fits exactly his manifest personality. The system and the man seem identical.

I got to know Carl Rogers quite well. As a graduate student at the University of Chicago (1953-1955) I was in contact with him as his client, and as a student. In later years I met him on many occasions socially and at professional meetings. Rogers, whether in his social life, as a teacher or as a therapist, was exactly the same. His system and he were identical.

I also got to know J. L. Moreno, the founder of Psychodrama quite well. I listened to him lecture many times, and often I was on the psychodrama stage with him, and I had a social relationship with him. There was no question at all about the congruence of Moreno's highly unique personality and his methodology. Again, the system and the man were identical.

Over the years I have met a considerable number of psychotherapy innovators, some listed on page 531 of chapter 14. In every single case, there was a close resemblance between the manifest personalities of these innovators and their systems. The conclusion is inescapable: people who develop systems of psychotherapy create them in their own image: a shy person develops a system in which he does not look others in the eye (Freud), a modest person develops a system in which he does a lot of agreeing with others (Rogers), a highly charged person develops a system with a lot of action (Moreno).

What is the implication of the above for the reader? I believe that if one is to go into the fields of counseling and psychotherapy then the best theory and methodology for one to use has to be one's own! The reader may not be either successful or happy using a method not suited to his or her own personality. The really successful therapist either adopts or develops a theory and methodology congruent with his or her own personality.

In reading these accounts, in addition to attempting to determine which school of psychotherapy seems most sensible, the reader should also attempt to find one that 'fits' his or her philosophy of life, one which seems most 'right' in terms of its theory, and one with a method of operation which appears most appealing in use.

A final further value of this book with its diversities of opinions lies in greater self-understanding that may be promoted by close reading. This book about psychotherapies may be psychotherapeutic for the reader. Close careful reading vertically (chapter-by-chapter) and then horizontally (section-by-section) may well lead to personal growth as well as better understanding of the current psychotherapies.

ANNOTATED BIBLIOGRAPHY

Adler, A. *What life should mean to you.* New York: Capricorn Books, 1958.

Adler has special meaning for me, since I am an Adlerian, and indeed the co-author of the first textbook on Adlerian psychology written in English (Manaster & Corsini, 1982). It so happens that the first book that I read written by Adler turned me off so thoroughly that it took well over twenty years before I read another. And it was *What life should mean to you* which helped convert me, even though by common consensus others of Adler's books are more important as one can tell by reading Harold Mosak's chapter in this book. I recommend this simple book as easy reading through which one can learn about a simple and good man and his penetrating thinking about topics of importance. You will learn that a good many so-called modern ideas about the sexes and the environment were topics of concern to Adler.

Corsini, R. J. *Handbook of innovative psychotherapies.* New York: John Wiley, 1981.

Much as I am loathe to advertise myself, there is no question that this book is the best source for in-depth understanding of current innovative psychotherapies. In close to 1000 double-columned pages, a total of 66 systems of psychotherapy are systematically summarized, as in *Current psychotherapies*, generally by the innovators of these various systems or by major interpreters. While in the present volume a dozen innovative systems are included, a much broader scope is found in the *Handbook*, which is aimed at the professional therapist rather than the student. The *Handbook* would follow quite well after *Current psychotherapies* for those who want a more complete and detailed understanding of psychotherapy as a whole.

Ellenberger, H. F. *The discovery of the unconscious.* New York: Basic Books, 1970.

Were I asked what is the single most important and necessary book for anyone to read to have a basic understanding of psychotherapy, without any question I would list Ellenberger's classic. One of the most readable and yet most thoroughly researched volumes, it is in my judgment the number one book in the field. Its subtitle: *The history and evolution of dynamic psychiatry* explains the book quite well. With close to 1000 tightly packed pages, any serious student of psychotherapy can only feel that it was too short. I recommend it without hesitation to all who enjoy reading good writing and who can be excited by the evolutionary history of psychotherapy as one of the greatest creations of the human mind.

Frank, J. D. *Persuasion and healing.* Baltimore: Johns Hopkins Press, 1961.

Of the literally thousands of books in psychotherapy of various kinds, Frank's book in my judgment stands out for its simplicity and good sense. Frank, who has both an M.D. and a Ph.D., and who is an outstanding therapist and researcher is, in my judgment, the leading figure in psychotherapy today. This book should be read by all who have any connection with psychotherapy on either side of the desk.

Freud, S. *The psychopathology of everyday life.* London: Complete psychological works of Sigmund Freud, (Vol. 6), 1901.

Whether one agrees with the validity of Freud's essential position (and I am not one of those who does), nevertheless it would be a major loss to anyone who is interested in psychotherapy not to read at least this volume, even if only to read a master expositor. Freud is thrilling to read, for one can almost see how he thinks: the clarity of his position and the forcefulness of his arguments have materially affected all people in the field of applied psychology, and in a sense practically every system in existence today owes its existence to psychoanalysis in that the new system was developed as an extension or as a reaction to Freud's thinking.

Rogers, C. R. *Counseling and psychotherapy.* Boston: Houghton-Mifflin, 1942.

I have a special affection for this book since it was the book which impelled me to attempt to become a psychotherapist. There is a joke about an imaginary book with the title *Brain surgery self-taught.* Well, no doubt thousands of other psychologists as well as myself began with Rogers' book in front of them while talking with clients. From being directive counselors we became non-directive therapists. In 1943, when I first read this book, as a prison psychologist, I was a psychometrician and a directive vocational and educational counselor. Within a few months of following the book I was in deep trouble in my attempt to be a therapist. I wrote to Carl Rogers who at that time was at Ohio State and who generously helped me. Later, I became his student at the University of Chicago. Over 40 years we have maintained our correspondence and our relationship. Regardless of one's position relative to Rogers, it is my judgment that this is still a fundamental book that every person interested in psychotherapy should read and understand. And to repeat what I have said earlier, no matter where one will move to later in one's career, there is no better way to begin as a psychotherapist than by following Rogers's direction as have many thousands.

REFERENCES

Ahnsen, A. *Eidetic psychotherapy.* Lahore, Pakistan: Nai Mat Booat, 1965.

Bach, G. R., & Goldberg, H. *Creative aggression.* Garden City, N.Y.: Doubleday, 1975.

Bindrim, P. Aqua-energetics. In R. J. Corsini (Ed.), *Handbook of innovative psychotherapies.* New York: John Wiley, 1981.

Bion, J. (Ed.). *Therapeutic social clubs.* London: Lewis, 1948.

Cautela, J. Covert conditioning. In R. J. Corsini (Ed.), *Handbook of innovative psychotherapies.* New York: John Wiley, 1981.

Corsini, R. J. Counseling and psychotherapy. In E. F. Borgatta & W. W. Lambert (Eds.), *Handbook of personality theory and research.* Chicago, Ill.: Rand McNally, 1968.

Corsini, R. J., Freud, Rogers and Moreno. *Group Psychotherapy,* 1956, *9,* 274-281.

Corsini, R. J. (Ed.). *Handbook of innovative psychotherapies.* New York: John Wiley, 1981.

Ellenberger, H. *The discovery of the unconscious.* New York: Basic Books, 1970.

Farrelly, F., & Brasma, J. *Provocative therapy.* Cupertino, Calif.: Meta, 1974.

Gazda, G. M. Multiple impact training. In R. J. Corsini (Ed.), *Handbook of innovative psychotherapies.* New York: John Wiley, 1981.

Horney, K. *Self-analysis.* New York: W. W. Norton, 1942.

Janov, A. *The primal scream.* New York: Vintage Books, 1970.

Lair, J., & Lair, J. C. *Hey, God, what should I do now?* New York: Doubleday, 1973.

Losoncy, L. *Encouragement therapy.* Englewood Cliffs, N.J.: Prentice-Hall, 1981.

Orr, L., & Ray, S. *Rebirthing in the new age.* Milbrae, Calif.: Celestial Arts, 1977.

Manaster, G. J., & Corsini, R. J. *Individual psychology.* Itasca, Ill.: F. E. Peacock Publishers, Inc., 1982.

Painter, G., & Vernon, S. Primary relationship therapy. In R. J. Corsini (Ed.), *Handbook of innovative psychotherapies.* New York: John Wiley, 1981.

Reik, T. *Listening with the third ear.* New York: Farrar and Strauss, 1948.

Schmidhoffer, E. Mechanical group therapy. *Science,* 1952, *115,* 120-123.

Shorr, J. E. *Psychoimagination therapy.* New York: Intercontinental Medical Book Co., 1972.

Shostrom, E. L., & Montgomery, D. *Healing love.* Nashville: Abingdon, 1978.

Simmel, E. War neuroses. In S. Lorand (Ed.), *Psychoanalysis today.* New York: International Universities Press, 1949.

van Kaam, A. *The dynamics of spiritual self-direction.* Denville, N. Y.: Dimension Books, 1976.

Wolpe, J. *Psychotherapy by reciprocal inhibition.* Stanford, Calif.: Stanford University Press, 1958.

Zaslow, R. W., & Menta, M. *Rage, resistance and holding.* San Jose, Calif.: State University Press, 1977.

2

Psychoanalysis

JACOB A. ARLOW

OVERVIEW

Psychoanalysis is a system of psychology derived from the discoveries of Sigmund Freud. Originating as a method for treating certain psychoneurotic disorders, psychoanalysis has come to serve as the foundation for a general theory of psychology. Knowledge derived from the treatment of individual patients has led to insights into art, religion, social organization, child development, and education. In addition, by elucidating the influence of unconscious wishes on the physiology of the body, psychoanalysis has made it possible to understand and treat many psychosomatic illnesses.

Basic Concepts

Basically, psychoanalysis is a psychology of conflict. According to Ernst Kris (1950), psychoanalysis may be defined as human nature seen from the vantage point of conflict. Psychoanalysis views the functioning of the mind as the expression of conflicting forces. Some of these forces are conscious; others, perhaps the major ones, are unconscious. As a system of psychology and as a method of therapy, psychoanalysis emphasizes the importance of unconscious forces in mental life.

Conflict is an inexorable dimension of the human condition. It reflects the contradiction inherent in man's dual nature as a biological animal and a social being. In a few short years, each human infant has to be civilized and acculturated; he has to incorporate and integrate the ideals and values, the inhibitions and the taboos, of his particular society. The primary instrument in this process is the family. After the age of five, the more formalized institutions of society take over much of the responsibility for acculturating the individual. In this development, frustration, anger, disappointment, and conflict are inevitable.

From its inception, the functioning of the mind is related to events in the body. The physiology of the body is the substrate of all psychology, including psychoanalysis. The basic responses to stimuli in terms of pleasure and pain (or unpleasure) are part of man's biological inheritance. These responses, phylogenetically determined, undoubtedly were of evolutionary significance in the struggle of the species to survive. A fundamental principle of psychoanalytic theory is that human psychology is governed by a tendency to seek pleasure and to avoid pain. This is referred to as the *pleasure principle* (Freud, 1911). Although this principle is operative throughout life, it is patently and overwhelmingly dominant in the first few years of existence. The earliest experiences of pleasure and pain (or one might say gratification and frustration) play a crucial role in shaping each individual's psychological structure. (The term *structure*, as used in psychoanalysis, pertains to the repetitive, relatively stable, organized forms of mental responses and functioning.) The impact of the earliest experiences is intensified in the case of the human infant, because in contrast to other animals, the human has a much longer period of dependence upon the adults in his environment. Without their care and solicitude over a period of several years, he could not survive. This fact of biology eventuates in an early and abiding attachment to others.

Freud's revolutionary perception of man's psychology represents a fusion of the most advanced humanistic and scientific ideas of the late nineteenth and early twentieth centuries. In psychoanalysis, he combined the liberal ideal of respect for the integrity of each individual with a rigorous attempt to establish a scientific method for studying the individual as a living, social entity. He emphasized that clinical observation is the foundation of psychoanalysis. Theory for Freud was a superstructure erected on clinical observation that could be altered by new findings. Accordingly, it was essential to establish an objective method by which reliable observations could be made. This prerequisite Freud met in his formulation of the psychoanalytic situation which is at the same time a form of therapy and a method of investigation.

Of all the forms of psychotherapy, psychoanalysis is founded on the most extensive, inclusive, and comprehensive system of psychology. It encompasses man's inner experience and outer behavior, his biological nature and his social role, how he functions as an individual and how he functions as a member of the group.

Essentially, psychoanalysis continues the rationalist spirit of Greek philosophy in its command to "know thyself." Knowing one's self, however, is understood in quite a different way. It is not to be found in the pursuit of formal, logical analysis of thinking. As far as the individual is concerned, the sources of his neurotic illness and suffering are by their very nature "unknowable." They reside outside the realm of consciousness, having been barred from awareness by virtue of their painful, unacceptable quality. By enabling the patient to understand how his neurotic symptoms and behavior represent derivatives of unconscious conflicts, psychoanalysis permits the patient to make rational choices instead of responding automatically. Thus, self-knowledge of a very special kind strengthens the individual's ability to control his fate and his happiness. For the successfully analyzed individual, freedom from neurotic inhibition and suffering is often experienced as a liberating, self-fulfilling transformation, which enables him not only to actualize his own potential but to contribute to the advancement and happiness of others. Thus, knowing one's self may have far-reaching social implications. It is important to bear this in mind, because even under the best of circumstances, because of practical difficulties, only a relatively small number of people at best can or will be analyzed.

Other Systems

Almost every form of modern psychotherapy owes some debt to psychoanalysis. As Leo Rangel¹ (1973) has shown, most forms of psychotherapy now widely practiced are based on some element of psychoanalytic theory or technique. Usually some procedure or a particular concept is borrowed from psychoanalysis and used as the rationale for a particular treatment. This is not to imply that other forms of therapy are invalid or ineffectual. Quite the contrary. Although there are many ways to treat neuroses, there is but one way to understand them— psychoanalysis (Fenichel, 1945). It has been stated in many quarters that psychoanalysts believe their method is the only worthwhile form of treatment. This is not true. There are many situations where a nonanalytic treatment is preferable to an analytic one. For many forms of mental illness, psychoanalysis is inadvisable or contraindicated. However, psychoanalysis is the only approach that makes clear what is going on in neurosis; it is the one theory that gives a scientific explanation to the effectiveness of all psychotherapies.

Historically, the line of descent of *Jungian analysis* and *Adlerian therapy* from psychoanalysis is clear. Both Carl Jung and Alfred Adler were students of Freud who broke with him early in the history of the psychoanalytic movement. Jung had serious differences with Freud concerning the nature of drives. His approach places less emphasis on maturational and developmental processes. Jung emphasized the significance of culturally determined, unconsciously transmitted symbolic representations of the principal themes of human existence. Behind the transformations of individual experience, Jung and his followers see the constant recurrence of mythic themes common to all mankind. Jung's concept of the transmission of unconscious fantasies through a collective unconscious has been

criticized as being too mystical. In some respects, Jung's views on the collective unconscious correspond to the Freudians' concept of primitive universal fantasy, but the latter regard these only as vehicles for derivatives of the instinctual drives of childhood rather than original determinants of behavior. They are secondary rather than primary factors in shaping personality. Some of Jung's concepts are particularly useful in elucidating the more regressed manifestations seen in schizophrenic patients (Jung, 1909).

Adler (Ansbacher & Ansbacher, 1956) believed the role of social and political pressures was underestimated by Freudian psychoanalysts. At the time, there was considerable validity to this criticism, analysts having concentrated primarily on the transformation of the derivatives of the energy of the sexual drive, the *libido*. To Adler, the cause of conflicts was more superficially determined by factors such as inferiority over social status, inadequate physical endowment, sexual weakness, and discrimination. Many of his concepts presaged later psychoanalytic contributions concerning the role of self-esteem, particularly in relation to the so-called narcissistic personality disorders.

Recent years have seen the burgeoning of many forms of therapy in which the central aspect of the treatment consists of self-expression, releasing emotion, overcoming inhibitions, and articulating in speech and behavior the fantasies or impulses previously suppressed. The *encounter movement* (Burton, 1969; Schultz, 1967) represents one such school. *Primal scream* is another. These forms of treatment represent exaggerations and caricatures of the principle of emotional catharsis that Freud advanced in his early studies of hysteria (Freud, 1895). At that time, he thought that discharge of pent-up emotion could have a beneficial therapeutic effect. Subsequent experience with the treatment of neurotic patients, however, convinced Freud that this method was limited and, in the long run, ineffectual, since it did not give sufficient weight to the needs of self-punishment and the various defenses the ego uses to ward off anxiety. In the expressive forms of treatment, the group experience plays an enormous role in mitigating anxiety. Expressing in the presence of others what is ordinarily inexpressible can go far in ameliorating a sense of guilt. The burden of guilt, furthermore, is lightened by the knowledge that other members of the group admit to the same or similar feelings and impulses. Everyone's guilt is no one's guilt (Sachs, 1942). The effect of such treatment, however, depends to a large extent on the continuity of contact with the group experience. Since no essential insight or psychological restructuring has taken place, the tendency for relapse once the group experience is discontinued is very strong. Furthermore, there are cases in which the temptation and the opportunity to express derivatives of forbidden impulses is perceived as so overwhelming a danger by the individual that he is unable to cope with it and in some instances may suffer a psychotic break.

Mitigating the influence of the superego on the total psychological equilibrium seems to be the essential feature of the *rational-emotive system* of Albert Ellis (1970). Ellis attempts to get the patient to change his values, particularly in regard to sexuality, helping relieve the patient of irrational guilt that may have inhibited many aspects of his life and behavior. When this treatment is effective, it can be understood in terms of the patient having made an identification with the therapist's personality and values. The therapist comes to serve as an auxiliary superego that may replace or alter the patient's patterns of judgment, self-evaluation and ideal aspirations. This is similar to what one observes in cases where individuals are "cured" of their difficulties through religious conversion, usually as the result of an attachment to some charismatic religious (sometimes political) figure.

As part of the psychoanalytic situation, the analyst listens patiently, sympathetically, uncritically, and receptively. This aspect of psychoanalytic technique forms the core of the nondirective listening of Carl R. Rogers (1951). In other forms of treatment, sympathetic listening may be combined with counseling, trying to guide the patient in a rational manner through the real and imaginary pitfalls of living. Otto Fenichel (1945) pointed out that verbalization of vaguely felt anxieties may bring relief since the individual can face concretized, verbalized ideas better than unclear, emotional sensations. Transference also plays a role. The fact that a therapist spends time, interest, and sympathy reawakens echoes of previous situations of having been helped by friends or relatives. For lonely people it can be a substantial relief to have someone to talk with. When the patient can see some connection between his worries and other patterns of behavior, he feels an accession of strength in relation to the deeper unconscious forces within his personality.

All the forms of therapy mentioned above make use of one or more of the fundamental features of psychoanalytic therapy, namely, a setting in which the patient can express his thoughts and feelings spontaneously and freely to an uncritical, receptive observer; the achievement of insight through interpretation; and finally, and perhaps most important, an awareness of the power of the transference relationship.

Other forms of therapy such as *Gestalt*

therapy (Perls, Hefferline & Goodman, 1951), *reality therapy* (Glasser, 1967), and *behavior therapy* (Wolpe, 1958) illustrate the principles just mentioned. Essentially, the therapist is unconsciously cast in the role of serving as a model or acting as the transference instrument in a desperate effort either to deny or project the effects of internal conflicts. The therapist unconsciously joins the patient in a pattern of playing out some derivative of the patient's childhood fantasies. Accordingly, such forms of therapy play into the tendency of patients to try to act out expressions of their unconscious conflicts. For this reason, one can expect that such forms of therapy can have only limited usefulness and short-termed effectiveness.

HISTORY

Precursors

Psychoanalysis, as originated by Sigmund Freud (1856-1939), represented an integration of the major European intellectual movements of his time. This was a period of unprecedented advance in the physical and biological sciences. A new liberal humanism was abroad, a humanism based on materialist philosophy and the free exercise of thought. These developments provided biologists with fresh concepts superseding the questionable theories of vitalism. The crucial issue of the day was Darwin's theory of evolution. A group of young biologists, deeply influenced by the teachings of Hermann Helmholtz (Berenfeld, 1944) took it as a matter of principle to explain biological phenomena solely in terms of physics and chemistry. One member of that group was Ernst Brücke (Jones, 1953), later chief of the biological research laboratories at the University of Vienna, where Freud went to pursue a career as a research biologist. Models borrowed from physics, chemistry, and the theory of evolution recur regularly throughout Freud's writings but most strikingly in his early psychological works.

Freud came to psychoanalysis by way of his interest in neurology. During his formative years, great strides were being made in neurophysiology and neuropathology. Freud himself contributed to the advancement of the science with original work on the evolution of the elements of the central nervous system, on aphasia, cerebral palsy, and on the physiological functions of cocaine. In fact, he came very close to formulating the neurone theory (Jones, 1953). In *The Interpretation of Dreams,* he offered a model of the human mind based on the physiology of the reflex arc.

This was also the time when psychology separated from philosophy and began to emerge as an independent science. Freud was interested in both fields. He knew the works of "the association" school of psychologists (J. F. Herbart, Alexander von Humboldt, and Wilhelm Wundt), and he had been impressed by the way Gustav Fechner (Freud, 1894) applied concepts of physics to problems of psychological research. Ernest Jones (1953) has suggested that the idea of using free association as a therapeutic technique may be traced to the influence of Herbart. There was, furthermore, an important field of investigation that bridged both neurology and psychiatry. In the midnineteenth century, there was great interest in states of split consciousness (Zilboorg & Henry, 1941). The French neuropsychiatrists had taken the lead in studying conditions such as somnambulism, multiple personalities, fugue states, and hysteria. Hypnotism was one of the principal methods used in studying these conditions. The leading figures in this field of investigation were Jean Charcot, Pierre Janet, Hippolyte Bernheim, and Ambrose Liebault. Freud had the opportunity to work with several of them and he was particularly influenced by Charcot.

Beginnings

Freud wrote two essays on the history of psychoanalysis: *The History of the Psychoanalytic Movement* (1914a) and *An Autobiographical Study* (1925). Both works concerned primarily how Freud's theories evolved. In what follows, this evolution is traced in sketchy form by organizing the developments around Freud's major works. Six key points are delineated in this process.

1. *Studies on Hysteria* (1895)
2. *The Interpretation of Dreams* (1900)
3. *On Narcissism* (1914b)
4. *Papers on Metapsychology* (1915a, 1915b)
5. *Dual Instinct Theory* (1920)
6. *Structural Theory* (1923, 1926)

Studies on hysteria

The history of psychoanalysis proper begins when Josef Breuer, a Viennese physician with research interests, told Freud about a remarkable experience he was having with a patient (Anna O.) who seemed to be curing herself of the symptoms of hysteria by means of talking. Breuer had observed that when he placed his patient into an hypnotic trance and had her relate what was oppressing her mind, she would tell of some highly emotional fantasy or event in her life. If the telling of this material was accompanied by a massive outburst of emotion, the patient would be relieved of her symptoms. Once awake, the patient was totally unaware of the "traumatic event" she had related or of its connection to her disability. Freud tried the same procedure on other patients and was able to confirm Breuer's findings. They summarized their findings in a publication entitled *Studies on Hysteria* (1895), in which they reasoned that the symptoms of hysteria were the result of an undischarged quantity of emotion, connected with a very painful memory. These memories have been split off from their connection with the rest of the mind but they continue to exert a dynamic, intrusive effect in the form of symptoms. The task of therapy was to bring about recollection of the forgotten event together with a cathartic abreaction of the undischarged emotion. Working independently, Freud came to the conclusion that the traumatic events involved in causing hysteria took place in childhood and were regularly of a sexual nature. Since at the time it was generally believed that children before the age of puberty had no sexual drives, Freud was led to the conclusion that the patients he observed had all been seduced by an older person. Further investigation demonstrated that this was not always true. Freud unknowingly had come upon the data that was to serve him as the basis for the discovery of childhood sexuality.

The interpretation of dreams (1900)

The second phase of Freud's discoveries concerned a solution to the riddle of the dream. The idea that dreams could be understood occurred to Freud when he observed how regularly they appeared in the associations of his neurotic patients. *Dreams* and *symptoms*, he came to realize, had a similar structure. They were both the end product of a compromise between two sets of conflicting forces in the mind, between unconscious childhood sexual wishes seeking discharge and the repressive activity of the rest of the mind.

In effecting this compromise, an inner censor disguised and distorted the representation of the unconscious sexual wishes from childhood. This process makes dreams and symptoms unintelligible. The kind of wishes that entered into the formation of dreams were connected with the pleasurable sensations that children get from stimulating the mouth, anus, skin, and genitals, and resembled the various forms of overt sexual activity typical for the perversions.

The Interpretation of Dreams was at the same time a partial record of Freud's own self-analysis. In it Freud first described the Oedipus complex, perhaps the most striking of his many ideas simultaneously destined to disturb the sleep of the world. In addition, in the concluding chapter of this work, Freud attempted to elaborate a theory of the human mind that would encompass dreaming, psychopathology, and normal functioning. The central principle of this theory is that mental life represents an unrelenting conflict between the conscious and unconscious parts of the mind. The unconscious parts of the mind contáin the biological, instinctual sexual drives, impulsively pressing for discharge. Opposed to these elements are those forces of the mind that are conscious or readily available to consciousness. This part of the mind functions at a logical, realistic, and adaptive levef. Because the fundamental principle of this conceptualization of mental functioning concerned the depth or "layer" of an idea in relationship to consciousness, this theory was called the *topographic theory*.

In the 10 years or so that followed the publication of *The Interpretation of Dreams,* Freud used the concepts of unconscious conflict, infantile sexuality, and the Oedipus complex to attain new insights into the psychology of religion, art, character formation, mythology, and literature. These ideas were published in a group of major contributions: *The Psychopathology of Everyday Life* (1901), *Jokes and Their Relationship to the Unconscious* (1905a), *Three Essays on Sexuality* (1905b), and, somewhat later, *Totem and Taboo* (1913).

On narcissism (1914)

The next phase in the development of Freud's concepts came when he attempted to apply methods of psychoanalysis to understanding the psychoses. Up to this point, Freud saw the major conflict in mental life as a struggle between the energy of the sexual drive (*libido*) which was directed towards preserving the species, opposed by the *ego,* the self-preservative drives. This frame of reference did not seem adequate to elucidate the symptoms of psychosis. These phenomena, Freud felt, could be better understood in terms of a conflict between libidinal energies vested in the self in opposition to libidinal energies vested in the representation of objects of the external world. The concept of *narcissism* proved useful, in addition, in explaining such phenomena as falling in love, pride in one's own children and group information (Freud, 1914a, 1921).

The metapsychological papers (1915)

From his clinical observations, Freud came to recognize certain inconsistencies in his topographical model of the mind. He noted, for example, that many unconscious mental contents were, in fact, anti-instinctual and self-punitive; clearly, a strict qualitative differentiation of mental phenomena accoraing to the single criterion of accessibility to consciousness was no longer tenable. In several papers, notably *Repression* (1915a) and *The Unconscious* (1915b), Freud tried to synthesize his psychological concepts under the heading of *metapsychology*. By this term he meant "describing a mental process in all of its aspects—dynamic, topographic, and economic." The papers written during this period represent a transitional phase in Freud's thinking before he embarked upon a major revision of his theory.

The dual-instinct theory (1920)

The role of aggression in mental life convinced Freud that he had to revise his theory of drives. He observed how self-directed aggression operated in depression, masochism, and generally, in the many ways people punish themselves. Individuals wrecked by success, persons who perform crimes out of a sense of guilt in the hope of being punished, and patients in therapy who respond negatively to the insight they achieve during treatment are typical of this category. In 1920, in his essay *Beyond the Pleasure Principle,* Freud extended his dualistic concept by putting forward the notion of two instincts, libido and aggression, both derived in turn from broader, all-pervading biological principles—an instinct of love (*Eros*) and an instinct towards death and self-destruction (*Thanatos*).

The structural theory (1923)

Having recognized that in the course of psychic conflict, conscience may operate at both a conscious and/or unconscious level, and having perceived that even the methods by which the mind protects itself from anxiety may be unconscious, Freud reformulated his theory in terms of a structural organization of the mind. Mental functions were grouped according to the role they played in conflict. The three major subdivisions of the psychic apparatus he called the ego, the id, and the superego. The *ego* comprises a group of functions that orient the individual toward the external world and mediates between it and the inner world. It acts, in effect, as an executant for the drives and correlates these demands with a proper regard for conscience and the world of reality. The *id* represents the organization of the sum total of the instinctual pressures on the mind, basically the sexual and aggressive impulses. The *superego* is a split-off portion of the ego, a residue of the early history of the individual's moral training and a precipitate of the most important childhood identifications and ideal aspirations. Under ordinary circumstances, there is no sharp demarcation among these three major components of the mind. Intrapsychic conflict, however, makes the differences and the demarcations stand out clearly.

One of the major functions of the ego is to protect the mind from internal dangers, that is, from the threat of a breakthrough into consciousness of conflict-laden impulses. The difference between mental health and illness depends upon how well the ego can succeed in this responsibility. In his monograph, *Inhibitions, Symptoms and Anxiety* (1926), Freud detailed that the key to the problem is the appearance of the unpleasant affective state of anxiety, perhaps the most common symptom of psychoneurosis. Anxiety serves as a warning signal alerting the ego to the danger of overwhelming anxiety or panic that may supervene if a repressed, unconscious wish emerges into consciousness. Once warned, the ego may undertake any of a wide array of defenses to protect itself. This new view had far-reaching implications for both theory and practice.

Current Status

Since Freud, developments in psychoanalysis have been many and varied. Under the leadership of Melanie Klein (1932), a so-called English school of psychoanalysis has emerged. It emphasizes the importance of primitive fantasies of loss (the *depressive* position) and persecution (the *paranoid* position) in the pathogenesis of mental illness. This school is particularly influential in Europe and South America.

When Nazi persecution forced many of the outstanding European analysts to migrate to this country, the United States became the world center for psychoanalysis. The leading figures in this movement were Heinz Hartmann, Ernst Kris, and Rudolf Loewenstein. These three collaborators (1946, 1949) tried to establish psychoanalysis as the basis for a general psychology. They did so by extending Hartmann's concepts of the adaptive function of the ego (Hartmann, 1939) and clarifying fundamental working hypotheses concerning the nature of the drives and the maturation and development of the psychic apparatus. Their theories integrated the invaluable contributions of Anna Freud (1936, 1951) derived from studies of long-term child development. In the course of these investigations, several questions concerning the sense of self were posed. How and when does the sense of self develop and what are the consequences to the individual if the process miscarries? Edith Jacobson (1954), D. W. Winnicott (1953), and John Bowlby (1958) were among those who contributed to the clarification of the problem. The most cogent studies in the field, however, come from the meticulous clinical and developmental observations conducted by Margaret Mahler (1975) and her co-workers. All of these studies underline the importance of the early attachment to the mother and the vicissitudes of the processes of separation and individuation.

These early experiences seem to play a crucial role in the development of self-esteem. Considerations of self-esteem are central in the psychology of narcissistic character disorders and borderline personalities. Clinical and theoretical illumination of these conditions were offered in the writings of Annie Reich (1973) and have been extended in an original way by Heinz Kohut (1971) and Otto Kernberg (1968).

The more recent developments in the field are too numerous to describe. David Rapaport (1951) and several of his students have integrated psychoanalytic theories with broad psychological principles and findings. Jacob Arlow and Charles Brenner (1964) have attempted to synthesize newer clinical findings into the framework of the structural theory. Other authors, critical of some of the propositions of psychoanalysis, are attempting to reformulate psychoanalytic theory in terms of communications theory (Peterfreund, 1971; Schafer, 1976) and neurophysiology (Rubinstein, 1967). Some authors have emphasized the importance of interpersonal relationships (Sullivan, 1953) and the role of identification and the transformations of the personality during the life cycle (Erikson, 1968). Karen Horney (1940) and Erich Fromm (1955) have stressed the social, political, and cultural factors in the development of the individual.

The American Psychoanalytic Association is the largest and most prestigious of organized psychoanalytic societies in the United States. It consists of almost 2,500 members and affiliates. It is comprised of 33 affiliate societies and conducts centers for the professional training of psychoanalysts in 26 institutes in the United States. With the exception of some recent changes, admission to training in affiliate institutes and to membership in the American Psychoanalytic Association is restricted to members of the medical profession. (This condition does not hold in the other affiliate societies of the International Psychoanalytical Association.) Standards for training in psychoanalysis are set by the Board on Professional Standards of the American Psychoanalytic Association. In addition to the requirement of an M.D. degree, a candidate must have had residency training in psychiatry. The course of study is from four to eight or more years and consists of three parts: (1) the training analysis, (2) formal courses in the literature and technique of psychoanalysis, and (3) the treatment of at least three or four patients under the supervision of a training analyst.

There are many other psychoanalytic organizations in the United States. The American Academy of Psychoanalysis is a scientific organization that has not in the past conducted programs of training. Although many of its members belong to the American Psychoanalytic Association, membership in the academy is not restricted to physicians. There are, in addition, several societies composed of physicians, psychologists, social workers, and other professionals who have received training at either the William Alanson White Institute or other centers for training in the United States. Perhaps the largest of these is the National Psychological Association for Psychoanalysis.

Recent years have witnessed a rich burgeoning of the psychoanalytic literature. In addition to the long-standing major publications in the field, such as the *American Psychoanalytic Association Journal,* the *International Journal of Psychoanalysis,* the *Psychoanalytic Quarterly, The Psychoanalytic Study of the Child,* the *Psychoanalytic Review,* and *Psychiatry,* many new journals have appeared, such as *The International Psychoanalytic Review, The Chicago Annual of Psycho-*

analysis, The International Journal of Psychoanalytic Psychotherapy, Psychoanalysis and the Contemporary Science, and *Psychological Issues.*

The 24-volume *Standard Edition of the Complete Works of Sigmund Freud* is the basic source for theory and instruction in psychoanalysis. In 1954 Fenichel wrote *The Psychoanalytic Theory of Neurosis,* the closest work to a textbook in psychoanalysis. Unfortunately, this valuable source book has not been brought up to date. The three volume biography of Freud by Ernest Jones (1953-57) contains a comprehensive overview of Freud's contributions. The most concise, accurate, and readable statement of current psychoanalytic theory is to be found in Charles Brenner's (1973) *An Elementary Textbook of Psychoanalysis.* Alexander Grinstein (1971) has been editing *The Index of Psychoanalytic Writings.* Consisting of 14 volumes, it covers all the psychoanalytic literature up to and including the year 1969. Currently, under the auspices of the American Psychoanalytic Association, a cumulative index of all psychoanalytic writings is being prepared.

PERSONALITY

Theory of Personality

The psychoanalytic theory of personality is based on a number of fundamental principles. The first and foremost of these is the principle of *determinism.* Psychoanalytic theory assumes that mental events are not random, haphazard, accidental, unrelated phenomena. Thoughts, feelings, and impulses are events in a chain of causally related phenomena. They result from antecedent experiences in the life of the individual. Through appropriate methods of investigation, the connection between current mental experience and past events can be established. Many of these connections are unconscious.

The second principle of psychoanalytic personality theory is the *topographic* viewpoint. Every mental element is judged according to its accessibility to consciousness. The process by which certain mental contents are barred from consciousness is called *repression*. This is an active process implying a persistent, repetitive effort to keep certain thoughts out of awareness, the motive being to avoid pain or unpleasure. Psychoanalytic investigation of normal and pathological phenomena has demonstrated the important role unconscious forces play in the behavior of the individual. Some of the most important decisions in one's life may be determined in a decisive way by unconscious motives.

The third basic approach to psychoanalytic personality theory is the *dynamic* viewpoint. This pertains to the interaction of the libidinal and aggressive impulses that are part of the human biological endowment. Because of their biological roots, these impulses have been loosely and inaccurately referred to as *instincts*. The correct term in psychoanalytic theory, translated from the German *Treib*, is *drives*. Since this has become common usage, *instinct and drive* will be used interchangeably in the rest of this chapter.

It is important to distinguish drives in the human from instinctive behavior in animals. *Instinct* in animals is a stereotyped response, usually with clear survival value evoked by specific stimuli in particular settings. As used in psychoanalysis, the *drive* is a state of central excitation in response to stimuli. This sense of central excitation impels the mind to activity, with the ultimate aim of bringing about the cessation of tension, a sense of gratification. Drives in humans are capable of a wide variety of complex transformations. Drive theory in psychoanalysis is intended to account for the psychological findings gathered in the clinical setting. Biology supports many of the formulations regarding the libidinal drive. This is not so in the case of the aggressive drive, a concept founded almost exclusively on psychological data (Brenner, 1971).

The fourth approach to personality theory has been called the *genetic* viewpoint, tracing the origins of later conflicts, character traits, neurotic symptoms, and psychological structure to the crucial events and wishes of childhood and the fantasies they generated. In contrast to the earlier concepts of determinism and the dynamic and topographic points of view, the genetic approach is not a theory; it is an empirical finding confirmed in every psychoanalysis. In effect, it states that in many ways, we never get over our childhood. We do not have a complete answer to the question why we fail to do so. One factor undoubtedly resides in the long period of biological dependence characteristic of the human infant. In addition, there seems to be a broad tendency in the higher forms of life for the earliest experiences to have a persistent and crucial effect on later development. Freud's observations about the crucial role of events in early childhood in shaping later behavior have been confirmed by ethologists in their studies of other forms of life (Lorenz, 1952; Tinbergern, 1951).

Personality evolves out of the interaction between inherent biological factors and the vicissitudes of experience. For any individual, given an average expectable environment, one may anticipate a more or less predictible sequence of events constituting the steps in the maturation of the drives and the other components of the psychic apparatus. Whatever happens to the individual—illness, accidents, deprivation, excess gratification, abuse, seduction, abandonment—in some way will alter and transform the native endowment and will contribute towards determining the ultimate personality structure.

The terminology used for describing the development of the drives originally applied only to the libidinal drives. Freud had conceptualized them first and did not postulate an independent aggressive drive until later. Furthermore, the early phases of the libidinal drives are quite distinct and clearly related to specific zones of the body. The somatic substrate of aggression is not so clearly defined. Psychoanalysis postulates that whenever drive activity is involved, some mixture or fusion of the sexual and the aggressive drive energies has taken place. Ordinarily one of the component elements is more dominant than the other.

Variety of Concepts

Oral phase

The earliest phase of instinctual life is the *oral phase*. It extends from birth to approximately 18 months. It is so called because the chief source of libidinal gratification centers around feeding and the organs connected with that function—the mouth, the lips, and the tongue. Gratification of oral needs in the form of satiety brings about a state of freedom from tension and induces sleep. Many disturbances of sleep seem to be connected with unconscious fantasies of an oral libidinal nature (Lewin, 1946, 1949). Biting and sucking are activities that serve both to gratify oral drives and to "explore" the world. During the oral phase, the basic orientation of the psychic ap-

paratus is to take in what is pleasurable and to expel what is unpleasant. According to Karl Abraham (1924), people whose early oral needs have been excessively frustrated turn out to be pessimists. On the other hand, individuals whose oral needs have been gratified tend to have a more optimistic view of the world.

Anal phase

Between the ages of 18 months to 3 years, the main source of pleasure and libidinal gratification comes from the activities connected with retaining and passing the feces. The fundamental instinctual orientation concerns what is to be retained and is therefore valuable, and what is to be expelled, and which ultimately becomes worthless. During the *anal phase*, interest in the bodily processes, in smelling, touching, and playing with feces, are paramount. Regarded for a while as an extruded portion of one's self, the feces are considered as a particularly valuable and highly prized possession. The disgust that those who train the child evince and the shame the child is made to feel may contribute toward a lowered sense of self-esteem. In reaction, the child may respond by stubborn assertiveness, contrary rebelliousness, and by the determination to be in control of whatever happens to him. Through a process known as *reaction formation*, the child may overcome his impulse to soil by becoming meticulously clean, excessively punctual, and quite parsimonious in handling his possessions (Freud, 1917).

Phallic phase

After the third year, the main area of libidinal gratification shifts to the genitals. For both boys and girls, the penis becomes the principal object of interest in the *phallic phase*. It is at this time that the clitoris, embryologically an analogue of the penis, begins to be appreciated for the pleasurable sensations evoked by stimulation. Recent investigations indicate that some awareness of the pleasure potential of the vagina is present at this phase in many little girls (Greenacre, 1967). Also prominent in the phallic phase are exhibitionistic and voyeuristic wishes.

By the time the child has reached the phallic phase, he has made marked advances in the complexity of his psychological structure. The basic orientation during this phase is therefore much more subtle and complicated. Although the child remains basically self-centered, his relations with others in the environment take on a rich texture. He loves and wants to possess those who give him pleasure; he hates and wants to annihilate those who stand in his way and frustrate him. He becomes curious about sexual differences and about the origin of life and in a primitive childlike way fashions his own answers to these important questions. He wants to love and to be loved, to be admired and to be like those he admires. He may overidealize himself or share a sense of power by feeling at one with those he idealizes. During this time, the child may entertain intensely hostile wishes with the penis serving as an instrument for aggression. This gives rise to intense fears of retaliation, usually directed against the penis. It is also the era of the discovery of the anatomical distinction between the sexes, a phase from which the fear of the female genital and envy of the male genital originate.

Three salient features in the development of the drives must be mentioned here. First is the concept of *autoerotism.* When gratification of a particular instinctual urge is not forthcoming, it is always possible for the child to gratify himself by stimulating the appropriate zones of his body, combining such activities with appropriate fantasies. This evolves into the more common forms of childhood masturbation. Second, it should be noted that as the individual passes from one libidinal phase to another, the interest in the gratification of the preceding phase is not completely surrendered. It is only partially superseded by the succeeding libidinal gratification. When there is a particularly strong and persistent attachment to libidinal gratification from a particular object of infancy, one speaks of *fixation.* Fixations are usually unconscious and often serve as a focus for symptom formation later in life. A third feature of libidinal development is the potentiality for *regression,* the reactivation of or the return to an earlier mode of libidinal gratification. Regressive reactivation of earlier modes of mental functioning are common and not necessarily pathological. Usually the regression reactivates some childhood libidinal impulse that had been involved in the process of fixation.

For each of the aforementioned phases of development, there is a characteristic danger. During the oral phase, the greatest danger is that the mother will not be available. This is usually referred to as the danger of *loss of the* (need satisfying) *object.* During the anal phase, after the concept of the mother as an independent entity has crystallized, *losing the mother's love* constitutes the danger. Typical of the phallic phase is fear of retaliation or punishment for forbidden sexual and aggressive wishes. The kind of punishment usually fantasied by both boys and girls takes the form of injury to the body, specifically to the genitals. For this reason, the danger characteristic of the phallic phase is referred to as the *fear of castration.* Later in life, after external prohibitions and threats of punishment have been internalized into the personality in the form of the superego, *fear of conscience* takes its place among the danger situations. Each one of these situations evokes anxiety as a signal alerting the ego to set in motion various mental maneuvers to eliminate or minimize the danger. These maneuvers Anna Freud (1936) called the *mechanisms of defense,* because they protect the rest of the personality from the unpleasant affect of anxiety.

The combined influence on the mind of the libidinal and aggressive wishes constitute the id. The other components of the mind are the ego and the superego. It will be possible to present only a few observations on the development of these psychological structures. The earliest psychological experience of the infant is most likely one of global sensory impingement (Spitz, 1955). There is no differentiation between his self and the rest of the world, between what is in his body and what is outside of it. The inherent capacities of man to perceive, to move, and later to speak mature gradually. The concept of the self as an independent entity develops over a period of two to three years (Jacobson, 1954; Mahler, 1975). There is evidence to suggest that for a certain period during the first year of life, the child is unable to distinguish between himself and the person who cares for him. Certain objects in the external world, for example, a blanket or a stuffed animal toy, may be experienced at times as being part of the self and at other times as part of the external world (Winnicott, 1953).

At first the instinctual drives center mainly on the self—a state called *narcissism.* As other people come to be appreciated as sources of sustenance, protection, and gratification, some of the energy of the libidinal drive settles (is vested) on mental representations of others. Technically, these others are referred to as *love objects,* or *objects* for short. At its core, the human personality retains a considerable compliment of childish self-centeredness. The capacity to need others, to love, to want to please, and to want to become like others is one of the most significant indicators of psychological maturity. In addition to constitutional factors, the quality of experience with objects during the early years is decisive in shaping the all-important capacity to love and identify with others. Disturbances in this process because of traumatic experiences or poor object relations contribute to the severe forms of pathology known as narcissistic character disorders, borderline states, and the psychoses.

Needing, wanting, and identifying with valued persons is fraught with the dangers of frustration, disappointment, and, inevitably, conflict. The imperious wishes of childhood can never be gratified in full. Inexorably, relations with the important objects become a mixture of love and hatred. Such feelings come to a climactic crisis with the Oedipal longings of the phallic phase. As a rule during the ages of three to six, the child develops intense erotic longings for the parent of the opposite sex and a hostile competitive orientation towards the parent of the same sex. Circumstances may induce enormous variations in this basic pattern, including a total inversion of the choice of sexual object. It is the responsibility of the ego to deal with these conflicts. Under favorable circumstances, the oedipal wishes are given up, repressed. They become unconscious. They are, however, not totally obliterated but continue as a potential source of instinctual pressure in the form of unconscious fantasies. Disguised versions of these fantasies may persist in consciousness as the familiar daydreams of childhood. They continue to exert an important influence on nearly every aspect of mental life: on the forms and objects of adult sexuality; on creative, artistic, vocational, and other sublimated activity; on character formation; and on whatever neurotic symptoms the individual may develop later (Brenner, 1973).

Under favorable circumstances, the child relinquishes most of the hostile and neurotic impulses of the Oedipus complex and identifies with the parent of the same sex, especially with his or her moral standards and prohibitions. This is the matrix of the moral part of the personality called the superego. This agency observes the self and judges its thoughts and actions in terms of what it considers right and wrong. It may prescribe punishment, reparation, or repentance for wrongdoing or may reward the self with heightened esteem and affection for virtuous thought and action. The superego is the seed of the conscience and the source of guilt. Under certain conditions, its functioning may be as impulsive and demanding as any primitive instinctual wish of the id. This is particularly true in states of depression.

Latency period

With the passing of the Oedipus complex and the consolidation of the superego, a relatively quiescent phase ensues, called the *latency period*. The child now can be socialized and he can direct his interests to the larger world where the process of education becomes a more formalized experience. This state prevails until the onset of *puberty and adolescence*. The transformations that take place during this period are crucial in establishing the adult identity. As a result of the physiological and psychological changes involved in assuming the adult role, the conflicts of childhood are evoked anew. Variations of fantasies that originally served as vehicles for the drives during childhood become the conscious concomitants of adolescent masturbation. The guilt over masturbation derives primarily from the unconscious wishes that find substitute expression in the masturbation fantasies. During the period of adolescence, a second attempt is made to master the conflicts arising from childhood wishes. (Through the successful resolution of these conflicts, the individual consolidates his adult identity about his sexual role, more responsibility, and choice of work or profession.)

Conflicts stemming from some phase of life are part of normal human development. Uncontrolled expression of certain instinctual impulses could have calamitous consequences for the individual. Free expression of the drives represents a major confrontation with one's morality and could, under certain circumstances, provoke a severe superego response in the form of guilt or self-punishment. It falls upon the ego to mediate the demands made upon it by the id and the superego with due consideration for the exigent needs of reality. All of mental life represents a shifting balance, a tenuously stable equilibrium between the pressures of the id, the superego, and reality. Presumably, the most effective way to deal with a conflict would be to bar the impulse permanently from consciousness. When this occurs, one may speak of successful repression. In most instances, however, the victory is by no means one-sided. By their very nature, unconscious wishes remain dynamic and from time to time threaten to overcome the repression instituted to constrain them. Such intrusion may precipitate attacks of panic or, in lesser form, anxiety. Under such circumstances, the ego undertakes fresh measures to ward off the unpleasant affect of anxiety. If successful repression cannot be maintained, various compromises have to be affected by calling into play the different mechanisms of defense which may become permanent features of the individual's character.

Unsuccessful resolution of intrapsychic conflicts eventuates in neurotic illness and neurotic character traits, inhibitions, sexual perversions, and patterns of behavior of a neurotic or self-defeating nature. In all these instances, a price has been paid in terms of suffering and restriction of the individual's capacities and freedom.

PSYCHOTHERAPY

Theory of Psychotherapy

The principles and techniques of psychoanalysis as therapy are based upon the psychoanalytic theory of neurosis. As the theory of neurosis changed, so did the technique of therapy. Originally, Freud felt that neurotic symptoms were the result of pent-up, undischarged emotional tension connected with the repressed memory of a traumatic childhood sexual experience. At first, he used hypnosis to bring about emotional catharsis and abreaction of the trauma. Since many of his patients could not be hypnotized, he dropped hypnosis in favor of forced suggestion, a technique of recollection fostered by the insistent demanding pressure of the therapist. Among other things, this technique produced artifacts in the form of sexual fantasies about childhood, which the patient offered the therapist as if they were recollections of actual events. Taking advantage of his new operational concepts of the dynamic unconscious and the principle of strict psychic determinism, Freud reduced the element of suggestion to a minimum by a new technical procedure in which he asked his patients to report freely and

without criticism whatever came into their minds. Thus, the technique of *free association* evolved.

During the period when the topographic model of the psychic apparatus was paramount in Freud's mind, the principal technical goal was to make the contents of the unconscious conscious. The patient's productions were interpreted according to principles very similar to those used in *The Interpretation of Dreams*. The most striking discovery Freud made during this period was the discovery of the *transference,* a highly emotional attitude the patient develops towards the analyst which represents a repetition of the individual's fantasy wishes concerning objects of the past, foisted onto the analyst. The discovery that the anti-instinctual forces of the mind, such as the defense mechanisms, guilt, and self-punishment, could operate at an unconscious level contributed to the elaboration of the structural theory. Applied to the technique of psychotherapy, the structural theory pointed to the need to analyze the functioning of the defense mechanisms and the self-punitive trends. Elucidating the nature of the unconscious danger and the quality of the anxiety attendant upon its appearance have since become central points of analytic technique.

In later years, in an attempt to apply psychoanalytic therapy to types of cases that have heretofore been refractory to treatment, newer techniques were suggested. Franz Alexander (1932) felt that since most patients had been traumatized by parental mismanagement during childhood, it was necessary for the analyst to arrange "a corrective emotional experience" to counteract the effects of the original trauma. A more recent elaboration of these ideas has been proposed by E. R. Zetzel (1970) and Ralph Greenson (1967) who emphasized particular measures required to instill confidence to create a proper alliance between therapist and patient. Greenson in particular emphasizes the importance of the real personality of the analyst. Some analysts influenced by the ideas of Melanie Klein see in the analyst's emotional reaction a mirror of what the patient is experiencing consciously or unconsciously (Racker, 1953; Weigert, 1970). Heinz Kohut (1971) has suggested several technical innovations aimed at strengthening the self-esteem of patients with narcissistic personality disorders. In addition, the combination of psychoanalysis with other modalities of treatment such as drugs, group therapy, and family interaction has been advanced.

Onset of neurosis

In the genesis of neurotic disorders, the conflicts of childhood are of critical importance. By far the most common and most significant conflicts are those that involve the wishes of the oedipal phase. All children have conflicts and most of them develop some kind of childhood neurosis. Usually *childhood neurosis* assumes the form of general apprehensiveness, nightmares, phobias, tics, mannerisms, or ritualistic practices. Most of the primary behavior disorders of children represent disguised forms of neurosis from which the element of manifest fear has disappeared. Phobia is probably the most frequent symptom of childhood neurosis. In most cases with the passage of the oedipal phase, the disturbances caused by the instinctual conflicts have been sufficiently ameliorated to permit the child to progress normally. In some cases, a childhood neurosis continues with relatively little change into adult life.

Neurosis in adults may develop anew when the balance between the pressures of the drives and the defensive forces of the ego is upset. There are three typical situations in which this may occur.

1. An individual may be unable to cope with the additional psychological burden that normal development places upon him. The unconscious significance of becoming an adult and assuming responsibilities of marriage and undertaking the competitive and aggressive challenges of maturity may prove too much for the ego.

2. Disappointment, defeat, loss of love, physical illness, or some other inevitable consequence of the human condition may lead an individual to turn away from current reality and unconsciously seek gratification in the world of fantasy. This usually involves a reactivation (regression) of the fantasy wishes of the oedipal phase. As these wishes are regressively reactivated, the conflicts and anxieties of childhood are revived and the process of symptom formation begins. The fantasy wishes that are regressively reactivated are the ones that earlier had been the subject of fixation.

3. By a combination of circumstances, an individual may find himself in adult life in a situation that corresponds in its essential features to some childhood trauma or conflict-laden fantasy. Current reality is then misperceived in terms of the childhood conflict and the individual responds as he did in childhood, by forming symptoms.

Process of Psychotherapy

The standard technical procedure of psychoanalysis for studying the functioning of the mind is known as the *psychoanalytic situation*. The patient is asked to assume a recumbent position on the couch, looking away from the analyst. The patient is asked to express in words whatever thoughts, images, or feelings come to mind, and to express these elements without distortion, censorship, suppression, or prejudgment concerning the significance or insignificance of any particular idea. Seated behind the couch, the analyst listens in an uncritical, nonjudgmental fashion, maintaining an attitude of benign curiosity. The analyst's values and judgments are strictly excluded from the therapeutic interaction.

From time to time the analyst interrupts the patient's associations. In doing so, he momentarily interferes with the patient's role as a passive reporter and makes him observe and reflect upon the significance and possible connections among his associations. The analyst's interventions momentarily change the patient's role from that of passive reporter to that of active observer and, at times, interpreter. The principle of free association is somewhat modified in connection with the interpretation of dreams. In this instance, the analyst may ask the patient to tell him whatever comes to mind in connection with this or that particular image of the dream.

The practical conditions of the treatment are also strictly regulated. A fixed schedule of fees and appointments is maintained. Any attempt on the part of the patient to deviate from the basic understanding of the analytic situation naturally becomes a subject for investigation and analysis. Changes in the basic conditions of the treatment are inadvisable and when necessary are effected by mutual consent between the patient and the analyst after the problem has been analyzed.

The analyst attempts to create a set of conditions in which the functioning of the patient's mind and the thoughts and images that emerge into consciousness are endogenously determined. The patient's thoughts and associations should come primarily from the stimulus of the persistent dynamic internal pressure of the drives as organized in unconscious fantasies. His thoughts and associations should not represent responses to external manipulation, exhortation, stimulation, or education. This is what is uniquely psychoanalytic in the therapeutic interaction. Under the conditions of the analytic situation, the influence of inner mental forces can be more easily and clearly observed than in more usual situations. It becomes possible for the material hitherto suppressed or repressed to be verbalized and examined. This presupposes the strictest adherence to professional principles on the part of the analyst. Everything he does must be in the interest of advancing the patient's insight through the process of analysis. Accordingly, there is no greater responsibility in the analytic situation than the strict preservation of the patient's confidentiality. Communication of any of the material of the analysis to whatever source is contrary to the spirit of the analytic situation, even when the patient believes a breach of confidentiality is in his own best interests.

Psychoanalysis involves a commitment to change through the process of critical self-examination. To maintain continuity of the analytic process, at least four sessions a week are indicated. Each session lasts at least 45 minutes. The course of treatment may run for several years. Undertaking psychoanalytic treatment involves considerable sacrifice in time, effort, and money. These are not conditions upon which one may enter lightly.

The psychoanalytic situation has been structured in this manner with the intention of making possible the accomplishment of the goal of psychoanalytic therapy, namely, to help the patient achieve a resolution of intrapsychic conflict through understanding his conflicts and dealing with them in a more mature manner. Since the analytic situation is relatively uncontaminated by the intrusion of ordinary interpersonal relationships, the interaction of the three components of the mind—the ego, the id, and the superego—may be studied in a more objective way, making it possible to demonstrate to the patient what parts of his thoughts and behavior are determined by inner wishes, conflicts, and fantasies and what part represents a mature response to objective reality.

Mechanisms of Psychotherapy

The treatment process may be divided into four phases:

1. The opening phase
2. The development of transference
3. Working through
4. Resolution of the transference

The opening phase

Psychoanalytic observation begins with the very first contact the patient makes with the analyst. Everything the patient says and does is noted for possible significance and use later in the treatment. The initial set of interviews is part of the opening phase. During these interviews, the nature of the patient's difficulty is ascertained and the decision is reached whether analysis is indicated. To determine this, it is necessary for the analyst to learn as much as possible about the patient; for example, his current life situation and difficulties, what he has accomplished, how he relates to others, and the history of his family background and childhood development. Formalized history taking, following a prescribed outline, is not encouraged. Priorities in the subjects to be discussed should be left to the patient's intuition. Much is learned

from how the patient approaches the practical task of making his problems known to the therapist and how he responds to the delineation of the analytic contract. The understanding of the analytical situation must be clearly defined from the very beginning and the respective responsibilities of both parties explicitly stated.

After a few sessions of face-to-face interviews, the second part of the opening phase begins when the patient assumes the couch. No two patients begin treatment in the same way. Some find it difficult to lie on the couch and say whatever comes to mind; others take readily to this new set of conditions. Everything the patient says and does, the position he assumes on the couch, the clothes he wears, his characteristic phrases, what he chooses to present as the opening statement of the session and whether he is on time for the appointment, are all clues to unconscious mental processes.

During the opening phase, the analyst continues to learn more about the patient's history and development. He gets to understand in broad outline the nature of the patient's unconscious conflicts and he has an opportunity to study the characteristic ways by which the patient resists revealing himself or becoming aware of repudiated thoughts and feelings. Gradually the analyst is able to detect a continuous thread of themes following relatively uniform sequences and becoming manifest repetitively in a variety of meaningful configurations. These productions of the patient can be understood in terms of the persistent, unconscious fantasy representing wishes from childhood, dynamically active in the patient's current life in disguised and distorted ways. In the early phases, the analyst deals amost exclusively with the superficial aspects of the patient's material. He tries to demonstrate to the patient significant correlations in the material presented but he restricts himself primarily to those elements that are readily accessible to consciousness and that are not too close to the patient's basic conflicts. In ordinary cases, the initial phase of the treatment lasts from three to six months.

The development of transference.
The next two phases of treatment, the transference and working through, constitute the major portion of the therapeutic work and actually overlap. At a certain stage in the treatment, when it appears the patient is just about ready to relate his current difficulties to unconscious conflicts from childhood concerning wishes over some important person or persons in his life, a new and interesting phenomenon emerges. Emotionally, the person of the analyst assumes major significance in the life of the patient. The patient's perceptions of and demands upon the analyst become quite inappropriate, out of keeping with reality. The professional relationship becomes distorted as he tries to introduce personal instead of professional considerations into their interaction. Understanding transference was one of Freud's greatest discoveries. He perceived that in the transference, the patient was unconsciously reenacting a latter-day version of forgotten childhood memories and repressed unconscious fantasies. *Transference*, therefore, could be understood as a form of memory in which repetition in action replaces recollection of events.

The analysis of the transference is one of the cornerstones of psychoanalytic technique. It helps the patient distinguish fantasy from reality, past from present, and it makes real to the patient the force of the persistent unconscious fantasy

wishes of childhood. Analysis of transference helps the patient understand how he misperceives, misinterprets, and misresponds to the present in terms of the past. In place of the automatic, uncontrolled, stereotyped ways through which the patient unconsciously responds to his unconscious fantasies, the patient is now able to evaluate the unrealistic nature of his impulses and anxieties and to make appropriate decisions on a mature and realistic level. In this way, analysis helps the patient achieve a major realignment in the dynamic equilibrium between impulse and conflict that ultimately leads to a satisfactory resolution of the pathogenic conflict once the patient comes to understand not only the nature of the fears that motivate his defenses, but the self-punitive trends as well. For the most part, these are also unconscious.

Working through
This phase of the treatment coincides with and continues the analysis of the transference. One or two experiences of insight into the nature of one's conflicts are not sufficient to bring about changes. The analysis of the transference has to be continued many times and in many different ways. The patient's insight into his problems by way of the transference is constantly deepened and consolidated by the process of working through, a process that consists of repetition, elaboration, and amplification. Working through acts as a kind of catalyst between analysis of transference and the overcoming of the amnesia for the crucial childhood experiences (Greenacre, 1956). Usually the experience of successful analysis of a transference phenomenon is followed by the emergence into memory of some important event or fantasy from the patient's past. Analysis of the transference facilitates recall. Recall illuminates

the nature of the transference. This reciprocal interplay between understanding the transference and recollecting the past consolidates the patient's insight into his conflicts and strengthens his conviction concerning the interpretive reconstructions made in the course of his treatment.

Resolution of the transference

The resolution of the transference comprises the termination phase of treatment. When the patient and the analyst are satisfied that the major goals of the analysis have been accomplished and the transference is well understood, a date is set for ending the treatment. Technically, the analyst's aim is to resolve the patient's unconscious neurotic attachment to him. There are a number of very striking features typical of this phase of the treatment. Most characteristic and dramatic is a sudden and intense aggravation of the very symptoms for which the patient sought treatment. It seems almost as if all the analytic work had been done in vain. Upon analysis, this interesting turn of events can be understood as a last-ditch effort on the part of the patient to convince the analyst that he is not yet ready to leave treatment and that he should be permitted to continue the relationship indefinitely. There are many motives for this unconscious attitude. In part, the patient is unwilling to surrender so gratifying and helpful a relationship. In part, it continues a continuation of some passive, dependent orientation from childhood. But most of all, it represents a last chance endeavor to get the analyst to fulfill the very unconscious, infantile fantasy wishes that were the source of the patient's conflicts to begin with.

Another interesting thing that happens during the termination phase of treatment is the emergence of hitherto repressed memories that confirm or elaborate the reconstructions and interpretations made earlier in the treatment. It is as if the patient presents new insight or findings to the analyst as a parting gift of gratitude. Unconsciously, it often has the significance of presenting the analyst with a child, a gift of new life, as a form of thanks for the new life that analysis has made possible for the patient.

Finally, during the closing phase of treatment, the patient may reveal a hitherto concealed group of wishes amounting to a desire to be magically transformed into some omnipotent or omniscient figure, a striving he had kept secret throughout the analysis but that he had quietly hoped would be fulfilled by the time the treatment was over. It is very important during this phase to analyze all the fantasies the patient has about how things will be after the analysis is over (Schmideberg, 1938). If one fails to deal with all the problems mentioned above, the possibilities of relapse remain very high.

APPLICATIONS

Problems

From the description of psychoanalysis as therapy, it should be clear that any potential patient must be able to fulfill certain objective as well as personal requirements. Essentially, he must be strongly motivated to overcome his difficulties by honest self-scrutiny. Because it is difficult at the beginning to predict in any definite way how long the treatment will last, the individual must be in a position to commit a considerable period in advance for the purpose of carrying the analysis through to successful termina tion. In addition, he must be able to accept the discipline of the conditions proposed by the psychoanalytic contract as outlined above. The psychoanalytic dialogue is a very unusual form of communication, inevitably entailing frustration of transference wishes. A patient must be able to accept such frustration and to express his thoughts and feelings in words rather than action. Impulsive, willful, self-centered, and highly narcissistic individuals may not be able to accommodate themselves to such structures. People who are basically dishonest, psychopathic, and pathological liars obviously will not be equal to the task of complete and unrelenting self-revelation. Furthermore, since cooperation with the analyst in an enterprise of self-exploration requires some degree of objectivity and reality testing, functions that are severely impaired in the psychoses, psychoanalysis can rarely be used in the treatment of such conditions except under very special circumstances.

Since psychoanalysis is a time-consuming, expensive, and arduous form of treatment, it is not indicated in those conditions when difficulties are minor. Genuine suffering and pain are the most reliable allies of the analytic process. Through insight, psychoanalysis hopes to enable the patient to overcome inner conflicts. This can be helpful only insofar as such insights can be put to constructive use in altering one's life situation. If the person's objective situation is so bad that there is nothing one can do about it, psychoanalysis will be of no avail. This can be seen for example in such cases where the analyst recognizes how the story the patient presents reflects a lifelong struggle against murderous, destructive, and self-destructive impulses, the psychological consequence of severe congenital deformity or crippling disease early in childhood. No psychological insight can compensate for the injustices of fate.

Because so much of psychoanalytic technique depends on the analysis of the transference, psychoanalysis is best suited for conditions in which transference attachments tend to be very strong. This is true in the classical psychoneurotic entities—hysteria, anxiety hysteria, obsessive-compulsive neurosis, and a variety of states characterized by anxiety. In actual practice, the symptomatology of the psychoneuroses tend to overlap. The diagnostic label attended to a particular condition usually reflects the major mechanism of defense characteristically employed to ward off anxiety. In hysteria, for example, by a process called *conversion,* the energy of a sexual wish which the ego was unable to repress successfully may be transformed into alterations of body functions like paralysis, absence of sensation, abnormal sensations, and so forth. An unconscious fantasy of sucking on a penis or swallowing it may become manifest consciously in the feeling that there is an abnormal lump in the throat that cannot be swallowed—the classical globus hystericus. A symptom is compromise formation. Unconsciously, it gratifies the wish and the need for punishment at the same time.

Phobias are typical of anxiety hysteria. The phobic patient wards off anxiety by treating some other external object or situation as the representative of the unconscious impulse. In one form of *agoraphobia,* a patient may become anxious whenever she goes out on the street, the street representing the place where it is possible to realize her unconscious wish to be a prostitute. The mechanism of defense is a double one. The internal (sexual) danger is projected onto the street, an external situation. By avoiding the external object, the patient controls an internal danger. The mechanisms of defense represent a combination of projection and avoidance.

Psychoanalysis is also applicable for character disorders that represent substitutes for psychoneurotic symptoms. For a person whose unconscious fantasies lead him unconsciously to misconstrue dancing as indulgence in dangerous sexual activity, it may prove much more acceptable just to avoid dancing than to experience blushing, palpitations, and sweating whenever he attempts it. Such a person may be diagnosed as suffering from phobic character disorders. There are many forms of character disorders of this type—hysterical, obsessive, compulsive, depressive, and so on. Arlow (1972) has demonstrated how certain character traits may represent transformations from what originally had been transient perversions. Petty liars, hoaxers, and unrealistic personalities may be said to be suffering from character perversions.

Sexual difficulties, like premature ejaculation, and psychoneurotic depressions are ordinarily quite amenable to psychoanalytic treatment. More generalized patterns of behavior that interfere with the patient's conscious goals for happiness and success can be traced to unconscious conflicts and can be treated psychoanalytically. Some men, for example, repeatedly fall in love with and marry the same kind of woman, although they know from previous experience that the marriage will end disastrously. Similarly, certain women seem incapable of choosing men other than those who will hurt, abuse, and humiliate them. Other people will unconsciously arrange their lives so any success is followed by an even greater

failure. In these cases, their normal way of life or choice of love object or self-engineered fate is the equivalent of a psychoneurotic disorder.

In recent years, many of the patients seeking psychoanalytic treatment seem to be suffering from masochistic character disorders or from narcissistic neuroses. Into this latter category fall those paradoxical combinations of low self-esteem and heightened grandiosity. Mood swings, depression, tendencies toward drug dependence, compulsive strivings for recognition and success, and patterns of promiscuous sexuality are not uncommon. Such patients often complain of inner emptiness, lack of goals, hypochondriasis, and an inability to make lasting attachments or love relationships. Because of new contributions to the technical management of these problems, the prognosis of their treatment by psychoanalysis seems much better today than it did in previous years.

There are a number of conditions that may be helped by psychoanalysis under specially favorable conditions. Among these are some cases of drug addiction, perversions, borderline personalities, and, on rare occasions, psychoses. Pioneering work applying psychoanalytic principles, if not the complete technique, to the treatment of psychotics has been done by Paul Federn (1952), Frieda Fromm-Reichmann (1950), H. Rosenfeld (1954) and H. F. Searles (1965).

Evaluation

Unfortunately, there exists no adequate study evaluating the results of psychoanalytic therapy. In a general way, this is true of almost all forms of psychotherapy. There are just too many variables to be taken into account to make it possible to establish a controlled, statistically valid study of the outcome of the therapy. Several attempts have been made in this direction beginning with Otto Fenichel (1930) and including studies by Fred Feldman (1968), H. J. Eysenck (1965), Julian Meltzoff and Melvin Kornreich (1970), R. S. Wallerstein and N. J. Smelser (1969), and A. Z. Pfeffer (1963), as well as several studies by the American Psychoanalytic Association. None of the findings of these studies has proven definitive and irrefutable. By and large, the number of "cures" range from 30 to 60 percent, depending on the studies and the criteria employed.

In any individual case, evaluation of the outcome of treatment has to be judged in a global fashion. Comparisons are made between the situation at the beginning of treatment and the alteration in the patient's life and symptoms at termination. He may have been cured of more conditions than he complained about when he first started; previously unforeseen possibilities of self-fulfillment may have been realized. On the other hand, unrecognized complicating difficulties and intercurrent events may have changed the total configuration of the patient's life. In the face of objective reality, the claims of psychoanalysis must be modest. At best, psychoanalysis tries to help the patient effect the best possible solution of his difficulties that circumstances will allow. It seeks to achieve for the patient the most stable equilibrium possible between the various forces at conflict in his mind. How well that equilibrium is sustained will also depend on how favorably life treats the patient during and after treatment. Freud himself was quite modest about the therapeutic claims of psychoanalysis (Freud 1937). The validity of what psychoanalysis has discovered concerning human nature and the functioning of the human mind are not necessarily related to the effectiveness of psychoanalysis as treatment. Nonetheless, the fact remains that when properly applied to the appropriate condition, psychoanalysis remains the most effective mode of therapy yet devised.

Treatment

In discussing the technical conduct of a psychoanalysis, Freud compared writing about the treatment to explaining the game of chess. It is easy to formulate the rules of the game, to describe the opening phases, and to discuss what has to be done to bring the game to a close. What happens in between is subject to infinite variation. The same is true of psychoanalysis. The analytic contract, the opening phase, and the tasks of termination can be described definitively. The analysis of the transference and the process of working through consist of countless bits of analytic work. Rudolf Loewenstein (1958) approached the problem by distinguishing between tactical and strategic goals in psychoanalytic technique. *Tactical* concerns involve the analysis of the immediate presenting material in terms of some conflict, usually involving the analyst. The *strategic* goal is to elucidate the nature of the unconscious childhood fantasy and to demonstrate the many ways in which it affects the patient in his current life.

How this appears in actual practice may be demonstrated in the following illustration. The patient is a middle-aged businessman whose marriage has been marked by repeated strife and quarrels. His sexual potency has been tenuous. At times he has suffered from premature ejaculation. At the beginning of one session, he began to complain about having to return to treatment after a long holiday weekend. He said "I'm not so sure I'm glad to be back in treatment even though I didn't enjoy my visit to my parents. I feel I just have to be free.'' He then continued with a description of his visit home, which he said had been depressing. His mother was bossy, aggressive, manipulative, as always. He feels sorry for his father. At least in the summertime, the father can retreat to the garden and work with the flowers, but the mother watches over him like a hawk. "She has such a sharp tongue and a cruel mouth. Each time I see my father he seems to be getting smaller and smaller; pretty soon he will disappear and there will be nothing left of him. She does that to people. I always feel that she is hovering over me ready to swoop down on me. She has me intimidated just like my wife.''

The patient continued, "I was furious this morning. When I came to get my car, I found that someone had parked in such a way that it was hemmed in. It took a long time and lots of work to get my car out. During the time I realized how anxious I was; the perspiration was pouring down the back of my neck.

"I feel restrained by the city. I need the open fresh air; I have to stretch my legs. I'm sorry I gave up the house I had in the country. I have to get away from this city. I really can't afford to buy another house now but at least I'll feel better if I look for one.

"If only business were better, I could maneuver more easily. I hate the feeling of being stuck in an office from nine until five. My friend Bob had the right idea—he arranged for retirement. Now he's free to come and go as he pleases. He travels, he has no boss, no board of directors to answer to. I love my work but it imposes too many restrictions on me. I can't help it, I'm ambitious. What can I do?''

At this point, the therapist called to the patient's attention the fact that throughout the material, in many different ways, the patient was describing how he feared confinement, that he had a sense of being trapped.

The patient responded, "I do get symptoms of claustrophobia from time to time. They're mild, just a slight anxiety. I begin to feel perspiration at the back of my neck, and I have a sense of restlessness. The hair seems to stand up on the back of my neck. It happens when the elevator stops between floors or when a train gets stuck between stations. I begin to worry about how I'll get out.''

The fact that he suffered from claustrophobia was a new finding in the analysis. The analyst noted to himself that the patient felt claustrophobic about the analysis. The conditions of the analytic situation imposed by the analyst were experienced by the patient as confining. In addition, the analyst noted, again to himself, these ideas were coupled with the idea of being threatened and controlled by his mother.

The patient continued, "You know I have the same feeling about starting an affair with Mrs. X. She wants to and I guess I want to also. Getting involved is easy. It's getting uninvolved that concerns me. How do you get out of an affair once you're in it?''

In this material, the patient associates being trapped in a confined space with being trapped in the analysis and with being trapped in an affair with a woman.

The patient continued, "I'm really chicken. It's a wonder I was ever able to have relations at all and to get married. No wonder I didn't have intercourse until I was in my twenties. My mother was always after me, 'be careful about getting involved with girls; they'll get you into trouble. They'll be after you for your money. If you have sex with them you can pick up a disease. Be careful when you go to public toilets; you can get an infection, etc., etc., etc.' She made it all sound dangerous. You can get hurt from this, you can get hurt from that. It reminds me of the time I saw two dogs having intercourse. They were stuck together and couldn't separate—the male dog was yelping and screaming in pain. I don't even know how old I was then, maybe five or six or perhaps seven, but I was definitely a child and I was frightened.''

At this point, the analyst is able to tell the patient that his fear of being trapped in an enclosed space is the conscious derivative of an unconscious fantasy in which he imagines that if he enters the woman's body with his penis, it will get stuck; he will not be able to extricate it; he may lose it. The criteria used in making this interpretation are clear: they consist of the sequential arrangement of the material, the contiguity of related themes, the repetition of the same or analogous themes, and the convergence of the different elements into one common hypothesis that encompasses all the data, namely, an unconscious fantasy of danger to the penis once it enters a woman's body. This is the tactical goal that can be achieved on the basis of this material. In this instance, it constitutes an important step toward the strategic goal, which, in this case, would consist of making the patient aware of childhood sexual strivings towards the mother, of a wish to have relations with her, and of a concomitant fear growing out of the threatening nature of her personality, and that, like a hawk, she would swoop down upon him and devour him. These interpretations would give him insight into the causes of his impotence and his stormy relations with

women, particularly his wife. The material also demonstrates how a neurotic person misperceives, misinterprets, and responds inappropriately to current experience in terms of his unconscious fantasy. To this patient, having to keep a definite set of appointments with the analyst, having his car hemmed in between two other cars, being responsible to authorities, and getting stuck in elevators or in trains were all experienced as dangerous situations that evoke the symptoms of anxiety. Consciously, he experienced restrictions by rules and confinement within certain spaces. Unconsciously, he was thinking in terms of experiencing his penis inextricably trapped inside a woman's body.

This is the essence of the neurotic process—the persistent unconscious fantasies of childhood serve to create a mental set according to which the individual in a selective and idiosyncratic way interprets everything that happens to him. Therefore, neurotic conflicts do not represent conflicts with reality. They are intrapsychic conflicts (Arlow, 1963).

The material of any one analytic session is by no means always so dramatic. Yet one must be careful not to prejudge the significance and possible ramifications of any event or session no matter how trivial it may appear at first. A seemingly insignificant interaction between the patient and the analyst may lead to very important discoveries illuminating the origins and the meaning of the neurosis. For the most part, however, the major portion of the analytic work is directed toward understanding the patient's defenses and overcoming his resistances. It is not always easy to distinguish between mechanisms of defense and resistances. Typically, the *mechanisms of defense* are repetitive, stereotyped, automatic means used by the ego to ward off anxiety. A *resistance* is any one of a wide range of phenomena distracting the patient from pursuing the requirements of the analytic situation.

It may seem strange that a patient who has made so serious a commitment to understanding himself should not follow the course of action in treatment that is intended to relieve him of his symptoms. On second thought, however, this is not at all unexpected. Since the mind characteristically turns away from or tries to repress unpleasant feelings and thoughts and since the neurotic process develops when it has been unable to accomplish this end successfully, it should come as no surprise that the endeavor to both fulfill and control forbidden impulses should continue into analytic experience. Herman Nunberg (1926) showed how the patient unconsciously brings into the analysis a wish to preserve intact those very infantile strivings that caused his difficulties in the first place.

The analysis of defenses and resistances is slow, piecemeal work. Nevertheless, from it, much can be learned about how the patient's character was shaped in response to the critical events and object relations of childhood. A particularly difficult resistance to overcome during treatment comes from the use of the mechanism known as *isolation*. This is the tendency for the patient to deal with his thoughts as if they were empty of feeling or unrelated to other ideas or to his behavior. A patient may begin a session, for example, by mentioning in two or three short sentences an incident that took place on his way to the session. He had passed a man on the street who suddenly, without cause or warning, extended his arm in such a way that he almost struck the patient. This reminded the patient of an incident some years earlier when he

saw someone actually being hit in this very same manner. On this occasion, as in the past, the patient, not a native New Yorker, shrugged the incident off with the reassuring judgment, "Well, that's New York for you. It's a good thing he didn't have a knife." All of this was stated in an even, flat, unemotional tone.

With no transition, the patient turned to matters of closer concern to him. He described at great length and again in an even-tempered way how his boss had criticized his work in front of his colleagues. Many of the criticisms, he felt, were unjustified, but mindful of his position, he had maintained a calm, respectful demeanor throughout the meeting. Even when recounting the incident, in the session, he showed little sign of anger. When this was called to his attention, he admitted that indeed he had been angry and was surprised that he had not transmitted that feeling to the therapist. At this point, the therapist made the connection for the patient between his opening report of a near-assault on the street and the experience with his boss. Actually, the patient had been saying, "There are dangerous people abroad. If one is not careful, they may strike you, even kill you. They have murderous impulses." The incident in the street served as a convenient locus onto which the patient projected his own murderous wishes to retaliate against the boss. He dealt with these impulses in an isolated way, an intellectual judgment he made about someone else's motives.

At this stage of the treatment, he could grasp only intellectually, by inference, the intensity of his vengeful wishes. Much could be learned from the analysis of this experience beyond illustrating how the patient manages to control and to suppress his feelings. This patient was particularly vulnerable to any assault on his pride, any humiliation of his narcissism, especially if it occurred as part of a public spectacle. Later in the analysis, it was possible to demonstrate the connection between these components of the patient's character and the feelings of defeat, insignificance, and humiliation he experienced during the oedipal phase while watching his parents having intercourse in the bedroom he shared with them.

It would be impossible to catalogue all the forms that resistance can take. Some of the more usual ones may be noted here. The most direct and unequivocal form of resistance occurs when the patient finds he has nothing to say. The patient may remain silent on the couch for minutes on end. Even a trivial lateness of a few minutes may carry some hidden meaning. Often a patient may miss sessions, forget them, or oversleep. He may be tardy in paying the bill for treatment, finding very realistic explanations to account for the tardiness. Sometimes patients will talk endlessly about the trivia of day-to-day events revealing little or nothing that can be used to understand their problems. A patient may introduce a dream at the beginning of a session and make no reference to it for the rest of the analytic hour. On the other hand, the patient may fill the entire session with dreams, making it impossible to learn more than the facade of what had been recorded of the night's experience. Some patients report how they have become ardent advocates of psychoanalysis, proselytizing their friends and relatives, urging all of them to enter into treatment, at the very time when they themselves are making little effort or progress in the analytic work.

The important principle governing all manifestations of resistance is that they must be analyzed like anything else that happens in the course of analysis. What must be understood is why the patient is behaving the way he is at a particular moment. What is the motive behind his unconscious wish to break off the analytic work? What conflict is he trying to evade? Exhortation, suggestion, encouragement, prohibitions, any of a number of educational procedures that in other forms of therapy may be introduced at such a time must be carefully avoided. No matter how provocative, frustrating, or irritating the patient's behavior may be, the analyst never departs from his responsibility to make the patient understand his behavior. His attitude must remain at all times analytic.

How the analyst works can best be understood by examining three aspects of his experience while treating the patient. These are empathy, intuition and introspection. An analyst must be capable of empathizing with his patient. *Empathy* is a form of "emotional knowing," the experiencing of another's feelings. It is a special mode of perceiving. It presupposes an ability on the analyst's part to identify with his patient and to be able to share the patient's experience affectively as well as cognitively. The empathic process is central to the psychotherapeutic relationship as it is also a basic element in all human interaction. It finds its highest social expression in the aesthetic experience of the artist and his audience as well as in religion and other group phenomena. It is based upon the dynamic effect of unconscious fantasies shared in common (Beres & Arlow, 1974). There are two distinguishing features to empathy. First, the identification with the patient is only transient. Second, the therapist preserves his separateness from the object (the person being analyzed). The analyst's empathy makes it possible for him to receive and perceive both the conscious and unconscious processes operating in the patient.

It is impossible for the analyst at any

one time to keep in the foreground of his thinking all the things the patient has told him. How then does he arrive at the understanding of his patient? This is done *intuitively*. The myriads of data communicated by the patient are organized in the analyst's mind into meaningful configurations outside the scope of consciousness. What the analyst perceives as his understanding of the patient is actually the end product of a series of mental operations he has carried out unconsciously. He becomes aware of this by the process of *introspection* when the interpretation comes to his mind in the form of a free association. Not everything that comes to the analyst's mind in the course of a session is necessarily the correct interpretation. If he is working properly, it is usually some commentary on the patient's material. After introspection presents to the analyst's consciousness the result of his intuitive work, he does not necessarily impart this information to the patient immediately. He checks his idea with what he has learned from the patient and judges its validity in terms of contiguity, repetition, coherence, consistency, and convergence of theme, as outlined earlier. Intuition gives way to *cognitive elaboration*. In the long run, the validity of the interpretation is confirmed by the dynamic impact it has upon the patient's productions, that is, how it affects the equilibrium between impulse and defense in the patient's mind.

Management

Much has been written about the analyst's emotional response to the patient. The analyst is not an unfeeling, neutral automaton as presented in caricatures of psychoanalysis. He does respond emotionally to the therapeutic interaction, but these responses he keeps to himself. He regards them as a form of affective monitoring of the patient's productions. He uses his feelings as clues to understanding the direction that the patient's thoughts are taking. If he feels angry, sexually aroused, or frustrated, he must always consider the possibility that this is precisely the mood the patient wants to generate in him. It behooves him then to uncover the patient's motive in doing so.

There is much disagreement in analytic literature about the analyst's emotional response to the patient. Sometimes this is referred to as *countertransference,* the counterpart of the patient's transference onto the analysis. These issues have been revived by Annie Reich (1960). Strictly speaking, countertransference should be reserved to those situations in which a patient and his productions evoke in the analyst conflicts relating to some unresolved childhood fantasy of his own, causing him to misperceive, misinterpret, and misrespond to the analysand in terms of his own difficulties. Some analysts see the therapist's feelings as the operation of a mechanism known as *projective identification* (Little, 1951; Tower, 1956). They interpret the analyst's feelings as identical with those the patient is experiencing and they feel it beneficial to the course of the analysis for the analyst to discuss these feelings with the patient. For some analysts, this is the principal mode of treatment. It is safe to say that most analysts in the United States do not agree with this point of view. They try to understand the significance of what they feel about the patient. They do not discuss it with the patient.

Neurotic countertransference to the patient on the part of the analyst can constitute a real problem. Ordinarily the analyst will try to analyze the problem for himself. If this is ineffective, he may seek a consultation with a colleague. If the problem persists, or if it can be demonstrated to be more pervasive than had been suspected before and to apply to other patients as well, it indicates a need for the analyst to undergo further psychoanalysis himself. When the analyst finds that he cannot control his countertransference responses, he discusses the issues honestly and frankly with the patient and arranges for transfer to another analyst.

CASE EXAMPLE

It is impossible to capture in any condensed presentation the essence of the psychoanalytic experience. The course of an analysis proceeds unevenly. Seemingly fragmented material, arduously assembled over long periods, incompletely comprehended, suddenly may be brilliantly illuminated in a few dramatic sessions, when thousands of disparate threads organize themselves into a tapestry of meaning. Accordingly, any effort to describe in an overall way the course of psychoanalysis inevitably must sound oversimplified and slick. For practical purposes, only the main trends and conclusions can be described. The taxing day-to-day struggle with resistances and defenses has to be inserted by one's imagination. With these warnings in mind, let us proceed to the description of a relatively uncomplicated case.

The patient, whom we will call Tom, was a junior faculty member in a prominent eastern university. At age 30 he was still unmarried, although recently he had begun to live with a woman who had studied under him when she was a graduate student. Although Tom was a popular and successful teacher, much admired and appreciated by his students, he was unable to advance professionally because he could not fulfill the requirements for the Ph.D. degree. He had passed the requisite courses and had completed his doctoral thesis except for a few notes and bibliographical references. The next step was to defend his thesis before the committee but he could not do so as long as he had not put the final touches on his thesis. This he seemed unable to do. Several years had gone by and he was afraid that all the work he had done might have been in vain.

Tom had another problem that concerned his difficulties with women. He did not seem to be able to maintain a long-term relationship with any woman. For almost a year, he had been really fond of a woman, whom we will call Anita, and at her urging, finally decided to let her live with him. That was four months ago, and since that time, he had become increasingly irritable and found himself quarreling with Anita, criticizing many of the things she did around the house. He would have liked to get her to move out but he was not quite sure how to tell her. Since she had moved in with him, his sexual performance had deteriorated. Whereas previously he had suffered from premature ejaculation after entry, in the past few months he had had difficulty getting and maintaining an erection. The only times he had been able to perform well sexually were with women he knew to be frigid.

Tom's father, a practical and industrious man, operated a small business. Through judicious and conservative investments, he was able to acquire a comfortable fortune. Although he was proud of Tom, he was unable to share his son's intellectual interests. Tom's mother, on the other hand, was a delicate, sensitive, somewhat hypochondriacal woman. As a child, she had had rheumatic fever, which had left her with a mild case of mitral stenosis. After she was married, her doctors had advised her not to have any children. But her wish for a child overcame her doctor's admonition, and after a rather difficult labor, which left her exhausted for several months, she gave birth to Tom. When Tom was five years old, she had a miscarriage. She was much concerned with Tom's development. She saw to it that he was well fed and clean. He was toilet trained by 18 months and seemed to thrive in all ways.

During the preliminary interviews, Tom stated that he was not aware of any neurotic problems he may have had in childhood. He recalled no phobias or nightmares but had been told that at the age of five he was something of a behavior problem. He had become contrary and disobedient towards his mother and had refused to let her kiss him goodnight. Once when his mother was out of the kitchen for a while, he had emptied the contents of the refrigerator on the kitchen floor. However, after a few months, he seemed to change. He reverted to the obedient child he had been before but now he became a finicky eater and remained so thereafter.

Tom was not happy about starting school. Since his mother was ill, a favorite aunt accompanied him on the first day. He was quite shy and fearful of the other children. Once he learned how to read, however, things began to change. He was clearly the best student in the class and was well liked because he generously helped the slower students with their work. Through various activities, he soon became the most popular student in each class. He could keep his classmates amused by inventing funny stories. At lunchtime, he would readily share his sandwiches with his friends. In spite of this, he was quite fearful of the other children. He shied away from contact sports and never got involved in a fistfight. He welcomed the frequent absences from school occasioned by repeated respiratory infections. He could stay in bed, munch crackers, and eat to his heart's delight.

Tom's academic progress was not as good as his teachers and parents had expected. Being naturally gifted, it was easy for him in the lower grades to be outstanding without exerting any real effort. In high school and college, he refused to be "a greasy grind." No one was going to accuse him of putting in extra effort just to get good marks. Repeatedly, his teachers informed him and his parents that he was not working up to his potential. When he had to recite in class, his heart would pound and his face would flush even though he knew the answers to the questions posed by the teacher. On two occasions in college, on crucial examinations, he made gross blunders in interpreting the questions. Ordinarily, he should have failed, but his teachers, cognizant of his abilities, after discussing the matter with him, gave him passing grades. In the Ph.D. program, he fulfilled the requirements at a satisfactory level. It was when he had to work independently that his performance faltered.

Although he liked girls, he never seemed to get along well with them. When he was five and one-half years old, he pinched the infant sister of a friend of his when no one was looking. When she began to cry, he disclaimed any knowledge of why she might be doing so. When he was 12 or 13, he recalled having a crush on a lovely girl who lived next door, but he never did anything about it. At 14 he was extremely disappointed when a girl he took to a party spent most of the evening in the company of his best friend. He never dated the girl again, but, surprisingly, his relationship with his friend remained unchanged. He felt a definite antagonism toward attractive girls, thinking they were all vain and self-centered. With those girls he did date, he maintained a haughty, condescending air. He would rupture the relationship through some seemingly inadvertent act that hurt the girl's feelings. He came to realize on his own that there was something malicious about his gaucherie. On several occasions, while talking to one girl, he would address her with the name of another, a slip of the tongue hardly flattering to the girl involved.

By the time Tom began his first sessions on the couch, he had broken up with Anita. At least he had told her to move out, although they remained friends. From the very beginning, he was a "good patient." He followed the rules of the analytic situation and was agreeable and deferential. He soon began to display the vast fund of knowledge he had on a great variety of subjects. In the course of some observation, I made a comment indicating some familiarity with one of the subjects Tom was discussing. This proved very upsetting to him. For a few days, he became anxious and depressed. Intellectually, he was convinced he was superior to everyone else, at least in the areas of his expertise. The only reason it was not generally acknowledged was that he did not try hard enough. He realized that he wanted me, as his analyst, to admire him, but he had not realized that behind his deferential facade, he was intensely competitive. A few days later, he reported a recurrent fantasy. He imagined what would happen if a holdup man confronted him with a gun. He would tell the villain, "My life is too important to me. Money doesn't mean anything to me—just don't hurt me," and he would passively hand over his wallet.

In the clothes closet, Tom noted a fur coat belonging to the patient who preceded him. He left the door of the waiting room open a fraction and placed his chair in a position where he could see the patient as she left the consulting room. She was an attractive woman with blonde ringlets, just the type he despised. In the sessions, he began to make disparaging comments concerning her. "How easy it is to be a woman. You just have to be attractive and everything is taken care of for you." He was certain that I was more interested in her and that I would be taken in by her self-centered complacency and smugness. It would be impossible for him to compete with her for my attention. She had the inside track. He began to realize some of the reasons for his antagonism towards such women. He felt that a woman so attractive would never pay any attention to him.

Tom began one session in a state of almost uncontrollable fury. I had begun his session seven minutes later than usual. Although this was due to my lateness in arriving at the office, he was certain that I had done so because I was too fascinated with what my previous patient was telling me to let her go on time. He began the session by saying that while he was in the clothes closet, he had had the impulse to take the coat belonging to the previous patient and throw it on the floor. On the way to his appointment that morning, the bus was very crowded and he had become quite anxious. People jostled him and he felt he could not breathe. He became so uncomfortable that he left the bus a few blocks earlier and walked the rest of the way to the office. He thought the city was getting too overcrowded with too many people on the relief rolls who have to be supported by hard-working citizens like himself. They were all parasites like my previous patient who probably lived luxuriously on her husband's hard-earned income.

In the ensuing weeks, he began to talk about his relationship with Anita. Her presence in his house was intrusive. She did not contribute sufficiently to the maintenance of the household. At night, after they had had intercourse, he would want to get as far away from her as possible. In fact, it would have been better if he could have told her to leave the bed completely. Several times he had a quick fantasy of choking her. In fact, he recalled a definite sense of pleasure when he saw her leaving the house. The thing that seemed to irritate him the most, however, was how careless Anita was with the food. She would take a portion of meat larger than she could eat, so much had to be thrown out. In addition, she used to leave the refrigerator door open for long periods. He would have to dispose of the milk that had gone sour. He did make the observation, "After all, I'm an only child. It never was easy for me to share." He remembered that when he was six years old, a friend of his and his friend's sister had received a toy log cabin for Christmas. The two of them were fighting over who should occupy the house. He then remembered reading in the Bible years later how Jacob and Esau had fought with each other inside their mother's womb.

During this phase of the analysis, he began to have nightmares. The following dream is typical. The patient reported, "I was swimming in the lake, the water was dark and murky. Suddenly, I was surrounded by a school of small fish, the kind I used to raise when I was a kid. They seemed prepared to lunge at me as if to bite me. I woke up gasping for breath."

Tom learned to swim late. He was most comfortable in a pool. In an ocean, he feared being bitten by a large fish or being stung by an eel. Worst of all was swimming in a lake where the reeds growing from the muddy bottom could tangle him, draw him down, and drown him. Between the ages of 8 and 12, he raised tropical fish. He was always careful to be present when the baby fish were hatched to remove them from the tank so the other fish would not eat them.

Shortly before he was five, his mother told him that he might be getting a baby sister or brother. She explained that his father had introduced something like an egg into her and that had hatched and a future baby was swimming around in a special fluid inside her body. Clearly this news did not please Tom for the story goes that he pointed his ray gun at his mother's abdomen. It was during the same period that he emptied the contents of the refrigerator onto the kitchen floor. The pregnancy did not come to term. A few months later, the mother began to bleed and she was taken to the hospital. Tom saw some of the blood on the bathroom floor. From the behavior of the grownups, Tom could conclude that something terrible was happening. His mother did not come home from the hospital with a baby. Tom was relieved that he had his mother back again and that he did not have to share her and the food with a younger sibling. But unconsciously, he imagined that he was responsible for the baby's death. He fantasied that when he was inside the mother's body, he had destroyed the potential sibling, lacerating it with his teeth. About this time, he developed an aversion to eating eggs or fish, a characteristic that persisted into his adult life. Unconsciously, he feared that these representatives of siblings whom he had destroyed within his mother's body would retaliate by destroying him from within his own body. The attractive patient in the consultation room, the grimy welfare recipients in the bus, and the sloppy Anita in his apartment all represented potential siblings he wanted to oust and destroy because they threatened to invade his territory and rob him of his mother's love and food. He feared they in turn would do to him exactly what he intended to do to them, namely, destroy them with his mouth. As he overcame these fears, he became more giving with Anita. He invited her to share his apartment again. Sexually, his potency began to improve.

His former rival, the attractive blonde with the fur coat, began to intrigue him. What kind of sexual life did she lead? Through the partially open doorway of the waiting room he observed her comings and goings. Perhaps the analyst was interested in her sexually. She seemed the type to go for older men.

Before his session one day, Tom went to the bathroom and forgot to lock the door. As he was standing urinating, the blonde patient entered. Surprised and embarrassed, she withdrew in great confusion. Somehow Tom found the incident amusing and gratifying.

A short time later, he had the following dream, "I get up at night and go to the bathroom. I sit on the toilet and masturbate looking at the pictures in some porno girlie magazine. Suddenly I notice that there are two sets of large French windows. They swing open, people are passing by on what seems to be a boardwalk. I'm angry and embarrassed because they're all looking in on me. In the background I hear the sounds of a choo-choo train going by."

Immediately, he related the dream to the experience with the previous patient. From the French windows, he could place the setting of the dream exactly. There were such windows in a room he and his parents had occupied in a rooming house at the Jersey shore where they had gone for a two-week vacation. He was four and one-half years old at the time and he was much intrigued by what was going on in the adjoining room at the rooming house. Two young women shared the room. It had a sliding door that did not close completely. Through the half-inch-wide space, little Tom tried to watch the girls getting undressed and he was especially curious when their boyfriends came to visit them over the weekend.

There had been a wreck on the Asbury Park railroad just before he and his parents had arrived at the seashore. Several people had been killed and the derailed cars had not yet been removed. He recalled for the first time that as a child he had had frequent nightmares in which he heard the huffing and puffing of a locomotive train, the volume and pitch of the noise increasing in unbearable intensity until he awoke in great anxiety. As it turned out, the room he used to occupy at home was next to his parents' bedroom and from time to time he had been aware of strange noises coming from their room.

Going to the bathroom in the dream reminded him of a number of "dirty habits" he had. After his bowels moved, he was not too meticulous about wiping himself, so frequently there were stains on his underwear. His mother used to scold him about this. When he undressed at night, he would let his dirty clothes pile up on the floor for his mother to pick up in the morning. Later when he began to masturbate, he would ejaculate onto the bedsheet, leaving a stain that his mother would have to notice when she changed the bedding. He did something similar when he began to entertain girlfriends in his bedroom. In no way did he try to conceal from his parents who often were home what was going on in his bedroom and if any doubt lingered in their minds, he left unambiguous evidence in the form of a rumpled bed and a stained sheet, making clear to them exactly what had been taking place. He defended his life-long pattern of masturbating. "To begin with," he said, "I'm completely in control. No girl can disappoint me; I have all the satisfaction I want and I get it by myself."

Working through the themes suggested in this material was very rewarding. It was clear that the patient had witnessed his parents having intercourse during that summer vacation. His response was as complex as it was long-lasting. He felt left out, betrayed, and humiliated. In his mind, his mother became a whore who did dirty things and who preferred his father because he was more powerful and had a bigger penis, while he was so small and insignificant. In his subsequent nightmares of the sounds of the locomotive, he feared his own wishes that his parents would die during the act as the people had perished in the railroad accident. He no longer trusted his mother and this affected his attitude toward all women, especially after his sweetheart had turned her affections to his best friend when he was 12 years old. He became convinced that no woman would be interested in him and he decided "to show them." He would grow up, become outstanding and famous, and would show that he had no use for them. He would take his vengeance by doing to his mother (and women in general) what she had done to him. He would flaunt before her the signs of his own dirty sexual activity and he would leave her and other women embarrassed, angered, and confused as he had left the blonde patient who had come into the bathroom while he was urinating. After some of these conflicts had been worked through, the blonde patient no longer seemed so haughty, and if Anita

did not close the door to the refrigerator so promptly, it no longer seemed catastrophic.

Tom's interests now turned to his professional work, which for a long time he had been treating lightly. He became more demanding of his students and less deferential to the chairman of his department. In fact, he realized how often he had thought of himself being the chairman. Behind his "good guy" affability, he could see how competitive and ambitious he really was. He decided that he was being underpaid, that he needed more money, and that the thing to do was to get on with his work and earn the Ph.D. degree. Without the Ph.D., he felt like a boy. It was time to become a man.

No sooner had he begun to work on his thesis than the old inhibition returned. He blocked on using key references from important authorities in the field. He thought that I would accuse him of being a plagiarist, stealing his teacher's ideas. Guilt over stealing was not a new theme in his life. During his latency years, for a few months, in the company of a friend, he went on a stealing spree. He took some of the small change his father had left on the dresser and went to his mother's pocketbook looking for bills he knew his father had put there. From the most popular boy in his class, a born leader, he stole a fountain pen, which he hid under his shirt. From a cousin whom he admired for his strong physique and athletic ability, he stole a textbook of an advanced grade. As he put it, "I devoured the book voraciously."

From childhood on, stealing was prominent in his fantasy life. His favorite story was "Jack and the Beanstalk." "I loved to hear again and again how Jack ran off with the giant's money." His favorite movie was *The Thief of Baghdad;* the most exciting part was where the thief,

Ali, goes to the mountains, climbs the great statue of the god, and steals from his forehead the largest jewel in the world, one that bestows on its owner magic, knowledge, and wealth. It reminded him of the myth of Prometheus who stole knowledge from the gods and of his own Promethean wish for omniscience. In this connection, he remembered that he had forgotten to return some books he had borrowed from the university library several years back. He recalled going with his father, at the age of four, to a turkish bath. He was awed by the gigantic size of his father's penis and wanted to reach up and touch it.

Coming a bit late for his session one day, he saw the blonde patient walking toward him on the street. He nodded to her and she acknowledged his greeting with a friendly smile. He felt he should have stopped to talk with her; perhaps he could have arranged for a date that ultimately could lead to an affair. As he entered the lobby of the building, he found himself caught up in a fantasy of a violent quarrel with me because I was forbidding him to have anything to do with the patient. Going up, he thought the elevator man seemed ominously threatening. This material led to the theme that I was standing in the way of his sexual freedom and of his achieving manhood, just as earlier in life, he had felt his father had stood in the way.

On two occasions, he lost the bill for the previous month's analysis and brought in a check for several sessions fewer than he was actually supposed to pay. He came to realize that he wanted to steal from me not just my money, but also my profession and my powers. He developed a craving for food before he came to the sessions; he was particularly fond of hot dogs and chocolate bars. For a while, he thought it would be a good idea to

become an analyst himself. He could do as well, if not better. During this time, he became increasingly irritable and anxious, and the work he had undertaken to complete his Ph.D. thesis came to a complete standstill.

The anxiety that appeared during this phase of the analysis was connected to three types of dreams or fantasies. They were (1) dreams in which there was a danger of being devoured by sharks, dogs, or lions roaming in the jungle; (2) fantasies of a confrontation with a holdup man (only now Tom would often see himself fighting back); and (3) fantasies and dreams of struggle with an adversary in an enclosed space: the lobby of my building, a tunnel, or the basement of his childhood home. He had several dreams in which he saw himself perched at the window of his basement with a gun ready to defend the house against assault by intruders.

From his associations, it became clear in time that the feared adversary who threatened to mutilate him physically represented at different times myself, his father, the chief of his department, and the man who was to serve as chairman of the oral examining board for the Ph.D. examination. An examination represented to him a bloody, competitive struggle, in which one either kills or is killed. It also had the unconscious significance of a trial where one is pronounced innocent or guilty. To pass the examination was to be permitted to enter the council of elders, to have the right to be sexual, to have a woman, and to become a father. He told Anita that until he got the Ph.D., he could not think of marrying her, but would do so as soon as he passed. Unconsciously he felt he could not become a husband or father as long as he was in analysis, which meant to him as long as his father was alive. Accordingly, successful termination of treatment had the unconscious significance of killing his father. Fear of retaliation for his murderous wishes against authority figures intensified. His impotence grew more severe; unconsciously he imagined that within the woman's vagina was the adversary who would kill or mutilate him. During this period, he recapitulated the events and fantasies of his childhood in which he competed with his father for his mother's attention. The experiences between the ages of four and five proved to be the crucial ones. They centered around the boy's hostility and envy of the father due to having slept in the same room with his parents at the Jersey coast. He recollected and reexperienced surges of tender loving feelings for his mother who risked her life giving birth to him. He felt he had to repay her in kind. If only he could restore her heart to its original condition. As a child, he would fantasize about giving her new life in the form of a child.

After many months of working through the anxieties of these unconscious fantasies of childhood, the patient began to make progress in his work and he became potent again. He was well prepared for his Ph.D. oral exam. The day before he took the examination, confident that he would pass, while giving a talk before a large audience in a lecture hall, he had the following fantasy: his eye had fastened on the elaborate chandelier that hung from the ceiling. He imagined himself reaching up with one hand and tearing the chandelier out of its roots from the ceiling. He recalled how as a child he had been greatly impressed when he saw his father, seemingly gigantic, standing on a ladder reaching up to the ceiling to change an electric bulb. His Promethean wish was about to be fulfilled. Indeed, he did succeed.

Tom married Anita after he got the Ph.D. Five years after finishing the analysis, he reported that he was doing well in his work. He had been promoted and would soon be eligible for tenure. He was the proud father of a daughter and his wife was expecting a second child. Anita continued to forget to close the refrigerator door.

SUMMARY

As a system of thought and a technique for dealing with mental illness, psychoanalysis has been developing and changing over the years. What seemed at first a monolithic theory is now being examined critically from many different points of view. Technical innovations and reformulations of theoretical concepts are appearing in ever-increasing numbers. In addition, the literature of psychoanalysis has expanded enormously and there are special volumes dedicated to psychoanalysis and sociology, anthropology, history of childhood, aesthetics, developmental psychology, religion, and biography. Clinical investigation in the therapeutic setting according to the rules of the psychoanalytic situation remains the fundamental base of psychoanalytic knowledge and will clearly continue to be so in the future. Many alternative forms of psychotherapy appear from time to time on the horizon, draw great attention to themselves, but soon fade from the scene. Psychoanalysis has remained a steady, reliable, and growing discipline.

Two points have to be borne in mind about the position of psychoanalysis as therapy and a system of thought. Not all forms of mental disturbance can or should be treated by psychoanalysis. Paradoxically, the demands of psychoanalysis require the cooperation of a patient with a fairly healthy ego, well motivated to change, and capable of facing himself honestly. For properly selected patients, psychoanalysis can offer the promise of helping the individual attain the best possible solution that can be realized from overcoming inner conflicts. It does not pretend to create supermen perfectly balanced, in harmony with themselves and the universe.

The second point to be emphasized is that the reliability of the conclusions of psychoanalytic investigation diminish the farther one gets away from the clinical base of the psychoanalytic situation. Whenever psychoanalytic knowledge and insights are applied outside the analytic situation, one must take into consideration the possibility of innumerable alternative hypotheses and influences.

Because of the changing nature of the psychopathology of our time, notably the great increase in patients suffering from narcissistic, neurotic, and character disorders, from mild perversions and addictions, one can anticipate new discoveries, fresh observations, original theoretical formulations, and innovative technical procedures.

ANNOTATED BIBLIOGRAPHY

For those who want to attain deeper and more immediate knowledge of psychoanalysis as theory and practice, the following books are recommended.

Brenner, C. *An elementary textbook of psychoanalysis.* New York: International Universities Press, 1973.

There is no better presentation of current psychoanalytic theory than this volume by Charles Brenner, which has become a world-wide introduction to psychoanalysis and has been translated into nine languages. It is the most comprehensive, systematic, and intelligible presentation of the subject, a worthy companion piece to Anna Freud's *The Ego and the Mechanisms of Defense.* The theoretical development flows smoothly, logically, and cautiously. In addition to the basic theory of psychoanalysis, the book describes the part played by unconscious forces in day-to-day living and surveys the remarkable contribution of psychoanalysis to human knowledge. Current trends in the field are assessed and problems still requiring exploration are examined.

Freud, A. *The ego and the mechanisms of defense.* (1936) *The writings of Anna Freud.* Vol. 2. New York: International Universities Press, 1966.

Perhaps the finest and clearest writing style in psychoanalysis belongs to Anna Freud. *The Ego and the Mechanisms of Defense* is an established classic for its lucidity in portraying the theoretical implications of the structural theory and its application to problems of technique. In a relatively small volume, the author offers a definitive presentation of the psychoanalytic concept of conflict, of the functioning of the anxiety signal and of the many ways in which the ego attempts to establish a stable homeostasis between impulse and defense. The sections on the origin of the superego, on identity, and on the transformations in adolescence afford the best picture of how the postoedipal child becomes an adult.

Freud, S. *Introductory lectures on psychoanalysis.* London: Hogart Press, 1915-1917.

These lectures comprise volumes 15 and 16 of *The Complete Psychological Works of Sigmund Freud.* The books constitute a set of lectures Freud gave at the University of Vienna. His lectures are a model of lucidity, clarity, and organization. Taking a new and complicated field of knowledge, Freud develops his thesis step by step, beginning with simple, acceptable, commonsense concepts, and advancing his argument consistently until the new and the startling ideas that he was to place before his audience seem like the inevitable and logical consequences of each individual's own reflection. *The Introductory Lectures on Psychoanalysis* remains to this day the easiest and most direct approach to the understanding of psychoanalysis.

Hartmann, H. *Essays on ego psychology.* New York: International Universities Press, 1964.

For the advanced reader who is interested in the broadest theoretical applications of psychoanalysis to psychology, science, and sociology, there is no more authoritative exposition than this book of essays by the outstanding American psychoanalytic theoretician of the twentieth century. Hartmann discusses the concept of health, rational and irrational action, and the application of psychoanalytic concepts to social science and developmental psychology. This is not an easy set of essays to read but the meticulous student who wants to be exposed to the broadest and highest level of analytic theory will be well rewarded for his or her efforts.

Jones, E. *The life and work of Sigmund Freud.* New York: Basic Books, 1953-57.

The three-volume biography of Freud is one of the great biographies of our time. It captures the intellectual and spiritual ambience of Freud's period in history. It is a remarkable portrayal of the personality and thought of a genius. In addition, this book contains an accurate and readable summary of almost all of Freud's important contributions. It traces the history and the personalities of the psychoanalytic movement to the death of Freud in 1939.

CASE READINGS

Arlow, J. A. Communication and character: A clinical study of a man raised by deaf mute parents. *Psychoanalytic Study of the Child,* 1976, *31,* 139-163.

Bornstein, B. The analysis of the phobic child, some problems of theory and technique in child analysis. *Psychoanalytic Study of the Child,* 1949, *4,* 181-226.

Freud, S. The rat man. In S. Freud, *Three case histories.* New York: Crowell-Collier, 1963. Reprinted in D. Wedding and R. J. Corsini (Eds.), *Great Cases in Psychotherapy.* Itasca, Il, F. E. Peacock, 1979.

Winnicott, D. W. (with A. Flarsheim). Fragment of an analysis. In P. L. Giovacchini, *Tactics and technique in psychoanalytic therapy.* New York: Science House, 1972, pp. 455-693.

REFERENCES

Abraham, K. The influence of oral erotism on character formation. *Selected papers of Karl Abraham, Vol. 1,* 393-496. London: Hogarth Press and the Institute of Psychoanalysis, 1924.

Alexander, F. *The medical value of psychoanalysis.* New York: Norton, 1932.

Ansbacher, H., & Ansbacher, R. (Eds.) *The individual psychology of Alfred Adler.* New York: Basic Books, 1956.

Arlow, J. A. Conflict, regression and symptom formation. *International Journal of Psychoanalysis,* 1963, *44,* 12-22.

Arlow, J. A. Character perversion. In I. M. Marcus (Ed.), *Currents in psychoanalysis.* New York: International Universities Press, 1972, *20,* 317-336.

Arlow, J. A., & Brenner, C. *Psychoanalytic concepts in the structural theory.* New York: International Universities Press, 1964.

Berenfeld, S. Freud's earliest theories and the school of Helmholtz. *Psychoanalytic Quarterly,* 1944, *13,* 341-362.

Beres, D., & Arlow, J. A. Fantasy and identification in empathy. *Psychoanalytic Quarterly,* 1974, *43,* 4-25.

Bowlby, J. The nature of the child's ties to the mother. *International Journal of Psychoanalysis,* 1958, *39,* 350-373.

Brenner, C. The psychoanalytic concept of aggression. *International Journal of Psychoanalysis,* 1971, *52,* 137-144.

Brenner, C. *An elementary textbook of psychoanalysis.* New York: International Universities Press, 1973.

Breuer, J., & Freud, S. *Studies on hysteria.* Standard edition of the complete psychological works of Freud. Vol. 2. London: Hogarth Press, 1895.

Burton, A. (Ed.), *Encounter*. San Francisco: Jossey-Bass, 1969.

Ellis, A. *Reason and emotion in psychotherapy*. New York: Lyle Stuart, 1970.

Erikson, E. *Identity, youth and crisis*. New York: Norton, 1968.

Eysenck, H. J. The effects of psychotherapy. *International Journal of Psychiatry*, 1965, *1*, 99-142.

Federn, P. *Ego psychology and the psychoses*. New York: Basic Books, 1952.

Feldman, F. Results of psychoanalysis in clinic case assignments. *Journal of the American Psychoanalytic Association*, 1968, *16*, 274-300.

Fenichel, O. *Zehn Jahre Berliner psychoanalytischer Institut*. Vienna: International Psychoanalytischer Verlag, 1930.

Fenichel, O. *The psychoanalytic theory of neurosis*. New York: Norton, 1945.

Freud, A. *The ego and mechanisms of defense*. New York: International Universities Press, 1936.

Freud, A. Observations on child development. *Psychoanalytic Study of the Child*, 1951, *6*, 18-30.

*Freud, S. *The neuropsychoses of defense*. Standard Edition, Vol. 3, 45-70, 1894.

Freud, S. *Studies on hysteria*. Standard Edition, Vol. 2, 1895.

Freud, S. *The interpretation of dreams*. Standard Edition, Vol. 4, 1900.

Freud, S. *The psychopathology of everyday life*. Standard Edition, Vol. 6, 1901.

Freud, S. *Jokes and their relationship to the unconscious*. Standard Edition, Vol. 8, 1905. (a)

Freud, S. *Three essays on sexuality*. Standard Edition, Vol. 7, 135-248, 1905. (b)

Freud, S. *Formulations regarding the two principles of mental functioning*. Standard Edition, Vol. 12, 218-228, 1911.

Freud, S. *Totem and taboo*. Standard Edition, Vol. 13, 1-161, 1913.

Freud, S. *The history of the psychoanalytic movement*. Standard Edition, Vol. 14, 7-66, 1914. (a)

Freud, S. *On narcissism, an introduction.*

Standard Edition, Vol. 14, 73-104, 1914. (b)

Freud, S. *Repression*. Standard Edition, Vol. 14, 143, 1915. (a)

Freud, S. *The unconscious*. Standard Edition, Vol. 14, 161, 1915. (b)

Freud, S. *On transformations of instinct as exemplified in anal erotism*. Standard Edition, Vol. 17, 125-34, 1917.

Freud, S. *Beyond the pleasure-principle*. Standard Edition, Vol. 18, 7, 1920.

Freud, S. *Group psychology and the analysis of the ego*. Standard Edition, Vol. 18, 69-144, 1921.

Freud, S. *The ego and the id*. Standard Edition, Vol. 19, 13-68, 1923.

Freud, S. *An autobiographical study*. Standard Edition, Vol. 20, 77-176, 1925.

Freud, S. *Inhibitions, symptoms and anxiety*. Standard Edition, Vol. 20, 87-128, 1926.

Freud, S. *Analysis terminable and interminable*. Standard Edition, Vol. 23, 216-254, 1937.

Fromm, E. *The sane society*. New York: Holt, Rinehart & Winston, 1955.

Fromm-Reichmann, F. *Principles of intensive psychotherapy*. Chicago: University of Chicago Press, 1950.

Glasser, W. *Reality therapy*. New York: Julian Press, 1967.

Greenacre, P. Re-evaluation of the process of working through. *International Journal of Psychoanalysis*, 1956, *37*, 439-444.

Greenacre, P. The influence of infantile trauma on genetic pattern. *Emotional Growth*, 1967, *1*, 216-299.

Greenson, R. *The technique and practice of psychoanalysis*. New York: International Universities Press, 1967.

Grinstein, A. (Ed.) *The index of psychoanalytic writings*. 14 vols. issued to date. New York: International Universities Press, 1971.

Hartmann, H. *Ego psychology and the problem of adaptation*. New York: International Universities Press, 1939.

Hartmann, H., & Kris, E. The genetic approach to psychoanalysis. *Psychoanalytic Study of the Child*, 1945, *1*, 11-30.

Hartmann, H., Kris, E., & Loewenstein, R. N. Comments on the formation of psychic structure. *Psychoanalytic Study of the Child*, 1946, *2*, 11-38.

Hartmann, H., Kris, E., & Loewenstein, R. N. Notes on the theory of aggression. *Psychoanalytic Study of the Child*, 1949, *4*, 9-36.

*All references to Freud are from the *Complete Psychological Works of Sigmund Freud*, edited by James Strachey, and published by Hogarth Press, London.

Horney, K. *New ways in psychoanalysis.* New York: Norton, 1940.

Jacobson, E. The self and the object world: Vicissitudes of their infantile cathexes and their influence on ideational and affective development. *Psychoanalytic Study of the Child,* 1954, *9,* 75-127.

Jones, E. *The life and work of Sigmund Freud.* New York: Basic Books, 1953.

Jung, C. *The psychology of dementia praecox.* New York & Washington: Nervous and Mental Disease Publishing Co., 1909.

Kernberg, O. The therapy of patients with borderline personality organization. *International Journal of Psychoanalysis,* 1968, *49,* 600-619.

Klein, M. *The psychoanalysis of children.* London: Hogarth Press, The Institute of Psychoanalysis, 1932.

Kohut, H. *The analysis of the self.* Monograph Series of the *Psychoanalytic Study of the Child.* No. 4. New York: International Universities Press, 1971.

Kris, E. Preconscious mental processes. *Psychoanalytic Quarterly,* 1950, *19,* 540-560.

Lewin, B. D. Sleep, the mouth and the dream screens. *Psychoanalytic Quarterly,* 1946, *15,* 419-434.

Lewin, B. D. Mania and sleep. *Psychoanalytic Quarterly,* 1949, *18,* 419-433.

Little, M. Countertransference and the patient's response to it. *International Journal of Psychoanalysis,* 1951, *32,* 321-340.

Loewenstein, R. Remarks on some variations in psychoanalytic technique. *International Journal of Psychoanalysis,* 1958, *39,* 202-210.

Lorenz, C. *King Solomon's ring.* New York: Crowell, 1952.

Mahler, M., Pine, F., & Bergman, A. *The psychological birth of the human infant.* New York: Basic Books, 1975.

Meltzoff, J., & Kornreich, M. *Research in psychotherapy.* New York: Atherton Press, 1970.

Nunberg, H. The will to recovery. *International Journal of Psychoanalysis,* 1926, *7,* 64-78.

Perls, F., Hefferline, R., & Goodman, P. *Gestalt therapy.* New York: Julian Press, 1951.

Peterfreund, E. Information systems and psychoanalysis. *Psychological Issues Monograph.* No. 25-26. New York: International Universities Press, 1971.

Pfeffer, A. Z. The meaning of the analyst after analysis: A contribution to the theory of therapeutic results. *Journal of the American Psychoanalytic Association,* 1963, *11,* 229-244.

Racker, E. A contribution to the problem of countertransference. *International Journal of Psychoanalysis,* 1953, *34,* 313-324.

Rangell, L. On the cacophony of human relations. *Psychoanalytic Quarterly,* 1973, *42,* 325-348.

Rapaport, D. *The organization and pathology of thought.* New York: Columbia University Press, 1951.

Reich, A. Further remarks on countertransference. *International Journal of Psychoanalysis,* 1960, *41,* 389-395.

Reich, A. *Psychoanalytic contributions.* New York: International Universities Press, 1973.

Rogers, C. *Client-centered therapy.* New York: Houghton Mifflin, 1951.

Rosenfeld, H. Consideration concerning the psychoanalytic approach to acute and chronic schizophrenia. *International Journal of Psychoanalysis,* 1954, *35,* 135-140.

Rubinstein, B. B. Explanation and mere description: A metascientific examination of certain aspects of the psychoanalytic theory of motivation in motives and thought. Psychoanalytic essays in honor of David Rapaport. R. R. Holt (Ed.), *Psychological Issues Monograph.* Nos. 18-19, 20-79. New York: International Universities Press, 1967.

Sachs, H. *The creative unconscious.* Cambridge, Mass.: Sci-Art Publishers, 1942.

Schafer, R. *A new language of psychoanalysis.* New Haven & London: Yale University Press, 1976.

Schmideberg, M. After the analysis. *Psychoanalytic Quarterly,* 1938, *7,* 122-142.

Schultz, W. C. *Joy.* New York: Grove Press, 1967.

Searles, H. F. *Collected papers on schizophrenia and related subjects.* New York: International Universities Press, 1965.

Spitz, R. The primal cavity: A contribution to the genesis of perception and its role in psychoanalytic theory. *Psychoanalytic Study of the Child,* 1955, *10,* 215-240.

Sullivan, H. S. *The interpersonal theory of psychiatry.* New York: Norton, 1953.

Tinbergern, N. *The study of instinct.* London: Oxford Universities Press, 1951.

Tower, L. E. Countertransference. *Journal of*

the *American Psychoanalytic Association,* 1956, *224,* 265.

Wallerstein, R. S., & Smelser, N. J. Articulations and applications. *International Journal of Psychoanalysis,* 1969, *50,* 693-710.

Weigert, E. *The courage to love.* New Haven: Yale University Press, 1970.

Winnicott, D. W. Transitional objects and transitional phenomena: A study of the first not-me possession. *International Journal of Psychoanalysis,* 1953, *34,* 89-97.

Wolpe, J. *Psychotherapy by reciprocal inhibition.* Stanford, Calif.: Stanford University Press, 1958.

Zetzel, E. R. *The capacity for emotional growth: Theoretical and clinical contributions to psychoanalysis.* New York: International Universities Press, 1970.

Zilboorg, G., & Henry, G. W. *A history of medical psychology.* New York: Norton, 1941.

3

Adlerian Psychotherapy

HAROLD H. MOSAK

OVERVIEW

Adlerian psychology (Individual Psychology), the personality theory and therapeutic system developed by Alfred Adler, views the person holistically as a creative, responsible, "becoming" individual moving toward fictional goals within one's phenomenal field. It holds that one's life-style is sometimes self-defeating because of inferiority feelings. The individual with "psychopathology" is discouraged rather than sick, and the therapeutic task is to encourage the person, to activate one's social interest, and to develop a new life-style through relationship, analysis, and action methods.

Basic Concepts

Adlerian psychology is predicated upon certain assumptions and postulates that differ in significant ways from the Freudian "womb" from which Adlerian psychology emerged. Adler throughout his lifetime credited Freud with primacy in the development of a dynamic psychology. His debt to Freud for explicating the purposefulness of symptoms and for expressing the notion that dreams were meaningful was consistently acknowledged. The influence of early childhood experiences in personality development

constitutes still another point of agreement. Freud emphasized the role of psychosexual development and the Oedipus complex while Adler focused upon the effects of children's perceptions of their family constellation and their struggle to find a place of significance within it.

Adlerian basic assumptions can be expressed as follows:

1. All behavior occurs in a social context. Man is born into an environment with which he must engage in reciprocal relations. The oft-quoted statement by the Gestalt psychologist Kurt Lewin that "behavior is a function of person and environment" bears a striking parallel to Adler's contention that people cannot be studied in isolation (1929).

2. A corollary of the first axiom is that Individual Psychology is an interpersonal psychology. How individuals interact with the others sharing "this crust of earth" (Adler, 1958, p. 6) is paramount. Transcending interpersonal transactions is the development of the feeling of being a part of a larger social whole, the feeling of being socially embedded, the willingness to contribute in the communal life for the common weal—movements that Adler (1964b) incorporated under the heading of *Gemeinschaftsgefühl*, or social interest.

3. Adlerian psychology rejects reductionism in favor of holism. Jan Smuts (1961), who introduced the concept of *holism*, and Adler engaged in a correspondence that unfortunately has never been published. The Adlerian demotes part-functions from the central investigative focus in favor of studying the whole person and how one moves through life. This renders the polarities of *conscious* and *unconscious, mind* and *body, approach* and *avoidance, ambivalence* and *conflict* meaningless except as subjective experiences of the whole person, that is, people behave *as if* the conscious mind moves in one direction while the unconscious mind moves in another. From the external observer's viewpoint all part functions are subordinate functions of the individual's goals and style of life.

4. *Conscious* and *unconscious* are both in the service of the individual who uses them to further personal goals. Adler (1963a) treats *unconscious* as an adjective rather than a noun, thus avoiding reifying the concept. That which is unconscious is the nonunderstood. With Otto Rank, Adler felt that man knows more than he understands. *Conflict*, defined as intrapersonal by others, is defined as a "one step forward and one step backward movement," the net effect being to maintain the individual at a point "dead center." Although he experiences himself in the throes of a conflict, unable to move, in reality he *creates* these antagonistic feelings, ideas, and values because he is unwilling to move in the direction of solving his problems (Mosak & LeFevre, 1976).

5. The understanding of the individual requires the understanding of one's *cognitive organization,* the life-style. The latter concept refers to the convictions the individual develops early in life to help him organize experience, to understand it, to predict it, and to control it. *Convictions* are conclusions derived from the individual's apperceptions, and they constitute a biased mode of apperception. Consequently, a *life-style* is neither right nor wrong, normal or abnormal, but merely the "spectacles" through which a person views himself in relationship to the way in which he perceives life. Subjectivity rather than so-called objective evaluation becomes the major tool for understanding the person. As Adler (1958) wrote, "We must be able to see with his eyes and listen with his ears" (p. 72).

6. Behavior may change throughout a person's lifespan in accordance with both the immediate demands of the situation and the long-range goals inherent in the life-style. The life-style remains relatively constant through life unless the convictions change through the mediation of psychotherapy. Although the definition of *psychotherapy* customarily refers to what transpires within a consulting room, a broader view of psychotherapy would include the fact that life in itself may be and is often psychotherapeutic.

7. According to the Adlerian conception, man is not pushed by causes, that is, one is not determined by heredity and environment. "Both are giving only the frame and the influences which are answered by the individual in regard to his styled creative power" (Ansbacher & Ansbacher, 1956). People move toward self-selected goals, which they feel will give them a place in the world, will provide them with security, and will preserve their self-esteem. Life is a dynamic striving. "The life of the human soul is not a 'being' but a 'becoming' " (Adler, 1963a, p. ix).

8. The central striving of human beings has been variously described as completion (Adler, 1958), perfection (Adler,

1964a), superiority (Adler, 1926), self-realization (Horney, 1951), self-actualization (Goldstein, 1939), competence (White, 1957), and mastery (Adler, 1926). Adler distinguishes between such strivings in terms of the direction a striving takes. If strivings are solely for the individual's greater glory, he considers them socially useless and in extreme conditions, characteristic of mental problems. On the other hand, if the strivings are for the purpose of overcoming life's problems, the individual is engaged in the striving for self-realization, in contributing to his fellowman, and in making the world a better place to live.

9. Moving through life, the individual is confronted with alternatives. Since Adlerians are either non determinists or soft determinists, the conceptualization of man as a creative, choosing, self-determined decision maker permits him to choose the goals he wants to pursue. He may select useful, socially contributive goals or he may devote himself to the useless side of life. He may choose to be task oriented or he may, as does the neurotic, concern himself with his own superiority, protecting himself from threats to his sense of personal worth.

10. The freedom to choose (McArthur, 1958) introduces the concepts of *value* and *meaning* into psychology, concepts anathema at the time (1931) that Adler wrote his *What Life Should Mean to You*. The greatest value for the Adlerian is *Gemeinschaftsgefühl,* or social interest (Ansbacher, 1968). Although Adler contends that it is an innate feature of man, at least as potential, acceptance of this criterion is not absolutely necessary. People possess the capacity for coexisting and interrelating with others. Indeed, the "iron logic of social living" (Adler, 1959) demands that we do so. Even in severe psychopathology, total extinction of social interest does not occur. Even the

psychotic retains some commonality with "normal" people.

As Rabbi Akiva noted two millennia ago, "The greatest principle of living is to love one's neighbor as oneself." If we regard ourselves as fellow human beings with fellow feeling, we are socially contributive people interested in the common welfare and, by Adler's pragmatic definition of *normality,* mentally healthy (Dreikurs, 1969; Shoben, 1957).

If my feeling derives from my observation and conviction that life and people are hostile and I am inferior, I may divorce myself from the direct solution of life's problems and strive for personal superiority through overcompensation, through wearing a mask, through withdrawal, through attempting only safe tasks where the outcome promises to be successful, and through other devices for protecting my self-esteem. Adler said the neurotic in terms of his movement displayed a "hesitating attitude" toward life (1964a). Also, the neurotic was described as a "yes-but" personality (Adler, 1934); at still other times, he was described as an "If only . . . " personality (Adler, 1964a). "If only I didn't have these symptoms, I'd. . . ." The latter provided the rationale for "The Question," a device Adler used for the purposes of differential diagnosis as well as for an understanding of the individual's task avoidance.

11. Since Adlerians are concerned with process, little diagnosis is done in terms of nomenclature. Differential diagnosis between functional and organic disorder does often present a problem. Since all behavior is purposeful, a *psychogenic* sympton will have a psychological purpose and an *organic* symptom will have a somatic purpose. An Adlerian would ask "The Question" (Adler, 1964a; Dreikurs, 1958, 1962), "If I had a magic wand or a magic pill which would eliminate your

symptom immediately, what would be different in your life?" If the patient answers, "I'd go out more often socially" or "I'd write my book," the symptom would most likely be psychogenic. If the patient responds, "I wouldn't have this excruciating pain," the symptom would most likely be organic.

An internist referred a woman to an Adlerian therapist because she complained of falling sensations. He thought it was an hysterical symptom. She told the therapist that the symptoms first occurred after breaking her engagement with her fiancé. She was asked "The Question." The patient said, "If I got better, then I wouldn't have these falling sensations." The therapist then asked the internist to reexamine the patient. She was given more tests; all were negative. The physician wanted to discharge her from the hospital and return her to the therapist who asked the internist to keep her in the hospital and continue the tests. Several days later, the physician telephoned, and asked, "How did you know my patient had Von Recklinghausen's disease?" The therapist not only did not know she had Von Recklinghausen's disease, he did not know what Von Recklinghausen's disease was. However, the patient was spared psychotherapy and received the medical treatment she required.

12. Life presents challenges in the form of the life tasks. Adler named three of these explicitly but referred to two others without specifically naming them (Dreikurs & Mosak, 1966). The original three tasks were those of *society, work,* and *sex.* We have already alluded to the first. However, since we exist in two sexes, we must also learn how to relate to that fact. We must define our sex roles, partly on the basis of cultural definitions and stereotypes, and train ourselves to relate to the *other*, not the *opposite*, sex. Other people, of either sex, do not represent the

enemy. They are our fellows with whom we must learn to cooperate. Third, since no person can claim self-sufficiency, we are interdependent. Each of us is dependent upon the labor of other people. In turn, they are dependent upon our contribution. Work thus becomes essential for human survival. The cooperative individual assumes this role willingly, and cheerfully accepts a part in the human enterprise.

A fourth (Dreikurs & Mosak, 1967) and fifth task (Mosak & Dreikurs, 1967) have been described. Although Adler alluded to the *spiritual,* he never specifically named it (Jahn & Adler, 1964). But each of us must deal with the problem of defining the nature of his universe, the existence and nature of God, and how one relates to these concepts. Finally, we must cope with ourselves. William James (1890) made the distinction between the self as subject and the self as object, and it is as imperative, for the sake of mental health, that good relations exist between the "I" and the "me" as between the "I" and other people.

13. Since life is bigger than we are and constantly provides challenges, living life demands courage (Neuer, 1936). Courage is not an *ability* one either possesses or lacks. Nor is courage synonymous with bravery, like falling on a grenade to save one's buddies from injury or death. *Courage* refers to the *willingness* to engage in risk-taking behavior when one either does not know the consequences or when the consequences might be adverse. Anyone is *capable* of courageous behavior provided the person is *willing*. Our willingness will depend upon many variables, internal and external, such as the life-style convictions, the degree of social interest, the extent of risk as the individual appraises it, and whether we are task oriented or prestige oriented. Since life offers few guarantees, all living re-

quires risk taking. It would require very little courage to live if we were perfect, omniscient, omnipotent. The question we must each answer is whether we have the courage to live despite the knowledge of our imperfection (Lazarsfeld, 1966).

14. Life has no intrinsic meaning. *We* give meaning to life, each of us in his own fashion. We declare it to be meaningful, meaningless, an absurdity, a prison sentence (cf., the adolescent's justification for doing as he pleases—"I didn't ask to be born"), a vale of tears, a preparation for the next world, and so on. Dreikurs (1957, 1971) maintained that the meaning of life resided in doing for others, in contributing to social life and to social change. Viktor Frankl (1963) believes the meaning of life lies in love, expressing a psychological variation of the 1950's popular song, "Nature Boy" in which the refrain went, "The greatest thing you'll ever learn is to love and be loved in return." The meaning we attribute to life will "determine" our behavior. We will behave *as if* life were really in accord with our perceptions, and, therefore, certain meanings will have greater practical utility than others. Optimists will live an optimistic life, take their chances, and not be discouraged by failure and adversity. They will be able to distinguish between failing and being a failure. Pessimists will refuse to be engaged with life, refuse to try, sabotage their efforts if they do attempt, and, through their methods of operation, endeavor to confirm their pre-existing pessimistic anticipations (Krausz, 1935).

Other Systems

Students often have asked, "Do you Adlerians believe in sex too?" The question is not always asked facetiously. Freud accorded sex the status of the master motive in behavior. Adler merely categorized sex as one of several tasks the individual was required to solve. Freud employed esoteric jargon and Adler favored common-sense language. One story has it that a psychiatrist took Adler to task after a lecture, denigrating his approach with the criticism, "You're only talking common sense," to which Adler replied, "I wish more psychiatrists did." We can place other differences between these two men in columnar form.

A more extended comparison of Freud's and Adler's concepts of man may be found in articles by H. W. von Sassen (1967) and Otto Hinrichsen (1913).

Adler and the neo-Freudians

Adler once proclaimed that he was more concerned that his theories survived than that people remembered to associate his theories with his name. His wish apparently was granted. In discussing Adler's influence upon contemporary psychological theory and practice, Henri Ellenberger (1970) comment, "It would not be easy to find another author from which so much has been borrowed from all sides without acknowledgement than Adler" (p. 645). Many neo-Freudians have credited Adler with contributing to and influencing their work. In her last book, Karen Horney (1951) wrote of "neurotic ambition," "the need for perfection," and "the category of power." "All drives for glory have in common the reaching out for greater knowledge, wisdom, virtue or powers than are given to human beings; they all aim at the *absolute*, the unlimited, the infinite" (pp. 34-35). Those familiar with Adler's writings on the neurotic's perfectionistic, godlike striving will immediately be struck with the similarity in viewpoint.

Horney (1951) rejected Freud's pessimism, "his disbelief in human

Freud	Adler
1. Objective	1. Subjective
2. Physiological substratum for theory	2. A social psychology
3. Emphasized causality	3. Emphasized teleology
4. Reductionistic. The individual was divided into "parts" which were antagonistic toward each other, e.g., id-ego-superego, Eros vs. Thanatos, conscious vs. unconscious.	4. Holistic. The individual is indivisible. He is a unity and all "parts" (memory, emotions, behavior) are in the service of the whole individual.
5. The study of the individual centers about the intrapersonal, the intrapsychic.	5. Man can only be understood interpersonally, a social being moving through and interacting with his environment.
6. The establishment of intrapsychic harmony constitutes the ideal goal of psychotherapy. "Where id was, there shall ego be."	6. The expansion of the individual, self-realization, and the enhancement of social interest represent the ideal goals for the individual.
7. Man is basically "bad." Civilization attempts to domesticate him for which he pays a heavy price. Through therapy the instinctual demands may be sublimated but not eliminated.	7. Man is neither "good" nor "bad," but as a creative, choosing human being, he may choose to be "good" or "bad" or both depending upon his life-style and his appraisal of the immediate situation and its payoffs. Through the medium of therapy man can choose to actualize himself.
8. Man is a victim of both his instinctual life and of his civilization.	8. Man, as chooser, can shape both his internal and external environment. Although he is not the complete master of his fate and cannot always choose what will happen to him, he can always choose the posture he will adopt toward life's stimuli.
9. Freud's description of child development was postdictive and not based upon direct observation of children but upon the free associations of adults.	9. Children were studied directly in families, in schools and in family education centers.
10. Emphasis upon the Oedipus situation and its resolution.	10. Emphasis upon the family constellation.
11. Men are enemies. They are our competitors, and we must protect ourselves from them. Theodore Reik (1948) quotes Nestroy, "If chance brings two wolves together, . . . neither feels the least uneasy because the other is a wolf; two human beings, however, can never meet in the forest, but one must think: That fellow may be a robber" (p. 477).	11. Other men are *mitmenschen,* fellow human beings. They are our equals, our collaborators, our cooperators in life.
12. Women feel inferior because they envy men their penises. Women are inferior. "Anatomy is destiny."	12. Women feel inferior because in our cultural milieu women are undervalued. Men have privileges, rights, preferred status although in the current cultural ferment, these roles are being reevaluated.
13. Neurosis has a sexual etiology.	13. Neurosis is a failure of learning, a product of distorted perceptions.
14. Neurosis is the price we pay for civilization.	14. Neurosis is the price we pay for our lack of civilization.

goodness and human growth," in favor of the Adlerian view that man could grow and could "become a decent human being" and that man's potentialities "deteriorate if this relationship to others and hence to himself is, and continues to be, disturbed."

Others have also remarked upon the resemblance between the theories of Horney and Adler; the reviewer of one Horney book wrote that Karen Horney had just written a new book by Alfred Adler (Farau, 1953).

Erich Fromm's theories also express views similar to those of Adler. According to Fromm, man makes choices. The attitude of the mother in child rearing is of paramount importance. Life fosters feelings of powerlessness and anxiety. Patrick Mullahy (1955) indicates that

The only adequate solution, according to Fromm, is a relationship with man and nature, chiefly by love and productive work, which strengthens the total personality, sustains the person in his sense of uniqueness, and at the same time gives him a feeling of belonging, a sense of unity and common destiny with mankind. (pp. 251-252)

Although Harry Sullivan places greater emphasis upon developmental child psychology than does Adler, Sullivan's "man" moves through life in much the same manner as does Adler's. Thus, Sullivan (1954) speaks of the "security operations" of the individual, a direct translation of Adler's and Lene Credner's (1930) "Sicherungen." His "good me" and "bad me" dichotomy, in expression if not in manner of development, is essentially the same as that described by Adlerians.

So many similarities between Adler and the neo-Freudians have been noted that Gardner Murphy (1947) concluded, "If this way of reasoning is correct, neurosis should be the general characteristic of man under industrialism, a point suspected by many Freudians and, in particular, by that branch of the Freudian school (Horney and her associates) that has learned most from Adler" (p. 569). A summary of such resemblances appears in Heinz and Rowena Ansbacher's *Individual Psychology of Alfred Adler* (1956) as well as in an article by Walter James (1947). Fritz Wittels (1939) has proposed that the neo-Freudians should more properly be called "neo-Adlerians" and a study by Heinz Ansbacher (1952) suggests that many traditional Freudians would concur.

Adler and Rogers

Although the therapies of Adler and Carl Rogers are diametrically opposed, their theories share many commonalities. Both are phenomenological, goal directed, and holistic. Each views people as self-consistent, creative, and capable of change. To illustrate, Rogers (1951) postulates the following:

1. The organism reacts as an organized whole to the phenomenal field . . . [p. 486].
2. The best vantage point for understanding behavior is from the internal frame of reference of the individual himself [p. 494].
3. The organism reacts to the field as it is experienced and perceived . . . [p. 484-85].
4. The organism has one basic tendency and striving—to actualize, maintain, and enhance the experiencing organism [p. 487].

Much of the early research on nondirective and client-centered therapy used as a criterion measure the discrepancy between *self-concept* and *self-ideal*. The Adlerian would describe this self-ideal self-congruence or discrepancy as a measure of inferiority feelings.

Adler and Ellis

Both cognitive psychologies, the two theories exhibit many points of convergence. What Adler calls "basic mistakes," Albert Ellis refers to as irrational beliefs or attitudes. Both accept the notion that emotions are actually a form of thinking, that people create or control their emotions by controlling their thinking. They agree that we are not victims of our emotions but their creators. In psychotherapy, they (1) adopt similar stances with respect to unconscious motivation, (2) confront patients with their irrational ideas (basic mistakes or internalized sentences), (3) counterpropagandize the patient, (4) insist upon action, and (5) constantly *encourage* patients to assume responsibility for the direction of their lives in more positive channels. The last phrase seems to reflect the major disagreement between Adler and Ellis, namely, what is "positive." Ellis (1957) argues,

Where Adler writes, therefore, that "All my efforts are devoted towards increasing the social interest of the patient," the rational therapist would prefer to say, "Most of my efforts are devoted towards increasing the self-interest of the patient." He assumes that if the individual possesses rational self-interest he will, on both biological and logical grounds, almost invariably tend to have a high degree of social interest as well. (p.43)

Adler and other systems

The many points of convergence and divergence between Adler and several of the existentialist thinkers have been noted by many writers (Birnbaum, 1961; Farau, 1964; Frankl, 1970). Phyllis Bottome had written in 1939 that "Adler was the first founder of an existence psychology" (p. 199). Since existential psychology is not a school but a viewpoint, it is difficult to make comparisons but the interested reader may discover for himself in an editorial by Ansbacher (1959) the lines of continuity between Adler and current existential thought.

The recognition of Adler as one of the earliest humanistic psychologists is clear. Ellis (1970) pays homage to Adler as "one of the first humanistic psychologists" (p. 32). Abraham Maslow (1962, 1970) published five papers in Adlerian journals over a period of 35 years. As we have already observed, many of Adler's ideas have been incorporated by the humanistic psychologists with little awareness of Adler's contributions. The parameter, "The model of man as a composite of part functions" that James Bugental (1963) questions has been repudiated by Adlerians for almost half a century. Bugental proposes: "That the defining concept of man basic to the new humanistic movement in psychology is

that *man is the process that supersedes the sum of his part functions.*" We may compare this proposal with that of Dreikurs (1960a), "The whole is more than a sum total of its parts; therefore, it cannot be explained by any number of qualities but only understood as an indivisible whole in motion toward a goal" (p. 194). Adlerian psychology is a value psychology (Adler wrote *What Life Should Mean to You* in 1931), as Viktor Frankl and Rollo May among others acknowledge in their debt to Adler. Frankl (1970) wrote, "What he [Adler] . . . achieved and accomplished was no less than a Copernican switch . . . . Beyond this, Alfred Adler may well be regarded as an existential thinker and as a forerunner of the existential-psychiatric movement" (p. 38); May (1970) expresses his debt as follows,

. . . I appreciate Adler more and more. . . Adler's thoughts as I learned them in studying with him in Vienna in the summers of 1932 and 1933 led me indirectly into psychology, and were very influential in the later work in this country of Sullivan and William Alanson White, etc. (p. 39)

Albert Ellis (1970, 1971) finds his rational-emotive psychology to parallel that of Adler's. Abraham Maslow (1970) wrote, "For me Alfred Adler becomes more and more correct year by year. As the facts come in, they give stronger and stronger support to his image of man. I should say that in one respect especially the times have not yet caught up with him. I refer to his holistic emphasis" (p. 39).

HISTORY

Precursors

Adler's insistence that people cannot be studied in isolation but only in their social context was previously expressed by

Aristotle who referred to man as a *zoon politikon,* a political animal (Adler, 1959). He related his description of personality types to Hippocrates's humoral theory but after 1927 made no further mention of it. Adler exhibits his affinity with the philosophy of stoicism as both Ellenberger (1970), and H. N. Simpson (1966) point out. Other commentators have noted the resemblance of Adler's writings to Kant's philosophy, especially with respect to the categorical imperative, private logic, and overcoming. Adler and Nietzsche have often been compared and much has been made of their common usage of the concept of the *will to power.* However, Adler spoke of it in terms of the normal strivings for competence while Nietzche's references to this concept referred to what Adler would call the "useless side of life." Nietzsche stressed the *Übermensch* (Superman) and Adler spoke of equality. Adler further stressed *social feeling*, a concept totally alien to the Nietzschian philosophy.

Throughout history, philosophers have struggled with the mind-body problem. At the dawn of the modern scientific era, the rationalistic and empirical schools of philosophy were providing explanations for the connections between mind and body. The issue lay relatively dormant within psychology and experienced a renaissance when psychologists and psychiatrists began to address themselves to the study of psychosomatic syndromes. Psychosomatic and somatopsychic hypotheses were advanced to explain how emotions could influence the production of symptoms and how bodily states might create emotional or mental illness. Adler rejected such divisions. Like Kurt Lewin (1935), he rejected categorization and dichotomies. Like Jan Smuts (1961), he was a holist; *Individual Psychology,* was not meant to describe the psychology of the individual. It referred rather to Adler's holistic stance, that a person could be understood only as a whole, an indivisible unity. To study people atomistically was to not capture fully the nature of humanity. For Adler, the question was neither "How does mind affect body?" nor "How does body affect mind?" but rather how does the individual use body and mind in the pursuit of goals? Although Adler's book, *Study of Organ Inferiority and Its Psychical Compensation* (1917), might seem to contradict the above statements in that Adler expresses a causalistic viewpoint, this highly original theory was formulated during the period when Adler was a member of the Freudian circle. Later he added the subjective factor,

It might be suggested, therefore, that in order to find out where a child's interest lies, we need only to ascertain which organ is defective. But things do not work out quite so simply. The child does not experience the fact of organ inferiority in the way that an external observer sees it, but as modified by his own scheme of apperception. (Adler, 1969)

Perhaps the greatest influence upon Adler was Hans Vaihinger's (1965) "philosophy" of 'as if.'" According to Vaihinger, a fiction is "a mere piece of imagination" that deviates from reality but that is nevertheless utilitarian for the individual. Both the concept of the world and the concept of the self are subjective, that is, fictional, and therefore in error. *Truth* is "only the most expedient error, that is, the system of ideas which enables us to act and to deal with things most rapidly, neatly, and safely, and with the minimum of irrational elements" (p. 108).

Finally, Adler's psychology has a religious tone (Adler, 1958; Jahn & Adler, 1964). His placement of social interest at the pinnacle of his value theory is in the tradition of those religions that stress men's responsibility for each other. Indeed, Adler (Rasey, 1956) maintained that "Individual Psychology makes good religion if you are unfortunate enough not to have another" (p. 254).

Beginnings

Adler was born near Vienna on February 7, 1870, and died while on a lecture tour in Aberdeen, Scotland, on May 27, 1937. Graduating from the University of Vienna in 1895, Adler entered private practice as an ophthalmologist in 1898. He later switched to general practice and then to neurology. During this period, Adler gave portents of his later social orientation by writing a book on the health of tailors (1898). In this respect, he may be regarded as the progenitor of industrial medicine.

In 1902, Adler, at Freud's invitation, joined in the latter's Wednesday evening discussion circle. Biographers agree that Adler wrote two defenses of Freud's theories that may have gained him the invitation. Although textbooks frequently refer to Adler as a student of Freud, Adler was actually a colleague who had already established his own place as a physician (Ansbacher, 1962; Ellenberger, 1970; Federn, 1963; Maslow, 1962). Through the next decade, Adler had one foot in and one foot out of the Freudian circle. Although his *Study of Organ Inferiority* won Freud's unqualified endorsement, Adler's introduction of the aggression instinct in 1908 met with Freud's disapproval. Not until 1923, long after Adler had discarded instinct theory, did Freud incorporate the aggressive instinct into psychoanalysis (Sicher & Mosak, 1967) at which time Adler declared, "I enriched psychoanalysis by the aggressive drive. I

gladly make them a present of it!" (Bottome, 1939, p. 63).

Adler's increasing divergence from Freud's viewpoint led to discomfort and disillusion in the Vienna Society. Adler criticized Freud's sexual stance; Freud condemned Adler's ego psychology. They disagreed on (1) the unity of neuroses, (2) penis envy (sexual) versus the masculine protest (social), (3) the defensive role of the ego in neuroses, and (4) the role of the unconscious. Freud did not think Adler had discovered anything new but had merely reinterpreted what psychoanalysis had already said. He believed that what Adler discovered was "trivial," and that it was "methodologically deplorable and condemns his whole work to sterility" (Colby, 1951). After a series of meetings where these issues were discussed in an atmosphere of fencing, heckling, and vitriol (Brome, 1968), Adler in 1911 resigned as president of the Vienna Psychoanalytic Society. Later that year, Freud forced the choice between Adler and himself. Several members of the circle expressed their sympathy for Adler by resigning and forming the Society for Free Psychoanalytic Research, the forerunner of the *Internationale Vereinigung für Individualpsychologie*. In 1914 they published the first issue of the *Zeitschrift für Individualpsychologie*.

During the next decade, with the exception of the war period, Adler and his co-workers developed the social view of the neuroses. Their focus was primarily clinical although Adler (1914) as early as 1908 had demonstrated an interest in children and in education. In 1922 Adler initiated what was perhaps the first community-outreach program, child-guidance centers within the community. These centers were located in public schools and conducted by psychologists who served without pay. The method, for which Adler drew much criticism, was that of public family education, a method still used in Adlerian family education centers. Twenty-eight such centers existed in Vienna until 1934 when with the advent of Nazism the centers were closed. This form of center was transported to the United States by Rudolf Dreikurs and his students (Dreikurs, Corsini, Lowe, & Sonstegard, 1959). The success of these centers motivated the Vienna School authorities to invite several Adlerians to plan a school along Adlerian lines and from this invitation emerged the school described in Oskar Spiel's *Discipline without punishment* (1962). The school emphasized encouragement, class discussions, democratic principles, the responsibility of children for themselves and for each other, educational methods that are still in use.

The social orientation of Individual Psychology inevitably led to interest in group methods and Adler's introduction of family therapy (1922). Dreikurs (1959) is credited with the first use of group psychotherapy in private practice.

Between World Wars I and II, Adlerian groups existed in 20 European countries and in the United States. In 1926 Adler was invited to the United States to lecture and demonstrate, and until 1934 when fascism took hold in Austria, he divided his time between the United States, where he was on the medical faculty of the Long Island College of Medicine, and abroad. Two of his children, Alexandra and Kurt, now practice psychiatry in New York City. With the march of Nazism, many Adlerians were forced to flee their European homelands, and after many hardships, Adlerians made the United States the center of their activities. Today Individual Psychology societies exist in the United States, England, Canada, France, Denmark, Switzerland, Germany,

Austria, the Netherlands, Greece, Italy, Israel, and Australia.

Current Status

The resurgence of the Adlerian school after the dispersion from Europe was an uphill effort. Personal hardships of refugee Adlerians were compounded by the existing psychological climate in this country. The economic depression still prevailed. The Freudian school held a near monopoly both in the treatment area and with respect to appointments in medical schools. Some Adlerians defected; others became crypto-Adlerians. However, others persevered in retaining their identity and their optimism. Local societies were founded and 1952 saw the formation of the American Society of Adlerian Psychology. Several journals appeared; the major American one is *Individual Psychology* formerly called the *Journal of Individual Psychology* which itself was the successor to the *Individual Psychology Bulletin* of which Dreikurs was for many years the editor. The International Association of Individual Psychology also publishes the *Individual Psychology Newsletter*.

Training institutes that offer certificates in psychotherapy, counseling, and child guidance are found in New York, Chicago, Minneapolis, Berkeley, St. Louis, Dayton, Toledo, Ft. Wayne, Cleveland, Vancouver, Montreal and Toronto. Individual courses and programs of study are offered at many universities, such as Oregon, Arizona, West Virginia, Vermont, Governors State, Southern Illinois, De Paul, and Rhode Island College. Masters degrees based on an Adlerian curriculum are offered by Bowie State College and by the Alfred Adler Institute of Chicago, and in 1984 the latter is to embark on a doctoral program in clinical psychology.

Although Adlerian psychology was once dismissed as moribund, superficial (i.e., an "ego psychology"), and as being suitable mainly for children, it is today a viable psychology that pioneered in the holistic, phenomenological, social, teleological view of man.

Today's Adlerian may operate as a traditional clinician. But he is still innovative. Joshua Bierer has been a pioneer in social psychiatry (1969) and a leader in the day-hospital movement (1951). Therapeutic social clubs are in operation at the Alfred Adler Mental Hygiene Clinic in New York and at Saint Joseph Hospital in Chicago. Dreikurs originated multiple psychotherapy (1950) and he, Harold Mosak, and Bernard Shulman have contributed to its development (1952a, 1952b, 1982). Rudolf Dreikurs, Asya Kadis, Helene Papanek, and Bernard Shulman have made extensive contributions to group therapy. In a joint research project with the Counseling Center (Rogerian) of the University of Chicago, John Shlien, Mosak, and Dreikurs (1962) investigated the effects of time limits in therapy. Since they prefer the goal of prevention to that of healing, Adlerians function extensively in the area of education. Manford Sonstegard, Raymond Lowe, Bronia Grunwald, Oscar Christensen, Raymond Corsini, and Loren Grey are among those responsible for applying Adlerian principles in the school situation. Mosak (1971) has participated in a program that introduced Adlerian methods into an entire school system. All these have been students of Dreikurs, who transported the tradition from Vienna, and who himself has made a great contribution in this area. In the Adlerian social tradition, Adlerians may be involved in community outreach programs or dedicating their efforts to the study of subjects such as drugs, aging, delinquency, religion, and poverty.

A new development in the field of education may be seen in the work of Corsini and his associates (1977, 1979). Corsini's Individual Education is a system which implements the philosophy of Adler in schooling. The contemporary Adlerian finds the growth model of personality infinitely more congenial than the sickness model. The Adlerian is not interested in curing sick individuals or a sick society, but in reeducating individuals and in reshaping society so all people can live together as equals in a free society.

PERSONALITY

Theory of Personality

Adlerian psychology is a psychology of use rather than of possession. This assumption decreases the importance of the questions: "How do heredity and environment shape the individual?" or "How much of intelligence is hereditary and how much is due to environment?" The functionalist, holistic Adlerian asks instead, "How does the individual *use* heredity and environment?"

For Adler, the family constellation constitutes the primary social environment for the growing child whose situation is comparable to that of an immigrant in a foreign country—unable to comprehend the language and unable to be understood. Ignorant of rules and customs, he discovers to his dismay that he cannot find his way about the territory until he learns the appropriate language and behavior. Parents, siblings, peers, institutions, and the culture exert influences in their efforts to socialize him. Until he learns what is expected of him, he is relatively helpless, incompetent, inferior. So he observes his environment, makes evaluations, and arrives progressively at various conclusions about himself, his worth, and his environment, what it demands of him, and how he can acquire "citizenship in the new world." Through observation, exploration, trial and error, and by getting feedback from his environment, he learns what gains approval and disapproval and how he can achieve significance. Aside from his perceptions and evaluations, the child is not a passive receptor of family influences. He actively and creatively is busy modifying his environment, training his siblings, and "raising" his parents (Mosak, 1980). He wants to belong, to be a part of, to count.

Whether this need to belong is biological or learned, every child searches for significance. He jockeys for position within his family constellation looking for a "place in the sun." One sibling becomes the "best" child, another the "worst" one. Being favored, being one of the favored sex within the family, adopting the family values, identifying or allying oneself with a parent or sibling may provide the grounds for the feeling of having a place. Handicaps, organ inferiorities, or being an orphan are other "position makers" for some children.

Of supreme importance for the child is the child's position in the family constellation. Thus, it would appear that the first child usually is a conservative, and the second is often a rebel. The baby is ordinarily either a prince or one who stands on the tips of his toes to see above his preceding siblings. If these general characteristics possess any validity, at best they exist as statistical probabilities and not as defining traits. Considering the family constellation in terms of birth order or ordinal position creates the problem of characterizing, let us say, the fifth child in the family. Although he is often

encountered in the therapy situation, he never receives any attention in the literature. Birth order, per se, also ignores the sexual position of the child. The children in two-sibling families in which the possible configurations are boy-boy, girl-girl, boy-girl, and girl-boy do not possess similar characteristics based upon ordinal position alone (Shulman & Mosak, 1977).

The Adlerian prefers to study the family constellation in terms of the *psychological* position. A simple example illustrates this point of view. Take two siblings separated in age by 10 years. In birth order research, these would be treated as a first child and a second child. From the Adlerian point of view the psychological position of each would *most likely* be that of an only child with *perhaps* the older child functioning as an additional parent figure for the younger. The italicized terms *most likely* and *perhaps* are used expressly to indicate that: (1) Adlerians do not recognize a causalistic, one-to-one relationship between family position and sibling traits; and (2) whatever relationship exists can only be understood in context, that is, when one knows the family climate and the total configuration of factors in the family constellation. Adler, whenever he generalized or ventured a prediction, was fond of reminding his students, "Everything could also be quite different."

The search for significance and the consequent sibling competition reflect the values of the competitive society in which we live. We are encouraged to be first, to excel, to be popular, to be athletic, to be a "real" man, to "never say die," that "practice makes perfect," and to "dream the impossible dream." Consequently, each child must stake out for himself a piece of "territory," which includes the attributes or abilities that he hopes will give him a feeling of worth. If through his evaluations of his own potency (abilities, courage, and confidence) he is convinced that he can achieve this place through useful endeavor, he will pursue "the useful side of life." Should he feel that he cannot attain the goal of having a "place" in this fashion, he will become discouraged and engage in disturbed or disturbing behavior in his efforts to find a place. For the Adlerian the "maladjusted" child is not a "sick" child. He is a "discouraged" child. Dreikurs (1947, 1948) classifies the goals of the discouraged child into four groups—attention getting, power seeking, revenge taking, and declaring deficiency or defeat. Dreikurs is speaking of immediate rather than long-range goals. These are the goals of children's "misbehavior," not of all children's behavior (Mosak & Mosak, 1975).

In the process of becoming a socialized human being, the child forms conclusions on the basis of his subjective experiences. Since judgment and logical processes are not highly developed in young children, many of their growing convictions contain errors or only partial "truths." Nevertheless, they accept these conclusions about themselves and others as if they were true even though they are "fictions." They are subjective evaluations, biased apperceptions of themselves and of the world, rather than objective "reality." Thus, one can be truly inferior without feeling inferior. Conversely, one can feel inferior without being inferior.

The child creates a cognitive map, the life-style that will assist "little" him, in coping with the "big" world. The life-style includes the aspirations, the long-range goals of the individual, a "statement" of the conditions, personal or social, that are requisite for the individual's "security." The latter are also fictions and are stated in therapy as "If only . . . , then I . . . ." Mosak (1954) divided life-style convictions into four groups:

1. The *self-concept*—the convictions I have about who I am.
2. The *self-ideal* (Adler coined this phrase in 1912)—the convictions of what I should be or am obliged to be to have a place.
3. The *Weltbild* or "picture of the world"—convictions about the not-self (world, people, nature, and so on) and what the world demands of me.
4. The *ethical convictions*—the personal "right-wrong" code.

When there is a discrepancy between self and ideal-self convictions ("I am short; I should be tall") *inferiority feelings* ensue. Although an infinite variety of inferiority feelings exist, one should be mentioned that Adler discussed while he was still in the Freudian Society, which eventuated in the rift between Adler and Freud. It assumes monumental importance in some circles today—the masculine protest. In a culture that places a premium on masculinity, some women feel inferior because they have not been accorded the prerogatives or privileges of men ("I am woman; I should be equal to man"). But men also suffered from the masculine protest because being a man is not sufficient to provide a "place" for some men ("I am a man; but I should be a *real* man"). Since Adler believed in the equality of the sexes, he could not accept these fictions (Mosak & Schneider, 1977). As the battle for equality between the sexes is now being fought, one observes confirmation of Wexberg's prediction (1929) that "The family in its present form will surely vanish in the constantly progressing process of woman's economic emancipation" (p. 203).

Lack of congruence between convictions in the self-concept and those in the *Weltbild* ("I am weak and helpless. Life is dangerous") also results in inferiority feelings. Discrepancies between self-concept and ethical convictions ("one should always tell the truth; I lie") lead to inferiority feelings in the moral realm. Thus, the guilt feeling is merely a variant of the inferiority feeling.

These variations of inferiority feelings in and of themselves are not "abnormal." It would be difficult to quarrel with Adler's observations that to live is to *feel* inferior. It is only when the individual acts *as if* he were inferior, develops symptoms, or behaves as "sick" that we see evidences of what in the medical model would be called *pathology* and what Adlerians call *discouragement* or the *inferiority complex*. To oversimplify, the *inferiority feeling* is universal and "normal"; the *inferiority complex* reflects the discouragement of a limited segment of our society and is usually "abnormal." The former may be masked or hidden from the view of others; the latter is an open demonstration of inadequacy, or "sickness."

Using his "map," the individual facilitates his movement through life. It permits him to evaluate and understand experience. It enables him to predict and to control experience. Lawrence Frank (1939) writes in this connection,

... the personality process might be regarded as a sort of rubber stamp which the individual imposes upon every situation by which he gives it the configuration that he, as an individual, requires; in so doing he necessarily ignores or subordinates many aspects of the situation that

for him are irrelevant and meaningless and selectively reacts to those aspects that are personally significant. (p. 392)

Although the life-style is the instrument for coping with experience, it is very largely nonconscious. The life-style comprises the cognitive organization of the individual rather than the behavioral organization. As an illustration, the conviction "I require excitement" may lead to the vocational choices of actor, racing car driver, explorer, or to "acting out behavior." Such a conviction may further lead to getting into jams or exciting situations, or engaging in creative acts, or discovery.

Within the same life-style, one can behave usefully or uselessly. The above distinction permits Adlerians (e.g., Dreikurs, 1961; Nikelly, 1971a) to distinguish between *psychotherapy* and *counseling*. The former, they maintain, has as its aim the change of life-style; the latter has as its goal the change of behavior within the existing life-style.

Since the Adlerian literature discusses the life tasks of occupation, society, and love so extensively, these tasks of life will not be elaborated upon here, except for some brief comments. Lewis Way (1962) points out that "The problems they pose can never be solved once and for all, but demand from the individual a continuous and creative movement toward adaptation" (pp. 179-80).

Love, as an emotion, is like other emotions, cognitively based. People are not "victims" of their emotions or passions. They create emotions to assist them in the attainment of their goals. Love is the conjunctive emotion we create when we want to move toward people.

Although the life tasks of love, occupation, and society demand solution, it is possible to avoid or postpone some if one can compensate in other areas. "Even successful persons fall into neurosis because they are not more successful" (Way, 1962, p. 206). The *neurotic symptom* is an expression of "I *can't* because I'm sick"; the person's movement betrays an "I *won't* because my self-esteem might get hurt" (Krausz, 1959, p. 112). Although the neurotic individual's movements are consonant with his "private logic" (Nikelly, 1971b), he still clings to the "common sense." He knows what he should do or feel, but he "can't." Adler referred to him as the "yes-but" personality. Eric Berne (1964) has graphically described his interpersonal maneuvers in the "Why don't you—Yes, but" game. The genesis of neurosis lies in discouragement. The individual avoids and postpones or takes circuitous routes to solutions so he can "save face." Even when he expects or arranges to fail, he tries to salvage some self-esteem. A student, fearful of failing an examination, will refrain from studying. In the event he does fail, he merely has to hold that he was lazy or neglectful but not stupid.

The *psychotic's* goal of superiority is often loftier than can be achieved by mortal man. "Individual Psychology has shown that the goal of superiority can only be fixed at such altitudes when the individual has, by losing interest in others, also lost interest in his own reason and understanding . . . common sense has become useless to him" (Adler, 1964a, pp. 128-29). Adler used "common sense" in much the same manner that Sullivan spoke of "consensual validation." In the pseudowork area, he elects himself superintendent of the mental hospital. In the pseudosocial area, the hypomanic patient resembles the cheerful extrovert and the more acutely manic patient becomes a "name dropper" and "swallows up" people (Shulman, 1962). The paranoid patient pictures people as threatening and manifests his "search for glory," to use Karen Horney's (1951) phrase, by his persecutory delusion that *they* are conspiring to do something to *me*. He is the center of the people's attention. The delusions of grandeur of the psychotic depressive patient ("I'm the *worst* sinner of all time") and of the schizophrenic who believes he is the Christ are some other "solutions" to the spiritual pseudotasks. The reifying hallucinations of talking with the Devil fall similarly in this category (Adler, 1963b; Mosak & Fletcher, 1973).

The *psychologically healthy* or *normal* individual is one who has developed his social interest, who is willing to commit himself to life and the life tasks without evasion, excuse or "sideshows" (Wolfe, 1932). He employs his energies in being a fellowman with confidence and optimism in meeting life's challenges. He has his place. He feels a sense of belonging and contributing, has his self-esteem and has the "courage to be imperfect," and possesses the serene knowledge that he can be acceptable to others, although imperfect. Above all, he rejects the faulty values his culture projects and enforces and attempts to substitute for them values more consonant with the "ironclad logic of social living." Such a person does not exist nor will any psychotherapy produce such a person. Yet this is the Adlerian ideal, and since Adler's intent was to substitute small errors for larger errors, many of these goals can be approximated in psychotherapy. Many fortunate people have the courage (Adler, 1928) and social interest to do this for themselves without therapeutic assistance.

Variety of Concepts

The simplicity of the Adlerian vocabulary renders definition and interpretation generally unnecessary. Yet some differences of opinion and emphasis about Adlerian concepts remain unresolved. In terms of *life-style*, Adlerians disagree with respect to what it describes—behavioral or cognitive organization. *Social interest* (Bickhard & Ford, 1976; Crandall, 1981; Edgar, 1975; Kazan, 1978) apparently is not a unitary concept but a cluster of feelings and behaviors (Ansbacher, 1968). Although social interest is often described as "innate," many Adlerians wonder what makes it "so" since it appears to be neither genetic nor constitutional. As one looks at the theories of Adler, Freud, and Jung, one is struck with the effort on the part of all three to "biologize" their theories. Perhaps it was the temper of the times. Perhaps it was because all three were physicians. Perhaps it resulted from the need to make their theories respectable during a period when psychoanalysis was held in low esteem. None of these theories would incur any great damage if "instincts," "social interest," and "racial unconscious" were treated as psychological constructs rather than as biological processes. Adler, having introduced the concept of *organ inferiority* with its consequent compensation, actually had proposed a biopsychological theory, but it must be recalled that this transpired during his "Freudian period." Later he substituted the *social inferiority feeling* for actual organ inferiority, and with the exception of one important article (Shulman & Klapman, 1968), Adlerians publish little on organ inferiority. Although people undoubtedly do compensate for organ inferiority, the latter is no longer the cornerstone of the Adlerian edifice.

Gardner Murphy (1947) took issue with Adler's use of compensation as the only defense mechanism. Literally, Adler's writings do read that way. On the other hand, if one reads more closely, compensation becomes an umbrella to cover all coping mechanisms. Thus, Adler speaks of safeguards, excuses, projection, the depreciation tendency, creating distance, and identification. Although a Freudian might view these as defense mechanisms the ego employs in its warfare with the instinctual drives, the Adlerian prefers to view them as problem-solving devices the person uses to protect his self-esteem, reputation and physical self rather than as defense mechanisms. Since Adlerians do not accept the concept of *the* unconscious, such mechanisms as repression and sublimation become irrelevant in the Adlerian framework. Adlerian theory has no room for instincts, drives, libido, and other alleged movers.

The *Journal of Individual Psychology* (now *Individual Psychology*) referred to itself as being "devoted to a holistic, phenomenological, teleological, field-theroetical, and socially oriented approach . . . ," placing it closer to Rogers, Maslow, the existential humanists, and some of the neo-Freudians than to the one-to-one (cause-effect, stimulus-response) psychologies. Because of the emphasis on behavior (movement), Adlerian psychology and behavior-modification theory have been equated. This is an error. Adlerians, although interested in changing behavior, have as their major goal not behavior modification, but motivation modification. Dreikurs (1963) writes, "We do not attempt primarily to change behavior patterns or remove symptoms. If a patient improves his behavior because he finds it profitable at the time, without changing his basic premises, then we do not consider that as a therapeutic success. We are trying to change goals, concepts, and notions" (p. 79).

PSYCHOTHERAPY

Theory of Psychotherapy

All scientific schools of psychotherapy have their shares of successes and failures. A considerable number of therapies based upon nonscientific foundations probably reach equal success levels. Consequently, we may conclude that the validity of a psychodynamic theory bears no direct relationship to its therapeutic effectiveness. Like their predecessors, modern theories may also vanish from practice to appear only in the textbooks of future generations. In any event, regardless of its validity or endurance, any theory must be implemented within the context of the therapist-patient relationship. As Fred Fiedler (1950) has shown, therapeutic success is a function of the expertness of the therapist rather than of the therapist's orientation. This may help to explain the successes of modern and primitive theories.

Since the underlying psychodynamic theory is not the crucial factor in therapy, perhaps it is the special techniques that contribute to therapeutic effectiveness. This would certainly seem to have been Rogers's early position before nondirective therapy became person-centered therapy. For the early nondirective school, the creation of a warm, permissive, nonjudgmental atmosphere, reflection of feeling, and avoidance of interpretation, advice, persuasion, and suggestion were paramount in the therapeutic situation.

The Freudian assigns central importance to transference but behavior modification therapists ignore it. To many directive therapists, content and manner of interpretation are crucial. The Adlerian emphasizes interpretation of the patient's life-style and his movement.

Criteria for "getting well" correspond to the particular therapeutic emphasis. Some therapists propose depth of the therapy as being the decisive factor. For most Adlerians, depth of therapy does not constitute a major concern, if any. In this connection, therapy is neither deep nor superficial except as the patient experiences it as such. In practice we observe patients who commend us for a particular interpretation, and when we discuss it with them, we learn that they have badly garbled it. In accordance with such arbitrariness, neither interpretative framework nor content nor depth is the decisive factor in curing patients.

If neither theory nor the use of prescribed techniques is decisive, is it the transference relationship that makes cure possible? Or the egalitarian relationship? Or the warm, permissive atmosphere with the nonjudgmental therapist accepting the patient as he is? Since all of these relationships are involved in various forms of both effective and noneffective therapy, we must hypothesize either that therapeutic effectiveness is a matter of matching certain therapeutic relationships to certain patients or that all therapeutic relationships possess common factors. These factors, variations on the Christian virtues of faith, hope, and love, appear to be necessary, but not sufficient, conditions of effective therapy.

Faith

D. Rosenthal and Jerome D. Frank (1956) discuss the implications of faith in the therapeutic process. Franz Alexander and Thomas French (1946) state:

As a general rule, the patient who comes for help voluntarily has this confidence, this expectation that the therapist is both able and willing to help him, before he comes to treatment; if not, if the patient is forced into treatment, the therapist must build up this feeling of rapport before any therapeutic change can be effected. (p. 173)

Many therapeutic mechanisms may enhance the patient's faith. A simple explanation clarifies matters for some patients, a complex interpretation for others. The therapist's own faith in himself, the therapist's appearance of wisdom, strength, and assurance, the therapist's willingness to listen without criticism, may all be used by the patient to strengthen his faith.

Hope

Patients seek treatment with varying degrees of hope running the gamut from complete hopelessness to hope for (and expectation of) everything, including a miracle. Because of the efficacy of the self-fulfilling prophecy, people *tend* to move in the direction of making their anticipations come true. Therefore, the therapist must keep the patient's hope elevated.

Since the Adlerian holds that the patient suffers from discouragement, a primary technique of the Adlerian therapist lies in encouragement. Expression of faith in the patient, noncondemnation, and avoidance of being overly demanding of him may give the patient hope. The patient may also derive hope from feeling understood. Accordingly, the construction of therapy as a "we" experience where the patient does not feel he stands alone, where he feels security in the strength and competency of his therapist, and where he feels some symptom alleviation may all prove helpful. He may also gain hope from attempting some course of action he feared or did not know was available to him. Humor assists in the retention of hope. Lewis Way (1962) comments, "Humour such as Adler possessed in such abundance, is an invaluable asset, since, if one can occasionally joke, things

cannot be so bad" (p. 267). Each therapist has faith in his methods for encouraging and sustaining hope. They are put to the most severe test in depressions and in suicide threats.

Love

In its broadest sense, the patient must feel that the therapist cares (Adler, 1963a, 1964a). The mere act of treating the patient may furnish such evidence by using techniques such as empathic listening, "working through" together, or having two therapists in multiple psychotherapy offering interest in the patient. Transfer of a patient to another therapist or from individual to group therapy may have a contrary effect unless it is "worked through."

But the therapist must avoid pitfalls such as infantilizing, oversupporting, or of becoming a victim of the patient when the patient accuses him of not caring enough. In Adlerian group therapy, the group is conceptualized as a "re-experiencing of the family constellation" (Kadis, 1956). Thus, the therapist may be accused of playing favorites, of caring too much for one or too little for another patient.

The Adlerian theory of psychotherapy rests on the notion that psychotherapy is a cooperative educational enterprise involving one or more therapists and one or more patients. The goal of therapy is to develop the patient's social interest. To accomplish this, therapy involves a changing of faulty social values (Dreikurs, 1957). The subject matter of this course in reeducation is the patient himself—his life-style and his relationship to the life tasks. Learning the "basic mistakes" in his cognitive map, he has the opportunity to decide whether he wants to continue in the old ways or move in other directions. "The consultee must under all circumstances get the conviction in relation to treatment that he is absolutely free. He can do, or not do, as he pleases" (Ansbacher & Ansbacher, 1956, p. 341). He can make the decision between self-interest and social interest. The educational process has as its goals:

1. The fostering of social interest.
2. The decrease of inferiority feelings and the overcoming of discouragement, and the recognition and utilization of one's resources.
3. Changes in the person's life-style, that is, perceptions and goals. The therapeutic goal, as has been mentioned, involves transforming big errors into little ones (as with automobiles, some persons need a "tune-up"; others require a "major overhaul").
4. Changing faulty motivation that underlies even acceptable behavior or changing values.
5. Encouraging the individual to recognize his equality among his fellowmen (Dreikurs, 1971).
6. Helping the person to become a contributive human being.

Should the "student" reach these educational objectives, he will feel belonging, acceptant of self and others. He will expect that others can accept him as he accepts himself. He will feel that the "motive force" lies within him, that he can arrange, within life's limits, his own destiny. He will feel encouraged, optimistic, confident, courageous, secure—and asymptomatic.

Process of Psychotherapy

The process of psychotherapy, as practiced by the Adlerian, has four aims: (1) establishing and maintaining a "good" relationship; (2) uncovering the dynamics of the patient, his life-style, his goals, and how they affect his life movement; (3) interpretation culminating in insight; and (4) reorientation.

Relationship

A "good" therapeutic relationship is a friendly one between equals. Both the Adlerian therapist and the patient sit facing each other, their chairs at the same level. Many Adlerians prefer to work without a desk since distancing and separation may engender undesirable psychological sets. Having abandoned the medical model, the Adlerian looks with disfavor upon casting the doctor in the role of the actor (omnipotent, omniscient, and mysterious) and the patient in the role of the acted-upon. Therapy is structured to inform the patient that a creative human being plays a role in creating one's problems, that one is responsible (not in the sense of blame) for one's actions, and that one's problems are based upon faulty perceptions, and inadequate or faulty learning, especially of faulty values. If this is so, one can assume responsibility for change. What has not been learned can be learned. What has been learned "poorly" can be replaced by better learning. Faulty perception and values can be altered and modified. From the initiation of treatment, the patient's efforts to remain passive are discouraged. The patient has an active role in the therapy. Although he may be in the role of student, he is still an active learner responsible for contributing to his own education.

Therapy requires cooperation, which means alignment of goals. Noncoincidence of goals may not permit the therapy "to get off the ground" as, for example, when the patient denies that he needs therapy and the therapist feels that he does. The initial interview(s) must not, therefore, omit the consideration of initial goals and expectations. The patient may wish to overpower the therapist, to put the therapist into his service, or to make the therapist powerful and responsible. The therapist's goal must be to avoid these traps. The patient may want to relinquish his symptoms but not his underlying convictions. He may be looking for a miracle. In each case, at least a temporary agreement upon goals must be arrived at before the therapy can proceed. Way (1962) cautions,

A refusal to be caught in this way [succumbing to the patient's appeals to the therapist's vanity or bids for sympathy] gives the patient little opportunity for developing serious resistances and transferences, and is indeed the doctor's only defence against a reversal of roles and against finding that he is being treated by the patient. The cure must always be a co-operation and never a fight. It is a hard test for the doctor's own balance and is likely to succeed only if he himself is free from neurosis. (p. 265)

Adler (1963a) offers similar warnings against role reversal.

Since the problems of resistance and transference are defined in terms of patient-therapist goal discrepancies, throughout therapy the goals will diverge and the common task will consist of realigning the goals so patient and therapist move in the same direction. The patient brings his life-style to therapy. Whatever factors influenced its creation, the life-style convictions give the patient a feeling of security. When the patient believes the therapist or questions or threatens these convictions, the patient must protect himself, must resist, even when he agrees with the therapist that it may be in his self-interest (Shulman, 1964). Take away his security—what does he have left? The goals go out of alignment again. The therapist advocates,

"Let go of the 'basic mistakes'" and the patient announces, "I can't" or "I won't" or "I'm scared" or "I'm not coming back" or "Let's talk about something else."

The patient, in bringing his life-style to therapy, expects from the therapist the kind of response he has trained himself from childhood to believe that people will give him. He may feel misunderstood, unfairly treated, or unloved and may anticipate that the therapist will exploit or dislike him. Often he unconsciously creates situations to invite the therapist to behave in this manner. For this reason, the therapist must be alert to what Adlerians call "scripts" and what Eric Berne (1964) calls "games" and foil the patient's expectations. A patient, for example, will declare, "Have you ever seen a patient like me before?" to establish his uniqueness and to challenge the therapist's competence to treat him. The therapist's response may just be a straight forward, but nonsarcastic, "Not since the last hour," and he may follow up with a discussion of uniqueness. Since assessment begins with the first moment of contact, the patient is generally given some interpretation, usually phrased as a guess, during the first interview. This gives the patient something to think about until the next interview. He may feel understood ("I never thought of it that way" or "I'm so relieved to learn that"). The therapist will soon find it possible to assess how the patient will respond to interpretation, to therapy, and to the therapist, and will gain some glimpse of the life-style framework. In playing the patient's game, the patient is the professional, having played it successfully since childhood (although often in self-defeating fashion), whereas the therapist is a relative amateur. The therapist does not have to *win* the game. He merely does not play it. To illustrate, only one side wins in a tug-of-war. However, if one side (the therapist) is disinterested in victories or defeats, he merely does not pick up his end of the rope. This renders the "opponent's" game ineffective and the two can proceed to play more productive, cooperative games.

The whole relationship process increases the education of the patient. For some patients it is their first experience of a good interpersonal relationship, a relationship of cooperation and mutual respect and trust. Despite occasional bad feeling, friction, the feeling of not being understood, the relationship can endure and survive. The patient learns that good and bad relationships do not merely happen; they are products of people's efforts. He learns that poor interpersonal relationships are products of or precipitated by misperceptions, inaccurate conclusions, and unwarranted anticipations incorporated in the life-style.

Analysis

Investigation of a patient's dynamics is divided into two parts. First, the therapist wants to understand the patient's life-style and, second, his aim is directed to understanding how the life-style affects his current function with respect to the life tasks. Not all suffering stems from the patient's life-style. Many patients with adequate life-styles develop problems or symptoms in the face of intolerable or extreme situations from which they cannot extricate themselves.

Analytic investigation begins with the first moment. The way a patient enters the room, his posture, and how and where he sits (especially important in family therapy) all provide clues toward the understanding of the patient. What the patient says and how he says it expand the therapist's understanding, especially when the therapist understands the patient's communications in interpersonal terms, or "scripts," rather than in descriptive terms. Thus, the Adlerian translates the descriptive statement, "I am confused" into the admonition, "Don't pin me down." "It's a habit," conveys the declaration, "And that's another thing you're not going to get me to change," as the patient attempts erroneously to convince the therapist that habits are unchangeable (Mosak & Gushurst, 1971). As therapy progresses, the therapist assesses, using processes similar to a detective except that he works toward a different goal since he is not attempting to establish culpability. He follows up clues, juxtaposes them in patterns, accepts some hypotheses, and rejects others in his efforts to understand the patient. As therapy progresses, the patient offers information one way or another, and the therapist pieces it together bit by bit like a jigsaw puzzle. Therapists vary in their treatment methods.

The life-style investigation

In formal assessment procedures, the patient's family constellation is explored to ascertain conditions prevailing when the child was forming his life-style convictions. We obtain glimpses of what position the child found in the family and how he went about finding his place within the family, in school, and among his peers. The second portion of the assessment consists of interpreting the patient's early recollections. An *early recollection* occurs in the period before continuous memory and may be inaccurate or a complete fiction. It represents a single event ("One day I remember . . .") rather than a group of events ("We used to . . ."). Adlerians refer to the latter as a *report* rather than a recollection. Recollections are treated as a projective technique (Mosak, 1958). If one understands the early recollections, one understands the patient's "Story of My Life" (Adler, 1958) since people selectively recollect from their past incidents consonant with their life-styles. The following recollection of Adler's (1947) may serve to illustrate the consonance between his earliest recollection and his later psychological views.

One of my earliest recollections is of sitting on a bench, bandaged up on account of rickets, with my healthy elder brother sitting opposite me. He could run, jump, and move about quite effortlessly, while for me movement of any sort was a strain and an effort. Everyone went to great pains to help me, and my mother and father did all that was in their power to do. At the time of this recollection I must have been about two years old. (p. 9)

In a single recollection, Adler refers to organ inferiority, the inferiority feeling, the emphasis upon "my desire to move freely—to see all psychic manifestations in terms of movements" (p. 10), and social feeling (Mosak & Kopp, 1973).

The summary of early recollections, the story of the patient's life, permits the derivation of the patient's "basic mistakes." The life-style can be conceived as a personal mythology. The individual will behave as if the myths were true because, for him, they are true. When the Greeks believed that Zeus lived on Olympus, they regarded it as truth and behaved as if it were true, although we have now consigned this belief to the realm of mythology. Although it was not true that Zeus existed, it is true that Olympus exists. So there are "truths" or partial "truths" in myths and there are myths we confuse with truth. The latter are *basic mistakes*.

Basic mistakes may be classified as follows:

1. *Overgeneralizations.* "People are hostile." "Life is dangerous."
2. *False or impossible goals of "security."* "One false step and you're dead." "I have to please everybody."
3. *Misperceptions of life and life's demands.* Typical convictions might be "Life never give me any breaks" and "Life is so hard."
4. *Minimization or denial of one's worth.* "I'm stupid" and "I'm undeserving" or "I'm *just* a housewife."
5. *Faulty values.* "Be first even if you have to climb over others."

Finally, the therapist is interested in how the patient perceives his assets.

A sample of life-style summary is presented. It is not intended to be a complete personality description but it does offer patient and therapist initial hypotheses as talking points for examination. Below is a typical *life-style summary*.

Summary of Family Constellation

John is the younger of two children, the only boy, who grew up fatherless after age nine. His sister was so precocious that John became discouraged. Since he felt he would never become famous, he decided perhaps he could at least be notorious, and through negative behavior brought himself to the attention of others. He acquired the reputation of a "holy terror." He was going to do do everything his way, and nobody was going to stop him. He followed the guiding lines of a strong, masculine father from whom he learned that the toughest man wins. Since notoriety came with doing the disapproved, John early became interested in and engaged in sex. This also reinforced his feelings of masculinity. Since both parents were handicapped and yet still "made it," John apparently decided that without any physical handicaps, the sky would be the limit for him.

Summary of Early Recollections

"I run scared in life, and even when people tell me there's nothing to be scared of, I'm still scared. Women give men a hard time. They betray them, they punish them, and they interfere with what men want to do. A real man takes no crap from anybody. Somebody always interferes. I am not going to do what others want me to do. Others call that 'bad' and want to punish me for it but I don't see it that way. Doing what I want is merely part of being a man."

"Basic Mistakes"

1. John exaggerates the significance of masculinity and equates it with doing what he pleases.
2. He is not on the same wavelength as women. They see his behavior as "bad"; he sees it as only "natural" for a man.
3. He is too ready to fight, many times just to preserve his sense of masculinity, and not because of the issue he is allegedly fighting over.
4. He perceives women as the enemy, even though he looks to them for comfort.
5. Victory is snatched from him at the last moment.

Assets

1. He is a driver. When he puts his mind to things, he makes them work.
2. He engages in creative problem solving.
3. He knows how to get what he wants.
4. He knows how to keep the world busy with him.
5. He knows how to ask a woman "nicely."

During the course of the treatment, other forms of analysis will occur. Since the therapist views the life-style as consistent, it will express itself in all of the patient's behavior—physical behavior, language and speech, fantasy productions, dreams, and interpersonal relations, past and present. Because of this consistency, the patient may choose to express himself in any or all of these media because they all express his life-style. The therapist observes behavior, speech, and language closely during each interview. Sometimes the dialogue will center on the present, sometimes on the past, often on the future. Free association and "chit chat," except when the latter serves a therapeutic purpose, are mostly discouraged. Although dream analysis is an integral part of psychotherapy, the patient who speaks only of dreams receives gentle dissuasion (Alexandra Adler, 1943). The analysis proceeds with an examination of the interplay between life-style and the life tasks—how the life-style affects the person's function and dysfunction vis-a-vis the life tasks.

Dreams

Adler saw the dream as a problem-solving activity with a future orientation in contrast to Freud's view that it was attempting to solve an old problem. The *dream* is seen by Adlerians as a rehearsal of possible future courses of action. If we want to postpone action, we forget the dream. If we want to dissuade ourselves from some action, we frighten ourselves with a nightmare.

The dream, Adler said, was the "factory of the emotions." In it we create moods that move us toward or away from the next day's activities. Commonly, people say, "I don't know why but I woke up in a lousy mood today." The day before Adler died, he told friends, "I woke smiling . . . so I knew my dreams were good although I had forgotten them" (Bottome, 1939, p. 240). Just as early recollections reflect long-range goals, the dream experiments with possible answers to immediate problems. In accord with the view of the individual's uniqueness, Adlerians reject the theory of fixed symbolism. One cannot understand a dream without knowing the dreamer, although

Adler (1936) and Erwin Wexberg (1929) do address themselves to some frequently encountered dream themes. Way (1962) admonishes,

One is reminded again of two boys, instanced by Adler [1964a, p. 150], each of whom wished to be a horse, one because he would have to bear the responsibility for his family, the other to outstrip all the others. This should be a salutary warning against making dictionary interpretations. (pp. 282-84)

The interpretation of the dream does not terminate with the analysis of the content but must include the purposive function. Dreams serve as a weathervane for treatment, bringing problems to the surface and pointing to the patient's movement. Dreikurs (1944) describes a patient who related recurrent dreams that were short and actionless, reflecting his life-style of figuring out "the best way of getting out of a problem, mostly without doing anything . . . When his dreams started to move and become active he started to move in his life, too" (p. 226).

Reorientation

All reorientation in all therapies proceeds from persuading the patient, gently or forcefully, that change is in his best interest. The patient's present manner of living accords him "safety" but not happiness. Since neither therapy nor life offers *guarantees,* would he risk some of his "safety" for the possibility of greater happiness, self-fulfillment, or for whatever he conceptualizes his goal to be? This dilemma is not easily solved. Like Hamlet, the patient wonders whether it is better to "bear those ills we have than fly to others that we know not of."

Insight

Analytic psychotherapists frequently assign central importance to insight, upon the assumption that "basic change" cannot occur in its absence. The conviction that insight must precede behavioral change often results in extended treatment, in encouraging some patients to become "sicker" to avoid or postpone change, and in increasing their self-absorption rather than their self-awareness. Meanwhile the patient relieves himself from the responsibility of living life until he has achieved insight.

A second assumption, treasured by therapists and patients alike, distinguishes between *intellectual* and *emotional* insight (Ellis, 1963; H. Papanek, 1959), a dualism the holistic Adlerian experiences difficulty in accepting. This and other dualisms such as conscious vs. unconscious undeniably exist in the patient's subjective experience. But these antagonistic forces are creations of the patient by which he can delay action. By creating "warring forces," he awaits the outcome of the battle before meeting the life tasks. Simultaneously he can maintain a good conscience since he is the victim of conflicting forces or an emotional block. Solving one's problems is relegated to the future while the patient pursues insight. *Insight,* as the Adlerian defines it, is understanding translated into constructive action. It reflects the patient's understanding of the purposive nature of his behavior and mistaken apperceptions as well as an understanding of the role both play in his life movement. So-called intellectual insight merely reflects the patient's desire to play the game of therapy rather than the game of life. He plays the game of "yes-but" (Adler, 1964b), as Adler called it. "Yes, I know what I should do, but . . . "

Interpretation

The Adlerian therapist facilitates insight mainly by interpretation. He interprets ordinary communications, dreams, fantasies, behavior, symptoms, the patient-therapist transactions, and the patient's interpersonal transactions. The emphasis in interpretation is upon purpose rather than upon cause, on movement rather than description, on use rather than possession. Through interpretation the therapist holds up a mirror to the patient so he can see how he copes with life.

The therapist relates past to present only to indicate the continuity of the maladaptive life-style, not to demonstrate a causal connection. He may use humor or illustrate with fables (Pancner, 1978), anecdotes, and biography. Irony may prove effective but it must be handled with care. He may "spit in the patient's soup," a crude expression for exposing the patient's intentions in such a way as to make them unpalatable so he can no longer maintain his current behavior with innocence or good conscience. The therapist may offer the interpretation directly or in the form of "Could it be that . . . ?" or may invite the patient to interpret for himself. Although timing, exaggeration, understatement, and accuracy are technical concerns of the therapist, they are not too important for the Adlerian therapist because he does not view the patient as fragile.

Other verbal techniques
Advice is often frowned upon by therapists. Hans Strupp (1972) relates, "It has been said that Freud, following his own recommendations, never gave advice to an analysand on the couch but did not stint with the commodity from the couch to the door" (p. 40). Wexberg (1970) frowns on giving advice to a patient but the Adlerian therapist does so as did Freud, taking care, however, not to encourage dependency. In practice the therapist may merely outline the alter-

natives and let the patient make the decision. This invitation develops faith in self rather than faith in the therapist. On the other hand, the therapist may offer direct advice, taking care to encourage the patient's self-directiveness and his willingness to stand on his own two feet.

Since the patient is considered by Adlerians as discouraged rather than sick, it is no surprise that they make extensive use of encouragement. Enhancing the patient's faith in himself, "accentuating the positive and eliminating the negative," and keeping up the patient's hope all contribute to counteracting the patient's discouragement. If he "walks and falls," he learns it is not fatal. He can pick himself up and walk again. Therapy also counteracts the patient's social values, thus altering his view of life and helping him to give meaning to it. Moralizing is avoided, although therapists must not deceive themselves into believing their system has no value orientation. The dialogue concerns "useful" and "useless," rather than "good" or "bad" behavior.

The therapist avoids rational argument and trying to "out-logic" the patient. These tactics are easily defeated by the patient who operates according to his *psychologic* (private logic) rather than the rules of formal logic. Catharsis, abreaction, and confession may afford the patient relief by freeing him from carrying the burden of "unfinished business," but as has been noted (Alexander & French, 1946), these may also be a test of whether one can place trust in the therapist. If the patient experiences relief or if the therapist passes the test, the patient may increase his readiness for change.

Action techniques
Adlerians regularly use role playing, talking to an empty chair (Shoobs, 1964), the

Midas technique (Shulman, 1962), the behind-the-back technique (Corsini, 1953), and other action procedures to assist the patient in reorientation. The extent of use is a function of therapist preference, the therapist's training, and his readiness to experiment with the novel.

Mechanisms of Psychotherapy

The therapist as model
The therapist represents values the patient may attempt to imitate. The Adlerian therapist represents himself as "being for real," fallible, able to laugh at himself, caring—a model for social interest. If the therapist can possess these characteristics, perhaps the patient can, too, and many patients emulate their therapists whom they use as a referent for normality (Mosak, 1967).

Change
There comes a time in psychotherapy when analysis must be abandoned and the patient must be encouraged to act in lieu of talking and listening. Insight has to give way to decisive action.

Some of the techniques Adlerians use to elicit change are described below. They are not panaceas nor are they used indiscriminately. The creative therapist will improvise techniques to meet the needs of the therapeutic moment, and remember, above all, people are more important than techniques and strategies. Losing sight of these cautions, the therapist is a technician who does all the "right" things but is never engaged in human encounter with another human being.

Acting "as if"
A common patient refrain in treatments is "If only I could . . . " (Adler, 1963a).

We often request of the patient that for the next week he act "as if." He may protest that it would only be an act and therefore phony, that underneath he would remain the same person. We show him that all acting is not phony pretense, that he is being asked to try on a role as one might try on a suit. It does not change the person wearing the suit but sometimes with a handsome suit of clothes, he may feel differently and perhaps behave differently, in which case he becomes a different person.

Task setting
Adler (1964a) gave us the prototype for task-setting in his treatment of depressives, writing:

To return to the indirect method of treatment: I recommend it especially in melancholia. After establishing a sympathetic relation I give suggestions for a change of conduct in two stages. In the first stage my suggestion is "Only do what is agreeable to you." The patient usually answers, "Nothing is agreeable." "Then at least," I respond, "do not exert yourself to do what is disagreeable." The patient, who has usually been exhorted to do various uncongenial things to remedy this condition, finds a rather flattering novelty in my advice, and may improve in behavior. Later I insinuate the second rule of conduct, saying that "it is much more difficult and I do not know if you can follow it." After saying this I am silent, and look doubtfully at the patient. In this way I excite his curiosity and ensure his attention, and then proceed, "If you could follow this second rule you would be cured in fourteen days. It is—to consider from time to time how you can give another person pleasure. It would very soon enable you to sleep and would chase away all your sad thoughts. You would feel yourself to be useful and worthwhile."

I receive various replies to my suggestion, but every patient thinks it is too difficult to act upon. If the answer is, "How can I give pleasure to others when I have none myself?" I relieve the prospect by saying, "Then you will need four weeks." The more transparent response, "Who gives *me* pleasure?" I encounter with what is probably the strongest move in the game, by saying, "Perhaps you had better train yourself a little thus: do not actually DO anything to please anyone else, but just think out how you COULD do it!" (pp. 25-26)

The tasks are relatively simple and are set at a level at which patients can sabotage the task but they cannot fail and then scold the therapist.

The patient must understand that not the physician but life itself is inexorable. He must understand that ultimately [he will have] to transfer to practical life that which has been theoretically recognized . . . But from the physician he hears no word of reproach or of impatience, at most an occasional kindly, harmless, ironical remark. (p. 101)

A 50-year-old man who professed "genuine" intention to get married but simultaneously avoided women was instructed to seek one meaningful contact with a woman (how to do so was up to him) every day. After raising many objections, he complained, "But it's *so* hard! I'll get so tired out I won't be able to function." The therapist good-humoredly relented and informed him, "Since God rested on the seventh day, I can't ask you to do more than God. So you need carry out the task only six days a week."

One form of task setting Adler introduced is called *antisuggestion* by Wexberg (1929) and *paradoxical intention* by Frankl (1963). This method used nonclinically by Knight Dunlap (1933) was labeled *negative practice*. The symptomatic patient unwittingly reinforces his symptoms by fighting them, by telling himself "Why did this have to happen to *me?*" He tries to divert his attention so he will not think about them and finds himself constantly thinking about them or watching himself. The insomniac keeps one eye open to observe whether the other is falling asleep, and then wonders why he cannot sleep. To halt this fight, the patient is instructed to intend and even increase that which he is fighting against.

Creating images

Adler was fond of describing patients with a simple phrase, for example, "The beggar as king." Other Adlerians give patients similar shorthand images that confirm the adage that "one picture is worth a thousand words." Remembering this image, the patient can remind himself of his goals, and in later stages he can learn to use the image to laugh at himself. One overambitious patient, labeled "Superman," one day began to unbutton his shirt. When the therapist made inquiry, the patient laughingly replied, "So you can see my blue shirt with the big 'S' on it." Another patient, fearing sexual impotence, concurred with the therapist's observation that he had never seen an impotent dog. The patient advanced as explanation, "The dog just does what he's supposed to do without worrying about whether he'll be able to perform." The therapist suggested that at his next attempt at sexual intercourse, before he made any advances, he should smile and say inwardly, "Bow wow." The following week he informed the members of his group, "I bow-wowed."

Catching oneself

When a patient understands his goals and wants to change, he is instructed to catch himself "with his hand in the cookie jar" as it were. The patient may catch himself in the midst of his old behavior but still feel incapable of doing anything about it at the moment. With additional practice, he learns to anticipate the situation and his behavior before their occurrence and, consequently, either to avoid or modify the situation or to change his behavioral approach.

The pushbutton technique

This method, effective with people who feel they are victims of their disjunctive emotions, involves requesting the patient to close his eyes, recreate a pleasant incident from his experience, and to note the feeling that accompanies this recreation. Then he is asked to recreate an unpleasant incident of hurt, humiliation, failure, or anger and to note the accompanying feeling. Following this the patient recreates the first scene again. The lesson Adlerians try to teach the client is that he can create whatever feeling he wishes merely by deciding about what he will think. He has the button in his hands and can push it at will to create any feeling, good or bad. He is the creator, not the victim, of his emotions. To be depressed, for example, requires *choosing* to be depressed. We try to impress the patient with his power for self-determination. This method, devised for clinical use by Mosak, has been the subject of experimental investigation by Brewer (1976) who found it the most effective technique in treating state depression.

The "aha" experience

As the patient gains awareness in treatment and increases his participation in life, he recurrently has "aha" or "eureka" experiences. "Hey, that makes sense." "Now I know how it works." "Wow, that was simpler than I thought." With this greater understanding, he generates self-confidence and optimism resulting in increased encouragement and willingness to confront life's problems with commitment, compassion, and empathy.

Posttherapy

The best part of therapy comes after therapy when the fledgling human being can leave the therapist's nest and try his wings on his own, nurturing himself, and flying like a free spirit in the universe. The patient can implement his newly acquired learnings in his own service and that of mankind. Operationally, the goal of therapy may be defined as that of making the therapist superfluous. If therapist and patient have both done their jobs well, the goal will have been achieved.

APPLICATIONS

Problems

Although Adler, like the other *Nervenärzte* ("nerve doctors") of his era, conducted one-to-one psychotherapy, his own social outlook moved him out of the consulting room and into the community. Although he never relinquished his clinical interests, he concurrently was an educator and social reformer. Joost Meerloo (1970), a Freudian, eulogizes Adler with his confession,

As a matter of fact, the whole body of psychoanalysis and psychiatry is imbued with Adler's ideas, although few want to acknowledge this fact. We are all plagiarists, though we hate to confess it . . . The whole body of social psychiatry would have been impossible without Adler's pioneering zest. (p. 40)

Clinical

All the early pioneers in psychotherapy treated neurotics. However, psychotics were considered not amenable to psychotherapy because they could not enter into a transference relationship. Adlerians, unencumbered by the concept of transference, treated psychotic patients regularly. Henri Ellenberger (1970) suggests that "among the great pioneers of dynamic psychiatry, Janet and Adler are the only ones who had personal clinical experience with criminals, and Adler was the only one who wrote something on the subject from his direct experience." Ernst Papanek (1971), of whom Claude Brown (1965) wrote so glowingly in his *Manchild in the Promised Land,* was director of Wiltwyck School (a reform school), and Mosak set up a group therapy program at Cook County Jail in Chicago employing paraprofessionals as therapists (O'Reilly, Cizon, Flanagan, & Pflanczer, 1965). The growth model implicit in Adlerian theory has prompted Adlerians to see human problems in terms of people realizing themselves, in becoming fellow human beings. Much "treatment" then is of "normal" people with "normal" problems. A therapy that does not provide the client with a philosophy of life, whatever else it may accomplish in the way of symptom eradication or alleviation, behavior modification, or insight, is an incomplete therapy. Hence the Adlerian concerns himself with his client's problems of living and his problems of existence. Deficiency, suffering, and illness do not constitute the price of admission to Adlerian therapy. One may enter therapy to learn about oneself, to grow, to actualize oneself.

Social

Adler's interests were rather catholic. In the area of education, he believed in prevention rather than cure and founded family education centers in the community where parents and teachers could receive direct advice on childrearing. Dreikurs and his students (Dreikurs et al., 1959) have founded family education centers throughout the world. Offshoots of these centers are the hundreds of parent study groups where parents can share problems and solutions with other parents under guidance of a paraprofessional leader (Soltz, 1967). In addition, professional therapists have used a variety of methods for teaching childrearing practices (Allred, 1976; Beecher & Beecher, 1966; Dreikurs, 1948; Dreikurs & Soltz, 1964).

Adler himself wrote on social issues and problems such as crime, war, religion, group psychology, Bolshevism, leadership, and nationalism. Among contemporary Adlerians [Angers (1960); Clark (1965, 1967a, 1967b); Elam (1969a, 1969b); Gottesfeld (1966); Hemming (1956); La Porte (1966); Lombardi (1969); and Nikelly (1971c)] the "newer" social problems of protest, race, drugs, social conditions, and the "newer" views of religion have been added to the Adlerians' previous interests.

Evaluation

Until very recently, little research had emerged from the Adlerian group. As was the case with most European clinicians, European Adlerians were suspicious of research based upon statistical methods. A complicating factor was the *idiographic* (case method) approach upon which Adlerians relied. Statistical methods are more appropriate for *nomothetic* (group) research. Even now statisticians have not developed appropriate sophisticated methods for idiographic studies. The research methods lent themselves well to studies of "causal" factors, but the Adlerian rejected causalism, feeling that causes can only be imputed (and therefore disputed) in retrospective fashion but that they contributed little to the understanding of man.

The most-often cited studies involving

Adlerian psychology were conducted by non-Adlerians. Fred Fiedler (1950) compared therapeutic relationships in psychoanalytic, nondirective, and Adlerian therapy. He found there was greater similarity between therapeutic relationships developed by experts of the three schools than between expert and less expert therapists within the same school. Recently Crandall (1981) has presented the first large-scale investigation of an Adlerian construct. Because of the number of ways social interest has been defined (Bickhard & Ford, 1976; Crandall, 1981; Edgar, 1975; Kazan, 1978), his study represents a valuable contribution to the understanding of this concept.

A joint research study conducted by the (Rogerian) Counseling Center of the University of Chicago and the Alfred Adler Institute of Chicago examined the effects of time limits in psychotherapy (Schlien, Mosak, & Dreikurs, 1962). Patients of both groups of therapists were given 20 interviews and the groups were compared with each other and with two control groups. The investigators reported changes in self-ideal correlations. These correlations improved significantly and, according to this measure, suggest that time-limited therapy "may be said to be not only *effective,* but also twice as *efficient* as time-unlimited therapy." Follow-up of these patients in both experimental groups indicated that the gains were retained when measured one year later.

Much of the research in family constellation has also been done by non-Adlerians. Charles Miley (1969), and Lucille Forer (1972) have compiled bibliographies of this literature. The results reported are contradictory probably because non-Adlerians treat birth order as a matter of ordinal position and Adlerians consider birth order in terms of

psychological position (Mosak, 1972). Walter Toman (1970) recognized this distinction in his many studies of the family constellation.

Ansbacher (1946) and Mosak (1958) have also distinguished between Freudian and Adlerian approaches to the interpretation of early recollections. Robin Gushurst (1971) provides a manual for interpreting and scoring one class of recollections. His reliability studies demonstrate that judges can interpret early recollection data with high interjudge reliability. He also conducted three validity studies to investigate the hypothesis that life goals may be identified from early recollections data, and found that he could do this with two of his three experimental groups. While Fiedler compared therapists of different orientations, Heine (1953) compared patients' reports of their experiences in Adlerian, Freudian, and Rogerian therapy.

Adlerian psychology would undoubtedly benefit from more research. With the shift in locus from Europe to the United States, with the accelerated growth of the Adlerian school in recent years, with the introduction of more American-trained Adlerians into academic settings, and with the development of new research strategies suitable for idiographic data, the integration of Adlerians into research activities already exhibits some signs of burgeoning.

Treatment

One can hardly identify a mode of treatment in which some Adlerian is not engaged. From a historical viewpoint the initial Adlerian modality was one-to-one psychotherapy. Many Adlerians still regard individual psychotherapy as the treatment of choice. But they did not accept some of the therapeutic conventions of the times and discounted the value of prognosis. Adlerians demonstrated willingness to undertake treatment with any who sought their services.

Dreikurs, Mosak, and Shulman (1952a, 1952b, 1982) introduced *multiple psychotherapy,* a format in which several therapists treat a single patient. It offers constant consultation between therapists, prevents the emotional attachment of a patient to a single therapist and obviates or dissolves impasses. Countertransference reactions are minimized. Flexibility in the number of therapist roles and models is increased. Patients are more impressed or reassured when two therapists independently agree. The patient also may benefit from the experience of observing disagreement between therapists and learn that people can disagree without loss of face. With respect to the patient the advantages are as follows:

1. Multiple therapy creates an atmosphere that facilitates learning.
2. The patient can interact with two different personalities with two different approaches.
3. Therapeutic impasses are avoided by the introduction of fresh viewpoints, thus accelerating the therapy.
4. Patients may view themselves more objectively, since they are both spectator and participant.
5. In the event that the therapist and patient do not "hit it off," the patient does not become a therapeutic "casualty" and is merely transferred to the second therapist.
6. The many problems related to dependency in treatment are solved more easily. These include the responsibility for the self, absence of the therapist, transference reactions, and termination.

7. Multiple therapy is an example of democratic social interaction and is thus a valuable lesson for the patient (Dreikurs, Mosak, & Shulman, 1952b, pp. 595-96).

An additional advantage of the method lies in its use for training therapists. The supervising therapist does not rely upon the candidate therapist's report, which may be distorted through retrospective falsification. Supervisors sit in with their trainees, observe their interventions, provide them with security and support, and can comment upon the observed behavior.

Dreikurs (1959) in the mid-1920s initiated group therapy in private practice. This application was a natural evolution from the Adlerian axiom that people's problems were always social problems. Group therapy finds considerable adherents among Adlerians. Some Adlerian therapists regard group therapy as the method of choice either on practical grounds (e.g., fees, large numbers of patients to be treated, etc.) or because they believe that since human problems are primarily social problems, they are most effectively handled in the group social situation. Others use group therapy as a preface to individual therapy or to taper patients off from intensive individual psychotherapy. A number of therapists combine individual and group psychotherapy in the conviction that this combination maximizes therapeutic effect (H. Papanek, 1954, 1956). Still other therapists visualize the group as assisting in the solution of certain selected problems or with certain types of populations. Co-therapist groups are very common among Adlerians.

An offshoot of group treatment is the therapeutic social club in a mental hospital as inititated by the British

Adlerian, Joshua Bierer. Similar clubs exist in New York (Mohr & Garlock, 1959) and at Saint Joseph Hospital in Chicago. Although these clubs possess superficial similarities to Abraham Low's Recovery groups (Low, 1952) and to halfway houses in that all attempt to facilitate the patient's reentrance into society, the therapeutic social club emphasizes "social" rather than the "therapeutic" aspects of life, taking the "healthy" rather than the "sick" model. Psychodrama has been used by Adlerians, sometimes as separate therapy, sometimes in conjunction with another therapeutic modality (Starr, 1977).

Marriage counseling has figured prominently in Adlerian activities. Adlerians defied the trend of the times and preferred to treat the couple as a unit rather than as separate individuals. To "treat" merely one mate may be compared to having only half the dialogue of a play. Seeing the couple together suggests that they have a joint relationship problem rather than individual problems and invites joint effort in the solution of these problems. The counselor can observe their interaction and point out to them the nature of their interaction (Mozdzierz & Lottman, 1973; Pew & Pew, 1972). Married couples group therapy (Deutsch, 1967) and married couples study groups constitute two more settings for conducting marriage counseling. Phillips and Corsini (1982) have written a self-help book to be used by married people who are experiencing trouble in their marriage.

In the early 1920s, Adler persuaded the Viennese school administration to establish child-guidance centers in the schools. The social group was the primary vehicle for treatment (Adler, 1963a; Alexandra Adler, 1951; Seidler & Zilahi, 1949). Dreikurs wrote several popular books and many articles (Dreikurs, 1948; Dreikurs & Grey, 1968; Dreikurs & Soltz, 1964) to disseminate this information to parents and teachers, and currently thousands of parents are enrolled in study groups where they obtain supplementary information on childrearing.

The preventive methods in schools as started by Adler were adopted by educators and school counselors who used them in individual classes, schools, and in one instance in an entire school system (Mosak, 1971a). The methods were originally applied in the Individual Psychological Experimental School in Vienna (Birnbaum, 1935; Spiel, 1962) and have been elaborated upon in this country by many educators (Corsini, 1977, 1979; Dreikurs, 1968, 1972; Dinkmeyer & Dreikurs, 1963; Dreikurs, Grunwald & Pepper, 1982; Grunwald, 1954).

With respect to broader social problems, Dreikurs devoted the last part of his life to the problem of interindividual and intergroup conflict resolution. Much of this work was performed in Israel and has not been reported in the literature. Kenneth Clark, a black psychologist and former president of the American Psychological Association, has devoted much of his career to studying and providing recommendations for solutions for problems of black people, as have Harry Elam (1969a, 1969b) and Jacqueline Brown (1976).

Management

The setting

Adlerians function in every imaginable setting: the private-practice office, hospitals, day hospitals, jails, schools, and in community programs. Offices do not need any special furnishing, but reflect either the therapist's aesthetic preferences or the condition of the institution's budget. No special equipment is used, except perhaps for special projects. Although voice recordings are a matter of individual choice, they are sometimes maintained as the patient's file. Some therapists ask their patients to listen to these recordings during or between interviews. Some voice recordings and videotape recordings have also been made for demonstration and teaching purposes.

In the initial interviews, the therapist generally obtains the following kinds of information (in addition to demographic information):

1. Was patient self-referred? If not, he may continue treatment only for the duration of his "sentence." A reluctant adolescent may punish his parents by failing to keep appointments for which he knows his parents must pay. For that matter, the patient who is sent may merely be the identified patient, so labeled by someone, usually parents. This is one reason why, when a child is referred, Adlerians prefer to see the entire family.

2. If the patient is reluctant, one must convert him into a patient if therapy is to proceed. Fourteen such "conversion techniques" appear in a therapy syllabus (Mosak & Shulman, 1963).

3. What does the patient come for? Does he seek treatment to alleviate suffering? If so, suffering from what? Does he make the implicit demand that the therapist legitimize or confirm an already made decision? Does he come to get others off his back? May he think that as long as he is in therapy, he does not have to accept responsibilities or make decisions? After all, he may be designated by himself or others as "sick" or "confused."

Some new patients are "supermarket shoppers." They inform you of the number of therapists who have helped them already. Their secret goal is to be perfect. Unless such a patient's fictional goal is disclosed and he is derailed from seeking it, you may be the latest of many therapists about whom he will be telling his next therapist. Adler describes such a person as belonging to the ruling type, one who must conquer. Others are scalp-collectors. They spend their lives defeating therapists, winning Pyrrhic victories. Therapists of any orientation will recognize many such recurring types (Mosak, 1971; Mosak & Shulman, 1963).

4. What are the patient's expectations about treatment? A patient may check his therapist's diplomas and credentials to make sure he is not a quack. If there is no couch in the room, he worries because in the movies an analyst has a couch. Controllers, persons with "verbal diarrhea," criers, and other such patients may not permit the therapist a word (and then thank him for being so helpful). Some viewers of psychological movies will think that free association is the order of the day.

5. What are the patient's expectations for himself? Does he expect to emerge from treatment perfect? Does he consider himself hopeless? Does he expect or demand a solution for a specific problem without any major personality alterations? Does he expect immediate cure?

6. What are the patient's goals in psychotherapy? We must distinguish between stated goals—to get well, to learn about himself, to be a better husband and father, to gain a new philosophy of life—and nonverbalized goals—to remain sick, to punish others, to defeat the therapist and sabotage therapy, to maintain good intentions without changing ("Look how hard I'm trying and the money I'm spending on therapy"). The importance of this determination cannot be overstated. The Adlerian defines resistance as that which occurs when the patient's goals and those of the therapist

do not coincide. Consequently, if the therapist fails to understand his patient's goals, they may be operating at cross-purposes, and the therapeutic effort may deteriorate into a vicious circle of resistance—overcoming resistance—resistance rather than the cooperative effort for which the Adlerian therapist aims. The best technique for handling resistance is to avoid fostering it, to listen attentively and empathically to the patient, to follow his movement in therapy, to understand his goals and strategies, and to encourage the development of therapy as a "we" endeavor.

The patient may resist to depreciate or defeat the therapist. He must defeat the therapist because he lacks the courage to live on the useful side of life and fears that the therapist might channel him in that direction. The intensification of such escape methods may become most pronounced during the termination phase of treatment when the patient realizes he must soon face the realistic tasks of life without the therapist's support and he is not sure of his own courage to embark on an independent venture of this magnitude.

Tests

Routine physical examinations are not required by Adlerians in view of the therapy's educational orientation. Nevertheless, many patients do have physiological problems and Adlerians are trained to be sensitive to the presence of these problems. Where the therapist suspects such problems, he will make referrals for physical examination.

Adlerians are divided on the issue of psychological testing. Most Adlerians avoid nosological diagnosis, except for nontherapeutic purposes such as filling out insurance forms. Labels are static descriptions and ignore the *movement* of

the individual. They describe what the individual *has,* but not how he *moves* through life.

Among the older, European-trained therapists, psychological testing was a dirty word. The older European psychological tradition included an anti-testing bias (Orgler, 1965), some notable exceptions being the Rorschach, the Binet, and the Word Association Test. Apparently Adler himself, although he developed the first projective test, Early Recollections, had little use for testing. Dreikurs was distrustful of tests, his opinion of them being that they were relatively unnecessary since "the test situation indicates what is probably true. Observation permits us to determine what is true. . . ." (Dinkmeyer & Dreikurs, 1963, p. 10). Dreikurs also felt tests were unreliable because they could provide deceptive results and, thus, might be harmful (Dreikurs, 1968, p. 7). Dreikurs did refer patients for testing nevertheless.

Regine Seidler (1967) placed more faith in projective testing than in so-called objective tests, maintaining that the latter are actually subjective tests since "The *subjective attitude* of each and every individual toward any given test necessarily renders the test non-objective" (p. 4). Objective tests were more useful to her as measures of test-taking attitude than of what the test was purportedly measuring.

Early recollections serve as a test for Adlerians, assisting them in the life-style assessment. Younger Adlerians employ many conventional tests and some nonconventional ones for diagnostic and differential diagnostic purposes as well as in the treatment of the patient.

The therapist

The Adlerian therapist ideally is an authentically sharing, caring person. Helene and Ernst Papanek (1961) write,

"The therapist participates actively. Without playing any sharply defined 'role,' he shows warmth toward and a genuine interest in the patient and encourages especially his desire for change and betterment. The relationship itself has a purpose: to help the patient help himself" (p. 117). Adler (1924) relates how he treated a mute schizophrenic patient who after three months of silence assaulted him and "I instantly decided not to defend myself. After a further attack, during which a window was smashed, I bound up his slightly bleeding wound in the friendliest way" (p. 24). Since the ideal goal in psychotherapy is to encourage the development of social interest, the therapist must be a model for social interest himself.

The Adlerian therapist remains free to have feelings and opinions and to express them. Such expression in a spontaneous way permits the patient to view therapists as human beings, discouraging any perceptions of omnipotence or perfection with which patients may invest them. If we therapists err, we err—but then the patient may learn the courage to be imperfect from this experience (Lazarsfeld, 1966). The experience may also facilitate therapy.

Therapists must not inject evaluation of their worth into the therapy, doing their therapeutic job without concern for prestige, not reveling in successes or becoming discouraged by failures. Otherwise, they may bounce like a rubber ball from therapy hour to therapy hour or perhaps even within the same hour. The therapist's worth does not depend upon external factors. The center of gravity, feeling of worth, lies within one's self. The therapist is task-oriented rather than self-oriented.

The therapist reveals himself as a person. Since the therapist is authentically himself, the patient has the opportunity to appraise him as a human being. These perceptions may combine realistic judgments as well as judgments stemming from the patient's life-style. The concept of the *anonymous therapist* is foreign to Adlerian psychology. Such a role would increase social distance between therapist and patient interfering with the establishment of an egalitarian, human relationship that Adlerians regard as indispensable. The "anonymous therapist" role was created to facilitate the establishment of a transference relationship and since the Adlerian rejects the transference concept, as Freud formulated it, the maintenance of such a posture is considered irrelevant if not harmful to the relationship the therapist wants to establish with his patient. Dreikurs (1961) deplored the prevalent attitude among therapists of not coming too close to patients because it might affect the therapeutic relationship adversely. Shulman (Wexberg, 1970, p. 88) defines the role of the therapist as that of "a helping friend." Self-revelation can only occur when therapists feel secure, at home with others, unafraid to be human and fallible, and thus unafraid of their patient's evaluations, criticism, or hostility (cf. Rogers' "congruence"). For these and other reasons, Adlerian training institutes customarily require a "didactic analysis" of their candidates.

Is the Adlerian therapist judgmental? In a sense all therapists are judgmental in that therapy rests upon some value orientation: a belief that certain behavior is better than other behavior, that certain goals are better than other goals, that one organization of personality is superior to another form of organization. Dreikurs (1961) states, "There is always a value and moral problem involved in the cure [in all therapy]" (p. 93). On the other hand, the patient who seeks help is often a discouraged human being. To criticize him would merely reinforce his discouragement, rob him of his residual sense of personal worth, and perhaps confirm some of his life-style convictions (e.g., "People are unfair" or "I am unlovable" or "I do everything wrong"). Since two cardinal principles of the Adlerian intervention are to win the patient and to encourage him, such judgments are best avoided.

Patient problems

If the therapist does not like the patient, it raises problems for a therapist of any persuasion (Fromm-Reichman, 1949). Some therapists merely do not accept such patients. Still others feel they ought not to have or ought to overcome such negative feelings and accept the patient for treatment, leading to both participants "suffering." It appears difficult to possess "unconditional positive regard" for a patient you dislike. Probably Adlerians meet this situation in the same manner other therapists do.

Seduction problems are treated as any other patient problem. The secure therapists will not be frightened, panic, or succumb. If the patient's activities nevertheless prevent the therapy from continuing, the patient may be referred to another therapist, a transfer easily accomplished in multiple psychotherapy. Flattery problems are in some ways similar and have been discussed elsewhere (Berne, 1964; Mosak & Gushurst, 1971).

Suicide threats are always taken seriously (Ansbacher, 1961, 1969). Alfred Adler warned, however, that our goal is "to knock the weapon out of his hand" so the patient cannot make us vulnerable and intimidate us at will with his threats. As an example, he narrates, "A patient once asked me, smiling, 'Has anyone ever taken his life while being treated by you?'

I answered him, 'Not yet, but I am prepared for this to happen at any time'" (Ansbacher & Ansbacher, 1956, pp. 338-39).

Kurt Adler (1961) postulates "an underlying rage against people" in suicide threats and that this goal of vengefulness must be uncovered. He "knocks the weapon out of the patient's hand" as follows:

Patients have tested me with the question, how I would feel, if I were to read of their suicide in the newspaper. I answer that it is possible that some reporter hungry for news would pick up such an item from a police blotter. But, the next day, the paper will already be old, and only a dog perhaps may honor their suicide notice by lifting a leg over it in some corner. (p. 66)

For an extended description of problems in psychotherapy, Alexandra Adler (1943), Lazarsfeld (1952-53) and Oscar Pelzman (1952) discuss problems beyond the scope of this chapter.

CASE EXAMPLE

Background

The patient was a 53-year old, Viennese-born man, in treatment almost continuously with Freudian psychoanalysts, here and abroad, since he was 17. With the advent of tranquilizers, he had transferred his allegiances to psychiatrists who treated him with a combination of drugs and psychotherapy and finally with drugs alone. When he entered Adlerian treatment, he was being maintained by his previous therapist on an opium derivative and Thorazine. He failed to tell his previous therapist of his decision to see us and also failed to inform us that he was still obtaining medication from his previous therapist.

The treatment process was atypical in the sense that the patient's "illness" hampered us from following our customary procedure. Having over the years become therapy-wise, he invested his creativity in efforts to run the therapy. Cooperative effort was virtually impossible. In conventional terms, the co-therapists, Drs. A and B, had their hands full dealing with the patient's resistances and "transference."

Problem

When the patient entered treatment, he had taken to bed and spent almost all his time there because he felt too weak to get up. His wife had to be constantly at his side or he would panic. Once she was encouraged by a friend to attend the opera alone. The patient wished her a good time, and then told her, "When you return, I shall be dead." His secretary was forced into conducting his successful business. Everyone was forced into "the emperor's service." The price he paid for this service was intense suffering in the form of depression, obsessive-compulsive behavior, phobic behavior, especially agoraphobia, divorce from the social world, somatic symptoms, and invalidism.

Treatment

The patient was seen in multiple psychotherapy by Drs. A and B, but both therapists were not present at each interview. We dispensed with the life-style assessment because the patient had other immediate goals. It seemed to us from the patient's behavior that he probably had been raised as a pampered child, and that he was using "illness" to tyrannize the world and to gain exemption from the life tasks. If these guesses were correct, we anticipated he would attempt to remain "sick," would resist giving up drugs, and would demand special attention from his therapists. As part of the treatment strategy, the therapists decided to wean him from medication, to give him no special attention, and not to be manipulated by him. Since he had undergone analysis over a period of more than three decades, the therapists thought he could probably produce a better analysis of his problems than they could. For this reason, interpretation was kept at a minimum. The treatment plan envisaged a tactical and strategic rather than interpretive approach. Some excerpts from the early part of treatment are reproduced below:

March 8

Dr. B wanted to collect lifestyle information but the patient immediately complained that he wanted to terminate. He said his previous therapist, Dr. C, had treated him differently. Therapist B was too impersonal. "You won't even give me your home phone number. You aren't impressed by my illness. Your treatment is well meaning but it won't help. Nothing helps. I'm going back to Dr. C and ask him to put me in the hospital. He gave me advice and you are so cruel by not telling me what to do."

March 19

Relatively calm. Compares B with Dr. C. Later compares B with A. Favors B over Dr. C because he respects former's strength. Favors B over A because he can succeed in ruffling latter but not former. Talk centers about his use of weakness to overpower others.

March 22

Telephones to say he must be hospitalized. Wife left him [untrue] and secretary left him [It turns out she went to lunch]. Would B come to his office to see him? B asks him to keep appointment in B's office. Patient races about office upset. "I'm sweating water and blood." When B remains calm, patient takes out bottle of Thorazine and threatens to take all. Next he climbs up on radiator, opens window (17th floor), jumps back, and says, "No, it's too high."

"You don't help me. Why can't I have an injection?" Then he informs B that B is a soothing influence. "I wish I could spend the whole day with you." He speaks softly to patient and patient speaks quietly. Patient asks for advice about what to do this weekend. B gives antisuggestion and tells him to try to worry as much as he can. He is surprised and dismisses it as "bad advice."

March 29

B was sick on 3-26 and patient saw A. "It was useless." No longer worried about state hospital. Will now wind up as bum because he got drunk last week. His secretary gave him notice but he hopes to keep her "by taking abuse. No one treats a boss like she treats me." Got out of bed and worked last week. Went out selling but "everyone rejected me." When B indicates that he seems to be better, he insists he's deteriorating. When B inquires how, he replies paradoxically, "I beat out my competitors this week."

April 2

Has habit of sticking finger down throat and vomiting. Threatens to do so when enters office today. B tells patient about the logical consequences of his act—he will have to mop up. Patient withdraws finger. "If you would leave me alone, I'd fall asleep so fast." B leaves him alone. Patient angrily declaims "Why do you let me sleep?"

April 9

Too weak even to telephone therapist. If wife goes on vacation, he will kill himself. How can he survive with no one to tell him to eat, to go to bed, to get up? "All I do is vomit and sleep." B suggests that he tyrannizes her as he did his mother and sister. He opens window and inquires, "Shall I jump?" B recognizes this as an attempt to intimidate rather than a serious threat and responds, "Suit yourself." Patient closes window and accuses, "You don't care, either." Asks whether he can see A next time and before receiving answer, says, "I don't want him anyway." Follows this with, "I want to go to the state hospital. Can you get me a private room?" At end of interview falls to knees and sobs, "Help me! Help me to be a human being."

April 12

Enters, falls to knees, encircles therapist's knees, whimpers, "Help me!" So depressed. If only he could end it all. B gives him Adler's suggestion to do one thing each day that would give someone pleasure. Patient admits behaving better. Stopped annoying secretary and let her go home early because of bad weather. Agitation stops.

April 15

Didn't do anything this weekend to give pleasure. However, he did play cards with wife. Took her for drive. Sex with wife for "first time in a long time." B gives encouragement and then repeats "pleasure" suggestion. He can't do it. Calm whole hour. Says his wife has told him to discontinue treatment. Upon inquiry, he says she didn't say exactly that but had said, "I leave it up to you."

April 19

Wants B to accompany him back to his

office because he forgot something. Wants shorter hour this week and longer one next week. "Dr. C let me do that." When B declines, he complains, "Doctor, I don't know what to do with you anymore."

April 23

Wouldn't consider suicide. "Perhaps I have a masochistic desire to live." B suggests he must be angry with life. He responds that he wants to be an infant and have all his needs gratified. The world should be a big breast and he should be able to drink without having to suck [probably an interpretation he had received in psychoanalysis]. Yesterday he had fantasy of destroying the whole city.

This weekend he helped his wife work in the garden. He asks for suggestions for weekend. B and patient play "yes-but." B does so deliberately to point out game (cf. Berne's "Why don't you . . . Yes But" [1964]) to patient. Patient then volunteers possibility of clay modeling. B indicates this may be good choice in that patient can mold, manipulate, and "be violent."

April 29

Had birthday last week and resolved to turn over new leaf for new year but didn't. Cries, "Help me, help me." Depreciates B. "How much would you charge me to come to my summer home? I'm so sick, I vomited blood." When B tells him if he's that sick, hospitalization might be advisable, he smiles and says, "For money, you'd come out." B and patient speak of attitude toward B and attitude toward his father. Patient depreciates both, possibly because he could not dominate either.

May 1

Didn't think he could make it today because afraid to walk on street. Didn't

sleep all night. So excited, so upset [he seems calm]. Perhaps he should be put in hospital but then what will happen to his business?

"We could sit here forever and all you would tell me is to get clay. Why don't you give me medicine or advice?" B points out that patient is much stronger than any medication as evidenced by number of therapists and treatments he has defeated.

He says he is out of step with world. B repeats an earlier interpretation by A that the patient wants the world to conform to him and follows with statement about his desire to be omnipotent, a desire that makes him feel weak and simultaneously compensates for his feelings of weakness. He confirms with "All Chicago should stand still so I could have a holiday. The police should stop at gunpoint anyone who wants to go to work. But I don't want to. I don't want to do anything anymore. I want a paycheck but I don't want to work." B remarks on shift from "I can't" to "I don't want to." Patient admits and says, "I don't want to get well. Should I make another appointment?" B refers decision back to him. He makes appointment.

May 6

"I'm at the end, dying with fear [enumerates symptoms]. Since 5 this morning I'm murdering ——— and ———. Such nice people and I'm murdering them and I'm electrocuted. And my secretary and wife can't stand it anymore. Take me to a state hospital. I don't want to go. Take me. I'm getting crazy and you don't help me. Help me, *Lieber Doktor!* I went into the ladies' room twice today to get my secretary and the girls complained to the building office. I'm not above the rules. I knew I violated them. My zipper was down again [he frequently "forgets"] and I just pull-

ed it up before you came in today." B
agrees that state hospital might be appropriate if he is becoming "crazier."
"Then my wife will divorce me. It's terrible. They have bars there. I won't go. I'm
not that bad yet. Why, last week I went
out and made a big sale!" B suggests he
"practice" his fears and obsessions.

May 8
Seen by A and B who did summary of his
family constellation. It was done very tentatively because of the sparsity of information elicited.

May 13
Complains about symptoms. He had
taken his wife to the movie but "was too
upset to watch it." He had helped with
the raking. Returns to symptoms and beg-
ging for Thorazine. "How will I live
without Thorazine?" B suggests they
ought to talk about how to live. He yells,
"With your quiet voice, you'll drive me
crazy." B asks, "Would you like me to
yell at you like your father did?" "I won't
talk to you anymore."

"Lieber Gott, liberate me from the evil
within me." Prays to everyone for help. B
counters with "Have you ever solicited
your own help?" Patient replies, "I have
no strength, I could cry. I could shout. I
don't have strength. Let me vomit."

May 15
Demands Thorazine or he will have heart
attack. B requests a future autobiography. "I don't anticipate anything" and
returns to Thorazine question. B points
out his real achievement in staying off
Thorazine. Patient mentions price in suffering. B points out that this makes it an
even greater achievement. Patient accepts
idea reluctantly. B points out that they are
at cross-purposes since patient wants to
continue suffering but have pills; B's goal

is to have him stop his suffering. "I want
pills." B offers clay. "Shit with your
clay."

May 20
Must have Thorazine. Has murderous
and self-castrating fantasies. Tells A that
he (A) doesn't know anything about
medicine. Dr. C did. Why don't we let
him go back to Dr. C? A leaves room with
patient following. After three to four
minutes he returns and complains, "You
call *this* treatment?" A points out demand of patient to have own way. He is a
little boy who wants to be big but doesn't
think he can make it. He is a pampered
tyrant and A refers to patient's favorite
childhood game of lying in bed with sister
and playing "Emperor and Empress."

Patient points out innate badness in
himself. A points out he creates it. Patient
talks of hostility and murder. A interprets
look on his face as taking pride in his bad
behavior. He picks up letter opener,
trembles, then grasps hand with other
hand but continues to tremble. A tells him
that this is a spurious fight between good
and evil, that he can decide how he will
behave.

He kneaded clay a little while this
weekend.

May 22
Last weekend he mowed lawn, tried to
read but "I'm nervous. I'm talking to you
like a human being but I'm not really a
human being." Raw throat. Fears might
have throat cancer. Stopped sticking
finger down throat to vomit as consequence. Discussion of previously expressed idea of "like a human being."
Fantasy of riding a boat through a storm.
Fantasy of A being acclaimed by crowd
and patient in fantasy asks B, "Are you
used to A getting all the attention?"

Complains about wife and secretary,

neither of whom will any longer permit tyrannization.

June 3

Relates fantasy of being magician and performing unbelievable feats at the White House. He asked the President whether he was happily married and then produced the President's ring. Nice weekend. Made love to wife at his initiative. Grudgingly admits enjoying it.

June 10

"Ignored my wife this week." Yet he took initiative and they had sex again. Both enjoyed it but he was afraid because he read in a magazine that sex is a drain on the heart. At work secretary is angry. After she checks things, he rechecks. Pledged his God today he wouldn't do it anymore. He'll only check one time more. Outlines several plans for improving business "but I have not the strength." Wants to cut down to one interview per week because he doesn't get well and can't afford to pay. B suggests that perhaps he is improving if he wants to reduce the number of interviews. Patient rejects and agrees to two interviews weekly.

June 24

Talks about fears. B tells him he will go on vacation next week. He accepts it calmly although he had previously claimed to be unendurably upset. Patient tells B that he has given up vomiting and masturbation, saying, "You have enormous influence on me." B encourages by saying patient made the decision by himself.

Sept. 4

[Patient was not seen during August because he went on a "wonderful" vacation.] He stopped all medication except for the occasional use of a mild tran-

quilizer his family physician prescribed. Able to read and concentrate again. He has surrendered his obsessive ruminations. He and his secretary get along without fighting although she doesn't like him. He is punctual at the office. He and wife get along well. He is more considerate of her. Both are sexually satisfied.

B and patient plan for treatment. He expresses reluctance, feeling that he has gone as far as he can. After all, one psychoanalyst said that he was hopeless, recommended a lobotomy, so this was marked improvement. B agreed, telling patient that if he had considered the patient hopeless, he would not have undertaken treatment nor would he now be recommending continuation. "What kind of treatment?" B tells him that no external agent (e.g., medicine, lobotomy) will do it, that his salvation will come from within, that he can choose to live life destructively (and self-destructively) or constructively. He proposes to come weekly for four weeks and then biweekly. B does not accept the offer.

Sept. 17

Since yesterday his symptoms have returned. Heart palpitations.

Sept. 25

Took wife to dinner last night. Very pleasant. Business is slow and his obligations are heavy but he is working. He has to exert effort not to backslide. B schedules double interview. Patient doesn't want to see A. It will upset him. He doesn't see any sense in seeing B either but since B insists . . . Heart palpitations disappeared after last interview. Expresses realistic concerns today and has dropped usual frantic manner. Wants biweekly interviews. B wants weekly. Patient accepts without protest.

As therapy continued, his discussion of symptoms was superseded by discussion of realistic concerns. Resistance waned. When he entered treatment, he perceived himself as a good person who behaved badly because he was "sick." During therapy, he saw through his pretenses and settled for being "a bad guy." However, once he understood his tyranny and was able to accept it, he had the opportunity to ask himself how he preferred to live his life—usefully or uselessly. Since the therapists used the monolithic approach (Alexander & French, 1946; Mosak & Shulman, 1963), after resolving the issue of his tyranny, therapy moved on to his other "basic mistakes," one at a time. The frequency of interviews was decreased and termination was by mutual agreement.

Follow-up

Patient improved, remaining off medication. Devoting himself to his business, it prospered to the point where he could retire early. He moved to a university town where he studied archaeology, the activity he liked best in life. The relationship with his wife improved and they traveled abroad. Because of the geographical distance between them, the therapists and the patient had no further contact.

SUMMARY

Adlerian psychology as a theory of personality may be described as follows:

1. Its approach is social, teleological, phenomenological, holistic, idiographic, and humanistic.

2. Its underlying assumptions are (*a*) tne individual is unique, (*b*) the individual is self-consistent, (*c*) the individual is responsible, (*d*) the person is creative, an actor, a chooser, and (*e*) people in a soft-deterministic way can direct their own behavior and control their destinies.

3. Its personality theory takes as its central construct the life-style, a system of subjective convictions held by the individual that contain his self-view and world-view. From these convictions, other convictions, methods of operations, and the goals of the person are derivative. The person behaves *as if* these convictions were true and uses his life-style as a cognitive map with which he explores, comprehends, prejudges, predicts, and controls the environment (the life tasks). Since the person cannot be understood *in vacuo* but only in his social context, the interaction between the individual and his life tasks, his line of movement, is indispensable for the purpose of fully comprehending the individual.

4. "Psychopathology," "mental illness," and similar nomenclature are reifications and perpetuate the nominal fallacy, "the tendency to confuse naming with explaining" (Beach, 1955). The "psychopathological" individual is a discouraged person. He had either never developed or lost his courage with respect to meeting the life tasks. With his pessimistic anticipations, stemming largely from his life-style, he creates "arrangements,"—evasions, excuses, sideshows, symptoms—to protect his self-esteem or he may "cop out" completely.

5. Since the person's difficulties emanate from faulty perceptions, learnings, values, and goals that have resulted in his discouragement, therapy consists of an educative or reeducative endeavor in which two equals cooperatively tackle the educational task. Many of the traditional analytic methods have been retained although they are understood, and sometimes used, differently by the Adlerian. The focus of the therapy is the encouragement of the individual, the experience of encouragement coming from many

avenues in the therapy. The individual learns to have faith in self, to trust, and to love. The ultimate, *ideal* goal of psychotherapy is to release the person's social interest so he may become a fellow human being, a cooperator, a contributor to the creation of a better society, a person who feels belonging and at home in the universe. This person can be said to have actualized himself. Since therapy is learning, theoretically at least, everyone can change. On the entrance door of the Guidance Clinic for Juvenile Delinquency in Vienna was the inscription, "IT IS NEVER TOO LATE" (Kramer, 1947).

From a rather shaky start, Adlerian psychology has become a viable, flourishing system. Neglected for several decades, it has in recent years acquired respectability. Training institutes, professional societies, family-education centers, and study groups continue to proliferate. With Adlerians being trained in universities rather than solely in institutes, they are writing more and doing research. Non-Adlerians are also engaged in Adlerian research. The previously rare Adlerian dissertation has become more commonplace. Currently Adlerians in greater numbers are moving out of the clinic and into society to renew their attention to the social issues and problems Adler raised 50 years ago—poverty, war, conflict resolution, aggression, religion, and social cooperation. As Way (1962) apprises, "We shall need not only, as Adler says, more cooperative individuals, but a society better fitted to fulfill the needs of human beings" (p. 360).

Complementing the Adlerians' endeavors are individuals and groups who have borrowed so heavily from Adler, often without acknowledgment and often without awareness. Adlerian formulations are so often discovered in the writing of non-Adlerians that they have become part of what Adler might have called "the common sense." Keith Sward (1947), for example, reviewed Alexander and French's *Psychoanalytic Therapy* (1946), writing,

—the Chicago group would seem to be Adlerian through and through. . . . The Chicago Institute for Psychoanalysis is not alone in this seeming rediscovery of Rank and Adler. Psychiatry and psychology as a whole seem to be drifting in the same direction. Adler has come to life in other vigorous circles, notably in the publications of the "Horney" school. (p. 601)

We observe glimpses of Adler in the Freudian ego-psychologists, in the neo-Freudians, in the existential systems, in the humanistic psychologies, in client-centered theory, in rational-emotive therapy, in integrity therapy, and in reality therapy. This is not an augury of the eventual disappearance of Adlerian psychology through absorption into other schools of psychology, for, as the motto of the Rockford, Illinois, Teacher Development Center, a school conducted along Adlerian lines as far as educational climate is concerned (Mosak, 1971a), proclaims, "Education is like a flame . . . you can give it away without diminishing the one from whom it came" (Teacher Development Center, n.d.). As Joseph Wilder writes in his introduction to *Essays in Individual Psychology* (Adler & Deutsch, 1959), ". . . most observations and ideas of Alfred Adler have subtly and quietly permeated modern psychological thinking to such a degree that the proper question is not whether one is Adlerian but how much of an Adlerian one is" (p. xv.).

ANNOTATED BIBLIOGRAPHY

Adler, A. *Social interest: A challenge to mankind.* (1929) New York: Capricorn Books, 1964.

This is the last exposition of Adler's

thought and provides an easily read overview of Adlerian psychology.

Adler, A. *Problems of neurosis: A book of case-histories.* (1929) New York: Harper Torchbooks, 1964.

Adler presents his theory of the neurotic process and neurotic development illustrating with many case examples. H. L. Ansbacher has written an excellent introduction to the paperback edition that concisely covers the basic theory of Adlerian psychology.

Ansbacher, H. L. Individual Psychology. In R. J. Corsini & A. J. Marsella (Eds.), *Personality theories, research and assessment.* Itasca, Ill.: F. E. Peacock, 1983.

Ansbacher's chapter is the twin of this one, compactly summarizing the theory of Individual Psychology while this chapter concentrates on Adlerian psychotherapy. Ansbacher's summary is probably one of the most satisfactory short explications of both the history and theory of Individual Psychology by one who is acknowledged to be the dean of Adlerian theoreticians.

Ansbacher, H. L., & Ansbacher, R. (Eds.). *The individual psychology of Alfred Adler.* New York: Basic Books, 1956, 1958; New York: Harper Torchbooks, 1964.

An almost encyclopedic collection of Adler's writings, this volume displays both the great variety of topics that commanded his attention and the evolution of his thinking through the years. Because of the nature of the construction of this book, it is imperative that the reader read the preface.

Dreikurs, R., & Soltz, V. *Children: The challenge.* New York: Duell, Sloan & Pearce, 1964.

Dreikurs and Soltz have written *the* Adlerian book on childrearing. It is the book most often studied in university training programs and parent study groups. While Adlerians have made extensive contributions to the fields of education and parent education, these are not within the purview of a chapter on Adlerian psychotherapy. Further references may be found in the two volumes of the Mosak & Mosak bibliography.

Manaster, G. J., & Corsini, R. J. *Individual psychology.* Itasca, Ill.: F. E. Peacock, 1982.

This is the first textbook of Adlerian psychology written in English by two students of Rudolf Dreikurs. Corsini was the former editor of the *Journal of Individual Psychology* and Manaster succeeded him. Written in a much simpler style than the Ansbacher & Ansbacher text (1956), this book covers more-or-less the same materials. Two features make it unique: it contains the single most complete Adlerian psychotherapy case summary published to date and there is a section abstracting the more important research studies published in the field of Adlerian psychology.

Mosak, H. H. (Ed.). *Alfred Adler: His influence on psychology today.* Park Ridge, N. J.: Noyes Press, 1973.

Written to commemorate the centennial year of Adler's birth, this volume contains chapters by Rudolf Dreikurs, Alexandra Adler, Lewis Way, Erwin Krausz, Willard and Marguerite Beecher, and others. These papers cover topics such as neurosis, black pride, Shakespeare, logical consequences, family therapy, the Oedipus myth, and sociometry.

Mosak, H., & Mosak, B. *A bibliography of Adlerian psychology.* Washington, D. C.: Hemisphere Publishing Corp., 1975.

This volume contains almost 10,000 references to the literature of Adlerian psychology and is valuable to the researcher in helping to locate Adlerian writings.

Mosak, B., & Mosak, H. H. *A bibliography of Adlerian psychology* (Vol. 2). Washington, D. C. Hemisphere Publishing, in press.

This second volume of this bibliography will cover all publications by Adlerians from 1973 to 1977.

CASE READINGS

Adler, A. *The case of Miss R: The interpretation of a life study.* New York: Greenberg, 1929.

Adler, A. The case of Mrs. A.: The diagnosis of a life style. In H. L. Ansbacher & R. R. Ansbacher (Eds.), *Superiority and social interest.* Evanston, Ill.: Northwestern University Press, 1964, pp. 159-90.

Ansbacher, H. L. Lee Harvey Oswald: An Adlerian interpretation. *Psychoanalytic Review,* 1966, *53,* 379-90.

Dreikurs, R. Case demonstrations. In R. Dreikurs, R. Lowe, M. Sonstegard, & R. J. Corsini, *Adlerian family counseling.* Eugene, Ore.: University of Oregon Press, 1959.

Mosak, Harold H. Life style assessment: A demonstration based on family constellation. *Journal of Individual Psychology,* 1972, *28,* 232-47.

REFERENCES

Adler, A. Problems in psychotherapy. *American Journal of Individual Psychology,* 1943, *3,* 1-5. (Also in K. A. Adler & D. Deutsch [Eds.], *Essays in individual psychology.* New York: Grove Press, 1959.)

Adler, A. Alfred Adler's viewpoint in child guidance. In E. Harms (Ed.), *Handbook of child guidance.* New York: Child Care Publications, 1951.

Adler, A. *Gesundheitsbuch für das Schneidergewerbe.* Berlin: C. Heymanns, 1898.

Adler, A. Das Zärtlichkeitsbedürfnis des Kindes. In A. Adler & C. Furtmuller (Eds.), *Heilen und Bilden.* München: Reinhardt, 1914.

Adler, A. *Study of organ inferiority and its psychical compensation.* New York: Nervous & Mental Disease Publishing Co., 1917.

Adler, A. Erziehungsberatungsstellen. In A. Adler & C. Furtmüller (Eds.), *Heilen und Bilden.* München: Bergmann, 1922.

Adler, A. Progress in individual psychology. *British Journal of Medical Psychology,* 1924, *4,* 22-31.

Adler, A. *The neurotic constitution.* Freeport, N. Y.: Books for Libraries Press, 1972. (Originally published in 1926.)

Adler, A. On teaching courage. *Survey Graphic,* 1928, *61,* 241-242.

Adler, A. Position in family influences life-style. *International Journal of Individual Psychology,* 1929, *3,* 211-227.

Adler, A. Individual psychology. In Carl Murchison (Ed.), *Psychologies of 1930.* Worcester, Mass.: Clark University Press, 1930.

Adler, A. Lecture to the Medical Society of Individual Psychology, London. *Individual Psychology Pamphlets,* 1934, *13,* 11-24.

Adler, A. On the interpretation of dreams. *International Journal of Individual Psychology,* 1936, *2,* 3-16.

Adler, A. How I chose my career. *Individual Psychology Bulletin,* 1947, *6,* 9-11. (Also in P. Bottome, *Alfred Adler: A biography.* New York: Putnam, 1939.)

Adler, A. *What life should mean to you.* New York: Capricorn Books, 1958.

Adler, A. *Understanding human nature.* New York: Premier Books, 1959.

Adler, A. *The practice and theory of individual psychology.* Paterson, N. J.: Littlefield, Adams, 1963. (a)

Adler, A. *The problem child.* New York: Capricorn Books, 1963. (b)

Adler, A. *Problems of neurosis.* New York: Harper & Row, 1964. (a)

Adler, A. *Social interest: A challenge to mankind.* New York: Capricorn Books, 1964. (b)

Adler, A. *The science of living.* New York: Doubleday Anchor Books, 1969.

Adler, K. A. Depression in the light of individual psychology. *Journal of Individual Psychology,* 1961, *17,* 56-67. (Also in H. D. Werner [Ed.], *New understandings of human behavior.* New York: Association Press, 1970.)

Adler, K. A., & Deutsch, D. *Essays in individual psychology.* New York: Grove Press, 1959.

Alexander, F., & French, T. M. *Psychoanalytic therapy.* New York: Ronald Press, 1946.

Allred, G. H. *How to strengthen your marriage and family.* Provo, Utah: Brigham Young University Press, 1976.

Angers, W. P. Clarifications toward the rapprochement between religion and psychology. *Journal of Individual Psychology,* 1960, *16,* 73-76.

Ansbacher, H. L. Adler's place today in the psychology of memory. *Journal of Personality,* 1946, *15,* 197-207. (Also in *Individual Psychology Bulletin,* 1947, *6,* 32-40, and *Internationale Zeitschrift für Individualpsychologie,* 1947, *16,* 97-111.)

Ansbacher, H. L. "Neo-Freudian" or "Neo-Adlerian?" *American Journal of Individual Psychology,* 1952, *10,* 87-88. (Also in *American Psychologist,* 1953, *8,* 165-166.)

Ansbacher, H. L. A key to existence. *Journal of Individual Psychology,* 1959, *15,* 141-142.

Ansbacher, H. L. Suicide: Adlerian point of view. In N. L. Farberow & E. S. Schneidman (Eds.), *The cry for help.* New York: McGraw-Hill, 1961.

Ansbacher, H. L. Was Adler a disciple of Freud? A reply. *Journal of Individual Psychology,* 1962, *18,* 126-135.

Ansbacher, Heinz L. Life style: A historical and systematic review. *Journal of Individual Psychology,* 1967, *23,* 191-212.

Ansbacher, H. L. The concept of social interest. *Journal of Individual Psychology,* 1968, *24,* 131-141.

Ansbacher, H. L. Suicide as communication: Adler's concept and current applications. *Journal of Individual Psychology,* 1969, *25,* 174-180. (Also in *Humanitas,* 1970, *6,* 5-13.)

Ansbacher, H. L., & Ansbacher, R. (Eds.). *The individual psychology of Alfred Adler.* New York: Basic Books, 1956.

Beach, F. A. The descent of instinct. *Psychological Review,* 1955, *62,* 401-410.

Beecher, W., & Beecher, M. *Parents on the run.* New York: Agora Press, 1966.

Berne, E. *Games people play.* New York: Grove Press, 1964.

Bickhard, M. H., & Ford, B. L. Adler's concept of social interest. *Journal of Individual Psychology,* 1976, *32,* 27-49.

Bierer, J. *The day hospital, an experiment in social psychiatry and synthoanalytic psychotherapy.* London: H. K. Lewis, 1951.

Bierer, J., & Evans, R. I. *Innovations in social psychiatry.* London: Avenue Publishing Co., 1969.

Birnbaum, F. The Individual-Psychological Experimental School in Vienna. *International Journal of Individual Psychology,* 1935, *1,* 118-124.

Birnbaum, F. Frankl's existential psychology from the viewpoint of Individual Psychology. *Journal of Individual Psychology,* 1961, *17,* 162-166.

Bottome, P. *Alfred Adler: A biography.* New York: Putnam, 1939.

Brewer, Deanna H. The induction and alteration of state depression: A comparative study. Ph.D. dissertation, University of Houston, 1976.

Brome, V. *Freud and his early circle.* New York: William Morrow, 1968.

Brown, C. *Manchild in the promised land.* New York: Signet Books, 1965.

Brown, J. F. Parallels between Adlerian psychology and the Afro-American value system. *Individual Psychologist,* 1976, *13,* 29-33.

Bugental, J. F. T. Humanistic psychology: A new breakthrough. *American Psychologist,* 1963, *18,* 563-567.

Clark, K. B. Problems of power and social change: Toward a relevant social psychology. *Journal of Social Issues,* 1965, *21,* 4-20.

Clark, K. B. *Dark ghetto.* New York: Harper Torchbooks, 1967. (a)

Clark, K. B. Implications of Adlerian theory for understanding of civil rights problems and action. *Journal of Individual Psychology,* 1967, *23,* 181-190. (b)

Colby, K. M. On the disagreement between Freud and Adler. *American Imago,* 1951, *8,* 229-238.

Corsini, R. J. The behind-the-back technique in group psychotherapy. *Group Psychotherapy,* 1953, *6,* 102-109.

Corsini, R. J. Let's invent a first-aid kit for

marriage problems. *Consultant,* 1967, *7,* 40.

Corsini, R. J. Individual education. In E. Ignas & R. J. Corsini (Eds.). *Alternative educational systems.* Itasca, Il: F. E. Peacock, 1979.

Corsini, R. J. Individual education. *Journal of Individual Psychology,* 1977, *33,* 295-349.

Crandall, J. E. *Theory and measurement of social interest.* New York: Columbia University Press, 1981.

Credner, L. Sicherungen. *Internationale Zeitschrift für Individualpsychologie,* 1930, *8,* 87-92. (Translated as "Safeguards," *International Journal of Individual Psychology,* 1936, *2,* 95-102.)

Deutsch, D. Group therapy with married couples. *Individual Psychologist,* 1967, *4,* 56-62.

Dinkmeyer, D., & Dreikurs, R. *Encouraging children to learn: The encouragement process.* Englewood Cliffs, N.J.: Prentice-Hall, 1963.

Dreikurs, R. The meaning of dreams. *Chicago Medical School Quarterly,* 1944, *3,* 4-6, 25-26. (Also in *Psychodynamics, psychotherapy and counseling.* Chicago: Alfred Adler Institute, 1967.)

Dreikurs, R. The four goals of children's misbehavior. *Nervous Child,* 1947, *6,* 3-11. (Also in *Child guidance and education: Collected papers.* Chicago: Alfred Adler Institute, 1974.)

Dreikurs, R. *The challenge of parenthood.* New York: Duell, Sloan & Pearce, 1948.

Dreikurs, R. Techniques and dynamics of multiple psychotherapy. *Psychiatric Quarterly,* 1950, *24,* 788-799. (Also in *Group psychotherapy and group approaches: Collected papers.* Chicago: Alfred Adler Institute, 1960.)

Dreikurs, R. Psychotherapy as correction of faulty social values. *Journal of Individual Psychology,* 1957, *13,* 150-158. (Also in *Psychodynamics, psychotherapy and counseling.* Chicago: Alfred Adler Institute, 1967.)

Dreikurs, R. A reliable different diagnosis of psychological or somatic disturbances. *International Record of Medicine,* 1958, *171,* 238-242. (Also in *Psychodynamics,* *psychotherapy and counseling.* Chicago: Alfred Adler Institute, 1967.)

Dreikurs, R. Early experiments with group psychotherapy. *American Journal of Psychotherapy,* 1959, *13,* 882-891.

Dreikurs, R. The current dilemma in psychotherapy. *Journal of Existential Psychiatry,* 1960, *1,* 187-206. (a)

Dreikurs, R. *Group psychotherapy and group approaches: Collected papers.* Chicago: Alfred Adler Institute, 1960. (b)

Dreikurs, R. The Adlerian approach to therapy. In Morris I. Stein (Ed.), *Contemporary psychotherapies.* Glencoe, Ill.: The Free Press, 1961.

Dreikurs, R. Can you be sure the disease is functional? *Consultant* (Smith, Kline & French Laboratories), August 1962.

Dreikurs, R. Psychodynamic diagnosis in psychiatry. *American Journal of Psychiatry,* 1963, *119,* 1045-1048. (Also in *Psychodynamics, psychotherapy and counseling.* Chicago: Afred Adler Institute, 1967.)

Dreikurs, R. *Psychology in the classroom.* New York: Harper & Row, 1968.

Dreikurs, R. Social interest: The basis of normalcy. *The Counseling Psychologist,* 1969, *1,* 45-48.

Dreikurs, R. *Social equality: The challenge of today.* Chicago: Henry Regnery, 1971.

Dreikurs, R. Technology of conflict resolution. *Journal of Individual Psychology,* 1972, *28,* 203-206.

Dreikurs, R., Corsini, R. J., Lowe, R., & Sonstegard, M. *Adlerian family counseling.* Eugene, Ore.: University of Oregon Press, 1959.

Dreikurs, R., & Grey, L. *Logical consequences.* New York: Meredith, 1968.

Dreikurs, R., Grunwald, B., & Pepper, F. C. *Maintaining sanity in the classroom.* (2nd ed.). New York: Harper & Row, 1982.

Dreikurs, R., & Mosak, H. H. The tasks of life I. Adler's three tasks. *Individual Psychologist,* 1966, *4,* 18-22.

Dreikurs, R., & Mosak, H. H. The tasks of life II. The fourth life task. *Individual Psychologist,* 1967, *4,* 51-55.

Dreikurs, R., Mosak, H. H., & Shulman, B.

H. Patient-therapist relationship in multiple psychotherapy. I. Its advantage to the therapist. *Psychiatric Quarterly,* 1952, *26,* 219-227. (a) (Also in *Group psychotherapy and group approaches: Collected papers.* Chicago: Alfred Adler Institute, 1960.)

Dreikurs, R., Mosak, H. H., & Shulman, B. H. Patient-therapist relationship in multiple psychotherapy. II. Its advantages for the patient. *Psychiatric Quarterly,* 1952, *26,* 590-596. (b) (Also in *Group psychotherapy and group approaches; Collected papers.* Chicago: Alfred Adler Institute, 1960.)

Dreikurs, R., Mosak, H. H., & Shulman, B. H. *Multiple psychotherapy.* Chicago: Alfred Adler Institute, 1982.

Dreikurs, R., & Soltz, V. *Children: The challenge.* New York: Duell, Sloan & Pearce, 1964.

Dunlap, K. *Habits: Their making and unmaking.* New York: Liveright, 1933.

Edgar, T. Social interest—another view. *Individual Psychologist,* 1975, *12,* 16-24.

Elam, H. Cooperation between African and Afro-American, cultural highlights. *Journal of the National Medical Association,* 1969, *61,* 30-35. (a)

Elam, H. Malignant cultural deprivation, its evolution. *Pediatrics,* 1969, *44,* 319-326. (b)

Ellenberger, H. F. *The discovery of the unconscious.* New York: Basic Books, 1970.

Ellis, A. Rational psychotherapy and Individual Psychology. *Journal of Individual Psychology,* 1957, *13,* 38-44.

Ellis, A. Toward a more precise definition of "emotional" and "intellectual" insight. *Psychological Reports,* 1963, *13,* 125-126.

Ellis, A. Humanism, values, rationality. *Journal of Individual Psychology,* 1970, *26,* 37-38.

Ellis, A. Reason and emotion in the Individual Psychology of Adler. *Journal of Individual Psychology,* 1971, *27,* 50-64.

Farau, A. The influence of Alfred Adler on current psychology. *American Journal of Individual Psychology,* 1953, *10,* 59-76.

Farau, A. Individual psychology and existentialism. *Individual Psychologist,* 1964, *2,* 1-8.

Federn, E. Was Adler a disciple of Freud? A Freudian view. *Journal of Individual Psychology,* 1963, *19,* 80-81.

Fiedler, F. E. A comparison of therapeutic relationships in psychoanalytic, nondirective and Adlerian therapy. *Journal of Consulting Psychology,* 1950, *14,* 436-445.

Forer, L. K. Bibliography of birth order literature of the 1970s. *Journal of Individual Psychology,* 1977, *33,* 122-141.

Frank, L. K. Projective methods for the study of personality. *Journal of Personality,* 1939, *8,* 389-413.

Frankl, V. E. *Man's search for meaning.* New York: Washington Square Press, 1963.

Frankl, V. E. Forerunner of existential psychiatry. *Journal of Individual Psychology,* 1970, *26,* 38.

Fromm-Reichman, F. Notes on personal and professional requirements of a psychotherapist. *Psychiatry,* 1949, *12,* 361-378.

Goldstein, K. *The organism.* New York: American Book Co., 1939.

Gottesfeld, H. Changes in feelings of powerlessness in a community action program. *Psychological Reports,* 1966, *19,* 978.

Grunwald, B. The application of Adlerian principles in a classroom. *American Journal of Individual Psychology,* 1954, *11,* 131-141.

Gushurst, R. S. The reliability and concurrent validity of an idiographic approach to the interpretation of early recollections. Ph.D. dissertation, University of Chicago, 1971.

Heine, R. W. A comparison of patient's reports on psychotherapeutic experience with psychoanalytic, nondirective, and Adlerian therapists. *American Journal of Psychotherapy,* 1953, *7,* 16-23.

Hemming, J. *Mankind against the killers.* London: Longmans, Green, 1956.

Hinrichsen, O. Unser Verstehen der seelischen Zusammenhänge in der Neurose und Freud's und Adler's Theorien. *Zentralblätter für Psychoanalyse,* 1913, *3,* 369-393.

Horney, K. *Neurosis and human growth.* London: Routledge & Kegan Paul, 1951.

Ignas, E., & Corsini, R. J. (Eds.). *Alternative educational systems.* Itasca, Ill.: F. E. Peacock, 1979.

Jahn, E., & Adler, A. Religion and Individual Psychology. In H. L. Ansbacher & R. Ansbacher (Eds.), *Superiority and social interest.* Evanston, Ill.: Northwestern University Press, 1964.

James, W. T., Horney, K., and Fromm, E. In relation to Alfred Adler. *Individual Psychology Bulletin,* 1947, *6,* 105-116.

James, W. *Principles of psychology.* New York: Holt, 1890.

Kadis, A. L. Re-experiencing the family constellation in group psychotherapy. *American Journal of Individual Psychology,* 1956, *12,* 63-68.

Kazan, S. Gemeinschaftsgefühl means caring. *Journal of Individual Psychology,* 1978, *34,* 3-10.

Kramer, H. C. Preventive psychiatry. *Individual Psychology Bulletin,* 1947, *7,* 12-18.

Krausz, E. O. The pessimistic attitude. *International Journal of Individual Psychology,* 1935, *1,* 86-99.

Krausz, E. O. The commonest neurosis. In K. A. Adler & D. Deutsch (Eds.), *Essays in individual psychology.* New York: Grove Press, 1959.

La Porte, G. H. Social interest in action: A report on one attempt to implement Adler's concept. *Individual Psychologist,* 1966, *4,* 22-26.

Lazarsfeld, S. Pitfalls in psychotherapy. *American Journal of Individual Psychology,* 1952-53, *10,* 20-26.

Lazarsfeld, S. The courage for imperfection. *Journal of Individual Psychology,* 1966, *22,* 163-165.

Lewin, K. *A dynamic theory of personality.* New York: McGraw-Hill, 1935.

Lombardi, D. M. The special language of the addict. *Pastoral Psychology,* 1969, *20,* 51-52.

Low, A. A. *Mental health through will training.* Boston: Christopher, 1952.

Manaster, G. J., & Corsini, R. J. *Individual psychology.* Itasca, Ill.: F. E. Peacock, 1982.

Maslow, A. H. Was Adler a disciple of Freud? A note. *Journal of Individual Psychology,* 1962, *18,* 125.

Maslow, A. H. Holistic emphasis. *Journal of Individual Psychology,* 1970, *26,* 39.

May, R. Myth and guiding fiction. *Journal of Individual Psychology,* 1970, *26,* 39.

McArthur, H. The necessity of choice. *Journal of Individual Psychology,* 1958, *14,* 153-157.

Meerloo, J. A. M. Pervasiveness of terms and concepts. *Journal of Individual Psychology,* 1970, *26,* 40.

Miley, C. H. Birth-order research 1963-1967: Bibliography and index. *Journal of Individual Psychology,* 1969, *25,* 64-70.

Mohr, E., & Garlock, R. The social club as an adjunct to therapy. In K. A. Adler & D. Deutsch (Eds.), *Essays in Individual Psychology.* New York: Grove Press, 1959.

Mosak, B., & Mosak, H. H. Dreikurs' four goals: The clarification of some misconceptions. *Individual Psychologist,* 1975, *12,* 14-16.

Mosak, H. H. The psychological attitude in rehabilitation. *American Archives of Rehabilitation Therapy,* 1954, *2,* 9-10.

Mosak, H. H. Early recollections as a projective technique. *Journal of Projective Techniques,* 1958, *22,* 302-311. (Also in G. Lindzey & C. S. Hall [Eds.], *Theories of personality: Primary sources and research.* New York: Wiley, 1965.)

Mosak, H. H. Subjective criteria of normality. *Psychotherapy,* 1967, *4,* 159-161.

Mosak, H. H. Strategies for behavior change in schools: Consultation strategies. *The Counseling Psychologist,* 1971, *3,* 58-62. (a)

Mosak, H. H. Lifestyle. In Arthur G. Nikelly (Ed.), *Techniques for behavior change.* Springfield, Ill.: Charles C Thomas, 1971, 77-81. (b)

Mosak, H. H. Life style assessment: A demonstration based on family constellation. *Journal of Individual Psychology,* 1972, *28,* 232-247.

Mosak, H. H. *A child's guide to parent rearing.* Chicago: Alfred Adler Institute, 1980.

Mosak, H. H., & Dreikurs, R. The life tasks III. The fifth life task. *Individual Psychologist,* 1967, *5,* 16-22.

Mosak, H. H., & Fletcher, S. J. Purposes of delusions and hallucinations. *Journal of Individual Psychology,* 1973, *29,* 176-181.

Mosak, H. H., & Gushurst, R. S. What patients say and what they mean. *American Journal of Psychotherapy,* 1971, *3,* 428-436.

Mosak, H. H., & Kopp, R. The early recollections of Adler, Freud, and Jung. *Journal of Individual Psychology,* 1973, *29,* 157-166.

Mosak, H. H., & LeFevre, C. The resolution of "intrapersonal conflict." *Journal of Individual Psychology,* 1976, *32,* 19-26.

Mosak, H. H., & Mosak, B. *A bibliography for Adlerian psychology.* Washington, D. C.: Hemisphere, 1975.

Mosak, H. H., & Schneider, S. Masculine protest, penis envy, women's liberation and sexual equality. *Journal of Individual Psychology,* 1977, *33,* 193-201.

Mosak, H. H., & Shulman, B. H. *Individual psychotherapy: A syllabus.* Chicago: Alfred Adler Institute, 1963.

Mozdzierz, G. J., & Lottman, T. J. Games married couples play: Adlerian view. *Journal of Individual Psychology,* 1973, *29,* 182-194.

Mullahy, P. *Oedipus: Myth and complex.* New York: Evergreen, 1955.

Murphy, G. *Personality: A biosocial approach to origins and structure.* New York: Harper, 1947.

Murphy, G., Murphy, L. B., & Newcomb, T. M. *Experimental social psychology* (Rev. ed.). New York: Harper, 1937.

Neuer, A. Courage and discouragement. *International Journal of Individual Psychology,* 1936, *2,* 30-50.

Nikelly, A. G. Basic processes in psychotherapy. In A. G. Nikelly (Ed.), *Techniques for behavior change.* Springfield, Ill.: Charles C Thomas, 1971. (a)

Nikelly, A. G. Developing social feeling in psychotherapy. In A. G. Nikelly (Ed.), *Techniques for behavior change.* Springfield, Ill.: Charles C Thomas, 1971. (b)

Nikelly, A. G. The protesting student. In A. G. Nikelly (Ed.), *Techniques for behavior change.* Springfield, Ill.: Charles C Thomas, 1971. (c)

O'Reilly, C., Cizon F., Flanagan, J., & Pflanczer, S. *Men in jail.* Chicago: Loyola University, 1965.

Orgler, H. *Alfred Adler: The man and his work.* New York: Capricorn Books, 1965.

Pancner, K. R. The use of parables and fables in Adlerian psychotherapy. *Individual Psychologist,* 1978, *15,* 19-29.

Papanek, E. Delinquency. In A. G. Nikelly (Ed.), *Techniques for behavior change.* Springfield, Ill.: Charles C Thomas, 1971, 177-183.

Papanek, H. Combined group and individual therapy in private practice. *American Journal of Psychotherapy,* 1954, *8,* 679-686.

Papanek, H. Combined group and individual therapy in the light of Adlerian psychology. *International Journal of Group Psychotherapy,* 1956, *6,* 136-146.

Papanek, H. Emotion and intellect in psychotherapy. *American Journal of Psychotherapy,* 1959, *13,* 150-173.

Papanek, H., & Papanek, E. Individual Psychology today. *American Journal of Psychotherapy,* 1961, *15,* 4-26.

Pelzman, O. Some problems in the use of psychotherapy. *Psychiatric Quarterly Supplement,* 1952, *26,* 53-58.

Pew, M. L., & Pew, W. Adlerian marriage counseling. *Journal of Individual Psychology,* 1972, *28,* 192-202.

Phillips, C. E., & Corsini, R. J. *Give in or give up.* Chicago, Il.: Nelson-Hall, 1982.

Rasey, M. I. Toward the end. In C. E. Moustakas (Ed.), *The self: Explorations in personal growth.* New York: Harper, 1956.

Reik, T. *Listening with the third ear.* New York: Farrar, Straus & Cudahy, 1948.

Rogers, C. R. *Client-centered therapy.* Boston: Houghton Mifflin, 1951.

Rosenthal, D., & Frank, J. D Psychotherapy and the placebo effect. *Psychological Bulletin,* 1956, *53,* 294-302.

Seidler, R. The individual psychologist looks at testing. *Individual Psychologist,* 1967, *5,* 3-6.

Seidler, R., & Zilahi, L. The Vienna child guidance clinics. In A. Adler & associates, *Guiding the child.* London: Allen & Unwin, 1949, 9-27.

Shlien, J. M., Mosak, H. H., & Dreikurs, R. Effect of time limits: A comparison of two psychotherapies. *Journal of Counseling Psychology,* 1962, *9,* 31-34.

Shoben, E. J., Jr Toward a concept of normal personality. *American Psychologist*, 1957, *12*, 183-189.

Shoobs, N. E. Role-playing in the individual psychotherapy interview. *Journal of Individual Psychology*, 1964, *20*, 84-89.

Shulman, B. H. A psychodramatically oriented action technique in group psychotherapy. *Group Psychotherapy*, 1960, *22*, 34-39.

Shulman, B. H. The meaning of people to the schizophrenic and the manic-depressive. *Journal of Individual Psychology*, 1962, *18*, 151-156.

Shulman, B. H. Psychological disturbances which interfere with the patient's cooperation. *Psychosomatics*, 1964, *5*, 213-220.

Shulman, B. H., & Mosak, H. H. Birth order and ordinal position. *Journal of Individual Psychology*, 1977, *33*, 114-121.

Shulman, B. H., & Klapman, H. Organ inferiority and psychiatric disorders in childhood. In E. Harms (Ed.), *Pathogenesis of nervous and mental diseases*. New York: Libra, 1968, 49-62.

Sicher, L., & Mosak, H. H. Aggression as a secondary phenomenon. *Journal of Individual Psychology*, 1967, *23*, 232-235. (Also in H. D. Werner [Ed.], *New understandings of human behavior*. New York: Association Press, 1970.)

Simpson, H. N. *Stoic apologetics*. Oak Park, Ill.: Author, 1966.

Smuts, J. C. *Holism and evolution*. New York: Viking Press, 1961.

Soltz, V. *Study group leader's manual.* Chicago: Alfred Adler Institute, 1967.

Spiel, O. *Discipline without punishment*. London: Faber & Faber, 1962.

Starr, A. *Psychodrama*. Chicago: Nelson-Hall, 1977.

Strupp, H. H Freudian analysis today. *Psychology Today*, 1972, *6*, 33-40.

Sullivan, H. S. *The psychiatric interview*. New York: Norton, 1954.

Sward, K. Review of Karen Horney, *Our inner conflicts*. *Science*, December 12, 1947, 600-601.

Toman, W. Never mind your horoscope, birth order rules all. *Psychology Today*, 1970, *4*, 45-49, 68-69.

Vaihinger, H. *The philosophy of "as if."* London: Routledge & Kegan Paul, 1965.

Von Sassen, H. W. Adler's and Freud's concepts of man: A phenomenological comparison. *Journal of Individual Psychology*, 1967, *23*, 3-10.

Way, L. *Adler's place in psychology*. New York: Collier Books, 1962.

Wexberg, E. *Individual Psychology*. London: Allen & Unwin, 1929.

Wexberg, E. *Individual psychological treatment*. Chicago: Alfred Adler Institute, 1970.

White, R. W. Adler and the future of ego psychology. *Journal of Individual Psychology*, 1957, *13*, 112-124.

Wittels, F. The neo-Adlerians. *American Journal of Sociology*, 1939, *45*, 433-445.

Wolfe, W. B. *How to be happy though human*. London: Routledge & Kegan Paul, 1932.

4

Analytical Psychotherapy

YORAM KAUFMANN

OVERVIEW

Analytical psychotherapy is an attempt to create, by means of a symbolic approach, a dialectical relationship between consciousness and the unconscious. The *psyche* is seen as a self-regulating system whose functioning is purposive with an internally imposed direction toward a life of fuller awareness. In psychotherapy a dialogue ensues, via dreams, fantasies, and other unconscious products, between the conscious state of the analysand and his personal, as well as the collective, unconscious.

Basic Concepts

The last millennium in Western culture can be characterized as a period of increased rationality. In the attempt to master nature and fate, humans have tried to discard fantasies, superstitions, and flights of fancy, replacing them with a more objective vision. The resulting viewpoint made possible technology and scientific knowledge that brought much material comfort. It was inevitable that this approach, therefore, gradually would outweigh all others. Freud's contribution to civilization was to suggest that rationality and consciousness form but one aspect of the totality of human ex-

perience, and to postulate another realm of the psyche, namely, the *unconscious.* This major assumption Jung shares with Freud. Neither of them sought to depreciate consciousness. Certainly the primary effort in life and in analysis is to become more conscious, to gain more awareness. But consciousness is but a small boat on the vast sea of the unconscious. We have to face the unpleasant fact that we are not masters in our own houses, but are ruled by forces and sources of energy operating through us, rather than ruled by us. These unconscious forces Jung saw as being both destructive and creative, but dangerous if ignored and unheeded. The unconscious is not just the sum total of everything that has been repressed in the course of one's development; it also contains wellsprings of creativity and sources of guidance and meaning.

Structurally, the *unconscious* and the *conscious* constitute two subsystems of the psyche. These two compensate one another; the more one-sided an attitude is in one system, the more pronounced is its opposite in the other. Thus, a young man very much steeped in religious and spiritual matters dreams: *A voice said to me, "the way to carry on for Christ is on the genitals."*

Obviously the extremely one-sided pre-

108

occupation with matters spiritual is at the expense of the instinctual aspect of life, of which fact the dreamer is here reminded in no uncertain terms. Conversely, if the instinctual side is overemphasized, the unconscious is quite likely to insist on a more spiritual attitude.

Jung postulated, in addition to the usual instincts of sex, aggression, hunger, and thirst, an instinct toward *individuation*. There exists within us, Jung believed, an autonomous force that persistently pushes us to acheive wholeness (not perfection!) much like the physiological force that guides our physical development. This force is constantly trying to launch us on a process of fulfilling our truest self, thereby finding our own wholeness and particular meaning in life. All our behavior is both consciously and unconsciously motivated. We behave partly because of reasons of which we are aware and partly because of reasons of which we are unaware. One could, therefore, explore the unconscious in the way we move, communicate, make love, and so on. One of the most fruitful ways to understand a person's unconscious is through his dreams. A dream is posited to contain a message to the dreamer's awareness from his unconscious. The message is not expressed in our everyday language, but is veiled. If the veil is lifted, the dream is said to be interpreted or translated. Analytical psychology attaches a great deal of importance to the interpretation of dreams. This process is usually the backbone of a person's analysis.

To the average modern rationalist, all this may seem ludicrous and foggy. To other civilizations, these ideas are a matter of course, an obvious aspect of life. The Naskapi Indian, for example, carries within himself, in his heart, an inner companion whom he calls the Great Man, who is immortal and toward whom an attitude of total honesty is required. He communicates with the Great Man via dreams and inner voices. Life is viewed as a deepening communication with this inner companion.

This view posits that the unconscious has an existence of its own not reducible to other modes of psychic activity such as sexuality, interpersonal relationships, or a striving for power. These play important roles in the development of the personality, but are not primary. They form only part of the warp and weft of a bigger totality. The guiding and directing quality imputed to the unconscious implies a prospective, teleological aspect. The past determines the present to a large extent, but primarily, our actions are geared with a view toward the future: we act not only because of (the past) but for the sake of (the future).

The unconscious is our storehouse of energy, the psychic sphere within which transformations and metamorphoses are made possible. One can decide to stop acting under compulsion but to no avail; no matter how resolute the decision, compulsion reappears. Take for example the case of a young man valiantly wrestling with a potential psychotic process. He has what seem to be psychotic episodes of a paranoid nature. He enters therapy with a competent therapist who helps the patient adjust to his reality. However, the patient still does not feel completely understood and still feels the threat of the psychosis. He then starts analytical therapy and it becomes clear that previous therapy had not reached his unconscious. He tells the following recurrent childhood dream:

I am standing along on a beach facing the Pacific Ocean. The ocean has huge waves, which come rolling on and engulf me.

The clinical picture is clear: The ego is

threatened by an invasion from the unconscious. A possibility of a psychotic process is indeed indicated. After several months of analysis in which close attention was given to unconscious material, the patient dreams:

I am on the beach in Acapulco with a lot of people around me having a good time. I sense turbulence in the ocean, but I know that it will not reach me; I sense very strongly the boundary between the ocean and the beach.

To *Acapulco* the patient associated the popular resort where everyone goes. The possibility of a transformation is indicated. Turbulence is still there but the patient (the dream-ego in Jungian terminology) feels more secure. Note the change from the lonely and isolated feeling of the childhood dream to this dream, which has the feeling of belonging. Later he brought in the following dream.

I am on a ship on a cruise. We are at the middle of the ocean. A plank is lowered, and we are invited to swim. The water is beautifully blue and clear. At first I am slightly anxious, but I jump in and swim, and then return safely to the ship.

The patient spontaneously added that he had always considered himself a borderline case but that he now felt he had crossed the border; he felt normal, grounded, and full of energy. Many changes were taking place in his life. He was able to finish some important tasks and had been appointed to a responsible and remunerative position.

What is the language of communication between consciousness and the unconscious? The unconscious is not directly available to consciousness. The only communication seemingly available is the symbol. Symbols are attempts to express something essentially unexplainable but nevertheless existing. One can have the greatest understanding of the cross as a symbol, but the cross itself, emerging in a dream, carries profound meaning to the dreamer unexplainable in rational terms. *It is a basic tenet of Jungian therapy that all products of the unconscious are symbolic* and can be taken as guiding messages. Thus, the symptoms, the neurosis itself, are not merely indications of psychic malfunctioning but show the way out of the conflict underlying them, if symbolically understood. If a man finds himself constantly attracted to mutilated women, he can infer that "his own inner woman," his feminine side, may be mutilated and crippled; that his awareness of this is needed to heal this area.

What is the source of power of the unconscious? Jung came to the conclusion that that part of the unconscious which is a direct result of each individual's particular life situation represents only a small though important part of a larger totality, which he named the *collective unconscious*. The first part is called the *personal* level of the unconscious, the second the *nonpersonal* (or transpersonal) level. What is meant here is that all human beings, from the most remote past to our present days and into the foreseeable future, share the same inherited predispositions for psychic functioning.

As an analogy, compare the libido with water and the unconscious to a flat plane. If the water were to cover that plane, there would be no differentiation in the way the water is distributed; it would also form a flat plane. If we assume, however, that the plane is covered with rocks, causing depressions and protrusions of various shapes and sizes, the water flow now is along certain *gradients*. These rocks and craters are somewhat akin to the *archetypes*. The archetypes are a priori ordering principles for potential reach of consciousness, but over the ages, personalities. Archetypes are out of the they have given rise to equivalent forms of imagery in myths, fairy tales, and works of art in many cultures. Motifs include transformation, death and rebirth, the hero struggle, the mother, the divine child. Archetypes exist in us as potentialities; our life circumstances (our particular culture, our family, and our environment) determine in which way and which of the archetypes are actualized. The archetype, or psychic propensity, has to be activated (or evoked) by an experiential reality, which endows it with its specific form. For instance, we all participate in the heroic struggle, but each of us experiences it differently according to talents, temperaments, and one's given environment.

The archetypes are carriers of energy; the emergence of an archetype brings forth an enormous amount of energy. Conversely, all genuine creativity is archetypal in nature (cf., Neumann, 1955). Under normal circumstances the archetypal images express contemporary motifs; modern man is not likely to dream about slaying a dragon (the archetypal imagery in Greek and Norse mythology), but rather about fighting with his mother-in-law, walking through a dark tunnel, and so on. The more archaic representations are usually activated when the life-force encounters a powerful obstruction, either through a life situation (loss of a leg, death of the beloved, a life situation that does not allow for an acceptable solution) or contrived through various methods of meditation. In both cases, a profound introversion results in a regression of the libido to more primitive levels. The archetypal realm, in its capacity as an ordering principle, provides us with a sense of meaning. If we understand all suffering as

a loss of meaning, the archetype can provide the healing-power principles.

Other Systems

The Jungian point of view accords easily with other contributions to the understanding of the psyche, such as the Gestalt theory, interpersonal and Adlerian theories, and even some aspects of behavior modification, especially as far as technique is concerned. But it is most edifying to contrast it with traditional psychoanalysis. To illustrate some of the differences between the Jungian and Freudian approaches, we have chosen examples of dreams discussed in Greenson's book, *The Technique and Practice of Psychoanalysis* (1968). It is dangerous to analyze dreams of patients one does not know, but nevertheless for heuristic purposes, some conclusions may be formulated. The first dream is that of a male patient (Greenson, 1968, p. 40):

I am waiting for a red traffic light to change when I feel that someone has bumped into me from behind. I rush out in fury and find out, with relief, it was only a boy on a bicycle. There was no damage to my car.

Greenson concludes that a comparison with his father in terms of sexual ability is involved. The boy on a bicycle is interpreted as masturbation and the red light as prostitution. Greenson comes to one conclusion that the patient has a wish-fulfilling fantasy that mother doesn't want sex with father who is not very potent. As Jungians, we would take the dream more phenomenologically. The red traffic light is taken to symbolize the laws of society, some general, conventional code, a collective prohibition; the little boy is an infantile, childish force within the dreamer, something not in full control; the being pumped, uncontrolled juvenile impatience, with no harm done. The message to the dreamer by the dream in terms of an analysis of the symbols is, therefore, "You are up against the need to control your childish, infantile side, which urges you to break accepted conventions that must be respected."

A woman patient in her fourth year of analysis dreams (p. 143):

(1) I am being photographed in the nude, lying on my back in different positions; legs closed, legs apart. (2) I see a man with a curved yardstick in his hand; it had writing on it which was supposed to be erotic. A red, spiny-backed little monster was biting this man with sharp, tiny teeth. The man was ringing a bell for help, but no one heard it but me and I didn't seem to care.

Greenson feels the dream points out the dreamer's resistance to her recognition of a deep-seated hostility to a man's penis and disgust towards her own vagina. With the red monster, she associates menstrual blood, a medieval fiend out of Hieronymus Bosch. We see this dream as possibly expressing criticism of the analysis. The patient feels she is being photographed in the nude in all positions, with special interest in the area between her legs: this seems to be her experiential feeling about her analysis. Dream (2) emphasizes this point even further: the man, with whom she later associates her analyst, is judging her by bookish (writing), distorted (curved), rigid (yardstick), and erotic standards. Furthermore, the analyst himself seems to be bitten, "bugged" as it were, by something out of Hieronymus Bosch. Bosch depicted in his paintings the two instincts that the Church, in the name of Christianity, was trying to suppress: sexuality and aggression, in their various forms. If a Jungian analyst were handed this dream, he would in all probability be asking himself whether the patient's unconscious was not picking up a sore spot of his own, namely, the analyst's repressed sexuality and/or aggression. This is not at all uncommon. We often get patients who hit us in our blind spots, and we end up treating our patients and ourselves at the same time.

If we want to be completely phenomenological and empirical, this interpretation is only a *possibility* suggested by the patient's association. The man in the dream is unknown. The patient could very well have dreamt the same dream with Dr. Greenson as the man holding the yardstick, and then we would have been more justified in our interpretation. As it is, it must be taken as a possible suggestive line of inquiry. We are on safer ground if we take this dream on a subjective level, taking the man with the yardstick as an inner man, an animus figure (see later). On that level, the dream has a paradoxical message indeed: The dreamer is excessively preoccupied with sexuality. This distorted, moralistic view of herself is in itself a result of a repression of deep-seated drive elements. Hence this interpretation would be in opposition to Greenson's formulation.

Sexuality, for Jung, is more than mere instinctuality; it is also creative power, a bridge between the sacred and the profane. In many religions, sexual symbolism is used to express man's complex relationship to God. With the advent of Christianity, this aspect of sexuality was repressed and what remained was mere body function. Rollo May (1961) gives an example in which church spires appearing in a dream were interpreted by a Freudian as phallic symbols and by a Jungian as spirituality.

Analytical psychotherapy strongly differentiates itself from other systems in its emphasis on the purposive, prospective functioning of the psyche. What it objects to in other dynamic systems of psychotherapy is the exaggerated emphasis on reductive, causal thinking. One can trace human behavior to genetic antecedents, but these account for only a portion of our nature; we not only react to our past, we live and relate in the present and take the future into account.

In its emphasis on the prospective and meaningful aspect of the psyche, analytical psychotherapy anticipated a lot of common ground with existential psychotherapy and logotherapy, perhaps most fundamentally in the fact that these therapies are philosophical rather than merely biological therapies. Although one cannot deal with the data of the human psyche without theories, one can minimize the theoretical restrictions imposed upon an interpretive system. Analytical psychology considers itself to be empirical and phenomenological in that the therapist is required to lay aside various preconceptions about human behavior and be ready to follow the vicissitudes and serpentine ways of the psyche wherever they might lead.

HISTORY

Precursors

C. G. Jung was born in Kesswil, Switzerland, and received most of his education in Basel. In contrast to Freud, who was primarily influenced by the scientific, positivistic, and materialistic philosophy of his time, Jung grew up in a cultural tradition that constituted a reaction to the Enlightenment movement.

The hallmark of the Enlightenment was its unswerving optimism. It sought to establish reason as the prime mover, admitting the existence of emotion but seeing it as an element primarily distracting to the rational process. It was believed that by the application of the analytical method all questions ultimately could be resolved.

Gradually, the Enlightenment gave way to a cultural climate that was in many ways its antithesis (Ellenberger, 1970). Reason began to be dethroned, and in contrast to the positing of a split between nature and man, the unity of the two was postulated, as well as the unity of reason and emotion. The world began to be seen as the arena for the interaction of polar oppositions, in chemistry and physiology as well as in philosophy and psychology. It followed naturally that consciousness could not be the only state extant in human beings. A hundred years after G. W. Leibnitz postulated it, the unconscious was again thrust into prominence; its manifestations were recognized as legitimate sources of inquiry, mysticism was not frowned upon, and parapsychology was earnestly studied. G. F. Creuzer (1810) published an exhaustive work on mythology and folktales, trying to understand them as symbolical productions rather than as undeveloped ways of thinking. Life was understood as a series of transformations from primordial phenomena and analogy was given a prominent place as a scientific tool. Outstanding and influential personalities of that time were the philosophers Friedrich Von Schelling, Eduard von Hartmann, and Arthur Schopenhauer, and the physician-psychologist Carl Gustav Carus. The latter especially influenced Jung's work. Not only did Carus treat the unconscious with the utmost respect, he also imputed to it a creative and healing ability (an essential element in Jungian psychology) and divided the unconscious into several parts, one of which, the "general unconscious," foreshadows Jung's concept of the collective unconscious.

Some of Jung's ideas can be traced even further back. His concept of the archetypes is adumbrated by Immanuel Kant's notion of a priori universal forms of perception. We can never perceive reality as it actually is, but have to impose upon the perceptual process a set of imperatives that determine what we actually see. Jung translated the concept of philosophical imperatives into archetypes in the psychological realm.

Dream interpretation, an important part of analytic psychotherapy, was used in ancient times. Particularly famous are Joseph's interpretation of his own dream (the first "self-analysis"), the dreams of his cell mates, and, finally, those of the Pharaoh. The Talmud also devotes a great deal of attention to dreams, and several dream books are known to us, notably the Egyptian, the Chaldean, and one by the Greek Artemidorus.

Beginnings

It is generally assumed that both Alfred Adler and Carl Jung began their psychoanalytic career with their association with Freud; that they started as his students, went with him some of the way and then "deviated" from orthodox psychoanalytic theory. (The reason this version persists is probably because it agrees with the myth of the rebellious son deposing the father.) In both cases, however, the situation was quite different. Both Adler and Jung had formulated some of their major ideas before they came to know Freud. At that time, Jung was writing his medical thesis on the

so-called occult phenomena (Jung, 1902). A careful reading of that initial statement of Jung's shows that it contains most of his major ideas in embryonic form.

It is ironic that Jung, later to be called vague, mystical, and abstruse, made as his next step a study bridging the gap between experimental and depth psychology. Jung was assigned by Eugen Bleuler (the head of the Burghölzli Clinic) the task of studying the association test, originally developed by Francis Galton. In this test, people are asked to respond to chosen words with the first word that comes spontaneously. Jung discovered that each person tended to respond to specific words, varying from person to person, either too quickly or too slowly, relative to an average response time for the rest of the words. From this Jung assumed that these particular words carried special meaning for that person—that the words led to some idea accompanied by affect, which Jung then called the *complex*. These complexes were usually unknown to the subject. Jung then postulated the notion that they were unconscious by virtue of repression. It seemed as if Jung had in this way adduced "proof" of the unconscious and the process of repression, both key concepts in Freud's budding theories. Moreover, it was an *empirical* confirmation, and it is important to note that all his life, Jung considered himself an empiricist, an observer of psychological data.

Not unnaturally, these discoveries resulted in a warm correspondence between Jung and Freud. The exchange of letters brought about in 1907 the meeting of Jung and Freud in Vienna. Freud was immediately captivated by Jung's tremendous energy and rich imagination. To the annoyance of his own inner circle, who felt that Jung would eventually go his own way, Freud appointed Jung the first president of the International Psychoanalytic Association.

Jung's next publication, *The Psychology of Dementia Praecox* (1907), considerably heightened his growing reputation and recognition. It was an application of psychoanalytic principles to schizophrenia, and although it contained serious misgivings about some of Freud's ideas, it was considered an important psychoanalytic contribution.

It was from a patient's report that Jung began to formulate an idea of the archetypes. One hallucination of a patient was the image of the sun as having a phallus that moved from side to side causing a wind. Jung was forcibly struck by the fact that this imagery was also used in ancient times, mentioned in sources of which this uneducated man had had no knowledge. This and similar incidents over a long period led Jung to postulate a level of primordial imagery in the unconscious common to all mankind. He called this the *collective unconscious,* and the primordial images were designated as *archetypes.* Note that Jung started out with empirical clinical data, and that theory followed. Jung thought the data were important and basic, whereas theory could be tentative and susceptible to change.

By identifying main themes in psychological material and amplifying them with parallel motifs culled from mythology, comparative religion, and literature, Jung forged a new way of looking at clinical material. He used this method first on a series of fantasies of a young woman, Miss Miller, reported by Theodore Flournoy in 1906. Out of this grew Jung's *Symbols of Transformation* (1911). This book marked a final break with Freud. Not only did it suggest a new method for a psychological approach to clinical material, it also challenged some of Freud's most basic ideas. Jung identified *libido* as general psychic energy rather than as sexual energy, thus dethroning sexuality as the all-encompassing causative element in things psychic. Disturbances in sexuality he viewed as the expression and reflection of more basic psychological conflicts—as the symptom, the outer manifestation, rather than the origin.

In contrast to the clear, persuasive writing of Freud, Jung's manner of writing presents problems to the uninitiated. Jung writes in the way he believes the psyche functions, and sometimes tends to assume all readers are familiar with the necessary background information. Furthermore, Jung believes the psychic realities he is trying to describe never can be completely grasped by consciousness. We can understand some of their manifestations, some of their characteristics, but inherently, they are beyond our ken. We cannot, therefore, delineate them precisely, but must be content with approximations and analogies. Jung's style is mosaiclike and allusive. One illustration leads to another. If, however, one follows his train of thought carefully, a definite pattern emerges, centering around a common theme, and the seeming digressions fall into place, elucidating and elaborating the main idea. The most rewarding way to read Jung is to let oneself actively associate to the images presented; the material then comes alive and becomes meaningful.

Current Status

The Jungian movement tended to attract, primarily, introverted people who shied away from proselytizing. Jung himself was extremely reluctant to give his assent for the establishment of an institute to teach and spread his ideas. New movements tend to attract unfavorable projections, and the Jungian movement has been no exception; until about 1960, it was virtually ignored in the United States. Jung's influence, however, has been enormous, although mostly unacknowledged, and recently there has been a reawakening to his ideas. Calvin Hall and Gardner Lindzey (1962) and Ruth Munroe (1955) include remarkably favorable chapters on Jung in their respective books; some existential therapists write and speak as underground Jungians. Three training institutes have been established in the United States in New York, Los Angeles, and San Francisco. The number of Jungian analysts has been steadily growing all over the world. There are important centers in Switzerland, Britain, Germany, Israel, France, and Italy. Since 1958, International Congresses have been held every two years, and several centers are publishing their own periodicals. The oldest of these is *Spring*, published by the New York Analytical Psychology Club; others are the annual *British Journal of Analytical Psychology, Psychological Perspectives* (Los Angeles), *Zeitschrift für Analytisch Psychologie und Ihre Grenzgebite* (Berlin), *La Rivista di Psicologia Analitica* (Rome), and *Quaternio* (Rio de Janeiro). In most centers, the emphasis is on work with adults, but in Israel and England, a considerable contingent of analysts works with children. Group work has only recently been introduced in New York, the West Coast, and Zurich, Switzerland.

Requirements for entry into the training institutes vary from place to place. Jung's original intention was to train any mature individual with an open relationship to his unconscious; he himself trained philosophers, philologists, artists, and mathematicians, recognizing that academic education contributes very little to one's ability to function as a therapist. The training institutes, however, consider that academic standards are necessary to give proof of seriousness of purpose as well as to meet outer standards of certification. Prospective analysts are allowed a range of related fields of academic endeavor, but the final criterion of acceptance as a candidate for training comes after at least 100 hours of qualified personal analysis, recommendation of the analyst, and interviews by three analysts of the training board. At present there are about 400 qualified Jungian analysts, members of the International Association for Analytic Psychology.

PERSONALITY

Theory of Personality

Analytical psychology does not possess a detailed personality theory equivalent to the topographic, genetic, economic, dynamic, and structural views of psychoanalytic theory. The psyche is viewed as composed of several subsystems, each autonomous, yet interdependent: the ego, the personal unconscious, and the nonpersonal (collective) unconscious.

The ego
The *ego* is the center of consciousness, the experiential being of the person. It is the sum total of thoughts, ideas, feelings, memories, and sensory perceptions.

The personal unconscious
This consists of everything that has been repressed during one's development. The *personal unconscious* is composed of elements that had once been conscious

and are relatively easily available to consciousness. These elements are clustered around complexes defined as emotionally toned ideas and behavioral impulses. The complex may be thought of as having a core, which is archetypal, and which therefore will lie outside the sphere of the personal unconscious; and a shell, which is the particular form it takes in a given individual. For instance, several people may have a father complex. The complex will take different guises with the different people.

The nonpersonal unconscious

This part of the unconscious includes the archetypes, which are inborn psychic predispositions to perception, emotion, and behavior. This layer of the unconscious is not directly amenable to consciousness, but can be observed indirectly through its manifestations in eternal themes in mythology, folklore and art. Some archetypes, due to their importance and frequency, have been documented more than others. For instance, Joseph Campbell (1956) has documented extensively the hero archetype. Other archetypes include rebirth, the Great Mother, the Wise Old Man, the trickster, the divine child, wholeness, and God. Not all of these archetypes are actualized at all times and with the same intensity. Some archetypes play an important role in the development of the personality—the persona, the shadow, the animus or anima, and the Self.

The persona. The *persona* is the archetype of adaptation. The word originally meant the actor's mask, but it is not used here in the negative sense. We need mediation between our inner psychic life and the outside world, as much as we need a skin for the same purpose for our physical being. It would be destructive if we behaved in the same way under all situations, as a teacher in front of a class, at a cocktail party, among close friends and in bed; this, indeed, is the case if we have not developed a viable persona. The persona may become rigid, as with the physician, lawyer, or minister who cannot stop being their roles. Ideally, the persona is flexible, that is, different circumstances evoke within us different qualities and aspects that are adaptive within the given context. People often mistake this phenomenon and take it to mean that they are different people in different places. A patient brings in the following initial dream:

I am with a lot of people, who are talking to each other. I try to talk, but I can't as I have a ball of hair in my throat.

The dreamer associated the ball of hair with the phenomenon of cats licking themselves. Very often a ball of hair is indeed formed and gets stuck in their throat. To the dreamer, this act was that of preening. That is, indeed, what she does herself. She is a model, a very beautiful young lady who uses her beauty professionally. The dream tells her that her own preening is a barrier to communication with other people. She is identified with her persona and as a result totally isolated. The persona is often symbolized in dreams by masks or clothes. A person whose adaptation of reality is very faulty might find himself dreaming that he is taking his coat off only to find underneath another coat, and so on (Whitmont, 1970).

The shadow. The *shadow* is our "other side," all that we would like not to be; it is the compensatory side to our conscious ego, as seen in the case of Dr. Jekyll and Mr. Hyde. It is all those things we would never recognize in ourselves, and what we are particularly allergic to in others. Since the shadow is unconscious, it is experienced as a *projection* onto others. Projection is the main mechanism of the psyche. The dynamics of projection seen this way are more encompassing than in the customary form; here, they do not necessarily involve an *erroneous* attribution of feelings or qualities to another person, but a mirror of ourselves. We might very well be correct in our perception (e.g., the other person might indeed be angry), but if it stirs strong emotions in us, that person reflects our own anger. An encounter with the shadow is the *sine qua non* of every analysis and is generally very painful. A patient who has been immobilized most of his adult life, unable to work or maintain any kind of meaningful relationship, brings the following dream.

I am walking, holding a leash in my hand, to which is attached a young man, who is very sweet and docile. All of a sudden, he turns into a ferocious beast, threatening to destroy me. I grab hold of him, and we attempt to fight, but it becomes apparent neither of us can win: the best I can do is keep him from destroying me.

Here, the dream-ego (the dreamer) is in deadly conflict with his shadow; no resolution is in sight. The dream seems to be telling the dreamer that as long as he maintains his "good" side on a leash, that is, as long as he is the "angel" his parents expect him to be, it will turn ferociously against him and he will be deadlocked.

Acceptance of the shadow is very difficult to achieve, but vitally important for adjustment. A young man who was in the throes of a very humiliating compulsion has been working for a long time on shadow aspects of his self, which he steadfastly refused to acknowledge. However, after a particularly painful experience in an encounter group he dreams:

I am on my way to find something which I know is very important. Suddenly, as I am about to turn a corner, I see a very shabbily dressed man who seems to be down in the dumps and appears very disgusting to me. He accosts me, and my first impulse is to shake him off, but all of a sudden I take pity on him and embrace him, to my own amazement.

The shadow, which very often appears in a dream as a derelict or "inferior" person, is here accepted. For this dreamer, it signaled the beginning of a conscious assimilation of his inferior side, which, in turn, made it possible for him to free himself slowly from his compulsion.

The shadow is always symbolized by figures of the same sex. As always in Jungian thought, the shadow is not all negative; if accepted and assimilated, it can become a source of creativity. In people whose conscious experience of themselves is very negative, the shadow, being a compensatory figure, will include all their positive qualities, and they will meet successful and talented men in their dreams.

The animus and anima. Two central elements in Chinese philosophy are the Yin and Yang. The *Yin* represents the feminine principle; it is the world of nature, creation and life, earthiness and concreteness, receptivity and yielding, the dark and containing, the collective and undifferentiated, the unconscious. The *Yang* is its opposite—the masculine principle, the driving energy, the creative and initiating, the light and hot, the penetrating, stimulating and dividing, the principle of separation and differentiation, restriction and discipline, the arousing and phallic, aggression and enthusiasm, spirit and heaven. These two principles do not oppose but complement each other. The Yin without the Yang is the status quo, inertia, and the Yang without the Yin is the enthusiastic rushing forward without the solid base of concreteness and solidity. Every element contains these two principles to varying degrees and proportions. These proportions are not unalterably fixed, they change with necessity; a given situation will require more of the Yin, and another will require more of the Yang.

The concept of anima and animus is similar to and is much harder to grasp than that of the shadow or the persona. Rationality fails us here, but the animus-anima experience is very real nonetheless, as we will try to illustrate.

Human beings are potentially bisexual, biologically as well as psychologically. During our development one side comes to predominate over the other, the other side existing in an inferior form. Thus, males have usually the preponderance of the Yang principle in their consciousness, women the Yin. Contrasexual aspects coexist in the unconscious; thus, the male has an unconscious Yin side, the *anima;* the woman has an unconscious Yang aspect, the *animus.* Thus, on the positive side, a woman's animus is responsible for her ability to discriminate and differentiate, to judge and to act, for discipline and aggressiveness. If a positive conscious relationship cannot be maintained toward the animus, we meet the notorious animus-ridden woman, whose hallmarks are argumentativeness, dogmatism, and behavior on the basis of prejudices and preconceived notions. Briefly, a woman's animus is the sum total of her expectations, a system of unconscious criteria with which the world is judged and experienced. The animus is symbolized by male figures appearing in a woman's dreams and fantasies, as a husband, son, father, lover, Prince Charming, the neighbor next door, and so on.

Conversely, for a man the anima embodies the Yin aspect. This accounts for a man's capacity for relatedness, emotionality, involvement with people and ideas, a spontaneous and unplanned approach to life and its experiences, sensuality, and instinctuality. The anima is symbolized by female figures in man's unconscious products, appearing as the beloved one, the princess, priestess, witch, prostitute, nymph. If the anima is not related to and consciously integrated, the man appears barren, abstract, and detached, as if lacking some vital element. On the other hand, an anima-possessed man is swayed by moods, depressions, and anxieties, and tends to be withdrawn and detached.

The animus and anima seem to operate like autonomous personalities. We experience them, but cannot control them. They are the guides to the collective unconscious, leading to the other side. Through painful encounter with them we gain some acquaintance with their mode of being, but never total control. Most of the mystery always remains. The directing and creative aspect of the anima is shown in the following dream, dreamt before the patient's starting analysis because of depression due to feelings of meaninglessness in his life:

I am standing, totally perplexed, in the midst of a Casbah-like city with serpentine and winding small streets, not knowing where to turn. Suddenly I see a young, mysterious woman whom I had never seen before, pointing the direction out with her hand. It had a very awesome quality to it.

The potentially destructive aspect of the anima can be gleaned from the following: A young man with pernicious compulsive behavior patterns that alienate and depress him, dreams:

A woman is coming after me with razor blades in her hands; she intends to kill me. I have no choice, so I go after her jugular vein, killing her instead.

This man experiences women as a tremendous threat; he feels used by them, and during intercourse has fantasies of being swallowed and smothered. He is subjected to violent moods and heavy drinking. The dream shows an archetypal situation with a disastrous relationship to the anima. The dreamer will have to learn, slowly and painfully, to come to terms with his feminine side. Otherwise, the anima will be continually projected onto the women he will meet and he will have to "kill" his own capacity for emotional response. The more unaware a man is of his undeveloped, inferior anima, the more likely he is to fall victim to an infatuation with a woman who embodies this unconscious anima.

The self. The archetype of the *Self* is an expression of man's inherent psychic predisposition to experience wholeness, centeredness, and meaning in life. The Self is our god within ourselves—although it must immediately be added that the psychological existence of such an element does not affirm or deny the metaphysical question of whether there is also a God outside of ourselves. It is the Great Man of the Naskapi Indian, the internal embodiment of ancient and timeless wisdom. We come in contact with the Self when we are faced with problems of eternal validity, with paradox, with absurd situations that admit of no rational solutions; when we are at the end of our tether as to what to do; when we have recognized that ego adaptation is not enough and have to surrender to a higher authority, transcending the ego. At the moment of birth, ego and Self appear as one; the first half of life is devoted to their separation, requiring heroic attitudes and ego reliance. Then the process reverses itself, as the ego attitude is revealed as incomplete and insufficient, and the striving for realization of the Self begins.

The process by which this goal is achieved is called individuation, separating oneself from the collective and finding one's own unique way. The Self is symbolized as the Wise Old Man, the figure of Christ, Buddha, the treasure hard to attain, the jewel, and the Philosopher's stone.

Variety of Concepts

Sexuality

Freud equated libido with sexual energy. To Jung, libido was *psychic energy* in any manifestation, including sexual and power drives. Psychic energy operates by archetypal fields analogous to the instincts on the biological level. Thus the archetypes pertain to the same realm as the instincts, while being at the same time paradoxically their polar opposites, because the instincts are energy carriers on the biological level, while the archetypes are energy carriers on the spiritual level.

Sexuality is the biological manifestation of the union of two opposites, male and female. The union of opposites, or their reconciliation, is the life goal; we have to reconcile good and evil, active and passive, life and death, and, most importantly, the personal and the transpersonal. The last pair, which can be formulated also as the union of the ego and the Self, means experiencing the religious dimension of the psyche. This is *not* to be understood as saying that religion is nothing but sublimation of sexuality; what it *does* mean is that both sexuality and religion are expressions of the phenomenon of the reconciliation of the opposites, two realms of experience expressing different levels of the same basic reality.

The Oedipus complex

Freud considered the Oedipal complex a central point of his theories. This refers to his observation that around the ages of three to five, boys want to possess their mother and dispose of their father. This wish is not carried out because the boy fears castration as punishment by the father. A normal "resolution" of this state of affairs is identification with the father. Freud initially came upon this concept from his own self-analysis; later he presumably found the same mechanism in his patients.

That the unconscious seems to have a mythological layer is one of the mainstays of Jungian psychology. The Oedipus story is seen as but one mythological pattern among many. The Jungian approach to mythology is symbolic, whereas Freud reduced the mythologem to a literal interpretation. From our point of view, Freud seems to have missed the point about this myth.

The story can carry quite a different flavor from that imputed to it by Freud. The main theme might be that *man cannot escape his fate.* Both Oedipus and his parents try to thwart fate, with disastrous results. Countless mythologems repeat that motif, for example, Jonah refuses to obey God's command, tries to escape, and is swallowed by the whale. In the oedipal myth, Oedipus is presented with a heroic task: He must face up to the mystery of his tragic fate, the mystery of the Sphinx—to murder his father, marry his mother—and *then consciously accept the inevitable tragic guilt!* Oedipus is thus a hero who has partially failed through his unconsciousness; this "blinds" him and makes him rejoin the Furies, the angry mothers. With respect to the Freudian emphasis, it is to be noted that the incest is only incidental to the main theme. Also, the incest itself is *not* desired by Oedipus, nor is he punished for it.

Racial unconscious

Jung never used this term. It was introduced by his opponents and detractors to imply a racist coloration to Jung's theories. As pointed out earlier, various archetypes are inherent in all of us but only a few are evoked in each of us, the others lying dormant in the deep reaches of the psyche. Which of the archetypes are actualized depends on a variety of factors: the historical period, the cultural environment, and the particular life situation of the individual. Jung used the term *collective unconscious* for the world of the archetypes; then the term *objective psyche* was introduced as a more accurate description of the idea, and finally the concept was termed the *transpersonal unconscious,* which we consider the most apt.

Organ inferiority

This Adlerian concept refers to the notion that most people have, or feel themselves subjectively to have, a part of the body that is inferior. This feeling of inferiority causes them to overcompensate and put much emphasis on the inferior organ. We have no quarrel with the fact that people tend to experience bodily parts as inadequate, and that this may bring about suffering leading to overcompensation; we contend, however, that the real or imagined deformity serves usually only as a hook for a projection. This projection will occur only if there exists an initial predisposition for it, that is, if there is an appropriate archetypal activation as can be seen from the fact that two people with the same deformity may react very differently to their problem. One might treat it purely as a physical handicap that must be overcome realistically and appropriately, and the other might see it in the source of all his troubles or an indication that life is against him. We would then say that in the first case, the deformity has not fallen within an activated archetype;

in the second case, we see the archetype of the victim (the martyr or the Isaac Complex).

Defense mechanism

The Jungian position generally views *defense mechanisms* as expressions of psychic necessity; based upon projections of judgmental or hostile dynamics upon the other person. Projection plays a crucial part in Jungian thinking, and to a lesser extent, so does identification; but both tend to be seen not as defenses against anxiety but as processes, inevitable because of a state of primary unconsciousness.

The pleasure principle

Jungians do not consider pleasure to be the ultimate drive, although we do not minimize its importance. It is seen as one drive among several.

Environment and conditioning

The analytical approach, despite what seems to be the general belief, places a great deal of importance on the effects of *environment* and *conditioning*. We stress that these two factors do not operate on a *tabula rasa,* but interact with the archetypal predispositions of the individual. The same environment will evoke different responses from different individuals. Given an archetypal constellation, conditioning can be very effective, but one cannot condition someone to a response that will run counter to his given predisposition, as has been convincingly demonstrated even in animals (Breland & Breland, 1961).

Psychopathology

Analytical psychology does not view psychopathology as a disease or a deviation from a "normal" state. Symptoms are considered to be unconscious messages to the individual that something is awry with him, presenting him with a task that demands to be fulfilled. He is not allowed to go on living comfortably but is summoned, as it were, by a voice within, urgently demanding to be heard. Why some people are called and others left alone is impossible to say. The explanation can be ascribed only partially to causal aetiological factors, for very often the same traumatic conditions affect one person in one way and another in a totally different way. The symptoms themselves, viewed symbolically, frequently provide the clue to precisely that which is missing and must be developed. Our infirmities, our inferior side, provide us ultimately with the way to meaning and wholeness.

PSYCHOTHERAPY

Theory of Psychotherapy

Analytical psychotherapy does not possess a theory to speak of, except in general terms. Jung conceived therapy variously as a process of self-knowledge, a reconstruction of the personality, or even as education. He emphasized the empirical, tentative nature inherent in any therapeutic approach, objecting strenuously to any premature attempt to cast psychotherapy into a fixed structure: "Theories in psychology are the very devil. It is true that we need certain points of view for orienting and heuristic value; but they should always be regarded as mere auxiliary concepts that can be laid aside any time" (Jung, 1954, p. 7). This is easier said than done. But Jung, for one, lived this principle as fully as possible. Jung is currently known for his revolutionary theoretical insights, but it is sometimes forgotten what a superb therapist he was as well. People who had doubts about his theoretical conceptualizations did not hesitate to consult him therapeutically. Jung as a therapist was unorthodox, doing one thing in a given case and doing the opposite in the next one, ready to modify, change, and create, constantly aware of the vagaries of human nature; he was a pragmatist whose motto was: "anything goes, as long as it works." Thus, when confronted in an initial interview by a woman whose main symptom was that she had not slept for several weeks, Jung sang a lullaby, putting her to sleep! In another case, faced with a woman unable to get in touch with her own inner religious function, Jung taught her the Scriptures, each session handing her an assignment and testing her the next session. In Jung's consulting room, people danced, sang, acted, mimed, played musical instruments, painted, and modeled with clay, the procedures limited only by Jung's inventiveness and ingenuity. It is not surprising, therefore, that Jung distrusted theory, endlessly cautioning against falling prey to its rigidities and limitations. "Learn your theories as well as you can, but put them aside when you touch the miracle of the living soul" (Jung, 1954). With this caveat firmly fixed in our minds, we will attempt to delineate several general principles applicable to the therapeutic procedure, always mindful that these should be overruled when the occasion arises.

As a general rule, therapy starts with a thorough investigation of the patient's conscious state. Since the unconscious is viewed as compensatory to the conscious state, the latter has to first be established. The same dream, for example, can have quite different interpretations with differing conscious attitudes. The investigation will include the past history of the patient, various important influences in his life, attitudes, values and ideas. The analyst

then is able to point out inconsistencies and contradictions, peculiar reactions, and behavior patterns. Most important, the patient is thus taught the slow and difficult road to one's inner world. Confronted with unexpected questions and observations, he finds many of his tacit assumptions challenged and questioned. He starts to learn to introspect. A not unusual result of this period is a sense of tremendous confusion, following the initial sense of relief that accompanies the onset of therapy.

With most people, dreamwork is then cautiously introduced. The patient is thus launched on the awesome encounter with his unconscious. If the patient is in any way receptive to this new way, he is soon confronted with the disagreeable realization that he is not master of his own house, and that he has to contend with forces over which he has little control. To the typical, rational Western man, this is a jarring proposition. With this encounter with the workings of his unconscious side, the patient becomes acquainted with the compensatory nature of the unconscious. No sooner has a firm attitude been established in consciousness than the unconscious seems to bring out the opposite one, and the patient soon finds himself caught between pairs of opposites. This position creates tension and anxiety, but also the possibility of transformation and the resolution of the opposites by the emergence of a third entity that transcends the two poles.

An important principle is that of the quasi-intentionality of the psyche. The person's unconscious products (dreams, fantasies, artistic productions) are interpreted not only in terms of antecedent causes—although this may also apply—but primarily as pointing out the way to further development. Thus, a patient brings in the following dream:

I am in a gym, performing various exercises, with some other men. They are arranged in a line, in which they perform the exercises. I try to join the line at the head, but am rejected; I then try for the second place, and am rejected again; I try one place after the other till coming to the end of the line, and am rejected from every one of them.

At first the dreamer has difficulty associating to the dream. The analyst points out that the dream seems to involve men only. The dreamer then realizes that the men in the dream were actually boys from his all-male Catholic primary school, a place dominated by "oughts" and "shoulds." With this come unpleasant memories of the gym class, which the dreamer hated passionately. The only reason he attended was because he was forced to; had it been left up to him, he would not have shown up at any of the classes. As an afterthought, he adds that his mother also thought "it was good for you." The imagery of the dream is direct and clear—the dreamer is being rejected from the line; he does not belong there.

Although for most people, the initial period of therapy is devoted to helping them get in touch with their inner world, for people who are overly absorbed in their introversion an attempt is made to put them in touch with external reality. The analysis always tries to compensate for attitudes that are too one-sided.

The major principle of analytical therapy is for the analyst to follow scrupulously the direction and guidance of the unconscious; to abandon, as far as possible, all preconceptions and fixed ideas. For instance, it might be an analyst's clinical judgment that a patient is caught in a mother problem, but the dreams might stress a problem with the older brother. For the analyst to put aside his own judgment is a tall order, since our

major way of coping with the unknown is to cling to ready-made formulas. In addition, the analyst may be presented with the necessity of not being judgmental towards lines of conduct that violate his or her inner moral code. By doggedly following the wisdom of the unconscious, the patient slowly learns to accept that within himself there exists a guiding force, the Self, that points the way, painful though it might be, to a mode of being more meaningful and more whole. This force may appear in the guise of a simple "solution" to a complicated situation (e.g., a way to overcome a nagging compulsion) or it may point to a considerable complication of what seems like a simple problem. It may tell the patient that there is a way out of his dilemma if he but changes his attitude, or, on the contrary, that nothing can be done about it, that he is "fated" to live with it. Dreams determine primarily the *timing* of what is being interpreted in addition to the content of the interpretation. The analyst is quite often aware of possibilities about what is going on in the patient long before the patient is. As a general rule, a Jungian analyst will refrain from introducing these interpretations unless a dream heralds the patient's readiness to assimilate them. Case management in general is based upon the direction of the unconscious.

Psychotherapy ideally takes into consideration three modes: the fate element (which determines, for instance, what cannot be changed but has to be accepted); skill (the sum total of techniques that can be consciously formulated, taught, and communicated); and art, that intangible something (related to intuition and feeling) that weaves everything together. An exclusive emphasis on fate is likely to lead to fortune telling and card reading; a stress on mere skill entails a typical mechanical and barren approach; if the art is overplayed, we get the "wild analyst."

Process of Psychotherapy

People who have only a vague familiarity with Jung, based primarily on his more theoretical writings, tend to have a rather distorted view of Jungian therapy. They conceive of it either as an endless concatenation of symbols leading far back to antiquity or as a spinning out of esoteric fantasies. Nothing is farther from the truth. People listening in on an analytic hour are liable to hear the most mundane issues being discussed, including one's budget, relationship with one's mother-in-law or one's boss, and so on. The cardinal rule in Jungian analysis is that *the basis of any analysis is experiencing; mere intellectual understanding is insufficient.* This is not to minimize the important role of intellectual understanding, but to emphasize the importance of experiencing a psychic reality. Thus, the analyst may discourage the attempt of a patient to do away with depression; rather, the patient will be asked to stay with the depression, to let it be, accepting it as an unconscious message.

Generally speaking, the therapeutic encounter in a Jungian setting involves an active interchange between analyst and patient. Depending on the patient's development, the state of the transference and various other factors, the analyst will exchange feelings, experiences, and even dreams. In principle, the nature of the interchange is limited only by the analyst's imagination. The mood of the hour may veer from being highly serious to humorous. The analyst may teach, suggest, cajole, give advice, reflect feelings, or give support. The main emphasis is on the conscious assimilation of the immediate experience, using as well techniques that have now become the stock in trade of Gestalt therapy and the encounter movement (breathing methods and what are now called sensitivity training activities were in use by Jungian analysts in the early twenties).

However, interpretation is the main work of the analytic process. *Interpretation* is the process of enlarging upon given data in a way that makes it possible for the patient to perceive connections, motivations, and feelings of which he has been unaware. The main thrust of the analytical process may be summarized as an attempt to make conscious as much as possible what has been unconscious. After the reality situation and the patient's phenomenological world have been established, dream interpretation is undertaken.

Dreamwork is the core of Jungian therapy. Individuals vary considerably in their capacity to remember dreams. There are some who never remember any, but they are rare in the typical patient population. The constant reinforcement of the importance attached to dreams by the analyst and the seriousness with which even the most trivial dream is treated, usually brings about a change even in those people who seem to have difficulty in remembering their dreams. We will focus here on dream interpretation, because all unconscious products (fantasies, paintings, daydreaming) are treated essentially in the same way.

Dream interpretation

The most profitable way to look at a dream is to see it as a metaphorical drama unfolding before our eyes. In a well-conceived play, the setting is first established, physically as well as psychologically; the mood is suggested and possible conflicts are hinted at. This may be called the *exposition*. Then a *crisis* develops and the conflict is thrust to the fore. The various forces hinted at in the exposition emerge fully and we have the unfolding of the drama. Then, as a general rule, a *solution* is introduced, sometimes in the form of there being no solution, but a stalemate, or an impasse. These dynamics apply equally well to any unconscious product, such as daydreams, fantasies, and fairy tales.

The main difference between a classical Freudian approach to a dream and a Jungian one is based on *repression*. To Freudians a dream is the result of the emergence of repressed contents from the unconscious. As a result, it is viewed, essentially, as a distortion that must be unravelled. Thus the actual drama of the dream is referred to as the *manifest* contents of the dream, behind which there lurks the *latent* content. A Jungian views the dream phenomenologically. The drama of the dream *is* the unconscious message expressed in symbolic form, a message not necessarily repressed or hidden, but rather trying to reveal.

Classically, in Freudian psychoanalysis, the dreamer would be asked to "free" associate to any given symbol in the dream. Assume, for instance, that a dream in which a wheel appears is reported. The dreamer might say that the wheel reminds him of a tractor, then a tractor toy he had in childhood; a whole slew of memories pertaining to that particular period might emerge, taking the dreamer farther and farther away from the original symbol, namely, the wheel. If the dreamer is persistent in his associative process, he will ultimately reach a painful point, concerning perhaps his mother, his older brother, or perhaps a homosexual experience. Naturally these are relevant domains for psychological inquiry, but in all probability they would have little to do with that specific dream.

A Jungian, on the other hand, would consider it of paramount importance that the specific symbol used by the unconscious is a wheel, not a tractor. The patient could have dreamt directly about the tractor, but did not. The symbol of the wheel emerged in his dream. The *association* to the tractor and that childhood period is, of course, not to be ignored. An *association* is a connection, not necessarily causal, by virtue of contiguity. Thus, the dreamer in Jungian analysis is asked to say what comes first to his mind when he thinks about, or pictures, the wheel of his dream. It could be his childhood tractor toy, his grandma's parakeet, or an ancient cart he had seen once in a movie. This is done for every symbol in the dream, for inanimate objects as well as for people. It is also done for the major occurrences in the dream. If, for instance, the dreamer is promised something in the dream, he will be asked to associate to a promise. Thus is the *associative context* of the dream established. But this is not sufficient for interpretation. The *amplifications* must be kept in mind as well. An amplification is what an object actually *is*. For example, the dreamer may associate his cousin to a lamp appearing in his dream, but essentially, a lamp is something that gives light in the darkness. Likwise, a pen might remind a dreamer of a penis (especially if he is a product of our culture), but primarily a pen is an instrument for writing. Amplification may come from yet another source. Because of the hypothesis of the archetypal nature of the unconscious, the analyst will bear in mind all possible parallels he can find (from mythology, fairy tales, literature, and so forth) to the various symbols and dramas featured in the specific dream. The more precise the equivalence, the more pertinent the amplification; amplifications that are too general can easily lead one astray.

Dreams have logic of their own. Usually it may be assumed that if the dream drama includes two events that follow each other, it is implied that the second happening occurred *because* of the first. A woman dreamt that she saw a snake on the ground, that she jeered at the snake and the snake then attacked her. We may conclude that the snake attacked her *because* she jeered at it. A more appropriate attitude would have been either to flee the scene as soon as possible or try to kill it. The dream implies that the dreamer is jeering at the very powerful unconscious content that, as a result of this attitude, is threatening to annihilate her. (In this specific case, the woman had just recently overcome a serious alcoholism problem. She was supremely confident of her ability not to succumb to it any more and was recklessly playing with dangerous temptations. The snake represents the addiction potentiality, which was still lurking.)

These examples, which were chosen for their relative clarity and simplicity, might easily mislead the uninitiated to believe that dreams are easily interpreted. This is far from the case. Every therapist is chagrined to discover that there are many leads and possibilities, and the ambiguity of dreams might very well allow for two completely contradictory understandings. This is why a dream *series* is of such paramount importance. A dream can be likened to a mathematical equation with many unknowns; the "solution," therefore, is at best tentative. A series of dreams supplies many more equations with the same unknowns and can be assumed to deal with the same conflict from many different angles. By finding parallels between dreams, one can often discern one's way in what might otherwise have been a jungle. At our present state of knowledge, dream interpretation is a trial-and-error process. The therapist is often aware that a dream may be understood along different, even contradictory lines. Sometimes the therapist needs to take a risk and follow one line of interpretation rather than another, and then wait for the following dream for corroboration or disproval.

A dream can be interpreted on the objective or the subjective level. The *objective level* refers to people (or events) outside of the dreamer; for instance, if one dreams about his wife, the dream is then taken to express something about the actual relationship between husband and wife. On the other hand, the *subjective level* entails relating to all figures and activities in the dreams as pertaining to the dreamer's "inner" psyche, that is, the inner wife, friend, boss, struggle, and so on.

For example, a young man is about to get married, although he is uncertain about his feelings about his future wife. He dreams he is about to embrace her passionately when a friend rings the doorbell; his wife-to-be answers the door and stays to talk with her friend, completely ignoring her fiancé, who is left frustrated and angry. On the objective level, this dream bodes ill for the relationship, the dream implying that she is far from being really related to him. On the subjective level, however, the dream seems to be saying that the dreamer and his feminine side are not well related; that is, he has difficulty relating to people and being intimate with them. Accordingly, interpretation on the objective level would thrust the burden of the problematic relationship onto the girl's shoulders; the subjective interpretation would implicate the dreamer's own capacity for relatedness.

Sometimes a dream that has to be understood subjectively is mistakenly taken on the objective level. A patient dreams that his wife has been sleeping with an ex-boyfriend of hers. The dreamer, impulsive and given to literal interpretations, gets furious and berates his wife for infidelity, to her utter bafflement, since she has not seen this boyfriend for years; moreover, he lives thousands of miles away. The next night our patient has the same dream, but this time it is not the boyfriend who is involved but some unknown man. Obviously the first dream was suggesting that his inner wife, the anima, was having an affair with someone else, rather than actually implicating his wife.

Let us consider another example. After six months in therapy, Miriam brings in the following dream:

I am in a classroom at my alma mater with Professor P. My father is standing beside me. Professor P. is explaining how to evaluate determinants. He says that a determinant always reduces to a fraction and another number, which he does not know whether to put in the numerator or the denominator. My father says it is not important where this number is put, while I passionately insist that it is very important indeed.

Miriam has a doctoral degree in mathematics, and the dream involves mathematical symbols. To the professor she associates the first course she took with him, on the functions of a real variable. The dream, therefore, is concerned with the determination and evaluation of reality. The professor, who is a loved and respected authority for her, explains that reality always reduces to a fraction, namely, to a situation where someone is above and someone below: That is, life is a power struggle or a battle for dominance (who is above and who under). Her father, an animus figure, claims that it should not matter. This brings to light Miriam's belief that an attempt to dominate and control is to be despised, an attitude forcibly inculcated into her by her rational, intellectual father. But the dreams bare her unconscious wish to dominate and control.

When the interpretation of the dream was offered to her, she burst into tears, and said that the previous night she and her husband had sexual intercourse, she being in the dominant position, and for the first time in ther life she really enjoyed herself, an experience that frightened her so much she had blocked it completely out of her memory until the interpretation recalled it to mind. She then recalled several instances in her life when her natural ambitions and assertiveness had been rudely repressed so that she was forced to adopt a passive-aggressive mode of behavior to avoid being crumbled and trodden upon by her environment.

Dream interpretation, regardless of how phenomenologically done, is still, unfortunately, a reductive procedure. The symbol is a mediator between consciousness and the unconscious, conveying much more than can be rationally expressed. When we interpret a dream we are, in effect, reducing a highly graphic and symbolic imagery to a verbal, that is, rational, statement. Something is lost in this reduction. It is incumbent, therefore, to make this statement more experiential to the dreamer. Miriam was asked to keep the imagery of the dream vividly in mind and to be reminded of it when confronted by a situation that seemed to her to involve issues of control and dominance. In therapy she might be asked to paint the dream or to carry on a conversation with the father figure in the dream. Other means might also be employed. The dream or fantasy might be enacted in a group, with various members taking different roles generating a psychodrama.

Mechanisms of Psychotherapy

Obviously the analytical process is not a simple one and does not lend itself to a clear explication. It is not easy to demonstrate precisely what factors are involved in a successful (or unsuccessful, for that matter) analysis. We can only try to establish tentative guidelines.

Acceptance

This is probably the *sine qua non* of any depth therapy. During the course of the therapy, it is essential that the patient feel accepted by the therapist. This is done not so much by what the therapist actually says as it is by his genuine openness. All Jungian analysts are required to undergo a thorough analysis. They therefore experience the difference between acceptance and nonacceptance by their own analysts and get a personal understanding of its profound importance. They learn that the relationship between the analyst and the analysand is not between the "healthy" and the "sick," but between someone who has delved into his own psyche and has come out of this experience not only unscathed but enhanced, and as a result has established an ongoing dialogue with his unconscious; and someone who has not undergone this voyage. This voyage, ideally, has not inflated the analyst and caused him to feel superior, but rather has gained for him an enormous respect for the intricacy and complexity of the human psyche and, consequently, a healthy humility in the face of hidden resources and potentialities inherent in the human being he is confronting.

The idea of psychic lameness may need to be acknowledged, but taken as a challenge to further psychic development and enrichment. One is crippled not so much because of what has happened in the past but because one is being called from within to enlarge one's horizons, to become more of a person.

A person's neurotic symptoms may present an important and difficult task; this is expressed in the mythologem of Jonah, called by God to prophesy doom to Nineveh. Jonah refused, and as a result was swallowed by a whale, or, psychologically stated, he was inflicted by a neurotic or psychotic depression. The neurotic is someone trying to escape his fate; but this fate, once recognized, accepted, assimilated, and actively participated in, could lead to a life of fuller meaning and greater wholeness—although not necessarily less suffering.

Relationship to the inner world

Western civilization, goal and achievement oriented, places a great deal of emphasis on the outside world. This is to the detriment of our other reality, the inner one, which is at least as important as the outer one. Most of the people applying for therapy have lost touch with their inner world; some of them are barely aware of its existence. One of the profound consequences of analytical therapy is the rebridging of the gap between the outer and inner worlds. The patient is gently but persistently encouraged to pay heed to and value his inner world. The power and vicissitudes of his inner psychic life are demonstrated to him over and over, and he comes to respect it.

On the other hand, some people seem to come for therapy not because they are out of touch with their inner world but because, or so it seems, they are too much in touch with it. In fact, they seem to be flooded with unconscious fantasies. Here the analytic task is different. To establish a viable dialogue between consciousness and unconsciousness, the two have to be clearly separated from each other. The integrity of an independent conscious position needs to be established. As with human beings, real communication exists only between distinctly different positions.

Transference

Transference is a special instance of the

more general phenomenon of projection. Unconscious contents, because unconscious, are subject to projection. The subject experiences that part of his psyche of which he is not aware by attributing it to the object. In general, this object can be both human as well as inanimate. *Transference* is the sum total of all the projections with which the patient endows his analyst. Jung's attitude toward the role that the transference plays during analysis underwent drastic changes. At the beginning, he tended to agree with Freud upon the all-important function of the transference for a therapeutic cure. As Jung became more and more involved with the archetypal nature of the psyche, however, he came to minimize the role of transference as an essential element in the therapeutic process. At this intermediate period, Jung maintained that therapy could go on comfortably without transference; that, in fact, it proceeded much more smoothly without it. It was a nuisance, he averred, and, moreover, it was a result of insufficient rapport between therapist and patient. Where this rapport has been established, he thought, there was no need for a transference. Yet ultimately Jung had to bow to the force of the clinical evidence and recognize the profound effect of the transference, as well as the therapeutic value of the analysis of the transference.

Countertransference is the analyst's projection on the patient. This phenomenon is not viewed as a hindrance to be avoided or minimized, but as a necessary concomitant, which may be fruitfully used by the therapist to guide him during the course of therapy. On a more general level, countertransference is the complementary part of the total archetype, which manifests itself in the guise of various polar opposites: guru-disciple, savior-sinner. The analyst can use his own reactions as a therapeutic tool. Those reactions provide him with information as to what is going on in the analytic process. If, for instance, the analyst perceives in himself a spontaneous urge to bully his patient, he will know the master-slave configuration is operating.

APPLICATIONS

Problems

Jung devoted a great deal of energy to religion. Religion is the expression of an archetypal need to endow our human existence with meaning. An understanding of the various archetypal form elements as expressed in the study of comparative religions, therefore, is crucial to a thorough understanding of how, for various peoples at different epochs, this need found its realization. Mythology in particular and folklore in general are domains in which archetypal imagery and archetypal motifs appear in practically "pure" form. Both myth and folktale are part of an essentially oral tradition that has handed these motifs down from generation to generation. That which survives such a prolonged process of erosion and distortion are the archetypal motifs in a clear and accessible form.

Art is another domain to which analytical psychology can contribute specific insights. All too often, artistic products are analyzed reductively, traced to the family constellation of the artist or to childhood traumata. Inspired art, however, is more than that. It is a personal expression of something universal and timeless, existing in each of us, the giving of a specific and personal form to an archetypal motif. It is a common hypothesis that creativity is the product of neurotic suffering—take away the neurosis and the art disappears. To this, analytic psychology takes exception. Creativity involves the ability to give realistic and visible expression to archetypal drives without being inundated by them. An artist is different from other people in that he is burdened, as it were, with the additional energy charge of archetypal forces that press for visible manifestation. He does not create because he is neurotic, but may be neurotic because he is creative and has to contend with powerful forces within himself. A genuine artist will not be robbed of his creativity by Jungian analysis; rather he will be more adequately able to contend with his potent resources. Only where "artistic" endeavours are used as cover-up or escape mechanisms will analysis undo them.

Evaluation

The Jungian analyst evaluates a prospective patient's readiness for therapy along the same lines used by other clinicians; the person's emotional maturity, the kind of adjustment he has made, his level of functioning, and so forth. He will, however, place primary importance on the person's relationship with his unconscious. Using his knowledge of archetypal patterns, he will often be able to gauge the patient's stage of development and base his decisions accordingly. Some examples will illustrate.

A highly intellectualized patient who seems to have difficulty in delving into himself and who experiences his being in analysis as a humiliating process brings, after several months, this initial dream:

I stand on the shore, under the watchful eye of the Queen and King. I am given to understand that a treasure is buried on the island facing us, and that I am to find it. I swim across to the island. On it there is a transparent wall that has to be climbed. It is covered by Venetian blinds. I peer through and see young children carrying guns. I recoil, and swim back to the mainland.

The atmosphere in the dream and the presence of the King and Queen clearly indicate the archetypal nature of this dream (the dreamer, musically inclined, associated Wagnerian figures to the King and Queen). Because this was an initial dream, it assumes an additional importance, possibly representing the life myth of the dreamer. Here he is presented with the hero's task, to uncover the "treasure hard to attain," a motif appearing in countless myths and fairy tales. As usual, the path to the treasure is not smooth; here, besides swimming to the island without apparent difficulties, our dreamer has to overcome a wall. As he looks through it, he sees that this would entail confronting his infantile aggressive impulses, and he draws back. Prognostically, this does not augur well for the analysis and the patient's ability or willingness to see it through. The treasure, which on the archetypal level is our very essence, seems to be beyond the reach of his effort. As a matter of fact, the patient stayed in therapy for six months, then took a job in another city and stopped therapy without having touched on any deep issue in himself.

Another example is of a different kind. The patient has come to therapy in a crisis situation and has made substantial progress both in solving his current conflicts as well as in bringing about what seems a real change in his personality. He is toying with the idea of terminating and "being on his own." Now, this is a classical dilemma for the therapist who has no objective standards to determine when the analysis is to be terminated. Is the patient's wish to leave the analysis a genuinely healthy decision, or is it an urge born out of the anticipatory anxiety of delving into deeper material? In the latter case, should the therapist let the patient go, hoping he will come back at a future time when he is more secure and ready, or should he confront the patient and analyze his "resistance"? In other words, is the patient requesting an honorable discharge, or is he shirking? In the actual case, the analyst presented the patient with the two alternatives, explained that he had no way of making the decision, and asked the patient to mull it over, bearing the alternatives in mind. The next session, the patient, not a prolific dreamer, brought the following dream:

I see a girl that I know. I want to approach her and talk to her, because I really like her, but when I half-heartedly attempt to do so, she suddenly vanishes.

To the girl he associates independence, autonomy, and self-reliance. Obviously the message of the dream is: "Your own independence, autonomy, and self-reliance still elude you." The therapist then took the stand that the patient's decision was precipitous and advised that he stay with the analysis.

Often, when the patient's grasp of reality is more or less tenuous, the therapist is involved in a different kind of problem. Thus, a patient who has been in therapy for several months dreams:

I am standing near the ocean. It is night, and there is a full moon. Suddenly, the moon starts swinging from side to side, in bigger and bigger arcs, until it falls into the ocean. There it explodes like a hydrogen bomb with a big mushroom. The radiation made me evaporate like powder.

The dream shows a tendency toward ego disintegration. A psychotic episode is foreshadowed. Indeed, upon further inquiry the therapist learned that on the day

before the dream, the patient felt he could not get up from a chair on which he had been sitting. Something was pulling him back and only the strongest effort managed to get him up. The therapist then confronted the patient with the fact that he was being threatened by a catatonic episode and both calmly discussed the alternatives involved, including hospitalization. They both finally decided to try to work at it together outside a hospital. For the next two weeks they were in close contact; it was touch and go whether the psychotic elements or the conscious ones would prevail. Fortunately, the latter won.

Treatment

Analytical psychology originally was considered applicable primarily for the person who had adjusted to the outer world very well, had accomplished what was expected of him by society, but who, entering the second half of life, found himself listless and dissatisfied. Thus, at its inception, analytical psychotherapy was an attempt to find meaning and was primarily geared for the "adjusted" middle-aged man or woman.

More than two-thirds of Jung's patients were in their second half of life. Most had paid society its due by raising a family and finding a vocation and were now confronted with the task of finding a meaning in their life. In his earlier writings, Jung stressed this division between the first "half" and the second "half" of life, maintaining that different modes of treatment were called for according to which "half" one is dealing with.

Group psychotherapy

It is useful to recall, whenever one deals with Jung, the background against which he practiced and wrote. The beginning of the twentieth century brought in its wake a psychology that defined normalcy in terms of a collective average. Pathology was still being conceptualized in terms of deviation from a statistical norm. Jung's basic Swiss temperament rebelled against this tendency toward conformity and collectivization, and during all his lifetime, he remained steadfastly a guardian of individuality.

It is not surprising, then, that Jung distrusted group therapy. To Jung, one of the most important aspects of the therapeutic process was the encounter with one's inner religion, one's sense of the divine within oneself. In a group, where so many emotions vie for attention, such an experience is harder to come by, unless the analyst is aware of this problem and takes direct actions to facilitate such experiences.

Yet there is nothing in Jung's psychotherapeutic concepts that is counterindicative of group analysis. Quite the opposite is the case; analytical concepts lend themselves admirably to the group process (Whitmont, 1964). Judiciously applied, they can turn the analytical group into a potent instrument yielding unexpected rewards.

Inherent in the group process is the enhancing of the experiential dimension. Instead of discussing the shadow abstractly in an individual hour, the shadow is lived and felt in the group. Something that may have been thrashed around for months in individual sessions becomes suddenly a gut experience in the group. Issues come to the fore that would be unlikely to arise in individual sessions. The group experience is, therefore, a complementary workshop experience to the individual analysis; each is enriched by the other.

The group experience often challenges one's relation to the mother archetype in its protecting or devouring aspect, thus reflecting one's relationship with one's personal mother. The group is also an excellent vehicle to constellate other archetypal dimensions. The transformation motif, death and rebirth, initiation, the twin brothers—all these can be evoked by various techniques as their possibilities arise spontaneously from the living situation. Psychodrama, Gestalt techniques, sensitivity training, and ritualizations may be employed. The analyst may be more active in group sessions than he could allow himself in individual sessions, and the transference to the analyst is lessened considerably. The analyst can be responded to more like the human being he is rather than the archetypal role into which he is thrust in individual analysis. Often this permits negative attitudes to surface in the group, attitudes of which the analysand was too frightened to raise individually.

Family therapy

Often analytic work with only one member of a couple will lead to the dissolution of the relationship. Although this is inevitable in some cases, it is destructive and unnecessary in others. Considerations like these may make it desirable that the same analyst work with the two members individually or even treat them as a couple. Very often the archetypal situation in which the patient finds himself lends itself to more effective handling in the family constellation, and then the entire family should be treated as a unit. With very severely disturbed people, family intervention may be indicated.

Management

Jungians do not, as a rule, differ to any marked degree from other therapists working within a dynamic depth-psychological framework as far as management is concerned.

The setting

The analyst may work in a clinic or an office, or often in his own home. No special trappings are necessary. The emphasis is on intimacy: the analyst may sit beside a desk, or a table, but nothing separates the analyst from the analysand, and they confront each other directly. The analyst may or may not take notes. In some cases the session takes place in a hospital. The patient is assured absolute confidentiality. Special equipment is rarely used, although in this electronic age some people express the desire to record the sessions so they can listen to them at home in leisure.

The intensity and effectiveness of the analysis is not a simple and direct function of the frequency of the sessions. One can work in depth even if one sees a patient once a month. Most analysts, however, prefer to see their patients once or twice a week, at least in the beginning. A growing number of analysts show a marked predilection for working on a once-a-week basis, increasing the number only if absolutely necessary.

Relationship

Analysts differ widely as to how they conduct the first interview. Some prefer to plunge into the thick of the problem, and others insist on a thorough anamnesis starting from earliest memories and going systematically and methodically through the various life stages and emotional development of the patient. Most analysts devote the first few sessions to a mutual evaluation of the patient and the therapist. A basic mutual liking and respect is necessary for a meaningful analysis. If the initial antagonism is too pronounced (on either side), the patient will be transferred. The analyst is aware that initial negative reactions are projections, and that attitude and feelings toward the patient will undergo a change. However, from his own personal analysis, the analyst has gained sufficient awareness of his own blind spots and knows that even in the most thorough analysis, these cannot be completely worked through. One is never perfect, and allowances for one's weaknesses are a crucial characteristic of a good therapist. As a general rule, it is not advisable to work in a relationship with an analysand who reminds the analyst forcibly of his mother or father, and this holds true even if the parental complex was thoroughly thrashed out during the analyst's own analytical work.

The major importance of the initial sessions lies in taking stock of the unconscious reactions of analyst and analysand to each other.

No routine demand for psychological testing or physical examination is usually made. If the analyst is presented with a symptom which might prove organic, a physical checkup is in order. Flexibility and an intuitive-feeling approach are the hallmarks of the good clinician.

The nature of the relationship between analyst and analysand is determined more by the nature of the two participants than by the specific school of thought to which the analyst belongs. Analysts differ in their personalities and temperaments. Some will tend to be more cerebral and aloof, others more feeling and warm; some more talkative, others more reticent, some more therapeutically active than others. Broadly speaking, however, an analyst would tend to be more a listener, less active and less sharing of himself at the early stages of analysis. It is by dint of cooperating fruitfully in the analytic process that a growing intimacy and a friendship are established. As time goes on the analyst generally shares more of self and the relationship becomes more of a peer confrontation, rather than a healer-patient one.

Patient problems

Very little can be said regarding the kind of patient behaviors likely to cause problems to the analyst. The way in which a given analyst reacts to a specific development is more a function of personality than it is of theoretical persuasion. Some therapists will exclude a certain category of patients on an a priori basis, such as alcoholics, drug addicts, suicidal risks. By these exclusions, the therapist recognizes his personal limitations. The analytical orientation as such does not preclude any given situation, and the way in which an analyst may deal with a particular kind of behavior, crying and severe depressive episodes, is determined by the analyst's personality, his understanding of the situation, and his relationship with the patient.

CASE EXAMPLE

Michael is in his early 20s, the third son in a midwestern family that had four sons. He is attractive, bright and introspective, and highly sensitive to the world around him. Mood and atmosphere affect him profoundly. This sensitivity allows him to feel the implicit and unexpressed needs of other people, a quality he is able to use creatively as well as destructively in a peer group. He tends to react in an extreme and absolutist fashion, betraying an inner insecurity that comes occasionally to the surface. He can be honest with himself and with others and is deeply committed to finding his true meaning.

Michael came to therapy because of his homosexuality. Refreshingly free from the common guilt feelings aroused by societal strictures (both his and his wife's families were aware of the state of affairs), he nevertheless had failed to find satisfaction in the homosexual world. Michael expected therapy to help him form lasting and meaning relationships in the homosexual or heterosexual world.

This was not Michael's first attempt at therapy. He had attempted to work through his problem in college, when his homosexual feelings intensified. The counselor refused to get involved with Michael's feeling and fantasy world, saying it was like a ball of yarn that was better left alone. He advised Michael to concentrate on his behavior rather than on his fantasies and attempted, as Michael experienced it, to "butch him up." As a result, he got married to a sexually shy girl, a virgin like himself. A baby girl was soon born, but the marriage rapidly deteriorated, resulting in a temporary separation. Michael came into the present therapy expecting to be told to "make a man of himself" and, in effect, to be rejected for what he was. That would have clinched his negative relationship toward the adult male world.

The first dream Michael presented was the following:

I am in the kitchen with my mother. Upstairs I can hear the sound of heavy chains clanking across the floor. Mother tells me not to worry, that father has gone insane, but that they had chained him upstairs so that he can't hurt me. She intimately places her hand over mine on the table and caresses it.

The dream seems to correspond to the actual family constellation. Michael experiences his father as weak, given to ineffectual violent rages that only emphasize his impotence. The mother stands always on the side of the children, effectively lessening any impact the father might have had. She is also seductive toward her children, especially towards Michael, her favorite. However, it would be a mistake to understand this dream as simply repeating the family psychology, the so-called oedipal character of which Michael is quite aware, for on that level the dream is adding nothing. What the dream is probably describing is the archetypal constellation of someone caught in the grips of homosexuality. The assertive capacity of the ego is under the seductive dominance of the mother archetype, hence his masculinity is chained and not trusted. The dream does not say anything about the outcome of this situation. That we are here dealing with a potentially difficult state of affairs is demonstrated in the second dream:

My father, brother, and I are peddling out to sea in water bikes. The water is choppy and threatening. I see my father dipping my baby into the shark-infested water.

Clearly, his anima is yet in an infantile ("baby") stage; that is, his feeling side, his capacity for emotional relatedness, is still undeveloped and threatened by the dangers of the deep, the regressive urges (sharks). He will have to derive masculine strength from an inner source, hopefully as a result of the analytical relationship. Indeed, sometime later we have the third dream:

I follow Y (the analyst) in climbing a difficult terraced mountain. Y is surprised that there is a physical side to my nature, and says he enjoys my company.

Michael, who had suppressed his physical side as a result of ridicule, or lack of trust, rediscovers it in the company of his spiritual guide. Climbing the mountain can be archetypically taken as the road of individuation, the analyst representing an aspect of the Self. A further progress is made when the symbolism is more personal in the fourth dream:

Keith boasts about how many girls he has dated. Under his braggadocio I sense his insecurity, to which I respond in a fatherly way. Suddenly, we are romantically kissing. We are equals. I am transported. Mother tries to find out what has happened between Keith and me.

Keith is a high school friend Michael had not seen since that time. He had idolized Keith, seeing in him that aspect of masculinity he himself so lacked. Here, Keith is to be taken as a positive shadow figure, and the dream foresees the possibility of Michael's getting in touch with his repressed masculinity. Now that this has happened, we can expect a new attitude toward the anima, the feminine side.

Fifth dream: I am teaching my baby girl to talk.

The anima is still a baby, but the ego is developing a positive relationship to her. In the meantime, Michael had decided to reestablish his relationship with his wife, and she returned to him. Michael had also joined a group run by his analyst. The atmosphere in the sessions became more and more charged. Obviously something is afoot.

Sixth dream: I am in the group and suddenly I discover to my horror that I am dressed in a way that looks very gay. I feel ridiculous and say so to one of the girls. She is not concerned and does not take my dress as an indication of my character, just an accident. She simply rolls down the sleeves and makes minor adjustments, and the clothes look normal. A guy who is sitting behind me is dressed in a gay manner. He tries to pull me away from the girl and embraces me. His clothing is full of curved needles that jut outward, and they pierce me. I struggle and free myself. The girl's clothing is also full of pins, but they are safety pins and they are closed.

The girl in question embodies to

Michael the essence of femininity, and her acceptance of him as a man is of prime importance. The conflict depicted here is between the homosexual and heterosexual sides in Michael. The homosexual side, although potent, proves to be "prickly" and disagreeable, according to our dream. We can conclude from it that potentially Michael is able to free himself from it. It is worthwhile to note that in this dream, the dream ego (the dreamer) has made an active choice, which involved a struggle he initiated and out of which he came victorious.

For Michael to be able actively to challenge the destructive aspect of the mother, he will have to get sustenance and support from the father world. In myths this usually takes the form of some "heavenly" intervention—Hercules is helped in his labors by Zeus, his divine father; Perseus is provided with the necessary gear (an invisible helmet and a shield) to fight the Gorgon (the Great Mother in her terrible aspect) who turns all who gaze upon her into stone. Consciously, Michael feels helpless. How will he be able to find his own masculinity when he has not had a strong father as a model? This is, indeed, difficult: Michael will have to find his father within himself, a search that will hopefully be aided by the relationship with the male analyst. In Michael's specific case, it means establishing contact with his spiritual side first, namely, broaching the religious question.

Seventh dream: The setting of this dream is a large church. In the rear Y (the analyst) is sitting behind an old wooden table reading from an ancient book. The letters are shaped like old German runes, long and narrow. But when I look close, I see that it could also be Chinese. Y is translating to a group of people, including me.

This dream had a profound effect on Michael. He was awed and puzzled by the church setting. His conflict with religion first arose when he came into puberty and started masturbating. In a characteristic absolutistic fashion, he decided that sex and religion were mutually exclusive, since the latter seemed to negate the former. He therefore discarded his religious beliefs and considered himself an atheist. Until the appearance of this dream, the religious function in him seemed to be successfully repressed. The dream imagery, however, awakened strong positive feelings, not necessarily for the collective form of institutionalized religion, but for an individual, inner experience. The dream casts the analyst as a translator and transmitter of ancient wisdom, both of Western (the runes) and Eastern tradition. There could hardly be a better description of the analytical process from a Jungian point of view. In a further scene in the dream (not reported here), a wind, a traditional symbol of the spirit, blows through the church. The symbolism is very rich and this made the analyst decide that the analytic sessions by themselves could not support the heavy symbolic load, since the duration of the sessions is too short to permit more than a hinting at the depth and amplitude of the issues raised by this dream. Up to this point, Michael did not know of the analyst's specific theoretical orientation. The issue had never arisen, as Michael did not come to him looking specifically for a Jungian analyst. No professional terminology was ever used. With Michael's intellectual bent, the analyst had decided that overemphasis on the intellectual side would be detrimental to the course of his analysis (with another patient it might prove important to introduce an intellectual framework at the outset of the therapy). The analyst now suggested several books having to do with the symbolism of church and spirit. In this he was also guided by considerations having to do with the archetypal nature of the dream. In Norse mythology, the runes (the alphabet, knowledge, consciousness) were given as a gift to Odin when he sacrificed himself on the ash tree as a symbol of transmittable culture and knowledge.

There is now a new element with which Michael must contend: the religious dimension, the spiritual side of the father archetype. The assimilation of a father figure on a more personal level will have to wait and will come only much later.

Eighth dream: I am with my father. A coarse brutish guy appears and insults my father. I wait confidently for my father to hit him but he is afraid; he is too weak. Thereupon I hit the guy.

Here the dreamer recognizes that he has to assume masculine qualities himself, rather than look for them in vain in other people who are unable to provide them. Meanwhile, on the level of outer reality, the changes that the unconscious heralds are taking place at a very slow rate. Michael is very anxious to get on with it and be "quickly transformed." He then has the following dream:

Ninth dream: It is a warm summery day. I find a cocoon hanging on a vine and pick it up. The covering is a delicate green color. Its transparency allows me to see the orange wings of the butterfly inside and I realize that it is a Monarch butterfly. I cup my hands together to provide warmth for the cocoon, hoping that the warmth of my hands will help it emerge sooner. Then I realize it won't help. I must simply wait for it to emerge by itself.

The graphic beauty of this dream is breathtaking. The dreamer is knowledgeable about butterflies and knows that the Monarch, a king, is a very unusual butterfly. In the fall, the Monarchs fly from all over together, congregating and mi-

grating thus to the South for the winter, after which they return. Butterfly is psyche in Greek and is an archetypal image for the Self, the goal of the individuation process. Michael spontaneously said that this is an initiation dream, in which he is initiated into manhood. To the Monarch he associated his masculinity "hang up," which, initially ugly, is transformed into something beautiful that is part of the collective sense of virility. But, says the dream, the process cannot be deliberately rushed; the natural rhythms of growth have to be respected.

We realize that our presentation of Michael's case is at best an abstraction. Any attempt to communicate an alive, intense, deep relationship between two people over a few pages is impossible; only a few broad strokes out of the whole picture can be delineated. We focused on a segment as it was reflected primarily in the unconscious process; we did not dwell on the outside reality nor on the vicissitudes of the analyst-analysand relationship. We depicted the most salient dreams, omitting scores of others, not all of which were understood. The overall pattern is discernible more in retrospect than *in situ;* certainly, no conscious plan was followed. Finally, let us again emphasize that dreams point to possibilities, not actualities. Michael's concrete problems are far from solved.

SUMMARY

Analytical psychotherapy attempts to deal with the human psyche in a phenomenological-existential way using a few basic assumptions as guideposts. The psyche includes consciousness, the center of which is the ego, and the unconscious, which comprises two spheres—the personal unconscious, the sum total of everything that has been repressed during one's lifetime, and the collective unconscious or nonpersonal psyche. Archetypes are instinctlike-ordering patterns of behavior, emotion, and perception. They can never be apprehended directly but are accessible to us through their effect on our behavior, feeling, or the emergence of image and representations in dreams, myths, folklore, and creative art.

Jung imputed to the psyche an inherent urge toward wholeness or individuation, the state of being what one was meant to become. The psyche is assumed to function in a purposive way toward the goal, and thus operates as a self-regulating compensatory system. All unconscious products are, therefore, interpreted as messages guiding us to that goal. The emphasis is not only on the inhibiting forces of the past, but primarily on the creative potential of the present.

The psyche contains several elements that are worthy of special consideration. The Self is the archetype of centeredness. It is the agency that directs the total functioning in a holistic way. The shadow is that part of the personality at variance with the ego ideal. The anima in men and the animus in women are our countersexual parts, the experience of the "other," the guide to what we might potentially be.

Jung has left us with theoretical foundations that, although far from exhausted, are firmly established and can be successfully applied in most cases. The technical side of psychotherapy, on the other hand, has not fared as well, and there is little doubt that this is the arena where future efforts must be directed. It has always been known, but is becoming increasingly more and more crucial, that an adequate interpretation and understanding of unconscious material, although of utmost importance, is, by itself, not enough. One is confronted more and more in one's clinical practice by instances where the dream, the fantasy, the drawing, the very nature of the problem is understood, both by the analyst as well as the analysand, and still no progress seems to be made. What we still sorely lack are effective means by which to translate the hard-won intellectual-theoretical understanding into an experiential phenomenon so that behavioral change is possible.

The verbal dimension by itself is decidedly not enough. The primitives intuited this and instituted rituals to enhance psychic phenomena. Analytical psychotherapy is also attempting to cope with this problem. To that effect, various non-verbal techniques are being incorporated into traditional practice; groups and movement, sensitivity training, and rituals are being employed so psychic facts can be experienced more deeply and hitherto unlocked doors may be thrust open.

ANNOTATED BIBLIOGRAPHY

Jung, C. G. *Modern man in search of a soul.* New York: Harcourt Brace & Co., 1933.

This is a collection of essays illustrating Jung's creative approach to psychotherapy, the role of dreams, and man's spiritual nature. It is written in a clear, engaging style, which makes for easy, enjoyable reading.

Jung, C. G. *Two essays on analytical psychology.* New York: Meridian Books, 1956.

This book, on a higher level of sophistication than *Man and His Symbols,* presents the core ideas of Jungian thought. These issues are the structure of the personal and transpersonal unconscious; the incompleteness of Freud's and Adler's viewpoints; persona, anima and animus; and Jung's psychotherapeutic approach.

Jung, C. G. *Memories, dreams, reflections.* Recorded and edited by Aniela Jaffe. New York: Pantheon Books, 1963.

This is the closest thing to an autobiography Jung ever wrote. It details the relationship between his inner, personal struggles and his discoveries. It is the least intellectual of his books; it is personal and warm and makes for absorbing reading.

Jung, C. G. *Man and his symbols.* Garden City, N. Y.: Doubleday, 1964.

This is the easiest of Jung's books to understand. Jung himself wrote only the first chapter, which he completed a few months before his death. It can, therefore, be taken as a final, authoritative statement of his ideas. The other chapters are written by his followers and students, under his supervision. In contrast to some of his other, specialized writings, this book is addressed to the intelligent lay reader. In the hardcover edition, there is a wealth of pertinent illustrations. The book presents Jung's basic ideas in an easily understandable way.

Whitmont, E. C. *The symbolic quest.* New York: Putnam, 1969.

This textbook presents a lucid exposition of Jung's major ideas, drawing upon clinical material for illustration. Particularly useful is the seventh chapter, which explains the way an archetypal theme is expressed in a person's life.

CASE READINGS

Adler, G. *The living symbol: A case study in the process of individuation.* New York: Pantheon Books, 1961.
A whole book devoted to an analysis of a woman suffering from claustrophobia. The material is used as a stepping stone for an examination of Jung's particular contribution to the process of analysis. It is worthwhile to gain the flavor of the experience in Jungian analysis.

Baynes, H. G. *Mythology of the soul: A research into the unconscious from schizophrenic dreams & drawings.* London: Riders & Company, 1969.

A massive book containing two case histories of people we would see today as belonging to the borderline syndrome. Written at a leisurely pace, this is a highly readable account of analytical psychotherapy in action by a very gifted teacher. One of the patients is an artist, thus providing for a case that is rare in the literature.

Hillman, J. Archetypal psychology. In A. Burton (Ed.), *Operational theories of personality.* New York: Brunner/Mazel, pp. 65-98.
A case history illustration for teaching purposes.

Lockhart, R. A. Mary's dog is an ear mother: Listening to the voices of psychosis. *Psychological Perspectives,* Vol. VI, Los Angeles, 1975.
An example of a brief, intensive psychotherapy with a young psychotic man who was hospitalized for hallucinations.

Rossi, E. L. *Dreams and the growth of personality: Expanding awareness in psychotherapy.* New York: Pergamon Press, 1972.
Part two of this book, pp. 23-130, contains a relatively full case history of a young woman. It is well written by a Jungian analyst who sees himself primarily as a "growth therapist."

Sullwood, E. Eagle eye. In Hilde Kirsch (Ed.), *The well-tended tree.* New York: Putnam, 1971, pp. 235-52.
A lovely analysis of a six-year-old Indian boy, an example of an analysis with children using a sandbox.

REFERENCES

Breland, K., & Breland, M. The misbehavior of organisms. *American Psychologist,* 1961, *16,* 681-684.

Campbell, J. *The hero with the thousand faces.* New York: Meridian, 1956.

Campbell, J. *The masks of gods.* New York: Viking Press, 1968.

Creuzer, G. F. *Symbolik und mythologie der alten völker.* Leipzig: Leske, 1810.

Ellenberger, H. F. *The discovery of the unconscious.* New York: Basic Books, 1970.

Flournoy, T. Miss Frank Miller "Quelque faits d'imagination creatrice subconsciente," *Archives de psychologie,* 1906, 36-51.

Greenson, R. R. *The technique and practice of psychoanalysis.* New York: International Universities Press, 1968.

Hall, C., & Lindzey, G. *Theories of personality.* New York: Wiley, 1962.

Jaffé, A. *From the life and work of C. G. Jung.* New York: Harper, 1971.

Jung, C. G. On the psychology and pathology of so-called occult phenomena. In *Psychiatric studies.* Collected Works. Vol. 1. Bollingen Series XX. Princeton, N. J.: Princeton University Press, 1957. (Originally published in 1902.)

Jung, C. G. The psychology of dementia praecox. In *The psychoanalysis of mental disease.* Collected Works. Vol. 3. Bollingen Series XX. Princeton, N. J.: Princeton University Press, 1960. (Originally published in 1907.)

Jung, C. G. *The development of personality.* Collected Works. Vol. 17. Bollingen Series XX. Princeton, N. J.: Princeton University Press, 1964. (Originally published in 1954.)

Jung, C. G. *Symbols of transformation.* Collected Works. Vol. 5. Bollingen Series XX. Princeton, N. J.: Princeton University Press, 1967. (Originally published in 1911.)

Jung, C. G. (1934) *The archetypes and the collective unconscious.* Collected Works. Vol. 9, Part 1. Bollingen Series XX. Princeton, N.J.: Princeton University Press, 1968.

May, R. (Ed.). *Existential psychology.* New York: Random House, 1961.

Munroe, R. *Schools of psychoanalytic thought.* New York: Holt, Rinehart & Winston, 1955.

Neumann, E. *The archetypal world of Henry Moore.* Bollingen Series LXI. Princeton, N. J.: Princeton University Press, 1955.

Whitmont, E. Group therapy and analytical psychology. *Journal of Analytical Psychology,* 1964, *9,* 1-21.

Whitmont, E. *The symbolic quest.* New York: Putnam, for the C. G. Jung Foundation for Analytic Psychology, 1970.

5

Person-Centered Therapy*

BETTY D. MEADOR and CARL R. ROGERS

OVERVIEW

Person-centered therapy, a continually developing approach to human growth and change, was developed originally by Carl Rogers in the 1940s. Its central hypothesis is that the growthful potential of any individual will tend to be released in a relationship in which the helping person experiences and communicates realness, caring, and a deeply sensitive nonjudgmental understanding. It is unique in being process oriented, in drawing its hypotheses from the raw data of therapeutic experience, and from recorded and filmed interviews. It has been determined to test all its hypotheses through appropriate research. It has application in every field of human endeavor where the healthy psychological growth of the individual is a goal.

*In 1974 Rogers and his colleagues changed the name of their approach from "client-centered" to "person-centered" therapy, believing this name to describe more adequately the human values their way of working incorporates.

This chapter was written by Dr. Betty Meador, but I have read the chapter with care, made some minor changes and additions, and believe it is a good and accurate presentation of what is an increasingly pervasive point of view. I am pleased she included my account of two interviews with "a silent young man." What I am saying is that this chapter has my full endorsement.—Carl R. Rogers.

Basic Concepts

The basic theory of person-centered therapy can be stated in the form of an "if—then" hypothesis. If certain conditions are present in the attitudes of the person designated "therapist" in a relationship, namely, congruence, positive regard, and empathic understanding, then growthful change will take place in the person designated "client." The hypothesis holds true, theoretically, in any relationship in which one person assumes attitudes of congruence, empathy, and positive regard, and the other person perceives these attitudes.

The hypothesis rests on an underlying view of man's nature. Person-centered theory postulates man's tendency toward *self-actualization.* "This is the inherent tendency of the organism to develop all its capacities in ways which serve to maintain or enhance the organism," says Rogers (1959b, p. 196).

The movement toward self-actualization is part of man's organismic nature. In this regard, Rogers quotes Lancelot Whyte:

Crystals, plants, and animals grow without any conscious fuss, and the strangeness of our own history disappears once we assume that the same kind of natural ordering process that guides their growth, also guided the development of man and of his mind and does so still! (Whyte, 1960)

The forces of self-actualization in the infant and child bump up against conditions that significant others in life impose. These "conditions of worth" tell him he is lovable and acceptable when he behaves in accordance with the imposed standards. Some of these conditions the child eventually assimilates into his self-concept. Then, according to Rogers, "he values an experience positively or negatively solely because of these conditions of worth which he has taken over from others, not because the experience enhances or fails to enhance his organism" (1959b, p. 209).

Even though the child has imposed restrictions on his organismic urges, he experiences them viscerally. An incongruence develops between the organismic forces of self-actualization and his ability to translate them into awareness and action.

The question that person-centered theory has sought to answer is this: How can an individual reclaim self-actualizing urges and acknowledge their wisdom? Broadly defined, *psychotherapy* is the "releasing of an already existing capacity in a potentially competent individual" (Rogers, 1959b, p. 221). If certain definable conditions are present, the individual gradually allows the self-actualizing capacity to overcome restrictions one has internalized in the conditions of worth. The definable conditions are that the individual perceive in the therapeutic relationship genuineness or congruence, accurate empathic understanding, and unconditional positive regard.

The three conditions are not distinct states of being from which an adept therapist intuitively selects. They are interdependent and logically related.

In the first place, the therapist must achieve a strong, accurate empathy. But such deep sensitivity to moment-to-moment "being" of another person requires that the therapist first accept, and to some degree prize, the other person. That is to say, a sufficiently strong empathy can scarcely exist without a considerable degree of unconditional positive regard. However, since neither of these conditions can possibly be meaningful in the relationship unless they are real, the therapist must be, both in these respects and in others, integrated and genuine within the therapeutic encounter. Therefore, it seems to me that genuineness or congruence is the most basic of the three conditions. (Rogers, 1959a, p. 184)

Genuineness or *congruence* is the basic ability of the therapist to read his own inner experiencing and to allow the quality of his inner experiencing to be apparent in the therapeutic relationship. That precludes his playing a role or presenting a facade. His words are consonant with his experiencing. He follows himself transparently. He follows the changing flow of his own feelings and presents himself transparently. He attempts to be fully present to his client; he is himself.

The concepts of genuineness and accurate, *empathic understanding* are closely related. The therapist, in the fullness of his own person, tries to immerse himself in the feeling world of his client to experience that world within himself. His understanding comes out of his own inner experiencing of his client's feelings, using his own inner processes of awareness for a referent. He actively experiences not only his client's feelings, but also his own inner responses to those feelings. Through this process he can often go beyond the words of the client to the surrounding, implicit feelings on the edge of the client's awareness.

Basic to his empathy for the client is a nonpossessive caring or acceptance of his individuality called *unconditional positive regard*. This attitude comes in part from the therapist's trust in the inner wisdom of the actualizing processes in the client, and in his belief that the client will discover for himself the resources and directions his growth will take. The therapist's caring does not take the form of advice or directions. He communicates his prizing of the client's individuality sometimes directly, often through his nonjudgmental understanding and genuine response.

Several studies have shown that client gain is significantly correlated with the attitudes of congruence, accurate empathy, and positive regard. Galatia Halkides found a positive correlation between the presence of the three attitudes and success in the clients (1958). A series of studies testing this hypothesis by Godfrey Barrett-Lennard (1959, 1962) found that clients who perceived more of the three attitudes in their therapists showed more positive gain in therapy than those who did not perceive these attitudes.

Later studies included the new theoretical dimension of person-centered therapy, the process conception of *client personality change.* The theory postulates that change takes place along a continuum, one end of which is represented by rigid, static, repetitive behavior, and the other end by behavior that changes and flows with the change and flow of inner experiencing. A study with hospitalized schizophrenic patients found patients whose therapists were high in the three attitudinal conditions show the greatest gain. Also, those patients who could interact in therapy at higher process levels showed greater gains than those whose behavior was relatively static and rigid (Rogers, 1967b).

In summary, individual positive change in a therapeutic relationship is precipitated when the client perceives the genuineness, empathy, and caring of his therapist. His personality change will oc-

cur in the direction of his being more and more aware of his inner experiencing, toward allowing his inner experiencing to flow and change, and toward behaving in congruence with his inner experiencing.

Other Systems

Rogers's attitude toward the future of the various systems of psychotherapy is stated in the following quotation in which he is speaking about research:

Its major significance, it seems to me, is that a growing body of objectively verified knowledge of psychotherapy will bring about the gradual demise of "schools" of psychotherapy including this one. As solid knowledge increases as to the conditions which facilitate therapeutic change, the nature of the therapeutic process, the conditions which block or inhibit therapy, the characteristic outcomes of therapy in terms of personality or behavioral change, there will be less and less emphasis upon dogmatic and purely theoretical formulations. Differences of opinion, different procedures in therapy, different judgments as to outcome, will be put to empirical test rather than being simply a matter of debate or argument. (Hart & Tomlinson, 1970, pp. 19-20)

The main thrust of person-centered therapy has been the empirical testing of those events that appear to facilitate growthful change in an individual. It has been the belief of those associated with person-centered therapy that the factors that precipitate growthful change are common, discoverable human events that pay no heed to the theoretical beliefs of the therapist. Characteristically, person-centered theorists have changed and expanded their theory and methods as they gained new insights from empirical testing.

It is not uncommon to find therapists of different persuasions exhibiting high levels of empathy, caring, and genuineness with their clients. The differences between person-centered therapy and other systems are frequently more apparent in the values each holds and their respective views of man in their methodology. The general discussion that follows considers these more basic value differences with full awareness that there is wide variation in actual practice among therapists in any given "school."

Directive techniques

Historically those associated with person-centered therapy have stood firmly against the therapist being directive with his client, as the original name, "non-directive therapy," suggests. *Directive therapy* includes any practice that views the therapist as an expert who knows the inner workings of human beings and is able to diagnose, prescribe, and cure the individuals who come to him for help.

Central to the person-centered point of view from the beginning was the belief in the self-directing capacity of the individual. Years of experience with clients and numerous research studies have confirmed this belief and developed it to the point where today, any interference by the therapist with his client's focus on his inner experiencing process is seen as counterproductive.

The person-centered therapist conveys his reliance on the client's resources in a number of ways. Any attitude or manipulation, such as the use of esoteric language, professionalism, or diagnostic testing, is avoided. These measures are seen as removing the process of therapy from the control of the client to the therapist, transferring the locus of evaluation from the client's hands to those of the therapist, and undermining the confidence of the client in his own ability to discover his pattern for growth. Any technique such as psychodrama, Gestalt therapy techniques, and bioenergetics likewise tends to put the therapist in the role of expert and

diminish the client's reliance on his own inner processes. "Psychotherapy is not the expert manipulation of a more or less passive personality" (Rogers, 1959b, p. 221).

Three forces in psychology

Rogers identifies himself with the so-called third force in psychology, a diverse group who come together under the name *humanistic psychology*. His identification with humanistic psychology is based on his advocacy of the dignity and value of the individual person in a search for growth, and on Rogers's interest in the development of a science of psychology that considers individual dignity and value as primary.

Rogers sums up the basic difference between the views held by psychoanalysis and by person-centered theory in this way:

I have little sympathy with the rather prevalent concept that man is basically irrational, and that his impulses, if not controlled, will lead to destruction of others and self. Man's behavior is exquisitely rational, moving with subtle and ordered complexity toward the goals his organism is endeavoring to achieve. (Rogers, 1961a, pp. 194-196)

Our defenses, he says, get in the way of our awareness of our organismic processes, which direct the individual toward positive growth. Man, when free from defensive distortion, lives in the flow of his inner experiencing, referring to the nuances of that organismic flow as guidelines for his behavior. Contrary to psychoanalytic thinking, Rogers sees the natural impulses of man, living out of his inner organismic experiencing, as constructive and conducive to health and fulfillment.

Psychoanalytic theory holds that by focusing on and understanding his past, the patient will, through the interpretations of his analyst, gain insight into his present behavior. Person-centered theory focuses on the present experiencing of the client, believing that the reestablishment of awareness of and trust in that experiencing provides the resources for growthful change.

In psychoanalysis, the analyst aims to interpret for his patient the connections between past and present. In person-centered therapy the therapist facilitates the client's discoveries of the meanings of his own current inner experiencing. The analyst in psychoanalysis takes the role of teacher in interpreting insights to the patient and encouraging the development of a transference relationship between the patient and himself, a relationship based on the neurosis of the patient. The therapist in person-centered therapy presents himself as honestly and transparently as he can, and attempts to establish a relationship in which he is simply the person he is, caring for and listening to another person.

In person-centered therapy, although beginnings of transference relationships occur, such relationships do not become full-blown (Rogers, 1951, p. 214). Rogers has postulated that perhaps transference relationships develop in an evaluative atmosphere where the client feels the therapist knows more about him than he knows himself, and therefore the client becomes dependent. The therapist in person-centered therapy tends to avoid any expression that could have evaluative connotations. He does not interpret meanings for the client, does not question in a probing manner, does not reassure, criticize, praise, or describe his client. Person-centered therapy has not found the transference relationship, central to psychoanalysis, a necessary part of a client's growthful change.

Differences between the person-centered point of view and behaviorism can be seen in the attitudes of each toward science and toward behavior change. Generally, *science* from a behavioristic stance is the observing, recording, and manipulation of observable phenomena. In this sense, it attempts to apply to behavior the ground rules of investigation of the physical sciences.

In this regard, the inner experiencing of persons is not subject to investigation since it is neither observable nor subject to controlled replication. Thus, a definite mind-set about what constitutes science determines what behavior can be investigated, how it can be understood, predicted, and controlled. Rogers has said there may be definite limits to the extent to which the experiential can be made part of the science of psychology, but to ignore it and its influence on behavior completely is indeed tragic (Hart & Tomlinson, 1970, p. 522). For Rogers, a science of the person must try to understand human beings in all their manifestations.

For behaviorism, *behavior change* comes about through external control of stimulus and reward. For person-centered theory, behavior change evolves from within the individual. Behavior therapy's goal is symptom removal. It is not concerned with inner experiencing of the symptom under consideration nor with the relationship between the person of the therapist and the person of the client. It seeks to eliminate symptoms as expeditiously as possible using the principles of learning theory. This point of view is quite contrary to person-centered therapy, which believes that the "fully functioning person" relies on inner experiencing for determining one's behavior.

HISTORY

Precursors

The American Heritage Dictionary defines a *precursor* as "One that precedes and indicates or announces someone or something to come." In that sense, it is doubtful that there would be any precursors of person-centered therapy. However, to set the person-centered point of view in historical perspective, person-centered therapy could probably best be traced to some Oriental thinkers. In Martin Buber's chapter about the "Teaching of the Tao" he explains the meaning of "Wu-Wei," a reasonable translation of which is "nonaction," a basic Taoist virtue. He quotes Lao-Tse:

To interfere with the life of things means to harm both them and one's self. He who imposes himself has the small, manifest might; he who does not impose himself has the great secret might. . . . The perfected man does not interfere in the life of beings, he does not impose himself on them, but he helps all beings to their freedom. (Buber, 1957, pp. 54-55)

Buber continues, "Through his unity, he liberates their nature and their destiny, he releases Tao in them."

This paragraph of Lao-Tse describes the person that the person-centered therapist would like to become. Much in the Zen tradition of insisting that the individual find the answers within himself is in accord with the thinking voiced by Rogers, although the methods are quite different.

Skipping a number of centuries, it is probably not accidental that Rogers used a quotation from Emerson as the first statement in *Client-Centered Therapy:* "We mark with light in the memory of the few interviews we have had, in the dreary years of routine and of sin, with souls that made our souls wiser; that spoke what we thought; that told us what we knew; that gave us leave to be what we inly were" (Emerson, 1838).

Rogers was influenced indirectly by John Dewey, particularly through the work of William H. Kilpatrick. Dewey's philosophy is clearly evident in books like *Freedom to Learn* (Rogers, 1969).

Another quite different influence was the work of Otto Rank. Rogers (1959b) helped organize a three-day institute with Otto Rank and had contact with the Philadelphia group of social workers and psychiatrists whom Rank had influenced. He says Rank's thinking, ". . . helped me to crystalize some of the therapeutic methods we were groping toward."

Still later, brought to his attention by the theological students at The University of Chicago, was the whole range of existentialist thinking. Martin Buber's and Soren Kierkegaard's ideas seemed most confirming of the person-centered point of view.

One can note similarities in theoretical background to Gestalt theory. Rogers's whole approach is that of field theory rather than the historical approach of Freudian psychology. It is thus based in the present, not in the past.

Probably lurking somewhere in the background is the individualism of the American frontier, the belief in self-reliance, the conviction that the individual could learn and do what was necessary for him to learn and do.

All of these influences, with the possible exception of Otto Rank, played no part in the development of person-centered therapy. Rogers learned about them later and felt confirmed by the points of view that had been expressed.

It can be said that through the centuries there have been many philosophers and some psychologists who expressed thoughts and ideas similar to those of Rogers. Yet in almost every case, his discovery of those ideas came after he had formulated his own mode of working and his own explanation of the process of therapy. For example, Samuel Tenenbaum, who wrote the definitive biography of William H. Kilpatrick, Dewey's follower, happened to be in a course with Rogers (Rogers, 1961a). It was his judgment that Kilpatrick and Dewey, too, would have been shocked by Rogers's willingness to give the student *real* freedom to make a choice. The idea that the student might reach a conclusion completely at odds with that of the instructor would doubtless have been quite unacceptable to Kilpatrick. Yet that was Rogers's conviction.

Perhaps these few paragraphs will set in some historical perspective the individuals who have in the past held similar points of view.

Although the growth of person-centered therapy has been shaped by many men and women who were students or colleagues of Carl Rogers, his dominance as its principal theorist and influence over more than four decades is uncontroverted.

Beginnings

Rogers was born January 8, 1902, into a close-knit, midwestern, Protestant family. When he was 12, the family moved to a farm. Part of the reason for the move was that his parents believed the values of honest work and Christian principles were more likely to germinate in their children if they were away from the influences of the city. On the farm, the young man's interest in and study of scientific agriculture developed in him a lasting respect for the scientific method.

Of early influences on his thinking, Rogers mentions a number of teachers from high school through graduate school who sanctioned and encouraged his ability to be original and unique and his penchant for the scholarly. His graduate education was varied and rich as he describes in the following passage:

Having rejected the family views of religion, I became interested in a more modern religious viewpoint and spent two profitable years in

Union Theological Seminary, which at that time was deeply committed to a freedom of philosophical thought which respected any honest attempt to resolve significant problems, whether this led into or away from the church. My own thinking led me in the latter direction, and I moved "across the street" to Teachers College, Columbia University. Here I was exposed to the views of John Dewey, not directly, but through William H. Kilpatrick. I also had my first introduction to clinical psychology in the warmly human and common-sense approach of Leta Hollingsworth. There followed a year of internship at the Institute for Child Guidance, then in its chaotic but dynamic first year of existence 1927-28. Here I gained much from the highly Freudian orientation of most of its psychiatric staff, which included David Levy and Lawson Lowrey. My first attempts at therapy were carried on at the Institute. Because I was still completing my doctorate at Teachers College, the sharp incompatibility of the highly speculative Freudian thinking of the Institute with the highly statistical and Thorndikean views at Teachers College was keenly felt. (Rogers, 1959b, p. 186)

Thus, Rogers began his work as a therapist having been exposed both to psychoanalytic thinking through the works of Freud and his modern interpreters, Karen Horney and Harry Stack Sullivan, and to psychology as it was developing in the United States with its emphasis on scientific method, operational definitions and the proof or disproof of hypotheses. His first position after completing his doctorate in 1931 was at the Child Study Department of a Rochester social agency. There his own ideas began to form as, from his experiences with clients, he began to sense the orderliness inherent in the experience of therapy.

About half way through his 12 years in Rochester, Rogers became acquainted with the thoughts of Otto Rank through social workers who had been trained in the Rankian method in Philadelphia. Rank's contention that the individual has self-directing capacities that emerge through therapy complemented Rogers's strong belief in the dignity of the individual as well as his accumulating experience with clients.

In some ways, Rank's thought strongly influenced person-centered therapy and in other ways it simply confirmed trends already emerging. This is evident in a brief look at Rank's ideas. He delineates three factors that influence psychotherapy: the individual, the therapist, and the relationship between them. The *individual* client, Rank says, is a moving cause, containing constructive forces within, which constitute a will to health. The *therapist* guides the individual to self-understanding and self-acceptance. The therapist as a human being is the remedy, not his technical skill. Of the *relationship*, Rank says the spontaneity and uniqueness of the experience of therapy lived in the present carry the patient toward health (Rank, 1936).

Seeds of Rogers's later ideas and some references to Rank and "passive therapy" appear in Rogers's first book, *The Clinical Treatment of the Problem Child*, written in 1937 and published in 1939. However, the real crystallization of the core of person-centered therapy took place between 1937 and 1941. The end of the precursor stage and beginning of person-centered theory development coincided with Rogers's move from Rochester to Ohio State University in January, 1940. Here Rogers's new methods of psychotherapy first came into public view, and the growth of person-centered therapy into a full-blown practice and theory began.

Rogers moved to Ohio State with the intention of training graduate students in the methods implicit in his way of working with clients. He thought at the time that his writings "were essentially attempts to distill out more clearly the principles which 'all clinicians' were using" (Rogers, 1959b), a pragmatic style determined by the orderliness of the client's

unfolding in the therapeutic experience. However, as he began to make his ideas explicit to graduate students, he realized his thinking was new to them and perhaps more of a new approach to psychotherapy than he had surmised. A paper presented at the Minnesota chapter of Psi Chi in December 1940, later included as chapter two of *Counseling and Psychotherapy* (Rogers, 1942), was his first attempt to develop in writing this line of thinking.

When Rogers published *Counseling and Psychotherapy* in 1942, the climate among counselors and psychotherapists was particularly receptive to a new way of working. Two major influences dominated the field of psychotherapy in the United States at the time. One was *psychoanalysis*. Although its practitioners were primarily medical doctors, nonmedical counselors and psychotherapists borrowed freely from the theories of Freud and his interpreters to explain human behavior and to derive techniques of therapy. The second influence was *directive counseling*. Basic to this technique is the view that the therapist is an expert who diagnoses his subject and on this basis selects the direction the client should take. Those theorists who emphasized diagnostic measures are included in this group. Both of these views were heavily dependent on the knowledge and skills of the therapist. The client was diagnosed, categorized, and explained with little reference to what he thought about himself. Disillusionment with these directive techniques inevitably occurred as counselors discovered that even though they "knew" what was wrong with a client and what he *should* do to help himself, neither this knowledge nor its communication was effective in changing his behavior.

In *Counseling and Psychotherapy*, Rogers proposed a counseling relationship whose characteristics were the warmth and responsiveness of the therapist, a permissive climate in which feelings could be freely expressed, and a freedom from all coercion or pressure. A client in such a relationship would gain understanding of himself that would "enable him to take positive steps in the light of his new orientation" (1942, p. 18). The therapist in the relationship was freed from the burden of scanning the system under which he worked to find the "right" diagnostic or interpretive category for his client at a given moment.

Originally the term *counseling* was chosen because it was a modest term, and because the word *therapy* immediately aroused a fight whenever it was used. Psychiatrists felt that therapy was their field. Consequently, the less emotion-arousing term, for both client and professional, was used. Still, *Counseling and Psychotherapy* is predominantly a technique-oriented book. Although the therapist was described as being warm, responsive, and permissive, he was not yet freed to be himself. This development was to come much later.

Rogers and his students at Ohio State had begun to make detailed analyses of counseling sessions, using for the first time verbatim transcripts of electrically recorded interviews. The first complete published therapeutic case appeared in *Counseling and Psychotherapy*. The invention of electrical recordings facilitated the kind of scrutiny of the counseling process that Rogers's continued concern for scientific definition and hypothesis testing demanded. The purpose of *Counseling and Psychotherapy*, he stated, was to stimulate research through the presentation of numerous explicit and implicit hypotheses.

From these beginnings, Rogers's emphasis has been on understanding how and why individuals change in the process of therapy, not primarily on theory development. *Theory development* grew naturally out of the testing of hypotheses that Rogers and his colleagues and students formed from their experience with clients. The changing character of person-centered therapy is due to Rogers's consistent insistence on looking at the facts and altering methods and theory whenever experience and research so dictated.

Rogers's move to the University of Chicago in 1945, where he organized the Counseling Center, began a decade of prolific research. The publication of *Client-Centered Therapy* in 1951 introduced the name change from "nondirective counseling" to "client-centered." The change was not merely semantic. It indicated a shift in emphasis from the negative, narrower statement, "nondirective," to the positive focus on the growth-producing factors in the individual client himself. (Footnote, page 000, describes the reason for the new name change to person-centered therapy.)

Emphasis in methodology and research in this era centered on the process of personality change. The repeated reference by clients in therapy to a "self" and its changingness led to theory formulation of the self-concept, first attempted at Ohio State by V. C. Raimy (1943). Further studies of the self-concept were greatly aided by the development of the Q-sort by William Stephenson (1953). From the self-concept research came a major theoretical formulation concerning personality change. "We came to see the troubled or neurotic individual," Rogers said, "as one whose self-concept had become structured in ways incongruent with his organismic experience" (1959a, p. 192). This new understanding led to methodological changes as therapists became more conscious of making explicit the organismic experience of their clients; whereas formerly they had responded to the client's words, reflecting what they heard, now they responded to the client's implicit as well as explicit affect. This required the therapists to get behind the words of the client and into his feeling world and precipitated a new look at accurate emphatic understanding.

This decade saw the publication of *Psychotherapy and Personality Change* in 1954, a report of a number of studies of change factors in therapy. It also saw the publication of several works on the maturing theory, beginning with *Client-Centered Therapy* (1951), and continuing with "A Theory of Therapy, Personality, and Interpersonal Relationships, as Developed in the Client-Centered Framework" (Rogers, 1959b) written around 1953-54. Two further important theory papers appeared in this decade. They were "The Necessary and Sufficient Conditions of Therapeutic Personality Change" (1957) and "A Process Conception of Psychotherapy" (1958).

Rogers moved to the University of Wisconsin in 1957 and found the opportunity to test a persistent question: Would the "necessary and sufficient conditions" and the newer process theory be applicable to hospitalized schizophrenics, as they were to the students, adults, and children who were clients at the University of Chicago Counseling Center? A five-year study sought to answer that question (Rogers, 1967b), and true to form, person-centered therapy and theory found itself incorporating changes as a result of the experience with schizophrenics. "It is already certain that the patients did a great deal to us," says one of the principal researchers, Eugene Gendlin. "I might say that our own improvement has been remarkable" (Hart & Tomlinson, 1970, p. 284).

This presentation has attempted to give the picture of person-centered therapy as a growing organism. Although Rogers has been the central figure in its development, he has had as students and colleagues many able individuals who have explored, independently, avenues of thought to which their experience and hypothesizing brought them. The characteristic close scrutiny of the actual therapeutic relationship plus the dogged refusal to be committed to any single formulation of the theory has opened those associated with person-centered therapy to the rich possibilities they have investigated. Rogers has by example and advocacy upheld the notion of science that he describes in the following passage:

It is my opinion that the type of understanding which we call science can begin anywhere, at any level of sophistication. To observe accurately, to think carefully and creatively—these activities, not the accumulation of laboratory instruments, are the beginnings of science. (Rogers, 1959b, p. 189)

Current Status

The central hypothesis of person-centered theory lends itself to application in any human relationship where either or both of the participants want genuine understanding or individual growth to unfold. The hypothesis states that if certain conditions are present in the attitude of the therapist, namely, genuineness, empathic understanding, and positive regard, then positive personality change will occur in the client (Rogers, 1957). The fleshing out of this hypothesis came with Rogers's publication of his process theory (1958) in which the orderly, sequential, positive changes an individual goes through in a therapeutic relationship were described.

Like rain off an umbrella, the influence

of person-centered theory has fallen in all directions. Because the theory relies on the inner attitudes of the person designated "helper" to facilitate positive change in the "other" in a relationship, it has been embraced by professional persons in a wide variety of fields. No longer is it necessary for complex diagnostic definitions, intricate webs of theory, or protocols of techniques to be applied to situations. The person who can be real, caring, and understanding can count on being an effective facilitator of growth in a helping relationship.

As Howard Kirschenbaum of Temple University and the New School of Social Research puts it:

Carl Rogers, the founder of the client-centered approach in psychotherapy, is still one of the leading figures in the fields of humanistic psychology and education. His theories, research, and methods have revolutionized our concept of the helping relationship—in therapy, in guidance, in education, in social work, in the ministry, and in many other professions. (Kirschenbaum, 1971)

To his list could be added the fields of psychiatry, industrial relations, organizational development, marriage and family counseling, speech therapy, the priesthood, and the use of nonprofessional workers in crisis centers such as "The Hot-Line"—and so on and on.

The acceptance of the fundamental hypotheses of person-centered therapy has not always been a smooth road. In the 1940s and 1950s this was a very controversial view indeed, and debates and highly critical reviews and articles were common. Recently, however, these views, especially in the helping relationship, have become imperceptibly woven into much of current thinking in all the fields mentioned.

Rogers himself has concentrated in re-

cent years on the application of person-centered theory and methods to enhance the growth and human relations abilities of normal individuals in a variety of settings. He has particularly explored the efficacy of the intensive small group or encounter group in facilitating individual and institutional change. Five of his books have the normal individual as the central concern: *On Becoming a Person* (1961a), *Freedom to Learn* (1969), *Carl Rogers on Encounter Groups* (1970), *On Becoming Partners: Marriage and Its Alternatives* (1972), *Carl Rogers on Personal Power* (1977), and *A Way of Being* (1980).

He began this work at Western Behavioral Sciences Institute in La Jolla, California, in 1964. In 1968 Rogers and the group of researchers who were working on a project for self-directed change in an educational system (Rogers, 1967a, 1969) formed the Center for Studies of the Person (CSP) in La Jolla.

As he entered these new fields, the criticisms cropped up again. Here are two quotations from reviews of *Freedom to Learn* showing how a new idea in education seems to be as polarizing as a new idea in psychotherapy. Professor R. S. Peters, an educator from the University of London, wrote (Peters, 1970):

What is surprising . . . is that an author who strongly advocates openness to the experiences of others should put together a collection of papers that are meant to be of general relevance to educational problems in such a seeming state of ignorance and innocence about educational theory and practice. Freedom is fine; and so is self-directed exploration. But there are other values, both in life and in education—truth, for instance, humility, and breadth of understanding.

To show a contrast in judgment, Dr. Samuel Tenenbaum reviewed the same book. Tenenbaum is a philosopher of education, the author of a definitive biography of William H. Kilpatrick, a teacher, and a therapist. Some excerpts from his review give its flavor (Tenenbaum, 1969):

Seldom does a book on education appear that so excites the imagination as to what is possible in education, so liberates the reader from viewing education in conventional ways. . . .

. . . Dr. Rogers sees the teacher as one who can release students as well as himself for growth. He, the teacher, also becomes a learner, eagerly seeking, as do his students, new meanings and insights. For Carl Rogers, education is not a mass of facts presented on examination papers, but a becoming process whose goal is ever richer and more meaningful living. In achieving these ends, the teacher is anything but an authoritarian figure, the processor of truth and wisdom, there to transmit it to students ignorant of this truth and wisdom. Each student in a good educational arrangement is given freedom to find his own truth and wisdom; and the adventure and the excitement lie in not knowing, in teacher and student finding out together. . . .

. . . In *Freedom to Learn,* one gains not only a philosophy and methodology of what is good education but also what is the good life to live.

This enormous discrepancy of judgment is similar to the judgments first made about person-centered therapy. Rogers hopes this phenomenon has the same meaning again—namely, that when vital new issues are raised in a professional field, violently opposing views are stirred up.

Person-centered theory is mature enough at this point that whatever growth or amplifications spring from its soil can do so independently of Rogers. The theory has moved, as Rogers predicted, toward a unified science of inner growth and of the conditions that facilitate it. The description of the sequential inner process that takes place as an individual undergoes positive personality change provides a basis for a common description of growth regardless of the school of psychology or the diagnosis of the client. The sequence of change in individuals needs further scrutiny, refinement, and testing as do the facilitating conditions, but the discoveries that those associated with person-centered therapy have made may lead to a unitary understanding of the process of personality change.

PERSONALITY

Theory of Personality

The development of a theory of personality has not been the primary concern of person-centered theorists:

Although a theory of personality has developed from our experience in client-centered therapy, it is quite clear to anyone closely associated with this orientation that this is not our central focus. Rather, the manner in which change comes about in the human personality has been the central core of our interest. . . .It seems to us that far more intelligent and answerable questions can be raised in regard to the *process* of personality change than in regard to the *causes* of the person's present personality characteristics. (Rogers, 1959b, p. 194)

Person-centered personality theory has grown out of clinical experience, research, and the theory of personality *change* developed by those associated with person-centered therapy (Holstock & Rogers, 1983).

Because the theoretical concepts grew out of an experience of process, it is a field theory, rather than a genetic theory such as Freud's. The significant forces are to be found in the immediate relationships, as in an electrical field of forces. Person-centered theory is primarily a theory of the conditions that bring about change. Hence the theory of personality is primarily inferred, and the propositions "are those which are furthest from the matrix of our experience and hence are most suspect" (Rogers, 1959b, p. 222).

The developing infant

Person-centered personality theory begins with certain postulates concerning the human at birth. The world of the infant is his own experiencing. His experiencing is his only reality. Within the world of his organism, the infant has one basic motivational force: a tendency toward self-actualization.

Along with this basic motivation, the infant has the inherent ability to value positively experiences he perceives as enhancing his organism, and to value negatively those experiences that appear contrary to his actualizing tendency. This, his "organismic valuing process," serves to direct his behavior toward the goal of his own self-actualization.

The self-concept

As the infant grows and develops, he begins to discriminate among his experiences and to "own" those that are part of his own being and functioning, and to assign ownership of other experiences to other persons and things in his environment. As his awareness of his own being and functioning develops, he acquires a sense of self made up of the experiences of his own being and functioning within his environment. This is his developing *self-concept.*

The development of a self-concept is strongly dependent on the individual's perception of his experiences in his environment influenced · by a need for positive regard, a universal need in human beings, pervasive and persistent (Rogers, 1959b, p. 223).

Out of the complex of experiences of satisfaction or frustration of his need for positive regard, the individual develops a sense of *self-regard,* a learned sense of self based on perception of the regard received from others. This sense of self-regard becomes a pervasive construct influencing the behavior of the whole organism and has a life of its own, independent of actual experiences of regard from others. The way in which this develops is explained by the individual's introjecting conditions of worth.

Conditions of worth

Inevitably, the child's need to retain the love of his parents gets at cross-purposes with the needs of his organism. The values he is aware of in his own organism are sometimes contrary to the values of his parents. His behavior, which springs out of his organismic needs and desires, is sometimes contrary to the behavior his parents find acceptable. When this occurs, he begins to take into his own system of self-regard the discrimination between experiences worthy of regard from significant others and those not worthy of their regard. He begins to avoid or to deny completely his organismic experiencings which he has learned are not worthy of positive regard.

These introjected conditions of worth become a part of his self-regard system. He experiences positive self-regard when his self-experiences are in accord with experiences for which he has received positive regard; he experiences negative self-regard when his experiences are those for which he has not received positive regard. His self-worth comes to depend on the conditions of worth that he has learned in his interaction with significant others in his world.

What happens to the actualizing tendency as conditions of worth develop in the self-regard system? The actualizing tendency remains the basic motivation for the individual. However, a conflict develops between organismic needs and self-regard needs, now containing conditions of worth. The individual, in effect, is faced with the choice between acting in accord with organismic sense or censoring the organismic urging and acting in accord with the condition of worth one has learned. To maintain his positive self-regard, and therefore maintain his feeling of worth and feeling of self-actualization, he chooses to act in accord with the condition of worth. In other words, his need for self-regard overpowers his organismic needs. At these choice points, he may come to believe that his organismic urges are "bad" and contrary to his being a "good" person, therefore, contrary to his self-actualization. Rogers says:

Estrangement of conscious man from his directional organismic processes is not a necessary part of man's nature. Instead, it is learned, and learned to an especially high degree in Western civilization. The satisfaction or fulfillment of the actualizing tendency has become bifurcated into incompatible behavior systems. This dissociation which exists in most of us is the pattern and basis of all psychological pathology in man. (Rogers, 1963, p. 24)

Fortunately, organismic urges do not cease upon being denied to awareness. However, their persistence poses a problem for the individual. He begins to perceive his experiences selectively according to their fitting or not fitting his concept of self, now defined in part by the conditions of worth.

Experiences which are in accord with his conditions of worth are perceived and symbolized accurately in awareness. Experiences which run contrary to the conditions of worth are perceived selectively and distortedly as if in accord with the conditions of worth, or are in part or whole, denied to awareness. (Rogers, 1959b, p. 226)

Whenever an individual's perception of his experience is distorted or denied, Rogers says, "a state of incongruence between self and experience, of psychological maladjustment and of vulnerability, exists to some degree" (Rogers, 1959b, p. 226).

Experiences not consistent with the individual's concept of self are conceived as a threat in that if such experiences were accurately symbolized in the individual's awareness, they would disturb the organization of his concept of self by being contrary to the conditions of worth he has incorporated. Thus, such experiences create anxiety in the person and arouse defense mechanisms that either distort or deny such experiences, thereby maintaining the individual's consistent perception of self. Because of the need to defend against accurate perception of experiences contrary to his conditions of worth, the individual develops a rigidity of perception in those areas.

Psychotherapy and personality change

The process of *therapy* is an intervention into the incongruence an individual has developed between his experiencing organism and his concept of self. In this relationship he may risk allowing into awareness previously distorted or denied experiences. In an atmosphere of nonjudgmental understanding, he may begin to allow previously denied organismic urges to be a part of his concept of self. Thus, in the process of therapy, ideally, the individual exchanges his conditions of worth for a trust and valuing of the wisdom of his developing organism in its entirety.

Variety of Concepts

Definitions of constructs

In person-centered theory, various systematic *constructs* have emerged, gradually acquiring sharper and more specific meaning. Also terms in common usage have gradually acquired somewhat specialized meanings in our theoretical statements.

Actualizing tendency

An *actualizing tendency* is the inherent tendency of the organism to develop in ways that serve to maintain or enhance the organism. It involves not only the tendency to meet what Abraham Maslow (1954) terms *deficiency needs* for air, food, water, and the like, but also involves development toward the differentiation of organs and of functions, expansion in terms of growth, expansion of effectiveness through the use of tools, and expansion and enhancement through reproduction. It is development toward autonomy and away from *heteronomy,* or control by external forces.

This basic actualizing tendency is the only motive postulated in this theoretical system. The organism as a whole, and only the organism as a whole, exhibits this tendency. There are no homunculi, no other sources of energy or action in the system. The self, for example, is an important construct in our theory, but the self does not *do* anything. It is only one expression of the general tendency of the organism to maintain and enhance itself.

Concepts such as *need-reduction, tension-reduction,* and *drive-reduction* are included in this concept. It also includes the seeking of pleasurable tensions, the tendency to be creative, the tendency to learn to walk and other self-actualizing tendencies.

Tendency toward self-actualization

Following the development of the self-structure, actualization expresses itself also in that portion of the experience of the organism symbolized in the self. If the self and the total experience of the organism are relatively congruent, the actualizing tendency remains relatively unified. If self and experience are incongruent, the organism may work at cross-purposes with the subsystem of that motive, the *tendency to actualize the self.*

Experience (noun)

The term *experience* includes all going on within the organism at any given moment that is potentially available to awareness. It includes events of which the individual is unaware, as well as all the phenomena in consciousness. Thus it includes the psychological aspects of hunger, even though the individual may be so fascinated by his work or play that he is completely unaware of the hunger; it includes the impact of sights and sounds and odors on the organism, even though these are not the focus of attention. It includes the influence of memory and past experience, as these are active in the moment, in restricting or broadening the meaning given to various stimuli. It also includes all in immediate awareness or consciousness. It does not include events such as neuron discharges or changes in blood sugar, because these are not directly available to awareness. *Experience* is thus a psychological, not a physiological, definition.

Experience (verb)

To experience means simply to receive in the organism the impact of the sensory or physiological events happening at any moment.

Often this process term is used in the phrase *to experience in awareness*, which means to symbolize in some accurate form at the conscious level the above sensory or visceral events. Since there are varying degrees of completeness in symbolization, the phrase is often *to experience more fully in awareness,* and thus indicates that it is the extension of this process toward more complete and accurate symbolization to which reference is being made.

Feeling, experiencing a feeling

The term *feeling* is heavily used in writings on person-centered therapy and theory. It denotes an emotionally tinged experience, together with its personal meaning. Thus it includes the emotion but also the cognitive content of the meaning of that emotion in its experiential context. It refers to the unity of emotion and cognition as they are experienced inseparably in the moment. It is perhaps best thought of as a brief theme of experience, carrying with it the emotional coloring and the perceived meaning to the individual.

Awareness, symbolization, consciousness

These three terms are defined as synonymous. *Awareness* is thus seen as the symbolic representation (not necessarily in verbal symbols) of some portion of our experience. This representation may have varying degrees of sharpness or vividness, from a dim awareness of something existing as ground, to a sharp awareness of something in focus as figure.

Availability to awareness

When an experience can be symbolized freely, without defensive denial and distortion, it is *available to awareness.*

Accurate symbolization

The *symbols* that constitute our awareness do not necessarily match, or correspond to, the "real" experience, or to "reality." Thus the psychotic is aware of electrical impulses in his body that do actually exist. It seems important to distinguish between those awarenesses that, in common-sense terms, are real or accurate and those that are not. But how can this be conceptualized if we are trying to think rigorously?

The most adequate way of handling this predicament seems to be to take the position that all perception is transactional in nature, a construction from our past experience and a hypothesis or prognosis for the future. If the psychotic were to check the electrical currents in his body, to see whether they have the same characteristics as other electric currents, he would be checking the hypothesis implicit in his awareness. Hence when we speak of accurate symbolization in awareness, we mean that the hypotheses implicit in the awareness will be borne out if tested by acting on them.

Perceive, perception

Perception is a hypothesis or prognosis for action that comes into being in awareness when stimuli impinge on the organism. When we *perceive* "this is a triangle," "that is a tree," "this person is my mother," it means we are making a prediction that the objects from which the stimuli are received would, if checked in other ways, exhibit properties we have come to regard, from our past experience, as being characteristics of triangles, trees, mother.

Thus we might say that *perception* and *awareness* are synonymous, perception being the narrower term, usually used when we want to emphasize the importance of the stimulus in the process, and awareness the broader term, covering symbolizations and meanings that arise from purely internal stimuli such as memory traces, visceral changes, and the like, as well as from external stimuli.

To define *perception* in this purely psychological fashion is not meant to deny that it can be defined in physiological fashion by referring to the impact of a pattern of light rays upon certain nerve cells, for example. For our purpose, however, the psychological definition seems more fruitful, and it is in this sense that the term is used in our formulations.

Subceive, subception

R. A. McCleary and R. S. Lazarus (1949) formulated this construct of *subception* to signify discrimination without awareness. They state that "even when a subject is unable to report a visual discrimination he is still able to make a stimulus discrimination at some level below that required for conscious recognition." Thus it appears that the organism can discriminate a stimulus and its meaning for the organism without using the higher nerve centers involved in awareness. This capacity in our theory permits the individual to discriminate an experience as threatening, without symbolization in awareness of this threat.

Self-experience

The term *self-experience,* coined by S. Standal (1954), is defined as being any event or entity in the phenomenal field discriminated by the individual that is also discriminated as "self," "me," "I," or related thereto. In general, self-experiences are the raw material of which the organized self-concept is formed.

Self, concept of self, self-structure

These terms refer to the organized, consistent conceptual Gestalt composed of perceptions of the characteristics of the "I" or "me" and the perceptions of the relationships of the "I" or "me" to others and to various aspects of life, together with the values attached to these perceptions. It is a Gestalt available to awareness although not necessarily in awareness. It is a fluid and changing process, but at any given moment it is a specific entity that is at least partially definable in operational terms by means of a Q-sort or other instrument or measure. The term *self* or *self-concept* is more likely to be used when we are talking of the person's view of himself, *self-structure* when we are looking at this Gestalt from an external frame of reference.

Ideal self

The *ideal self* (or *self-ideal*) denotes the self-concept the individual would most like to possess, upon which one places the highest value for self. In all other respects, it is defined in the same way as the self-concept.

Incongruence between self and experience

A discrepancy frequently develops between the self as perceived and the actual experience of the organism. Thus the individual may perceive himself as having characteristics *a, b,* and *c,* and experiencing feelings *x, y,* and *z.* An accurate symbolization of his experience would, however, indicate characteristics *c, d,* and *e,* and feelings *v, w, x.* When such a discrepancy exists, there is an *incongruence between self and experience.* This state is one of tension and confusion, since in some respects the individual's behavior will be regulated by the actualizing tendency, and in other respects by the self-actualizing tendency, thus producing discordant or incomprehensible behaviors. What is commonly called neurotic behavior is one example, the neurotic behavior being the product of the actualizing tendency, whereas in other respects, the individual is actualizing the self. Thus the neurotic behavior is incomprehensible to the individual himself, since it is at variance with what he consciously "wants" to do, which is to actualize a self no longer congruent with experience.

Vulnerability

The term *vulnerability* refers to the state of incongruence between self and experience. The term is used to emphasize the potentialities of this state for creating psychological disorganization. When incongruence exists, and the individual is unaware of it, he is potentially vulnerable to anxiety, threat, and disorganization. If a significant new experience demonstrates the discrepancy so clearly that it must be consciously perceived, the individual will be threatened, and his concept of self disorganized by this contradictory and unassimilable experience.

Anxiety

Phenomenologically, *anxiety* is a state of uneasiness or tension whose cause is unknown. From an external frame of reference, anxiety is a state in which the incongruence between the concept of self and the total experience of the individual is approaching symbolization in awareness. When experience is *obviously* discrepant from the self-concept, a defensive response to threat becomes increasingly difficult. Anxiety is the response of the organism to the "subception" that such discrepancy may enter awareness, thus forcing a change in the self-concept.

Threat

A *threat* exists when an experience is perceived or anticipated (subceived) as incongruent with the structure of the self. It may be regarded as an external view of the same phenomenon that, from the internal frame of reference, is anxiety.

Psychological maladjustment

A state of *psychological maladjustment* exists when the organism denies to awareness, or distorts in awareness, significant experiences that consequently are not accurately symbolized and organized into the Gestalt of the self-structure, thus creating an incongruence between self and experience.

Defense

A *defense* is the behavioral response of the organism to threat, the goal of which is the maintenance of the current structure of the self. This goal is achieved by the perceptual distortion of the experience in awareness to reduce the incongruity between the experience and the structure of the self, or by the denial to awareness of an experience, thus denying any threat to the self.

Distortion in awareness, denial to awareness

Material significantly inconsistent with the concept of self cannot be directly and freely admitted to awareness. To explain this, the construct of *denial* or *distortion* has been developed. When an experience is dimly perceived (*subceived* is perhaps the better term) as being incongruent with the self-structure, the organism appears to react with a distortion of the meaning of the experience (making it consistent with the self) or with a denial of the existence of the experience, to preserve the self-structure from threat. It is perhaps most vividly illustrated in those occasional moments in therapy when the therapist's response, correctly heard and understood, would mean that the client would necessarily perceive openly a serious inconsistency between his self-concept and a given experience. In such a case, the client may respond, "I can hear the words you say, and I know I should understand them, but I just can't make them convey any meaning to me." Here the relationship is too good for the meaning to be distorted by rationalization, but at the same time, the meaning is too threatening to be received. Hence the organism denies meaning in the communication. Such outright denial of experience is much less common than the phenomenon of distortion. Thus if the concept of self includes the characteristic "I am a poor student," the experience of receiving a high grade can be easily distorted to make it congruent with the self by perceiving in it meanings such as, "That professor is a fool", "It was just luck", and so on.

Intensionality

This term is taken from general semantics. If the person is reacting or perceiving in an *intensional* fashion, he tends to see experience in absolute and unconditional terms, to overgeneralize, to be dominated by concept or belief, to fail to anchor his reactions in space and time, to confuse fact and evaluation, to rely upon abstractions rather than upon reality testing. This term covers the frequently used concept of rigidity but includes perhaps a wider variety of behaviors than are generally thought of as constituting rigidity.

Congruence, congruence of self and experience

These basic concepts have grown out of therapeutic experience, in which the individual appears to be revising his concept of *self* to bring it into *congruence* with his *experience*, accurately symbolized. Thus he discovers that one aspect of his experience, if accurately symbolized, would be hatred for his father; another would be strong homosexual desires. He reorganizes the concept he holds of himself to include these characteristics, which would previously have been inconsistent with self.

Thus, when self-experiences are accurately symbolized, and are included in the self-concept in this accurately symbolized form, the state is congruent of self and experience. If this is true of all self-experiences, the individual would be a fully functioning person. If it is true of some specific aspect of experience, such as the individual's experience in a given relationship or in a given moment of time, we can say that the individual is to this degree in a state of congruence. Other terms generally synonymous with congruence are *integrated, whole, genuine.*

Openness to experience

To be *open to experience* is the polar opposite of defensiveness. The term may be used in regard to some area of experience or in regard to some area of experience of the organism. It signifies that every stimulus, whether originating within the organism or in the environment, is freely relayed through the nervous system without being distorted or channeled off by any defensive mechanism. There is no need of the mechanism of "subception" whereby the organism is forewarned of experiences threatening to the self. On the contrary, whether the stimulus is the impact of a configuration of form, color, or sound in the environment on the sensory nerves, or a memory trace from the past, or a visceral sensation of fear, pleasure, or disgust, it is completely available to the individual's awareness. In the hypothetical person completely open to his experience, his concept of Self would be a symbolization in awareness completely congruent with his experience.

Psychological adjustment

Optimal *psychological adjustment* exists when all experiences are assimilated on a symbolic level into the Gestalt of the self-structure. Optimal psychological adjustment is thus synonymous with complete congruence of self and experience or complete openness to experience. Improvement in psychological adjustment progresses toward this end point.

Extensionality

This term is taken from general semantics. A person reacting or perceiving in an *extensional* manner tends to see experience in limited, differentiated terms, to be aware of the space-time anchorage of facts, to be dominated by facts, not by concepts, to evaluate in multiple ways, to be aware of different levels of abstraction, to test inferences and abstractions against reality.

Maturity

The individual exhibits *mature* behavior when he perceives realistically and in an extensional manner, is not defensive, accepts the responsibility of being different from others, accepts responsibility for his own behavior, evaluates experience in terms of the evidence coming from his own senses, changes his evaluation of experience only on the basis of new evidence, accepts others as unique individuals different from himself, prizes himself, and prizes others.

Conditions of worth

The self-structure is characterized by a *condition of worth* when a self-experience or set of related self-experiences is either avoided or sought solely because the individual discriminates it as being less or more worthy of self-regard.

This important construct developed by Standal (1954) takes the place of "introjected value," a less exact concept used in earlier formulations. A condition of worth arises when the positive regard of a significant other is conditional, when the individual feels in some respects prized and in others not. Gradually this same attitude is assimilated into one's own self-regard complex, and one values an experience positively or negatively solely because of these conditions of worth which one has taken over from others, not

because the experience enhances or fails to enhance one's organism.

This last phrase deserves special note. When the individual has experienced unconditional positive regard, a new experience is valued or not, depending on its effectiveness in maintaining or enhancing the organism. But if a value is "introjected" from a significant other, this condition of worth is applied to an experience without reference to the extent to which it maintains or enhances the organism. It is an important specific instance of inaccurate symbolization, the individual valuing an experience positively or negatively, *as if* in relation to the criterion of the actualizing tendency, but not actually in relation to it. An experience may be perceived as organismically satisfying, when in fact this is not true. Thus a condition of worth, because it disturbs the valuing process, prevents the individual from functioning freely and with maximum effectiveness.

Locus of evaluation

This term indicates the source of evidence concerning values. Thus an internal *locus of evaluation* within the individual means he is the center of the valuing process, the evidence being supplied by his own senses. When the locus of evaluation resides in others, their judgment as to the value of an object or experience becomes the criterion of value for the individual.

Organismic valuing process

This concept describes an ongoing process in which values are never fixed or rigid, but experiences are being accurately symbolized and continually and freshly valued in terms of the satisfactions *organismically* experienced; the organism experiences satisfaction in those stimuli or behaviors that maintain and enhance the organism and the self, both in the immediate present and in the long range. The actualizing tendency is thus the criterion.

Internal frame of reference

This is all of the realm of experience available to the awareness of the individual at a given moment. It includes the full range of sensations, perceptions, meanings, and memories, available to consciousness.

The *internal frame of reference* is the subjective world of the individual. Only he knows it fully. It can never be known to another except through empathic inference and then can never be perfectly known.

Empathy

The term *empathy* refers to the accurate perception of the internal frame of reference of another with the emotional components and meanings that pertain thereto, as if one were the other person, but without ever losing the "as if" condition.

External frame of reference

To perceive solely from one's own subjective internal frame of reference without empathizing with the observed person or object is to perceive from an *external frame of reference*. The "empty organism" school of thought in psychology is an example of this. Thus the observer says that an animal has been stimulated when the animal has been exposed to a condition that, in the observer's subjective frame of reference, is a stimulus. There is no attempt to understand empathically whether this is a stimulus in the animal's experiential field. Likewise the observer reports that the animal emits a response when a phenomenon occurs that, in the observer's subjective field, is a response.

These concepts continue to be useful in describing the process of therapy in a person-centered framework.

PSYCHOTHERAPY

Theory of Psychotherapy

Rogers stated, "Therapy is of the essence of life, and is to be so understood" (1951, p. x). Person-centered therapy calls upon the whole range of the ongoing inner dynamics of the therapist and the client. The interacting of two persons out of an awareness of their individual inner responses is the dynamics of the therapeutic relationship in person-centered therapy. The focus is on the direct experiencing in the relationship:

> The process is not seen as primarily having to do with the client's memory of his past, nor with his exploration of the problems he is facing, nor with the perceptions he has of himself, nor the experiences he has been fearful of admitting into awareness. The process of therapy is, by these hypotheses, seen as being synonymous with the experiential relationship between client and therapist. Therapy consists in experiencing the self in a wide range of ways in an emotionally meaningful relationship with the therapist. The words—of either client or counselor—are seen as having minimal importance compared with the present emotional relationship which exists between the two. (Rogers, 1951, p. 172)

Person-centered theory has settled on three attitudes necessary and sufficient to effect change in clients. The theory does not stress the technical skills or knowledge of the therapist. It asks him to be *(a)* genuine or congruent, *(b)* to be empathic or understanding, and *(c)* to be unpossessively caring or confirming. These attitudes are the catalytic agent in the person-centered therapeutic relationship. If the client perceives these attitudes and if he is uncomfortable with himself, he will engage in the process of positive personality change. This is the basic hypothesis of person-centered therapy.

Briefly, the therapist wants to convey his sincere acceptance and caring for his client. For the client to trust his caring, the client must see the therapist's realness or genuineness. These attitudes set the climate for the primary work of the therapist, his accurate, empathic understanding. A closer look at the three therapists' attitudes will demonstrate their interdependence.

Empathy

For the therapist to *understand* his client, he must focus on the client's phenomenal world. Person-centered therapists throughout the four decades of its development have continually reaffirmed this basic tenet: Understanding the world of the client *as he* (the client) *sees it* is primary in effecting therapeutic change. "This exclusive focus in therapy on the present phenomenal experience of the client is the meaning of the term 'client-centered'" (Rogers, 1959a, p. 191).

Understanding the phenomenal world of the client requires more of the therapist than merely understanding the client's words. The therapist attempts to "get into the shoes" of his client, to "get under his skin." He not only listens to the client's words, but immerses himself in the client's world. His comments reflect not only what the client is saying, but also reflect the hazy area at the edge of the client's awareness. Through the therapist's communicating his understanding of the client's felt meanings, those meanings not yet conceptualized into awareness, the client broadens his understanding of himself and allows into his awareness more of his organismic experiencing. The confirmatory experience of feeling understood seems to give substance and power to the client's expanding self-concept. It is as though the client affirms, "It is OK to be me, even this tentative new me which is emerging." The therapist does not focus on the present experiencing of the client's world to make an interpretation or diagnosis. He believes it is the experience of feeling understood itself that effects growthful change.

Positive regard

For the therapist genuinely to maintain unconditional *positive regard,* means that he will avoid any behavior overtly or covertly judgmental. He does not probe unnecessarily; he does not express approval or disapproval; he does not interpret. He genuinely accepts the client with all the understanding he can muster, and he completely trusts the client's resources for self-understanding and positive change. The more sincerely the therapist relies on the client to discover himself and to follow his own processes of change, the more freely the client will do just that. The client sees, "Here is someone who repeatedly tells me in one way or another that he believes in my ability to find my way in the process of growth. Perhaps I can begin to believe in myself."

Unconditional positive regard and accurate understanding act together to provide a climate in the therapeutic relationship in which the client is gradually able to allow into his awareness and behavior those portions of his inner experiencing inconsistent with his self-concept, portions around which he has built strong defenses. As he verbalizes these formerly unallowable feelings, he receives the confirmation of genuine understanding from another person and the positive acceptance of his changing, new self.

Genuineness

For the therapist to be genuine or congruent, he relies on moment-to-moment felt experiencing in his relationship with the client. His *genuineness* permeates his attitudes of understanding and positive regard as well as guides his verbalization of his own understanding and experiencing.

In his effort to understand his client, he lets his imagination experience the experiencing his client reports. By allowing his client's experiences to be his own for a moment, he has available to himself his own visceral responses to being in the situation of the client. His understanding is not only intellectual, but also organismic, to the extent that he can "feel" what it would be like to live the experiencing of the client. Genuineness and empathy combine as he reports his felt meanings after putting himself in his client's shoes.

In the same way, positive regard is not an intellectual attitude nor a saccharine optimism toward humanity. It is a reality-based trust in the actualizing potential of the individual and is expressed in an unwillingness to interfere, direct, or evaluate the ongoing processes of another human being. Congruence in the attitude of positive regard is the therapist's insistent focus on the phenomenal world of the client, repeatedly returning to the moment-to-moment experiencing of the client as the resource for his positive change.

Congruence in the therapist's own inner self is his sensing of and reporting his own felt experiencing as he interacts in the relationship. The therapist trusts his own organismic responses in the situation and conveys those feelings of his that he intuitively believes have relevance in the relationship. His willingness and consistency in being real in the relationship provide the client a reality base he can

trust and take away some of the risk of sharing himself with another.

Summary

This section has presented the three therapist attitudes that research has confirmed are necessary and sufficient in a therapeutic relationship to effect positive change in the client. It should be stressed that the basis of person-centered therapy is the "forward moving tendency of the human organism" (Rogers, 1951, p. 489). Person-centered theorists believe they have discovered the conditions for the actualization processes to free themselves of whatever strictures were holding them back. Whenever a therapist is congruent, understanding, and caring toward his client, the actualizing potential of the client will be released and the client will begin to change and grow.

Process of Psychotherapy

Rogers's manner of working has probably never been better expressed than in a section of the book reporting the research with schizophrenics (1967b, p. 401-6), entitled "A Silent Young Man." It is reprinted here with a few simplifying changes.

A Silent Young Man

It would surely be desirable, if it were possible, to give the reader some experience of the process of therapy as it was lived by each therapist in his interaction with his schizophrenic clients. Yet long descriptions of therapy in a variety of cases tend to be unconsciously distorted; the transcription of a whole case would be much too long for presentation (and misleading in its omission of voice qualities); and consequently some other solution must be found.

What I propose to do in this section is to present, in transcribed form, two significant and I believe crucial interviews in the therapy with James Brown (pseudonym, of course) together with my comments as therapist on this experience. This seems to be a doubly valuable approach since the two interviews presented here are available in tape recorded form to any professional worker through the Tape Library of the American Academy of Psychotherapists.[1] Thus the person who is seriously interested in the interaction in this case can read and study these two interviews and my presentation of the meanings I see in them, and can listen to the two interviews in order to judge the quality of the interaction for himself.

Let me give a few of the facts which will introduce James Brown. He was 28 years old when I first began to see him as a part of the research. A coin toss had selected him as the member of a matched pair to receive therapy. He had been hospitalized three times, the first time for a period of three months when he was 25. He had been hospitalized for a total of 19 months when I first began to see him, and for two and one-half years at the time of these interviews. He is a person of some intellectual capacity, having completed high school and taken a little college work. The hospital diagnosis was "schizophrenic reaction, simple type."

Some readers will be disappointed that I am not presenting any of the facts from his case history. A superficial reason for this is that it might be identifying of this individual. A deeper reason is that I myself, as his therapist, have never seen

his case history and do not know its contents. I should like to state briefly my reasons for this.

If I were trying to select the most promising candidates for psychotherapy from a large group, then an examination of the case histories by me—or by someone else—might be helpful in making such a selection. But in this instance Brown had been selected by the impersonal criteria of our research as a person to whom a relationship was to be offered. I preferred to endeavor to relate to him as he was in the relationship, as he was as a person at this moment, and not as a configuration of past historical events. It is my conviction that therapy (if it takes place at all) takes place in the immediate moment-by-moment interaction in the relationship. This is the way in which I encountered Mr. Brown, and I am asking the reader to encounter him in the same way.

At the time of these two interviews, I had been seeing Mr. Brown on a twice a week basis (with the exception of some vacation periods) for a period of 11 months. Unlike many of the clients in this research the relationship had, almost from the first, seemed to have some meaning to him. He had ground privileges, so he was able to come to his appointments, and he was almost always on time, and rather rarely forgot them. The relationship between us was good. I liked him and I feel sure that he liked me. Rather early in our interviews he muttered to his ward physician that he had finally found someone who understood him. He was never articulate, and the silences were often prolonged, although when he was expressing bitterness and anger he could talk a bit more freely. He had, previous to these two interviews, worked through a number of his problems, the most important being his facing the fact that he was entirely rejected by his stepmother, rela-

[1] We are very grateful to "Mr. Brown" for his permission to make professional use of this material. The address of the Tape Library of the American Academy of Psychotherapists is 585 3rd Avenue, Salt Lake City, Utah 84103. In their listing this is "The Case of Mr. VAC."

tives, and worst of all, by his father. During a few interviews preceding these two he had been even more silent than usual, and I had no clue to the meaning of this silence. As will be evident from the transcript his silences in these two interviews were monumental. I believe that a word count would show that he uttered little more than 50 words in the first of these interviews! (In the tape recording mentioned above, each of the silences has been reduced to 15 seconds, no matter what its actual length.)

In the two interviews presented here I was endeavoring to understand all that I possibly could of his feelings. I had little hesitancy in doing a good deal of empathic guessing, for I had learned that though he might not respond in any discernible way when I was right in my inferences, he would usually let me know by a negative shake of his head if I was wrong. Mostly, however, I was simply trying to be my feelings in relationship to him, and in these particular interviews my feelings I think were largely those of interest, gentleness, compassion, desire to understand, desire to share something of myself, and eagerness to stand with him in his despairing experiences.

To me any further introduction would be superfluous. I hope and believe that the interaction of the two hours speaks for itself of many convictions, operationally expressed, about psychotherapy.

The Interviews

Tuesday

T: I see there are some cigarettes here in the drawer. Hm? Yeah, it is hot out. [Silence of 25 seconds]

T: Do you look kind of angry this morning, or is that my imagination? [Client shakes head slightly.] Not angry, huh? [Silence of 1 minute, 26 seconds]

T: Feel like letting me in on whatever is

going on? [Silence of 12 minutes, 52 seconds]

T: [*softly*] I kind of feel like saying that "If it would be of any help at all I'd like to come in." On the other hand if it's something you'd rather—if you just feel more like being within yourself, feeling whatever you're feeling within yourself, why that's O.K. too—I guess another thing I'm saying, really, in saying that is, "I do care. I'm not just sitting here like a stick." [Silence of 1 minutes, 11 seconds]

T: And I guess your silence is saying to me that either you don't want to or can't come out right now and that's O.K. So I won't pester you but I just want you to know, I'm here. [Silence of 17 minutes, 41 seconds]

T: I see I'm going to have to stop in a few minutes.[2] [Silence of 20 seconds]

T: It's hard for me to know how you've been feeling, but it looks as though part of the time maybe you'd rather I didn't know how you were feeling. Anyway it looks as though part of the time it just feels very good to let down and—relax the tension. But as I say I don't really know—how you feel. It's just the way it looks to me. Have things been pretty bad lately? [Silence of 45 seconds]

T: Maybe this morning you just wish I'd shut up—and maybe I should, but I just keep feeling I'd like to—I don't know, be in touch with you in some way. [Silence of 2 minutes, 21 seconds] [*Jim yawns.*]

T: Sounds discouraged or tired. [Silence of 41 seconds]

C: No. Just lousy.

T: Everything's lousy, huh? You feel lousy? [Silence of 39 seconds]

---

[2]Long experience had shown me that it was very difficult for Jim to leave. Hence I had gradually adopted the practice of letting him know, 10 or 12 minutes before the conclusion of the hour, that "our time is nearly up." This enabled us to work through the leaving process without my feeling hurried.

T: Want to come in Friday at 12 at the usual time?

C: [*Yawns and mutters something unintelligible.*] [Silence of 48 seconds]

T: Just kind of feel sunk way down deep in these lousy, lousy feelings, hm?—Is that something like it?

C: No.

T: No? [Silence of 20 seconds]

C: No. I just ain't no good to nobody, never was, and never will be.

T: Feeling that now, hm? That you're just no good to yourself, no good to anybody. Never will be any good to anybody. Just that you're completely worthless, huh?—Those really are lousy feelings. Just feel that you're no good at *all*, hm?

C: Yeah. [*Muttering in low, discouraged voice*] That's what this guy I went to town with just the other day told me.

T: This guy that you went to town with really told you that you were no good? Is that what you're saying? Did I get that right?

C: M-hm.

T: I guess the meaning of that if I get it right is here's somebody that—meant something to you and what does he think of you? Why, he's told you that he thinks you're no good at all. And that just really knocks the props out from under you. [*Jim weeps quietly.*] It just brings the tears. [Silence of 20 seconds]

C: [*rather defiantly*] I don't care though.

T: You tell yourself you don't care at all, but somehow I guess some part of you cares because some part of you weeps over it. [Silence of 19 seconds]

T: I guess some part of you just feels, "Here I am hit with another blow, as if I hadn't had enough blows like this during my life when I feel that people don't like me. Here's someone I've begun to feel attached to and now *he* doesn't like me. And I'll say I don't care. I won't let it

make any difference to me—But just the same the tears run down my cheeks."

C: [*Muttering*] I guess I always knew it.

T: Hm?

C: I guess I always knew it.

T: If I'm getting that right, it is that what makes it hurt most of all is that when he tells you you're no good, well shucks, that's what you've always felt about yourself. Is that—the meaning of what you're saying? [*Jim nods slightly, indicating agreement.*] —M-hm. So you feel as though he's just confirming what—you've already known. He's confirming what you've already felt in some way. [Silence of 23 seconds]

T: So that between his saying so and your perhaps feeling it underneath, you just feel about as no good as anybody could feel. [Silence of 2 minutes, 1 second]

T: [*Thoughtfully*] As I sort of let it soak in and try to feel what you must be feeling—It comes up sorta this way in me and I don't know—but as though here was someone you'd made a contact with, someone you'd really done things for and done things with. Somebody that had some meaning to you. Now, wow! He slaps you in the face by telling you you're just no good. And this really cuts *so* deep, you can hardly stand it. [Silence of 30 seconds]

T: I've got to call it quits for today, Jim. [Silence of 1 minute, 18 seconds]

T: It really hurts, doesn't it? [This is in response to his quiet tears.] [Silence of 26 seconds]

T: I guess if the feelings came out you'd just weep and weep and weep. [Silence of 1 minute, 3 seconds]

T: Help yourself to some Kleenex if you'd like—Can you go now? [Silence of 23 seconds]

T: I guess you really hate to, but I've got to see somebody else. [Silence of 20 seconds]

T: It's really bad, isn't it? [Silence of 22 seconds]

T: Let me ask you one question and say one thing. Do you still have that piece of paper with my phone numbers on it and instructions, and so on? [*Jim nods.*] O.K. And if things get bad, so that you feel real down, you have them call me. 'Cause that's what I'm here for, to try to be of some help when you need it. If you need it, you have them call me.[3]

C: I think I'm beyond help.

T: Huh? Feel as though you're beyond help. I know. You feel just completely hopeless about yourself. I can understand that. I don't feel hopeless, but I can realize that you do.[4] Just feel as though nobody can help you and you're really beyond help. [Silence of 2 minutes, 1 second]

T: I guess you just feel so, so down that—it's awful. [Silence of 2 minutes]

T: I guess there's one other thing too. I, I'm going to be busy here this afternoon 'til four o'clock and maybe a little after. But if you should want to see me again this afternoon, you can drop around about four o'clock. O.K.?—Otherwise, I'll see you Friday noon. Unless I get a call from you. If you—If you're kind of concerned for fear anybody would see that you've been weeping a little, you can go out and sit for a while where you waited for me. Do just as you wish on that. Or go down and sit in the waiting

room there and read magazines— I guess you'll really have to go.

C: Don't want to go back to work.

T: You don't want to go back to work, hm?

This is the end of the interview. Later in the day Rogers saw Mr. Brown on the hospital grounds. He seemed much more cheerful and said that he thought he could get a ride into town that afternoon. The next time Rogers saw Mr. Brown was three days later, on Friday. This interview follows.

Friday

T: I brought a few magazines you can take with you if you want.[5] [Silence of 47 seconds]

T: I didn't hear from you since last time. Were you able to go to town that day?

C: Yeah. I went in with a kid driving the truck.

T: M-hm. [Voices from next office are heard in background.] [Silence of 2 minutes]

T: Excuse me just a minute. [Goes to stop noise.] [Silence of 2 minutes, 20 seconds]

T: I don't know why, but I realize that somehow it makes me feel good that today you don't have your hand up to your face so that I can somehow kind of see you more. I was wondering why I felt as though you were a little more here than you are sometimes and then I realized well, it's because—I don't feel as though you're hiding behind your hand, or something. [Silence of 50 seconds]

---

[3]Two words of explanation are needed here. He seemed so depressed that I was concerned that he might be feeling suicidal. I wanted to be available to him if he felt desperate. Since no patient was allowed to phone without permission, I had given him a note which would permit a staff member or Jim himself to phone me *at any time* he wished to contact me, and with both my office and home phone numbers.

[4]This is an example of the greater willingness I have developed to express my own feelings of the moment, at the same time accepting the client's right to possess *his* feelings, no matter how different from mine.

[5]I had, on several occasions, given magazines and small amounts of money to Mr. Brown and loaned him books. There was no special rationale behind this. The hospital environment was impoverished for a man of Brown's sort, and I felt like giving him things which would relieve the monotony.

T: And I think I sense, though I could be mistaken, I think I do sense that today just like some other days when you come in here, it's just as though you let yourself sink down into feelings that run very deep inside you. Sometimes they're very bad feelings like the last time and sometimes probably they're not so bad, though they're sort of—I think I understand that somehow when you come in here it's as though you do let yourself down into those feelings. And now—

C: I'm gonna take off.

T: Huh?

C: I'm gonna take off.[6]

T: You're going to take off? Really run away from here? Is that what you mean? Must be some—what's the—what's the background of that? Can you tell me? Or I guess what I mean more accurately is I know you don't like the place but it must be that something special came up or something?

C: I just want to run away and die.

T: M-hm, m-hm, m-hm. It isn't even that you want to get away from here *to* something. You just want to leave here and go away and die in a corner, hm? [Silence of 30 seconds]

T: I guess as I let that soak in I really do sense how, how deep that feeling sounds, that you—I guess the image that comes to my mind is sort of a——a wounded animal that wants to crawl away and die. It sounds as though that's kind of the way you feel that you just want to get away from here and, and vanish. Perish. Not exist. [Silence of 1 minute]

C: [*almost inaudibly*] All day yesterday and all morning I wished I were dead. I even prayed last night that I could die.

T: I think I caught all of that, that—for

[6]Clearly my empathic guessing in the two previous responses was completely erroneous. This was not troublesome to me, nor, I believe, to him. There is no doubt, however, that my surprise shows.

a couple of days now you've just *wished* you could be dead and you've even prayed for that—I guess that—One way this strikes me is that to live is such an awful thing to you, you just wish you could die, and not live. [Silence of 1 minute, 12 seconds]

T: So that you've been just wishing and wishing that you were not living. You wish that life would pass away from you. [Silence of 30 seconds]

C: I wish it more'n anything else I've ever wished around here.

T: M-hm, m-hm, m-hm. I guess you've wished for lots of things but boy! It seems as though this wish to not live is deeper and stronger than anything you ever wished before. [Silence of 1 minute, 36 seconds]

T: Can't help but wonder whether it's still true that some things this friend said to you—are those still part of the thing that makes you feel so awful?

C: In general, yes.

T: M-hm. [Silence of 47 seconds]

T: The way I'm understanding that is that in a general way the fact that he felt you were no good has just set off a whole flood of feeling in you that makes you really wish, *wish* you weren't alive. Is that—somewhere near it?

C: I ain't no good to nobody, or I ain't no good for nothin', so what's the use of living?

T: M-hm. You feel, "I'm not any good to another living person, so—why should I go on living?" [Silence of 21 seconds]

T: And I guess a part of that is that—here I'm kind of guessing and you can set me straight, I guess a part of that is that you felt, "I tried to *be* good for something as far as he was concerned. I really tried. And now—if I'm no good to him, if he feels I'm no good, then that proves that I'm just no good to anybody." Is that, uh—anywhere near it?

C: Oh, well, other people have told me that too.

T: Yeah. M-hm. I see. So you feel if, if you go by what others—what several others have said, then, then you are *no good*. No good to anybody. [Silence of 3 minutes, 40 seconds]

T: I don't know whether this will help or not, but I would just like to say that—I think I can understand pretty well—what it's like to feel that you're just *no damn good* to anybody, because there was a time when—I felt that way about *myself*. And I know it can be *really rough*.[7] [Silence of 13 minutes]

T: I see we've got only a few more minutes left. [Silence of 2 minutes, 51 seconds]

T: Shall we make it next Tuesday at eleven, the usual time? [Silence of 1 minute, 35 seconds]

T: If you gave me any answer, I really didn't get it. Do you want to see me next Tuesday at eleven?

C: Don't know.

T: "I just don't know." [Silence of 34 seconds]

T: Right at this point you just don't know—whether you want to say "yes" to that or not, hm?—I guess you feel so down and so—awful that you just don't know whether you can—can see that far ahead. Hm? [Silence of 1 minute, 5 seconds]

T: I'm going to give you an appointment at that time because *I'd* sure like to see *you* then. [*Writing our appointment slip.*] [Silence of 30 seconds]

T: And another thing I would say is that—if things continue to stay so rough for you, don't hesitate to have them call

me. And if you should decide to take off, I would very much appreciate it if you would have them call me and—so I could see you first. I wouldn't try to dissuade you. I'd just want to see you.

C: I might go today. Where, I don't know, but I don't care.

T: Just feel that your mind is made up and that you're going to leave. You're not going *to* anywhere. You're just—just going to leave, hm? [Silence of 53 seconds]

C: [*muttering in discouraged tone*] That's why I want to go, 'cause I don't care what happens.

T: Huh?

C: That's why I want to go, 'cause I don't care what happens.

T: M-hm, m-hm. That's why you want to go, because you really don't care about yourself. You just don't care *what* happens. And I guess I'd just like to say—I care about you. And *I* care what happens.[8] [Silence of 30 seconds] [*Jim bursts into tears and unintelligible sobs.*]

T: [*tenderly*] Somehow that just—makes all the feelings pour out. [Silence of 35 seconds]

T: And you just weep and weep and weep. And feel so badly. [Jim continues to sob, then blows nose and breathes in great gasps.]

T: I do get some sense of how awful you feel inside—You just sob and sob. [He puts his head on desk, bursting out in great gulping, gasping sobs.]

T: I guess all the pent-up feelings you've been feeling the last few days just—just come rolling out. [Silence of 32 seconds, while sobbing continues]

T: There's some Kleenex there, if you'd like it—Hmmm. [*sympathetically*] You

---

[7]This is a most unusual kind of response for me to make. I simply felt that I wanted to share my experience with him—to let him know he was not alone.

[8]This was the spontaneous feeling which welled up in me, and which I expressed. It was certainly not planned, and I had no idea it would bring such an explosive response.

just feel kind of torn to pieces inside. [Silence of 1 minute, 56 seconds]

C: I wish I could die. [*sobbing*]

T: You just wish you could die, don't you. M-hm. You just feel so awful, you wish you could perish. [Therapist laid his hand gently on Jim's arm during this period. Jim showed no definite response. However, the storm subsided somewhat. Very heavy breathing.] [Silence of 1 minute, 10 seconds]

T: You just feel so awful and so torn apart inside that, that it just makes you wish you could pass out. [Silence of 3 minutes, 29 seconds]

T: I guess life is so tough, isn't it? You just feel you could weep and sob your heart away and wish you could die.⁹ [Heavy breathing continues.] [Silence of 6 minutes, 14 seconds]

T: I don't want to rush you, and I'll stay as long as you really need me, but I do have another appointment, that I'm already late for.

C: Yeah. [Silence of 17 minutes]

T: Certainly been through something, haven't you? [Silence of 1 minute, 18 seconds]

T: May I see you Tuesday?

C: [*inaudible response.*]

T: Hm?

C: Don't know. [*almost unintelligible*]

T: "I just don't know," M-hm. You know all the things I said before, I mean very much. I want to see you Tuesday and I want to see you before then if you want to see me. So, if you need me, don't hesitate to call me. [Silence of 1 minute]

T: It's really rough, isn't it? [Silence of 24 seconds]

C: Yes.

T: Sure is. [*Jim slowly gets up to go.*] [Silence of 29 seconds]

T: Want to take that too? [*Jim takes appointment slip.*] [Silence of 20 seconds]

There's a washroom right down the hall where you can wash your face. [Jim opens the door; noise and voices are heard from corridor.] [Silence of 18 seconds] [*Jim turns back into the room.*]

C: You don't have a cigarette, do you? [Therapist finds one.]

T: There's just one. I looked in the package but—I don't know. I haven't any idea how old it is, but it looks sort of old.

C: I'll see you. [*hardly audible*]

T: O.K. I'll be looking for you Tuesday, Jim.

Commentary

What has happened here? I am sure there will be many interpretations of this material. I would like to make it plain that what follows is my own perception of it, a perception which is perhaps biased by the fact that I was a deeply involved participant.

Here is a young man who has been a troublesome person in the institution. He has been quick to feel mistreated, quick to take offense, often involved in fights with the staff. He has, by his own account, no tender feelings, only bitter ones against others. In these two interviews he has experienced the depth of his own feelings of worthlessness, of having no excuse for living. He has been unsupported by his frequently felt feelings of anger, and has experienced only his deep, deep despair. In this situation something happens. What is it, and why does it occur?

In my estimation, I was functioning well as a therapist in this interaction. I felt a warm and spontaneous caring for him as a person, which found expression in several ways—but most deeply at the mo-

---

⁹As I have listened to the recording of this interview, I wish I had responded to the relief he must have been experiencing in letting his despair pour out, as well as to the despair itself.

ment when he was despairing. I was continuously desirous of understanding his feelings, even though he gave very few clues. I believe that my erroneous guesses were unimportant as compared to my willingness to go with him in his feelings of worthlessness and despair when he was able to voice these. I think we were relating as two real and genuine persons. In the moments of real encounter the differences in education, in status, in degree of psychological disturbance, had no importance—we were two persons in a relationship.

In this relationship there was a moment of real, and I believe irreversible, change. Jim Brown, who sees himself as stubborn, bitter, mistreated, worthless, useless, hopeless, unloved, unlovable, *experiences* my caring. In that moment his defensive shell cracks wide open, and can never again be quite the same. When someone *cares* for him, and when he feels and experiences this caring, he becomes a softer person whose years of stored up hurt come pouring out in anguished sobs. He is not the shell of hardness and bitterness, the stranger to tenderness. He is a person hurt beyond words, and aching for the love and caring which alone can make him human. This is evident in his sobs. It is evident too in his returning to the office, partly for a cigarette, partly to say spontaneously that he will return.

In my judgment what we have here is a "moment of change" in therapy. Many events are necessary to lead up to such a moment. Many later events will flow from it. But in this moment something is experienced openly which has never been experienced before. Once it had been experienced openly, and the emotions surrounding it flow to their natural expression, the person can never be quite the same. He can never completely deny these feelings when they recur again. He can

never quite maintain the concept of self which he had before that moment. Here is an instance of the heart and essence of therapeutic change.

An Objective Look at the Process

If we look at the few client expressions in these interviews in terms of the hypotheses of this research, we can see that being deeply in therapy does not necesssarily involve a ready flow of words. Let us take some of the feeling themes Brown expresses and look at them in terms of the process continuum we have conceptualized.

My feelings are lousy.
I ain't no good to nobody.
I think I'm beyond help.
I don't want to go back to work.
I just want to run away and die.
I ain't no good, so what's the use of living?
I don't care what happens.
I wish I could die.

Compare these themes with brief descriptions of the process continuum at stages 3, 4, 5 and 6 of the seven stages of the original Process Scale (first version, described in the following section).

Stage 3. "There is much description of feelings and personal meanings which are not now present." "The experiencing of situations is largely described in terms of the past." "Personal constructs are rigid but may at times be thought of as constructs."

Clearly Mr. Brown's manner of expression does not fit this stage in any respect except that his concept of himself as no good is held in rigid fashion.

Stage 4. "Feelings and personal meanings are freely described as present objects owned by the self. . . . Occasionally feelings are expressed in the present but this occurs as if against the individual's wishes." "There is an unwilling fearful recognition that one is experiencing things—a vague realization that a disturbing type of inner referent does exist." "The individual is willing to risk relating himself occasionally to others on a feeling basis."

It is evident that this matches more closely Mr. Brown's experience in these hours.

Stage 5. "In this stage we find many feelings freely expressed in the moment of their occurrence and thus experienced in the immediate present." "This tends to be a frightening and disturbing thing because it involves being in process." "There is a desire to be these feelings, to be 'the real me.'" This stage seems to catch even more the quality of the experiencing in these interviews.

Stage 6. "Feelings which have previously been denied to awareness are now experienced with immediacy and acceptance. . . not something to be denied, feared, or struggled against." "In the moments of movement which occur at this stage there is a dissolving of significant personal constructs in a vivid experiencing of a feeling which runs counter to the constructs."

While some aspects of Jim's experiencing in these interviews come close to this description, it is clear that he is not acceptant of the feelings which well up in him. It appears that ratings of the stage he has reached in these interviews would probably cluster modally around stage 5, with some elements rated 4 or 6.

Perhaps this will give the reader some feeling for both the strengths and inadequacies of our conceptualizing of the process continuum and our attempts to cap-

ture it in a objective rating scale. It is relevant to what has occurred in these interviews, yet Brown's unique expression of his feelings is certainly not fully contained in the descriptions supplied by the original Process Scale, or the further separate scales developed from it (Rogers, 1967b).

This examination of the process aspect of these interviews may help to explain something which has mystified colleagues who have listened to the interviews. They often marvel at the patience I displayed in sitting through a silence of say, 17 minutes. The major reason I was able to do so was that when Jim said something it was usually worth listening to and showed real involvement in a therapeutic process. After all, most therapists can listen to talk, even when the talk is saying very little and indicates that very little that is therapeutic is going on. I can listen to silence, when I think that the silence is likely to end with significant feelings. I should add, however, that when I ceased to be patient, or ceased to be acceptant of the silence, I felt free to express my own feelings as they were occurring in me at the moment. There are various examples of this in these interviews. I do recognize, however, that it is easier for me to be patient than it is for a number of my colleagues. I have my style, and they have theirs.

Later Events

If one expects some quick and miraculous change from such a moment of change as we saw in the Friday interview, he will be disappointed. I was, myself, somewhat surprised that in the next interview it was as though these two had never happened—Jim was inarticulate, silent, uncommunicative, and made no reference to his sobbing or to any other portion of the interviews. But over the next months the change showed. Little by little he became willing to risk himself in a positive approach to life. Yet even in this respect he would often revert to self-defeating behaviors. Several times he managed to make all the necessary arrangements for leaving the hospital to attend school. Always at the last moment he would become involved in violent altercations (completely the fault of the other person, naturally!) which caused the hospital staff to confine him and which thus destroyed all the carefully laid arrangements. Finally, however, he was able to admit that he himself was terrified of going out—afraid he couldn't make good. When I told him that this was something to decide within himself—that I would see him if he chose to stay in the hospital, and that I would continue to see him if he chose to leave—he tentatively and fearfully moved out toward the world. First he attended school, living at the hospital. Then he worked through many realistic problems regarding a suitable room, finally found a place for himself in the community, and fully moved out.

As he could permit others to care for him, he was able to care for others. He accepted friendly gestures from members of the research staff, and it meant much to him to be treated as a person by them. He moved out to make friends of his own. He began to live his own life, apart from any hospital or therapy influence.

The best evidence of the change is in a letter to me, a little more than two years after these interviews. At the time I was away for an academic year. I was seeing him very infrequently at the time I left, but I made arrangements for him to see another therapist (whom he knew slightly) if at any time he wished to do so. A few months after I left, I received the following letter from him:

Hi Doc,

I suppose you thought I had died, but I'm still here.

I've often thought of you and have been wanting to write but I'll use the old excuse that I've been busy.

Things are moving along pretty fast. I'm back in school, but things have changed slightly there. Mr. B. decided to quit teaching, so everything I had planned with him fell through.

(There followed three paragraphs about the courses he is taking and his pleasure at having been given—through the rehabilitation officer—an expensive tool of his trade. He also speaks of his part-time job which is continuing. Unfortunately, this material is too identifying to quote. He continues on a more personal note):

. . . I had a wonderful summer. Probably the best in years. I sure hate to see it come to an end.

I've met lots of people and made lots of friends. I hardly saw any of the kids from school all summer, and I didn't go out to the hospital all summer. Now, when I look back, it was like going down a different road. A very enjoyable one at that.

Also I haven't seen G. S. (substitute therapist in therapist's absence) at all this summer so far. As far as I could see it was good not seeing anybody, nor having to think about hospitals, doctors, and being out there. It was more or less like being free as a bird.

In fact, Doc, I was suppose to have gone up to the university and write those tests again. Some Mrs. N. has been calling and it irritates me because *I* think I did good and all that going up there will do is spoil the effect more or less. I don't mind seeing you, Doc. That's not the point. I still want to see you when you get back, but it is a good feeling not having to have to see anybody.

I can't really explain it, so I won't try.

I sure wish I was out there at this time. It's been down in the low 40's every night here lately and it's starting to rain a lot.

By the way, I finally went home. That was last Wednesday. I got there at noon and I could hardly wait to get back. Back to Madison, back to my room, back to my friends and civilization.

Well, Doc, I guess I've talked enough about myself and I guess about half way back, I'd have let you do all of it. Right?

All in all things couldn't be too much better for me, compared to what they have been. It sure feels good to be able to say, "To hell with it," when things bother me.

I'll write later when I have "time," Doc. Maybe I'll be mean and won't write until you do, because I did wonder how come I never heard from you before I did.

Bye for now, Doc.
Sincerely,
JIM.

In his newfound independence he has refused to see Mrs. N. and to take the follow-up tests which were so important to our research. The statistical measures at follow-up would have been definitely improved had Jim been included. But his refusal is very thought-provoking (as well as a bit amusing). Perhaps when people accept themselves as persons, they refuse to be regarded as "objects" no matter how important this is to the researcher. It is a challenging, and in some deep sense a positive, thought.

An Eight-Year Follow-up

Eight years after these interviews I received a phone call from far across the country. It opened with the familiar voice I had come to know so well: "Hi Doc, remember me?" Jim went on to tell of several efforts he had made to reach me, mistakenly thinking I was in another city. His main message that he wanted to get across was that he was "sassy, ornery, and liberal." He is still working for the same firm, though his attitudes occasionally get him labeled as an agitator. He is still living in the same rooming house ("I'm in love with my landlady," he said, in what I *think* was a facetious remark.) He is a solid employed citizen, living a rather limited social life, but content. The fact that he wished to let me know how much our relationship had meant to him during eight long years of separation was, for me, very meaningful.

Mechanisms of Psychotherapy

Thus far, this chapter has dealt primarily with the therapist conditions or attitudes necessary for constructive change to take place in the client. These conditions form one half of the equation of psychotherapy, which is the basis of person-centered therapy. That equation has been stated by Rogers in this way: "The more the therapist is perceived by the client as being genuine, as having an empathic understanding, and an unconditional regard for him, the greater will be the degree of constructive personality change in the client" (Rogers, 1961b, p. 32).

This section will deal with the other half of the equation, namely, the "constructive personality change" that takes place in the client in a person-centered therapeutic relationship.

The interest of the researchers and theorists who worked in the development of person-centered therapy has always been the process of personality change rather than in static descriptions of personality or personality formation. It was in the search for understanding the process of change that Rogers immersed himself for a period of several months in the recordings of numerous person-centered cases judged successful by multiple criteria. He began to note a consistent pattern of change in all the cases. Personality movement was from rigidity to flow, from stasis to changingness. Rogers describes the continuum of change:

. . . it commences at one end with a rigid, static, undifferentiated, unfeeling, impersonal type of psychologic functioning. It evolves through various stages to, at the other end, a level of functioning marked by changingness, fluidity, richly differentiated reactions, by immediate experiencing of personal feelings, which are felt as deeply owned and accepted. (1961b, p. 33)

Out of Rogers's study of the process of change emerged seven behavior strands within which behavior changes could be described. The strands are feelings and personal meanings, manner of experiencing, degree of incongruence, communication of self, manner in which experience is construed, relationship to problems, and manner of relating. Rogers and R. A. Rablen (1958) developed a scale to measure the stage on the process continuum at which a client was operating.

Brief and partial descriptions of each of these different stages of process are as follows:

First stage. Communication is about externals. There is an unwillingness to communicate self. Feelings and personal meanings are neither recognized as such nor owned. Constructs are extremely rigid. Close relationships are construed as dangerous.

Second stage. Feelings are sometimes *described* but as unowned past *objects* external to self. The individual is remote from his subjective experiencing. He may voice contradictory statements about himself somewhat freely on nonself topics. He may show some recognition that he has problems or conflicts but they are perceived as external to the self.

Third stage. There is much *description* of feelings and personal meanings which are not now present. These distant feelings are often pictured as unacceptable or bad. The *experiencing* of situations is largely described as having occurred in the past or is cast in terms of the past. There is a freer flow of expression about self as an *object*. There may be communication about self as a reflected object, existing primarily in others. Personal constructs are rigid but may at times be thought of as constructs, with occasionally a questioning of their validity. There is a beginning recognition that any problems that exist are inside the individual rather than external.

Fourth stage. Feelings and personal meanings are freely described as present objects owned by the self. Feelings of an intense sort are still described as not now present. There is a dim recognition that feelings denied to awareness may break through in the present, but this is a frightening possibility. There is an unwilling, fearful recognition that one is *experiencing* things. Contradictions in experience are clearly realized and a definite concern over them is experienced. There is a beginning loosening of personal constructs. It is sometimes discovered that experience has been *construed* as having a certain meaning but this meaning is not inherent nor absolute. There is some expression of self-responsibility for problems. The individual is occasionally willing to risk relating himself to others on a feeling basis.

Fifth stage. Many feelings are freely expressed in the moment of their occurrence and are thus experienced in the immediate present. These feelings are owned or accepted. Feelings previously denied now tend to bubble through into awareness though there is fear of this occurrence. There is some recognition that experiencing with immediacy is a referent and possible guide for the individual. Contradictions are recognized as attitudes existing in different aspects of the personality as indicated by statements such as, "My mind tells me this is so but I don't seem to believe it." There is a desire to be the self-related feelings, "To be the real me." There is a questioning of the validity of many personal constructs. The person feels that he has a definite responsibility for the problems which exist in him.

Sixth stage. Feelings previously denied are now experienced both with immediacy and *acceptance*. Such feelings are not something to be denied, feared, or struggled against. This experiencing is often vivid, dramatic, and releasing for the individual. There is full acceptance now of experiencing as providing a clear and usable referent for getting at the implicit meanings of the individual's encounter with himself and with life. There is also the recognition that the self is now becoming this process of experiencing. There is no longer much awareness of the self as an object. The individual often feels somewhat "shaky" as his solid constructs are recognized as construings taking place within him. The individual risks being himself in process in the relationship to others. He takes the risk of being the flow that is himself and trusting another person to accept him as he is in this flow.

Seventh stage. The individual lives comfortably in the flowing process of his experiencing. New feelings are experienced with richness and immediacy, and this inner experiencing is a clear referent for behavior. Incongruence is minimal and temporary. The self is a confident awareness of this process of experiencing. The meaning of experiencing is held loosely and constantly checked and rechecked against further experiencing. (Rogers & Rablen, 1958)

Studies using the Process Scale or its derivatives show that significant behavior variations are discernible over the course of individual or group therapy using the process variables. The initial validation studies (Tomlinson, 1962; Tomlinson & Hart, 1962; Walker, Rablen & Rogers, 1960) showed that prejudged more successful and less successful individual counseling cases, using a multiple criteria of judgment, were highly distinguishable when "blind" ratings of segments from them were made on the Process Scale. In later studies, the Process Scale has distinguished individual process movement in encounter groups (Clark & Culbert, 1965; Culbert, 1968; Meador, 1971). In all cases interjudge reliability has been satisfactory.

Examples are given below of individual movement within each strand. These examples are taken from the eight individuals in a weekend encounter group. In a study of this group, Meador (1971) found that each of the eight individuals made significant (p < .01) positive process movement during the 16 hours that the group met. That is, each individual moved from the process level at which he entered the group along the continuum toward more flexibility, toward being better able to express his feelings as they occurred, toward more awareness of his inner experiencing, greater congruence, toward relating to others in the immediacy of the present.

Feelings and personal meanings

Change in the way a client relates to his feelings and personal meanings has to do with the degree to which he is aware of his feelings, the degree to which he owns his feelings as his, and the degree to which he can express his feelings in the moment of their occurrence. Early in a group one of the participants says:

Keith: . . . If I am going to be a member of the group, I must contribute. I don't know what, but if you're going to be part of it, you've got to contribute to the well-being of the group.

Therapist: If you knew what it was you would do it.

Keith: Yes, I would do it and sort of do it and get it over with if I had the magic formula. I guess this is what was worrying me this afternoon. I don't believe that there is a magic answer. I seem to get from you that I should try a little harder.

This is an example of someone remote from his feelings, looking outside himself for a "magic formula," a clue from others to show him how to behave in this situation. This represents behavior low on the process continuum. Gradually, Keith begins to own his feelings and to talk about them in the past tense, representative of the middle of the continuum:

Keith: There are times I am afraid, and you said yesterday "why don't you just tell everybody what you think and let it go." There are times I don't seem to be able to do that. There are other times when I can. I don't, to my knowledge, turn these on and off as a mechanism or anything like that. It happens.

Therapist: Can you get any closer at all to what it's like when you are afraid? If that clicks, I just wonder if you could just let us sink in and let us know a little more of what it seems like inside when you feel that way?

Keith: What it feels like inside when I am afraid is like your first speech in front of a large audience. Your stomach feels like a used lemon rind. It churns.

Later, Keith expresses his feelings in the moment of their occurrence in the following example,

Keith: . . . You made me a bit mad with your emptiness. I don't know whether you made me mad because maybe I am empty, or you made me mad because I don't like the idea because I don't think that it is applicable over here. . . .

Joe: Yes it is.

Keith: Well maybe, but I don't see it!

To summarize the strand of feelings and personal meanings, on the lower end of the continuum the person is remote from his feelings and disowns them. Gradually he comes to recognize that he has feelings and is able to talk about having them in the past. Later he may fearfully express his feelings as they occur, representing a higher stage on the continuum. Finally, he is able to allow his feelings to flow freely, acknowledging them and expressing them as they occur and change from moment to moment.

Manner of experiencing .

In psychotherapy the individual moves from a remoteness from his inner experiencing through the process of becoming aware of it, to a point where he uses his changing inner experiencing as a referent for behavior. For example, early in the group, Jerry says, "I would like to get an honest feeling about myself, period, and act this way in all cases." This statement indicates that he has some awareness of the changingness of his inner experience of himself, and that he would like that changingness to cease, to be more dependable, more static. Later he begins to distinguish the characteristics of his inner experiencing, although he is still holding himself at arm's length from it:

Jerry: It's an odd thing. I remember starting off thinking about this openness and I . . . I don't feel that I've been open. It's a desire to be open, and yet I seem to still be back here listening to you other people and trying to really get into it, but I . . . I can't seem to do it. Of course this empty expression to me is kind of a horrifying thought. And when you said it to Karl I immediately thought of it in relation to myself and wondered just how empty I was.

Toward the end of the group, Jerry is allowing his inner experiencing to flow and is able to move with its changingness as in this statement:

Jerry: "I find weeping is good, and . . . and a cleansing thing, and if . . . uhh . . . by somebody's action in this group, like Roz . . . uhh . . . how this has a welling up of making you feel a part of the group even though it's done by an individual of the group; it seemed to make me feel a part of everybody here, and which I'll forever be indebted to you, Roz, for. And . . . uhh . . . I had no embarrassment in coming back into the room.

Therapist: I noticed that.

Jerry: But then a wave of sadness comes over, and . . . and . . . at least I feel . . . uhh . . . which is the thing that Beth and I were discussing . . . is, well, what happens from this point on. And it's frightening, and it's . . . it's . . . uh . . . a real dilemma. The thing that you get is that there are people that could care, and so therefore it may not be a really hopeless situation.

In this statement, Jerry mentions several aspects of his inner experiencing and translates these into meanings for his own self-understanding. This speech is representative of behavior on the upper end of the process continuum.

Personal constructs
Another aspect of the process continuum is the way in which an individual construes his experiences. At one end of the continuum, his meanings for experiences are very rigid and seem to be placed on his experiences from the outside as though meanings were absolute truths. Beth relates her construing of male-female relationships in this way.

Beth: What amazes me is the fact that I have always felt that a man-woman relation was just sexual and that there . . . it couldn't be a love or anything beyond a superficial feeling for any other man. And it has affected me very deeply that I have moved him. But it did not occur to me to go and put my arms around him because to me this is wrong to kiss, or embrace, or love a man that I am not married to or don't feel that way towards.

Gradually the individual begins to question his personal constructs particularly as he begins to trust his inner experiencing and to find his meaning there. Later in the group, Beth is using her own feelings as referents for meaning as in this statement:

Beth: Well, I really do think that you like me now. I told you that, you know, that you weren't reaching me. I don't remember how far back it was, now, but

that I wasn't digging you or reading you. You weren't, but I think you do really like me now. I feel this. So I feel we have made, at least you and I have made, contact.

Therapist: You can really believe the guy inside.

Beth: Uh-huh. Besides getting his handkerchief. I thought for a minute he was going to cuddle up, and I was going to tell him I wouldn't give it back to him, only if I could have it back again, because I want to take it home with me.

Beth can now allow the caring she feels for another man to be expressed, to value and prize her affection as she experiences it, rather than squelching her feelings in favor of a meaning she was imposing upon herself.

Communication of self
Change can be seen in the individual over the course of psychotherapy in the way in which he talks about himself. At one end of the continuum, he is unwilling to talk about himself or talks about himself only in terms of external events. At the midpoint of the continuum, the individual talks about himself as an object he hardly seems related to. Gradually, he begins to own himself and his feelings and experiencing and to communicate himself in that way. At the beginning of the group, Carlene exemplifies the lower end of the continuum when she says, "I think that there is need for keeping some of self to self." Slowly, she begins to communicate herself, but still speaks of herself in the third person, "You're not seeing Carlene in that, or maybe I'm not projecting Carlene, and you're questioning this." Her movement in communicating herself is clear when she says, "I am enjoying myself here to the extent of . . . to the point where I am finding so many things out about me, and I really . . . I think

that I have grown greatly since I have been here and I have found a lot of things out that I never really accepted before.'' Although in this statement she speaks of experiences that are not occurring at the moment, she is communicating about very recent and implicitly ongoing experiencing. Finally, Carlene exemplifies the upper end of the process continuum when, weeping, she communicates herself to another in the midst of her strong feelings about herself:

Carlene: I wanted so badly to reach out to you Jerry. . . . Uhmmm . . . I was just kind of boiling inside, and I couldn't do it. . . . And I was sitting here after Roz came over to you, and then after you left, and I wanted to go out then, and I couldn't do that either.

As Carlene came to trust the others in the group, she changed the way she talked about herself from being very remote and hidden in her communication to being open, claiming the self she was communicating.

Congruence

Another strand on which an individual changes during psychotherapy is the continuum from incongruence to congruence. *Congruence* refers to the individual's being what he feels inside, being aware of his inner experiencing and translating that into his behavior. *Incongruence* refers to his playing a role designed to cover up or hide his inner self. References to congruence often include phrases such as "taking off the mask" or "tearing down the wall." Another member of the group, Joe, speaks of his awareness of the difference between inner feelings and outward actions in these two segments. The first is from early in the group:

Joe: Aren't we always giving off cues? And if I do not like you, Beth, I am sure that you would sense it. Just like at the cocktail party you were talking about. If I come up to you and say a few pleasant words, and then go to the other side of the room, that's one thing. But if I am really warm to you, somehow we would be tearing bricks down from this wall between us. I guess what I am trying to say is that we are really more open with people, we get these cues, more than we seem to think.

In this speech, Joe speaks of a hypothetical situation and in the inclusive "we" thus avoiding making this statement his own personal belief; he does not own the belief as an experience of his. Much later in the group, Joe expresses his experience of incongruence in a more personal way:

Therapist: We want you to say what is hard for you to say now. That was hard for you to say, "Don't forget about me," wasn't it?
Joe: Uh-huh.
Therapist: Can you finish that?
Joe: I don't want you to forget about me, and I also don't want you to remember me as just, . . . I guess I've been a nice guy because I do smile a lot. That's only a part of me. And I think, there *is* something in here, and I want you to know this guy, too.
Therapist: What is it?
Joe: I don't know. It's the guy that's inside of me. It isn't too easy to know him. I don't know . . . I can't . . . This guy has got sweaty palms right now even though he is sitting here very calm.

Here Joe is much closer to his own experiencing and expresses his awareness of the difference between his outward behavior and his inner feelings. Becoming aware of incongruence is the intermediate step toward allowing one's inner experiencing to flow outward, shaping one's behavior. The unbroken flow between inner experiencing and outward behavior is characteristic of high-process level.

Relationship to problems

Another strand on which individuals show movement in psychotherapy is how they talk about their *problems*. At the lower end of the continuum, the individual is either unaware of having problems or sees his problems as outside himself. As he moves on the process continuum, he begins to talk about his problems in the past, as Winnie, in this excerpt, tells how she dealt with her brother's anger: "I listened when he got mad. That was the only time that he ever expressed any hostility at all. And it was a very real moment." Movement on this strand can be seen as the individual begins to own his part in contributing to the problem, although he still speaks of problems in the past. Winnie says, "Why was I so irritated at you? What was it? Was it really the reasons that I was giving you all: and then I thought, you act like my brother.... Then I knew what was at the bottom of the problem, but it would take me so long to get there. But then at least I know something now that I didn't know this morning." The upper portion of the continuum is represented by behavior in which the individual has immediate access to his problems as he senses them in his experiencing. He understands that the problems are *his* and seeks the solution within himself, as in this excerpt:

Winnie: This feeling in myself has come in and has just sort of barred everything else out temporarily. It isn't that I don't feel. ... If I stop and think about it, I feel the way about all of you that I did this morning; but this is immediate, and it is right now, and it is a problem for me, and it is something I'm going to have to work out. I just don't know quite how.

Interpersonal relationships

The final strand on the process continuum has to do with the way in which the individual relates to others. At the lower end of the continuum the person is very fearful of close relationships and wants to know how he should behave in the situation as Keith expressed, "If I knew what to do, I would do it and get it over with." The midpoint of the continuum is represented by behaviors in which the individual cautiously tests the relationship, frequently rationalizing why it is unsafe still to trust the relationship. Roz exemplifies this point in the following excerpt:

Roz: Well, this is how I've always been. I've formed relationships at one point, and then there's a wall there, and I think it's for the same reasons as you have said. Maybe if he sees too much of me, he'll see these things about me that I don't like and he won't like, and by his not liking it he'll just make it that much clearer to myself. ... But I'm not satisfied with relationships that end just there.

As the individual moves toward the upper end of the continuum, he is able to express his feelings in a relationship as they occur. Roz says at the end of the group:

Roz: I love you [because] you have responded so warmly to me and you have given me love. I sort of put you up here because of that. I think when I walk away from here I know that you will be a part of me, and I'll always remember you and the experience.

A person's words are one manifestation of his inner self that we can record and analyze. His inner feelings, the nuances of his experiencing, are not directly available to us. The *process theory* is an attempt to identify inward processes through the quality or type of verbalization, the way an individual reports himself. Studies using the Process Scale have reliably correlated process movement in therapy with outcome, as well as correlating positive process movement with the presence of the three therapist conditions: genuineness, caring, and understanding. The theory is a beginning toward understanding human growth and change, and hopefully these descriptions will generate investigations into their refinement.

APPLICATIONS

Problems

The person-centered approach is theoretically applicable to any relationship where the persons want to understand each other and want to be understood; where the persons are willing to reveal themselves to some degree; and where the persons want to enhance their own growth. These characteristics are present in a wide variety of relationships, and consequently the person-centered principles are being used in more and more situations. The elements of genuineness, empathic understanding, and positive regard promote and enhance a healthy relationship regardless of the circumstances in which they are present. Because they are simple, understandable attitudes, available at least to some degree to any human being, they can be practiced by anyone and are not the exclusive acquisi-

tion of professionals through long years of training. The fact that they are simple and understandable does not mean they are easy to achieve; their acquisition is not guaranteed by professional training and in fact may take much longer than professional training.

Four categories contain most of the situations in which the person-centered principles are applied. These four are *(a)* counseling situations, *(b)* human-relations training situations, *(c)* small group situations, and *(d)* projects on institutional change. There is some overlapping of these four, but they are considered separately.

Counseling and psychotherapy

The person-centered approach was developed as an approach to *counseling* troubled individuals, and this probably remains the most widespread application of the theory. It has been used successfully in individual counseling with all diagnostic groups: normals, neurotics, and psychotics. It is used extensively in pastoral counseling and in school counseling. It has been used in play therapy with children and in speech therapy, and in marriage and family counseling.

Human-relations training

Person-centered principles are used extensively in training professionals and nonprofessionals who work with people. This includes all levels of workers in the schools. It includes social workers, nurses, physicians, and aides to all these professions. It includes volunteer workers like those in the Peace Corps and VISTA and volunteers for various charitable agencies, particularly the newer agencies that do telephone counseling with troubled persons and that frequently serve persons in crisis situations. It includes training programs for leadership in many areas.

Small groups

Another application of person-centered principles is in groups such as personal growth groups or encounter groups and in groups whose goal is tension reduction in a given situation. Sometimes the participants have their work field in common, such as groups for teachers, business executives, or ministers. Other groups are formed for married couples, families, women, or students, groups whose members have a common interest. Tension-reduction groups have been formed for labor-management disputes, black-white and other ethnic relations, student-faculty concerns, and other polarized situations. In all these groups, the emphasis is on honest communication and understanding.

Institutional change

A fourth area in which the person-centered approach is used is in institutions seeking either orderly change or enhancement of human relations. This has included an entire school system made up of elementary schools, high schools, and a college. It has included faculties of individual schools and of an entire inner-city school system. It has included industrial plants, businesses, churches, institutions such as the YWCA/YMCA and the Boys Club. It has included government agencies at many levels.

Evaluation

This section does not pretend to be a complete review of the research on person-centered therapy. An overview of person-centered research and its influence on theory and therapy has been published (Shlien & Zimring, 1970). A few historical highlights given here will demonstrate the interaction of the factors mentioned above in the evaluation of the person-centered approach.

Rogers in 1940 was the first to use electrical recording of entire cases for study and training. This was before tape recordings were invented. With recordings, the person-centered group was able to make detailed studies of client change and therapist response and of the relationship between the two.

An outgrowth of recordings was the monumental study *Psychotherapy and Personality Change* (Rogers & Dymond, 1954), which reports an intensive, multifaceted look at the complete recordings plus pre-, post-, and follow-up testing of 25 clients and controls.

The satisfaction of the theory and methods with disturbed or neurotic individuals led to a five-year study with schizophrenic patients in a state mental hospital. The results are reported in *The Therapeutic Relationship with Schizophrenics* (Rogers, 1967b). The therapists found that in working with schizophrenics, they were forced to rely more heavily on their own experiencing in the relationship. They began to state what they were feeling during the therapy hour, and frequently their reporting seemed to precipitate movement in their clients. This has been illustrated in the earlier portion of this chapter, "A Silent Young Man." Later, research evidence confirmed that those therapists who were more able to be genuine than others had clients who made significantly more positive gain in therapy and who operated at higher process levels. This influenced person-centered therapists in general to enlarge their concept of genuineness to a more active, intuitive self-reporting.

Rogers then investigated the effect of person-centered principles in relationships with normal individuals. The vehicle for his study was the intensive small group or encounter group. Rogers sent questionnaires to over 500 persons who had participated in encounter groups under his direction. The results of his investigation are reported in *Carl Rogers on Encounter Groups* (1970). The obvious potency of the experience in an encounter group led Rogers to consider the effect such groups would have on an institution. A person-centered group carried out a three-year research study of intensive small groups on educational institutions (Rogers, 1969).

Interest in the changes institutions in our society are undergoing led this group to form in 1968 an experimental institution, the Center for Studies of the Person. This is a group of some 40 members, including psychologists, sociologists, anthropologists, and journalists. They are more a psychological community than a working community. Each individual is responsible for his own income. The weekly "staff" meetings provide for exchange of ideas on the wide variety of projects members are engaged in, for personal exploration, and for touching base with the family group. One of the goals of CSP is to provide an atmosphere in which members can create and carry out the most imaginative projects possible, without the restrictions of traditional institutions.

The pattern that emerges in this description is one of natural growth. A group of researchers immerse themselves in one area of application of person-centered theory. The area is thoroughly researched, spawning new aspects of theory and method. The study reaches a natural completion, and the group moves to another area. The years of searching for explanations and understanding of the phenomena of individual therapeutic change were amply rewarded by the refinements of research discoveries. The legacy of person-centered therapy is embodied in the studies of the scores of researchers who have been associated with Rogers.

Treatment

In the earlier section on "Problems," four areas of the application of person-centered theory were considered. This section describes some specific examples of ways in which the theory is translated into practical application in those four areas.

Counseling and psychotherapy

The primary emphasis in individual therapy is the ongoing experiencing of the client. The therapist focuses on that experiencing to understand empathically the client's internal frame of reference. At the same time, he is aware of his own inner self and genuinely communicates those feelings. He seeks to maintain a balance between his understanding and caring for his client and communication of his own experiencing of the relationship, a balance that is optimally facilitative of the client's awareness of his inner self. The balance is determined by the therapist's intuitive grasp of the relationship and depends on his own creative ability to be fully present.

Personal growth group

The person-centered therapist's behavior in a personal growth group is not unlike his activity in an individual setting. His attitudes toward the group members convey empathic understanding, nonpossessive caring, and genuine expression of his own ongoing feeling process. He does not "play" himself; he *is* genuinely himself, bringing all of his knowledge, experience, and his affective humanness to the relationships in the group.

The group has a wide and varied application. Participation in an intensive small group appears to facilitate therapeutic movement. In a study by Betty Meador (1971), a group of normal individuals, initially strangers, met for 16 hours over the period of a weekend. Blind ratings by independent judges found that each individual moved closer to his inner experiencing, became more able to express congruently what he was feeling, and became more real in his relationships.

The La Jolla Program: Human-relations training

The La Jolla Program is a training experience for persons who lead small groups in their work. Participants come from a variety of professions, but the majority have been school counselors, ministers, priests, nuns, social workers, teachers, administrators, and psychotherapists. Three aspects of the program convey its basic character. First, there is an emphasis on the participants having firsthand experience in a variety of groups; second, the model of leadership is that the individual rely on himself as a person, not on his expertise; and, third, the 100 or more participants experience the building of a community among themselves.

The Project for Educational Innovation: Institutional change

The Project for Educational Innovation sought to apply person-centered principles in an educational system that was seeking positive, productive change, which included several elementary schools, a high school, and a college. A plan was designed that proposed holding intensive small groups for faculties of the individual schools, for students, for parents, for administrators, and then for mixtures of these categories (Rogers, 1967a). The plan included a research component. The hypothesis of the study was that participation in the small groups would release the creative potential of the participants and enhance their human relationships, and that results would be seen in the human relations and creativity in the classroom, in the curriculum, and in the attitudes of all groups toward the school and toward each other.

Space does not permit a more detailed description of this project and its results. It can be found in Rogers's book *Freedom to Learn* (1969) and in Morton Shaevitz and Don Barr's chapter "Encounter Groups in a Small College" (1972). The results, although complex, were generally positive. There was a loosening of the categories "student," "faculty," "administrator" and more communication among individuals in all these groups. There was more student participation in decision making at all levels and more student-centered teaching. There was more experimentation and innovation by teachers in the classroom. After the project was finished, some of the school personnel themselves obtained a grant to continue the small groups, using some of the facilitators from the research group and some from other sources. Their desire to continue having the groups was a confirmation both of the value the school personnel placed on the groups and of their willingness and ability to continue the process of change on their own.

The four situations described in this section to which the person-centered approach has been applied—individual therapy, group therapy, human-relations training, and institutional change—reflect the broadening definition of the concept *psychotherapy*. Person-centered theory holds that the process of human growth is potentially ongoing in the most withdrawn schizophrenic and in the most productive "normal" member of society. The three conditions of person-centered therapy (Rogers, 1969, p. 14) have been found to be conducive to growth in many different situations and appear to be generally applicable whether the client is an extremely troubled individual or a teacher in an elementary school. In any case, the goal of the person-centered therapy is the same: the release of the self-actualizing forces in the individual.

Management

The following is a brief account of the *management* of therapy under the headings "the setting," "relationships," and "patient problems."

The setting

Because the person-centered approach is used in a wide variety of situations, no one typical physical setting would be generally applicable. The setting for a one-to-one client-therapist relationship might be a traditional office, and a group of Peace Corps Volunteers might meet in a trailer on an Indian reservation. Generally, person-centered therapists do not have specific requirements for the physical setting other than minimal needs for comfort and quiet. The setting chosen for a particular activity depends on the activity and the persons involved, whether individual or group therapy, and whether the clients are students, businessmen, women, a group of faculty, administrators, couples, and so forth.

Relationships

The relationship between client and therapist in person-centered therapy has been amply described in the preceding sections. Perhaps a word could be said about how a therapist might open an interview with a client or with a group.

In beginning an interview with an individual, the therapist speaks out of his attitude of being immediately present to the client. He might say, "This is our first hour together. I hope we can get to know each other a little bit in some meaningful way today." His emphasis in whatever he says is on the relationship and not on the "problem" of the client. Thus he immediately establishes himself as a person relating to another, not as an expert with answers.

A person-centered therapist beginning a group would speak out of the same attitude of presence to the immediate situation. His remarks come from himself, his awareness at the moment. He might say, "We have sixteen hours to spend together. We can make of that time whatever we want. I don't know what is going to happen. I am looking forward to our interacting with one another, to our getting to know each other." In beginning a group, the therapist relies on himself, his ongoing, inner experiencing, as the resource for his participation, just as he depends on this resource throughout the group.

Patient problems

The only patient problem discussed in this section is suicide threat. There are, perhaps, certain generalizations that can be drawn from the manner of handling such threats, which can be applied to other "patient problems."

Rogers has reported on the way in which suicide threats were handled at the Counseling Center at The University of Chicago. When a counselor reported that one of his clients threatened suicide, the counselor was asked, "Are you comfortable in your relationship with your client?" His answer might be, "Yes, but I realize that the Counseling Center will be held responsible if anything happens." Rogers would then answer, "If you are comfortable in the relationship, OK. Deal with your client as a person. I will stand behind you if anything happens." On the other hand, if the counselor said he felt worried and uneasy, the client would be transferred to another counselor or psychiatrist.

Of the thousands of clients seen at the Chicago Counseling Center, there never was a single suicide by a client in therapy.

These guidelines can be applied to

whatever "problem" a client presents. If he feels comfortable in the relationship, he should treat his client as a person, not as the problem he is presenting, and the therapist should honestly react to the person with his intuitive awareness.

CASE EXAMPLE

Introduction

In 1964 Carl Rogers was filmed in a half-hour interview with a woman client for a film series, *Three Approaches to Psychotherapy* (1965). That interview contains many of the elements of person-centered therapy discussed in this chapter and is a typical example of the person-centered way of working. Since the film is available for rental or purchase (Rogers, 1965), it also gives the reader an opportunity to see and hear person-centered therapy in action.

Rogers had never seen the woman before the interview and knew his contact with her would be limited to the half hour before the cameras. In his filmed introduction to the interview, he describes the way he will hope to be with her. He says he will, if he is fortunate, first of all, be real, try to be aware of his own inner feelings and to express them in ways that will not impose these feelings on her. Second, he hopes he will be caring of her, prizing her as an individual, accepting her. Third, he will try to understand her inner world from the inside; he will try to understand not just the surface meanings, but the meanings just below the surface. Rogers says if he is successful in holding these three attitudes, he expects certain things to happen to the client, expectations based on his experience and his research. He expects she will move from a remoteness from her inner experiencing to a more immediate awareness and expres-

sion of it; from disapproving of parts of her self to greater self-acceptance; from a fear of relating to relating to him more directly; from holding rigid, black and white constructs of reality to holding more tentative constructs; and from seeing the locus of evaluation outside herself to finding the locus of evaluation in her own inner experiencing.

The fact that the interview lasted for only one-half hour and the client was seen by the therapist only this one time emphasizes that the person-centered approach depends on the here-and-now attitudes of the therapist, attitudes as valid and constant in a brief interaction as over a long period. If the person-centered equation predicts a change in the way of being of a client, theoretically that change could be apparent even in a half-hour interview. A look at this brief interview supports the person-centered prediction.

The Interview

The interview is with a young woman, Gloria, a 30-year-old divorcee. The first portion of the interview concerns the problem Gloria presents initially, that she has not been honest with her nine-year-old daughter Pammy about the fact that she has had sexual relationships with men since her divorce. Gloria has always been honest with her children and is feeling great conflict over having lied to Pammy. She wants to know whether telling Pammy the truth about her sexual relationships will affect Pammy adversely.

At the very beginning Gloria tells Rogers, "I almost want an answer from you. I want you to tell me if it would affect her wrong if I told her the truth, or what." Later, on two occasions, she asks again for a direct answer to her question. Clearly, she wants an "authority" to tell her what to do. Rogers's responses assure her that he understands her dilemma and guides her to her own resources for answering. After each time that she asks the question and hears the response, Gloria explores her own feelings a little more deeply.

To her first request, Rogers replies, "And it's this concern about her (Pammy) and the fact that you really aren't—that this open relationship that has existed between you, now you feel it's kind of vanished?" and after Gloria's reply he says, "I sure wish I could give you the answer as to what you should tell her." "I was afraid you were going to say that," she says. Rogers replies, "Because what you really want *is* an answer."

Gloria begins to explore her relationship with Pammy and concludes that she feels real uncertainty whether or not Pammy would accept her "devilish" or "shady" side. Gloria finds she is not certain she accepts that part of herself. Again she asks Rogers for an answer: "You're just going to sit there and let me stew in it and I want more." Rogers replies, "No, I don't want to let you just stew in your feelings, but on the other hand, I also feel this is the kind of very private thing that I couldn't possibly answer for you. But I sure as anything will try to help you work toward your own answer. I don't know whether that makes any sense to you, but I mean it." Gloria says she can tell he really does mean it and again begins to explore her feelings, this time focusing more on the conflict she herself feels between her actions and her inner standards. Shortly, she again says, "I want you very much to give me a direct answer. . . ." Rogers replies:

I guess, I am sure this will sound evasive to you, but it seems to me that perhaps the person you are not being fully honest with is you, because I was very much struck by the fact that

you were saying, "If I feel all right about what I have done, whether it's going to bed with a man or what, if I really feel all right about it, then I do not have any concern about what I would tell Pam or my relationship with her."

To this Gloria answers:

Right. All right. Now I hear what you are saying. Then all right, then I want to work on accepting me then. I want to work on feeling all right about it. That makes sense. Then that will come natural and then I won't have to worry about Pammy. . . .

This statement indicates that Gloria has assimilated a real insight, an understanding that the solution to her problem is in herself rather than in an authoritative opinion on how knowledge of her sex life will affect Pammy.

From this point in the interview she focuses on her inner conflict. She tells Rogers what she "wishes he would tell her" and then says she can't quite take the risk of being the way she wants to be with her children "unless an authority tells me that. . . ." Rogers says with obvious feeling, "I guess one thing that I feel very keenly is that it's an awfully risky thing to *live*. You'd be taking a chance on your relationship with her and taking a chance on letting her know who you are, really." Gloria says she wishes very strongly that she could take *more risks*, that she could act on her own feelings of rightness without always needing encouragement from others. Again she says what she'd like to do in the situation with Pammy, and then adds, "Now I feel like 'now that's solved'—and I didn't even solve a thing; but I feel relieved."

Gloria: I do feel like you have been saying to me—you are not giving me advice, but I do feel like you are saying, "You know what pattern you want to follow,

Gloria, and go ahead and follow it." I sort of feel a backing up from you.

Rogers: I guess the way I sense it, you've been telling me that you know what you want to do, and yes, I do believe in backing up people in what they want to do. It's a little different slant than the way it seems to you.

Gloria's expressing the feeling, "Now that's solved—and I didn't even solve a thing but I feel relieved," exemplifies an awareness of inner experiencing, a felt meaning she has not yet put into words. She "feels relieved" as though her problem is solved. Therapeutic movement has occurred in her inner self before she understands its explicit meaning. It is interesting that she says in the same speech, "I feel a backing up from you." She *feels* the support of Rogers's empathic understanding and acceptance of her. From the person-centered point of view there is a relationship between her feeling understood and valued and her movement from seeking the locus of evaluation outside herself to depending on her own inner feeling of "rightness" for a solution to her problem.

The next portion of the interview involves Gloria's experience of her own inner valuing processes and the conflicts she sometimes feels. She explains her use of the word *utopia*, which refers to times she is able to follow her inner feelings:

When I do follow a feeling and I feel this good feeling inside of me, that's sort of utopia. That's what I mean. That's the way I like to feel whether it's a bad thing or a good thing. But I feel right about *me*.

Whether the action she takes might be thought of as "good" or "bad," if she feels right about it, that's "utopia." Rogers's response that in those moments she must feel "all in one piece" brings tears to Gloria's eyes, for those moments are all too few. In the midst of her weeping, she says:

You know what else I was just thinking? I . . . a dumb thing . . . that all of a sudden while I was talking to you, I thought, "Gee, how nice I can talk to you and I want you to approve of me and I respect you, but I miss that my father couldn't talk to me like you are." I mean, I'd like to say, "Gee, I'd like you for my father." I don't even know why that came to me.

Rogers: You look to me like a pretty nice daughter. But you really do miss the fact that you couldn't be open with your own dad.

Gloria is now quite close to her inner experiencing, allowing her tears to flow as she thinks of rare moments of "utopia" and then expressing a feeling that comes into awareness of positive affection for Rogers. She then explores her relationship with her father, maintaining the same closeness to her inner feelings, as she says, "You know, when I talk about it, it feels more flip. If I just sit still a minute, it feels like a great big hurt down there."

Gloria looks at and feels her deep inner hurt over her relationship to her father. She has moved significantly from seeking a solution outside herself to a problem with her children to looking inward at a painful hurt. She says she tries to soothe the hurt through relationships with fatherly men, pretending they are her father, as she is doing with Rogers.

Rogers: I don't feel that's pretending.
Gloria: Well, you're *not* really my father.
Rogers: No. I meant about the real close business.
Gloria: Well, see, I sort of feel that's

pretending too, because I can't expect you to feel very close to me. You don't know me that well.

Rogers: All I can know is what I am feeling, and that is I feel close to you in this moment.

Here Rogers presents himself as he really is, offering Gloria the experience of genuine caring from another, an experience she has felt deprived of in the relationship with her real father. Shortly after this exchange, the interview ends.

Evaluation

In Rogers's filmed introduction to the interview he says he hopes to be real, caring, and understanding with his client. If he succeeds, he says, he expects Gloria will make therapeutic movement in certain explicit ways. Examples from the excerpts quoted in the previous paragraphs demonstrate the therapist's attitudes as well as the client's process.

First, Rogers hopes to be his real self, to be aware of his inner feelings and express them in ways that will not impose them on Gloria. Several examples of the therapist's genuineness occur. In Gloria's insistence on his answering her question, he maintains his belief in *her* ability to find the answer within herself. His strong inner feeling that he repeatedly expresses is that he does not have the answer for her. Still, in blocking this road, he opens another in which he just as firmly believes. He offers repeatedly to help her find the answer in herself.

The intensity of his genuineness and presence in the relationship is readily apparent from watching the film. The strength of his feelings comes through when he says, ". . . it's an awfully risky thing to *live*," or when he clearly expresses his inner self, "All I can know is

what I am feeling, and that is I feel close to you in this moment." The quality of the therapist's genuineness is pervasive throughout this interview. The attitude of genuineness is not to be turned on and off, but is a state of presence and awareness of oneself that is constantly there.

Rogers expresses his caring for his client both directly and indirectly. He tells her directly, when she says she'd like him for her father, "You look to me like a pretty nice daughter." Indirectly, his attitude is one of attentiveness and acceptance of all she says. He makes himself openly available to her to facilitate her search for an answer, an offer that implies his confidence in her potential. Gloria is aware of his acceptance when she says, "I sort of feel a backing up from you." Her awareness of his caring is as necessary to her movement as his expression of the attitude.

In being understanding, Rogers says he hopes to understand not just the surface meanings but the meanings below the surface of the client's awareness. He says to Gloria, "It seems to me that perhaps the person you are not being fully honest with is you. Because I was very much struck by the fact that you were saying, 'If I feel all right about what I have done, whether it's going to bed with a man or what, if I really feel all right about it, then I do not have any concern about what I would tell Pam or my relationship with her.' " Gloria at this point becomes aware of her outward-directed search for an answer and turns to look inside herself. Rogers, in understanding her inner struggle with accepting herself, makes explicit what Gloria has been implying. Her hearing his statement precipitates a real insight for her, as though a light turns on and she understands where she must go for answers, namely, into herself. Another clear example of the therapist's understanding precipitating movement occurs as Rogers replies to Gloria's description of her "utopia" feeling. He says, "I sense that in those utopian moments, you really feel kind of whole. You feel all in one piece." Gloria becomes very tearful, lets her feelings flow, and is surprised by the warmth she feels toward Rogers and the hurt she feels in her relationship with her father. In these examples, the importance of the therapist's understanding for the client's growth becomes apparent. Still, understanding without genuineness and caring seems sterile, and the interrelatedness of the three attitudes is again clear.

The therapeutic movement the client makes follows the direction and manner that Rogers initially described. First, he says she will move from a remoteness from her feelings to an immediate awareness and expression of them. She does in fact begin the interview wanting an answer to a troubling question and does move to a point toward the end where her feelings are flowing into awareness and she is expressing them as they occur. At one point she says, concerning her wanting a father like Rogers, "I don't even know why that came to me." She is allowing her feelings to come into expression without censoring, questioning, or even knowing where they are coming from.

Rogers says she will move from disapproving of herself toward self-acceptance. At the beginning, Gloria says she is not sure she accepts her 'shady" or "devilish" side. Later, she very explicitly asks to work on accepting herself and spends much of the remaining time exploring the nuances of her self-acceptance.

Another strand on which she moves is from a fear of relating to the therapist to relating more directly. Initially Gloria says, "I wish I weren't so nervous," and holds Rogers at a distance by making him in her eyes an expert, an authority. Her attitude softens to the point toward the end when she can say, "I wish I had you for a father."

Her search for an authoritative answer exemplifies another strand on which she shows therapeutic movement, her construing of reality. Initially, she believes there is a true answer that will solve her problem. She construes reality in this black and white fashion. Later, she tentatively considers relying on her own inner experiencing for solutions, as she says, "I *wish* I could take *more risks*." Finally, she describes the utopian experience of feeling so sure of herself that whatever she does come out of her inner experience and feels "right." This same example demonstrates the therapeutic process on the final strand Rogers mentions, that of moving from finding the locus of evaluation outside oneself to finding it in one's inner self.

The quality of this interview is like a piece of music, which begins on a thin persistent note and gradually adds dimensions and levels until the whole orchestra is playing. The intuitive interaction and response of the therapist is not unlike the interplay in a creative improvisation. Whatever wisdom science can bring to how the instruments are made and which combinations make for harmony and growth will greatly enrich the players, but may we never lose sight of the primacy of the creative human beings making the music.

There is a postscript to this brief interview. Almost 20 years have passed since the film was made. Once or twice each year, Gloria has written Rogers telling him of important events in her life, of times she felt lost or sad as well as fulfilled and growing. Her memory of the interview is of a warm, real, human contact, moments shared that were fulfilling. Rogers once answered a counseling student who asked what you do if you only have a short time with a client, "If you have only thirty minutes, then give thirty minutes worth."

SUMMARY

The theoretical base of person-centered therapy is a belief in the "exquisite rationality" of human growth under optimal conditions. The actualizing tendency in man is a powerful force equipped with its own rhythm and direction.

The task of the therapist is to facilitate the client's awareness of and trust in his own actualizing processes. The primary discovery of person-centered therapy is that of the attitudes of the therapist that create the optimal climate in which the client can allow his own growth to unfold. The process of therapy is truly centered in the client whose inner experiencing dictates the pace and direction of the therapeutic relationship.

The attitude of uncompromising trust in the growth processes of individuals is as much a value system as it is a guide for therapy. As such, it is contrary to the prevailing values of the schools, the family, the church, business, and other institutions in this country. The predominant attitude in these institutions is one of cautious delimitation and an implicit skepticism of the process of human growth. One has only to imagine a family or school that might adopt an attitude of uncompromising trust in the growth process of its members in an atmosphere of genuineness, caring, and understanding to appreciate the contrast with the majority of families and schools.

It is possible that the influence of person-centered theory will be felt to a greater extent on the institutions of this country in the future, more than in the profession of psychotherapy. This is already true to some extent. The number of individuals in education and religion, for example, who are adopting person-centered principles is apparently increasing each year.

The tentative conclusion one could draw is that three decades of person-centered therapy, research, and writing offer ample statement of a rather radical value stance, one that advocates complete trust in individual growth and development under stated conditions. As such, person-centered theory presents a compelling invitation, not only to the therapist in a client-therapist relationship, but to human clusters of all shapes, sizes, and persuasions.

ANNOTATED BIBLIOGRAPHY

Rogers, C. R. *Client-centered therapy.* Boston: Houghton Mifflin, 1951.

This book is the first major formulation of the person-centered point of view. It covers earlier views on the three therapist attitudes, the therapy relationship as experienced by the client, and the process of therapy itself. It indicates how person-centered therapy principles can be applied in play therapy, group therapy, administration, and teaching. There is a chapter on the training of therapists. The final chapter contains an initial formulation of the theory of therapy and personality. It is a good first reading.

Rogers, C. R. A theory of therapy, personality, and interpersonal relationships, as developed in the client-centered framework. In S. Koch (Ed.), *Psychology: A study of a science,* Vol. III. *Formulations of the person and the social context.* New York: McGraw-Hill, 1959, pp. 184-256.

This is not easy reading. It is a tightly woven, comprehensive statement of the conditions for and the outcomes of effective therapy, a theory of the development of personality, and a general theory of interpersonal relationships. Because it is stated in carefully defined terms, the theory as stated in this article has been the source of many research hypotheses. Also, the article contains a plea for the development of a science more suited to the study of the whole person.

Rogers, C. R. *On becoming a person.* Boston: Houghton Mifflin, 1961.

This is Rogers's best known book. It contains much personal material, the often-reprinted chapter on the characteristics of the helping relationship, and a careful formulation of the process of therapy. It presents the philosophy behind the person-centered point of view. It faces squarely the dilemmas involved in conducting the scientific investigation of subjective phenomena. Other material includes teaching and learning and the relevance of the approach to family and group tensions. Questions are raised about the place of the individual in the world view being developed in the behavioral sciences. Readers respond especially to the highly personal character of some of the material and to the excerpts from recorded case material.

Rogers, C. R. *Carl Rogers on personal power: Inner strength and its revolutionary impact.* New York: Delacorte Press, 1977.

In this book, the person-centered approach is presented as bringing about a quiet revolution in the helping professions, education, marriage and family relationships, and administration. It has developed beginning models for resolving intercultural tensions. One of the most widely read chapters presents a complete picture of a 16-day, intensive person-centered workshop from the planning stages to outcome. There is a case example of a quiet revolution in a day camp. There is also a chapter describing the struggles and successes of a couple involved in an open marriage. A political

base for the person-centered approach is found in the actualizing tendency that provides a theoretical underpinning. An important chapter presents the emerging person as spearhead of the quiet revolution. This book more than any of the others shows the far-reaching implications of the person-centered approach.

Rogers, C. R., & Dymond, R. (Eds.). *Psychotherapy and personality change.* Chicago: University of Chicago Press, 1954.

This is a full report of a major research project on the outcomes of person-centered therapy. The chapters are written by many of the research staff who participated in the project. It includes the first major use of the Q Sort in measuring change in self-concept. The project involved the use of carefully selected control groups, the transcription of all interviews in all the research cases, and the assembling of large amounts of data from various personality and behavior measures. The study was outstanding in presenting data on one case of effective psychotherapy and equally complete data on a failure case. The book is regarded as a landmark in psychotherapy research.

CASE READINGS

Rogers, C. R. *Counseling and psychotherapy.* Boston: Houghton Mifflin, 1942.

A classic in the field of psychotherapy. Rogers spends a good deal of the contents of this book in the analysis of the treatment of a college student.

Rogers, C. R. The case of Mrs. Oak. In C. R. Rogers and R. F. Dymond (Eds.), *Psychotherapy and personality change.* Chicago: University of Chicago Press, 1954. (Also found in abridged form in C. R. Rogers, *On becoming a person.* Boston: Houghton Mifflin, 1961. Also in D. Wedding & R. J. Corsini [Eds.], *Great cases in psychotherapy.* Itasca, Ill.: F. E. Peacock Publishers, 1979.)

Another classic case with more mature analysis showing how Rogers perceives therapy and his insightfulness in dealing with clients.

REFERENCES

Barrett-Lennard, G. Dimensions of perceived therapist response related to therapeutic change. Doctoral dissertation, University of Chicago, 1959.

Barrett-Lennard, G. Dimensions of therapist response as causal factors in therapeutic change. *Psychological Monographs,* 1962, *76,* Whole No. 562.

Buber, M. *Pointing the way.* New York: Harper & Row, 1957.

Cartwright, D. Annotated bibliography of research and theory construction in client-centered therapy. *Journal of Counseling Psychology,* 1957, *4,* 82-100.

Clark, J. V., & Culbert, S. A. Mutually therapeutic perception and self-awareness in a T-group. *Journal of Applied Behavioral Science,* 1965, *1,* 180-194.

Culbert, S. A. Trainer self-disclosure and member growth in two T-groups. *Journal of Applied Behavioral Science,* 1968, *4,* 47-73.

Emerson, R. W. "Divinity School Address," 1838.

Halkides, G. An experimental study of four conditions necessary for therapeutic personality change. Doctoral dissertation, University of Chicago, 1958.

Hart, J. T., & Tomlinson, T. M. (Eds.), *New directions in client-centered therapy.* Boston: Houghton Mifflin, 1970.

Holdstock, T. L., & Rogers, C. R. Person-centered theory. In R. J. Corsini & A. J. Marsella (Eds.), *Personality theories, research, and assessment.* Itasca, Ill.: F. E. Peacock Publishers, Inc., 1983.

Kirschenbaum, H. Application to the Guggenheim Foundation. Document prepared for the Guggenheim Foundation, December 1971.

McCleary, R. A., & Lazarus, R. S. Autonomic discrimination without awareness. *Journal of Personality,* 1949, *18,* 171-179.

Maslow, A. H. *Motivation and personality.* New York: Harper, 1954.

Meador, B. D. Individual process in a basic encounter group. *Journal of Counseling Psychology,* 1971, *18,* 70-76.

Peters, R. S. Review of C. R. Rogers, Freedom to Learn. *Interchange,* 1970, *1,* 111-114.

Raimy, V. C. The self-concept as a factor in counseling and personality organization. Doctoral dissertation, Ohio State University, 1943.

Rank, O. *Will therapy.* New York: Knopf, 1936.

Rogers, C. R. *The clinical treatment of the problem child.* Boston: Houghton Mifflin, 1939.

Rogers, C. R. *Counseling and psychotherapy.* Boston: Houghton Mifflin, 1942.

Rogers, C. R. *Client-centered therapy.* Boston: Houghton Mifflin, 1951.

Rogers, C. R. *Psychotherapy and personality change.* Chicago: University of Chicago Press, 1954.

Rogers, C. R. The necessary and sufficient conditions of therapeutic personality change. *Journal of Consulting Psychology,* 1957, *21,* 95-103.

Rogers, C. R. A process conception of psychotherapy. *American Psychologist,* 1958, *13,* 142-149.

Rogers, C. R. Client-centered therapy. In Silvano Arieti (Ed.), *American handbook of psychiatry,* Vol. 3. New York: Basic Books, 1959. (a) (Vol. 3, a *Supplement to the handbook,* published by Basic Books, 1966, pp. 183-200.)

Rogers, C. R. A theory of therapy, personality, and interpersonal relationships, as developed in the client-centered framework. In S. Koch (Ed.), *Psychology: A study of a science,* Vol. III. *Formulations of the person and the social context.* New York: McGraw-Hill, 1959, pp. 184-256. (b)

Rogers, C. R. *On becoming a person.* Boston: Houghton Mifflin, 1961. (a)

Rogers, C. R. The process equation of psychotherapy. *American Journal of Psychotherapy,* 1961, *15,* 27-45. (b)

Rogers, C. R. The actualizing tendency in relation to "motives" and to consciousness. In M. Jones (Ed.), *Nebraska symposium on motivation,* 1963. Lincoln, Neb.: University of Nebraska Press, 1963, pp. 1-24.

Rogers, C. R. Client-centered therapy, Film No. 1. In Everett Shostrom (Ed.), *Three approaches to psychotherapy.* (Three 16 mm. color motion pictures.) Santa Ana, Calif.: Psychological Films, 1965.

Rogers, C. R. A plan for self-directed change in an educational system. *Educational Leadership,* 1967, *24,* 717-731. (a)

Rogers, C. R. (Ed.) *The therapeutic relationship and its impact: A study of psychotherapy with schizophrenics.* With E. T. Gendlin, D. J. Kiesler, and C. Louax. Madison, Wisc.: University of Wisconsin

Press, 1967. (b)

Rogers, C. R. *Freedom to learn: A view of what education might become.* Columbus, Ohio: Charles E. Merrill, 1969.

Rogers, C. R. *Carl Rogers on encounter groups.* New York: Harper & Row, 1970.

Rogers, C. R. *On becoming partners: Marriage and its alternatives.* New York: Delacourte, 1972.

Rogers, C. R. *Carl Rogers on personal power.* New York: Delacorte, 1977.

Rogers, C. R. *A way of being.* Boston: Houghton Mifflin, 1980.

Rogers, C. R., & Dymond, R. F. (Eds.). *Psychotherapy and personality change.* Chicago: University of Chicago Press, 1954.

Rogers, C. R., & Rablen, R. A. A scale of process in psychotherapy. Manuscript, University of Wisconsin, 1958. (Available in mimeo form from Center for Studies of the Person, La Jolla, California.)

Shaevitz, M., & Barr, D. Encounter groups in a small college. In Lawrence Solomon and Betty Berzon (Eds.), *New perspectives on encounter groups.* San Francisco: Jossey-Bass, 1972.

Shlien, J. M., & Zimring, F. M. Research directives and methods in client-centered therapy. In J. T. Hart & T. M. Tomlinson (Eds.), *New directions in client-centered therapy.* Boston: Houghton Mifflin, 1970, 33-57.

Standal, S. The need for positive regard: A contribution to client-centered theory. Doctoral dissertation, University of Chicago, 1954.

Stephenson, W. *The study of behavior: Q-technique and its methodology.* Chicago: University of Chicago Press, 1953.

Tenenbaum, S. Review of *Freedom to learn. Education Leadership,* 1969, *27,* 1, 97-99.

Tomlinson, T. M. Three approaches to the study of psychotherapy: Process, outcome, and change. Doctoral dissertation, University of Wisconsin, 1962.

Tomlinson, T. M., & Hart, J. T., Jr. A validation study of the process scale. *Journal of Consulting Psychology,* 1962, *26,* 74-78.

Walker, A. M., Rablen, R. A., & Rogers, C. R. Development of a scale to measure process changes in psychotherapy. *Journal of Clinical Psychology,* 1960, *16,* 79-85.

Whyte, L. *The unconscious before Freud.* London: Tavistock Publications, 1960.

6

Rational-Emotive Therapy

ALBERT ELLIS

OVERVIEW

Rational-emotive therapy (RET), a theory of personality and a method of psychotherapy developed by Albert Ellis, a clinical psychologist, in the 1950s holds that when a highly charged emotional consequence (*C*) follows a significant activating event (*A*), *A* may seem to, but actually does not, cause *C*. Instead, emotional consequences are largely created by *B*—the individual's *belief system*. When an undesirable emotional consequence occurs, such as severe anxiety, this can usually be traced to the person's irrational beliefs, and when these beliefs are effectively disputed (at point *D*), by challenging them rationally, the disturbed consequences disappear and eventually cease to recur. From its inception, RET has viewed cognition and emotion integratively, with thought normally including and being sparked by some degree of desire or feeling and with feeling significantly including cognition (Ellis, 1962). It is therefore a comprehensive cognitive-affective behavioral theory and practice of psychotherapy.

Basic Concepts

The main propositions of rational-emotive therapy (RET) are:

1. People are born with a potential to be rational as well as irrational. They have predispositions to be self-preserving, to think about their thinking, to be creative, to be sensuous, to be interested in their fellows, to learn by mistakes, and to actualize their potentials for life and growth. They also have propensities to be self-destructive, to be short-range hedonists, to avoid thinking things through, to procrastinate, to repeat the same mistakes, to be superstitious, to be intolerant, to be perfectionistic and grandiose, and to avoid actualizing their potentials for growth.

2. People's tendency to irrational thinking, self-damaging habituations, wishful thinking, and intolerance is frequently exacerbated by their culture and their family group. Their suggestibility (or conditionability) is greatest during their early years, and consequently they are then most influenced by family and social pressures.

3. Humans tend to perceive, think, emote, and behave simultaneously. They therefore, at one and the same time, are cognitive, conative, and motoric. They rarely act without also cognizing, since their present sensations or actions are apprehended in a network of prior experiences, memories, and conclusions. They seldom emote without thinking, since their feelings include, and are usually triggered by, an appraisal of a given situation and its importance. They rarely act without perceiving, thinking, and emoting, since these processes provide them with

reasons for acting. Just as their "normal" behavior is a function of their perceiving, thinking, emoting, and acting, so, too, is their disturbed behavior. To understand self-defeating conduct, therefore, we had better understand how people perceive, think, emote, and act. To help them change their malfunctioning, it is usually desirable to use a variety of perceptual-cognitive, emotive-evocative, and behavioristic-reeducative methods in a full therapeutic armamentarium (Ellis, 1971, 1973b, 1976a, 1977a, 1982; Ellis & Grieger, 1977).

4. Although all the major psychotherapies employ a variety of cognitive, emotive, and desensitizing techniques, and although all (including many unscientific methods like witch doctoring and Christian Science) may help individuals who have faith and who work at applying them, they are probably not equally effective in terms of time and effort nor in terms of the elegance and long lastingness of the "solutions." Highly cognitive, active-directive, homework-assigning, and discipline-oriented therapies like RET are likely to be more effective, usually in briefer periods and with fewer sessions, than therapies that include less cognitive-active-disciplining methodologies.

5. Rational-emotive therapists do not believe a warm relationship between counselee and counselor is a necessary or a sufficient condition for effective personality change. They believe it is desirable for therapists to accept clients but criticize and point out the deficiencies of their *behavior*. RET therapists accept clients as fallible humans without necessarily giving *personal* warmth. They may use a variety of impersonal therapeutic methods, including didactic discussion, behavior modification, bibliotherapy, audiovisual aids, and activity-oriented homework assignments. To keep clients from becoming and remaining unduly dependent, RET therapists often deliberately use hardheaded methods of convincing clients that they had damned well better resort to more self-discipline.

6. Rational emotive therapists use role playing, assertion training, desensitization, humor, operant conditioning, suggestion, support, and a whole bag of other "tricks." As A. A. Lazarus (1981) points out in presenting "multimodal" behavior therapy, such wide-ranging methods are most effective in helping the client achieve a deep-seated cognitive change. RET is not really oriented toward symptom removal, except when it seems that this is the only kind of change likely to be accomplished with clients. It is primarily designed to induce people to examine and change some of their most basic values—particularly those values that keep them disturbance prone. If clients have a serious fear of failing on the job, the rational-emotive therapist does not merely help them to give up this particular symptom. Instead, the therapist usually tries to show them how to minimize their basic catastrophizing tendencies. The usual goal of RET, therefore, is not merely to eliminate clients' presenting symptoms but to help rid them of other symptoms as well and, more importantly, to modify their underlying symptom-creating propensities. There are really two basic forms of RET: (1) general RET, which is almost synonymous with cognitive-behavior therapy; and (2) preferential RET, which includes general RET but which also emphasizes cognitive or philosophic restructuring and which strives for the most elegant kind of solution to emotional disturbance. General RET tends to teach clients rational or appropriate behaviors. Preferential RET teaches them how to dispute irrational ideas and inappropriate behaviors and to internalize rules of logic and scientific method.

7. RET holds that virtually all serious

emotional problems directly stem from magical, empirically unvalidatable thinking; and that if disturbance-creating ideas are vigorously disputed by logico-empirical thinking, they can be eliminated or minimized and will ultimately cease to reoccur. No matter how defective people's heredity may be, and no matter what trauma they may have experienced, the *main* reason they now overreact or underreact to obnoxious stimuli (at point *A*) is because they *now* have some dogmatic, irrational, unexamined beliefs (at point *B*). Because these beliefs are unrealistic, they will not withstand objective scrutiny. They are essentially deifications or devil-ifications of themselves or others; and when empirically checked and logically assailed, they tend to evaporate. Thus, a woman with severe emotional difficulties does not merely believe it is *undesirable* if her love partner is rejecting. She tends to believe, also, that (1) it is *awful*; (2) she *cannot stand* it; (3) she *should not*, must not be rejected; (4) she will *never* be accepted by any desirable partner; (5) she is a *worthless person* because one lover has rejected her; and (6) she *deserves to be damned* for being so worthless. Such common covert hypotheses are nonsensical and devoid of empirical referents. They can be elicited and demolished by any scientist worth his or her salt; and the rational-emotive therapist is exactly that: an exposing and nonsense-annihilating scientist.

8. Rational-emotive psychology asserts that insights often do not lead to major personality change since, at best, they help people see that they do have emotional problems and that these problems have dynamic antecedents—presumably in the experiences that occurred during childhood. According to RET theory, this kind of insight is largely misleading. It is not the activating events (*A*) of people's life that "cause" dysfunctional emotional consequences (*C*); it is that they interpret these events unrealistically, and therefore have irrational beliefs (*B*) about them. The "real" cause of upsets, therefore, is themselves and not *what happens* to them (even though the experiences obviously have some influence over what they think and feel). In RET, insight no. 1—namely, that the person's self-defeating behavior is related to antecedent and understandable causes—is duly stressed; but clients are led to see these antecedents largely in terms of their own beliefs and not in terms of past or present activating events. Their therapist, moreover, also presses them to see and to employ two additional insights.

Insight no. 2 is the understanding that although they became emotionally disturbed (or, more accurately, *made* themselves disturbed) in the past, they are *now* upset because they *keep indoctrinating themselves* with the same kind of magical beliefs. These beliefs do not continue because people were once "conditioned" and so hold them "automatically." No! They still, here and now, *actively reinforce them*, by mixed-up thinking and foolish actions (or inactions); and it is their own present active self-propagandizations that truly keep them alive. Unless they fully admit and face their own responsibilities for the continuation of these irrational beliefs, it is unlikely they will uproot them.

Insight no. 3 is people's acknowledgment that since it is their own tendency to think crookedly that created emotional malfunctioning, and that since it is their own continuous reindoctrinations and habituations that keep this magical thinking extant *only hard work and practice* will correct these irrational beliefs—and keep them corrected. They had better admit that insights nos. 1 and 2 are not enough! Only repeated rethinking of their irrational beliefs and repeated actions designed to undo them are likely to extinguish or minimize them.

Other Systems

RET, which is different from most other schools of psychotherapy, largely eschews free association, much gathering of material about the client's past history, and dream analysis, all of which are considered to be mostly sidetracking and thus ineffectual. RET is not concerned with the presumable sexual origins of disturbance, nor with the Oedipus complex. When transference does occur in therapy, the rational therapist is likely to attack it, showing clients that transference phenomena tend to arise from the irrational belief that they must be loved by the therapist (and others), and that they had better surrender this foolish belief. Although RET practitioners are much closer to modern neoanalytic schools, such as those of Karen Horney, Erich Fromm, Wilhelm Stekel, Harry Stack Sullivan, and Franz Alexander, than to the Freudian school, they employ considerably more persuasion, philosophical analysis, activity homework assignments, and other directive techniques than practitioners of these schools generally use.

RET overlaps significantly with Adlerian theory, but departs from the Adlerian practice of stressing early childhood memories, of making considerable use of dream material, of insisting that social interest is the heart of therapeutic effectiveness. RET is much more specific than Adler's individual psychology in disclosing, analyzing, and attacking the concrete internalized beliefs that clients keep telling themselves to create and perpetuate their disturbance; and so it is closer in this respect to general semantic theory and to philosophical analysis than it is to individual psychology.

Adler contends that people have basic fictional premises and goals and that they generally proceed quite logically on the basis of these false hypotheses. RET, on the other hand, holds that people, when disturbed, may have both irrational premises and illogical deductions from these premises. Thus, in individual psychology, a male who has the unrealistic premise that he *should* be the king of the universe, but actually has only mediocre abilities, is shown that he is "logically" concluding that he is an utterly inferior person. But in RET this same individual, with the same irrational premise, is shown that in addition to this "logical" deduction he may also be making several other illogical conclusions: for example, (1) he should be king of the universe because he was once king of his own family; (2) his parents will be impressed by him only if he is outstandingly achieving and *therefore* he must achieve outstandingly; (3) if he cannot be king of the universe, he might as well do nothing and get nowhere in life; and (4) he deserves to suffer for not being the noble king that he *should be.*

RET has much in common with parts of the Jungian therapeutic outlook, especially in that it views clients holistically rather than only analytically; holds that the goal of therapy would better be growth and achievement of potential as well as relief of disturbed symptoms; and emphasizes individuality. In practice, however, RET deviates radically from Jungian treatment, because the Jungians are fairly psychoanalytic and are preoccupied with dreams, fantasies, symbol productions, and the mythological or archetypal contents of their clients' thinking—most of which the RET practitioner deems a waste of time, since these techniques are not too effective in showing clients what their irrational philosophic assumptions are and how these can be radically challenged and changed.

RET is in close agreement with person-centered or relationship therapy in one—and perhaps only one—way: They both emphasize what Stanley Standal and Carl Rogers call *unconditional positive regard* and what in rational-emotive psychology is called *full acceptance* or *tolerance*. Harry Bone (1968) points out that both RET and client-centered therapy have basically the same goal: helping people to refuse to condemn themselves even though they may be utterly unenthusiastic about some of their behavior. Rational therapists differ radically from the Rogerian therapist in that they actively *teach* (1) that blaming is the core of emotional disturbance; (2) that it leads to dreadful results; (3) that it is possible, although difficult, for humans to learn to avoid rating them*selves* even while continuing to rate their *performances*; and (4) that they can give up self-rating by challenging their magic-based (*must*urbatory), self-evaluating assumptions and by deliberately risking (through homework activity assignments) possible failures and rejections. The rational-emotive practitioner is more persuading, more didactic, and more information giving than the person-centered practitioner; and in these respects they are probably almost at opposite ends of the therapeutic continuum.

RET is in many respects an existential phenomenologically-oriented therapy, since rational-emotive goals overlap with the usual existentialist goals of helping clients to define their own freedom, cultivate individuality, live in dialogue with others, accept their experiencing as highly important, be fully present in the immediacy of the moment, and learn to accept limits in life. Many who call themselves existential therapists, however, are rather anti-intellectual, prejudiced against the technology of therapy, and confusingly nondirective, while RET makes much use of incisive logical analysis, clear-cut techniques (including behavior modification procedures), and a great deal of directiveness and teaching by the therapist.

RET has much in common with conditioning-learning therapy or behavior modification. Many behavior therapists, however, are mainly concerned with symptom removal and ignore the cognitive aspects of conditioning and decondical forms of operant conditioning or ditioning. RET is therefore closer to "broad-spectrum" or "multimodal" behavior modifiers—such as A. T. Beck (1976), M. R. Goldfried and G. C. Davison (1976), A. A. Lazarus (1981), M. J. Mahoney (1974), and D. H. Meichenbaum (1977)—than to therapists who mainly stick to classical forms of operant conditioning or symptom desensitization.

HISTORY

Precursors

The philosophic origins of rational-emotive therapy (RET) go back to the Stoic philosophers, particularly Epictetus and Marcus Aurelius. Although most early Stoic writings have been lost, their main gist has come down to us through Epictetus, who in the first century A.D. wrote in *The Enchiridion*: "Men are disturbed not by things, but by the view which they take of them."

The modern psychotherapist who was the main precursor of RET was Alfred Adler. "I am convinced," he stated, "that *a person's behavior springs from his ideas*" (Adler, 1964a. Italics in original). And:

"The individual ... does not relate himself to the outside world in a predetermined manner, as is often assumed. He relates himself always according to his own interpretation of himself and of his present problem. .... It is his attitude toward life which determines his relationship to the outside world" (Adler, 1964b). Adler (1931) put the A-B-C or S-O-R theory of human disturbance very neatly: "No experience is a cause of success or failure. We do not suffer from the shock of our experiences— the so-called *trauma*—but we make out of them just what suits our purposes. We are *self-determined* by the meaning we give to our experiences; and there is probably something of a mistake always involved when we take particular experiences as the basis of our future life. Meanings are not determined by situations, but we determine ourselves by the meanings we give to situations." In his first book on individual psychology, Adler's motto was *omnia ex opionione suspensa sunt* (Everything depends on opinion). It would be hard to state the essential tenets of RET more succinctly and accurately.

Other important precursors of the rational-emotive approach are Paul Dubois, Jules Dejerine, and Ernest Gaukler who used persuasive forms of psychotherapy with their clients. Alexander Herzberg was one of the inventors of homework assignments. Hippolyte Bernheim, Andrew Salter, and a host of other therapists have employed hypnosis and suggestion in a highly active-directive manner. Frederick Thorne created what he once called directive therapy. Franz Alexander, Thomas French, John Dollard, Neal Miller, Wilhelm Stekel, and Lewis Wolberg all practiced forms of psychoanalytically oriented psychotherapy that actually diverged so far in practice from the mainstays of Freudian theory that they more properly can be classified in the active-

directive therapy column and can in many ways be identified with RET.

In addition, a large number of individuals during the early 1950s, when RET was first being formulated, independently began to arrive at some theories and methodologies that significantly overlap with the methods subsequently outlined by Ellis (1957, 1962, 1971). These include Eric Berne, Rogelio Diaz-Guerrero, Jerome Frank, George Kelly, Abraham Low, E. Lakin Phillips, Julian Rotter, and Joseph Wolpe.

Beginnings

After practicing classical psychoanalysis and psychoanalytically oriented psychotherapy for several years, during the late 1940s and early 1950s, Ellis discovered that no matter how much insight his clients gained, or how well they seemed to understand the events of their early childhood and to be able to connect them with their present emotional disturbances, they rarely lost their presenting symptoms, and when they did, they still retained strong tendencies to create new ones. He eventually realized this was because they were not merely indoctrinated with irrational, mistaken ideas of their own worthlessness when they were very young (as virtually all the psychoanalytic theories of personality hold), but that they actively *reindoctrinated themselves* with the original taboos, superstitions, and irrationalities they had picked up (and *invented* as well as easily learned) during their childhood.

Ellis also discovered that as he pressed his clients to surrender the few basic irrational premises that invariably seemed to underlie their disturbed symptoms, they often tended to resist giving up these ideas. This was not, as the Freudians hypothesized, because they hated the therapist, or wanted to destroy themselves, or were still resisting parent images, but because they *naturally*, one might say *normally*, tended to *mus*turbate: to absolutistically demand (1) that they do well and win others' approval; (2) that people act considerately and fairly, and (3) that environmental conditions be unfrustrating and gratifying. Ellis concluded that humans are *self-talking* and *self-evaluating* and *self-sustaining*. They frequently take simple preferences—such as desires for love, approval, success, and pleasure—and misleadingly define them as needs. They thereby inevitably get into "emotional" difficulties.

Ellis thus found that people are not exclusively the products of social learning but rather that their so-called pathological symptoms are the result of *bio*social learning. *Because they are human* (and not because they are reared in specific family-centered ways), they tend to have strong, irrational, empirically unvalidatable ideas; and as long as they hold on to these ideas—which nearly all of them fairly consistently do—they tend to be what is commonly called "neurotic." These main irrational ideologies are not infinitely varied or hard to discover. They can be listed under a few simple headings; and once understood, they can be quickly uncovered by the rational-emotive way of classifying them.

Ellis also discovered these irrational assumptions were not effectively unblocked by most current psychotherapeutic techniques because they were so biosocially deep-rooted and so difficult for the average individual to surrender that weak methods were unlikely to budge them. Passive, nondirective methodologies (such as reflection of feeling and free association) rarely changed them. Warmth and support often helped clients live more "happily" with unrealistic notions. Suggestion or "positive thinking" sometimes enabled them to cover up and

live more "successfully" with underlying negative self-evaluations but seldom helped them get rid of these silly notions. Abreaction and catharsis frequently helped them to feel better but tended to reinforce rather than to eliminate these demands. Classic desensitizing sometimes relieved clients of anxieties and phobias but did not elegantly undermine their anxiety-arousing, phobia-creating fundamental philosophies.

What would work effectively, Ellis found in the early days of RET, to help rid a client of irrationalities was an active-directive, cognitive-emotive-behavioristic attack on major self-defeating value systems—not directed against clients but against their *unrealistic beliefs*. The essence of effective psychotherapy according to RET is full tolerance of people *as individuals* combined with a ruthless campaign against their self-defeating *ideas*, *traits*, and *performances*. Paraphrasing Clarence Darrow, "We respect the individual, but not his ideas."

As Ellis abandoned his previous psychoanalytic approaches, to become much more philosophical rather than psychological in his discussions of his clients' problems, and to push his clients to work actively against their major irrational premises, he found he obtained significantly better results (Ellis, 1962). Other therapists who began to employ RET in their own practice also found that when a difficult client, with whom various methods had been ineffectively employed, switched to rational-emotive procedures, more progress was made in a few weeks than in months or even years of the prior treatment. When RET methods were used with new clients, they frequently became significantly improved after as few as 3 to 10 sessions, even though they might have had serious disturbances of long-standing duration (Ellis & Abrahms, 1978).

Current Status

The Institute for Rational-Emotive Therapy, Inc., a nonprofit scientific and educational organization, was founded in 1959 to teach the principles of rational living. In 1968 The Institute for Rational-Emotive Therapy was chartered by the Regents of the University of the State of New York. With headquarters in New York City and branches in several cities in the United States and other countries, it conducts activities to disseminate the rational-emotive approach, including (1) adult education courses for adults in the principles of rational living; (2) postgraduate training programs; (3) moderate cost clinics for individual or group therapy; (4) special workshops, seminars, practica, and training marathons for professionals given regularly in various parts of the world, often in conjunction with scientific meetings; and (5) the publication of books, monographs, pamphlets, and a journal, *The Journal of Rational-Emotive Therapy*, in which the latest developments in the field of cognitive-emotive therapy are published.

The Institute for Rational-Emotive Therapy, 45 East 65th Street, New York, N.Y. 10021, has a register of hundreds of psychotherapists who have received training in RET. In addition, hundreds of other therapists mainly follow RET principles, and a still greater number use some of the major aspects of RET in their work. Cognitive restructuring, employed by almost all cognitive-behavior therapists today, mainly consists of RET.

Research studies
Many experiments have validated the main therapeutic hypotheses of RET. Ellis found the vast majority of these studies support important RET contentions. For example, (1) clients tend to receive more effective help from a highly active-directive than from a more passive psychotherapeutic approach. (2) Effective therapy importantly includes the therapist's strong challenge to clients' irrational philosophies and persuading them to adopt less self-defeating beliefs. (3) Efficient therapy includes activity-oriented homework assignments. (4) Abreaction and catharsis of dysfunctional emotions like anger may have temporary palliative effects but often prove iatrogenic in that they tend to reinforce the beliefs that people use to create these feelings; the rational disputing of these philosophies gives better and more lasting effects. (5) People largely choose to disturb themselves and can intentionally choose to surrender these disturbances. (6) Self-control has very strong cognitive, as well as behavioral, elements and effective therapy often consists of helping clients use cognitive-related self-management principles. (7) Helping clients believe they can cope with conditions of distress and stress constitute effective methods of psychotherapy. (8) A great deal of psychotherapy consists of cognitive diversion or distraction, which can be used for significant, if often inelegant, personality change. (10) Helping clients modify their beliefs helps them to make significant changes, which are more enduring than those achieved through other methods of therapy. (11) Effective psychotherapy provides clients, in a variety of ways, with information that can help them understand how they have disturbed themselves and what they can do to make themselves less disturbed. (12) Many effective methods of cognitive therapy exist, including modeling, roleplaying, skill training, and problem solving.

In addition, hundreds of clinical and research papers have appeared that present empirical evidence of the validity of RET's main theories of personality. Most of the experimental studies in this area have been done by psychologists who have no stake in substantiating RET. Many of these studies are reviewed and listed in Ellis (1982) and Ellis and Whiteley (1979). These research studies substantiate the following hypotheses: (1) Human thinking and emotion do not constitute two disparate or different processes, but significantly overlap. (2) Although activating events (*A*) significantly contribute to emotional and behavioral consequences (*C*), people's beliefs (*B*) about *A* more importantly and more directly "cause" *C*. (3) The kinds of things people say to themselves, as well as the form in which they say these things, significantly affect their emotions and behavior and often lead them to feel emotionally disturbed. (4) Humans not only think and think about their thinking but also think about thinking about their thinking. Whenever they have strong feelings at *C* (consequence) after something has happened in their lives at *A* (activating events), they tend to make *C* into a new *A*— to perceive and think about their emotions (and emotional disturbances), and thereby significantly escalate, diminish, or otherwise modify these emotions and create new ones. (5) People not only think about what happens to them in words, phrases, and sentences but also do so by images, fantasies, dreams, and other kinds of pictorial representations. These nonverbal cognitions contribute significantly to their emotions and behaviors and can be used to change such behaviors. (6) Just as cognitions importantly contribute to emotions and actions, emotions also significantly contribute to or "cause" cognitions and actions; and actions contribute to or "cause" cognitions and emotions. When people change one of these three modalities of behaving they concomitantly tend to change the other two. (7) By

focusing on, and cognizing about their physiological somatic processes, people can often change these dramatically. (8) Humans have strong innate as well as acquired tendencies to think, emote, and behave in certain ways, although virtually none of their behavior stems solely from instinct and practically all of it has powerful environmental and learning factors that contribute to its "causation." (9) When people expect that something will happen or expect that others will act in a certain way, they act significantly differently than when they have other kinds of expectancies. (10) When people view situations, others' reactions, and their own behavior as within their control they act significantly differently than when they view them as stemming from external sources. (11) Humans attribute motives, reasons, and causes to other people and to external events and to internal physical states; and they significantly influence their own emotions and behaviors by these attributions, even when based on false or misleading perceptions and conceptions.

PERSONALITY

Theory of Personality

Physiological basis of personality

Unlike most modern systems of psychotherapy, RET emphasizes the biological aspects of human personality. Obliquely, most other systems do this, too, since they say, at bottom, something like this: "Humans are easily influenced by their parents during early childhood and thereafter remain similarly influenced for the rest of their lives, unless some intervention, such as years of psychotherapy, occurs to enable them to give up this early ingrained influenceability and to start thinking much more independently." If what these psychotherapeutic systems implicitly contend is actually true, they have stated an "environmentalist's" position, which is really highly physiologically and genetically based, since only a *special, innately predisposed* kind of animal would be so prone to be "environmentally determined."

Rational-emotive psychology specifically acknowledges that humans are often "naturally" inclined to do *x* rather than *y*, that the family and cultural group in which they are reared unwittingly or wittingly goes along with this "natural" disposition, and that only with enormous countereffort does the individual or the culture radically change. Because, moreover, such change requires an almost incredible amount of effort, it is usually not accomplished or it is achieved through unplanned, "artificial" developments, such as technological "advances" (e.g., the Industrial Revolution).

Although RET holds that people have vast untapped resources for growth and that in many important ways are able to change their social and personal destiny, it also holds that they have exceptionally powerful innate tendencies to think irrationally and to harm themselves (Ellis, 1976b).

Most of these tendencies of humans may be summarized by stating that humans are born with an exceptionally strong tendency to want and to insist that everything happens for the best in their life and to roundly condemn (1) themselves, (2) others, and (3) the world when they do not immediately get what they want. They consequently think "childishly" (or "humanly") all their lives and only with enormous difficulty are able to achieve and maintain "mature" or realistic behavior. This is not to deny, as Abraham Maslow, Carl Rogers, and many leaders have pointed out, that humans have impressive self-actualizing capacities. They

have, and these are strong inborn propensities, too. But, alas, they frequently defeat themselves by their inborn and acquired self-sabotaging ways.

Social aspects of personality

Humans are reared in social groups and spend much of their lives trying to impress, to live up to the expectations of, and to outdo the performances of other people. On the surface, they are "ego oriented," "identity seeking," or "self-centered." Even more importantly, however, they usually define their "selves" as "good" or "worthwhile" when they are successfully other-directed—that is, when they believe that others accept and approve of them. It is realistic and sane for people to find or fulfill "themselves" in their interpersonal relations and to have a considerable amount of what Adler calls "social interest." For, as John Donne beautifully expressed it, practically no one is an island unto himself. The healthy individual *does* find it enjoyable to love and be loved by significant others and to relate reasonably well to almost everyone he or she encounters. In fact, the better one's interpersonal relations are, the happier one is likely to be.

However, what we call *emotional disturbance* is frequently associated with people's caring too much about what others think and stems from their believing they can accept themselves only if others think well of them. When disturbed, they escalate their desire for others' approval, and the practical advantages that normally go with such approval, into an absolutistic, dire need to be liked; and, doing this, they can hardly avoid becoming anxious and prone to depression. Since we have our being-in-the-world, as the existentialists point out, it is quite *important* that others to some degree value us. But it is not *all*-important that they regard us very highly; and it is our tendency to exaggerate the importance of others' acceptance that often causes our inappropriate emotions.

Psychological aspects of personality

How, specifically, do people become psychologically disordered? According to RET, they usually needlessly upset themselves as follows:

When individuals feel upset at point *C*, after experiencing an obnoxious occurrence at point *A*, they almost always convince themselves of highly inappropriate, irrational beliefs (*iB's*) like: "I *can't stand* this Activating Event! *It is awful* that it exists! It *shouldn't* exist! I am a *worthless person* for not being able to ward it off or immediately get rid of it. And you are a louse for inflicting it on me!" This set of beliefs is irrational because (1) people *can* stand the noxious activating event, even though they may never like it. (2) It is hardly *awful*, since *awful* is an essentially undefinable term, with surplus meaning and no empirical referent. By calling the noxious activating event *awful*, the disturbed individual means (*a*) it is highly inconvenient; and (*b*) it is *more than* inconvenient, disadvantageous, and unbeneficial. But what noxious stimulus can be, in point of fact, *more than* inconvenient, disadvantageous, and unbeneficial? (3) By holding that the noxious happening in their lives *should not* exist, people really contend that they have Godly power; and that whatever they *want* not to exist *should* not. This hypothesis is, to say the least, highly unprovable! (4) By contending that they are *worthless persons* because they have not been able to ward off an unfortunate activating event, people hold that they should be able to control the universe, and that because they are not succeeding in doing what they cannot do,

they are obviously worthless. They thereby posit *two* unvalidatable premises.

The basic tenet of RET is that emotional *upsets*, as distinguished from feelings of sorrow, regret, annoyance, and frustrations, are caused by irrational beliefs. These beliefs are irrational because they magically insist that something in the universe *should, ought,* or *must* be different from the way it indubitably is. Although, then, these irrational beliefs are ostensibly connected with reality (the activating events at point *A*), they are magical ideas beyond the realm of empiricism and are established by arbitrary fiat. They generally take the form of the statement, "Because I *want* something it is not only desirable or preferable that it exist, but it absolutely *should*, and it is *awful* when it really doesn't!" No such proposition, obviously, can ever be validated; and yet, oddly enough, such propositions are devoutly held, every day, by literally billions of human beings. That is how incredibly disturbance-prone people are!

Once people become emotionally upset —or, rather, upset themselves!—another peculiar thing frequently occurs. Most of the time, they know they are anxious, depressed, or otherwise agitated, and also generally know that their symptoms are undesirable and (in our culture) socially disapproved. For who approves or respects highly agitated or "crazy" people? They therefore make their emotional consequence (*C*) or symptom into another activating event (A^2) and create a secondary symptom (C^2) about this new *A*!

Thus, if you originally start with something like "(*A*) I did poorly on my job today; (*B*) Isn't that horrible!" you will wind up with (*C*) feelings of anxiety, worthlessness, and depression. You may now start all over: (A^2): "I feel anxious and depressed, and worthless!" (B^2): "Isn't *that* horrible!" Now you end up with (C^2): even greater feelings of anxiety, worthlessness, and depression. In other words, once you become anxious, you frequently make yourself anxious about *being* anxious; once you become depressed, you make yourself depressed about being depressed; and so on. You now have two consequences or symptoms for the price of one; and you often go around and around, in a vicious cycle of (1) condemning yourself for doing poorly at some task; (2) feeling guilty or depressed because of this self-condemnation; (3) condemning yourself for your feelings of guilt and depression; (4) condemning yourself for condemning yourself; (5) condemning yourself for seeing that you condemn yourself and for still not stopping condemning yourself; (6) condemning yourself for going for psychotherapeutic help and still not getting better; (7) condemning yourself for being more disturbed than other individuals; (8) concluding that you are indubitably hopelessly disturbed and that nothing can be done about it; and so on, in an endless spiral.

No matter what your original damning is about—and it hardly matters what it is about, since the activating event (*A*) is not really that important—you eventually tend to end up with a chain of disturbed reactions only obliquely related to the original "traumatic events" of your life. That is why the psychoanalytic psychotherapies are quite misleading—they wrongly emphasize these "traumatic events" rather than your self-condemnatory attitudes *about* these events—and that is why these therapies are virtually powerless to help you with any secondary disturbance, such as anxiety about being anxious. Most major psychotherapies also concentrate either on *A*, the activating events in the individual's life, or on *C*, the

emotional consequences experienced subsequent to the occurrence of these events. But this is precisely what people wrongheadedly overfocus on, *A* and/or *C*, and rarely deeply consider *B*, the belief system, which is the vital factor in the creation of disturbance.

Even assuming, moreover, that the activating events in people's lives and the emotional consequences are important, there is not too much we can do by concentrating our therapeutic attention on these two things. The activating events belong to the past by the time we see the clients. Sometimes it was many years ago that they were criticized by their parents, rejected by their mates, or lost a series of jobs. There is nothing that anyone can do to *change* those prior happenings.

As for clients' present feelings, the more we focus on them, the worse they are likely to feel. If we keep talking about their anxiety, getting them to reexperience this feeling, they can easily become more anxious. The most logical point to interrupt their disturbed process is to get them to focus on their anxiety-creating belief system—point *B*.

If, for example, a male client feels anxious during a therapy session and the therapist reassures him that there is nothing for him to be anxious about, he may become more anxious or may achieve a palliative "solution" to his problem by convincing himself, "I am afraid that I will act foolishly right here and now, and wouldn't that be awful! No, it really wouldn't be awful, because *this* therapist will accept me, anyway."

Or the therapist can concentrate on the activating events in the client's life, which are presumably making him anxious—by, for instance, showing him that his mother used to point out his deficiencies in making an impression on others; that he was always afraid his teachers would criticize him for reciting poorly; that he is still afraid of speaking to authority figures who might disapprove of him; and that, *therefore*, because of all his prior and present fears, in situations A^1, A^2, A^3 . . . A^n, he is *now* anxious with the therapist. Whereupon the client might convince himself, "Ah! Now I see that I am generally anxious when I am faced with authority figures. No wonder I am anxious even with my own therapist!" In which case, he might feel much better and temporarily lose his anxiety.

It would be much better for the therapist to show this client that he was anxious as a child and is still anxious with various kinds of authority figures not because they are authorities or do have some power over him, but because he has always believed, and still believes, that he *must* be approved, that it is *awful* when an authority figure disapproves of him, and that he will be destroyed if he is criticized.

Whereupon the anxious client would tend to do two things: (1) He would become diverted from A (criticism by an authority figure) and from C (his feelings of anxiety) to a consideration of B (his irrational belief system). This diversion would help him become immediately nonanxious—for when he is focusing on "What am I telling myself (at B) to *make* myself anxious" he cannot too easily focus upon the self-defeating, useless thought, "Wouldn't it be terrible if I said something stupid to my therapist and if even he disapproved of me!" (2) He would begin actively to dispute (at point D) his anxiety-creating irrational beliefs; and not only could he then temporarily change them (by convincing himself, "It would be *unfortunate* if I said something stupid to my therapist and he disapproved of me; but it would hardly be *terrible* or *catastrophic!*"),

but he would also tend to have a much weaker allegiance to these self-defeating beliefs the next time he was with an authority figure and risked criticism by this individual. So he would obtain, by the therapist's getting him to focus primarily on B rather than on A and C, curative and preventive, rather than palliative, results in connection with his anxiety.

This is the basic personality theory of RET: Human beings largely (although not entirely) create their own emotional consequences; they are born with a distinct proneness to do so and learn, through social conditioning, to exacerbate (rather than to minimize) that proneness; they nonetheless have considerable ability to understand what they are foolishly believing to cause their upsetness (because they have a unique talent for thinking about their thinking) and to train themselves to change or eliminate their self-sabotaging beliefs (because they also have a unique capacity for self-discipline or self-reconditioning). If they *think* and *work* hard at understanding and contradicting their magical belief systems, they can make amazing palliative, curative, and preventive changes in their disturbance-creating tendencies; and if they are helped to zero in on their crooked thinking and inappropriate emoting and behaving by a highly active-directive, didactic, philosophic, homework-assigning therapist (who may or may not have a warm, personal relationship with them), they are much more likely to change their symptom-creating beliefs than if they mainly work with a dynamically oriented, client-centered, conventional existentialist, or classical behavior-modification-centered therapist.

Although RET is mainly a theory of personality change, it is also a personality theory in its own right (Ellis, 1974, 1978).

Many of its hypotheses have been validated by scores of controlled experiments as indicated in the *research studies* section of this chapter.

Variety of Concepts

RET largely tends to agree with the views of Sigmund Freud and Adolf Meyer that there are important biological aspects to personality disturbance; with Freud, that the pleasure principle (or short-range hedonism) tends to run most people's lives; with Karen Horney and Erich Fromm, that cultural influences as well as early family influences tend to play a significant part in bolstering people's irrational thinking; with Alfred Adler, that fictive goals tend to order and to run human lives; with Knight Dunlap and Gordon Allport, that once individuals begin to think and act in a certain manner, habituation or functional autonomy tends to take over, so they find it very difficult to think or act differently even when they want strongly to do so; with Ivan Pavlov, that although lower animals are responsively or reflexly conditioned in accordance with their primary signaling system, humans' much larger cerebral cortex provides them with a secondary signaling system through which they usually become cognitively conditioned; with Hippolyte Bernheim and Jerome Frank, that people are exceptionally prone to the influence of suggestion; with Jean Piaget, that active teaching is much more effective than passive learning; with Freud and his daughter Anna, that instead of actively and honestly condemning themselves for errors, people frequently refuse to acknowledge their mistakes and resort to all kinds of defenses and rationalizations that cover up underlying feelings of shame and self-deprecation; and with

Abraham Maslow and Carl Rogers, that human beings, however disturbed they may be, have great untapped growth forces.

On the other hand, RET has serious objections to certain aspects of many popular personality theories:

1. It opposes the Freudian concept that people have clear-cut libidinous instincts, which if thwarted must lead to emotional disturbances. It also objects to the views of William Glasser and a whole host of psychological and social thinkers, who insist that all humans have needs to be approved and to succeed—and that if these are blocked, they cannot possibly accept themselves or be happy. RET, instead, thinks in terms of human desires and tendencies, which only become needs or necessities when people foolishgly *define* them as such.

2. RET places the Oedipus complex as a relatively minor subheading under people's major irrational belief that they absolutely have to receive the approval of their parents (and others), that they *must not* fail (at lusting or almost anything else), and that when they are disapproved and when they fail, they are totally worthless. Virtually all so-called sexual problems—such as impotence, frigidity, compulsive homosexuality, and nymphomania—partly result from people's irrational beliefs that they *utterly need* approval and success.

3. RET holds that humans' environment, particularly childhood parental environment, *reaffirms* but does not *create* strong tendencies to think irrationally and to over- or underemote. Parents and culture usually teach children *which* superstitions, taboos, and prejudices to abide by; but they do not originate their basic tendency to superstitiousness, ritualism, and bigotry.

4. RET looks skeptically at anything mystical, religious, transpersonal, or magical, when these terms are used in the strict sense. It believes that reason itself is limited, ungodlike, and unabsolute (Ellis, 1968). It holds that humans may in some ways transcend themselves or experience altered states of consciousness—for example, hypnosis—that may enhance their ability to know themselves and the world and to solve some of their problems. But it does not believe that people can transcend their humanness and become in any way more than or greater than human —that is, superhuman. They can become more adept, competent, intelligent; but they still remain *fallible* and in no way godly. RET especially holds that minimal disturbance is correlated with the individuals' surrendering all pretensions to superhumanness and with fully accepting their and the world's intrinsic limitations.

5. RET believes that no part of the human being is to be reified into an entity called the unconscious, although it holds that people have many thoughts, feelings, and even acts of which they are dimly or almost completely unaware. These "unconscious" thoughts and feelings are, for the most part, slightly below the level of consciousness, are not often deeply repressed, and can usually be brought to consciousness by some brief, incisive probing. Thus, if a wife is more angry at her husband than she is aware of, and if her anger is motivated by the unconscious grandiose thought, "After all I've done for him, he *should be* having sex with me more frequently!" a rational-emotive therapist (who is aware of these unconscious feelings and thoughts of the client because RET theory indicates, when the client gives him certain evidence, that they probably exist) can usually induce her to (1) *hypothesize* that she is angry with her husband and look for some evidence with

which to test that hypothesis and (2) *check* herself for grandiose thinking whenever she feels angry. In the majority of instances, without resorting to free association, dream analysis, analyzing the transference relationship, hypnosis, or other presumably "depth-centered" techniques for revealing unconscious processes, rational-emotive practitioners can reveal these processes in short order—sometimes in a matter of minutes. They continually show the client her unconsciously held or unawarely subscribed to attitudes, beliefs, and values and, in addition, teach the client methods of bringing these somewhat hidden ideas to consciousness quite rapidly and of actively disputing them, when they are inimical to her appropriately emoting and behaving, until she minimizes or eliminates them.

People often see how RET differs significantly from psychoanalysis, Rogerianism, Gestalt therapy, and orthodox behavior therapy but have difficulty seeing how it differs from more closely related schools, such as Adler's individual psychology and Glasser's reality therapy. RET agrees with almost all of Adlerian theory but has a much more hardheaded and behavior-oriented practice (Ellis & Bernard, 1984). Reality therapy appears to be similar to RET (which antedated it by almost 10 years) and, like RET, emphasizes that humans are responsible for their own feelings and actions; that they'd better not be condemned for their foolish behavior; that they have inherent tendencies toward growth and change; that they easily make themselves into short-range hedonists and had better, instead, adopt longer range hedonism; and that the psychotherapeutic process had best stick with the here-and-now instead of the past, include skill training and problem solving, show the clients alternate ways of helping themselves, be active-directive, confront and pin down elusive and resistant clients, waste virtually no time with dream analysis, and employ a good deal of humor (Ellis, 1977a, 1977b, 1977c).

RET, however, has several important theoretical differences with reality therapy: (1) It does not believe that humans have a strong love *need* but only a powerful *desire*, which they self-defeatingly define as a "need" or "necessity." (2) It also holds that people *had better* accomplish things but not that they *have to*; and that they can truly accept themselves whether or not they receive recognition or success. (3) Reality therapy insists that humans have a need for an individual identity interrelated with their social identity. RET, again, sees this "need" as a strong desire and emphasizes the desirability of being oneself over the desirability of gaining "identity" or "ego" from one's social group. (4) Reality therapy stresses the immorality or irresponsibility of certain behaviors and implies that one *is* an irresponsible or bad *person* if one continues to behave immorally. RET shows people how their *acts* may be quite irresponsible but how *they* are never condemnable—no matter what! (5) Reality therapy emphasizes schools without failure and thinks children will grow up to hate themselves unless the system is arranged so they practically never fail. RET teaches children (and adults) that they can fail and fail and fail—and still accept themselves with their failures. (6) Reality therapy encourages therapists to show clients that they really care and believe a warm therapist is necessary for client change. RET gives therapists leeway to give caring and warmth to clients if they wish to do so, but also holds that highly effective therapy can be done without such warmth, as long as therapists fully accept (but not necessarily like) their clients. In several important respects, reality therapy seems to be a more indulgent, less hardheaded, less elegant form of RET; and it largely omits the rigorous logico-empirical disputing found in RET.

PSYCHOTHERAPY

Theory of Psychotherapy

According to the theory of RET, emotional disturbance occurs when individuals *demand, insist,* and *dictate* that they must have their wishes satisfied. Thus, they *demand* that they succeed and be approved; they *insist* that others treat them fairly; and they *dictate* that the universe be more pleasant. If people's demandingness (and not their desirousness) gets them into emotional trouble, they can alleviate their pain in several inelegant and elegant ways.

Distraction

Just as a whining child can be temporarily diverted by giving him a piece of candy, so can adult demanders be transitorily sidetracked by distraction. Thus, a therapist who sees a man who is afraid of being rejected (that is, *demands* that significant others accept him) can try to arrange things so he is diverted into activities such as sports, aesthetic creation, a political cause, yoga exercises, meditation, therapizing his friends, preoccupation with the events of his childhood, and so on. While the individual is so diverted, he will hardly have the time, or inclination, to demand acceptance by others and to make himself anxious. Distraction techniques are mainly palliative, since the individual still is underlyingly a demander and as soon as he is not diverted he will probably return to his childish dictating all over again.

Satisfying demands

If a woman's insistences are always

catered to, she will tend to feel better (but not necessarily get better). To arrange this kind of "solution," a therapist can give her love and approval, provide her with pleasurable sensations (for example, put her in an encounter group where she is hugged or massaged), teach her methods of succeeding in getting her demands, or give her reassurance that she eventually, and preferably soon, will be gratified. Many clients will feel immensely better when given this kind of treatment; but most will probably have their demandingness reinforced rather than minimized by such procedures.

Magic

A boy who demands frequently can be assuaged by magic: by, for example, his parents saying that a fairy godmother will soon satisfy these demands. Similarly, adolescent and adult demanders can be led to believe (by a therapist or someone else) that God will help them; that if they suffer enough on this earth they will indubitably go to heaven and have all their demands satisfied there; that even though they are deprived in one way (say, by being rejected), they are really a *better person* than their rejector and that therefore they can tolerate rejection; that their therapist is a kind of magician who will take away their troubles merely by their telling him or her what bothers them; that they are members of a superior group (such as the Aryan race) and that consequently they will ultimately triumph. These magical solutions sometimes work beautifully by getting the true believer to feel better and to give up disturbed symptoms; but they rarely work for any length of time and they frequently lead to eventual disillusionment (and sometimes suicide).

Giving up demandingness

The most elegant solution to the problems that result from irrational demandingness is to induce the individual to become less commanding, godlike, or dictatorial. Normal children in maturing become less childish, less insistent that they must have their desires immediately gratified. This is what the rational psychotherapist tries to induce clients to acquire: minimal demandingness and maximum tolerance. RET practitioners may, at times, use temporary therapeutic "solutions," such as distraction, satisfying the client's "needs," and even (on very rare occasions) magic. But if they do they realize that these are low-level, inelegant, palliative solutions, mainly to be used with clients with whom there is little or no chance that they will accept a more elegant and permanent resolution of their basic demandingness. Preferably, the rational-emotive therapist strives for the highest order solution: radical minimization of *mus*turbation, perfectionism, grandiosity, and intolerance. This kind of radical solution was also attempted by religious leaders such as Buddha, Jesus, and St. Francis of Assisi; but because they refused to stay with logico-empiric methods, they strayed into irrational pathways.

In RET, the attempt to help clients minimize their dictatorial, dogmatic, absolutistic core philosophy is attempted in three main therapeutic ways: cognitive, emotive, and behavioristic.

1. *Cognitive therapy* attempts to show clients that they had better give up perfectionism if they want to lead a happier, less anxiety-ridden existence. It teaches them how to recognize their *shoulds, oughts,* and *musts*; how to separate rational (non-absolutistic) from irrational (absolutistic) beliefs; how to use the logico-empirical method of science in relation to themselves and their own problems; and how to accept reality, even when it is pretty grim. It assumes that clients can think, can think about their thinking, and can even think about thinking about their

thinking; and it consequently helps them to hone and sharpen their cognitive processes. Information-giving, explicatory, and didactic, RET is oriented toward helping people with emotional disturbances philosophize more effectively and thereby uncreate these disturbances. It not only employs a one-to-one Socratic-type dialogue between the client and the therapist; but it also, in group therapy, encourages other members of the group to discuss, explain, and reason with the ineffectually thinking client. It teaches logical and semantic precision—that a man's being rejected does not mean he will *always* be rejected, and a woman's failing does not mean she *cannot* succeed. It helps clients to keep asking themselves whether even the worst things that might happen would be really as bad as they melodramatically fantasize that they would be.

2. *Emotive-evocative therapy*, when used to help change clients' core values, employs various means of dramatizing truths and falsehoods so they can clearly distinguish between the two. Thus, the therapist may employ *roleplaying*, to show the clients exactly what their false ideas are and how they affect relations with others; *modeling*, to show clients how to adopt different values; *humor*, to reduce disturbance-creating ideas to absurdity; *unconditional acceptance*, to demonstrate that they are acceptable, even with their unfortunate present traits, and that they can accept themselves fully; *exhortation*, to persuade people to give up some of their crazy thinking and replace it with more efficient notions. The therapist may also direct clients, either in individual or group counseling, to take risks (for example, telling another group member what they really think of him) that will prove it is really not that risky; to reveal themselves (for example, give the details of their impotency or homosexuality), to convince themselves that others can accept them

with their failings; to get in touch with their "shameful" feelings (such as hostility), so they can zero in on the exact things they are telling themselves to create these feelings. The therapist may also use pleasure-giving techniques, such as sensory awareness and being cuddled by another group member, not merely to satisfy clients' unreasonable demands for immediate gratification, but to show them they are capable of doing many pleasant acts that they think, wrongly, they *cannot* do, and that they *can* guiltlessly seek mere pleasure for the sake of pleasure, even though others may frown upon them for so doing.

3. *Behavior therapy* is employed in RET not only to help clients change their dysfunctional symptoms and to become habituated to more effective ways of performing, but also to help change their *cognitions*. Thus their demandingness that they perform beautifully may be whittled away by the therapist's giving them assignments, such as to take risks (for example, ask a member of the other sex for a date); to deliberately fail at some task (for example, make a real attempt to speak badly in public); to imagine themselves in failing situations; to throw themselves into unusual activities that they consider especially dangerous. Clients' demandingness that others treat them fairly and the world be kind may be challenged by the therapist's inducing them to stay in poor circumstances and teach themselves, at least temporarily, to accept them; to take on hard tasks (like enrolling in college); to imagine themselves having a rough time at something and not feeling terribly upset or having to "cop out" of it; to allow themselves to do a pleasant thing, such as go to a movie or see their friends, only after they have done unpleasant but desirable tasks, such as study French or finish a report for their boss; and so on. RET often employs operant conditioning

to reinforce peoples' changing behavior (e.g., smoking or overeating) or changing irrational thinking (e.g., condemning themselves when they smoke or overeat).

The RET theory of psychotherapy asserts that there are many kinds of psychological treatment, and that most of them work to some degree. An efficient system of therapy includes (1) economy of time and effort, (2) rapid symptom reduction, (3) effectiveness with a large percentage of different kinds of clients, (4) depth of solution of the presenting problems, and (5) lastingness of the therapeutic results. A therapy with these elements may be labeled "elegant"—that is, approaching the ideal of psychotherapy Clinical and experimental evidence now exists that RET works better than other psychotherapies now extant (DiGiuseppe, Miller, & Trexler, 1979; Ellis, 1982; Ellis & Grieger, 1977; Ellis & Whiteley, 1979; Smith & Glass, 1977). Philosophically, RET more intensively combats absoluteness than any other system. Realistic and unindulgent, RET gets to the core of and ruthlessly persists at undermining childish demandingness—the main element of serious emotional disturbance.

Process of Psychotherapy

The many roads taken in RET are aimed at one major goal: minimizing the client's central self-defeating outlook and acquiring a more realistic, tolerant philosophy of life. Since some of its methods are similar to methods used by other therapists, they are not detailed in this chapter. Most of the space here is devoted to the cognitive-persuasive aspects of RET, its most distinguishing characteristic.

Rational-emotive therapists generally do not spend a great deal of time listening to the client's history, encouraging long tales of woes, sympathetically getting in tune with emotionalizing, or carefully and incisively reflecting feelings. They may at times use all these methods; but they usually make an effort to keep them short, since they consider most long-winded dialogues of this nature a form of indulgence therapy, in which the client may be helped to *feel* better but rarely is aided in *getting* better. Even when these methods work, they are often highly inefficient, sidetracking, and unhelpful.

Similarly, the rational-emotive therapist makes little use of free association, dream analysis, interpretations of the transference relationship, explanations of the client's present symptoms in terms of past experiences, disclosure and analysis of the so-called Oedipus complex, and other "dynamically" directed interpretations or explanations. When these are employed at all, they are briefly employed to help clients see some of their basic irrational ideas.

Thus, if a male therapist notes that a female client rebels against him, just as she previously rebelled against her father during her childhood, he will not interpret the present rebelliousness as stemming from the prior pattern, but will instead probably say something like:

It looks like you frequently hated your father because he kept forcing you to follow certain rules you considered arbitrary and because you kept convincing yourself: "My father isn't being considerate of me and he *ought* to be! I'll fix his wagon!" I think you are now telling yourself approximately the same thing about me. But your angry rebelliousness against your father was senseless because (1) he was not a *total bastard* for perpetrating a bastardly *act*; (2) there was no reason why he *ought* to have been considerate of you (although there were several reasons why *it would have been preferable* if he had been); and (3) your getting angry at him and trying to "fix his wagon" would not, probably, encourage him to act more kindly, but actually to be more cruel.

You consequently confused—as most children will—being displeased with your father's *behavior* with being "righteously" angry at *him*; and you foolishly and needlessly *made yourself* upset about his supposedly unfair treatment of you. In my case, too, you are probably doing much the same thing; you are taking the restrictions that I place on you and insisting they are *too* onerous (when in point of fact, they are only onerous); and, after assuming that I am wrong in placing them on you (which I indeed may be), you are condemning me for my supposedly wrong deeds. Moreover, you are quite possibly assuming that I am "wrong" and a "louse" for being wrong because I resemble, in some ways, your "wrong" and "lousy" father.

But this is another illogical conclusion (that if I resemble your father in *some* ways, I must resemble him in all ways) and an irrational premise (that I, like your father, am a *bad person* if I do a wrong *act*). So you are not only *inventing* a false connection between me and your father, but you are creating today, as you have done for many years now, a renewed *demand* that the world be an easy place for you and that everyone *ought to* treat you fairly. Now, how are you going to challenge your irrational premises and illogical deductions?

Rational-emotive practitioners mainly employ a fairly rapid-fire active-directive-persuasive-philosophic methodology. In most instances, they quickly pin the client down to a few basic irrational ideas. They challenge the client to validate these ideas; show that they contain extralogical premises that cannot be validated; logically analyze these ideas and make mincemeat of them; vigorously show why they cannot work and why they will almost inevitably lead to renewed disturbed symptomatology; reduce these ideas to absurdity, sometimes in a highly humorous manner; explain how they can be replaced with more rational theses; and teach clients how to think scientifically, so they can observe, logically parse, and minimize any

subsequent irrational ideas and illogical deductions that lead to self-defeating feelings and behaviors.

Lest it be thought that this picture of what the therapist does in RET is exaggerated, a verbatim typescript from the recording of the first part of an initial session with a 25-year-old single woman who works as the head of a computer programmer section is presented:

T-1 [reading from the biographical information form that the clients at the Institute for Rational-Emotive Therapy in New York City fill out before their first session]: Inability to control emotions; tremendous feelings of guilt, unworthiness, insecurity; constant depression; conflict between inner and outer self; overeating; drinking; diet pills.

T-1: All right, what would you want to start on first?

C-1: I don't know. I'm petrified at the moment!

T-2: You're petrified—of what?

C-2: Of you!

T-3: No, surely not of me—perhaps of yourself!

C-3: [laughs nervously]

T-4: Because of what I am going to do to you?

C-4: Right! You are threatening me, I guess.

T-5: But how? What am I doing? Obviously, I'm not going to take a knife and stab you. Now, in what way am I threatening you?

C-5: I guess I'm afraid, perhaps, of what I'm going to find out—about *me*.

T-6: Well, so let's suppose you find out something *dreadful* about you—that you're thinking foolishly, or something. Now why would that be awful?

C-6: Because I, I guess I'm the most important thing to me at the moment.

T-7: No. I don't think that's the answer. It's, I believe, the opposite! You're really the *least* important thing to you. You are prepared to beat yourself over the head if I tell you that you're acting foolishly. If you were not a self-*blamer*, then you wouldn't care what I said. It would be important to you—but you'd just go around correcting it. But if I tell you something really negative about you, you're going to beat yourself mercilessly. Aren't you?

C-7: Yes, I generally do.

T-8: All right. So perhaps *that's* what you're really afraid of. You're not afraid of me. You're afraid of *your* own self-criticism.

C-8: [sighs] All right.

T-9: So why do you have to criticize yourself? Suppose I find you're the worst person I ever met? Let's just suppose that. All right, now *why* would you have to criticize yourself?

C-9: [pause] I'd have to. I don't know any other behavior pattern, I guess, in this point of time. I always do. I guess I think I'm just a shit.

T-10: Yeah. But that, that isn't so. If you don't know how to ski or swim, you could learn. You can also learn not to condemn yourself, no matter what you do.

C-10: I don't know.

T-11: Well, the answer is: you don't know how.

C-11: Perhaps.

T-12: I get the impression you're *saying,* "I *have* to berate myself if I do something wrong." Because isn't that where your depression comes from?

C-12: Yes, I guess so. [silence for awhile]

T-13: Now, what are you *mainly* putting yourself down for right now?

C-13: I don't seem quite able, in this point of time, to break it down very neatly. The form gave me a great deal of trouble. Because my tendency is to say *everything.* I want to change everything; I'm depressed about everything; *et cetera.*

T-14: Give me a couple of things, for example.

C-14: What I'm depressed about? I, uh, don't know that I have any purpose in life. I don't know what I—what I am. And I don't know in what direction I'm going.

T-15: Yeah. But that's—so you're saying, "I'm ignorant!" [client nods] Well, what's so awful about being ignorant? It's too bad you're ignorant. It would be nicer if you weren't—if you *had* a purpose and *knew* where you were going. But just let's suppose the worst: for the rest of your life you didn't have a purpose, and you stayed this way. Let's suppose that. Now, why would *you* be so bad?

C-15: Because everyone *should* have a purpose!

T-16: Where did you get the *should?*

C-16: 'Cause it's what I believe in. [silence for a while]

T-17: I know. But think about it for a minute. You're obviously a bright woman; now, where did that *should* come from?

C-17: I, I don't know! I'm not thinking clearly at the moment. I'm too nervous! I'm sorry.

T-18: Well, but you *can* think clearly. Are you now saying, "Oh, it's hopeless! I can't think clearly. What a shit I am for not thinking clearly!" You see: you're blaming yourself for *that.*

(From C-18 to C-26 client upsets herself about not reacting well to the session but the therapist shows her this is not overly important and calms her down.)

C-27: I can't imagine existing, uh, or that there would be any reason for existing without a purpose!

T-28: No, but the vast majority of human beings don't have much purpose.

C-28: [angrily] All right, then. I should not feel bad about it.

T-29: No, no, no! Wait a minute, now. You just *jumped.* [Laughs] You jumped from one extreme to another! You see, you said a sane sentence and an *insane* sentence. Now, if we could get you to separate the two—which you're perfectly able to do—you would solve the problem. What you really mean is: "*It would be better* if I had a purpose. Because I'd be happier." Right?

C-29: Yes.

T-30: But then you magically jump to: "Therefore I *should!*" Now do you see the difference between, "*It would be better* if I had a purpose," and "I *should, I must,* I've *got to*"?

C-30: Yes, I do.

T-31: Well, what's the difference?

C-31: [laughs] I just said that to agree with you!

T-32: Yes! See, that won't be any good. We could go on that way forever, and you'll agree with me, and I'll say, "Oh, what a great woman! She agrees with me." And then you'll go out of here just as nutty as you were before!

C-32: [laughs; this time with genuine appreciation and good humor]

T-33: You're perfectly able, as I said, to think—to stop giving up. That's what you've done most of your life; that's why you're disturbed. Because you refuse to think. And let's go over it again: (1) "It would be better if I had a purpose in life; if I weren't depressed, *et cetera, et cetera.* If I had a good, nice, enjoyable purpose." We could give reasons why it would be better. "It's fairly obvious why it would be better!" Now, why is that a magical statement, that "I *should* do what would be better"?

C-33: You mean, why do I feel that way?

T-34: No, no. It's a belief. You feel that way because you believe that way.

C-34: Yes.

T-35: If you believed you were a kangaroo, you'd be hopping around; and you'd *feel* like a kangaroo. Whatever you *believe,* you feel. Feelings come from your beliefs. Now, I'm temporarily forgetting about your feelings, because we really can't change feelings without changing beliefs.

So I'm showing you: you have two beliefs—or two feelings, if you want to call them that. One, "It would be better if I had a purpose in life." Do you agree? [client nods] Now that's perfectly reasonable. That's quite true. We could prove it. Two, "Therefore, I *should* do what would be better." Now those are two different statements. They may seem the same, but they're vastly different. Now, the first one, as I said, is sane. Because we could prove it. It's related to reality. We can list the advantages of having a purpose—for almost anybody, not just for you.

C-35: [calm now, and listening intently to T's explanation]: Uh-huh.

T-36: But the second one, "therefore, I *should* do what would be better" is crazy. Now, why is it crazy?

C-36: I can't accept it as a crazy statement.

T-37: Because who said you *should?*

C-37: I don't know where it all began! Somebody said it.

T-38: I know, but I say whoever said it was screwy!

C-38: [laughs] All right.

T-39: How could the world possibly have a *should?*

C-39: Well, it does.

T-40: But it *doesn't!* You see, that's what emotional disturbance is: believing in *shoulds, oughts,* and *musts* instead of *it would be betters.* That's exactly what makes people disturbed! Suppose you said to yourself, "I wish I had a dollar in my pocket right now," and you had only ninety cents, how would you feel?

C-40: Not particularly upset.

T-41: Yes; you'd be a little disappointed. "*It would be better* to have a dollar." But now suppose you said, "I *should,* I *must* have a dollar in my pocket at all times," and you found you had only ninety cents. Now, how would you feel?

C-41: Then I would be terribly upset, following your line of reasoning.

T-42: But not because you had only the ninety cents.

C-42: Because I thought I *should* have a dollar.

T-43: THAT'S RIGHT! The *should*. And what's more, let's just go one step further. Suppose you said, "I must have a dollar in my pocket at all times." And you found you had a dollar and ten cents. Now how would you feel?

C-43: Superb, I guess.

T-44: No!—anxious.

C-44: [laughs] You mean I'd be guilty: "What was I doing with the extra money?"

T-45: No.

C-45: I'm sorry, I'm not following you. I—

T-46: Because you're not *thinking*! Think for a minute. Why, if you said, "I *must* have a dollar, I *should* have a dollar," and you had a dollar and ten cents, would you still be anxious? *Anybody* would be. Now why would anybody be anxious if they were saying, "I've got to have a dollar!" and they found they had a dollar and ten cents.

C-46: Because it violated their *should*. It violated their rule of what they thought was right, I guess.

T-47: Well, not at the moment. But they could easily lose twenty cents.

C-47: Oh! Well.

T-48: Yeah! They'd still be anxious. You see, because *must* means, "At *all* times I must—"

C-48: Oh, I see what you mean! All right. I see what you mean. They could easily lose some of the money and would therefore feel insecure.

T-49: Yeah. All anxiety comes from *musts*.

C-49: [long silence] Why do you create such an anxiety-ridden situation initially for someone?

T-50: I don't think I do. I see hundreds of people and you're one of the few who *makes* this so anxiety provoking for your-

self. The others may do it mildly; but you're making it very anxiety provoking. Which just shows that you carry *must* into *everything*, including this situation. Most people come in here very relieved. They finally got to talk to somebody who knows how to help them, and they're very happy that I stop the horseshit, and stop asking about their childhood, and don't talk about the weather, *et cetera*. And I get *right away* to what bothers them. I tell them in five minutes. I've just explained to you the secret of all emotional disturbance. If you really followed what I said, and used it, you'd never be disturbed about practically anything for the rest of your life!

C-50: Uh-huh.

T-51: Because everytime you're disturbed, you're changing *it would be better* to a *must*. That's all disturbance is! Very very simple. Now, why should I waste your time and not explain this—and talk about irrelevant things?

C-51: Because perhaps I would have followed your explanation a little better, if I hadn't been so threatened initially.

T-52: But then, if I pat you on the head and hold back, *et cetera*, then you'll think for the rest of your life you have to be patted on the head! You're a bright woman!

C-52: All right—

T-53: That's another *should*. "He *should* pat me on the head and take it slowly—*then* a shit like me can understand! But if he goes *fast*, and makes me *think*, oh my God I'll make an error—and that is awful!" More horseshit! You don't have to believe that horseshit! You're perfectly able to follow what I say—if you stop worrying about "I *should* do perfectly well!" For that's what you're basically thinking, sitting there. Well, why *should* you do perfectly well? Suppose we had to go over it twenty times before you got it?

C-53: I don't *like* to appear stupid!

T-54: No. See. Now you're lying to yourself! Because you again said a sane thing— and then you added an insane thing. The sane thing was "I don't like to appear stupid, because *it's better* to appear bright." But then you immediately jumped over to the insane thing. "And it's *awful* if I appear stupid—"

C-54: [laughs appreciatively, almost joyously]

T-55: "—I *should* appear bright!" you see?

C-55: [with conviction] Yes.

T-56: The same crap! It's always the same crap. Now if you would look at the crap—instead of "Oh, how stupid I am! He hates me! I think I'll kill myself!" then you'd get better right away.

C-56: You've been listening! [laughs]

T-57: Listening to what?

C-57: [laughs] Those wild statements in my mind, like that, that I make.

T-58: That's right! Because I know that you have to make those statements—because I have a good *theory*. And according to my theory, people couldn't get upset *unless* they made those nutty statements to themselves.

C-58: I haven't the faintest idea why I've been so upset—

T-59: But you *do* have the faintest idea. I just told you.

C-59: All right; I know!

T-60: Why are you upset? Repeat it to me.

C-60: I'm upset because I know, I—The role that I envisioned myself being in when I walked in here and what I [laughs, almost joyously] and what I would do and should do—

T-61: Yeah?

C-61: And therefore you forced me to violate that. And I don't like it.

T-62: "And isn't it *awful* that I didn't come out greatly! If I had violated that *beautifully*, and I gave him the *right* answers immediately, and he beamed, and

said 'Boy, what a bright woman this is!' then it would have been all right."

C-62: [laughing good-humoredly] Certainly!

T-63: Horseshit! You would have been exactly as disturbed as you ae now! It wouldn't have helped you a bit! In fact, you would have got nuttier! Because then you would have gone out of here with the same *philosophy* you came in here with: "That when I act well and people pat, uh, when they pat me on the head and say 'What a great woman am I!' then everything is rosy!" It's a nutty philosophy! Because even if I loved you madly, the next person you talk to is likely to hate you. So I like brown eyes and he likes blue eyes, or something. So you're then dead! Because you really think: "I've got to be *accepted!* I've got to act intelligently!" Well, why?

C-63: [very soberly and reflectively] True.

T-64: You see?

C-64: Yes.

T-65: Now, if you will learn that lesson, then you've had a very valuable session. Because you *don't* have to upset yourself. As I said before: if I thought you were the worst shit who ever existed, well that's my *opinion.* And I'm entitled to it. But does it make you a turd?

C-65: [reflective silence]

T-66: *Does* it?

C-66: No.

T-67: *What* makes you a turd?

C-67: *Thinking* that you are.

T-68: That's right! Your *belief* that you are. That's the only thing that could ever do it. And you never have to believe that. See? You control your thinking. I control *my* thinking—*my* belief about you. But you don't have to be affected by that. You *always* control what you think. And you believe you don't. So let's get back to the depression. The depression, as I said before, stems from self-castigation. That's where it comes from. Now what are you castigating yourself for?

C-68: Because I can't live up to—There's a basic conflict in what people appear to think I am and what I think I am.

T-69: Right.

C-69: And perhaps it's not fair to blame other people. Perhaps I thrust myself into a leader's role. But, anyway, my feeling right now is that all my life I've been forced to be something that I'm not, and the older I get the more difficult this *facade*, huh, this *appearance*, uh—That the veneer is coming thinner and thinner and thinner, until I just can't do it any more.

T-70: Well, but really, yeah, I'm afraid you're a little wrong. Because, oddly enough, almost the opposite is happening. You are thrust into this role. That's right: the role of something of a leader. Is that correct?

C-70: Yes.

T-71: And *they* think you're filling it.

C-71: Everyone usually does.

T-72: And it just so happens they're *right*.

C-72: But it's taking more and more out of me.

T-73: Because you're not doing something else. You see, you *are* fulfilling their expectations of you. Because, obviously, they wouldn't think you are a leader, they'd think you were a nothing if you *were* acting like a nonleader. So you are filling their expectations. But you're not fulfilling your own idealistic and impractical expectations of leadership.

C-73: [verging on tears] No, I guess I'm not.

T-74: You see that's the issue. So therefore you *are* doing okay by them—by your job, *et cetera*. But you're not being an angel; you're not being *perfect!* And you should be, to be a real *leader*. And therefore you're a *sham!* You see? Now, if you give up those nutty expectations of yourself, and

go back to their expectations, you're in no trouble at all. 'Cause obviously you're doing all right by them, and *their* expectations.

C-74: Well, I haven't been. I had to, to give up one very successful situation. And, uh, when I left they thought it was still successful. But I just could not go on—

T-75: "Because I must, I must *really* be a leader in *my* eyes, be pretty *perfect.*" You see. "If I satisfy the world, but I know I did badly, or less than I *should*, then I'm a slob! And they haven't found me out, so that makes me a *double* slob. Because I'm pretending to them to be a nonslob when I really am one!"

C-75: [laughs in agreement; then soberly] True!

T-76: But it's all your silly *expectations*. It's not *them*. And oddly enough, you are— even with your *handicap*, which is depression, self-deprecation, *et cetera*—you're doing remarkably well. Imagine what you might do *without* this nutty handicap! You see, you're satisfying them while you're spending most of your time and energy flagellating yourself. Imagine what you might do *without* the self-flagellation! Can you see that?

C-76: [stopped in her self-blaming tracks: at least temporarily convinced. Very meaningfully] Yes!

Mechanisms of Psychotherapy

From the foregoing partial protocol (which consumed about 15 minutes of the first session with the client), it can be seen that the therapist tries to do several things:

1. No matter what *feelings* the client brings out, the therapist tries to get back to her main irrational *ideas* that most probably lie behind these feelings—especially her ideas that contend that it would be *awful* if someone, including him, disliked her.

2. The therapist does not hesitate to contradict the client, using evidence from her own life and from his knowledge of people in general.

3. He usually is a step *ahead* of her—tells her, for example, that she is a self-blamer before she has said that she is. Knowing, on the basis of RET *theory*, that she has *shoulds*, *oughts*, and *musts* in her thinking if she is becoming anxious, depressed, and guilty, he forces her to admit these *shoulds* and then attacks them (T-16; T-17).

4. He uses the strongest philosophic approach he can think of. "Suppose," he keeps saying to her, "the *worst* thing happened and you really did do badly and others hated you, would you *still* be so bad?" (T-15). He assumes if he can convince her that *none* of her behavior, no matter how execrable, denigrates *her*, he has helped her to make a *deep* attitudinal change.

5. He is not thrown by her upsetness (C-17), is hardly sympathetic about these feelings, but *uses* them to try to prove to her that, right now, she still believes in foolish ideas and thereby upsets herself. He does not dwell on her "transference" feelings, the way she accuses him of acting toward her. He interprets the *ideas* behind these feelings, shows her why they are self-defeating, and indicates why his acting sympathetically would probably reinforce instead of help change her demanding philosophy.

6. He is fairly stern with her, but also shows full acceptance and demonstrates confidence in her abilities by insisting that she can do better in her thinking and her behaving if she stops berating herself (T-20; T-33).

7. Instead of merely *telling* her that her ideas are irrational, he keeps trying to get her to see this for herself (T-36). He does, however, *explain* some relevant psycho-logical processes, such as that her *feelings* come from her *thinking* (T-35; T-68).

8. He deliberately, on several occasions, uses strong language (T-18; T-50; T-53; T-56; T-63; T-65). This is done (1) to help loosen up the client; (2) to show that even though he is a professional, he is also a down-to-earth human being; (3) to give her an emotive jolt or shock, so his words may take more dramatic effect. Note that in this case the client *first* called herself a "shit" (C-9).

9. Although hardly sympathetic to her ideas, he is really quite empathic: for he is listening hard to what she is probably telling herself. In this sense, rational-emotive therapists are very empathic, since they are usually attuned to the client's unexpressed concepts (her negative ideas about herself and the world) rather than to her *superficial* feelings (her perceptions that she is doing poorly or that others are abusing her).

10. The therapist keeps *checking* the client's ostensible understanding of what he is teaching her (T-65; T-67), to make sure she truly does understand and can repeat back his message in her own words.

11. Although a meaningful dialogue obviously takes place, the therapist—as is common in early sessions of RET—does most of the talking and explaining. He gives her plenty of opportunity to express herself, but uses her responses as take-off points for further teaching. At times, he almost seems to be lecturing her. But he tries to make each "lecture" brief and trenchant and to relate it specifically to her problems and feelings. Also, at times he stops to let ideas sink in.

As can be seen from the first part of this initial RET session, the client does not receive feelings of love and warmth from the therapist. Transference and countertransference spontaneously occur, but they are quickly analyzed, the philosophies behind them revealed, and they tend to evaporate in the process. The client's deep feelings (shame, self-pity, weeping, anger) clearly exist; but the client is not given too much of a chance to revel in these feelings or to abreact strongly to them. As the therapist points out and attacks the ideologies that appear to underlie these feelings, they swiftly change and are sometimes almost miraculously transformed into other, contradictory feelings (such as humor, joy, and reflective contemplation). On the whole, because of the therapist's "coolness," philosophizing, and insistence that the client can feel otherwise than anxious and depressed, she tends to change her destructiveness into constructive feelings minutes after the session starts.

What the client does seem to experience, as the session proceeds, are: (1) full acceptance of herself, in spite of her poor behavior both during the session and in her external life; (2) renewed confidence, that she can do certain things—especially, think for herself—that at first she seems to think she cannot do; (3) a new concept, that never or rarely seems to have occurred to her before, namely, that it is her own perfectionistic *shoulds* that are upsetting her and not the attitudes of others (including the therapist); (4) reality testing, in her starting to see that even though she performs inefficiently (with the therapist and with some of the people she works with), she can still recover, try again, and probably do better in the future; (5) reduction of some of her defenses, in that she can stop blaming others (such as the therapist) for her anxiety and can start to admit that she is doing something herself to cause it.

For the 15 minutes that the session chronicled above proceeds, the client is getting only *glimmerings* of these constructive thoughts and feelings. The RET intent, however, is that she will *keep* getting

insights—that is, *philosophic* rather than merely *psychodynamic* insights—into her self-causation of her disturbed symptoms; that she will use these insights to change some of her most enduring and deep-seated ways of thinking about herself, about others, and about the world about her; and that she will thereby eventually become ideationally, emotionally, and behaviorly much less self-defeating. Unless she finally makes a thorough-going *attitudinal* (as well as symptom-reducing) change as a result of rational-emotive therapy, although helped considerably, she will still be far from the ideal RET goal of basic personality change.

APPLICATIONS

Problems

It is easier to state what kind of problems are *not* handled than the kind that *are* handled in RET. Individuals who are out of contact with reality, in a highly manic state, seriously autistic or brain injured, and in the lower ranges of mental deficiency are not normally treated. They are referred for physical treatment, for custodial or institutional care, or for behavior therapy along operant conditioning lines.

Most other individuals with difficulties are treated with RET. These include (1) clients with maladjustment, moderate anxiety, or marital problems; (2) those with sexual difficulties; (3) run-of-the-mill "neurotics"; (4) individuals with character disorders; (5) truants, juvenile delinquents, and adult criminals; (6) borderline psychotics; (7) overt psychotics, including those with delusions and hallucinations, when they are somewhat in contact with reality; (8) individuals with higher grade mental deficiency; (9) clients with psychosomatic problems.

Although innumerable kinds of individuals with varying types of problems are treated with RET, no claim is made that they are treated with equal effectiveness. As is the case with virtually all psychotherapies, the rational-emotive approach is significantly more effectual with mildly disturbed individuals or with those having a single major symptom (such as sexual inadequacy) than with seriously disordered clients (Ellis, 1962). This conforms to the prediction of RET theory that states that the tendency toward emotional upset is largely inborn, and not merely acquired, that individuals with serious aberrations are more innately predisposed to have rigid and crooked thinking than those with lesser aberrations, and that consequently they are likely to make lesser advances. Moreover, RET emphasizes hard work at changing one's thinking and at doing activity homework assignments; and it is clinically observable that many of the most dramatically symptom-ridden individuals (such as those who are severely depressed) tend to do considerably less work and more shirking (including shirking at therapy) than those with milder symptoms. Nevertheless, virtually all seasoned RET practitioners claim they get better results with a wide variety of clients than do therapists from other schools.

RET is rightly applicable for preventive purposes. Rational-emotive procedures are closely connected to the field of education and have enormous implications for emotional prophylaxis. A number of clinicians and other professionals have shown how they can prevent normal children from eventually becoming seriously upsettable. Evidence shows that when nondisturbed grade school pupils are given, along with regular elements of an academic education, a steady process of rational-emotive education, they can learn to understand themselves and others and to live more rationally and happily in this difficult world (Ellis, 1969a, 1973a, 1982; Ellis & Bernard, 1984; Gerald & Eyman, 1981; Knaus, 1974).

Evaluation

RET has directly or indirectly inspired scores of experimenters to test its clinical and personality theories; and there now are hundreds of research studies that tend to validate its hypotheses (Ellis & Whiteley, 1979). More than 200 outcome studies have been published, showing that RET is effective in changing the thoughts, feelings, and behaviors of groups of individuals with various kinds of disturbances— including anxiety, depression, hostility, addiction, sex problems, phobias, and other kinds of difficulties. These have been listed and summarized by DiGiuseppe, Miller and Trexler (1979); and Ellis, (1982). Smith and Glass (1977), doing a meta analysis of hundreds of outcome studies of psychotherapy, found RET to have a higher index of effectiveness than any of the major systems reviewed.

In addition, scores of other outcome studies have been done by other cognitive therapists and their associates—particularly by Bandura (1977) and Beck, Rush, Shaw, and Emery (1979)—that also support the clinical hypotheses of RET. Finally, more than 200 other researches have shown that the irrationality scales derived from Ellis's original list of irrational ideas significantly correlate with virtually all the diagnostic disorders with which these scales have been tested (Ellis, 1982). This impressive research showing of RET, as a theory and a practice of psychotherapy, is a tribute to its effort to state its hypotheses in a clear and highly testable form.

Considering its relative newness in the field of psychotherapy, RET has made an enormous impact on both professionals and the public in recent years. In addition to the texts of Ellis and his collaborators, several other textbooks have appeared, including those by Bard (1980), Grieger and Boyd (1980), Grieger and Grieger (1982), Morris and Kanitz (1975), Walen, DiGiuseppe, and Wessler (1980), Wessler and Wessler (1980), and Wolfe and Brand (1977). Many rationality scales incorporating Ellis's basic ideas have been created and validated (Ellis, 1982). RET books have been published in many different fields, including adolescence (Tosi, 1974); assertion training (Lange & Jakubowski, 1976); child therapy (Bernard & Joyce, 1984; Ellis & Bernard, 1984); law and criminality (Church, 1975; Ellis & Gullo, 1972); religion (Hauck, 1972); executive leadership (Ellis, 1972); children's literature (Bedford, 1974; Garcia & Pellegrini, 1974; Waters, 1981); music (Ellis, 1977b); (Wolfe, 1976a, 1976b); philosophy (Ellis, 1968); and parenting (Ellis, Wolfe, & Moseley, 1966).

RET has been significantly incorporated into scores of self-help books. These include books by David Burns, Wayne Dyer, Albert Ellis, Robert Harper, Paul Hauck, Maxie Maultsby, Jr., John Powell, and Howard Young.

Individual evaluations
RET therapists may use various diagnostic instruments and psychological tests; and they especially employ tests of irrationality, such as the rational beliefs inventories of Jones (1968), Kassinove, Crisci and Tiegerman (1977), Baisden (1980), Shorkey and Whiteman (1977), and Zingle (1965). Many of these tests have been shown to have considerable reliability and validity in controlled experiments (Ellis, 1982; Zingle & Mallett, 1976).

Treatment

RET employs virtually all forms of individual and group psychotherapy. Some of the main methods are these:

Individual therapy
Most clients with whom RET is practiced are seen for *individual* sessions, usually on a once-a-week basis, for from 5 to 50 sessions. They generally start off their sessions by telling their most upsetting feelings or consequences (C) during the week. RET therapists then discover what activating events (A) occurred before clients felt so badly and help them to see what rational beliefs (rB) and what irrational beliefs (iB) they held in connection with the activating events. They teach clients to dispute (D) their irrational beliefs and often give them concrete activity homework assignments to help with this disputing. They then check up the following session, sometimes with the help of a Rational Self-Help Form or other homework report to see how they have tried to use the RET approach during the week; and they keep teaching clients how to dispute their irrational beliefs and keep giving them new homework assignments, until they not only start to lose their presenting symptoms but acquire a saner, more tolerant attitude toward life.

In particular, RET therapists try to show clients how (1) to rid themselves of anxiety, guilt, and depression by fully accepting themselves, as human beings, *whether or not* they succeed at important tasks and performances and *whether or not* significant people in their lives approve or love them; (2) to minimize their anger, hostility, and violence by becoming quite tolerant of other *people* even when they find these people's *traits* or *performances* unappetizing and unfair; and (3) to reduce their low frustration tolerance and inertia by working hard to change unpleasant reality but learning gracefully to stand it when it is truly inevitable.

Group therapy

RET is particularly applicable to *group therapy*, because in groups, members are taught to apply RET principles to the other members of the group; so they thereby are able to help these others learn the principles better themselves and get practice (under the direct supervision of the group leader) in applying them. In group work, moreover, there is usually more opportunity for the members to be given homework assignments (some of which are to be carried out in the group itself); to get assertion training; to engage in roleplaying; to interact with other people; to take verbal and nonverbal risks; to learn by the experiences of others; to interact therapeutically and socially with each other in after-group sessions; to have their behavior directly observed by the therapist and other group members (Ellis, 1973a, 1973b).

Marathon encounter groups

Although RET is one of the most cognitively oriented therapies, it has been successfully modified for what Ellis (1969b) calls "A Weekend of Rational Encounter." In a *rational-emotive marathon*, the first several hours are spent in having members of the marathon group go through a series of exercises designed to get them to know each other intimately, to relate verbally and nonverbally, to bring out some of their most harrowing and "shameful" experiences, to take unusual risks, and to have intense one-to-one personal encounters. During these first hours, problem-solving is deliberately eschewed. Then, when the members of the

marathon group have gotten to know each other and given up some of their defenses, many hours are spent delving into their deepest problems in the usual RET cognitive-probing manner, so most of them come to understand the philosophic sources of their emotional problems and how they can change themselves by altering these cognitions. Other verbal and nonverbal exercises to encourage encountering and intensive therapy are performed. Specific homework assignments are given to each of the marathon group members. Finally, there are closing exercises. The entire marathon lasts from 14 to 24 hours. A reunion is usually held for several hours six to eight weeks later, to check on progress and on the homework assignments. In some cases, follow-up therapy is recommended. This kind of an intensive experience with RET-oriented encounter methods has proven to be an unusually enjoyable experience, as well as an effective introduction or addition to rational-emotive therapy.

Brief therapy

RET is naturally designed for *brief therapy*. It is preferable that individuals with severe disturbances come to individual and/or group sessions for at least six months or one year, so they have an opportunity to practice what they are learning. But for individuals who are going to stay in therapy for only a short while, RET can teach them, in from 1 to 10 sessions, the A-B-C method of understanding any emotional problem, seeing its main philosophic source, and how to start to work to change fundamental disturbance-creating attitudes (Ellis & Abrahms, 1978).

This is particularly true for the person who has a specific problem—such as hostility toward a boss or sexual impotency—and who is not too *generally* disturbed.

Such an individual can, with the help of RET, be almost completely "cured" in a few sessions. But even clients with long-standing difficulties may be significantly helped as a result of brief therapy using the rational-emotive approach. They are frequently able to keep using the principles they learned during relatively few sessions and to treat themselves, often with the help of supplementary reading of R-E materials, so they not only quickly improve but also augment their improvement as the months and years go by.

Two special devices often employed in RET with regular clients can help speed the therapeutic process and make most series of sessions relatively brief. The first of these is to tape the entire session. These recordings are then listened to, usually several times, by the clients in their own home, car, or office; so they can more incisively see their problems and the rational-emotive way of handling them. Many clients who have difficulty in hearing what goes on during the face-to-face sessions (because they are too intent on talking themselves, are easily distractable, or are too anxious) are able to get more from listening to a recording of these sessions than from the original encounter with the therapist.

Second, a Rational Self Help Form or homework report is frequently used with RET clients, which helps teach them how to use the method whenever assailed with any emotional problems in between therapy sessions or after therapy has ended. This form is reproduced on pages 228-230.

Marriage and family therapy

From its very beginnings, RET has been extensively used in marriage and family counseling (Ellis, 1957, 1962, 1965, 1977a, 1982; Ellis & Harper, 1961, 1975). Usually marital or love partners are seen together. RET therapists listen to their complaints about each other, then try to show that even if the complaints are justified, upsetness is not. Work is done with either or both the participants to minimize anxiety, depression, guilt, and—especially—hostility; and a kind of small-group session ensues. As they begin to learn and apply the RET principles, they usually become much less disturbed about their differences, often within a few sessions; and as they become less disturbed, they are much better able to minimize their incompatibilities and to maximize their compatibilities. Sometimes, of course, they decide that they would be better off separated or divorced; but usually they decide to work at their individual and collective problems, to tackle some of their basic disturbances, and to achieve a happier marital arrangement. They are frequently taught contracting, compromising, communication, and other relating skills. The therapist is concerned with each of them as individuals who can be helped emotionally, whether or not they decide to stay together. But the more they work at helping themselves, the better their relationships tend to become.

In family therapy, rational-emotive practitioners sometimes see all the members of the same family together; or they may see the children in one session and the parents in another; or they may see them all individually. Some joint sessions are usually held, to see what the interactions among family members actually are; but there is no fetishistic sticking *only* to joint sessions. Whether together or separately, parents are frequently shown how to accept their children and to stop condemning *them*, no matter how execrable their *behavior* may be; and children are similarly shown that they can accept their parents and their siblings even when their traits and deeds are highly disappointing. The general rational-emotive principles of tolerance for oneself and for others are repeatedly taught; and as these are imbibed and applied, family relationships tend to become remarkably improved. As is common in RET procedures, bibliotherapy supplements counseling, and the family participants often significantly help themselves by reading RET materials like *A New Guide to Rational Living* (Ellis & Harper, 1975), *A Rational Counseling Primer* (Young, 1974), *How to Live with—and without—Anger* (Ellis, 1977a), *How to Live with a "Neurotic"* (Ellis, 1957), *A Guide to Successful Marriage* (Ellis & Harper, 1961), *The Art and Science of Love* (Ellis, 1969c), *How to Raise an Emotionally Healthy, Happy Child* (Ellis, Wolfe, & Moseley, 1966), and *The Rational Management of Children* (Hauck, 1967).

Management

The *setting* of rational-emotive sessions is much like that for other types of therapy. Most individual sessions take place in an office, but there may well be no desk between the therapist and the client, and RET therapists tend to be informally dressed and use down-to-earth language. Because they presumably have relatively few ego hangups and because they do not care too much what others, including clients, think of them, they tend to be more open, authentic, and less "professional" than the average therapist. The main special equipment used is a cassette tape recorder, with the client being encouraged to bring his own cassette, to make a recording of the session, and to take it home for replaying.

Relationships between client and therapist are somewhat different in RET than in many other forms of therapy. Rational-emotive therapists are highly active; give their own views without hesitations; usually answer direct questions about their

personal life; do a good deal of the speaking, particularly during early sessions; and are quite energetic and often directive in group therapy. At the same time, they may engage in considerable explaining, interpreting, and "lecturing"; may be objective and not overly warm to many clients; and may easily work with clients they personally do not like, since they are much more interested in helping them with their emotional problems than relating personally to them. Because they tend to have complete tolerance for all individuals, no matter how execrable their behavior, RET therapists are often seen as "warm" and "caring" by clients, even though they may have relatively little personal interest in them.

Resistance is usually handled by showing clients that they resist changing their outlook and behavior because they would like a magical easy solution rather than to work at changing themselves. Resistance is not usually interpreted as their particular feelings about the therapist. If a female client tries to seduce a male therapist, this is not usually explained in terms of "transference" but in terms of (a) her dire needs for love; (b) her normal attraction for a helpful person; and (c) the natural sex urges of two people who have intimate mental-emotional contact. If the therapist is attracted to the client, he usually admits his attraction, but explains why it is unethical for him to have sex relations with her.

Client problems

No matter what the presenting problem, RET therapists do not become over-interested in *it*, nor devote too much time and energy to trying to induce the client to fully *express* it or the emotions surrounding it. Rather, they almost always try to get the client to see and to tackle the basic ideas or philosophies that underlie it. This

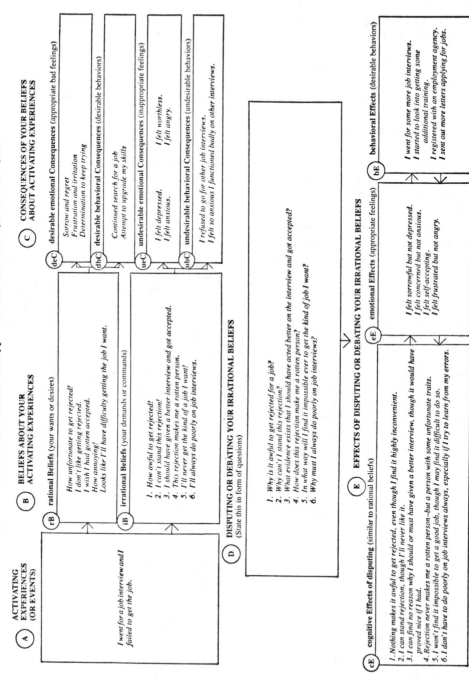

SAMPLE RATIONAL SELF HELP FORM
Institute for Rational-Emotive Therapy   45 East 65th Street, New York 1Q021

(A) ACTIVATING EXPERIENCES (OR EVENTS)

I went for a job interview and I failed to get the job.

(B) BELIEFS ABOUT YOUR ACTIVATING EXPERIENCES

(rB) rational Beliefs (your wants or desires)

How unfortunate to get rejected!
I don't like getting rejected.
I wish I had gotten accepted.
How annoying!
Looks like I'll have difficulty getting the job I want.

(iB) irrational Beliefs (your demands or commands)

1. How awful to get rejected!
2. I can't I stand this rejection!
3. I should have given a better interview and got accepted.
4. This rejection makes me a rotten person.
5. I'll never get the kind of a job I want!
6. I'll always do poorly on job interviews.

(C) CONSEQUENCES OF YOUR BELIEFS ABOUT ACTIVATING EXPERIENCES

(deC) desirable emotional Consequences (appropriate bad feelings)

Sorrow and regret
Frustration and irritation
Determination to keep trying

(dhC) desirable behavioral Consequences (desirable behaviors)

Continued search for a job
Attempt to upgrade my skills

(ueC) undesirable emotional Consequences (inappropriate feelings)

I felt depressed.   I felt worthless.
I felt anxious.   I felt angry.

(ubC) undesirable behavioral Consequences (undesirable behaviors)

I refused to go for other job interviews.
I felt so anxious I functioned badly on other interviews.

(D) DISPUTING OR DEBATING YOUR IRRATIONAL BELIEFS
(State this in form of questions)

1. Why is it awful to get rejected for a job?
2. Why can't I stand this rejection?
3. What evidence exists that I should have acted better on the interview and got accepted?
4. How does this rejection make me a rotten person?
5. In what way will I find it impossible ever to get the kind of job I want?
6. Why must I always do poorly on job interviews?

(E) EFFECTS OF DISPUTING OR DEBATING YOUR IRRATIONAL BELIEFS

(cE) cognitive Effects of disputing (similar to rational beliefs)

1. Nothing makes it awful to get rejected, even though I find it highly inconvenient.
2. I can stand rejection, though I'll never like it.
3. I can find no reason why I should or must have given a better interview, though it would have proved nice if I had.
4. Rejection never makes me a rotten person—but a person with some unfortunate traits.
5. I won't find it impossible to get a good job, though I may find it difficult to do so.
6. I don't have to do poorly on job interviews always, especially if I try to learn from my errors.

(eE) emotional Effects of disputing (appropriate feelings)

I felt sorrowful but not depressed.
I felt concerned but not anxious.
I felt self-accepting.
I felt frustrated but not angry.

(bE) behavioral Effects (desirable behaviors)

I went for some more job interviews.
I started to look into getting some additional training.
I registered with an employment agency.
I sent out more letters applying for jobs.

RATIONAL SELF HELP FORM

Institute for Rational-Emotive Therapy 45 East 65th Street, New York 10021

INSTRUCTIONS: Please fill out the **ueC** section (undesirable emotional Consequences) and the **ubC** section (undesirable behavioral Consequences) **first.**
Then fill out all the A-B-C-D-E's. PLEASE PRINT LEGIBLY. BE BRIEF!

(A) ACTIVATING EXPERIENCES (OR EVENTS)

(B) BELIEFS ABOUT YOUR ACTIVATING EXPERIENCES

(rB) rational Beliefs (your wants or desires)

(iB) irrational Beliefs (your demands or commands)

(C) CONSEQUENCES OF YOUR BELIEFS ABOUT ACTIVATING EXPERIENCES

(deC) desirable emotional Consequences (appropriate bad feelings)

(dbC) desirable behavioral Consequences (desirable behaviors)

(ueC) undesirable emotional Consequences (inappropriate feelings)

(ubC) undesirable behavioral Consequences (undesirable behaviors)

(D) DISPUTING OR DEBATING YOUR IRRATIONAL BELIEFS
(State this in the form of questions)

(E) EFFECTS OF DISPUTING OR DEBATING YOUR IRRATIONAL BELIEFS

(cE) cognitive Effects of disputing (similar to rational beliefs)

(eE) emotional Effects (appropriate feelings)

(bE) behavioral Effects (desirable behaviors)

1. FOLLOW-UP. What new GOALS would I now like to work on? ....

....

....

....

What specific ACTIONS would I now like to take?...

....

....

2. How soon after feeling or noting your undesirable emotional CONSEQUENCES (ueC's) or your undesirable behavorial CONSEQUENCES (ubC's) of your irrational BELIEFS (iB's) did you look for these iB's and DISPUTE them?................

....

....

How vigorously did you dispute them? ....

....

If you didn't dispute them, why did you not do so?...

....

3. Specific HOMEWORK ASSIGNMENT(S) given you by your therapist, your group or yourself: ... .

....

....

4. What did you actually do to carry out the assignment(s)? ....

....

5. How many times have you actually worked at your homework assignments during the past week?...........................

....

6. How many times have you actually worked at DISPUTING your irrational BELIEFS during the past week?................

....

7. Things you would now like to discuss with your therapist or group ....

....

....

is notably shown in the course of the workshops and seminars for executives. In the course of these workshops, the participating executives constantly bring up business, management, organizational, personal, and other problems. But they are shown that whatever these specific problems are, they invariably have a problem about the problem; and it is *this* (emotional or philosophic) problem that the rational-emotive method zeroes in on and helps the individual quickly and effectively solve. Then he or she usually has little difficulty in solving the original, objective problem (Ellis, 1972).

The one main exception to this rule are individuals who are so inhibited or defensive that they do not permit themselves to feel, and who therefore may not even be aware of some of their underlying problems. Thus, the successful businessman, who only comes for psychological help because his wife insists they have a poor relationship, and who claims that nothing really bothers him other than his wife's complaints, may have to be jolted out of his complacency by direct confrontation by the rational-emotive therapist or group, and may be able to see that he really has a problem mainly by such powerful confrontation. RET marathon group therapy may be particularly helpful for such an individual, and may so shake him up that he finally expresses underlying anxieties and resentments and begins to acknowledge he has problems he can work on.

Extreme emotionalism in the course of RET sessions—such as crying, psychotic behavior, and violent expressions of suicidal or homicidal intent—are naturally difficult to handle. But the therapist is bolstered in handling them by his own presumably rational philosophy of life and of therapy, which includes these ideas: (1) Client outbursts make things difficult, but they are hardly *awful, terrible,* or *catastrophic.* It is merely too bad that they occur. (2) Behind each outburst is some concrete, irrational idea. Now, what is this idea? How can it be forcefully brought to the client's attention and what can be done to help change it? (3) No therapist can possibly help every client all the time. If this particular client cannot be helped and has to be referred elsewhere or lost to therapy, that is unfortunate. But it does not mean that the therapist is a failure with a capital F, and that he or she cannot go on to help others.

Profound depressions are usually handled by the rational-emotive therapist by showing the clients, as quickly, directly, and vigorously as possible, that they are probably causing their depression by (1) blaming themselves for what they have done or not done; (2) castigating themselves for being depressed and inert; and (3) bemoaning their fate because of the hassles and harshness of environmental conditions. This self-condemnation is not only revealed but energetically attacked; and, in the meantime, the therapist may give clients reassurance and support, may refer them for supplementary medication, may speak to their relatives or friends to enlist their aid, and may recommend temporary withdrawal from some involved activities. Through an immediate and direct assailing of clients' extreme self-deprecation and self-pity, the therapist often helps deeply depressed and suicidal people in a short period.

The most difficult clients are usually the chronic avoiders or shirkers, who keep looking for magical solutions. These individuals are forthrightly shown that no such magic exists; that if they do not want to work hard to get better, it is their privilege to keep suffering; that they are entitled to goof, are not *terrible persons* for goofing, but that they could live much more enjoyably if they worked at helping themselves; and that to help them get going a form of people-involved therapy, such as group therapy, is frequently a method of choice. Results with these kinds of individuals are still relatively poor in RET (and virtually all other therapies); but persistence and vigor on the part of the therapist often finally overcome this kind of resistance.

CASE EXAMPLE

This section is relatively brief, since it concerns the case of the 25-year-old computer programmer, part of whose initial session was given earlier in this chapter. Other case material on this client follows.

Background

Sara R. came from an orthodox Jewish family. Her mother died in childbirth, when Sara was two years of age, and she was raised by a loving, but strict and somewhat remote, father and tyrannical paternal grandmother. She did well in school, but had few friends up to and including college. Although fairly attractive, she was always ashamed of her body, did little dating, and occupied herself mainly with her work. At the age of 25, she was head of a section in a data processing firm. She was highly sexed, masturbated several times a week; but only had intercourse with a male once, when she was too drunk to know what she was doing. She had been overeating and overdrinking steadily, since her college days. She had three years of fairly classical psychoanalysis, thought her analyst was "a very kind and helpful man," but got little or no help from the process. She was quite disillusioned about therapy as a result of this experience, and only came to see the present therapist because the president of her company,

who liked her a great deal, told her that he would no longer put up with her constant drinking and insisted that she come to see the writer.

Treatment

Rational-emotive treatment continued for six sessions, along the same lines as indicated in the verbatim transcript included previously in this chapter, followed by 24 weeks of RET group therapy and 1 weekend of rational encounter.

Cognitively, the client was repeatedly shown that her central problem was that she devoutly believed she *had to be* almost perfect and that she *must not* be criticized in any major way by significant others. She was persistently taught, instead, to refrain from rating her *self* but only to measure her *performances*; to see that she could never be, except by arbitrary definition, a worm even if she never rid herself of her overeating, her compulsive drinking, and her other foolish symptoms; to see that it was highly desirable but not necessary that she relate intimately to a man and to win the approval of her peers and her bosses at work; and first to accept herself *with* her hostility and then to give up her childish *demands* on others that led her to be so hostile to them. Although she devoutly believed in the "fact" that she and others *should* be extremely efficient and follow strict disciplinary rules, and although she time and again resisted the therapist's and the group members' assaults against her moralistic *shoulds,* she was finally induced to replace them, in her vocabulary as well as in her internalized beliefs, with *it would be betters.* She claimed to have completely overthrown her original religious orthodoxy; but she was shown that she had merely replaced it with an inordinate demand for certainty in her personal life and in world affairs; and she was finally induced to give this up, too.

Emotively, Sara was fully accepted by the therapist *as a person,* even though he ruthlessly assailed many of her *ideas* and sometimes humorously reduced them to absurdity. She was assertively confronted by some of the group members, who took her to task for condemning other members of the group for their stupidities and for their shirking; and she was helped to relate to these people in spite of their inadequacies. The therapist and some of the others in her group and in the marathon weekend of rational encounter in which she participated used vigorous, down-to-earth language with her, which she first got "shook up" about but which she later began to use to some extent herself. When she went on a drinking bout for a few weeks and felt utterly depressed and hopeless, two of the group members brought out their own previous difficulties with alcohol and drugs and showed how they had managed to get through that almost impossible period of their lives; another member gave her steady support through many phone calls and visits. At times, when she clammed up or sulked, the therapist and other group members forced her to open up and voice her real feelings; then they went after these defenses, with RET analyses, and revealed her foolish ideas (especially the idea that she had to be terribly hurt if others rejected her) and how these could be uprooted. During the marathon, she was able, for the first time in her life, to let herself be really touched emotionally by a male who, up to that time, was a perfect stranger to her, and this showed her that she could afford to let down her long-held barriers to intimacy and to let herself love.

Behavioristically, Sara was given home-work assignments of talking to attractive males in public places and thereby overcame her fears of being rejected. She was shown how to stay on a long-term diet (which she had never done before) by only allowing herself rewarding experiences (such as listening to classical music) when she had first kept to her diet for a certain number of hours. Through the use of role-playing with the therapist and other group members she was given training in being assertive with people at work and in her social life, without being hostile.

Resolution

Concomitant with her individual and group therapy, and probably as a result of the combination of cognitive, emotive, and behavioristic approaches, Sara progressed in several ways: (1) She stopped drinking completely, lost 25 pounds, and appeared to be maintaining both her sobriety and her weight loss. (2) She became considerably less condemnatory of both herself and others and began to make some close friends. (3) She had satisfactory sex relations with three different males and began to go steadily with the second one of the three. (4) She only rarely made herself guilty or depressed, accepted herself with her failings, and began to focus much more on enjoying than on rating herself.

Follow-up
Sara had RET individual and group sessions for six months—and occasional follow-up sessions for the next year. She married her steady boyfriend about a year after she had originally begun treatment, having two premarital counseling sessions with him following their engagement. Two and one-half years after the close of therapy, she and her husband visited one of

the regular Friday night workshops given by the therapist at the Institute for Rational-Emotive Therapy in New York City and they reported that everything was going well in their marriage, at her job, and in their social life. Her husband seemed particularly appreciative of the use she was making of RET principles, and noted that "she still works hard at what she learned with you and the group and, frankly, I think that she keeps improving, because of this work, all the time." She smilingly and enthusiastically agreed.

SUMMARY

Rational-emotive therapy (RET) is a comprehensive system of personality change that includes a large variety of cognitive, emotive, and behavior therapy methods. It is not merely an eclectically or pragmatically oriented form of psychological treatment but is based on a clearcut theory of emotional health and disturbance: The many techniques it employs are used in the light of that theory. Its major hypotheses also relate to childrearing, education, social and political affairs, and for the extension of people's intellectual-emotional frontiers and the abetting of their unique potential for growth. Rational-emotive psychology is hardheaded, empirically oriented, rational, and nonmagical. It fosters the use of reason, science, and technology in the straightforward interest of man and woman. It is humanistic, existentialist, and hedonistic; it makes growth and happiness the relevant core of a person's intrapersonal and interpersonal life.

RET theory holds that people are biologically and culturally predisposed to choose, to create, to relate, and to enjoy, but that they are also just as strongly predisposed to conform, to be suggestible, to

hate, and arbitrarily to block their enjoying. Although they have remarkable capacities to observe, to reason, and imaginatively to enhance their experiencing and to transcend some of their own essential limitations, they also have an incredibly facile and easy propensity to ignore reality, to misuse reason, and rigidly and intolerantly to invent gods and demons that frequently sabotage their health and happiness. In the course of their refusals to accept reality, their continual *mustur*bation, and their absorption in deifying and devilifying themselves and others, they almost always wind up with fairly severe manifestations of what is called "emotional disturbance."

More specifically, when noxious stimuli occur in peoples' lives at point A (the activating event), they usually observe these events fairly objectively and conclude, at point rB (their rational belief), that this event is unfortunate, inconvenient, and disadvantageous, and that they wish it would change for the better or disappear, and they appropriately feel, at point C (the consequence), sad, regretful, frustrated, or annoyed. These appropriate feelings usually help them to try to do something about the noxious activating event, so they feel a new consequence, namely, neutrality or joy. Their inborn and acquired hedonistic orientation thereby encourages them to have, in regard to noxious or unpleasant activating events (or activating experiences), thoughts ("I don't like this; let's see what I can do to change it") and feelings (sorrow and annoyance) that enable them to reorder their environment and to live more enjoyably.

Very often, however, when similar noxious activating events occur in people's lives, they observe these events intolerantly and grandiosely and conclude, at point iB (their irrational beliefs), that they are awful, horrible, and catastrophic; that they *must* not exist; and that they absolutely cannot stand them. They then inappropriately feel the consequence, at point *C*, of worthlessness, guilt, anxiety, depression, rage, and inertia. Their inappropriate feelings usually interfere with their doing something constructive about the noxious activating events, and they tend to condemn themselves for their unconstructiveness and to experience more feelings of shame, inferiority, and hopelessness. Their inborn and acquired person-downing, antihumanistic, god-and-devil-inventing philosophy encourages them to have, in regard to noxious or unpleasant activating events, foolish thoughts ("How awful this is and I am! There's nothing I can do about it!") and inappropriate feelings (hatred of themselves, of others, and of the world) that drive them to whine and rant and to live less enjoyably.

RET is a cognitive-emotive-behavioristic method of psychotherapy uniquely designed to enable people to observe, to understand, and persistently to attack their irrational, grandiose, perfectionistic *shoulds, oughts,* and *musts.* It employs the logico-empirical method of science to encourage people to surrender magic, absolutes, gods, and devils; to acknowledge that nothing is sacred or all-important (although many things are quite important) and nothing is "awful" or "terrible" (although many things are exceptionally unpleasant and inconvenient); and to gradually teach themselves and to practice the philosophy of desiring rather than demanding and of working at changing what they can change and gracefully lumping what they cannot.

In conclusion, rational-emotive therapy is a method of personality change that quickly and efficiently helps people resist their tendencies to be too conforming, suggestible, and unenjoying. It actively and didactically, as well as emotively and behaviorally, shows people how to abet and enhance one side of their humanness while simultaneously changing and living more happily with (and not repressing or squelching) another side of their humanity. It is thus realistic and practical, as well as idealistic and future oriented. It helps individuals more fully to actualize, experience, and enjoy the here and now; but it also espouses long-range hedonism, which includes planning for their own (and others') future. It is what its name implies: rational *and* emotive, realistic *and* visionary, empirical *and* humanistic. As, in all their complexity, are humans.

ANNOTATED BIBLIOGRAPHY

Ellis, A. *How to live with a "neurotic."* New York: Crown Publishers, 1957. (Revised edition, 1975.)
This first book published on RET shows how almost anyone can use it to cope with and to help disturbed individuals at home or on the job. Also the first psychology book using a new linguistic device called E-prime language, or "semantic therapy," which eliminates the use of any form of the verb "to be," allowing no implication that human behavior remains fixed or unalterable.

Ellis, A. *Reason and emotion in psychotherapy.* New York: Lyle Stuart, 1962. Paperback edition, Secaucus, N.J.: Citadel, 1977.
The first book presenting RET in textbook form, mainly written for therapists and clinicians but also widely used by people who want to help themselves overcome their emotional problems.

Ellis, A. *Growth through reason: Verbatim cases in rational-emotive therapy.* Palo Alto, Calif.: Science and Behavior Books; and Hollywood: Wilshire Books, 1971.
Verbatim dialogues between rational-

emotive therapists and their clients, with Dr. Ellis stopping the tape, so to speak, at frequent intervals to explain what is happening—what techniques of RET the therapist is using and what growth is taking place. Two of Dr. Ellis's therapy dialogues are included, as well as those by other therapists using RET: Drs. Ben N. Ard, Jr., H. Jon Geis, John M. Gullo, Paul A. Hauck, and Maxie C. Maultsby, Jr.

Ellis, A. *Humanistic psychotherapy: The rational-emotive approach.* New York: Crown Publishers and McGraw-Hill Paperbacks, 1973.

Presents, for the public and the profession, an up-to-date version of RET that emphasizes both its humanistic and its active-directive aspects. Places humans squarely in the center of the universe and shows how they have full responsibility for choosing to make or not make themselves emotionally disturbed.

Ellis, A., & Grieger, R. *Handbook of Rational-emotive therapy.* New York: Springer, 1977.

A sourcebook of some of the most salient and classic writings on RET, with sections on the theoretical and conceptional foundations of RET, the dynamics of emotional disturbance, primary techniques and basic process of rational-emotive therapy, and RET with children.

Ellis, A., & Harper, R. A. *A new guide to rational living.* Englewood Cliffs, N.J.: Prentice-Hall; and Hollywood: Wilshire Books, 1975.

A completely revised and rewritten version of the RET self-help classic. One of the most widely read self-help books ever published and the one most often recommended by cognitive-behavior therapists to their clients. A succinct, straightforward approach to RET based on self-questioning and homework.

CASE READINGS

Ellis, A. A twenty-three-year-old woman, guilty about not following her parents' rules. In A.

Ellis, *Growth through reason: Verbatim cases in rational-emotive therapy.* Palo Alto, Calif.: Science and Behavior Books; and Hollywood: Wilshire Books, 1971, pp. 223-86.

Ellis presents a verbatim protocol of the first, second, and fourth sessions with a woman who comes for help because she is quite self-punishing, impulsive and compulsive, afraid of males, has no goals in life, and is guilty about her relations with her parents. The therapist quickly zeroes in on her main problems and shows her that she need not feel guilty about doing what she wants to do in life, even if her parents keep upsetting themselves about her beliefs and actions.

Maultsby, M. C., Jr. A relapsed client with severe phobic reactions. In A. Ellis, *Growth through reason: Verbatim cases in rational-emotive therapy.* Palo Alto, Calif.: Science and Behavior Books; and Hollywood: Wilshire Books, 1971, pp. 179-222.

Maultsby presents a verbatim first session and parts of subsequent sessions with a 24-year-old undergraduate student who had been previously hospitalized for a psychotic episode, who had 30 sessions of traditional psychotherapy, who reported significant improvement in most of his problems after 50 sessions of group rational-emotive therapy, but a year later reported that his gains were being whittled away, that he was becoming afraid of having a concussion and a consequent major loss of his intelligence, that he again felt stupid in his school work, and that he blamed many of his personal failings on an automobile accident. Maultsby deals with this relapsed client in an active-directive manner and in relatively few additional sessions helps him get to the point where he no longer feels disturbed.

Ellis, A. Verbatim psychotherapy session with a procrastinator. In A. Ellis & W. J. Knaus, *Overcoming procrastination.* New York: New America Library, 1977, pp. 152-67.

Ellis presents a single verbatim session with a procrastinator who was failing to finish her doctoral thesis in sociology. He deals with her problems in a direct, no-nonsense manner typical of rational-emotive therapy; and as a result of a single session, she later reports she finished her thesis although she had previously been procrastinating on it for a number of years.

REFERENCES

Adler, A. *What life should mean to you.* New York: Blue Ribbon Books, 1931.

Adler, A. *Superiority and social interest.* Ed. by H. L. Ansbacher & R. R. Ansbacher. Evanston, Ill.: Northwestern University Press, 1964. (a)

Adler, A. *Social interest: A challenge to mankind.* New York: Capricorn Books, 1964. (b)

Baisden, H. E. *Irrational beliefs: A construct validation study.* Ph.D. thesis, University of Minnesota, 1980.

Bandura, A. *Social learning theory.* Englewood Cliffs, N. J.: Prentice-Hall, 1977.

Bard, J. A. *Rational emotive therapy in practice.* Champaign, Ill.: Research Press, 1980.

Beck, A. T. *Cognitive therapy and the emotional disorders.* New York: International Universities Press, 1976.

Beck, A. T.; Rush, A. J., Shaw, B. F., & Emery, G. *Cognitive therapy of depression.* New York: Guilford, 1979.

Bedford, S. *Instant replay.* New York: Institute for Rational Living, 1974.

Bernard, M. E., & Joyce, M. R. *Rational-emotive therapy with children and adolescents.* New York: Wiley, 1984.

Bone, H. Two proposed alternatives to psychoanalytic interpreting. In E. Hammer (Ed.), *The use of interpretation in treatment.* New York: Grune & Stratton, 1968.

Church, V. A. *Behavior, law and remedies.* Dubuque, Ia.: Kendall/Hunt, 1975.

DiGiuseppe, R., Miller, N., & Trexler, L. A. review of rational-emotive psychotherapy outcome studies. In A. Ellis and J. M. Whiteley (Eds.), *Theoretical and empirical foundations of rational-emotive therapy.* Monterey, Calif.: Brooks/Cole, 1979.

Ellis, A. *How to live with a "neurotic"* (rev. ed.). New York: Crown Publishers, 1957. (Rev. ed., 1975.)

Ellis, A. *Reason and emotion in psychotherapy.* Secaucus, N. J.: Lyle Stuart and Citadel Books, 1962.

Ellis, A. *Sex without guilt* (rev. ed.). New York: Lyle Stuart and Hollywood: Wilshire Books, 1965.

Ellis, A. *Is objectivism a religion?* New York: Lyle Stuart, 1968.

Ellis, A. Teaching emotional education in the classroom. *School Health Review,* November 1969. (a)

Ellis, A. A. weekend of rational encounter. In A. Burton (Ed.), *Encounter.* San Francisco: Jossey-Bass, 1969. (b)

Ellis, A. *The art and science of love* (rev. ed.). New York: Lyle Stuart and Bantam Books, 1969. (c)

Ellis, A. *Growth through reason: Verbatim cases in rational-emotive therapy.* Palo Alto, Calif.: Science and Behavior Books; and Hollywood: Wilshire Books, 1971.

Ellis, A. *Executive leadership: A rational approach.* New York: Institute for Rational Living, 1972.

Ellis, A. Emotional education with groups of normal school children. In M. M. Ohlsen (Ed.), *Counseling children in groups.* New York: Holt, Rinehart & Winston, 1973. (a) Reprinted: New York: Institute for Rational Living, 1973.

Ellis, A. *Humanistic psychotherapy: The rational-emotive approach.* New York: Crown Publishers and McGraw-Hill Paperbacks, 1973. (b)

Ellis, A. Rational-emotive theory. In A. Burton (Ed.), *Operational theories of personality.* New York: Brunner/Mazel, 1974.

Ellis, A. *Sex and the liberated man.* Secaucus, N. J.: Lyle Stuart, 1976. (a)

Ellis, A. The biological basis of human irrationality. *Journal of Individual Psychology,* 1976, *32,* 145-168. (b)

Ellis, A. *How to live with—and without—anger.* New York: Reader's Digest Press, 1977. (a)

Ellis, A. *A garland of rational songs.* New York: Institute for Rational Living, 1977. (b)

Ellis, A. *Fun as psychotherapy.* Cassette recording. New York: Institute for Rational-Emotive Therapy, 1977. (c)

Ellis, A. Toward a theory of personality. In R. J. Corsini (Ed.), *Readings in current personality theories.* Itasca, Ill.: F. E. Peacock Publishers, Inc., 1978.

Ellis, A. Rational-emotive family therapy. In A. M. Horne & M. M. Ohlsen, *Family counseling and therapy.* Itasca, Ill.: F. E. Peacock Publishers, Inc., 1982. (a)

Ellis A. *Rational-emotive therapy and cognitive behavior therapy.* New York: Springer, 1982. (b)

Ellis, A., & Abrahms, E. *Brief psychotherapy in medical and health practice.* New York: Springer, 1978.

Ellis, A., & Bernard, M. E. (Eds.) *Rational-emotive approaches to childhood.* New York: Plenum, 1984.

Ellis, A., & Grieger, R. (Eds.) *Handbook of rational-emotive therapy.* New York: Springer,

1977.

Ellis, A., & Gullo, J. M. *Murder and assassination.* Secaucus, N. J.: Lyle Stuart, 1972.

Ellis, A., & Harper, R. A. *A guide to successful marriage.* Hollywood: Wilshire Books, 1961.

Ellis, A., & Harper, R. A. *A new guide to rational living.* Englewood Cliffs, N. J.: Prentice-Hall; and Hollywood, Cal.: Wilshire Books, 1975.

Ellis, A., & Whiteley, J. M. (Eds.) *Theoretical and empirical foundations of rational-emotive therapy.* Monterey, Cal.: Brooks/Cole, 1979.

Ellis, A., Wolfe, J. L., & Moseley, *How to raise an emotionally healthy, happy child.* Hollywood, Cal.: Wilshire Books, 1966.

Garcia, E., & Pellegrini, N. *Homer the homely hound dog.* New York: Institute for Rational-Emotive Therapy, 1974.

Gerald, M., & Eyman, W. *Thinking straight and talking sense: An emotional education program.* New York: Institute for Rational-Emotive Therapy, 1981.

Goldfried, M. R., & Davison, G. C. *Clinical behavior therapy.* New York: Holt, Rinehart & Winston, 1976.

Grieger, R., & Boyd, W. *Rational-emotive therapy: A skills based approach.* New York: Reinhold, 1980.

Grieger, R., & Grieger, I. *Cognition and emotional disturbance.* New York: Human Sciences, 1982.

Hauck, P. *The rational management of children.* New York: Libra, 1967.

Hauck, P. *Reason in pastoral counseling.* Philadelphia: Westminster Press, 1972.

Jones, R. G. *A factored measure of Ellis' irrational belief system with personality and malajustment correlates.* Ph.D. thesis, Texas Technological College, 1968.

Kassinove, H., Crisci, R., & Tiegerman, S. Developmental trends in rational thinking: Implications for rational-emotive, school mental health programs. *Journal of Community Psychology,* 1977, *5,* 266-274.

Knaus, W. Rational-Emotive education. New York: Institute for Rational-Emotive Therapy, 1974.

Lange, A., & Jakubowski, P. *Responsible assertion training.* Champaign, Ill.: Research Press, 1976.

Lazarus, A. A. *The practice of multimodal therapy.* New York: McGraw-Hill, 1981.

Mahoney, M. J. *Cognition and behavior modification.* Cambridge, Mass.: Ballinger, 1974.

Maultsby, M. C., Jr. *Help yourself to happiness.* New York: Institute for Rational-Emotive Therapy, 1975.

Meichenbaum, D. H. *Cognitive behavior therapy.* New York: Plenum, 1977.

Morris, K. T., & Kantiz, H. M. *Rational-emotive therapy.* Boston: Houghton-Mifflin, 1975.

Shorkey, C. T., & Whiteman, V. L. Development of the Rational Behavior Inventory. *Educational and Psychological Measurement,* 1977, *37,* 527-534.

Smith, M. L., & Glass, G. V. Meta analysis of psychotherapy outcome studies. *American Psychologist,* 1977, *32,* 752-760.

Tosi, D. J. *Youth: Toward personal growth, a rational-emotive approach.* Columbus, Ohio: Charles Merrill, 1974.

Walen, S. R., DiGiuseppe, R., & Wessler, R. L. *A practitioner's guide to rational-emotive therapy.* New York: Oxford, 1980.

Waters, V. *Rational stories for children.* New York: Institute for Rational-Emotive Therapy, 1981.

Wessler, R. A., & Wessler, R. L. *The principles and practice of rational-emotive therapy.* San Francisco: Jossey-Bass, 1980.

Wolfe, J. L. *How to be sexually assertive.* New York: Institute for Rational-Emotive Therapy, 1976. (a)

Wolfe, J. L. Rational-emotive therapy as an effective feminist therapy. *Rational Living,* 1976, *1,* 2-7. Reprinted: New York: Institute for Rational Living, 1976. (b)

Wolfe, J., & Brand, E. (Eds.) *Twenty years of rational therapy.* New York: Institute for Rational-Emotive Therapy, 1977.

Young, H. S. *A rational counseling primer.* New York: Institute for Rational Living, 1974.

Zingle, H. W. *Therapy approach to counseling underachievers.* Ph.D. thesis, University of Alberta, 1965.

Zingle, H. W., & Mallett, M. *A bibliography of R-E-T materials and theses from the University of Alberta.* Edmonton, Canada: University of Alberta, 1976.

7

Behavior Therapy

G. TERENCE WILSON

OVERVIEW

Behavior therapy is a relative newcomer on the psychotherapy scene. Not until the late 1950s did it emerge as a systematic approach to the assessment and treatment of psychological disorders. In its early stages of development, behavior therapy was defined as the application of modern learning theory to the treatment of clinical problems. The phrase *modern learning theory* then referred to the principles and procedures of classical and operant conditioning. Behavior therapy was seen as the logical extension of behaviorism to complex forms of human activities.

In little more than the two decades since its inception, behavior therapy has undergone significant changes in both nature and scope. This rapid change and growth is one of the striking features of behavior therapy which has been responsive to advances in experimental psychology and innovations in clinical practice. It has grown increasingly more complex and sophisticated. As a result, behavior therapy can no longer be simply defined as the clinical application of classical and operant conditioning theory.

Behavior therapy today is marked by a diversity of views. There is now a broad range of heterogeneous procedures with different theoretical rationales, and open debate about conceptual bases, method-

ological requirements, and evidence of efficacy (Kazdin & Wilson, 1978). As behavior therapy has expanded, the degree of overlap with other psychotherapeutic approaches has increased. Nevertheless, the basic concepts characteristic of the approach are clear and its commonalities with and differences from nonbehavioral therapeutic systems can be identified.

Basic Concepts

The various approaches in contemporary behavior therapy include (*a*) *applied behavior analysis*, (*b*) *a neobehavioristic mediational stimulus-response model*, (*c*) *social learning theory*, and (*d*) *cognitive behavior modification*. Basically, these four approaches differ in the degrees to which they use cognitive concepts and procedures. At one end of this continuum is *applied behavior analysis*, which focuses exclusively on observable behavior and rejects all cognitive mediating processes. At the other end are *social learning theory* and *cognitive behavior modification*, which rely heavily on cognitive theories.

Applied behavior analysis
This approach is a direct extension of Skinner's (1953) radical behaviorism, relying on operant conditioning, the fundamental assumption of which is that behavior is a function of its consequences.

Accordingly, treatment procedures are based on altering relationships between overt behaviors and their consequences. Applied behavior analysis makes use of techniques based on reinforcement, punishment, extinction, stimulus control, and other procedures derived from laboratory research. Cognitive processes are considered private events and are not regarded as the proper subjects of scientific analysis. Applied behavior analysis is also distinguished by its methodology for evaluating treatment effects. The focus is on the intensive study of the individual subject.

The neobehavioristic mediational stimulus-response model

This approach features the application of the principles of classical and avoidance conditioning. It derives from the learning theories of Ivan Pavlov, E. R. Guthrie, Clark Hull, O. H. Mowrer, and N. E. Miller. Unlike the operant approach, the S-R model is mediational, with intervening variables and hypothetical constructs prominently featured. Exemplifying the mediational nature of this approach is the central importance assigned to anxiety. The treatment techniques of systematic desensitization and flooding, which are most closely associated with this model, are both directed toward the extinction of the underlying anxiety that is assumed to maintain phobic disorders. Private events, especially imagery, have been an integral part of this approach, including systematic desensitization and covert conditioning techniques such as covert sensitization. The rationale behind all these methods is that covert processes follow the laws of learning that govern overt behaviors.

Social learning theory

The social learning approach to behavior therapy depends on the theory that be-

havior is based on three separate but interacting regulatory systems (Bandura, 1977). They are (*a*) external stimulus events, (*b*) external reinforcement, and (*c*) most importantly, cognitive mediational processes.

In the social learning approach, the influence of environmental events on behavior is largely determined by cognitive processes, which govern what environmental influences are attended to, how they are perceived, and how the individual interprets them. Social learning theory is based on a reciprocal determinism model of causal processes in human behavior. Psychological functioning, according to this view, involves a reciprocal interaction among three interlocking sets of influences: behavior, cognitive processes, and environmental factors. Bandura (1977) put it as follows:

Personal and environmental factors do not function as independent determinants; rather they determine each other. Nor can "persons" be considered causes independent of their behavior. It is largely through their actions that people produce the environmental conditions that affect their behavior in a reciprocal fashion. The experiences generated by behavior also partly determine what individuals think, expect, and can do, which in turn, affect their subsequent behavior. (p. 345)

In social learning theory the person is the agent of change: The theory emphasizes the human capacity for self-directed behavior change.

Cognitive behavior modification

This fourth approach encompasses a number of diverse procedures, some of which have developed outside the mainstream of behavior therapy. The techniques most characteristic of cognitive behavior modification are referred to as cognitive restructuring. One form of cognitive restructuring is Ellis's (1962) rational-emotive therapy (RET), as described in Chapter 6 of this volume. The basic assumption of this approach is that it is not experience itself, but the person's interpretation of that experience which produces psychological disturbance. Therapy consists of persuasion and argument directed toward altering irrational ideas. Specific behavioral tasks are also used to modify faulty perceptions and interpretations of important life events.

Common characteristics

Although the four preceding behavior therapy approaches often involve conceptual differences, behavior therapists subscribe to a common core of basic concepts. Two major assumptions are (1) a learning model of human behavior that differs fundamentally from the traditional intrapsychic, psychodynamic, or quasi-disease model of mental illness; and (2) a commitment to the scientific method.

The emphasis on the psychological as opposed to quasi-disease model of abnormal behavior has the following consequences:

a. Many types of abnormal behavior formerly regarded as illnesses in themselves or as signs and symptoms of illness are better construed as nonpathological "problems of living" (key examples include anxiety reactions, sexual deviance, and conduct disorders).
b. Most abnormal behavior is assumed to be acquired and maintained in the same manner as normal behavior; it can be treated through the application of behavioral procedures.
c. Behavioral assessment focuses on the current determinants of behavior rather than on the analysis of possible historical antecedents. Speci-

ficity is the hallmark of behavioral assessment and treatment, and it is assumed that the person is best understood and described by what the person does in a particular situation.
d. Treatment requires a prior analysis of the problem into components or subparts and then procedures are targeted at specific components systematically.
e. Treatment strategies are individually tailored to different problems in different individuals.
f. Understanding the origins of a psychological problem is not essential for producing behavior change. Conversely, success in changing a problem behavior does not imply knowledge about its etiology.
g. Behavior therapy involves a commitment to the scientific approach. This includes the following: an explicit, testable conceptual framework; treatment either derived from or at least consistent with the content and method of experimental-clinical psychology; therapeutic techniques that can be described with sufficient precision to be measured objectively and which can be replicated; the experimental evaluation of treatment methods and concepts; and the emphasis on innovative research strategies that allow rigorous evaluation of specific methods applied to particular problems instead of global assessment of ill-defined procedures applied to heterogeneous problems.

Other Systems

Behavior therapy shares many commonalities with other psychological therapies, particularly those that tend to be briefer and more directive. The broader and more complex behavior therapy has become, the greater has been the overlap. In some cases, behavior therapy has "borrowed" treatment concepts and methods from other systems. For example, behavioral marital therapy places great emphasis on communication skills (Jacobson & Margolin, 1979). The reliance upon communication analyses of interpersonal behavior in the treatment of marital conflict was derived not from an operant conditioning viewpoint, but from the clinical tradition of client-centered therapy (Knudson, Gurman, & Kniskern, 1979).

Some concepts of Albert Ellis's rational-emotive therapy form part of cognitive restructuring methods in cognitive-behavioral treatment (Kendall & Hollon, 1979). While such approaches within behavior therapy are proving useful in conceptualizing therapeutic mechanisms, the evidence shows that the behavioral procedures are the most effective methods for producing psychological change—broad change that includes subjective, emotional, as well as actual behavioral components (Bandura, 1982).

In terms of clinical practice, behavior therapy and multimodal therapy are similar. The majority of the techniques that Arnold Lazarus (1981) lists as the most frequently used in multimodal therapy are standard behavior therapy strategies. This is not surprising since Lazarus (1971) was one of the pioneers of clinical behavior therapy, helping to broaden its conceptual bases and introducing innovative clinical methods. Whether or not the multimodal techniques that receive no attention in behavior therapy (e.g., time projection, the empty chair technique) add to therapeutic efficacy is unclear, since there are no controlled studies or even acceptable uncontrolled clinical trials to help decide the issue.

Either therapists are guided in their formulations and treatment of different problems on the basis of clearly stated principles or they act as a result of personal experience and intuition. Behavior therapy represents an attempt to move beyond idiosyncratic practices and to base clinical practice on more secure scientific foundations. Of course, this does not mean that the clinical practice by behavior therapists is always based on solid empirical evidence. Behavior therapists, not unlike therapists from other approaches, have developed their own clinical lore, much of which owes nothing to experimental research. Lacking sufficient information and guidelines from research, behavior therapists often adopt an informed trial-and-error approach to difficult or unusual problems. This, quite literally, is the current state of the art and science in behavior therapy. Nonetheless, behavior therapy is clearly linked to a specifiable and testable conceptual framework.

Behavior therapy differs fundamentally from some psychodynamic approaches to treatment. Based on a learning or educational model of human development, behavior therapy rejects the quasi-disease model of psychoanalytic therapy in which abnormal behavior is viewed as a symptom of underlying unconscious conflicts. Psychoanalytic therapy has difficulty in explaining the well-documented successes of behavior therapy that directly contradict basic concepts that psychoanalysts claim are crucial for therapeutic change. Some psychodynamic therapists have predicted that behavioral treatment will result in symptom substitution because behavioral treatment allegedly overlooks the "real" cause of the problem. Yet the evidence is clear that symptom substitution does not occur as a sequel of successful behavior theory. (e.g., Sloane, Staples, Cristol, Yorkston, & Whipple, 1975).

Family and systems therapists assert

that problems of an individual can best be understood and successfully treated by changing the entire interpersonal system within a family. Behavior therapy has increasingly emphasized the importance of other family members in treatment, especially in the maintenance of therapeutic improvement. However, behavior therapists reject the assumption that every problem requires a broad-scale intervention in the family system. The findings of well-controlled outcome studies clearly show that this is not always necessary (Mathews, Gelder, & Johnston, 1981). For example, not only does individual behavior therapy for agoraphobics produce long-term improvement in phobic fear and avoidance behavior, but it often also results in increases in marital satisfaction and other aspects of interpersonal functioning (Marks, 1981). Data such as these discredit some of the claims of the family systems theorists.

Most forms of psychotherapy tend to be limited to specific populations of patients. Traditional psychoanalytic therapy, for instance, has focused predominantly on white, well-educated, socially and economically advantaged, neurotic patients. Behavior therapy is more broadly applicable to the full range of psychological disorders than traditional psychotherapy (Kazdin & Wilson, 1978). In the Sloane et al. (1975) study, for example, behavior therapy appeared to be more effective than traditional psychotherapy, particularly with the more complex problems in the more severely disturbed patients. Areas of successful application of behavior therapy procedures are found in education, rehabilitation, and even medicine (Franks, Wilson, Kendall & Brownell, 1982; Kazdin, 1978b). Finally, there is evidence showing that behavior therapy is the preferred treatment for certain problems, such as phobic and obsessive disorders, sexual dysfunction,

and a number of childhood disorders. Overall evaluation of the comparative efficacy of behavior therapy versus other psychotherapies continues to be uncertain. Nevertheless, in no comparative outcome study to date has behavior therapy been shown to be less effective than any alternative form of psychotherapy (Kazdin & Wilson, 1978). The evidence, unsatisfactory as it still is, indicates that behavior therapy may be more effective than psychoanalytic and other verbal psychotherapies (see Andrews & Harvey, 1981; Kazdin & Wilson, 1978; Shapiro & Shapiro).

HISTORY

Precursors

Two historical events overshadow all others in the development of behavior therapy. The first was the rise of behaviorism in the early 1900s. The key figure in the United States was J. B. Watson who criticized the subjectivity and mentalism of the psychology of the time and put forward behaviorism as the basis for the objective study of behavior. Watson's emphasis on the overriding importance of environmental events, his rejection of covert aspects of the individual, and his claim that all behavior could be understood as a result of learning became the formal bases of behaviorism.

Watson's extremist position has been widely rejected, and more refined versions of behaviorism have been developed. Preeminent in this regard has been B. F. Skinner whose radical behaviorism has had a significant impact not only on behavior therapy (particularly applied behavior analysis) but also on psychology in general. Like Watson, Skinner insisted that overt behavior is the only acceptable subject of scientific investigation and rejected mentalistic concepts.

The second event was experimental research on the psychology of learning. In Russia, around the turn of the century, Ivan Pavlov, a Nobel Laureate in physiology, established the foundations of classical conditioning. About the same time in the United States, pioneering research on animal learning by E. L. Thorndike showed the influence of consequences (rewarding and punishing events) on behavior. Beginning in the late 1930s, instrumental learning was elaborated upon by Skinner in his research on operant conditioning.

Research on conditioning and learning principles, conducted largely in the animal laboratory, became a dominant part of experimental psychology in the United States following World War II. Workers in this area, in the traditions of Pavlov and Skinner, were committed to the scientific analysis of behavior using the laboratory rat and pigeon as their prototypic subjects. Among the early applications of conditioning principles to the treatment of clinical problems were two particularly notable studies. In 1924, Mary Cover Jones described the use of different behavioral procedures for overcoming children's fears. Later, in 1938, O. Hobart Mowrer and E. Mowrer extended conditioning principles to the treatment of enuresis. The method that resulted from their work is now a demonstrably effective and widely used treatment (Ross, 1981). These isolated and sporadic efforts had scant impact on psychotherapy then, partly because conditioning principles, demonstrated with animals, were rejected as too simplistic and irrelevant to the treatment of complex human problems. Conditioning treatments were rejected as superficial, mechanistic, and naive. A schism existed between academic-experimental and clinical psychologists. The former were trained in scientific methods,

with an emphasis on controlled experimentation and quantitative measurement. The latter concerned themselves with the "soft" side of psychology, including uncontrolled case studies, speculative hypotheses, and psychodynamic hypotheses about unconscious motivation. Some efforts were made to integrate conditioning principles with psychodynamic theories of abnormal behavior, but these eclectic formulations had little effect and only obscured crucial differences between the respective behavioral and psychodynamic approaches. Dollard and Miller (1950), for example, translated psychodynamic therapies into the language of Hullian learning theory but with little consequence for any clinical innovation since they were merely reinterpreting psychotherapy as it was, rather than advocating different concepts and procedures. The advent of behavior therapy was marked by its challenge of the prevailing status quo and the presentation of a systematic and explicitly formulated clinical alternative that attempted to bridge the gap between the laboratory and the clinic.

Beginnings

The formal beginnings of behavior therapy can be traced to separate but related developments in the 1950s in three countries.

Joseph Wolpe (1958), in South Africa, presented procedural details and results of his application of learning principles to adult neurotic disorders. Wolpe introduced several therapeutic techniques based on Pavlov's conditioning principles, Hull's stimulus-response (S-R) learning theory, and his own experimental research on fear reduction in laboratory animals. Anxiety was regarded as the causal agent in all neurotic reactions; it was defined as a persistent response of the autonomic nervous system acquired through the process of classical conditioning. He developed specific techniques designed to extinguish these conditioned autonomic reactions, including systematic desensitization, one of the most widely used methods of behavior therapy. A particularly controversial statement found in Wolpe's book was his claim that 90 percent of his patients were either "cured" or "markedly improved." Moreover, this unprecedented success rate was apparently accomplished, not after years and years of therapy as posited to be necessary by psychoanalysis, but within a few months, or even weeks. Wolpe influenced A. A. Lazarus and S. Rachman, both of whom became leading figures in the development of behavior therapy. Wolpe's pioneering use of different conditioning techniques in therapy was consistent with similar proposals that had been put foward by Andrew Salter (1949) in New York.

Another landmark in the development of behavior therapy as an alternative approach to the traditional psychoanalytic model was the research and writings of Hans J. Eysenck and his students at the Institute of Psychiatry of London University. In a seminal paper published in 1959, Eysenck defined behavior therapy as the application of modern learning theory to the treatment of behavioral and emotional disorders. Eysenck emphasized the principles and procedures of Pavlov and Hull, as well as learning theorists such as Mowrer (1947) and Miller (1948). In Eysenck's formulation, behavior therapy was an applied science, the defining feature of which was that it is testable and falsifiable. A testable theory can be specified with sufficient precision for experimental investigation. A falsifiable theory specifies experimental conditions that can result in the theory being disproved or falsified. In 1963 Eysenck and Rachman established the first journal devoted exclusively to behavior therapy— *Behaviour Research and Therapy*. As a result of the continuing research and writings of Eysenck and Rachman and their colleagues at the Institute of Psychiatry of London, this institute has remained one of the foremost centers of behavior therapy in the world.

A major force in the emergence of behavior therapy was the growth of operant conditioning in the United States and the extension of operant conditioning principles to clinical problems. This development was spurred by the publication in 1953 of Skinner's book, *Science and Human Behavior*, in which he criticized psychodynamic concepts and reformulated psychotherapy in behavioral terms. The most important initial clinical application of operant conditioning was with children, work carried out under the direction of Sidney Bijou at the University of Washington. The broad application of operant conditioning to the whole range of psychiatric disorders reached full expression in the influential publication of Leonard Ullmann and Leonard Krasner's book, *Case Studies in Behavior Modification* in 1965. This book presented contrasting descriptions of medical and psychological models of treatment, and illustrated how learning principles, particularly operant conditioning, could be used to modify diverse clinical problems. In 1968, the *Journal of Applied Behavior Analysis* was published, providing the premier outlet for research on the modification of socially significant problems through the use of operant conditioning procedures.

Toward the end of the 1960s the theoretical and research bases of behavior therapy began to be expanded by drawing more broadly upon areas of experimental research and psychological theory beyond classical and operant conditioning principles. Increasingly, behavior therapists turned to current developments in areas such as social, personality, and developmental psychology for different ways of conceptualizing their activities and as a source of innovative therapeutic strategies. Particularly noteworthy in this regard was Bandura's (1969) social learning theory, with its emphases on vicarious learning (modeling), symbolic processes, and self-regulatory mechanisms. The 1970s witnessed an increased emphasis on cognitive processes and procedures in behavior therapy, as noted in the preceding section. (See Kazdin [1978a] for a detailed history of behavior therapy.)

Current Status

Within the space of only two decades, behavior therapy has established itself as a major form of psychological therapy. It has helped to transform graduate training in clinical psychology in the United States. Several doctoral training programs are predominantly behavioral in orientation (e.g., programs at Pennsylvania State University, Rutgers University, State University of New York at Stony Brook). Few training programs in clinical psychology have no behavioral training component. Counseling programs in schools of education and doctoral programs in schools of psychology also reflect the influence of behavior therapy. In a recent survey of a random sample of clinical and counseling psychologists, Smith (1982) concluded that "No single theme dominates the present development of professional psychotherapy. Our findings suggest, however, that cognitive-behavioral options represent one of the strongest, if not *the* strongest, theoretical emphases today" (p. 808). The impact of behavior therapy on psychiatry has been

far less (Brady & Wienckowski, 1978), although the American Psychiatric Association issued a report concluding that "behavioral principles . . . have reached a stage of development where they now unquestionably have much to offer informed clinicians in the service of modern clinical and social psychiatry" (Birk, Stolz, Brady, Brady, Lazarus, Lynch, Rosenthal, Skelton, Stevens, & Thomas, 1973, p. 64).

The Association for Advancement of Behavior Therapy (AABT) is the major behavior therapy organization in North America. It is a professional, interdisciplinary organization with over 3,000 members. Membership is open to professionals and students in disciplines such as psychology, psychiatry, social work, medicine, nursing, dentistry, rehabilitation, and education. The majority of members are clinical psychologists with doctoral degrees. Participation in AABT activities is open to qualified nonmembers. AABT does not certify or license behavior therapists. AABT publishes two major journals, *Behavior Therapy* and *Behavioral Assessment*, produces a monthly newsletter called *The Behavior Therapist*, and holds annual conventions. Behavior therapy is well represented throughout Europe, particularly in Great Britain, the Netherlands, West Germany, and Scandanavia. The umbrella organization there is the European Association of Behaviour Therapy. The British Association of Behaviour Therapy alone has over 1,100 members and published *Behavioural Psychotherapy*, an interdisciplinary international journal for the helping professions.

The practice of behavior therapy is developing in Latin America, with active organizations in Bolivia, Chile, Columbia, Mexico, Peru, and Venezuela, among other countries. The federated association representing Central and South America is the Latin American Association for the

Analysis and Modification of Behavior (ALOMOC). Brownell (1981) provides an informative analysis of behavior therapy organizations around the world.

The explosion of literature on behavior therapy has been dramatic. At present there are at least nine journals devoted exclusively to behavior therapy: *Advances in Behaviour Research and Therapy, Behaviour Research and Therapy, Behavior Therapy, Behavioral Assessment, Behavioural Psychotherapy, Behavior Modification, Journal of Behavior Therapy and Experimental Psychiatry, Journal of Behavioral Assessment,* and *Journal of Applied Behavior Analysis.* A 10th, *Cognitive Therapy and Research,* is an outlet for the cognitive connection in cognitive behavior modification, while *Biofeedback and Self-Regulation* and *Journal of Behavioral Medicine* overlap greatly with traditional behavior therapy research and practice. Behavior therapists are also significant contributors to and editorial board members of journals, such as *Journal of Consulting and Clinical Psychology,* the most widely distributed clinical journal in the United States. In 1973 C. M. Franks and G. T. Wilson edited the first volume of *Annual Review of Behavior Therapy: Theory and Practice,* while M. Hersen, R. Eisler, and P. Miller (1973) began the annual series *Progress in Behavior Modification.* Books abound in behavior therapy, to the point where Rachman and Wilson (1980) noted that it "is no exaggeration to say that a major text on the subject is published virtually every month" (p. 3).

PERSONALITY

Theory of Personality

There are specific theoretical differences within the broad framework of contemporary behavior therapy. These differences are most noticeable in person-

ality theories on which the respective approaches are based. Eysenck (1967) has developed an elaborate trait theory of personality. Briefly, Eysenck classifies people on two major personality dimensions. The first, *introversion-extraversion,* refers to characteristics normally associated with the words *introverted* and *extraverted.* The second dimension is *neuroticism-emotional stability,* ranging from moody and touchy at one extreme to stable and even-tempered at the other. These personality dimensions are believed by Eysenck to be genetically determined. According to Eysenck's theory, introverts are more responsive to conditioning procedures than extraverts, so that where a client is classified on this dimension predicts how he or she will respond to treatment. Aside from Eysenck's own work and that of some of his students, this personality theory appears to have had little impact on clinical behavior therapy. Classifying clients on introversion-extraversion and neuroticism-stability dimensions has not proved useful in designing therapeutic interventions or in predicting outcome. Behavior therapists in general have rejected trait theories of personality.

Applied behavior analysis, derived directly from Skinner's radical behaviorism, restricts itself to the study of overt behavior and environmental conditions that presumably regulate the behavior. Covert unobservable elements such as needs, drives, motives, traits, or conflicts that are assumed by some to underlie and direct behavior, are disregarded. Behaviorists criticize such typical personality concepts such as drive as being vague pseudo-explanations of behavior. Skinner's analyses of behavior are couched in terms of conditioning processes such as reinforcement, discrimination, and generalization.

However, radical behaviorism, with its

emphasis on the overriding importance of environmental control of behavior, has been criticized for losing sight of the importance of the person—and lacking a theory of personality. The objection from humanistic psychologists is that applied behavior analysts treat people as though they were externally controlled only by situational forces rather than being free, self-directed agents responsible for their own growth and actions. A solution to this clash between two extreme viewpoints is to recognize that the characteristics of the environment *interact* with the nature of the people in it, and both commonsense and experimental findings show how unwise it is to ignore either side of this crucial interaction. A social learning framework of personality development and change provides a detailed and sophisticated analysis of this interaction between person and situation (Bandura, 1969; Mischel, 1968, 1981).

Much debate has centered on the question of whether the person or the situation is more important in predicting behavior. This question is misguided and unanswerable. In terms of a social learning analysis, the relative importance of individual differences and situations will depend on the situation selected, the type of behavior assessed, the particular individual differences sampled, and the purpose of the assessment (Mischel, 1973).

Consider the varying influence of different situations on different behavior. Evidence clearly shows that an individual's behavioral patterns are generally stable and consistent over time. Nevertheless, studies also reveal that behavioral patterns are not highly generalized in different situations. The specificity or discriminativeness of behavior in different situations poses a significant problem for trait theories of personality. The central assumption of such theories is that people possess stable and generalized personality traits which determine behavioral consistency across a wide variety of different situations. Yet as Mischel (1968) has pointed out, with the exception of activities closely related to intelligence and certain forms of problem solving, the correlations between different measures of the same trait are usually very low and there is little consistency in behavior patterns across different stimulus situations.

Some psychodynamic conceptualizations of personality assume that the underlying personality structure is stable irrespective of the situation. Apparent inconsistencies or discriminativeness in behavior are explained away as the surface or symptomatic manifestations of the "real" underlying motives. Overt behavior is of interest for them only to the extent that the behavior provides signs of deep-seated, generalized personality traits. It is said that behavior cannot be taken at face value but must be interpreted symbolically because the personality's defense mechanisms disguise and distort the "real" motivations being expressed in observed behavior. This practice of disregarding the importance of the patient's behavior in real-life situations in favor of a search for hidden motivational states is defensible only if the underlying motives can be reliably inferred and then shown to be useful for selecting specific treatment techniques. However, "the accumulated findings give little support for the utility of clinical judgments .... Clinicians guided by concepts about underlying genotypic dispositions have not been able to predict behavior better than have the person's own direct self-report, simple indices of directly relevant past behavior, or demographic variables" (Mischel, 1973, p. 254).

Social learning theory readily accounts for the discriminativeness of human behavior. A person would be predicted to act consistently across situations only to the extent that similar behavior leads, or is expected to lead, to similar consequences across those conditions. Since it is rare to find the same behavior reinforced across situations, it is not surprising that people make subtle discriminations and behave differently in different settings. An illustration from Mischel (1976) will help clarify this key concept:

Consider a woman who seems hostile and fiercely independent some of the time but passive, dependent, and feminine on other occasions. What is she really like? Which one of these two patterns reflects the woman that she really is? Is one pattern in the service of the other, or might both be in the service of a third motive? Must she be a really aggressive person with a facade of passivity—or is she a warm, passive-dependent woman with a surface defense of aggressiveness? Social learning theory suggests that it is possible for her to be all of these—a hostile, fiercely independent, passive, dependent, feminine, aggressive, warm person all in one. Of course which of these she is at any particular moment would not be random and capricious; it would depend on discriminative stimuli—who she is with, when, how, and much, much more. But each of these aspects of herself may be a quite genuine and real aspect of her total being (p. 86).

The difference between the behavioral and psychodynamic approaches in explaining the development of abnormal behavior can be illustrated with reference to Freud's Little Hans. The child developed a phobia for horses, which Freud attributed to castration anxiety and Oedipal conflict. In their reinterpretation of this case, Wolpe and Rachman (1960) point out that Little Hans had recently experienced four incidents in which horses were associated with frightening events that could have created a classically conditioned phobic reaction, the most striking being an accident in which he was terrified by seeing a horse drawing a loaded cart

knocked down and apparently killed. From a psychodynamic viewpoint, these external stimuli (what Little Hans saw) had little effect on the phobia; the fear of horses per se was less significant than the underlying conflict. As Freud put it, "the anxiety originally had no reference to horses but was transposed onto them secondarily." This interpretation does not account for the discriminative pattern of the boy's reactions. For example, he was fearful of a single horse pulling a loaded cart (viewed by Freud as a symbol of pregnancy) but not of two horses; of a large rather than a small horse; and of rapidly moving horse-drawn carts more than slowly moving ones, and so on. How is this pattern predicted by a global, internal construct such as an Oedipus conflict? In the accident that the boy witnessed, a single, large horse, moving rapidly, was believed to have been killed. A conditioning explanation emphasizes that specific stimulus elements elicit particular responses, and therefore accounts plausibly for the discriminative fear responses of Little Hans.

Trait theories emphasize differences among people on some dimension selected by the clinician. For some purposes, such as gross screening (e.g., administering an MMPI to a client to explore further the extent of his or her psychopathology) or group comparisons, a trait approach is useful. But it does not aid the therapist in making treatment decisions about a particular individual. Take the traits of introversion-extraversion. According to Eysenck's theory, particular treatments will have different effects on clients that vary along these dimensions. In a well-controlled study, Paul (1966) correlated performance on a range of paper and pencil personality tests measuring extraversion, emotionality, and anxiety among other traits, with the therapeutic success obtained by treating public speaking anxiety with systematic desensitization. His results revealed no relationship whatsoever between global personality measures and therapeutic outcome. This result is typical of other outcome studies.

The social learning approach, however, is person-centered and focuses on describing the individual in relation to the particular psychological conditions of one's life. The heart of this approach is an analysis that investigates covariations between changes in the individual and changes in the conditions of his or her life. The interest here is not in how people compare to others, but in how they can move closer to their own goals and ideals if they change their behavior in specific ways as they interact with the significant people in their lives. In this sense, the social learning approach captures the richness and uniqueness of individual clients' lives.

Variety of Concepts

Learning principles

The case of Little Hans, described above, illustrates the role of classical conditioning. When a previously neutral stimulus is paired with a frightening event (the unconditioned stimulus), it can become a conditioned stimulus (CS) that elicits a conditioned response (CR) such as anxiety. Current analyses of classical conditioning have moved away from the once popular notion that what was learned consisted of simple stimulus-response (S-R) bonds. Rather, learning of correlational or contingent relationships between the CS and US defines the conditioning process. Classical conditioning is no longer seen as the simple pairing of a single CS with a single US on the basis of temporal contiguity. Instead, correlations between entire classes of stimulus events can be learned. People may be exposed to trau-matic events (contiguity) but not develop phobic reactions unless a correlational or contingent relationship is formed between the situation and the traumatic event.

Operant conditioning emphasizes that behavior is a function of its environmental consequences. Behavior is strengthened by positive and negative reinforcement; it is weakened by punishment. Positive reinforcement refers to an increase in the frequency of a response followed by a favorable event. Reinforcement involves a contingency between behavior and the reinforcing event. An example would be a teacher or parent praising a child for obtaining a good report card. *Negative* reinforcement refers to an increase in behavior as a result of avoiding or escaping from an aversive event that one would have expected to occur had the escape behavior not been emitted. For example, an agoraphobic, fearing that she will lose control and experience a panic attack in a crowded shopping mall, will escape this aversive prospect by staying at home. She now experiences relief from anxiety by having avoided this panic and thereby finds it increasingly difficult to leave her house. In *punishment*, an aversive event is contingent on a response; the result is a decrease in the frequency of that response. If a child is criticized or punished by his parents for speaking up, he is likely to become an inhibited and unassertive adult. *Extinction* refers to the cessation or removal of a response. Thus the family of an obsessive-compulsive client might be instructed to ignore requests for reassurance from the client that he has not done something wrong. The reinforcer that is no longer presented is inappropriate attention.

Discrimination learning occurs when a response is rewarded (or punished) in one situation but not in another. Behavior is then under specific *stimulus control*. This process is particularly important in explaining the flexibility or discriminativeness of human behavior under different physical and social conditions. For example, an obese client who goes on eating binges may show good food self-control under some circumstances but lose control in predictable situations (e.g., being alone and feeling frustrated or depressed). *Generalization* refers to the occurrence of behavior in situations other than that in which it was acquired. A therapist might help a client to become more assertive and expressive during treatment sessions. But the goal of therapy is for the client to act more assertively in real-life situations—in other words, it is important for generalization to occur.

Social learning theory recognizes the importance of awareness in learning and of the person's active cognitive appraisal of environmental events. Learning is facilitated when people are aware of the rules and contingencies governing the consequences of their actions. Reinforcement does not involve an automatic strengthening of behavior. Learning from response consequences is attributable to the informative and incentive functions of rewards. By observing the consequences of behavior, the person learns what action is appropriate in what situation. By symbolic representation of anticipated future outcomes of behavior, the person helps to generate the motivation to initiate and sustain current actions (Bandura, 1977). Often, people's expectations and hypotheses about what is happening to them may affect their behavior more than the objective reality of the rules and contingencies associated with the behavior. Clinical practice provides numerous instances that our subjective perception of the external world rather than objective reality frequently determines behavior. Clinical problems often arise when a significant discrepancy between a person's perception of events and objective reality develops. This is one of the reasons for the growing importance of cognitive restructuring methods in behavior therapy.

The importance social learning theory attaches to *vicarious learning (modeling)* is consistent with its emphasis on cognitive processes. In this form of learning, people acquire new knowledge and behavior by observing other people and events, without engaging in the behavior themselves and without any direct consequences to themselves. Vicarious learning may occur when people watch what others ("models") do, or when they attend to the physical environment, to events, and to symbols such as words and pictures. The influence of vicarious learning on human behavior is pervasive, and this concept greatly expands the power of social learning theory to account for the great complexity of psychological functioning.

Person variables

People do not passively interact with situations with empty heads or an absence of feelings. Rather, they actively attend to environmental stimuli, interpret them, encode. them, and selectively remember them. Mischel (1973) has spelled out a series of person variables that explain the interchange between person and situation. These person variables are the products of each person's social experience and cognitive development that, in turn, determine how future experiences influence him or her. Briefly, they include the individual's *competencies* to construct (generate) diverse behaviors under appropriate conditions. In addition, there is the person's *encoding* and *categorization* of events and people, including the self. To understand how and what a person will perform in particular situations also requires attention to his or her *expectancies,* the *subjective values* of any expected outcomes, and the individual's *self-regulatory systems and plans.*

A full discussion of these person variables is beyond the scope of the present chapter, but some illustrative examples may be given. Take the role of *personal constructs.* A common clinical phenomenon is the client who constantly "puts himself down" considering himself incompetent even though it is clear to the objective onlooker that he is competent and that he is distorting reality. In cases like these, behavior is mainly under the control of internal stimuli rather than environmental events. Different people might respond differently to the same objective stimulus situation depending on how they subjectively perceive or interpret what is happening to them. Therapy should concentrate on correcting such faulty cognitive perceptions. But the behavior therapist must also assess a client's cognitive and behavioral *competencies* to ascertain whether he or she really *can* engage in a particular response. A client may be depressed not because he misperceives the situation but because he actually lacks the appropriate skills and behavior necessary to secure rewards which are important to him. A case in point would be a shy, under-assertive college freshman who is motivated to date girls, but realizes that he does not have the social skills needed to meet and befriend members of the opposite sex. Therapy in this case would be geared to overcoming his behavioral deficit, helping the freshman to acquire the requisite interpersonal skills.

Self-efficacy is assessed simply by asking the person to indicate the degree of confidence that he or she can do a particular task which is described in detail.

Such person variables differ from traits in that they do not assume broad cross-situational consistency. Instead, they depend on specific contexts. Constructs such as generalized expectancies have not proved fruitful in predicting behavior. However, specific evaluations of individuals' efficacy expectations with respect to particular tasks are useful.

Applied behavior analysts, given their rejection of cognitive mediating processes in assessment and modification of behavior, find little use for the person variables described so far. They agree that the environment interacts with the person, but, as radical behaviorists, contend that the role of the person is best explained in terms of *past history of reinforcement.* To illustrate the differences between the social learning and the radical behaviorist positions, imagine a client who is phobic about flying. This client typically becomes highly anxious when he hears a sudden noise at takeoff due to the normal retracting of the plane's landing gear. A therapist with a cognitive social learning view might attribute this anxiety reaction to the client's perception that something is wrong. The radical behaviorist would suggest that the client is reacting, not only to the present environment (the sudden noise), but also to stories he has heard in the past about engines falling off and planes crashing. Rachlin (1977) summarizes this view by stating that "Inferences about past experiences may be as speculative about present cognitions, but at least they are potentially observable." This example makes it clear that radical behaviorism is not free from inferential reasoning, as is commonly supposed. The question is not whether inferences will be made in trying to account for human behavior, but what sort of inference is the most useful. And there is now evidence to demonstrate that taking person variables into account improves prediction about behavior and enhances therapeutic efficacy (Wilson & O'Leary, 1980).

PSYCHOTHERAPY

Theory of Psychotherapy

Cognitive learning

Behavior therapy emphasizes corrective learning experiences in which clients variously acquire new coping skills and improved communication competencies, or learn how to break maladaptive habits and overcome self-defeating emotional conflicts. In contemporary behavior therapy these corrective learning experiences involve broad changes in cognitive, affective, and behavioral spheres of functioning; they are not limited to modifications of narrow response patterns in overt behavior. These corrective learning experiences are the product of a wide range of different strategies continually being modified and refined on the basis of research and clinical findings. These therapeutic strategies are implemented during and between formal treatment sessions.

The learning that characterizes behavior therapy is carefully structured. Perhaps more than any other form of treatment, behavior therapy involves asking a patient to do something such as practice relaxation training, self-monitor daily caloric intake, engage in assertive acts, confront anxiety-eliciting situations, and refrain from carrying out compulsive rituals. The high degree to which behavior therapists emphasize the client's activities in the real world between therapy sessions is one of the distinctive features of the behavioral approach. Behavior therapy is not a one-sided influence process by the therapist to effect changes in a client's beliefs and behavior. It is a dynamic process of interaction between therapist and client and then—it is directed work on the part of the client. A crucial factor in therapy is the client's motivation, the willingness to cooperate in the arduous and challenging task of making significant changes in real-life behavior. Resistance to change or lack of motivation are common reasons for treatment failures in behavior therapy. Much of the art in therapy involves coping with issues of this sort (Lazarus & Fay, 1982).

The therapeutic relationship

Behavior therapy demands considerable therapist skill, sensitivity, and clinical acumen. Brady (1980) underscores the importance of the therapeutic relationship as follows:

There is no question that qualitative aspects of the therapist-patient relationship can greatly influence the course of therapy for good or bad. In general, if the patient's relationship to the therapist is characterized by belief in the therapist's competence (knowledge, sophistication, and training) and if the patient regards the therapist as an honest, trustworthy, and decent human being with good social and ethical values (in his own scheme of things), the patient is more apt to invest himself in the therapy. Equally important is the quality and tone of the relationship he has with the therapist. That is, if he feels trusting and warm toward the therapist, this generally will facilitate following the treatment regimen, will be associated with higher expectations of improvement, and other generally favorable factors. The feelings of the therapist toward the patient are also important. If the therapist feels that his patient is not a desirable person or a decent human being or simply does not like the patient for whatever reasons, he may not succeed in concealing these attitudes toward the patient, and in general they will have a deleterious effect. There are some exceptions to these generalizations, however. Some patients will feel frightened and vulnerable with a therapist toward whom they feel attracted, particularly if from past experience they perceive such relationships as dangerous (danger of being hurt emotionally). With such a patient, a somewhat more distant and impersonal relationship may be more desirable in that it will facilitate the patient's involvement in the treatment, following the treatment regimen, etc. (pp. 285-286).

A survey of behavior practitioners indicated that among the treatment procedures most frequently reported were methods aimed at improving the therapeutic relationship (Swan & MacDonald, 1978). O'Leary, Turkewitz, and Tafel (1973) found that virtually all parents whose children were treated at the Stony Brook child guidance clinic rated their behavior therapists as understanding, warm, sincere, and interested. Similarly, in a study of marital therapy by Turkewitz and O'Leary (1981), clients' ratings of their behavior therapists were very positive.

There are important theoretical and practical differences between behavior therapy and traditional psychotherapies in the way in which the relationship in psychotherapy is conceptualized. As opposed to the neutral and detached role that the psychoanalytically therapist is taught to assume, the behavior therapist is more directive and more concerned —a problem-solver and a coping model who tries to instigate behavioral change in the client's natural environment, and who serves as a source of personal support. In their comparative study of behavior therapy and psychoanalytically oriented psychotherapy, Staples, Sloane, Cristol, Yorkston, and Whipple (1975) concluded that:

Differences between behavior therapy and analytically-oriented psychotherapy . . . involved the basic patterns of interactions between patient and therapist and the type of relationship formed. Behavior therapy is not psychotherapy with special "scientific techniques" superimposed on the traditional therapeutic paradigm; rather, the two appear to represent quite different styles of treatment although they share common elements (p. 1521).

The behavior therapists were rated as more directive, more open, more genuine, and more disclosing than their psychoanalytically oriented counterparts. An early criticism was that behavior therapy would result in "symptom substitution." However, recent research has shown that this is not true. Both behavioral and psychodynamic treatments attempt to modify underlying causes of behavior; the difference is what proponents of each approach regard as causes. Behavior analysts look for current variables and conditions which control behavior. Some psychodynamic approaches ask: "How did he become this kind of person?" (Psychoanalysis.) Others ask: "What is this person trying to achieve?" (Adlerian psychotherapy.) Behavioral approaches ask: "What is causing this person to behave in this way right now, and what can we do right now to change that behavior?"

Careful treatment outcome research shows that symptom substitution does not occur (Kazdin & Wilson, 1978; Sloane et al., 1975). The latter investigators summarize their findings as follows: "Not a single patient whose original problems had substantially improved reported new symptoms cropping up. On the contrary, assessors had the informal impression that when a patient's primary symptoms improve, he often spontaneously reported improvement of other minor difficulty" (p. 100).

Ethical issues

In behavior therapy the client is encouraged to participate actively. Consider, for example, the important issue of who determines the goals of therapy. Because it is fundamental to behavior therapy that the client should have the major say in setting treatment goals, it is important that the client is fully informed, and consents to and participates in setting goals. A distinction is drawn between how behavior is to be changed—in which the therapist is presumably expert—and the objectives. The latter must ultimately be determined by the client. The client controls *what*, we control *how*. The major contribution of the therapist in this regard is to assist clients by helping them to generate alternative courses of action and to analyze the consequences of pursuing various goals. Since this process involves an expression of the therapist's own values, the therapist should identify his or her values and explain how they might affect the therapist's analysis of therapeutic goals.

Selecting goals is far more complicated in the case of disturbed clients (such as institutionalized psychotics) who are unable to participate meaningfully in deciding treatment objectives. To ensure that treatment is in the client's best interests, it is important to monitor program goals and procedures through having conferences with other professionals (Risley & Sheldon-Wildgen, 1982).

All forms of therapy involve social influence. The critical ethical question is whether therapists are aware of this influence. Behavior therapy entails an explicit recognition of the influence process and emphasizes specific, client-oriented behavioral objectives. Behavior therapists have formulated procedures to guarantee protection of human rights and personal dignity of clients, including homosexuals, the retarded, mental hospital patients, and school children, among others (Stolz, 1978; Wilson & O'Leary, 1980).

Process of Psychotherapy

Problem identification and assessment

The initial task of behavior therapists is to identify and understand the client's presenting problem(s). The therapist using behavioral theory seeks detailed information about the specific dimensions of problems, such as when they began, how severe they are, and how frequently they occur. What has the client done to cope with the problems? What does the client think about his or her problem, and any previous therapeutic contacts? Obtaining answers to such searching questions, which the client might find distressing or embarrassing, is facilitated by first building a relationship of trust and mutual understanding. To achieve this, the therapist is attentive, tries to be emotionally objective, and ideally is an empathic listener. The therapist then proceeds to make a functional analysis of the client's problem, attempting to identify specific environmental and person variables that are soon to be maintaining maladaptive thoughts, feelings, or behavior. The emphasis on variables currently maintaining the problem does not mean that the client's past history is ignored. However, past experiences at any time in life are focused upon only to the degree that they are still active in directly contributing to the client's present distress.

Assessment methods

In the behaviorally oriented interview the therapist seldom asks the client *why* questions; for example, "Why do you become anxious in crowded places?" Questions starting with *how, when, where,* and *what* are more useful in identifying relevant personal and situational variables currently maintaining the client's problems. The therapist does not necessarily take everything the client says at face value, and is constantly on the lookout for inconsistencies, evasiveness, or apparent distortions. Nevertheless, the therapist relies heavily on clients' self-reports, particularly in assessing thoughts, fantasies, and feelings. Self-report has often proved to be a superior predictor of behavior compared to clinicians' judgments or scores on personality tests (Mischel, 1981). Of course, therapists must ask the right questions if they are to get meaningful answers. Given the tendency of most people to describe themselves in terms of broad personality labels, therapists may have to guide clients in finding specific behavioral referents of global subjective impressions.

Guided imagery

A useful method for assessing clients' reactions to particular situations is to have them symbolically recreate a problematic life situation. Instead of asking clients simply to talk about an event, have them imagine it actually happening to them. When clients have conjured up an image of a situation they are then asked to verbalize any thoughts that come to mind, a particularly useful way of uncovering the specific thoughts associated with particular events.

Roleplaying

Another alternative is to ask clients to role-play a situation rather than to describe or imagine it. This method lends itself well to the assessment of interpersonal problems, with the therapist adopting the role of the person with whom the client reports problems. Roleplaying provides the therapist with a sample of the problem behavior, albeit under somewhat artificial circumstances. If the therapist is assessing a client couple, the two partners are asked to discuss chosen issues that enable the therapist to observe firsthand the nature of their interpersonal skills and ability to resolve conflict.

Physiological recording

Technological progress in monitoring different psychophysiological reactions has opened up possibilities of objectively measuring a number of problems, although these sophisticated resources are often available only in some clinics or hospital settings. Monitoring a client's sexual arousal in response to specific stimuli that cause changes in penile or vaginal blood flow (Rosen & Keefe, 1978) is an example of how physiological recording instruments can be used in behavioral assessment and treatment strategies.

Self-monitoring

Clients are typically instructed to keep detailed, daily records of particular events or psychological reactions. Obese clients, for example, are asked to self-monitor daily caloric intake, the degree to which they engage in planned physical activities, the conditions under which they eat and overeat, and so on. In this way it is possible to detect behavioral patterns in clients' lives functionally related to their problems, patterns of which they might be unaware.

Behavioral observation

Assessment of overt problem behavior, ideally, is based on actual observation of the client's behavior in the natural environment in which it occurs. Accordingly, behavior therapists have developed sophisticated behavioral observation rating procedures for measuring behavior directly. These procedures have most often been used with children either in the classroom or at home, or with hospitalized patients. Parents, teachers, nurses, and hospital aides have been trained as behavioral observers. Once these individuals have learned to observe behavior they can then be taught how to make a behavioral analysis of the problem and then instructed in how to alter their own behavior so as to modify the problem behavior.

Psychological tests and questionnaires

In general, behavior therapists do not use standardized psychodiagnostic tests, which are often based on questionable assumptions of personality trait theory. Tests such as the MMPI may be useful providing an overall picture of the client's personality profile but they do not yield the kind of information necessary for a functional analysis or for the development of a strategy of therapeutic interventions. Projective tests are widely rejected in view of their assumptions of psychodynamic theory and the lack of acceptable evidence for their validity or utility (Mischel, 1968). Behavior therapists do use checklists and questionnaires. Some examples in the assessment of adult disorders are: the Marks and Mathews (1979) Fear Questionnaire; self-report scales of depression—the Beck Depression Inventory (Beck, Rush, Shaw, & Emery, 1979); assertion inventories—the Rathus (1973) questionnaire; and paper and pencil measures of marital satisfaction—the Locke and Wallace (1959) inventory of marital adjustment. These assessment devices are not sufficient for carrying out a functional analysis of the determinants of the problem, but are useful in establishing the initial severity of the problem and for charting therapeutic efficacy over the course of treatment.

Treatment techniques

Behavior therapy offers a wide range of different treatment methods. Rather than artificially molding the client's problems to suit the therapist's preconceived theoretical notions, behavior therapy attempts to tailor the principles of social learning theory to each individual's unique problem. Some techniques are more appropriate with some problems and clients than with others. In selecting treatment techniques, the behavior therapist relies heavily on available empirical evidence about the efficacy of that technique applied to the particular problem. This information is frequently not sufficient for guiding therapeutic interven-

tions, and in many cases the empirical evidence is unclear or largely nonexistent. Here the therapist is influenced by accepted clinical practice (the state of the art) and the basic logic and philosophy of a social learning approach to human behavior and its modification. In the process, the therapist must often use intuitive skill and clinical savvy in deciding not only on the appropriate treatment methods, but also the important matter of timing—when to use any specific technique. Both science and art enter into informed clinical practice, and the most effective therapists are those aware of the advantages and limitations of each.

The following are some selective illustrations of the varied methods the typical behavior therapist is likely to employ in clinical practice.

Imagery-based techniques

In systematic desensitization, after isolating specific events that trigger unrealistic anxiety, the therapist constructs a stimulus hierarchy in which different situations that the client fears are ordered along a continuum from mildly stressful to very threatening. The client is instructed to conjure a clear and vivid image of each item while he or she is deeply relaxed. Wolpe (1958) adapted from Jacobson (1938) the method of progressive relaxation training as a means of producing a response incompatible with anxiety. Briefly, this consists of training clients to concentrate on systematically relaxing the different muscle groups of the body, which results in lowered physiological arousal and a comfortable subjective feeling of calmness. In the event that any item produces much anxiety, the client is instructed to cease visualizing the particular item and to restore feelings of relaxation. The item is then repeated, or the hierarchy adjusted, until the client can visualize the scene without experiencing anxiety. Only then does the therapist present the next item of the hierarchy.

Symbolically generated aversive reactions are used to treat unwanted problems including alcoholism and sexual disorders such as exhibitionism. In this procedure the client is asked to imagine the aversive consequence. An alcoholic might be asked to imagine experiencing nausea at the thought of a drink. As illustrated in "Case Example," an exhibitionist might be asked to imagine being apprehended by the police. This method is often referred to as covert sensitization (Cautela, 1967). A hierarchy of scenes that reliably elicit the problem urge or behavior is developed and each scene systematically presented until the client gains control over the problem.

Cognitive restructuring

The treatment methods in this category are based on the assumption that emotional disorders result from maladaptive thought patterns. The task of therapy is to alter these faulty cognitions. Ellis's (1962) RET may be viewed as a cognitive-behavioral approach to cognitive restructuring. Another widely used method is Meichenbaum's (1977) self-instructional training which involves the following steps: (a) the client is trained to identify and become aware of maladaptive thoughts (self-statements); (b) the therapist models appropriate behavior while verbalizing effective action strategies; these verbalizations include an appraisal of task requirements, self-statements that stress personal adequacy and counteract worry over failure, and self-reinforcement for successful performance; (c) the client then performs the target behavior first while verbalizing aloud the appropriate self-instructions and then by covertly rehearsing them Beck's (1976) cognitive therapy is a particularly useful form of cognitive restructuring that combines cognitive with behavioral methods.

Assertiveness and social skills training

A common clinical problem is presented by unassertive clients who are unable to express their emotional feelings and who do not stand up for their legitimate rights. They are often taken advantage of by others, feel anxiety in social situations, and suffer from a low sense of self-esteem. In behavior rehearsal the therapist may model the appropriate assertive behavior and may ask the client to engage repeatedly in a graduated sequence of similar actions. Attention is focused on developing nonverbal as well as verbal features of expressive behavior (e.g., body posture, voice training, and eye contact). The therapist then encourages the client to carry out assertive actions in the real world to ensure generalization. Behavior therapy is frequently conducted on a group as well as an individual basis (Upper & Ross, 1981). Behavior rehearsal for assertiveness training is well suited to group therapy, since group members can provide more varied sources of educative feedback than can a single therapist and can also offer a diversified range of modeling influences.

Aside from enhancing assertiveness, the instructional, modeling, and feedback components of behavior rehearsal facilitate a broader range of communication competencies, including active listening, giving personal feedback, and building trust through self-disclosure. These communication principles, drawn from nonbehavioral approaches to counseling but integrated within a behavioral framework, are an important ingredient of behavioral marital therapy (Jacobson & Margolin, 1979).

Self-control procedures

In behavioral treatment programs, both child and adult clients are taught that they must play an active part in determining their treatment goals and in implementing the treatment program. Behavior therapists use a number of self-control procedures (Bandura, 1977; Kanfer, 1977). Fundamental to successful self-regulation of behavior is self-monitoring, a process to make clients more aware of their specific problems and actions. The therapist helps the client to set goals or standards that guide behavior. In the treatment of obesity, for example, daily caloric goals are mutually worked out that enable the client to lose weight safely and effectively. Behavioral research has identified certain properties of goals that increase the probability of successful self-control. For example, one should set highly specific, unambiguous, and short-term goals, such as consumption of no more than 1,200 calories each day. Compare this to the goal of "cutting back" on eating for the "next week." Failure to achieve such vague goals elicits negative self-evaluative reactions by clients, whereas successful accomplishment of goals produces self-reinforcement that increases the likelihood that the self-regulatory behavior will be further maintained.

Self-instructional training, described above, is often used as a self-control method for coping with problems such as impulsivity, stress, excessive anger, and pain. Similarly, progressive relaxation training is widely applied as a self-control method for reducing different forms of stress, including insomnia, tension headaches, and hypertension (O'Leary & Wilson, in press). Biofeedback methods used to treat a variety of psychophysiological disorders also fall under the category of self-control procedures (Yates, 1980).

Real-life performance-based techniques

The foregoing techniques are applied during treatment sessions, and most are routinely coupled with instructions to clients to complete homework assignments: namely, specific tasks carried out *between* therapy sessions in the real world. In addition, some treatment methods are to be implemented primarily in the client's natural environment. The behavioral treatment of agoraphobia, as described in the section "Treatment" is an example of a real-life performance-based technique.

The diversity of behavioral treatment methods, including radical departures from conventional practice, is seen in the application of operant conditioning principles in settings ranging from classrooms to institutions for the retarded and the insane. An excellent illustration is the use of *token economy*. The main elements of a token reinforcement program can be summarized as follows: (*a*) carefully specified and operationally defined target behaviors, (*b*) backup reinforcers, the "good things in life" or what people are willing to work for, (*c*) tokens which represent the backup reinforcers, and (*d*) rules of exchange which specify the number of tokens required to obtain backup reinforcers.

A token economy in a classroom might consist of the teacher, at regular intervals, making ratings in special books on each child's desk indicating how well the student had behaved both academically and socially. At the end of the day the ratings would be exchangeable for various small prizes. These procedures reduce disruptive social behavior in the classroom and can improve academic performance (O'Leary & O'Leary, 1977). In the case of psychiatric patients on a mental hospital ward the staff might make tokens contingent upon improvements in self-care activities, on reductions in belligerent acts, and on cooperative problem-solving behavior (Kazdin, 1977).

The behavior therapist designs the token economy and monitors its implementation and efficacy. The procedures themselves are implemented in real-life settings by teachers, parents, nurses, psychiatric aides—whoever has most direct contact with the patient. Ensuring that these psychological assistants are well trained and supervised is the responsibility of the behavior therapist.

Length of treatment

Much of behavior therapy is short-term treatment, but therapy lasting from 25 to 50 sessions is commonplace, and still longer treatment is not unusual. Therapy in excess of 100 sessions, however, is relatively rare. There are no established guidelines for deciding on the length of therapy in any a priori fashion. The usual approach in clinical practice is to carry out a detailed behavioral assessment of the problem(s) and to embark upon interventions as rapidly as possible. Assessment is an ongoing process, as the consequences of initial treatment interventions are evaluated against therapeutic goals. Unless treatment is explicitly time limited from the start, the length of therapy and the scheduling of the treatment sessions are contingent upon the patient's progress.

Typically, a behavior therapist might contract with the patient to pursue a treatment plan for two to three months (approximately 8-12 sessions) and reevaluate progress at that point. The relative absence of any discernible improvement is cause for the therapist to reevaluate whether he or she conceptualized the problem accurately, whether he or she is using the appropriate techniques or needs to switch tactics, whether there is some personal problem with him or her as the therapist, or whether a referral to another therapist or another form of treatment might be called for.

In terminating a successful case, the behavior therapist usually avoids an abrupt end. A typical procedure is to lengthen gradually the time between successive therapy sessions, from weekly to fortnightly to monthly and so on. These concluding sessions which progressively phase out the therapist's active involvement may be shorter than earlier ones, with telephone contacts occasionally interspersed among them.

Mechanisms of Psychotherapy

Research on behavior therapy has not only demonstrated that particular treatment methods are effective, but also identified what components of multifaceted treatment methods and programs are responsible for therapeutic success. For example, the preceding section described the use of the token economy. Empirical evidence has established that the changes produced by token reinforcement programs are due to the learning principles of operant conditioning on which they are based (Kazdin, 1977).

Learning processes

A pioneering token reinforcement program with predominantly schizophrenic patients on a psychiatric hospital ward was reported by Ayllon and Azrin (1965). The target behaviors in this investigation were self-care and improved capacity for productive work. Rewards were made contingent on improvement in these two areas. The decisive role of the response-reinforcement contingency in producing significant increases in working habits was shown by using an ABA design in which each patient served as her own control. Following a period during which the job assignments of all 44 patients on the entire ward were rewarded contingently (phase A), tokens were administered on a noncontingent basis (phase B). In this phase B procedure, patients were given tokens each day regardless of their performance which broke the contingency between reinforcer and response without eliminating the reinforcer completely. This ensured that the amount of social interaction between the attendants and ward staff who administered the tokens and the patients remained unchanged. Any deterioration in performance is then directly attributable to the precise functional relationship between behavior and reinforcement. In other words, any observed improvement in the patients' functioning during the reinforcement phase could not be attributed to increases in attention from the hospital staff or other uncontrolled factors. Phase C marked a return to contingent reinforcement as in phase A. The results showed that "free" reinforcement (phase B) was totally ineffective in maintaining the work performance of the patients. Similarly, the complete withdrawal of all tokens resulted in their job performance decreasing to less than one fourth of the rate at which it had previously been maintained by contingently rewarding the patients with tokens.

The theoretical mechanisms that account for therapeutic success vary, depending on treatment methods and problems. No single, monolithic theory encompasses the diverse methods and applications of the different behavior therapies. Although operant conditioning principles explain the efficacy of a broad range of behavioral procedures, they do not account for the success of a number of other methods. Numerous studies, using innovative methodological strategies, have identified the critical element of this multicomponent technique in treating fears. Neither the therapist-patient relationship, the training in progressive relaxation training, nor any other placebo value of the method is essential for success. The necessary (and usually sufficient) therapeutic component is repeated exposure to the fear-eliciting object or situation. Relaxation training and the use of a carefully graded hierarchy facilitate exposure and hence contribute indirectly to treatment success. Real-life exposure, where possible, is more powerful than imaginal processes.

Why does systematic, repeated exposure work? The answer to this question remains elusive. Originally, the explanation was based on Mowrer's (1947) two-factor theory of learning, according to which repeated exposure to anxiety-eliciting situations, as in systematic desensitization, resulted in the extinction of classically conditioned anxiety that mediates phobic avoidance behavior. However, recent research (Bandura, 1977) casts doubt on the validity of this explanation.

Cognitive mechanisms

In terms of social learning theory, exposure leads not to the extinction of any underlying anxiety drive state, but rather to modification of the client's expectations of self-efficacy (Bandura, 1982). Self-efficacy refers to clients' beliefs that they can cope with formerly feared situations. Self-efficacy itself is really a capsule summary construct comprising several specific cognitive processes, including the type of attributions the client makes. For efficacy expectations to change, the client must make a self-attribution of behavioral change. For example, it is not uncommon for an agoraphobic client to approach situations she has avoided without increases in self-efficacy or reductions in fear. The explanation seems to be that some clients do not credit themselves for the behavioral change. The agoraphobic might say that she was "lucky" that she did not have a panic attack, or that she just happened to have one of those rare "good days." The therapist must anticipate this frequent occurrence and be prepared to help the client, using cognitive methods, attribute changes to herself so that her sense of personal efficacy increases.

Initial studies with phobic subjects have generally provided empirical support for self-efficacy theory, although some of the findings are mixed (Rachman, 1978). Experiments by Bandura and his associates have shown that efficacy expectations accurately predicted reductions in phobic avoidance behavior regardless of whether they were created by in vivo exposure or symbolic modeling, covert modeling, or systematic desensitization. Moreover, measures of personal efficacy predicted differences in coping behavior by different individuals receiving the same treatment, and even specific performance by subjects in different tasks. Consistent with the theory, participant modeling, a performance-based treatment, produced greater increases in level and strength of efficacy expectations and in related behavior change (Bandura, 1982).

APPLICATIONS

Problems

As noted in the "Overview" section, behavior therapy is applicable to a full range of psychological disorders in different populations (Kazdin & Wilson, 1978). It also has broad applicability to problems in education, medicine, and community living (Franks et al., 1982; Kazdin, 1978a). The following are some selected examples of problems in different domains for which behavior therapy appears to be an effective treatment.

Anxiety disorders

Evidence from controlled clinical investi-gations in a number of different countries has convincingly demonstrated the efficacy and efficiency of behavior therapy in the treatment of phobic disorders, including the often complex cases of agoraphobia. It can be argued that behavior therapy is the treatment of choice for phobias (Marks, 1981; Mathews et al., 1981). The main technique is systematic exposure possibly supplemented with additional cognitive-behavioral strategies (e.g., cognitive restructuring, behavioral marital therapy, and so on) in the case of some agoraphobic disorders. Despite the evidence that behavior therapy provides the most cost-effective treatment, results still leave something to be desired. Although the majority of clients are successfully treated, and this improvement is maintained in follow-ups five to nine years later, therapeutic failures (figures that range from roughly 10 percent to 40 percent with agoraphobics) remain a problem (Munby & Johnston, 1980).

Depression

Combined cognitive and behavioral treatment programs have shown promising results in the treatment of unipolar depression. In one study, A. T. Beck's cognitive-behavioral therapy produced greater improvement and fewer dropouts from treatment than pharmacotherapy which is widely regarded as the most powerful therapy for depression (Beck et al., 1979). The clients in this study were depressed outpatients between the ages of 18 and 65 years. On average, they had been chronically or intermittently depressed for about nine years, 75 percent reported suicidal ideas and 12 percent had a history of previous suicide attempts. The majority had had previous psychotherapy without success and 22 percent had been hospitalized as a result of their depression. MMPI profiles indicated that these subjects were severely disturbed. It is too soon to tell whether cognitive-behavioral therapy is more effective than pharmacotherapy in certain types of depression. It is not recommended for bipolar affective disorders. Nevertheless, current findings indicate that it is well suited to a large number of mildly to severely depressed outpatients.

Sexual disorders

There is now general consensus, even among psychodynamically oriented authorities, that behavior therapy is the preferred treatment for male and female sexual problems, such as impotence, premature ejaculation, orgasmic dysfunction, and vaginismus (LoPiccolo & LoPiccolo, 1978). Masters and Johnson's (1970, 1979) two-week rapid treatment program is the best known example of short-term behavioral treatment of sexual dysfunction in heterosexual and homosexual men and women. Consistently successful results, comparable to those of Masters and Johnson's, have been reported by other groups of investigators using these and other brief behavioral methods. In many cases of sexual dysfunction that are uncomplicated by interpersonal and communication problems, brief self-help behavioral programs, ranging from 6 to 15 sessions, have proved to be an efficient and cost-effective treatment strategy. In less straightforward cases requiring intensive behavioral marital therapy or other cognitive-behavioral interventions as a prelude to, or in addition to specific sex therapy, treatment may take anywhere from 20 to 50 sessions.

A variety of other sexual disorders, the paraphilias, which include exhibitionism, transvestism, and sado-masochism, are commonly treated with different cognitive-behavioral methods as the "Case Example" illustrates.

Interpersonal and marital problems

Social skills training and assertiveness training are used to treat a broad range of interpersonal problems, ranging from limited social-behavioral repertoires to social anxieties. Behavioral marital therapy is a relatively recent development, the central focus of which is helping partners to learn more positive and productive means of achieving desired behavioral changes in one another (Jacobson & Margolin, 1979). As in the case of anxiety and sexual disorders, specialized behavior marital therapy clinics are now in operation. Behavior therapy has shown clear promise as an effective and efficient method for dealing with marital problems, but comprehensive investigations of severely distressed couples, with lengthier follow-ups, are necessary before definitive conclusions can be reached.

Behavioral treatments for intervening in entire family systems have yet to be developed.

Psychotic disorders

Behavior therapy is not useful in treating acute psychotic reactions. Most behavior therapists would favor pharmacotherapy as the treatment of choice for schizophrenic disorders. Yet behavioral programs are clearly indicated for treating the chronically mentally ill. In a study by Paul and Lentz (1977) of chronic mental patients, all of whom were diagnosed as process schizophrenic, were of low socioeconomic status, had been confined to a mental hospital for an average of 17 years, and had been treated previously with drugs and other methods without success, approximately 90 percent were being maintained on drugs at the onset of the study. Their level of self-care was too low and the severity of their bizarre behavior too great to permit community placement despite the best efforts of the hospital administrators. According to Paul and Lentz, these subjects were "the most severely debilitated chronically institutionalized adults ever subjected to systematic study" (p. v). In the most detailed, comprehensive, and well-controlled evaluation of the treatment of chronic mental hospital patients ever conducted, Paul and Lentz (1977) produced a wealth of objective data, including evidence of cost effectiveness, showing that behavioral procedures (predominantly a sophisticated token reinforcement program) are the treatment of choice.

Childhood disorders

Children with problems varying in type and severity have been treated from the earliest days of behavior therapy. Treatment programs have addressed problems ranging from circumscribed habit disorders in children whose behaviors are otherwise "normal" to multiple responses of children who suffer all-encompassing excesses, deficits, or bizarre behavior patterns (e.g., autism). Conduct problems, including such behaviors as aggressive acts, truancy, theft, and noncompliance with adults, have been among the behaviors treated. Hyperactivity is widely treated by behavioral methods, such as token reinforcement programs. The documented success of the behavioral approach, particularly in improving the academic performance of these children, suggests that it be used to complement widespread use of medication for controlling hyperactivity, or even as an alternative to drug treatment in some cases (O'Leary, 1980).

Delinquency is a major conduct problem treated in institutions and in home-style, community-based behavioral programs. One of the most elaborate and well-investigated treatment models involves adjudicated children who participate in a family-style facility with a few other delinquent youths (Phillips, Phil-

lips, Fixsen, & Wolf, 1971). A highly trained couple, "teaching parents," administer an incentive system that encompasses virtually all aspects of everyday life. Programs have typically focused on altering academic behaviors and social interaction as well as self-care. Evidence suggests that recidivism may be decreased and school performance after treatment may be enhanced through intensive behavioral treatment relative to traditional institutional care or probation.

Childhood psychoses, characterized by such symptoms as lack of affect, performance of repetitive and self-stimulatory behavior, severe withdrawal, and muteness or echolalia, have also been treated with behavioral techniques. Self-stimulatory and self-destructive behavior such as biting and head-banging have been eliminated with aversive procedures. Positive behaviors have been developed to improve language and speech, play, social interaction and responsiveness, and basic academic skills (O'Leary & Carr, 1982).

One of the most effectively treated childhood problems has been enuresis. The well-known bell-and-pad method has produced improvement rates greater than 80 percent in many reports. Toileting accidents have been effectively altered with other behavioral procedures (Ross, 1981).

Behavioral medicine

Behavioral medicine, a recent but already influential development, has been defined as the "interdisciplinary field concerned with the development and integration of behavioral and biomedical science knowledge and techniques relevant to health and illness and the application of this knowledge and these techniques to prevention, diagnosis, treatment and rehabilitation" (Schwartz & Weiss, 1978, p. 250). Behavior therapy has helped to catalyze the rapid growth of this field, in which the procedures of behavior modification are used to treat illness-related behavior and to promote improved personal health care.

Prevention and treatment of cardiovascular disease

Specific behavior patterns have been identified that appear to increase the risk of needless or premature cardiovascular disease. Modification of these behavior patterns or life-styles is likely to produce significant reductions in cardiovascular disease. Among the risk factors that have been the target of behavioral treatment programs are cigarette smoking, obesity, lack of exercise, stress, hypertension, and excessive alcohol consumption. Substance abuse is typically treated with a combination of the self-control procedures. Stress and hypertension have been successfully treated using methods such as relaxation training. Behavior intervention methods have been applied not only to identified clients in both individual and group therapy sessions, but also to essentially healthy individuals in the workplace and the community in programs designed to prevent cardiovascular disease. An illustration of the latter is the Stanford Three Community Study (Maccoby, Farquhar, Wood, & Alexander, 1977). A multimedia campaign was conducted for two years, in two Northern California communities, in one of which it was supplemented by an intensive-instruction program with high-risk individuals. A third community served as a control. Results from a sample survey of the populations showed that both interventions produced substantial increases in knowledge about health care, alteration in unhealthy behavior patterns, and change in the estimated risk of cardiovascular disease.

Other applications

Behavioral techniques have also been successfully applied to such diverse health-related problems as tension headaches, different forms of pain, eating disorders such as anorexia nervosa and bulimia, asthma, epilepsy, sleep disorders, nausea reactions in cancer patients that are associated with radiation therapy, and children's fears about being hospitalized and undergoing surgery (Melamed & Siegel, 1980). Finally, cognitive-behavioral principles show promise in increasing compliance with medical treatments.

Evaluation

Evaluation of therapy outcome must be guided by the question "What treatment, by *whom*, is most effective for *this* individual with that specific problem and under *which* set of circumstances?" (Paul, 1967, p. 111). We should also add "on what measures" and "at what cost" round off this appeal to specificity of therapy outcome evaluation. The issue of "what problems" behavior therapy is appropriate for has been addressed in the immediately preceding section.

What treatment methods?

Behavior therapy consists of a broad range of different techniques, some of which are differentially effective for different problems. Hence it is difficult to evaluate some global entity called "behavior therapy"—evaluation must be directed at specific methods applied to particular problems.

What measures should be used to evaluate therapy outcome?

A major contribution of behavior therapy to the evaluation of therapy outcome has been the development of a wide range of measurement strategies for the assessment and modification of various disorders. Examples of these innovations in the objective measurement of psychological change are the following: behavioral measures of phobic avoidance and compulsive rituals; coding systems for direct behavioral observation of diverse behaviors across different situations (for example, patients' level of functioning on a hospital ward, unhappy spouses discussing a problem, or parents interacting with their child); and psychophysiological systems for anxiety and sexual disorders. Adequate assessment of treatment outcome will necessarily require multiple objective and subjective measures. In the treatment of anxiety-related disorders, for example, it is now clear that measures of three response systems—avoidance behavior, physiological arousal, and self-report—are necessary. The correlations among these systems are often low. Thus, simply measuring one dimension might miss important changes in the other two. Moreover, there is evidence that these response systems may change at different speeds and be differentially reactive to different treatment methods.

Treatment at what cost?

Behavior therapy can be a relatively cost-effective method. Paul and Lentz (1977) found that their behavioral treatment program was less expensive than either of the two alternative approaches with which it was compared: namely, milieu therapy and traditional psychiatric care typical of state hospitals in the United States. This benefit, added to the significantly greater efficacy of the behavioral program, make it the cost-effective choice. In England, Marks (1981) and his colleagues improved on the cost-effectiveness of the behavioral treatment of agoraphobics and obsessive-compulsives by using nurses as therapists instead of more highly trained clinical psychologists and psychiatrists. No falloff in efficacy was observed.

Evaluating therapy outcomes

Behavior therapists have developed various research strategies for addressing different issues related to therapy outcome. Some brief examples can be mentioned. Single-case experimental designs are particularly important because they enable cause-effect relationships to be drawn between treatments and outcome in the individual case. There are several single-case experimental designs. The ABA or reversal design was illustrated in the Ayllon and Azrin study described in the section, "Problems." In the multiple-baseline design, different responses are continuously measured. Treatment is then applied successively to each in turn. If the desired behavior changes maximally only when treated, then a cause-effect relationship can be inferred. Among the advantages of single-case experimental designs are that individual clinical problems can be studied that are unsuitable for group designs and innovative treatments can be developed efficiently before being tested in group outcome studies. Limitations of single-subject methodology include the inability to examine the interaction of subject variables with specific treatment effects and difficulty in generalizing findings to other cases.

Several different types of between-group designs are used in the evaluation of treatment outcome, each design having its particular advantages and limitations, depending on the question being asked. Laboratory-based studies make possible the evaluation of specific techniques applied to particular problems under tightly controlled conditions; for example, evaluating fear reduction methods with snake-phobic subjects (Bandura, 1982). The advantages of this methodology include the use of multiple objective measures of outcome, the selection of homogeneous subject samples and therapists, and the freedom to assign subjects to experimental and control groups. Limitations include the possibility that findings with only mildly disturbed subjects might not be generalizable to more severely disturbed clients.

The treatment package strategy evaluates the effect of a multifaceted treatment program. If the package proves to be successful, its effective components are analyzed in subsequent research. One way of doing this is using the dismantling strategy, in which components of the treatment package are systematically eliminated and the associated decrement in treatment outcome measured. The relative contributions of each component can then be evaluated.

The comparative research strategy is directed toward determining whether some therapeutic techniques are superior to others. Comparative studies are appropriate after specific techniques have been shown to be effective in single-subject or laboratory-based research, and the parameters that maximize their efficacy are known. Different group designs require different control groups depending on the research question addressed. The no-treatment control group controls for the possible therapeutic effects of assessment of outcome, maturation, and other changes in clients' behavior that occur independently of formal treatment. Attention-placebo control groups are used to parcel out the contribution to treatment effects of factors that are common to all forms of therapy. These factors include the relationship between therapist and client, expectations of therapeutic progress, suggestion, and others.

Treatment

Some clinical details of a cognitive-behavioral approach to therapy may be illustrated by the treatment of agoraphobia, a complex anxiety disorder. Initially, the therapist carries out a careful assessment of the nature of the problem and the variables that seem to be maintaining it. Subsequent treatment may vary, depending on the particular case, but it is probable that some form of in vivo exposure method will be a central part of therapy. Together, therapist and client work out a hierarchy of increasingly fear-eliciting situations that the client has been avoiding. The behavioral basis of the treatment is repeated and systematic exposure to these situations occurs until avoidance is eliminated and fear decreased. Cognitive principles and procedures feature prominently in preparing the client for these corrective learning experiences.

Clients are given an explanation of the treatment procedures and their rationales, together with an interpretation of their problem as a learned fear/avoidance reaction that can be overcome by guided relearning experiences. The therapist is careful to distinguish systematic exposure treatment from the unsystematic and ill-considered attempts clients have typically made to enter feared situations too quickly. Preparation for each exposure experience involves anticipating the inevitable fearful reactions and teaching clients appropriate coping skills. This includes recognizing and accepting feelings of fear; identifying cognitive distortions that elicit or exacerbate fear; and counteracting cognitive distortions. Instead of catastrophizing (e.g., "Oh no! Here I go again; I'm really in trouble; I must get out of here fast"), they learn coping self-instructions (e.g., "this anxiety is distressing but not dangerous"; "It'll pass; concentrate on what you need to do now"; "one step at a time"). These preparatory coping responses are often rehearsed in imagery.

The therapist might accompany the client during in vivo exposure sessions, providing encouragement, support, and social reinforcement. Although empathic about the discomfort the agoraphobic might experience, the therapist remains firm about the necessity for systematic exposure. Once clients enter the feared situation, the golden rule is no leaving it until anxiety has decreased. Clients are allowed to withdraw if absolutely necessary, but in a manner mutually agreed upon in advance planning. First, abrupt withdrawal is strongly discouraged; clients are to try to remain in the situation as long as possible, even though they experience considerable discomfort. Second, if they cannot remain in the situation, they follow a preplanned withdrawal instead of fleeing the scene. If the situation is a supermarket, for example, they move to the least crowded area of the store and try to calm themselves. If that fails, they exit from the store, but instead of rushing to the car and going home to "safety," they try to reenter the supermarket as soon as possible.

Following the exposure, therapist and client analyze what happened. This provides the therapist with an opportunity to see how the clients interpret their experience and to uncover any faulty cognitive processing. For example, agoraphobics tend to discount positive accomplishments, do not always attribute success experiences to their own coping ability, and therefore do not develop greater self-efficacy (Bandura, 1982).

Clients are given specific instructions about exposure homework assignments between therapy sessions and are asked to keep detailed daily records of what they attempted, how they felt, and what problems they encountered. These self-recordings are reviewed by the therapist at the beginning of the next session. In addition to providing the therapist with information on the clients' progress (or lack of progress), these daily records facilitate the process of changing clients' cognitive sets about their problems. For example, because of their negative thinking, clients often bemoan their perceived lack of improvement and dwell on the difficulties of completing exposure assignments. Usually the therapist can point to specific successes as indicated in the weekly behavioral recordings that these clients had not taken seriously enough. By directing their attention to the records of their own experience, the therapist helps clients to gain a more objective and balanced view of their problems and progress.

Homework assignments typically require the active cooperation of the client's spouse (or some other family member). The therapist invites the spouse to one or more therapy sessions to assess his or her willingness and ability to provide the necessary support and to explain what is required. Mathews et al. (1981) have developed treatment manuals for both the agoraphobic and the spouse in which they detail each step of in vivo exposure treatment and describe mutual responsibilities. In many cases, these manuals can greatly reduce the number of sessions the couple need spend with the therapist.

Not uncommonly agoraphobics fail to complete homework assignments. There are several possible reasons for lack of compliance, ranging from poorly chosen homework assignments to resistance to change by the agoraphobic. All of these potential problems need to be considered as the therapist begins to analyze the causes of noncompliance. Another possibility is that the spouse is uncooperative or even tries to sabotage therapy. One of the advantages of including the spouse in treatment is that this resistance to progress is rapidly uncovered and can be directly addressed in the therapy sessions. Marital therapy might be necessary to resolve interpersonal conflict that may block the agoraphobic's progress.

Additional techniques might be needed to supplement in vivo exposure, as indicated above. These are usually in the service of helping clients cope more constructively with different sources of stress. Some, for example, might need assertiveness training to overcome the stress of interpersonal conflicts, whereas others might need to acquire ways of coping with suppressed anger. Finally, before terminating successful treatment, the therapist works on relapse prevention training with clients. Briefly, clients are told that it is possible that they might experience an unexpected return of some fear at unpredictable points in the future. Using imagery to project ahead to such a recurrence of fear, clients learn to cope with their feelings by reinstituting previously successful coping responses. They are reassured that these feelings are quite normal, that they will pass, and do not necessarily signal a relapse. Clients learn that it is primarily the way they interpret these feelings that determines whether or not they experience a relapse. Specifically, the therapist tries to inoculate them against such anxiety-inducing cognitive errors as catastrophizing, selective focus on an isolated anxiety symptom, and so on.

Management

Behavior therapists work in a variety of different settings—private clinical practice, clinics, mental health centers, hospitals, institutions for the retarded, schools, and even industry. In their typical practice, behavior therapists function quite similarly to other psychotherapists. For instance, they have emulated the treatment format and scheduling of the more traditional psychotherapies in sticking to the standard 50-to 60-minute session on a weekly basis. Occasionally, alternative treatment formats are used. For example, there is some tentative evidence that longer, more intensive sessions may be more effective with agoraphobic clients.

Behavior therapy sessions may often be different from psychotherapy, however. Thus the therapist might accompany the client on some in vivo assignment (e.g., going with an agoraphobic to a shopping mall). In some instances, particularly with children's problems, the therapist might go to the client's home or school to observe or intervene. Behavior therapists are actively concerned with what occurs between therapy sessions, and intermittent telephone contacts with clients and psychological assistants such as family members and teachers are common. Similarly, even after therapy has ended successfully, the therapist frequently keeps in touch with clients through the telephone or mail, a strategy designed to facilitate maintenance of improvement, particularly in problems with a high probability of relapse.

The clients that behavior therapists treat come from diverse sources. Many clients are referrals from the medical community or from other mental health professionals. It was once the case that the majority of clients seen by behavior therapists were the failure of the then dominant psychoanalytically oriented psychotherapy. This still happens, but to a much lesser extent. Today a growing number of clients enter into behavioral treatment as their first therapy experience. Whereas most clients once consulted behavior therapists for treatment of specific problems (e.g., phobias or habit disorders), modern clientele suffer from the full range of problems, from the simple to the complex, including those that are well-defined and those that are shadowy and ambiguous. Occasionally, clients who are in some form of long-term, psychoanalytically oriented psychotherapy consult a behavior therapist for concurrent help with a specific problem. In some cases these clients are referred by their psychotherapists, in other cases these clients initiate behavioral treatment themselves, with or without the knowledge of their psychotherapist. The feasibility of this sort of arrangement depends on the details of the individual client, the particular problem, and, of course, the attitudes of the therapists involved.

CASE EXAMPLE[1]

Mr. B was a 35-year-old man, married, with two sons aged eight and five, from a successful, middle-class family. He was a persistent exhibitionist whose pattern over the past 20 years had been to expose his genitals to unsuspecting adult women as often as five or six times a week. Fifteen years of intermittent psychoanalytic treatment, several hospitalizations at psychiatric institutions in the United States, and a six-year prison sentence for his deviant sexual behavior had failed to help Mr. B change his apparently uncontrollable behavior. He was currently under grand jury indictment for exposing himself to an adult woman in the presence of

1. This case example, with minor modifications, is taken from G. T. Wilson and K. D. O'Leary, *Principles of Behavior Therapy* (Englewood Cliffs, N.J.: Prentice-Hall, 1980). Reprinted with permission.

a group of young children. There was every prospect that he would receive a life sentence in view of his repeated offenses and numerous failures to show improvement as a result of lengthy and costly psychiatric treatment. At least one psychiatrist had diagnosed him as untreatable and had advocated a lifelong removal from free society. Shortly before coming to trial, Mr. B's psychoanalyst referred him to a behavior therapist as a last resort to see if behavior therapy might succeed where traditional forms of treatment had failed.

Mr. B was hospitalized and treated on a daily basis for six weeks, a total of about 50 hours of direct therapist contact. After spending some time to develop a trusting personal relationship so that Mr. B would feel comfortable in disclosing intimate details about his problems, the therapist conducted a series of intensive interviews to ferret out the specific environmental circumstances and psychological factors that were maintaining Mr. B's deviant behavior. With his permission, his parents and wife were also interviewed to obtain more information and to corroborate aspects of his own description of the development and present status of the problem. To obtain a sample of his actual exhibitionist behavior, a situation was arranged in a hospital office that closely resembled the conditions under which Mr. B would normally expose himself in real life. Two attractive female professional colleagues of the therapist were seated in a simulated doctor's waiting room, reading magazines, and the patient was instructed to enter, sit across from them, and expose himself. Despite the artificial setting, he proceeded to expose himself, became highly aroused, and nearly masturbated to orgasm. This entire sequence was videotaped, and objective measures of his response to this scene as well as to various other adult sexual stimuli were obtained by recording the degree of penile erection he showed while observing the videotape and selected other erotic filmed material.

On the basis of this behavioral assessment, a detailed picture was developed of the chain or sequence of internal and external stimuli and responses that preceded his acts of exposure. For example, a woman standing alone at a bus stop as he drove past in his car often triggered a pattern of thoughts and images that caused him to circle the block and eventually expose himself. Alternatively, the anger he experienced after a heated argument with his father, which he could not handle, could also elicit the urge to expose himself. The more Mr. B thought about exposing himself, the more obsessed he became with a particular woman and her anticipated reactions. Since he tuned out everything except his immediate feelings and intentions, he became oblivious to the consequences of his actions. His behavior was out of control. Mr. B hoped that his victim would express some form of approval, either by smiling or making some sexually toned comment. Although this did happen periodically, most women ignored him, and some called the police.

Not atypically, Mr. B's idea about behavior therapy was that he would be passively "conditioned" so that his problem would disappear. The therapist systematically disabused him of this notion by explaining that success could be achieved only with his active cooperation in all phases of the treatment program. He was told that there was no automatic "cure" for his problem, but he could learn new behavioral self-control strategies, which, if practiced conscientiously and applied at the right time, would enable him to avoid further deviant behavior.

As in most complex clinical cases, treatment was multifaceted, meaning that a number of different techniques were employed to modify different components of the disorder. His own beliefs about his problem were that he was suddenly seized by a desire, which he could not consciously control, and that his subsequent actions were "involuntary." Analysis of the sequence of events that always preceded exposure altered Mr. B's expectation that he was unable to control his behavior. He was shown how he himself was instrumental in transforming a relatively weak initial urge into an overpowering compulsion to expose because he attended to inappropriate thoughts and feelings and engaged in behaviors that increased, rather than decreased, the temptation. It was explained that the time to break this behavioral chain, to implement the self-control strategies he would acquire as a result of treatment, was at the beginning when the urge was weakest. In order to do this, he would have to learn to be aware of his thoughts, feelings, and behavior, and to recognize the early warning danger signals.

Specific tension states had often precipitated exposure. Accordingly, Mr. B was trained to reduce this tension through the procedure of progressive relaxation. Instead of exposing himself, he learned to relax, an activity incompatible with exposure behavior. Assertion training was used to help Mr. B cope constructively with feelings of anger and to express them appropriately, rather than to seek relief through deviant behavior. Using roleplaying, the therapist modeled an appropriate reaction and then provided Mr. B with reinforcing feedback as he rehearsed progressively more effective ways of responding to anger-inducing events. In covert modeling Mr. B was taught to imagine himself in a range of situations that customarily had resulted in exposure, and to see himself engaging in alternative responses to exposure; for example, relaxing away tension, expressing anger appropriately, reminding himself of the consequences of being caught, or simply walking away from a tempting situation.

Aversion conditioning was used to decrease the positive appeal exposure had for him. During repeated presentations of the videotape of his exposure scene, a loud, subjectively aversive police siren was piped over earphones he was wearing on an unpredictable schedule. Whereas Mr. B initially found watching the videotape pleasurable and sexually arousing, he progressively lost all sexual interest in it. He reported that he experienced marked difficulty in concentrating on the scene because he began to anticipate the disruptive—and given his personal social learning history, an understandably frightening—police siren in connection with thoughts of exposure. The siren was also paired systematically with a range of fantasies of different situations in which he would expose himself. In addition to the siren, Mr. B learned how to associate self-administered aversive cognitive events with deviant thoughts or images. For example, imagery of an aversive event, such as being apprehended by the police, was coupled with thoughts of exposure. Periodically, Mr. B's sexual arousal to the videotape was assessed directly by measuring penile erection to provide an evaluation of his progress.

Following every session with the therapist, Mr. B was given specific homework assignments to complete. These included self-monitoring and recording any urges to expose himself, so as to ensure awareness about any signs of reverting back to old habits. Other assignments involved (*a*) practicing relaxation exercises and recording the degree to which the relaxation was associated with reduced tension; (*b*) rehearsing the association of aversive imagery with fantasies of exposure, recording the intensity of the aversive imagery and the clarity of the exposure fantasies on 10-point rating scales; and (*c*) engaging in assertive behavior where appropriate during interactions with other patients and staff on his assigned ward. Direct observation of his interpersonal behavior on the hospital ward provided an index of his utilization of assertive behavior.

Finally, after speaking with the therapist about cooperation and apparent progress in the treatment program, Mr. B's wife agreed to several joint therapy sessions which used behavioral methods for improving marital communication and interaction. Although the behavioral assessment had indicated that Mr. B's exhibitionist behavior was not directly caused by an unhappy marriage or lack of sexual satisfaction from his wife, the rationale was that improvement in these spheres of functioning would help consolidate and support his self-control over deviant sexual behavior acquired through the rest of the treatment program.

On leaving the hospital at the end of treatment, Mr. B continued to self-monitor any thoughts or feelings about exposing himself, to relax systematically, to assert himself, and to rehearse the pairing of aversive imagery with thoughts of exposure. Every week he mailed these records to the therapist for analysis, a procedure designed to generalize treatment-produced improvement to the real world and to maintain self-control over time. Another facet of this maintenance strategy was a series of booster sessions scheduled approximately four months after therapy in which he returned to the hospital for a week of intensive treatment along the same lines as described above.

In large part owing to the therapist's strong recommendation, the court gave him a suspended sentence. A five-year follow-up showed that Mr. B had refrained from any exhibitionism, had experienced very few such desires, and felt confident in his newly found ability to control any urges that might arise.

SUMMARY

Behavior therapy is a young field that is still developing. The future will witness continued development and change in its theoretical foundations, research evidence, and practical applications. As the theoretical bases of behavior therapy are broadened, there will be renewed interest in identifying the commonalities among different therapies and in bringing about a rapprochement between behavior therapy and other forms of psychotherapy (Goldfried, 1980). Other behavior therapists contend that this proposal is premature (Wilson, 1982). Alternatively, behavior therapists might better devote their energies to developing replicable, testable, and effective methods of therapeutic change within the general social learning framework of behavior therapy and invite other theoretical orientations to do the same. There will be time enough to discuss common principles of change when different approaches can show convincing evidence of what they can and cannot accomplish.

The advent of behavior therapy has resulted in a dramatic increase in the quantity and quality of treatment research. Nevertheless, the preponderance of outcome studies has been with mildly disturbed subjects, usually in laboratory-based or analogue research. Controlled studies of patient populations with complex disorders have been underrepresented. Yet this sort of clinical research seems necessary if the gap between research and practice is to be closed. Confronted with substantial changes of obvious clinical relevance obtained with

"real" patients, by using clearly described and replicable methods under realistic conditions of clinical practice, the practitioner is more likely to take notice. Happily, there are indications that clinical research in behavior therapy is on the increase (Agras & Berkowitz, 1980).

Future developments in behavior therapy will have to be evaluated within the context of fundamental changes that are beginning to occur in the field of clinical psychology as a whole. In the United States the movement toward professionalism, for better or worse, is well under way. As the number of applicants to scientist-practitioner training programs appears to be decreasing, the applications to at least some of the new professional schools are increasing. Behavior therapy has always been rooted in the scientist-practitioner model of training, but, in principle, the practitioner model need not be inconsistent with behavior therapy. There are different levels of analysis and training along the continuum from basic scientific research to clinical practice, and each has its unique and necessary place in the overall development of an applied clinical science. Clinical researchers will necessarily be trained at the scientist-practitioner level, whereas full-time clinicians may be sensibly trained at the practitioner level of the professional school. Acceptable professional schools should be part of a university, and reflect the relationship between the clinic and science by being closely tied to an academic department of psychology. The faculty should be capable of teaching applied psychology, and the school should offer appropriate courses in related behavioral and biological sciences that are directed to the future clinician and applied researcher. Active programs of applied research should be pursued by the faculty of such schools.

Another major challenge facing clinical psychology and psychiatry is the increasing demand for accountability and evidence of treatment efficacy by government, insurance companies, and the consumer movement. Some suggest that psychotherapy is facing a crisis, while others refer to an attack from outside the system. Behavior therapists, however, view this demand for accountability as an important opportunity to promote the use of empirically based treatments wherever possible. It can be argued that procedures that are grounded in empirical research are used sparingly, if at all, in general clinical practice, whereas unsupported and even discredited methods continue to flourish. The implications are obvious. To quote Liberman (1980),

After almost 20 years of behavioral analysis and therapy, workers in the field must realize that political, personal, and social factors determine upwards of 90% of the success and survival of technical procedures. . . . Implementation, survival, and dissemination of empirically validated interventions require much more than data and journal publications. . . . If we want our work to live beyond a library bookshelf, we will have to jump into the political mainstream and get our feet wet as administrator researchers. (pp. 370-71)

Ideally, in the near future, behavior therapists, possibly through the AABT, will join with other organizations in supporting reasonable legislation that seeks to make reimbursable only those mental health services that are safe and effective, and to guarantee the appropriate recognition of psychologists and other professionals as independent health providers.

ANNOTATED BIBLIOGRAPHY

Beck, A., Rush, J., Shaw, B., & Emery, G. *Cognitive therapy of depression.* New York: Guilford Press, 1979.

An excellent clinical guide on the use of cognitive restructuring with adult dis-

orders that draws attention to seminal clinical issues in all forms of psychotherapy and gives actual protocols that illustrate particular cognitive-behavioral techniques. The book focuses specifically on depression and provides the most detailed and sophisticated account of the treatment of this disorder using cognitive-behavioral methods.

Franks, C. M., Wilson, G. T., Kendall, P., & Brownell, K. D. *Annual review of behavior therapy: Theory and practice,* Vol. 8. New York: Guilford Press, 1982.

The latest volume in an annual review series begun in 1973. Broad coverage of virtually all aspects of theory, research, and application in behavior therapy, with critical commentary by the authors. Perhaps the most up-to-date and comprehensive overview of the field on a year-to-year basis.

Goldstein, A., & Foa, E. (Eds.) *Handbook of behavioral interventions: A clinical guide.* New York: Wiley, 1980.

An edited volume with chapters of specific behavioral techniques applied to anxiety and sexual disorders. By remaining close to the clinical data, including the generous use of transcripts from individual therapy sessions, the authors provide a flavor of the clinical practice of behavior therapy.

Kazdin, A. E. *Behavior modification in applied settings* (rev. ed.). Homewood, Ill.: The Dorsey Press, 1980.

A clearly written, comprehensive review of primarily operant-conditioning principles and procedures in behavior modification. The focus is on applications of learning principles in applied settings (e.g., classrooms and institutions for the retarded and psychiatric patients).

O'Leary, K. D., & Wilson, G. T. *Behavior therapy: Application and outcome,* 2d. ed. Englewood Cliffs, N.J.: Prentice-Hall, in press.

Detailed description and evaluation of cognitive-behavior treatment of a wide range of childhood and adult disorders.

Aside from traditional psychiatric disorders (e.g., anxiety, addictive, and schizophrenic disorders), areas covered include interpersonal and marital problems, behavioral medicine and preventive health care, and various educational and clinical problems in children.

Rhoades, L. J. *Treating and assessing the chronically ill: The pioneering research of Gordon L. Paul.* Rockville, Md.: U.S. Department of Health and Human Services, 1981.

One of the *Science Reports* series published by the National Institute of Mental Health, explaining significant achievements in mental health services and directed at the general scientific, academic and professional communities. A clearly written, nontechnical summary account of the detailed Paul and Lentz (1977) book, describing the treatment procedures and important findings of the most thorough study of chronic mental hospital patients ever conducted.

CASE READINGS

Bachrach, A. J., Erwin, W. J., & Mohr, J. P. The control of eating behavior in an anorexic by operant conditioning techniques. In L. P. Ullmann & L. Krasner (Eds.), *Case studies in behavior modification.* New York: Holt, Rinehart & Winston, 1965.

Melamed, B., & Siegel, L. Self-directed in vivo treatment of an obsessive-compulsive checking ritual. *Journal of Behavior Therapy and Experimental Psychiatry,* 1975, *6,* 31-35.

Novaco, R. Stress inoculation: A cognitive therapy for anger and its application to a case of depression. *Journal of Consulting and Clinical Psychology.* 1977, *45,* 600-608.

Wolf, M. M., Risley, T., & Mees, H. Application of operant conditioning procedures to the behavior problems of an autistic child. In L. P. Ullmann & L. Krasner (Eds.), *Case studies in behavior modification.* New York: Holt, Rinehart & Winston, 1965.

REFERENCES

Agras, W. S., & Berkowitz, R. Clinical research in behavior therapy: Halfway there? *Behavior Therapy,* 1980, *11,* 472-487.

Andrews, G., & Harvey, R. Does psychotherapy benefit neurotic patients? *Archives of General Psychiatry,* 1981, *38,* 1203-1208.

Ayllon, T., & Azrin, N. H. The measurement and reinforcement of behavior of psychotics. *Journal of the Experimental Analysis of Behavior,* 1965, *8,* 357-383.

Bandura, A. *Principles of behavior modification.* New York: Holt, Rinehart & Winston, 1969.

Bandura, A. *Social learning theory.* Englewood Cliffs, N.J.: Prentice-Hall, 1977.

Bandura, A. Self-efficacy mechanisms in human agency. *American Psychologist,* 1982, *37,* 122-147.

Beck, A. T. *Cognitive therapy and the emotional disorders.* New York: International Universities Press, 1976.

Beck, A. T., Rush, A. J., Shaw, B. F., & Emery, G. *Cognitive therapy of depression.* New York: Guilford Press, 1979.

Birk, L., Stolz, S. B., Brady, J. P., Brady, J. V., Lazarus, A. A., Lynch, J. J., Rosenthal, A. J., Skelton, W. D., Stevens, J. B., & Thomas, E. J. *Behavior therapy in psychiatry.* Washington, D.C.: American Psychiatric Association, 1973.

Brady, J. P., & Wienckowski, L. A. Update on the teaching of behavior therapy in medical student and psychiatric resident training. *Journal of Behavior Therapy and Experimental Psychiatry,* 1978, *9,* 125-127.

Brady, J. P. In M. Goldfried (Ed.). Some views on effective principles of psychotherapy. *Cognitive Therapy and Research,* 1980, *4,* 271-306.

Brownell, K. D. Report on international behavior therapy organizations. *The Behavior Therapist,* 1981, *4,* 9-14.

Cautela, J. Covert sensitization. *Psychological Reports,* 1967, *20,* 459-468.

Dollard, J., & Miller, N. E. *Personality and psychotherapy.* New York: McGraw-Hill, 1950.

Ellis, A. *Reason and emotion in psychotherapy.* New York: Lyle Stuart, 1962.

Eysenck, H. J. Learning theory and behavior therapy. *British Journal of Medical Science,* 1959, *105,* 61-75.

Eysenck, H. J. *The biological basis of personality.* Springfield, Ill.: Charles C Thomas, 1967.

Franks, C. M., & Wilson, G. T. *Annual review of behavior therapy: Theory and practice* (Vol. 1). New York: Brunner/Mazel, 1973.

Franks, C. M., Wilson, G. T., Kendall, P., & Brownell, K. *Annual review of behavior therapy: Theory and practice.* (Vol. 8). New York: Guilford Press, 1982.

Gelder, M. G., Bancroft, J. H. J., Gath, D., Johnston, D. W., Mathews, A. M., & Shaw, P. M. Specific and non-specific factors in behavior therapy. *British Journal of Psychiatry*, 1973, *123*, 445-462.

Goldfried, M. R. Toward the delineation of therapeutic change principles. *American Psychologist*, 1980, *35*, 991-999.

Hersen, M., Eisler, R., & Miller, P. *Progress in behavior modification.* (Vol. 1). New York: Academic Press, 1973.

Jacobson, E. *Progressive relaxation.* Chicago: University of Chicago Press, 1938.

Jacobson, N., & Margolin, G. *Marital therapy.* New York: Brunner/Mazel, 1979.

Jones, M. C. The elimination of children's fears. *Journal of Experimental Psychology*, 1924, *7*, 382-390.

Kanfer, F. H. The many faces of self-control, or behavior modification changes its focus. In R. B. Stuart (Ed.). *Behavioral self-management.* New York: Brunner/Mazel, 1977.

Kazdin, A. E. *The token economy.* New York: Plenum, 1977.

Kazdin, A. E. The application of operant techniques in treatment, rehabilitation, and education. In S. L. Garfield, & A. E. Bergin (Ed.). *Handbook of psychotherapy and behavior change.* 2d. ed. New York: Wiley, 1978. (*a*)

Kazdin, A. E. *History of behavior modification.* Baltimore, Md.: University Park Press, 1978. (b)

Kazdin, A. E., & Wilson, G. T. *Evaluation of behavior therapy: Issues, evidence and research strategies.* Cambridge, Mass.: Ballinger, 1978.

Kendall, P., & Hollon, S. (Eds.). *Cognitive-behavioral interventions: Theory, research, and procedures.* New York: Guilford Press, 1979.

Knudson, R. M., Gurman, A. S., & Kniskern, D. P. Behavioral marriage therapy: A treatment in transition. In C. M. Franks & G. T. Wilson (Eds.). *Annual review of behavior therapy: Theory and practice.* (Vol. 7). New York: Brunner/Mazel, 1979.

Lang, P. J. A bio-informational theory of emotional imagery. *Psychophysiology*, 1979, *16*, 495-512.

Lazarus, A. A. *Behavior therapy and beyond.* New York: McGraw-Hill, 1971.

Lazarus, A. A. *The practice of multimodal therapy.* New York: McGraw-Hill, 1981.

Lazarus, A. A., & Fay, A. Resistance or rationalization? A cognitive-behavioral perspective. In P. L. Wachtel (Ed.). *Resistance: Psychodynamic and behavioral approaches.* New York: Plenum, 1981.

Liberman, R. P. Review of: Psychosocial treatment for chronic mental patients by Gordon L. Paul and Robert J. Lentz. *Journal of Applied Behavior Analysis*, 1980, *13*, 367-372.

Locke, H. J., & Wallace, K. M. Short marital adjustment and prediction tests: Their reliability and validity. *Marriage and Family Living*, 1959, *21*, 251-255.

LoPiccolo, J., & LoPiccolo, L. (Eds.). *Handbook of sex therapy.* New York: Plenum, 1978.

Maccoby, N., Farquhar, J., Wood, P. D., & Alexander, J. Reducing the risk of cardiovascular disease: Effects of a community-based campaign on knowledge and behavior. *Journal of Community Health*, 1977, *3*, 100-114.

Mahoney, M. J. Psychotherapy and the structure of personal revolutions. In M. J. Mahoney (Ed.). *Psychotherapy process.* New York: Plenum, 1980.

Marks, I., & Mathews, A. Brief standard self-rating for phobic patients. *Behaviour Research and Therapy.* 1979, *17*, 263-267.

Marks, I. M. *Cure and care of the neuroses.* New York: Wiley, 1981.

Masters, W., & Johnson, V. *Human sexual inadequacy.* Boston: Little Brown, 1970.

Masters, W. & Johnson, V. *Homosexuality in perspective.* Boston: Little Brown, 1979.

Mathews, A. M., Gelder, M. G., & Johnston, D. W. *Agoraphobia: Nature and treatment.* New York: Guilford, 1981.

Meichenbaum, D. *Cognitive behavior modification.* New York: Plenum, 1977.

Meichenbaum, D., & Cameron, R. Cognitive behavior modification: Current issues. In G. T. Wilson & C. M. Franks (Eds.). *Contemporary behavior therapy: Conceptual and empirical foundations.* New York: Guilford Press, 1982.

Melamed, B., & Siegel, L. *Behavioral medicine.* New York: Springer, 1980.

Miller, N. E. Studies of fear as an acquirable drive: I. Fear as motivation and fear reduction as reinforcement in the learning of new responses. *Journal of Experimental Psychology,* 1948, *38,* 89-101.

Mischel, W. *Personality and assessment.* New York: Wiley, 1968.

Mischel, W. Toward a cognitive social learning reconceptualization of personality. *Psychological Review,* 1973, *80,* 252-283.

Mischel, W. *Introduction to personality.* New York: Holt, Rinehart & Winston, 1976.

Mischel, W. A cognitive social learning approach to assessment. In T. V. Merluzzi, C. R. Glass, & M. Genest (Eds). *Cognitive assessment.* New York: Guilford Press, 1981.

Mowrer, O. H. On the dual nature of learning—A reinterpretation of "conditioning" and "problem solving." *Harvard Educational Review,* 1947, *17,* 102-148.

Mowrer, O. H., & Mowrer, E. Enuresis: A method for its study and treatment. *American Journal of Orthopsychiatry,* 1938, *4,* 436-459.

Munby, M., & Johnston, D. W. Agoraphobia: The long-term follow-up of behavioural treatment. *British Journal of Psychiatry,* 1980, *137,* 418-427.

Nelson, R. O. Realistic dependent measures for clinical use. *Journal of Consulting and Clinical Psychology,* 1981, *49,* 168.

O'Leary, K. D. Pills or skills for hyperactive children. *Journal of Applied Behavior Analysis,* 1980, *13,* 191-204.

O'Leary, K. D., & Carr, E. G. Childhood disorders. In G. T. Wilson & C. M. Franks (Eds.). *Contemporary behavior therapy: Conceptual and empirical foundations.* New York: Guilford, 1982.

O'Leary, K. D. & Wilson, G. T. *Behavior therapy: Application and outcome* (2nd ed.). Englewood Cliffs, N. J.: Prentice-Hall, in press.

O'Leary, K. D., & O'Leary, S. G. *Classroom management.* New York: Pergamon Press, 1977.

O'Leary, K. D., Turkewitz, H., & Tafel, S. Parent and therapist evaluation of behavior therapy in a child psychological clinic. *Journal of Consulting and Clinical Psychology,* 1973, *41,* 289-293.

Paul, G. L. *Insight versus desensitization in psychotherapy.* Stanford: Stanford University Press, 1966.

Paul, G. L. Outcome research in psycho-therapy. *Journal of Consulting Psychology,* 1967, *31,* 109-188.

Paul, G. L., & Lentz, R. J. *Psychological treatment of chronic mental patients.* Cambridge, Mass.: Harvard University Press, 1977.

Phillips, E. L., Phillips, E. A., Fixsen, D., & Wolf, M. M. Achievement place: The modification of the behaviors of predelinquent boys within a token economy. *Journal of Applied Behavior Analysis,* 1971, *4,* 45-59.

Rachlin, H. A. Review of *Cognition and Behavior Modification* by M. J. Mahoney. *Journal of Applied Behavior Analysis,* 1977, *10,* 369-374.

Rachman, S. (Ed.). Perceived self-efficacy: Analyses of Bandura's theory of behavioural change. *Advances in Behaviour Research and Therapy,* 1978, *1,* 139-269.

Rachman, S., & Hodgson, R. *Obsessions and compulsions.* Englewood Cliffs, N. J.: Prentice-Hall, 1980.

Rachman, S., & Wilson, G. T. *The effects of psychological therapy.* Oxford: Pergamon Press, 1980.

Rathus, S. A. A 30-item schedule for assessing assertive behavior. *Behavior Therapy,* 1973, *4,* 398-406.

Risley, T., & Sheldon-Wildgen, J. Invited peer review: The AABT experience. *Professional Psychology,* 1982, *13,* 125-131.

Rosen, R. C., & Keefe, F. J. The measurement of human penile tumescence. *Psychophysiology,* 1978, *15,* 366-376.

Ross, A. *Child behavior therapy.* New York: Wiley, 1981.

Salter, A. *Conditioned reflex therapy.* New York: Farrar, Straus, 1949.

Schwartz, G. E., & Weiss, S. M. Behavioral medicine revisited: An amended definition. *Journal of Behavioral Medicine,* 1978, *1,* 249-252.

Shapiro, D. A., & Shapiro, D. Meta-analysis of comparative therapy outcome research: A critical appraisal. *Behavioural Psychotherapy,* 1983, *10,* 4-25.

Skinner, B. F. *Science and human behavior.* New York: Macmillan, 1953.

Sloane, R. B., Staples, F. R., Cristol, A. H., Yorkston, N. J., & Whipple, K. *Psychotherapy versus behavior therapy.* Cambridge, Mass.: Harvard University Press, 1975.

Smith, D. Trends in counseling and psycho-therapy. *American Psychologist,* 1982, *37,*

802-809.

Staples, F. R., Sloane, R. B., Whipple, K., Cristol, A. H., & Yorkston, N. Differences between behavior therapists and psychotherapists. *Archives of General Psychiatry*, 1975, *32*, 1517-1522.

Stolz, S. G. *Ethical issues in behavior modification*. San Francisco, Jossey-Bass, 1978.

Swan, G. E., & MacDonald, M. D. Behavior therapy in practice: A national survey of behavior therapists. *Behavior Therapy*, 1978, *9*, 799-807.

Turkewitz, H., & O'Leary, K. D. A comparative outcome study of behavioral marital and communication therapy. *Journal of Marital and Family Therapy*, 1981, *7*, 159-169.

Ullmann, L. P., & Krasner, L. *Case studies in behavior modification*. New York: Holt, Rinehart & Winston, 1965.

Upper, D., & Ross, S. M. (Eds.) *Behavioral group therapy*. Champaign, Ill.: Research Press, 1981.

Wilson, G. T. Psychotherapy process and procedure: The behavioral mandate. *Behavior Therapy*, 1982, *13*, 291-312.

Wilson, G. T., & Evans, I. M. The therapist-client relationship in behavior therapy. In R. S. Gurman & A. M. Razin (Eds.). *The therapist's contribution to effective psychotherapy: An empirical approach*. New York: Pergamon Press, 1977.

Wilson, G. T., & O'Leary, K. D. *Principles of behavior therapy*. Englewood Cliffs, N. J.: Prentice-Hall, 1980.

Wolpe, J. *Psychotherapy by reciprocal inhibition*. Stanford: Stanford University Press, 1958.

Wolpe, J., & Rachman, S. Psychoanalytic evidence: A critique based on Freud's case of Little Hans. *Journal of Nervous and Mental Disorders*, 1960, *131*, 135-145.

Yates, A. J. *Biofeedback and the modification of behavior*. New York: Plenum, 1980.

8

Gestalt Therapy*

JAMES S. SIMKIN and GARY M. YONTEF

Gestalt therapy is a form of phenomenological-existential therapy founded by
Frederick (Fritz) S. Perls and Laura P.
Perls in the 1940s and subsequently developed by many others. The methodology
of Gestalt therapy is phenomenological
and dialogic, focusing on bringing immediate present experience into greater
clarity and increasing awareness. Explanations and interpretations are considered less reliable than what is directly
perceived and felt. Gestalt therapy treats
with equal respect the immediate experience of both patient and therapist. Discrepancy between the experiences of the
participants becomes the focus of experimentation and dialogue. The goal is for
clients to become aware of what they are
doing, how they are doing it and, at the
same time, to learn to accept and esteem
themselves.

Gestalt therapy focuses on *process* (what
is happening) rather than *content* (what is
being discussed). Process refers to the
observable development of behavior that
occurs during the therapy hour. The emphasis is on *what is*, rather than on *what
was, might be, could be* or *should be*. Attention is given to process: the patient's, the
therapist's, and the interaction between
them.

*The authors appreciate the assistance of Jeffrey
Hutten, Ph.D., and of Lynne Jacobs, Ph.D.

OVERVIEW

Basic Concepts

The phenomenological perspective
Phenomenology is a systematic exploration that takes as genuine knowledge only
what is immediately given in the experience of the perceiver. Rather than infer an
absolute reality which underlies and
causes "mere appearances," Gestalt therapy trusts immediate awareness.

All immediate experience is considered
equally valid. The systematic observation
of behavior and other "objective" exteroceptive experience is as inherent a part of
phenomenology as "subjective" or "feeling" experiences.

Customary modes of thought, especially
metaphysical biases and exclusionary
beliefs about what data are important, are
"put in brackets." A Gestalt exploration
attempts to increase the clarity of immediate, "naive" perception "undebauched by
learning" (Wertheimer, 1945, p. 331).
Stepping back from assumptions and
ordinary ways of looking enables the
separation of immediate experience from
old learning (Idhe, 1977).

The objective of Gestalt phenomenological exploration is awareness or insight.
"Insight is a patterning of the perceptual
field in such a way that the significant
realities are apparent; it is the formation

of a gestalt in which the relevant factors fall into place with respect to the whole" (Heidbreder, 1933, p. 355, from Kohler). Insight in Gestalt therapy is defined in terms of awareness that is clear about the structure of the situation being studied. The *Aha!* is not defined as apprehension of the genetic cause of current transference distortions as in psychoanalysis. Insight in Gestalt therapy is a field concept.

Immediate awareness without systematic study is not ordinarily sufficient to develop insight. Therefore, Gestalt therapy uses focused awareness and experimentation.

How one becomes aware is crucial to any phenomenological investigation. As the content of each awareness is noted, the phenomenologist also studies the awareness process itself. From this the patient learns a tool: being aware of his or her own awareness. How the phenomenologist/therapist and the patient experience (are aware of) their relationship is of special interest in Gestalt therapy (Yontef, 1976, 1981b, 1982).

The field theory perspective

Field theory is a method of exploring that describes the whole field of which the event is currently a part rather than analyzing the event in terms of a class to which it belongs by its "nature" (e.g., Aristotelian classification) or a unilinear, historical, cause-and-effect sequence (e.g., Newtonian mechanics).

The field is a whole in which the parts are in immediate relationship and responsive to each other and no part is uninfluenced by what goes on elsewhere in the field. The field replaces the notion of discrete, isolated particles. The person in his or her life space constitutes a field.

In field theory no action is at a distance; that is, what has effect must touch that which is effected in time and space.

Gestalt therapists work in the here-and-now, and are sensitive to how the here-and-now includes residues of the past, such as body posture, habits and beliefs.

The phenomenological field is defined by the observer and is meaningful only when one knows the frame of reference of the observer. The observer is necessary since what one sees is somewhat a function of how and when one looks.

Field approaches are descriptive rather than speculative, interpretive, or classificatory. The emphasis is on observing, describing, and explicating the exact structure of whatever is being studied. In Gestalt therapy, data unavailable to direct observation by the therapist are studied by phenomenological focusing, experimenting, and reporting of participants and by dialogue (Yontef, 1981b, 1982).

The existential perspective

Existentialism is based on the phenomenological method. Existential phenomenologists, including Gestalt therapists, focus on the *act*—the perceiving person. The chief focus is the person who does the experiencing, his joys and suffering, *as experienced.*

The existential view of humankind is that people are endlessly remaking or discovering themselves. There is no essence to be discovered "once and for all." There are always new horizons, new problems, and new opportunities. Any concept of the absolute "nature of man" is put in brackets.

People operate in an unstated context of conventional thought that obscures or avoids acknowledging how the world *is.* This is true especially of oneself, of one's relations in the world, and of one's choices. This, as a *self*-deception, creates such feelings as dread, guilt or anxiety. This self-deception is the basis of living inauthentically; it is not based on the truth of oneself in the world. Gestalt therapy provides a way of living authentically and of being meaningfully responsible for oneself. By becoming aware, one becomes able to choose and to organize one's own existence in a meaningful manner (Jacobs, 1978; Yontef, 1981b, 1982).

Dialogue

People exist in relation to environments, especially to each other. As an existential therapy, Gestalt therapy emphasizes relationships in its personality theory and in its therapeutic methodology. The basic unit of relationship is contact. Contact is defined as the experience of the boundary between "me" and "not me." It is the experience of a connection with the not-me, while maintaining a sense of being separate from the not-me.

Much of the work in Gestalt therapy deals with the development of appropriate support for desired contact or withdrawal (L. Perls, 1976, 1978). Support refers to anything that makes contact or withdrawal possible, including energy, body support, breathing, information, concern for others, language, and so forth. Supporting is the process of mobilizing resources for contact or withdrawal. For example, to support the excitement accompanying contact, a person must have an adequate support of oxygen. Thus if a person begins to express anger, he or she will need to breathe deeply. Cutting off one's breath would change the feeling of anger to anxiety.

Psychotherapeutic relations are built on contact marked by caring. Dialogue is the particular form of contact most appropriate to a phenomenological-existential psychotherapeutic relationship. In Gestalt therapy, caring, warmth, and acceptance are manifested through an I-Thou dialogue relationship.

Martin Buber states the "I" only has meaning in the I of an I-Thou or I-It contact. I-It is a relating in which the other person is manipulated rather than experienced. Dialogue, the I-Thou relation, embodies authenticity and responsibility. In I-Thou the Other is treated as a Thou—as a person. The other person is treated as an end and not as a means to an end. In a true dialogue one manifests the true self, one says what one means and means what one says.

In Gestalt therapy the dialogic relation has five characteristics.

1. Inclusion. This is putting oneself as fully as possible into the experience of the other without judging, analyzing, or interpreting while simultaneously retaining a sense of one's separate, autonomous presence. This is an existential and interpersonal application of the phenomenological trust in immediate experience. Inclusion provides an environment of safety for the patient's phenomenological work and, by communicating an understanding of the patient's experience, helps sharpen the patient's self-awareness.

2. Presence. The Gestalt therapist expresses her self to the patient. Regularly, judiciously, and with discrimination she expresses observations, preferences, feelings, personal experience, and thoughts. Thus, the therapist can share her perspective by modeling phenomenological reporting thereby aiding the patient's learning about the trust and use of immediate experience to raise awareness. If the therapist relies on theory-derived interpretation, rather than personal presence, she leads the patient into relying on phenomena not in his or her own immediate experience as the tool for raising awareness.

3. Commitment to dialogue. Contact is more than something two people do to each other. Contact is something that happens between people, something that arises from the interaction between them. In Gestalt therapy dialogue the therapist surrenders herself to this interpersonal process. This is *allowing* contact to happen rather than *making* contact and controlling the outcome.

4. No exploitation. Any form of exploitation is at variance with the dialogic relationship. Exploitation influences the patient's experience to adjust to a goal of the therapist rather than protecting the integrity of the patient's actual experience.

5. Dialogue is lived. Dialogue is something done rather than talked about. "Lived" emphasizes the excitement and immediacy of doing. The mode of dialogue can be dancing, song, words, or any modality that expresses and moves the energy between or among the participants. An important contribution of Gestalt therapy to phenomenological experimentation is enlarging the parameters to include explication of experience by nonverbal expressions. However, the interaction is limited by ethics, appropriateness, therapeutic task, and so on.

Other Systems

Yontef (1969) notes that:

The theoretical distinction between Gestalt Therapy, behavior modification and psychoanalysis is clear. In behavior modification, the patient's behavior is directly changed by the therapist's manipulation of environmental stimuli. In psychoanalytic theory, behavior is caused by unconscious motivation which becomes manifest in the transference relationship. By analyzing the transference the repression is lifted, the unconscious becomes conscious. In Gestalt Therapy the patient learns to fully use his internal and external senses so he can be self-responsible and self-supportive. Gestalt Therapy helps the patient

regain the key to this state, the awareness of the process of awareness. Behavior modification conditions [by] using stimulus control, psychoanalysis cures by talking about and discovering the cause of mental illness [The Problem], and Gestalt Therapy brings self-realization through Here-and-Now experiments in directed awareness. (pp. 33-34)

Behavior modification and other therapies that primarily try for direct control over symptoms (for example, chemotherapy, ECT, hypnosis, etc.) contrast with both Gestalt therapy and psychodynamic therapies in that the latter systems foster change primarily by the patient learning to understand him/herself in the world through insight.

The methodology of Gestalt and psychodynamic therapy uses an accepting relationship and a technology to help the patient change via emotional/cognitive self-understanding. In psychoanalysis the basic patient behavior is free association; the chief tool of the analyst is interpretation. To encourage transference the analyst withholds any direct expression of his personhood (no "I" statements) and practices the "Rule of Abstinence"; that is, he does not gratify any of the patient's wishes. This approach is true of all psychodynamic schools: classical, object relations, ego psychological, Kohutian, Jungian. The psychodynamic therapist isolates her person in order to encourage a relationship based explicitly on transference (rather than contact).

Gestalt therapy works for understanding by using the active, healing presence of the therapist *and the patient* in a relationship based on true contact. Transference, explored and worked through as it arises, is not encouraged by the Gestalt therapist (Polster, 1968). Characterological issues are *explicitly dealt with in Gestalt therapy* via the dialogic and phenomenological method.

In Gestalt therapy the immediate experience of the patient is actively used. Rather than free associate, while passively awaiting the therapist's interpretation and subsequent change, the patient is seen as a collaborator who is to learn how to heal himself. The patient "works" rather than free associates. "What can I do to work on this?" is a frequent question in Gestalt therapy and frequently there is an answer. For example, a couple with sexual difficulties might be asked to practice sensate focusing.

More than any other therapy, Gestalt therapy emphasizes that whatever exists is here and now and that experience is more reliable than interpretation. The patient is taught the difference between *talking about* what occurred five minutes ago (or last night or 20 years ago) and *experiencing* what is now.

Psychoanalyst S. A. Applebaum (1976) observes that:

In Gestalt Therapy the patient quickly learns to make the discrimination between ideas and ideation, between well-worn obsessional pathways and new thoughts, between a statement of experience and a statement of a statement. The Gestalt goal of pursuing experience and not explanations, based on the belief that insight which emerges as the Gestalt emerges is more potent than insight given by the therapist, does help the patient and the therapist draw and maintain these important distinctions. (p. 757)

Systems relying on interpretation are not effective in teaching this. Therapies such as behavior modification, reality therapy, and rational emotive therapy do not work with the *patient's* experience enough to do this. In Rogerian therapy the passivity imposed on the therapist severely narrows the range or power of the therapy to teach these distinctions.

The practice of most therapy systems encourages intellectualizing, that is, talking about the irrationality of patient beliefs, talking about behavior changes the therapist believes that the patient should make, and so forth. The Gestalt therapy methodology utilizes active techniques that clarify experience (and are not designed to directly modify behavior, though they often have the effect).

In no other systematic therapy does the therapist have as wide a range of responses to choose from. The psychoanalyst can only use interpretation. The Rogerian can reflect and clarify. Gestalt therapists may use any techniques or methods they know, as long as (1) they are aimed toward increasing awareness, (2) they emerge out of dialogue and phenomenologic work, and (3) they are within the parameters of ethical practice.

Experimentation helps patients learn to discriminate which behavior satisfies needs. But unlike most other therapies, in Gestalt therapy the *process* of discovery through experimentation *is* the end point rather than the feeling or idea or content discovered.

The Gestalt therapy belief is that the power and responsibility for the present is in the hands of the patient and that in the past the patient was psychologically in mutual interaction with his environment and not a passive recipient of trauma. Thus the patient may have received shaming messages from his parents, but swallowing the message and coping by self-blame was his own, as was the continuation of the shaming internally from then until now. This point of view is at variance with psychodynamic attitudes, but consonant with Adler's and Ellis's views.

This viewpoint enables the patient to be more responsible for his own existence, including his therapy, and for both patient and therapist to know that. When the therapist believes that the past causes the present and that the patient is controlled by unconscious motivation not readily available to the patient, the patient is encouraged to rely on interpretations of the therapist rather than being autonomous.

In therapies in which the therapist undertakes to directly modify the patient's behavior, the immediate experience of the patient and therapist are not honored. This is what separates Gestalt therapy from most other therapies. A resentful patient may increase his awareness by expressing his resentment. If the therapist suggests this as a means of catharsis it is different than the phenomenological focusing of Gestalt therapy.

In Gestalt therapy there are no "shoulds." Instead of emphasizing what should be, Gestalt therapy stresses awareness of what is. *What is, is.* This contrasts with any therapist who "knows" what the patient "should" do. For example, A. T. Beck (cognitive behavior modification), Albert Ellis (rational emotive therapy), and William Glasser (reality therapy) all try to modify the patient's irrational or irresponsible or unreal attitudes. They judge what is irrational. For example, Ellis "disputes" the client's "irrational beliefs."

Even though Gestalt therapy discourages interrupting the organismic assimilating process by focusing on cognitive explanatory intellectualizations, Gestalt therapists do work with belief systems. Clarifying thinking, explicating beliefs, mutually deciding what "fits" for the patient, are all part of Gestalt therapy. Gestalt therapy de-emphasizes thinking that avoids experience (obsessing) rather than thinking that supports experience. Gestalt therapy excludes the therapist narcissistically teaching the patient rather than being contactful and expediting the patient's self discovering through use of his feeling and sensing faculties.

Many persons claim they practice "TA [transactional analysis] and Gestalt," having combined transactional analysis with Gestalt therapy. Usually these people use the TA *theory* and some Gestalt therapy *techniques*. The techniques are not the important aspect of Gestalt therapy. When used in an analytic, cognitive style these techniques are not Gestalt therapy! Such a combination often aborts, prevents or neutralizes the organismic awareness work of the phenomenological-existential method. A better combination would be integrating the concepts of TA into a Gestalt therapy framework. Thus the parent/adult/child ego states, crossed transactions, and life scripts can be translated into Gestalt process language and worked with experimentally and dialogically.

Another difference between Gestalt therapy and other therapies is Gestalt therapy's genuine regard for holism and multidimensionality. People manifest their distress in how they behave, think, and feel. "Gestalt therapy views the entire biopsychosocial field, including organism/environment, as important. Gestalt therapy actively uses physiological, sociological, cognitive, motivational variables. No relevant dimension is excluded in the basic theory" (Yontef, 1969, pp. 33-34). Clinically, direct usage of multidimensional and holistic techniques, that is, body work, would raise grave questions in any therapy relying on transference and interpretation. In fact, it is often interpreted as acting out.

HISTORY

Precursors

The history of Gestalt therapy starts with the professional development of Fritz Perls, its principal founder, and the Zeitgeist he lived in. After acquiring the

M.D. degree, Perls went to Frankfurt-am-Main in 1926 as an assistant to Kurt Goldstein at Goldstein's Institute for Brain Damaged Soldiers. Here he was exposed to Professors Goldstein and Adhemar Gelb and he met his future wife, Laura, the following year. At that time Frankfurt-am-Main was a center of intellectual ferment and Perls was directly and indirectly exposed to leading Gestalt psychologists, existential philosophers and psychoanalysts.

Fritz Perls became a psychoanalyst. He was influenced directly by Karen Horney and Wilheim Reich, and indirectly by Otto Rank and others. Perls was especially influenced by Wilhelm Reich, who was Perls's analyst in the early 1930s, and "who first directed my [Perls] attention to a most important aspect of psychosomatic medicine—to the function of the motoric system as an armour" (F. Perls, 1947, p. 3).

Three influences on his intellectual development should be noted. One was the philosopher, Sigmund Friedlander. From Friedlander's philosophy, Perls incorporated the concepts of differential thinking and creative indifference, spelled out in Perls's first book, *Ego, Hunger and Aggression* (1947). Perls was also influenced by Jan Smuts. Smuts was the prime minister of South Africa when Perls moved there with his family (having first escaped from Nazi Germany and then Nazi-occupied Holland). Before becoming prime minister, Smuts had written a major book on holism and evolution that, in effect, examined the broader ecological world from a Gestalt perspective. Smuts coined the word "holism." Third, Alfred Korzybski, the semanticist, was an influence on Perls's intellectual development.

Laura Posner Perls was a co-founder of Gestalt therapy. Her influence on Perls was generally known and she wrote several chapters of *Ego, Hunger and Aggression*. She was a psychology student at the time she met Perls, receiving the D.Sc. degree from the University of Frankfurt in 1932. She was knowledgeable in the field of general psychology and more specifically the emerging impactfulness of Gestalt psychology. She had contact with and was influenced by the existentialist theologians Martin Buber and Paul Tillich. Much of the Gestalt phenomenological and existential influence in Gestalt therapy is through her, although credit and influence were limited by how little she wrote (under her name) (Rosenfeld, 1978).

Although Perls was a training psychoanalyst, he was among those who chafed under the dogmatism of classical Freudian psychoanalysis. The 1920s, 30s and 40s were periods of great ferment and rebellion against Newtonian positivism. This was true in science (for example, Einstein's field theory), theater and dance, philosophy, art, architecture, and existentialism. Both Laura and Fritz lived in a Zeitgeist permeated by phenomenological-existentialist influence. These later became integrated into Gestalt therapy (Kogan, 1976).

Among the ideas that were "in the air" that laid the foundation for the establishment of Gestalt therapy were the Gestalt psychology phenomenological and field ideas connected with direct experience and the whole Gestalt. Included were the concepts that we perceive in differentiated wholes; that the whole field had principles not formed from a mere atomistic summation of constituent parts; that the whole is segregated from a background and internally differentiated into parts; that perception is a function of the whole person (especially the central nervous system) and not of the peripheral sense organs; that the person is *not* a passive recipient of meaningless stimuli that people are taught how to interpret; that the situation has inherent organization not created by the observer; and the here-and-now field emphasis. Among the existential ideas were acknowledgement of responsibility and choice in creating one's personal existence, the primacy of existence over essence, and the existential dialogue.

Beginnings

Ego, Hunger and Aggression was written in 1941-42. In its first publication in South Africa in 1946, it was subtitled *A Revision of Freud's Theory and Method*. The subtitle of the book when it appeared in 1966 was changed to *The Beginning of Gestalt Therapy*. The actual term *Gestalt Therapy* was first used as the title of a book written by Fritz Perls, Ralph Hefferline, and Paul Goodman (1951). Shortly after the New York Institute for Gestalt Therapy was organized, headquartered in the apartment of Fritz and Laura Perls in New York City. This apartment was used for seminars, workshops, and groups. Among those who studied with Perls at that time were Paul Weisz, Lotte Weidenfeld, Buck Eastman, Paul Goodman, Isadore From, Elliot Shapiro, Leo Chalfen, Iris Sanguilano, James Simkin, and Kenneth A. Fisher.

During the 1950s, intensive workshops and study groups were established throughout the country. Before the American Psychological Association meeting, which was held in New York City in 1954, a special intensive workshop limited to 15 qualified psychologists was given over a three-day period. Similar workshops were held in Cleveland, Miami, and Los Angeles. In 1955 the Cleveland study group formed the Gestalt Institute of Cleveland.

Fritz Perls moved to the West Coast in 1960 at which time Simkin arranged a Gestalt therapy workshop for him. Perls, Walter Kempler, and James Simkin offered the first Gestalt therapy training workshops at the Esalen Institute during the summer of 1964. These training workshops continued under the leadership of Perls and Simkin through 1968. After Perls moved to Canada, Simkin along with Irma Shepherd, Robert W. Resnick, Robert L. Martin, Jack Downing, and John Enright continued to offer Gestalt therapy training there through 1970.

During this beginning period, Gestalt therapy pioneered many ideas which have subsequently been accepted into eclectic psychotherapy practice. The excitement of direct contact between therapist and patient, emphasis on direct experience, the use of active experimentation, the emphasis on the here and now, responsibility of the patient for him/herself, the awareness principle, trust in organismic self-regulation, the ecological interdependence of person and environment, the principle of assimilation and other such concepts were new, exciting, and shocking to a conservative establishment. In this period the practice of psychotherapy was dichotomized between the older, traditional approach of psychoanalytic drive theory and the ideas pioneered largely by Gestalt therapy. This was a period of expansion with integration of the principles with each other and the elucidation and enucleation of the principles left for the future. Thus, for example, Gestalt therapy pioneered the use of the active presence of the therapist in a contactful relationship, but did not consider in detail what constituted a healing dialogic presence.

Current Status

There are (1982) some 53 Gestalt therapy institutes and the list continues to grow. Virtually every major city in the United States has at least one Gestalt institute. In New York City, where Gestalt therapy training has continued since the early 1950s, there are four institutes. There are also institutes in Europe and other continents. Some institutes are organized around one or two persons. For example, Simkin has been offering training in Gestalt therapy since 1972 at Big Sur, California. Other institutes have a large faculty and multiple programs. For example, the Gestalt Therapy Institute of Los Angeles, started in 1969, has an ongoing training program with a variety of didactic, professional, clinical, and experiential offerings, a summer residential training program, and a low-fee public clinic.

No national organization has been established. As a result, there are no established standards for institutes, trainers, and trainees. Each institute has its own criteria for training, membership, selection, and so on. Attempts in the recent past to organize a nationwide conference for establishing standards for trainers have not been successful. There are no agreed-upon standards for what constitutes good Gestalt therapy or a good Gestalt therapist. Therefore, it is incumbent on Gestalt therapy consumers to carefully evaluate the educational, clinical, and training background of people calling themselves "Gestalt therapists," or who give training in Gestalt therapy (see Yontef, 1981a, 1981c).

Two journals have been established. *The Gestalt Journal* is devoted primarily to articles on Gestalt therapy. *Gestalt Theory* publishes articles on Gestalt psychology including some on Gestalt therapy. Bibliographic information can be obtained from Kogan (1980) and Rosenfeld (1981).

As experience doing Gestalt therapy has grown, earlier therapeutic practices have been altered. For example, earlier Gestalt therapy practice often stressed the clinical use of frustration, a confusion of self-sufficiency with self-support, and an abrasive attitude if the patient was interpreted by the therapist as manipulative. This approach tended to enhance the shame of shame-oriented patients. There has been a movement toward more softness in Gestalt therapy practice, more direct self-expression by the therapist, more of a dialogic emphasis, decreased use of stereotypic techniques, increased emphasis on description of character structure (with utilization of psychoanalytic formulations), and increased use of group process.

Thus a patient is more likely to encounter, among Gestalt therapists who are involved in the newer mode, an emphasis on self-acceptance, a softer demeanor by the therapist, more trust of the patient's phenomenology, and more explicit work with psychodynamic themes.

Along with the stress of clarity about the qualities of a good Gestalt therapy relationship there has been an increase in emphasis on group process, including relation between group members, and decrease in formal, one-to-one work. There is also an increased attention to theoretical instruction, theoretical exposition, and work with cognition in general.

PERSONALITY

Theory of Personality

Ecological interdependence: The organism/environment field

People are differentiated out of the organism/environment field. Every human process is both internal and interpersonal.

A person exists by differentiating self and other and by connecting self and other. These are the two functions of a boundary. To make good contact with one's world, it is necessary to risk reaching out and discovering one's own boundaries. Effective self-regulation includes contact in which one is aware of novelty in the environment that is potentially nourishing or toxic. That which is nourishing is assimilated and all else is rejected. This kind of differentiated contact inevitably leads to growth (Polster & Polster, 1973, p. 101).

Mental metabolism

In Gestalt therapy, the food metabolism process is used as a metaphor for psychological functioning. Organisms undergo a constant metabolic cycle of expending energy with the outside based on an internal sense of need and preference and external sense of available nutrients. People grow through biting off an appropriate-sized piece (be this food or ideas or relationships) and chewing it (considering), discovering whether it is nourishing or toxic. If nourishing, through chewing and swallowing, the organism assimilates it and makes it part of itself. If toxic the organism spits it out (rejects). This requires a person to be willing to trust his taste and judgment. Discrimination requires *actively* sensing outside stimuli and processing this exteroceptive stimulus along with interoceptive data.

Regulation of the boundary

The boundary between self and environment must be kept permeable to allow exchanges and firm enough for organismic autonomy. The environment includes toxic elements to be screened out. Even what is nourishing needs to be discriminated according to what is the dominant present need. Metabolic processes are governed by the laws of homeostasis. Ideally the most urgent need energizes the organism until the need is met or is superseded by a more vital need. Living is a progression of needs, met and unmet, achieving homeostatic balance and going on to the next moment and new need.

Disturbances of the contact boundary

When the boundary between self and other becomes unclear, lost, or impermeable, this results in a disturbance of the distinction between self and other, a disturbance of both contact and awareness (see Perls, 1973; Polster & Polster, 1973).

Confluence (fusion) is absence of a distinction of self and other. *Isolation* is a loss of connection between self and other. *Withdrawal* is a boundary phenomenon in the rhythm of contact withdrawal, while isolation is a loss of boundary. In withdrawal, the boundary is maintained although the person's awareness is on "me" rather than "not-me." Isolation is somewhat like living behind a high wall.

Retroflection is a split within the self, a resisting of aspects of the self by the self. This substitutes self for environment, as in doing to self what one wants to do to someone else or doing for self what one wants someone to do for self. This is the mechanism that achieves isolation. The illusion of self-sufficiency is one example of retroflection as it substitutes self for environment. Although one can do one's own breathing and chewing, the air and food must come from the environment. Introspection is a form of retroflection; Gestalt awareness is a connection with the environment. Retroflection can be pathological or healthy. For example, resisting the impulse to express anger may serve to cope with a dangerous environment. In such a situation biting one's lip may be more functional than saying something biting.

Through *introjection* foreign material is absorbed without discriminating or assimilating. Swallowing whole creates an "as if" personality and rigid character. Introjected values and behavior are imposed on self. As in all contact boundary disturbances, swallowing whole can be healthy or pathological depending on the circumstances and degree of awareness. For example, students taking a lecture course may, with full awareness that they are doing so, copy, memorize, and regurgitate material without full "digestion," making it possible to complete the course and to go back and assimilate it at a future time. To introject without such awareness or where not fitting the situation, would be pathological.

Projection is a confusion of self and other by attributing to the outside something that is truly self. An example of healthy projection is art. Pathological projection is a way of not acknowledging (contacting or being aware of and responsible for) that which is projected. Example: A man is angry and resists his own anger. He wrongly imagines his friend is angry at him.

Deflection avoids contact and awareness by turning aside, as by being polite instead of direct. The deflection can be accomplished by not expressing directly or by not receiving. In the latter case, the person usually feels untouched; in the former case the person is often ineffective and baffled about not getting what is wanted. Deflection can be very useful where, with awareness, it meets the needs of the situation (e.g., where the situation needs cooling down). Other techniques include not looking at the person, verbosity, vagueness, understating, and talking about rather than *to* (Polster & Polster, 1973, pp. 89-92).

Organismic self-regulation

Human regulation is to varying degrees either organismic, that is, based on a relatively full and accurate acknowledgement of *what is*, or "shouldistic," that is based on the arbitrary imposition of what some controller thinks should or should not be. This applies to intrapsychic regulation, to the regulation of interpersonal relations, and to the regulation of social groups.

"There is only one thing that should control: the *situation*. If you understand the situation you are in and let the situation you are in control your actions, then you learn to cope with life" (F. Perls, 1976, p. 35). Perls explicated the above with an example of driving a car. Instead of a preplanned program, "I want to drive 65 miles per hour," a person cognizant of the situation will drive a different speed at night or differently when in traffic, or still differently when tired, and so on. Here Perls makes it clear that "let the situation control" means regulating through awareness of the contemporary context, including one's wants, rather than through what was thought "should" happen.

In organismic self-regulation, choosing and learning happen holistically, that is, with a natural integration of mind and body, thought and feeling, and spontaneity and deliberateness. In shouldistic regulation, cognition reigns and there is no felt, holistic sense. Impulsive self-regulation is a nonholistic regulation in which there is neither cognitive restraint nor the support of the holistic integration of mind and body.

Obviously, everything relevant to boundary regulation cannot be in full awareness. Most transactions are handled by automatic, habitual modes with minimal awareness. Organismic self-regulation requires that the habitual becomes fully aware as needed. When awareness does not emerge as needed and/or does not organize the necessary motor activity, psychotherapy is a method of increasing awareness, and gaining meaningful choice and responsibility.

Awareness

Awareness and dialogue are the two primary therapeutic tools in Gestalt therapy. Awareness is a form of experience which may be loosely defined as being in touch with one's own existence, with *what is.*

Laura Perls (1973) states:

The aim of Gestalt Therapy is the *awareness continuum*, the freely ongoing Gestalt formation where what is of greatest concern and interest to the organism, the relationship, the group or society becomes Gestalt, comes into the foreground where it can be fully experienced and coped with (acknowledged, worked through, sorted out, changed, disposed of, etc.) so that then it can melt into the background (be forgotten or assimilated and integrated) and leave the foreground free for the next relevant Gestalt. (p. 2)

Full awareness is the process of being in vigilant contact with the most important event in the individual/environment field with full sensorimotor, emotional, cognitive, and energetic support. Insight, a form of awareness, is an immediate grasp of the obvious unity of disparate elements in the field. Aware contact creates new, meaningful wholes and thus is in itself an integration of a problem.

Effective awareness is grounded in and energized by the dominant present need of the organism. It involves not only self-knowledge, but a direct knowing of the current situation and how the self is in that situation. Any denial of the situation and its demands or of one's wants and chosen response in the situation is a disturbance of awareness. Meaningful awareness is of self in the world, in dialogue with the world, and with awareness of Other—it is not an inwardly focused introspection. Awareness is accompanied by *owning*, that is, the process of knowing one's control over, choice of, responsibility for, one's own behavior and feelings. Without this the person may be vigilant to his own experience and life space, but not to what power he has and does not have. Awareness is cognitive, sensory, and affective. The person who acknowledges

verbally his situation but does not really *see* it, *know* it, *react* to it, *feel* in response to it, is not fully aware, and is not in full contact. The person who is aware knows *what* he does, *how* he does it, that he has alternatives, and that he *chooses* to be as he is.

The act of awareness is always here and now, although the content of awareness may be distant. The act of remembering is now; what is remembered is not now. When the situation calls for an awareness of the past or anticipation of the future, effective awareness takes this into account.

Example

P: [Looking more tense than usual.] I don't know what to work on.

T: What are you aware of right now?

P: I am glad to see you, but I'm tense about a meeting tonight with my boss. I have rehearsed and prepared and I've tried to support myself as I wait.

T: What do you need right now?

P: I thought of putting her in the empty chair and talking to her. But I am so tense I need to do something more physical—I need to move, breathe, make noise.

T: [Looks but remains silent.]

P: It's up to me, huh? [Pause. Patient gets up, starts stretching, yawning. The movements and sounds become more vigorous. After a few minutes he sits down. Looks more soft and alive.] Now I'm ready.

T: You look more alive.

P: Now I am ready to explore what had me so uptight about tonight.

Self-rejection and full awareness are mutually exclusive. Rejecting of self is a distortion of awareness since it is a denial of who one is. Self rejection is simultaneously a confusion of who "I am" and a self-deception or "bad faith" attitude of being above that which is ostensibly being acknowledged (Sartre, 1966). Saying "I am" as if it were an observation of another person, or as if the "I" were not chosen, or without knowing how one creates and perpetuates that "I am" is bad faith rather than insightful awareness.

Responsibility

People, according to Gestalt therapy, are responsible (response-able), that is, the primary agent in determining their own behavior. When people confuse responsibility with blaming and shoulds they pressure and manipulate themselves, they "try" and are not integrated and spontaneous. In such instances one's true wants, needs, responses to environment and choices in the situation are ignored and one overcomplies or rebels against shoulds.

Gestalt therapy believes in the importance of a clear distinction between what one chooses and what is given. People are responsible for what they choose to do. For example, people are responsible for their action on behalf of the environment. Blaming outside forces (genetics, parents, environment) for what one chooses is self-deception. Taking "responsibility" for what one did not choose, a typical shame reaction, is also a deception.

People are responsible for moral choices. Gestalt therapy helps patients discover what is moral according to their own choice and values. Far from advocating "anything goes," Gestalt therapy places a most serious obligation on each person: choosing and valuing.

Variety of Concepts

Gestalt therapy personality theory has evolved primarily out of clinical experience. The focus has been a theory of personality that supports our task as psychotherapists rather than an overall theory of personality. The constructs of Gestalt therapy theory are field theoretical rather than genetic, and phenomenological rather than conceptual.

Although Gestalt therapy is phenomenological, it also deals with the unconscious, that is, with what systematically does not enter into awareness when needed. In Gestalt therapy awareness is conceived as being in touch and unawareness as being out of touch. Unawareness can be explained by a variety of phenomena, including learning what to attend to, repression, cognitive set, character, and style, a healthy and needed inattention to one thing to attend to something else. Simkin (1976) envisions personality like a floating ball—at any given moment only a portion is exposed while the rest is submerged: unawareness is the result of the organism not being in touch with its external environment due to its being mostly submerged in its own internal environment or fantasies (pp. 17-18), or not being in touch with its inner life due to fixation on the external.

Gestalt therapy theory of change

Children swallow whole (introject) ideals and behavior that do not suit them. This results in an enforced morality rather than an organismically compatible morality. As a result, people frequently feel guilt when they behave in accordance with their wants as opposed to their shoulds. In some people, an enormous amount of energy is invested in maintaining the split between shoulds and wants—the resolution of which requires a recognition of one's own morality as opposed to an introjected one. Shoulds sabotage the person and the more the person pushes to be what he or she is not, the more resistance is set up, and no change occurs.

Beisser advanced the theory that change takes place when a person becomes what he is, and not by trying to become what he is not. Thus change is thought not to occur by a "coercive attempt by the individual or by another person to change him," but does happen if the person puts in the time and effort to be "what he is," "to be fully in his current position" (Beisser, 1970, p. 70). When the therapist rejects the change agent role, change that is orderly and also meaningful is possible. Part of the rationale is that by standing in one place one can have "firm footing" as support to move, and that without this support movement is difficult or impossible.

The Gestalt therapy notion is that awareness (including owning, choice, and responsibility) and contact bring natural and spontaneous change. Forced change is an attempt to actualize an image rather than to actualize the self. With awareness, self-acceptance, and concomitantly the knowledge of the right to exist *as is*, the organism can grow. Forced intervention retards this process.

The Gestalt psychology principle of Prägnanz states that the field will form itself into the best Gestalt that global conditions will allow. So, too, Gestalt therapy believes that people have an innate drive to health. This propensity is found in nature and people are part of nature. Awareness of the obvious, the awareness continuum, is the tool that a person can deliberately use which channels this spontaneous drive for health.

Differentiation of the field: Polarities versus dichotomies

A dichotomy is a split whereby the field is considered not as a whole differentiated into different and interlocking parts, but rather as consisting of competing (either/or) and unrelated forces. Dichotomous thinking interferes with organismic self-regulation. Dichotomous thinking tends to be intolerant of diversity between persons and paradoxical truths about a single person.

Organismic self-regulation leads to integrating parts with each other and into a whole which encompasses the parts as integral. The field is often differentiated into *polarities*; that is, parts that are opposites that complement or explicate each other. The positive and negative poles of an electrical field are the prototypical mode for this differentiation in a field theoretical way. The concept of polarities treats the opposites as part of one whole, as yin and yang.

With this polar view of the field, differences are accepted and integrated. Lack of genuine integration creates splits such as body-mind, self-external, infantile-mature, biological-cultural, unconscious-conscious, and so on. Through dialogue there can be an integration of parts, into a new whole in which there is a differentiated unity. Dichotomies such as the self-ideal and the needy self, thought and impulse, social requirements and personal needs, can be healed by integrating into a whole differentiated into natural polarities (Perls, 1947).

Definition of health I: The good Gestalt as polarity

The goal in Gestalt therapy is an awareness process with qualities of a good Gestalt organized by the dominant organismic need at each moment. The "good Gestalt" describes a perceptual field organized with clarity and good form. A well-formed figure clearly stands out against a broader and less distinct background. The relation between that which stands out (figure) and the context (ground) is meaning. In the good Gestalt the meaning is clear. The good Gestalt gives a content-free definition of health.

In health, the figure changes as needed; that is, shifts to another focus when the need is met or superseded by a more urgent need. It does not change so rapidly as to prevent satisfaction (as in hysteria) nor so slowly that new figures have no room to assume organismic dominance (as in compulsivity). When figure and ground are dichotomized, one is left with a figure out of context or a context without focus (F. Perls et al., 1951). In health, awareness accurately represents the dominant need of the whole field. Need is a function of external factors (physical structure of the field, political activity, acts of nature, and so on) and internal factors (hunger, fatigue, interest, past experience, and so forth).

Example. I am tired, hungry, and want time alone—my son has not seen me all day. He has had an upsetting day and wants my attention. In health, the dominant need arises from recognition of these and other relevant factors (how much time will I be at home, when does my child go to sleep, how fatigued am I, how long do I need to recover, who else is present who can meet the need, is this child one who usually develops self-support, or is it a child who is chronically overdependent?)

The figure and ground form a polarity that differentiates the field. The process of good Gestalt formation constitutes a culture-free, content-free definition of health. With good Gestalt formation comes flexibility, responsiveness to need, lack of internal conflict and self-support.

Definition of health II: The polarity of creative adjustment

Adjustment of the individual to society versus creating something new or molding the external world to the will of the individual are polar opposites. The Gestalt therapy concept of healthy functioning includes *creative adjustment.* A psychotherapy that only helps patients adjust creates conformity, stereotypy. A psychotherapy that only led people to impose themselves on the world without considering others would engender pathological narcissism, and a world-denying realization of self isolated from the world.

Self and other are polarities that form a whole. A person who shows creative interaction takes responsibility for the ecological balance between self and surroundings.

This is the theoretical context (F. Perls et al., 1951) within which some seemingly individualistic and even anarchistic statements of Gestalt therapy are most accurately considered. The individual and environment form a polarity. The choice is not between the individual and society, but between organismic and arbitrary regulation.

Resistance is part of a polarity consisting of an impulse, and a resistance of being aware of and expressing it. Seen as a dichotomy, resistance is often treated as "bad," and in such a context often turns out to be nothing more than the patient following his dictates rather than the therapist's. Seen as a polarity, resistance is as integral to health as the trait being resisted.

Appelbaum (1976) says: "The Gestalt emphasis on helping the patient discover 'the mechanism by which he alienates part of his self-process and thereby avoids awareness of himself and environment' is a 'serviceable definition of resistance' " (p. 763).

Gestalt therapists attend to both the working process of consciousness and the resistance process of consciousness. Many Gestalt therapists avoid the word *resistance* because of its pejorative dichotomized connotation which frames the process as a power battle between therapist and patient rather than as the self-conflict of the patient that needs integrating into a harmoniously differentiated self.

Impasse

An impasse is a situation in which external support is not forthcoming and the person believes he cannot support himself. The latter is due in large part to the person's strength being divided between impulse and resistance. The most frequent method of coping with this is to manipulate others.

An organismically self-regulating person knows he can support himself and takes responsibility for what is done for self, what is done by others for self, and what is done for others by self. The person exchanges with the environment but the basic support for regulation of one's existence is by self. When the individual does not know this, external support becomes a replacement for self-support rather than a source of nourishment for the self.

In most psychotherapy the impasse is gotten through with external support by the therapist, and the patient does not find that his self-support is sufficient. In Gestalt therapy, patients can get through the impasse because of the emphasis on loving contact without doing the patient's work, that is, without *rescuing* or infantilizing.

PSYCHOTHERAPY

Theory of Psychotherapy

Goal of therapy

In Gestalt therapy, *the goal is always awareness and only awareness.* This includes greater awareness in a particular area and also greater ability for the patient

to be able to bring automatic habits into awareness as needed. In the former sense awareness is a content, in the latter sense it is a process. Both awareness as content and awareness as process progress to deeper levels as the therapy proceeds. At all levels awareness includes knowing the environment, responsibility for choices, self-knowledge and self-acceptance, and the ability to contact. It includes knowing and accepting what one is doing and how, and what is being done to one and how.

Beginning patients are chiefly concerned with the solution of problems. The issue for the Gestalt therapist is how patients support themselves in solving problems. Gestalt therapy facilitates problem solving through increased self-regulation and self-support by the patient. As therapy goes on, the patient and therapist turn more attention to general personality issues of the patient. By the end of successful therapy the patient directs much of the work and is able to integrate problem solving, characterological themes related to this, relationship issues with the therapist, and means of regulating one's own awareness.

Gestalt therapy is most useful for patients open to working on self-awareness, who want natural mastery of their awareness process. Although some people claim they are interested in changing their behavior most people seeking psychotherapy mainly want relief from discomfort. Their complaint may be generalized malaise, specific discomforts, or dissatisfaction in relationships. Patients often expect that relief will result from their therapist doing the work rather than through their own efforts.

Psychotherapy is most appropriate for persons who create anxiety, depression, and so forth by rejecting themselves, alienating aspects of themselves, deceiving themselves. In short, people who do not know how they further their own unhappiness are prime candidates, providing they are open to awareness work, especially awareness of self-regulation. Gestalt therapy is especially appropriate for those who know intellectually about themselves and yet don't grow beyond a stuck point.

Those who, after exposure to the awareness method, want symptom relief without doing awareness work may be better candidates for behavior modification, medication, biofeedback, and so on. The direct methods of Gestalt therapy facilitate patients making this choice early in the therapy. However, the patient's difficulty in doing the contact or awareness work should not automatically be interpreted as meaning that the patient does not want to work. Respect for the total person enables a Gestalt therapist to help the patient become clear about the differences between "can't" and "won't" and to know how internal barriers or resistance such as prior learning, anxiety, shame, and sensitivity to narcissistic injury, inhibit awareness work.

No shoulds

There are no shoulds in Gestalt therapy. We do not know what the patient "should" be. In Gestalt therapy a higher value is placed on the autonomy and the self-determination of the patient than on other values. This is not a "should," but a preference. The "no-should" ethic takes precedence over the therapist's goals for the patient and leaves the responsibility and sanctioning of the patient behavior to the patient (of course, the injunctions and requirements of society are not suspended because the patient is in Gestalt therapy).

Simkin often starts workshops with a statement such as:

I believe that there are no "shoulds" in Gestalt therapy. What you do is what you do. What I do is what I do. I do have a preference. I prefer that you be straight with me. *Please* remember, this is a preference, not a should. If you feel that you *should* honor my preference, then that's *your* should. When I ask you, "Where are you?" and the like, my preference is that you tell me—or tell me that you're not willing to tell me. Then our transaction is straight. Any time that you want to know where I am, please ask me. I will either tell you, or tell you that I am unwilling to tell you—so that our transaction will be straight.

How is the therapy done?

Gestalt therapy is an exploration rather than a direct modifying of behavior. The goal is growth and autonomy through an increase in consciousness. The Gestalt therapy method involves contacting and focusing of awareness. The therapist actively engages with the patient. Rather than maintaining distance and interpreting, the Gestalt therapist meets the patient and guides active awareness work. The therapist's active presence is alive and excited (hence warm), honest, and direct. As appropriate, patients can see, hear, and be told how they are experienced, what is seen, how the therapist feels, what the therapist is like as a person. Growth occurs from real contact between real people. Patients learn how they are seen and how their awareness process is limited not primarily from talking about their problems, but how they and the therapist engage each other around the process.

The focusing runs the range from simple inclusion or empathy (i.e., the therapist communicating how he understands the patient's phenomenology) to exercises arising mostly from the therapist's phenomenology while with the patient. The experiments and exercises may be done in the therapy hour or at home. The attitude in either case is the same: direct experience, not interpretation, is primary. Everything is secondary to the direct experience of both participants.

The general approach of Gestalt therapy is to facilitate exploring in such a way as to maximize what continues to develop after the session and without the therapist. Rather than finishing the Gestalt of each piece of work, the patient is often left unfinished but thoughtful or "opened up," or with an assignment. This is like a roast that cooks after being removed from the oven. This is in part how Gestalt therapy can be so intensive on fewer sessions per week. We cooperate with growth occurring without us; we initiate where needed. We give the degree of facilitation necessary, desired by the patient, and that fosters patient self-improvement. We foster growth rather than complete a cure process.

Perls believed that the ultimate goal of psychotherapy was the achievement of "that amount of integration which facilitates its own development" (1948, pp. 572-573). An example of this kind of facilitation is the analogy of a small hole cut into an accumulation of snow. Once the draining process begins, the base that began as a small hole enlarges by itself.

Successful psychotherapy achieves *integration*. Integration requires identification with *all* vital functions—not only with *some* of the patient's ideas, emotions, and actions. Any rejection of one's own ideas, emotions, or actions results in alienation. Reowning allows the person to be whole as opposed to having gaps or holes. The task, then, in therapy is to have the person become aware of previously alienated parts and taste them, consider them and assimilate them if they are ego-syntonic, or reject them if they prove to be ego-alien. Simkin (1968) has used the simile of a cake in encouraging patients to reown the parts of themselves that they have considered noxious or otherwise unacceptable: just as the oil, or flour, or baking powder by themselves can be distasteful—as a part of

the whole cake they are indispensable to insure its success.

Three descriptive principles: I and Thou, What and How, and *Here and Now.*

The I-thou relation

This principle contrasts with the relationship of the transference-inducing withheld presence of the analyst, the master reconditioner stance of the behavior modifier, the guru, master/discipline relationship of cults, some encounter groups, and some spiritual disciplines.

Gestalt therapy focuses on the patient, as any therapy system does. However, the relationship is dialogic or horizontal, thus differing in several ways from the traditional therapy relationship. For one thing, in Gestalt therapy the therapist and patient speak the same language, the language of present centeredness emphasizing direct experience of both participants. Therapists as well as patients in Gestalt therapy show their full presence.

Since its beginning, Gestalt therapy has emphasized the patient's experience as well as the therapist's *observation* of what is not in the patient's awareness. This allows the patient to act as an equal having full access to the data of his own experience so he can directly experience from inside what is *observed* by the therapist. In an interpretive system the patient is an amateur and does not have the theoretical foundation for the interpretation. It is assumed that the important, internal data is unconscious and not experienced.

The I-Thou relation emphasizes not only the polar presence of patient and therapist, but especially what is between them.

An important aspect of the Gestalt therapy relationship is the question of responsibility. In Gestalt therapy we emphasize that both the therapist and patient are self-responsible. When therapists regard themselves as responsible for patients, they collude with patients not feeling self-responsible and thereby reinforce the necessity for manipulation due to the belief that patients are unable to support and regulate themselves. However, it is *not enough for the therapist to be responsible for self and patient for self*—there is also an alliance of patient and therapist that must be carefully, constantly, and competently attended to.

Therapists are responsible for the quality and quantity of their presence, for knowledge about themselves and the patient, for maintaining a nondefensive posture, and for keeping their awareness and contact processes clear and matched to the immediate environment, that is, the patient. They are responsible for the consequences of their own behavior. The therapist is responsible for establishing and maintaining the therapeutic atmosphere.

The awareness of what and how

In Gestalt therapy there is a constant and careful emphasis on what the patient does and how, through direct and immediate sharing of observations and directing the patient's attention. Does the patient notice what he is doing? What did the patient think he was doing? What does the patient experience when attention is called to what he is doing? Exactly how does this patient do what he is doing? How does the patient scare himself, or keep himself uninvolved and bored?

The emphasis is on the patient's direct experience of what is being done by and to the patient. What does the patient face? What choices does the patient have? Does the patient self-support or resist? Direct experience is the tool and it is expanded

beyond what is at first experienced by continuing to focus deeper and broader. The techniques of *Gestalt therapy are experimental tasks. They are a means of expanding direct experience. These are not designed to get the patient somewhere, to change the patient's feelings, to recondition, to foster catharsis, and so on.*

Here and now

In a phenomenological therapy "now" starts with the present awareness of the patient. What happens first is not childhood, but what is experienced now. Awareness is a sensory experience and takes place now. Prior events may be the object of present awareness, but the awareness process (e.g., remembering) is now.

Contact also takes place now. *Now* I can contact the world around me, or *now* I can contact memories of the past or expectations of the future. Not knowing the present, not remembering or not anticipating are all disturbances. The present is an ever-moving transition between the past and future. Frequently patients do not know their current behavior. In some cases patients live in the present as if they had no past. Most patients live in the future as if it were now. All these are disturbances of time awareness.

In Gestalt therapy "now" refers to this moment. In the hour, when the patients refer to their lives out of the hour, or earlier in the hour, that is *not* now. In Gestalt therapy we orient more to the now than in any other form of psychotherapy. Experiences of the past few minutes, days, years, or decades that are of present importance are dealt with. We attempt to move from talking about to directly experiencing. For example, talking *to* a person who is not physically present rather than talking about mobilizes more direct experience of feelings.

Themes of childhood are dealt with in Gestalt therapy if the individual Gestalt therapist knows psychodynamics, is receptive to this work, and knows her own characterological material. Then the characterological work can be done using the phenomenological-existential method if the Gestalt therapist also knows the essence of Gestalt therapy and not just techniques. Some Gestalt therapists know how to make contact, but because of training, background, personality, their own therapy, etc., are not able to do significant characterological work.

Example. A 30-year-old female patient is in group therapy. She is in the middle phase of therapy. She says she is very angry at a man in the group. The man is a provocative, 40-year-old obsessive who judges and is emotionally unresponsive. One legitimate and frequent Gestalt approach is: "Say it to him." Instead the therapist took a different tack:

T: You sound not only angry but something more.

P: [Looks interested.]

T: You sound and look like you are enraged.

P: I am, I would like to kill him.

T: You seem to feel impotent.

P: I am.

T: Impotence usually accompanies rage. What are you impotent about?

P: I can't get him to acknowledge me.

T: [The therapist's observations of her previous encounters with the man agree with that statement.] And don't accept that.

P: No.

T: And there is an intensity to your rage that seems to be greater than the situation.

P: [Nods and pauses.]

T: What are you experiencing?

P: I am thinking about a lot of men in my life who have been like that.

T: Like your father. [Comes from prior work with patient and not a shot in the dark. The work proceeded into a re-experiencing the narcissistic injury from her father who was never responsive to her.]

Process of Psychotherapy

What Gestalt therapy "looks like" depends on the modality of therapy and style of the therapist. Gestalt therapy probably has a greater range of styles and modalities than any other system. It is practiced in individual therapy, groups, workshops, couples, families, and with children. It is practiced in clinics, family service agencies, hospitals, private practice, growth centers, and so on. The styles in each modality vary drastically on many dimensions: degree and type of structure, quantity and quality of techniques used, frequency of sessions, abrasiveness-ease of relating, focus on body, cognition, feelings, interpersonal contact, knowledge of and work with psychodynamic themes, degree of personal encountering, and so forth.

All styles and modalities of Gestalt therapy have in common the general principles we have been discussing, that is, emphasis on direct experience and experimenting (phenomenology), use of direct contact and personal presence (dialogic existentialism), emphasis on the field concepts of what and how and here and now. Within these parameters, interventions are patterned according to context and personality of the therapist and the patient.

At the heart of the methodology is the emphasis on the difference between "work" and other activities, especially "talking about." Work has two meanings. First, it refers to a deliberate, voluntary, and disciplined commitment to use phenomenologically focused awareness to increase the scope and clarity of one's experience and achieve greater awareness of one's life. When one moves from talking about a problem or being with someone in a general way to studying what one is doing, especially being aware of how one is aware, one is working. Second, in a group, it means being the primary focus of the therapist's and/or group's attention and working in the sense of the first definition.

Differences in techniques are not important, although the quality and type of therapeutic contact and a fit between the attitude and emphasis of the therapist and the patient's needs are important and the differences between interventions in these regards may be vital. Techniques per se do not distinguish between Gestalt therapy and other therapies or between styles of Gestalt therapy. Techniques are just techniques: the overall method, relationship established, and attitude are the vital aspects.

Nevertheless a discussion of some techniques or tactics might elucidate the overall methodology. These are only illustrative of what is possible.

Techniques of patient focusing

All techniques of patient focusing are elaborations of: "What are you aware of (experiencing) now?" and "Try this experiment and see what you become aware of (experience or learn)." Many interventions are as simple as asking what the patient is aware of, or more narrowly, "What are you feeling." "What are you thinking?"

One: "Stay with it." A frequent technique upon finding out what the patient is aware of is: "Stay with it," or "Feel it out."

"Stay with it," encourages the patient to continue with the same feeling that is being reported, building the patient's capacity to deepen and work a feeling through to completion consciously and voluntarily.

Example: Patient looks sad.

T: What are you aware of?

P: I am sad.

T: Stay with it.

P: [Tears well up, then the patient tightens and looks away and starts to look thoughtful.]

T: [If quick enough to say so while patient is still with the sadness.] Stay with it.

Alternative:

T: I see you are tightening. What are you aware of?

P: I don't want to stay with the sadness.

T: Stay with the not wanting to. Put words to the not wanting to. (This intervention is likely to bring awareness of the patient's resistance to melting. The patient might respond: "I won't cry here—I don't trust you" or "I am ashamed," or "I am angry and don't want to admit I miss him.")

Two: Enactment. Here the patient is asked to put feelings or thoughts into action. For example, "say it to the person" (if present) or some kind of roleplaying enactment (such as empty chair and psychodrama if the person is not present). "Put words to it" is another example. The patient with tears in his eyes might be asked to "put words to it." Enactment is intended as a way of increasing awareness, *not* as a form of catharsis. It is *not* a universal remedy. Exaggeration is a special form of enactment. A person is asked to exaggerate some feeling, thought, movement, etc., in order to feel the more intense (albeit, artificial) enacted or fantasied vision. Enactment into movement, sound, art, poetry, etc., can stimulate creativity as well as being therapeutically powerful.

Example: A man who has been talking about his mother without being in touch with any unfinished business is asked to describe her. Out of this description came the suggestion to move like her. As the patient adopted her posture and movement, intense feelings came back into awareness and could then be worked with.

Three: Guided Fantasy Visualization. Sometimes a patient can bring an experience into the here and now more efficiently by visualizing than by enacting.

Example:

P: I was with my girl friend last night. I don't know how it happened but I was impotent. [Patient gives more detail and some history.]

T: Close your eyes. Imagine it is last night and you are with your girl friend. Say out loud what you experience at each moment.

P: I am sitting on the couch. My friend sits next to me and I get excited. Then I go soft.

T: Let's go through that again in slow motion, in more detail. Be sensitive to every thought or sense impression.

P: I am sitting on the couch. She comes over and sits next to me. She touches my neck, it feels so warm and soft. I get excited, you know, hard. She strokes my arm, and I love it. [Pause, looks startled.] Then I thought, I had such a tense day, maybe I won't be able to get it up.

This patient became aware of how he created anxiety and impotence. This fantasy was recreating an event that happened in order to get in better touch with it. The fantasy could be of an expected event, a metaphorical event, and so forth.

Example: In working on shame and self-rejection, the patient is asked to

imagine, to create, a perfectly accepting mother, a mother who says and means "I love you just the way you are." As the fantasy is given detail the patient attends to his or her experience. This fantasy helps the patient become aware of the possibility of good self-mothering and can serve as a transition to integrate good self-parenting. The image can be used to work between sessions or used as a meditation. It also raises feelings about experiences with abandonment, loss, bad parenting, etc.

Four: Loosening and Integrating Techniques. Often the patient is so fettered by the bonds of the usual ways of thinking that alternate possibilities, other ways of experiencing are not allowed into awareness. This includes traditional mechanisms such as denial or repression, but also cultural and learning factors affecting ways of thinking. One technique is just to ask the patient to imagine something, for example, the opposite of whatever he believes to be true.

Integrating techniques bring together processes the patient doesn't bring together or actively keeps apart (splitting). The patient might be asked to put words to a negative process such as tensing, crying, or twitching. Or when the patient verbally reports a feeling, that is, an emotion, he might be asked to locate it in his body. Another example is asking a patient to express positive *and* negative feelings about the same person.

Five: Body Techniques. These include any techniques that bring patients' awareness to their body functioning, or help them to be aware of how they can use their bodies to support excitement, awareness and contact.

Example: A patient is tearful and clamping his jaw tight.

T: Would you be willing to try an experiment? [Patient nods.] Take some deep, deep breaths, and on each exhale let your jaw loosely move down. [The patient breathes deeply, lets his jaw drop on the exhale.] Stay with it. [The patient starts melting, crying, then sobbing.]

Techniques of therapist disclosure

The Gestalt therapist is encouraged to make "I" statements and discouraged from relying on interpretations. Such "I" statements are used to facilitate both the therapeutic contact and the patient's focusing and are made discriminately and judiciously. Using the "I" to facilitate therapeutic work requires even more technical skill, personal wisdom, and self-awareness on the therapist's part than other interventions. Therapists may share what they see, hear, or smell. They can share how they are affected. The personal experience of the therapist may be shared. Facts the therapist is aware of and the patient is not are shared, especially if the information is unlikely to be spontaneously discovered in the phenomenological work during the hour yet is believed important to the patient.

Mechanisms of Psychotherapy

Old deficits, new strengths

The child needs a parental relationship with a nurturant organismic/environmental ecological balance. For example, between them, the mother and child must see that the child's needs are met and the development of its potentialities facilitated. The child needs the warm, nurturing, joy-at-the-child kind of mirroring. And the child also needs room to struggle, be frustrated, to fail. The child also needs limits; for example to experience the consequences of behavior. When parents cannot meet these needs of the child because of need for a dependent child, or because of insufficient inner resources, the child develops distorted contact boundaries, awareness, and lowered self-esteem.

Unfortunately, children are too often shaped only to meet the approval of parents and society, without equal emphasis on their own needs. This involves the crippling of some inherent attitudes and exaggeration of others. As a result, the spontaneous personality is superseded by an artificial one. On the other hand, some children are allowed to believe they can have their own needs met by others without consideration for the autonomy of others. This results in the formation of the polar opposite, that is, impulsive character rather than spontaneity.

Patients need a therapist who will relate in a healthy, contactful manner, neither losing self by indulging the patient at the expense of exploration and working through nor by creating excessive anxiety, shame, and frustration by not being respectful, warm, receptive, direct, honest, and instead trying to "shape up" the patient.

Patients who enter psychotherapy with decreased awareness of their needs and strengths, of their resisting rather than supporting their organismic self, are in pain. They try to obtain from the therapist what is missing, try to get the therapist to do for them what they believe they cannot do for themselves. When therapists go along with this, patients do not reown and integrate their lost or never developed potential. Therefore they still cannot operate with organismic self-regulation, being responsible for themselves. They do not find out if they have the strength to exist autonomously because the therapist met their needs without strengthening their awareness and ego boundaries (see Resnick, 1975).

As Gestalt therapy proceeds and patients learn to be aware and responsible and contactful, their current ego functioning improves. As they do this they gain tools for deeper exploration. The childhood experiences of the formative years can then be explored without the regression and overdependency necessary in regressive treatment and without the temporary loss of competence that a transference neurosis entails. Childhood experiences are brought into present awareness without the assumption that patients in the present are determined by past events. Patients actively project transference material on the Gestalt therapist thereby giving opportunities for deeper exploration.

The following two examples show patients with different defenses, needing different treatment, but with similar underlying issues.

Example (Need for Softness): A 45-year-old man in the helping professions was proud of his intelligence, self-sufficiency, and independence. He was not aware that he had unmet dependency needs and that he resented not being given to. This affected his marriage in that his wife felt unneeded and inferior since she was in touch with needing and showed it. This man's self-sufficiency required respect— it met a need, was in part constructive and the patient's self-esteem was built on it. So without disrespecting this trait the therapist responded with a soft and giving attitude.

P: [With pride.] When I was a little kid my mom was so busy I just had to learn to rely on myself.

T: I appreciate your strength, and when I think of you as such a self-reliant kid I want to stroke you and give you some parenting.

P: [Tearing a little.] No one has been able to do that for me.

T: You seem sad.

P: I am remembering when I was a kid . . .

[Exploration led to awareness of a shame reaction to unavailable parents and a compensatory self-reliance.]

Example (Need for Firmness): A 45-year-old man in the helping professions. Patient felt shame and isolated himself in reaction to any criticism, rejecting any response that was not "soft and fuzzy." He was in touch with needing and responded positively to any invitation to regress and be dependent. He did not know how nor was he inclined to experiment with self-nourishment.

P: I don't know what to do today. [Whiny voice.]

T: [Looks and does not talk.]

P: I could talk about my week. [Looks questioningly at therapist.]

T: I feel pulled on by you right now. I imagine you want me to direct you.

P: Yes. What's wrong with that?

T: Nothing. I prefer not to direct you right now.

P: Why not?

T: You *can* direct yourself. I believe you are directing us away from your inner self right now. I don't want to cooperate with that. [Silence.]

P: I feel lost.

T: [Looks and does not talk.]

P: You are not going to direct me are you?

T: No.

P: Well, let's work on my believing I can't take care of myself. [Patient directs a fruitful piece of work that leads to awareness of abandonment anxiety, and feelings of shame in response to unavailable parents.]

Frustration and support

Gestalt therapy balances frustration and support. The therapist explores rather than gratifies the patient's wishes—and this is frustrating for the patient. Providing contact is supportive, although honest contact frustrates manipulation. The Gestalt therapist expresses herself and emphasizes exploring, including exploring desire, frustration, and indulgence. The therapist responds to manipulations by the patient *without reinforcing them,* without judging and without being purposely frustrating. A balance of warmth and firmness is important. Without frustration many patients will cling or isolate; without horizontal, mutual respectful warmth the patient's self-rejection will be reinforced.

The paradoxical theory of change

Patients are in conflict with at least two warring internal factions. There is a constant moving between "what should be" and what "is," without fully identifying with either. Paradoxically, the more one tries to be who one is not, the more one stays the same. The Gestalt therapist asks the person to invest fully in conflicting roles, one at a time. The patient is asked what he or she is at each moment (Beisser, 1970, pp. 70-78). When the patient can be aware of both roles during a piece of work, integrating techniques are used to create a whole encompassing both and transcending this dichotomy.

The Gestalt therapist uses paradoxes not to trick the patient into change, but to be aware of what is. Polster and Polster say that there are two axioms in Gestalt therapy: "What is, is," and "one thing leads to another" (Polster & Polster, 1973). *The medium of change is a relationship with a therapist who shows who he or she is and understands and accepts who the patient is.*

Awareness of "what is" leads to spontaneous change. When the person manipulating for support finds a therapist who is contactful and accepting and does not collude with the manipulation he may become aware of what he is doing. This *Aha!* is a new gestalt, a new outlook, a taste of a new possibility: I can be with someone and not manipulate or be manipulated. When such a person meets "therapeutic" collusion, derision, mind games, game busting, and so on, this increase in awareness is unlikely to happen.

At each and every point along the way this new *Aha!* can occur. As long as the therapist or the patient can see new possibilities and the therapist can facilitate, and the patient wants to learn, new *Ahas* are possible and with them new growth.

The *Aha!* is a reorganization of the field. The field consists of ideas, physical forces, physiological forces, sensing, emoting, social forces, and so forth. The awareness work can start anywhere the patient is willing, if the therapist is aware and connects it to the whole. The ensuing process in Gestalt therapy leads to changes everywhere in the field. The more thorough the investigation, the more intense the reorganization. Some changes can only be appreciated years later. So, too, some iatrogenic exacerbation of psychological dysfunction by the therapist's activities may only be realized years later.

Patients in Gestalt therapy are seen as in charge of their lives. The therapist facilitates attention to opening restricted awareness and areas of constricted contact boundaries and bringing firmness and limits to areas with poor boundaries. As sensing increases in accuracy and vividness, and breathing becomes fuller and more relaxed and patients make better contact, patients bring the skills of therapy into their lives. Sometimes the intimacy and work improvements follow

Gestalt work like an act of grace without the patient connecting the increase to the work done in therapy. But the organism does grow with awareness and contact. One thing does lead to another.

APPLICATIONS

Problems

A good rule of thumb is that Gestalt therapy can be used effectively with any patient population that the Gestalt therapist understands and is reasonably comfortable with. If the therapist can relate to the patient as well as conditions allow, the Gestalt therapy principles of dialogue and direct experiencing can be applied. With each patient *these general principles must be adapted to the particular clinical situation.* If the patient's treatment is made to conform to "Gestalt therapy" rather than Gestalt therapy adapting to the patient's clinical needs, treatment can be ineffective or harmful. A schizophrenic, sociopath, a borderline, and an obsessive-compulsive neurotic all need a different approach. Thus, *the competent practice of Gestalt therapy requires a background in more than Gestalt therapy.* A knowledge of diagnoses, personality theory, psychodynamic theory, and so forth, is also needed.

The individual clinician has a great deal of discretion in Gestalt therapy. Modifications are made by the individual therapist according to his style, personality, diagnostic considerations, and so on. This encourages and requires individual responsibility by the therapist. Gestalt therapists are encouraged to have a firm grounding in personality theory, psychopathology, theories and application of psychotherapy, and so on, as well as adequate clinical experience. Participants in the therapeutic encounter are encouraged by the therapist to experiment with new

behavior and then share cognitively and emotionally what the experience was like.

Gestalt therapy has traditionally been considered most effective with "overly socialized, restrained, constricted individuals" (e.g., anxious, perfectionistic, phobic, and depressed clients), whose inconsistent or restricted functioning is primarily a result of "internal restrictions" (Shepherd, 1970, pp. 234-235). Such individuals usually show only a minimal enjoyment of living.

Although Shepherd's statement accurately delineates a population Gestalt therapy is effective with, current clinical practice of Gestalt therapy includes treatment of a much wider range of problems.

Gestalt therapy in the "Perlsian," workshop style is of more limited application than Gestalt therapy in general (Dolliver, 1981; Dublin, 1976). In Shepherd's discussion of limitations and cautions she notes restrictions that apply to any therapist, but should especially be noted in a workshop setting, as well as by therapists not well trained or experienced with disturbed patient populations.

Work with psychotic, disorganized or other severely disturbed people is more difficult and calls for "caution, sensitivity, and patience." Shepherd advises against doing such work where it is not feasible to make a "long-term commitment" to the patient. Disturbed patients need support from the therapist and at least a minimal amount of faith in their own natural healing capacity before they can explore deeply and experience intensely the "overwhelming pain, hurt, rage, and despair" that underlie the psychological processes of disturbed patients (Shepherd, 1970, pp. 234-235).

Working with more disturbed populations requires clinical knowledge of how to balance support and frustration, knowledge of character dynamics, need for auxiliary support (such as day treatment and medication) and so forth. Some statements which seem to make sense in a workshop encounter are obvious nonsense when applied in a broader context. Consider for example, the "do your own thing" cliché in the context of treatment with acting out patients!

A perusal of the Gestalt therapy literature such as *Gestalt Therapy Now* (Fagan & Shepherd, 1970), *The Growing Edge of Gestalt Therapy* (Smith, 1976), and the *Gestalt Journal*, will show Gestalt therapy is used for crisis intervention, ghetto adults in a poverty program (Barnwell, 1968), interaction groups, psychotics, and almost any group imaginable. Unfortunately the literature provides examples (and a small number at that) without sufficient explication of necessary alterations in focus and without discussing negative results.

Gestalt therapy has also been successfully employed in the treatment of a wide range of "psychosomatic" disorders including migraine, ulcerative colitis, and spastic neck and back. Gestalt therapists have successfully worked with couples, with individuals having difficulties coping with authority figures, and with a wide range of intrapsychic conflicts. Gestalt therapy has been effectively employed with psychotics and severe character disorders.

Because of the impactfullness of Gestalt therapy and the ease with which strong, frequently buried affective reactions can be reached, it is necessary to establish what Simkin calls "safety islands" to which both the therapist and patient can comfortably return. It is also imperative for the therapist to stay with the patient until he or she is ready to return to these "safety islands."

As an example of the above, after an especially strong emotionally laden experience, the Gestalt therapist asks the patient whether he can see her or (if in a group) see members of the group. Patients are encouraged to make visual, tactile, or other contact with the therapist or with one or more group members and report what his experience in making contact is like. Another "safety" technique is to have the patient shuttle back and forth between making contact in the now with the therapist or group members and with the emotionally laden unfinished situation that the patient was experiencing, until all of the affect has been discharged and the unfinished situation worked through.

From its beginnings, Gestalt therapy has been used with individuals displaying a wide variety of emotional problems ranging from neuroses through psychotic states. Gestalt therapy has also been applied to the problems of individuals and groups where psychopathology was not the dominant feature.

Some of the earliest workshops (from 1952 on) in Gestalt therapy were offered to diverse specific groups such as educators, dentists, actors, and physicians. The purpose of these workshops was to augment the professional skills of the participants through the experiential learning and application of Gestalt therapy.

The Gestalt therapy emphasis on personal responsibility, interpersonal contact, and increased clarity of awareness of what is, could be of great value in meeting the problems of the present. Unfortunately, a discussion of the extension of Gestalt therapy and the implications of Gestalt therapy in various areas and for research has barely begun. One example is application of Gestalt therapy in schools (Brown, 1970; Lederman, 1970).

Evaluation

Gestalt therapists are singularly unimpressed with formal psychodiagnostic evaluation and nomothetic research methodology. No statistical approach can tell the individual patient or therapist what works for him. What is shown to work for most does not tell what works for a particular individual. This does not mean that Gestalt therapists are not in favor of research. No case against research is made in the Gestalt therapy literature. One institute (Gestalt Therapy Institute of Los Angeles) has offered grants to subsidize research. It is true that Perls offered no quantified, statistical evidence that Gestalt therapy works. He did say: "... we present nothing that you cannot verify for yourself in terms of your own behavior..." (F. Perls et al., 1951, p. 7). In the publication *Gestalt Therapy* a series of experiments are provided that can be used to test for oneself the validity of Gestalt therapy.

In the Gestalt therapy approach each session is seen as an experiment, an existential encounter in which both the therapist and the patient engage in calculated risk taking (experiments) involving exploration of heretofore unknown or forbidden territories. The patient is aided in using phenomenological focusing skills and dialogic contact to evaluate what is and is not working. Thus, constant, idiographic research takes place. Gestalt therapy has "sacrificed exact verification for the value in ideographic experimental psychotherapy" (Yontef, 1969, p. 27).

A survey of the Gestalt therapy literature reported in *Psychological Abstracts* of 1979 and early 1980 revealed the publication of over 20 doctoral dissertations out of some 65 entries under Gestalt therapy. Some dissertations include research studies which specifically test basic Gestalt therapy theory. In addition there is an increasing number of research studies being published (primarily in psychology journals).

The following studies are fairly typical of the type of research that has been generated around the beginning of the 1980s:

1. Resolving splits: Use of the two-chair technique

L. S. Greenberg (1979) defines a split as "a verbal performance pattern in which a client reports a division of the self process into two partial aspects of the self or tendencies." He concludes that "two-chair operations conducted according to the principles ... [of his study] ... have been found to facilitate an increase in the Depth of Experiencing and index of productive psychotherapy ... and to lead to resolutions of splits with populations seeking counseling ..." (p. 323).

2. A study called the "*Effects of Two-Chair Dialogues and Focusing on Conflict Resolution*" by L. S. Greenberg and H. M. Higgins (1980) found that "Two-chair dialogue appeared to produce a more direct experience of conflict ... [split] ... and encouraged the client in a form of self-confrontation that helped create a resolution to the conflict" (p. 224).

3. Verbal therapeutic behavior of expert psychoanalytically oriented, Gestalt, and behavior therapists

Brunnink and Schroeder (1979) found that "Gestalt therapists were very different from the other two types. [They] ... provided more direct guidance, less verbal facilitation, less focus on the client, more self-disclosure, greater initiative and less emotional support." They also found that the "... interview content of Gestalt therapists tended to reflect a more experiential or subjective approach to therapy" (p. 572).

No claim is made in the Gestalt therapy literature that Gestalt therapy is demonstrated to be the "best." There is theoretically no reason why "Gestalt therapy" should be more generally effective than therapies under other names that follow the principles of good psychotherapy. General outcome research may yield less useful results than process research looking at behavior, attitude, and consequences. An example of this is Simkin's assessment of the effectiveness of Gestalt therapy in workshops ("massed learning") as contrasted with "spaced" weekly therapy sessions. He finds evidence for his preference for massed learning (Simkin, 1976).

Some Gestalt therapy viewpoints on what constitutes good therapy is supported by general research. The research on experiencing within the Rogerian tradition demonstrated the effectiveness of an emphasis on direct experience by any therapist. In Gestalt therapy there is also the emphasis on personal relating, presence, and experience rather than charismatic guruship. Unfortunately, some therapists regularly and blatantly violate the principles of good psychotherapy according to the Gestalt therapy model, but call themselves "Gestalt therapists" (Lieberman, Yalom, & Miles, 1973).

Treatment

Ongoing individual Gestalt therapy

Although Gestalt therapy has acquired a reputation of being primarily applicable to groups it has been used right from its inception, and is still extensively used, with individuals. Individual treatment is actually the mainstay of Gestalt therapy. Several examples can be found in *Gestalt Therapy Now* (Fagan & Shepherd, 1970). An annotated bibliography of case readings can be found in Simkin (1979, p. 299).

Gestalt therapy begins with the first contact. Ordinarily assessment and screening are done as a part of the ongoing relationship rather than as a separate period of diagnostic testing, social history taking, and so on. The data for the assessment is obtained by beginning the work, for example, by therapeutic encounter. This assessment includes the patient's willingness and support for work within the Gestalt therapy framework, match of patient and therapist, as well as the usual professional diagnostic and characterological discriminations, decisions on frequency of sessions, need for adjunctive treatment, need for medical consultation, and so forth.

An average frequency for sessions is once per week. Using the Gestalt methodology an intensity equivalent to psychoanalysis can often be achieved at this frequency. Often individual therapy is combined with group therapy, workshops, conjoint or family therapy, movement therapy, meditation or biofeedback training. Sometimes patients can utilize more frequent sessions, but often they need the interval to digest material and more frequent sessions may result in overreliance on the therapist. Besides the question of time for digestion, the question of frequency of sessions depends on such issues as how long the patient can go between sessions without loss of continuity, decompensation, or lesser forms of relapse. The range of frequency of sessions varies from five times per week to every other week. Less frequently than every week obviously diminishes intensity unless combined with a weekly group with the same therapist. More than twice a week is ordinarily not indicated except with psychotics, and is definitely contraindicated with borderline personality disorders.

All through the therapy the patient is encouraged and aided in doing the decision making for himself. When to start, stop, whether to do an exercise, what adjunctive therapies to use, and so on are all discussed together, but the competence and ultimate necessity for the patient to make these choices is supported.

Group models

Gestalt therapy groups vary from one and one-half to three hours in length with an average length of two hours. A typical two-hour group has up to 10 participants. Gestalt therapists usually experience maximal involvement with heterogeneous groups, with a balance of men and women. Participants need to be screened. Any age is appropriate for Gestalt therapy, but an ongoing private practice group would typically range from 20-65 with the average between 30 and 50.

Many Gestalt therapists follow Perls's lead in doing one-on-one therapy in the group setting and use the "hot seat" structure (see Levitsky & Simkin, 1972).

"According to this method, an individual expresses to the therapist his interest in dealing with a particular problem. The focus is then on the extended interaction between patient and group leader (I and Thou)" (Levitsky & Simkin, 1972, p. 140). One-on-one episodes average 20 minutes, but range from a couple of minutes to 45 minutes. During the one-on-one work the other members remain silent; after the work they give feedback on how they were affected and what they observed and their own experiences similar to those the patient worked on. In recent years the one-on-one work has been expanded to include awareness work that is not focused around a particular "problem."

In the early 1960s Perls wrote a paper in which he said:

Lately, however, I have eliminated individual sessions altogether except for emergency cases. As a matter of fact, I have come to consider that all individual therapy is obsolete and should be replaced by workshops in Gestalt Therapy. In my workshops I now integrate individual and group work. (Perls, 1967, p. 306)

This opinion was not then shared by most Gestalt therapists and is not currently recognized Gestalt theory or practice.

Some critics of Gestalt therapy have described the Gestalt therapist's style of group work as doing individual therapy in a group setting. To some extent this criticism has been valid since many Gestalt therapists have used the model just discussed and do not emphasize or deal with the group dynamics, nor strive for the development of group cohesiveness. However, this is only one style of Gestalt therapy—many Gestalt therapists do emphasize group dynamics.

Greater use of the larger field (i.e., the group) is certainly within the Gestalt methodology and is increasingly done by Gestalt therapists (Enright, 1975; Feder & Ronall, 1980; Zinker, 1977). This includes greater involvement of group members when an individual is doing one-to-one work, working on individual themes by everyone in the group, emphasis on interrelationships (contact) in the group, and working with group processes per se. The varied degree and type of structure provided by the leader includes structured group exercises or no structured group exercises, observing the group evolving to its own structure, encouraging one-on-one work, and so on. Often Gestalt groups begin with some exercise to help participants to make the transition into working by sharing here and now experience.

A frequently used model is one that encourages both gaining awareness through focus on contact between group members and one-on-one work in the group (with other members encouraged to participate during the work). This encourages greater fluidity and flexibility.

Workshop style

A good deal of the work done in Gestalt therapy is conducted in workshops, which are scheduled for a finite period, some for as short as one day. Weekend workshop may range from 10 to 20 or more hours. Longer workshops range from a week through several months in duration. A typical weekend workshop membership consists of one Gestalt therapist and 12-16 people. Given longer periods (ranging from one week up to a month or longer) as many as 20 people can be seen by one therapist. Usually if the group is larger than 16 participants, cotherapists are used.

Since workshops have a finite life and there are just so many hours available to the participants, usually there is high motivation to "work." Sometimes, rules are established so no one can work a second time until every other participant has had an opportunity to work once. At other times, no such rules are set. Thus depending on a person's willingness, audacity, and drive, some people may get intense therapeutic attention several times during a workshop.

Although some workshops are arranged with established groups most assemble people for the first time. As in ongoing groups, the ideal practice is to screen patients before the workshop. An unscreened workshop requires a clinician experienced with the range of severe pathology and careful protection for possibly vulnerable group members. Confrontive or charismatic Gestalt styles are particularly likely to exacerbate existing mental illness in some participants (Lieberman et al., 1973).

Other treatment modalities

The application of Gestalt therapy to working with families has been most extensively elaborated by Walter Kempler (1973, pp. 251-286). The most complete description of Kempler's work appears in his *Principles of Gestalt Family Therapy* (1974).

Gestalt therapy has also been used in short-term crisis intervention (O'Connell, 1970), as an adjunct treatment for visual problems (Rosanes-Berret, 1970), for awareness training of mental health professionals (Enright, 1970), with behavior problem children (Lederman, 1970), with staff training for a day-care center (Ennis & Mitchell, 1970), with "Teaching Creativity to Teachers and Others" (Brown, 1970), with a dying person (Zinker & Fink, 1966), and with organization development (Herman, 1972).

Management

Case management by a Gestalt therapist tends to be quite practical and guided by the goal of supporting the person-to-person relationship. Appointments are usually arranged over the telephone by the therapist directly. Office decor reflects the personality and style of the therapist and is not purposely neutral. The offices are designed and furnished to be comfortable and without desk or table between therapist and patient. Typically the physical arrangement leaves room for movement and experimentation. The therapist's dress and manner are usually quite informal. Typically the patient enters the waiting room, presses a button that turns on a light in the waiting room and consultation room. He or she is ushered from the waiting room by the therapist personally.

Arrangement of fees varies with the individual and there is no particular Gestalt style, except straightforwardness. Fees are discussed directly with the patient and usually collected by the therapist.

Clarity of boundaries is stressed with each responsible for attending to the task at hand. The "work" or therapy starts from the first moment. No notes are taken during the session as it interferes with contact. The therapist takes personal responsibility for note taking after the session if needed, and for safeguarding notes, video or tape recordings and other clinical material. The therapist sets down conditions of payment, cancellation policy, and so forth. Violations or objections are directly discussed. Decisions are made together and agreements are expected to be kept by both. The therapist arranges the office to protect it from invasion and where possible soundproofs the office.

The evaluation process occurs as a part of the therapy and is mutual. Some of the considerations involved in the evaluation process include deciding on individual and/or group therapy; estimating the capacity on the part of the therapist to establish a trusting, caring relationship; and letting the patient decide on an adequate sample basis if he finds the therapist and the therapy suitable for him. If either the therapist or the patient decides to discontinue because of interpersonal conflicts and/or an inability to deal with the specific psychopathology, referrals to other psychotherapists are offered before termination.

Problems arising in the relationship are discussed directly both in terms of dealing with the concrete problem and in terms of exploring any related characterological life-styles or relationship processes that would be fruitful for the patient to explore. Always the needs, wishes, and direct experience of both participants guide the exploration and problem solving.

CASE EXAMPLE

Peg was originally seen in a Gestalt training workshop where she worked on the grief and anger she felt toward her husband who had committed suicide. His death left her with the full responsibility of raising their children and beginning a career outside the home to support herself and her family. She was in her late 30s at the time.

With considerable courage and initiative, Peg had organized a crisis clinic sponsored by a prominent service organization in the large Southern California city in which she resided. She was one of 11 people who participated in making a Gestalt therapy training film with Simkin (1969). The following is excerpted from the film, *In the Now:*

Peg: I have a . . . recurring dream. I'm standing on the ground, up by Camp Pendleton. There's an open, rolling countryside. Wide dirt roads crisscrossing all over it. A series of hills and valleys and hills and valleys. . . . And off to my right I see a tank, like in the army—marine tanks with the big tracks . . . and there's a series of them and they're all closed tight and they're rumbling over these hills and valleys in a line, all closed up. And I'm standing beside this road and I'm holding a platter of Tollhouse cookies. And they're hot cookies. And they are just on the platter—I'm just standing there, and I see these tanks coming by one at a time. And as the tanks come past, I stand there and I watch the tanks. And as I look to my right I see one—and there's a pair of shiny black shoes, running along between the treads of the tank as it comes over the hill. And just as it gets in front of me . . . the man bends down and the tank goes on, and he comes over toward me and it's my best friend's husband. And I always wake up. I always stop my dream . . . and I laughed. It doesn't seem so funny anymore.

Jim: True. What are you doing?

Peg: Trying to stop my teeth from chattering.

Jim: What's your objection?

Peg: I don't like the feeling of anxiety and fear I have now.

Jim: What do you imagine?

Peg: Ridicule.

Jim: Okay. Start ridiculing.

Peg: Peg, you're ridiculous. You're fat . . . you're lazy. You're just comic. You're pretending to be grown up and you're not. Everybody looking knows that you're a kid inside, masquerading as a 39-year-old woman and . . . it's a ridiculous disguise. You haven't any business being 39. A ridiculous age. You're comic. You have a job you don't have the remotest idea how to do. You're making all kinds of grandiose plans that you haven't brains enough to carry through and people are going to be laughing at you.

Jim: Okay, now please look around and note how people are laughing at you.

Peg: I'm scared to. [Looks around, slowly.] They appear to be taking me quite seriously.

Jim: So who is laughing at you?

Peg: I guess . . . only my fantasy . . . my . . .

Jim: Who creates your fantasy?

Peg: I do.

Jim: So who's laughing at you?

Peg: Yeah. That's so. I . . . I'm really laughing at what's not funny. I'm not so damned incompetent. [Pause]

Jim: What are you really good at?

Peg: I'm good with people. I'm not judgmental. I'm good at keeping house. I'm a good seamstress, good baker, I . . .

Jim: Maybe you'll make somebody a good wife.

Peg: I did.

Jim: Maybe you'll make somebody a good wife again.

Peg: I don't know.

Jim: So say that sentence. "I don't know if I'll ever make somebody a good wife again."

Peg: I don't know if I'll ever make someone a good wife again.

Jim: Say that to every man here.

Peg: I don't know if I'll make someone a good wife again.... [Repeats the sentence five more times.]

Jim: What do you experience?

Peg: Surprise. Boy . . . I assumed I would never make anybody a good wife again.

Jim: Right.

Jim: What do you experience right now?

Peg: Satisfaction. Pleasure. I feel good. I feel done.

Although Peg's "ticket of admission" was a dream, what became foreground was her anxiety and fantasies of being ridiculed. The dream served as a vehicle for starting and, as is frequently the case, the work led to a most unpredictable outcome.

At the weekend workshop during which the training film was made, Peg met a man to whom she was attracted and who, in turn, was attracted to her. They began to date and within a few months they married.

A second sample of Gestalt therapy follows, selectively excerpted from a book to illustrate some techniques (Simkin, 1976, pp. 103-118). The following is a condensed transcript of a two-hour workshop in a TV studio with six volunteers at Bradley University, Peoria, Illinois, May 1971. The morning session included a lecture-demonstration and film showing.

Jim S: I'd like to start with saying where I am and what I'm experiencing at this moment. This seems very artificial to me, all of these lights and the cameras and the people around. I feel breathless and burdened by the technical material, the equipment, etc. and I'm much more interested in getting away from the lights and the cameras and getting more in touch with you. [Inquires as to the names of participants of the group and introduces himself.]

I am assuming that all of you were in the audience this morning, that you saw the film and the demonstration; and my preference would be to work with you as you feel ready to work. I'll reiterate our contract, or agreement. In Gestalt therapy the essence of the contract is to say where you are, what you are experiencing at any given moment; and, if you can, to stay in the continuum of awareness, to report where you are focusing, what you are aware of.

* * * * * *

I'd like to start first with having you say who you are and if you have any programs or expectations.

Jim 2: Right now I'm a little tense, not particularly because of the technical equipment because I'm kind of used to that. I kind of feel a little strange about being in a situation with you. This morning I was pretty upset because I didn't agree with a lot of the things you were talking about, and I felt pretty hostile to you. Now I more or less accept you as another person.

Jim S: I'm paying attention to your foot now. I'm wondering if you could give your foot a voice.

Jim 2: My foot a voice? You mean how is my foot feeling? What's it going to say?

Jim S: Just keep doing that, and see if you have something to say, as your foot.

Jim 2: I don't understand.

Jim S: As you were telling me about feeling hostile this morning, you began to kick and I'm imagining that you still have some kick coming. .

Jim 2: Uh, yeah. I guess maybe I do have some kick left, but I really don't get

the feeling that that's appropriate.

* * * * * *

Lavonne: Right now I'm feeling tense.

Jim S: Who are you talking to, Lavonne?

Lavonne: I was just thinking about this morning. I was feeling very hostile. I still think I am somewhat hostile.

Jim S: I am aware that you are avoiding looking at me.

Lavonne: Yes, because I feel that you are very arrogant.

Jim S: That's true.

Lavonne: And as if I might get into a struggle with you.

Jim S: You might.

Lavonne: So the avoidance of eye contact is sort of a putoff of the struggle. I have some things that I'd like to work on. I don't know whether they can be resolved.

Jim S: Would you be willing to tell me what your objections are to my arrogance?

Lavonne: Well, it's not very comforting. If I have a problem and I talk to you about it and you're arrogant, then that only makes me arrogant.

Jim S: You respond in kind is what you are saying. Your experience is you respond that way.

Lavonne: Yes. Right on. Then at this university I feel that I must be arrogant and I must be defensive at all times. Because I'm black, people react to me in different ways . . . different people . . . and I feel that I have to be on my toes most of the time . . .

Mary: I want to work on my feelings for my older son and the struggle that I have with him—only, I suspect it is really a struggle I'm having with myself.

Jim S: Can you say this to him? Give him a name and say this to him.

Mary: All right. His name is Paul.

Jim S: Put Paul here [empty chair] and say this to Paul.

Mary: Paul, we have a lot of friction. Every time you go out of the drive on your own, independent, I hate you for it. But...

Jim S: Just a moment. Say the same sentence to Mary. Mary, each time you go out the drive, independent, I hate you for it.

Mary: That fits. Mary, each time you go out the drive, independent, I hate you for it, because you are not being a good mother.

Jim S: I don't know about your because.

Mary: No. That's my rationale. That's the same I do to myself doing yoga.

Jim S: You sound identified with Paul.

Mary: I am. I know this. I envy his freedom, even from the time he was a little kid and went to the woods. I envied his ability to go to the woods.

Jim S: Tell Paul.

Mary: Paul, even when you were a little boy and you would go for all day Saturday, and not tell me where you were going but just go, I envied you for it. I envied you very much, and I felt hurt because I couldn't do it too.

Jim S: You couldn't, or you wouldn't?

Mary: I would not do it. I wanted to, but I would not do it.

Jim S: Yeah. For me to have somebody around that keeps reminding me of what I can do and don't really pisses me off.

Mary: This is what I do to myself. I keep reminding myself of what I can do and won't do. And then I don't do anything. I'm at a standstill. Firmly planted.

Jim S: I'd like you to get in touch with your spitefulness. Put your spitefulness out here and talk to Mary's saboteur.

Mary: You idiot. You've got the time to do your work. You also have the energy to do your work ... which you dissipate. You get involved in umpteen dozen things

so you will have an excuse not to do your work, or to do anything else ... [Pause] You just spend time making yourself miserable and complicating your life.

Jim S: What's going on here? [Points to Mary's hand.]

Mary: Yes. Tight-fisted ... won't do.

Jim S: Are you tight-fisted?

Mary: Yes, I think I am.

Jim S: O.K. Can you get in touch with the other part of you—your generous self?

Mary: I don't really know my generous self very well.

Jim S: Be your tight-fisted self just saying, "Generous self, I have no contact with you, I don't know you, etc."

Mary: Generous self, I don't know very much of you. I think you try every now and then when you give presents to people instead of giving yourself. You withhold an awful lot that you could give.

Jim S: What just happened?

Mary: I rehearsed. I just wasn't talking to my generous self. I was talking to ... you primarily. I was withholding part.

Jim S: I have difficulty imagining you as a withholding person. You came on in the beginning as very vibrant and alive ... to me, very giving.

Mary: I don't know whether I really am giving or not.

Jim S: Say that again please.

Mary: I don't know whether I really am giving or not. Sometimes I feel like I do give and what I give is not accepted as a gift. And sometimes I want to give and I can't. And I feel sometimes I have given too much and I shouldn't have.

Jim S: Yeah. This is what I'm beginning to sense. Some hurt. You look like you've been hurt—in the past. That you've been vulnerable and somehow hurt in the process.

Mary: To some degree I'm hurting.

Jim S: To me you look like you're

hurting now, especially around your eyes.

Mary: I know that, and I don't want to do that . . . I don't want to show that.

Jim S: O.K. Would you be willing to block?

Mary: [Covering her eyes] When I do that, I can't see you.

Jim S: That's true.

Mary: When I do that, I can't see anyone.

Jim S: Very true. When I block my hurt, no one exists for me. This is my choice.

Mary: I made it my choice too.

Jim S: I am enjoying looking at you. To me you are very generous at this moment.

Mary: You are very generous to me. I feel that you are. I hear you respond to me and I feel that I'm responding to you. . .

Jim S: I'm curious if you can come back to Paul for a moment now. Encounter him and explore what happens.

Mary: Paul, I want to be warm to you, and I want to be generous to you, and I think I might hurt you by being so. You're six feet tall now and sometimes I very much want to come up to you and just give you a kiss goodnight or just put my arms around you and I can't do it anymore.

Jim S: You can't?

Mary: I won't. I won't, because, uh . . . I've been shoved away.

Jim S: You've been hurt.

Mary: Yeah, I've been hurt. Paul, I think it's your own business if you want to shove me away, but that doesn't stop me from being hurt.

Jim S: I like what, I believe, Nietzsche once said to the sun, "It's none of your business that you shine at me."

Mary: I keep hoping that, Paul, when you're 25 or if you go to the Army or whatever . . . that I can kiss you goodbye. [Pause] I'll try to remember what Nietzsche said to the sun.

Jim S: O.K. I enjoyed working with you.

Mary: Thank you.

SUMMARY

Fritz Perls prophesied three decades ago that Gestalt therapy would come into its own during the 1960s and become a significant force in psychotherapy during the 1970s. His prophecy has been more than fulfilled.

In 1952, there were perhaps a dozen people seriously involved in the movement. In 1983 there were scores of training institutes, hundreds of psychotherapists who have been trained in Gestalt therapy, and many hundreds of nontrained or poorly trained persons who call themselves "Gestaltists." Thousands of people have been exposed to experiencing Gestalt therapy—many with quite favorable results—others with questionable or poor outcomes.

Because of the unwillingness on the part of Gestalt therapists to set rigid standards for the selection and training of psychotherapists there is a wide range of criteria for the selection and training of Gestalt therapists. Some people having experienced a weekend consider themselves amply equipped to do Gestalt therapy. Other psychotherapists spend months and years in training as Gestalt therapists and have an enormous respect for the simplicity and infinite innovativeness and creativity that Gestalt therapy requires and engenders.

Despite the fact that Gestalt therapy attracts some people who are looking for shortcuts, it also has attracted a substantial number of solid, experienced clinicians who have found in Gestalt therapy not only a powerful psychotherapy but also a viable life philosophy.

Those looking for quick solutions and shortcuts will go on to greener pastures.

Gestalt therapy will take its place along with other substantive psychotherapies in the next several decades. It will continue to attract creative, experimentally oriented psychotherapists for many years to come.

Gestalt therapy has pioneered many useful and creative innovations in psychotherapy theory and practice. These have been incorporated into general practice without credit. Now Gestalt therapy is moving into further elaboration and refinement of these principles. Regardless of label, the principles of existential dialogue, use of the direct phenomenological experience of patient and therapist, trust of organismic self-regulation, emphasis on experimentation and awareness to test what fits for the person, the "no should" attitude by the therapist, responsibility of the patient and therapist for their own choices all form a model of good psychotherapy that will continue to be used by Gestalt therapists and others.

To summarize, a quote from Levitsky and Simkin (1972) seems appropriate:

If we were to choose one key idea to stand as a symbol for the Gestalt approach, it might well be the concept of authenticity, the quest for authenticity.
If we regard therapy and the therapist in the pitiless light of authenticity, it becomes apparent that the therapist cannot teach what he does not know.
A therapist with some experience really knows within himself that he is communicating to his patient his [the therapist's] own fears as well as his courage, his defensiveness as well as his openness, his confusion as well as his clarity. The therapist's awareness, acceptance, and sharing of these truths can be a highly persuasive demonstration of his own authenticity. Obviously such a position is not acquired overnight. It is to be learned and relearned ever more deeply not only throughout one's career but throughout one's entire life.

ANNOTATED BIBLIOGRAPHY

Fagan, J., & Shepherd, I. L. (Eds.). *Gestalt therapy now*. Palo Alto, Calif.: Science

and Behavior Books, 1970. (Also, New York: Harper & Row, Harper Colophon Books [Paperback], 1971.)

This classic collection of articles on the theory, techniques, and applications of Gestalt therapy incorporates original articles by F. S. Perls, Erving Polster, Walter Kempler, James Simkin, I. L. Shepherd, Abraham Levitsky, and other leading Gestalt therapists. Each section has an introduction by the authors and the appendix has a bibliography of books, articles, tape recordings, and films that were available in 1970 when the book was first published. A more recent collection of articles is *The Growing Edge of Gestalt Therapy*, E. W. L. Smith (Ed.). New York: Brunner/Mazel, 1976. Note especially articles by Smith, L. Perls, Shepherd, and Dublin.

Hatcher, C., & Himelstein, P. (Eds.). *The handbook of Gestalt therapy*. New York: Jason Aronson, 1976.

Some of the articles in this collection appear here for the first time. Others have appeared in other sources. Although this volume is marred by a number of typographical errors and several poor selections, it contains the most up-to-date bibliography in existence (Chapter 32) as of 1976 and several outstanding contributions such as Appelbaum's, "A Psychoanalyst Looks at Gestalt Therapy"; Gerald Kogan's, "The Genesis of Gestalt Therapy"; and Miriam Polster's, "Women in Therapy: A Gestalt Therapist's View." It contains the first section of *Gestalt Therapy Verbatim* (Moab, Utah: Real People Press, 1969). This section deals primarily with the theory of Gestalt therapy in a seminar style with interspersed questions from participants. The bulk of *Gestalt Therapy Verbatim* is not included in the *Handbook* and consists of specific verbatim transcripts of Perls' Gestalt therapy work with people who attend a weekend dreamwork seminar and excerpts from audio tapes of a four-week, intensive workshop.

Perls, F. S. *In and out the garbage pail*. Moab, Utah: Real People Press, 1969

(Bantam, 1971).

This is Fritz Perls's autobiography, written over a period of three months in 1969, about one year before he died. It has a wide-ranging, free-floating style that includes poetry and prose, tragedy and humor, seriousness and lightness, and a host of other polarities that characterized the primary founder of Gestalt therapy. For those individuals never having had the opportunity to meet him in person, this book is the next best thing.

Perls, F. *The Gestalt approach.* Palo Alto: Science & Behavior Books, 1973 (Bantam, 1976).

Perls's last general statement on Gestalt therapy and his clearest. Especially good on contact boundaries.

Perls, F., Hefferline, R., & Goodman, P. *Gestalt therapy.* New York: Dell Books, 1951.

This book has two parts. Volume I contains an important introduction and a series of 18 graduated experiments (phenomenological exploration exercises), and comments of students taking the experiments. Many find this very useful in self-exploration. The second volume is a major theoretical source in Gestalt therapy. Unfortunately, it is very difficult reading. A must for the serious scholar or therapist, but not a good book for an easy introduction.

Polster, E., & Polster, M. *Gestalt therapy integrated: Contours of theory and practice.* New York: Brunner/Mazel, 1973.

This is a scholarly, penetrating, and well-written book. It covers topics such as The Now Ethos; Figure and Ground; Resistance; Contact-Boundary, Contact Functions and Contact Episodes; Awareness; Experiment; and a description of working with a variety of groups in a section labeled Beyond One to One. Chapters on Contact (Chapters 4-6) are especially noteworthy.

Simkin, J. S. *Gestalt therapy mini-lectures.* Millbrae, Calif.: Celestial Arts, 1976.

The first section contains an introductory chapter on Gestalt therapy in groups. The second section—*Theoretical and Practical Issues*—consists of short minilectures covering a range of concepts and constructs popular in Gestalt therapy. The third section deals with techniques. Section four is an extensive example of working with a dream in Gestalt therapy and the fifth section—*Clinical Work*—is a condensed transcript of a two-hour workshop at a midwestern university in the early 1970s. A total of 41 references are included.

CASE READINGS

Fagan, J. Three sessions with Iris. *The Counseling Psychologist,* 1974, *4,* 42-59. (Also in C. Hatcher & P. Himelstein [Eds.], *The handbook of Gestalt therapy.* New York: Jason Aronson, 1976, pp. 673-721.)

Dr. Fagan describes her work with Iris as "being an example of good, hard, routine work with a resistant patient in individual therapy in a heavily Gestalt style" (1976, p. 674). The patient was a volunteer for a doctoral dissertation and had agreed to be videotaped and had had no previous experience with Gestalt therapy.

Perls, F. S. Jane's three dreams. In *Gestalt therapy verbatim.* Moah, Utah: Real People Press, 1969, pp. 251-272.

Three dreams, labeled Jane I, Jane II, and Jane III, are presented verbatim. In the section called Jane III, Jane continues to work on an unfinished part of the dream she had worked on in Jane II. (Portions of this material are also found in D. Wedding & R. J. Corsini [Eds.], *Great cases in psychotherapy.* Itasca, Ill.: F. E. Peacock, 1979.)

Perls, L. P. Two instances of Gestalt therapy. *Case reports in clinical psychology.* Kings County Hospital, Brooklyn, New York, 1956. (Also found in P. D. Pursglove (Ed.), *Recognition in Gestalt therapy.* New York: Funk & Wagnalls, 1968, pp. 42-68.)

Laura Perls presents the case of Claudia, a 25-year-old black woman who comes from a lower middle-class West Indian background, and the case of Walter, a 47-year-old Central European Jewish refugee.

Simkin, J. S. *Individual Gestalt therapy.* A. A. P.

tape library (50 minutes), Orlando, Florida, 1967.

The 11th hour with a 34-year-old actor. Emphasis is on the present, nonverbal communications leading to production of genetic material. The use of fantasy dialogue is also illustrated in this piece of work.

Simkin, J. S. The use of dreams in Gestalt therapy. In C. J. Sager & H. S. Kaplan (Eds.), *Progress in group and family therapy.* New York: Brunner/Mazel, 1972, pp. 95-104.

A verbal transcript of a patient working on a dream concerning his youngest daughter. He tells this dream in a group workshop in which he has worked with several of the group's members before.

REFERENCES

Appelbaum, S. A. A psychoanalyst looks at Gestalt therapy. In C. Hatcher & P. Himelstein (Eds.), *The handbook of Gestalt therapy.* New York: Jason Aronson, 1976.

Barnwell, J. E. Gestalt methods and techniques in a poverty program. In J. S. Simkin (Ed.). *Festschrift for Fritz Perls.* Los Angeles, 1968.

Beisser, A. R. The paradoxical theory of change. In J. Fagan & I. L. Shepherd (Eds.), *Gestalt therapy now.* Palo Alto, Calif.: Science and Behavior Books, 1970.

Brown, G. I. Teaching creativity to teachers and others. *Journal of Teacher Education,* 1970, *21,* 210-216.

Brunnink, S., & Schroeder, H. Verbal therapeutic behavior of expert psychoanalytically oriented, Gestalt and behavior therapists. *Journal of Consulting and Clinical Psychology,* 1979, *47,* 567-574.

Dolliver, R. Some limitations in Perls' Gestalt therapy. *Psychotherapy, Research and Practice,* 1981, *8,* 38-45.

Dublin, J. Gestalt therapy. Existential-Gestalt therapy and/versus "Perls-ism." In E. Smith (Ed.), *The growing edge of Gestalt therapy.* New York: Brunner/Mazel, 1976.

Ennis, K., & Mitchell, S. *Staff training for a day care center.* In J. Fagan & I. L. Shepherd (Eds.), *Gestalt therapy now.* Palo Alto, Calif.: Science and Behavior Books, 1970.

Enright, J. B. Awareness training in the mental health professions. In J. Fagan & I. L. Shepherd (Eds.), *Gestalt therapy now.* Palo Alto, Calif.: Science and Behavior Books, 1970.

Enright, J. B. Gestalt therapy in interactive groups. In F. D. Stephenson (Ed.), *Gestalt therapy primer: Introductory readings in Gestalt therapy.* Springfield, Ill.: Charles C Thomas, 1975.

Fagan, J. Gestalt techniques with a woman with expressive difficulties. In J. Fagan & I. L. Shepherd (Eds.), *Gestalt therapy now.* Palo Alto, Calif.: Science and Behavior Books, 1970.

Fagan, J. Personality theory and psychotherapy. *The Counseling Psychologist,* 1974, *4,* 4-7.

Fagan, J., & Shepherd, I. L. (Eds.). *Gestalt therapy now.* Palo Alto, Calif.: Science and Behavior Books, 1970.

Feder, B., & Ronall, R. (Eds.). *Beyond the hot seat.* New York: Brunner/Mazel, 1980.

Greenberg, L. S. Resolving splits: Use of the two-chair technique. *Psychotherapy: Theory, Research and Practice,* 1979, *16,* 316-324.

Greenberg, L. S., & Higgins, H. M. Effects of two-chair dialogues and focusing on conflict resolution. *Journal of Counseling Psychology,* 1980, *27,* 221-224.

Hatcher, C., & Himelstein, P. (Eds.). *The handbook of Gestalt therapy.* New York: Jason Aronson, Inc., 1976.

Heidbreder, E. *Seven psychologies.* New York: Century Company, 1933.

Herman, S. N. The Gestalt orientation to organizational development. In *Contemporary organization development.* Bethel, Maine: National Institute of Applied Behavioral Science, 1972.

Idhe, D. *Experimental phenomenology.* New York: G. P. Putnam & Sons, Capricorn Books, 1977.

Jacobs, L. I-thou relations in Gestalt therapy. Unpublished doctoral dissertation, California School of Professional Psychology, 1978.

Kempler, W. Gestalt therapy. In R. J. Corsini (Ed.), *Current psychotherapies.* Itasca, Ill.: F. E. Peacock, 1973.

Kempler, W. *Principles of Gestalt family therapy.* Costa Mesa, Calif.: Kempler Institute, 1974.

Kogan, G. The genesis of Gestalt therapy. In C. Hatcher & P. Himelstein (Eds.), *The handbook of Gestalt therapy.* New York: Jason Aronson, 1976.

Kogan, J. *Gestalt therapy resources* (3d ed.).

Berkeley, Calif.: Transformation Press, 1980.

Lederman, J. Anger and the rocking chair. In J. Fagan & I. L. Shepherd (Eds.), *Gestalt therapy now*. Palo Alto, Calif.: Science and Behavior Books, 1970.

Levitsky, A., & Simkin, J. S. Gestalt therapy. In L. N. Solomon & B. Berzon (Eds.), *New perspectives on encounter groups*. San Francisco: Jossey-Bass, 1972.

Lieberman, M., Yalom, I., & Miles, M. *Encounter group: First facts*. New York: Basic Books, 1973.

O'Connell, V. F. Crisis psychotherapy: Person, dialogue and the organismic approach. In J. Fagan & I. L. Shepherd (Eds.), *Gestalt therapy now*. Palo Alto, Calif.: Science and Behavior Books, 1970.

Perls, F. S. *Ego, hunger and aggression*. London: Allen & Unwin, 1947. (San Francisco: Orbit Graphic Arts, 1966.)

Perls, F. S. Theory and technique of personality integration. *American Journal of Psychotherapy*, 1948, *2*, 656-686.

Perls, F. S. Group vs. individual therapy. *ETC*, 1967, *24*, 306-312.

Perls, F. S. *Gestalt therapy verbatim*. Moab, Utah: Real People Press, 1969.

Perls, F. S. *The Gestalt approach*. Palo Alto: Science and Behavior Books, 1973 (Bantam, 1976).

Perls, F. S. Resolution. In J. O. Stevens (Ed.), *Gestalt is*. Moab, Utah: People Press, 1975.

Perls, F. S. Gestalt therapy verbatim: Introduction. In C. Hatcher & P. Himelstein (Eds.), *The handbook of Gestalt therapy*. New York: Jason Aronson, 1976.

Perls, F. S., Hefferline, R. F., & Goodman, P. *Gestalt therapy*. New York: Julian Press, 1951.

Perls, L. Some aspects of Gestalt therapy. Manuscript presented at Annual Meeting of the Orthopsychiatric Association, 1973.

Perls, L. Comments on the New Directions. In E. Smith (Ed.), *The growing edge of Gestalt therapy*. New York: Brunner/Mazel, 1976.

Perls, L. Concepts & misconceptions of Gestalt therapy. *Voices*, 1978, *14*, 31-36.

Polster, E. A. A contemporary psychotherapy. In P. D. Pursglove (Ed.), *Recognitions in Gestalt therapy*. New York: Funk & Wagnalls, 1968.

Polster, E., & Polster, M. *Gestalt therapy integrated*. New York: Brunner/Mazel, 1973.

Resnick, R. Chicken soup is poison. *Voices*, 1970, *6*, 75-78. Also in F. D. Stephenson (Ed.), *Gestalt therapy primer*. Springfield, Ill.: Charles C Thomas, 1975.

Rosanes-Berret, M. M. Gestalt therapy as an adjunct treatment for some visual problems. In J. Fagan & I. L. Shepherd (Eds.), *Gestalt therapy now*. Palo Alto, Calif.: Science and Behavior Books, 1970.

Rosenfeld, E. An oral history of Gestalt therapy: Part I: A conversation with Laura Perls. *The Gestalt Journal*, 1978, *1*, 8-31.

Rosenfeld, E. The Gestalt bibliography. *The Gestalt Journal*, 1981, *1*, 8-31.

Sartre, J. P. *Being and nothingness*. New York: Washington Square Press, 1966.

Shepherd, I. L. Limitations and cautions in the Gestalt approach. In J. Fagan & I. L. Shepherd (Eds.), *Gestalt therapy now*. Palo Alto, Calif.: Science and Behavior Books, 1970.

Simkin, J. S. (Ed.). *Festschrift for Fritz Perls*. Los Angeles, Calif.: Author, 1968.

Simkin, J. S. *In the now*. A training film. Beverly Hills, Calif.: 1969.

Simkin, J. S. Mary: A session with a passive patient. In J. Fagan & I. L. Shepherd (Eds.), *Gestalt therapy now*. Palo Alto, Calif.: Science and Behavior Books, 1970.

Simkin, J. S. *Gestalt therapy mini-lectures*. Millbrae, Calif.: Celestial Arts, 1976.

Simkin, J. S. Gestalt therapy. In R. J. Corsini (Ed.), *Current psychotherapies* (2nd ed.). Itasca, Ill.: F. E. Peacock, 1979.

Smith, E. *The growing edge of Gestalt therapy*. New York: Brunner/Mazel, 1976.

Wertheimer, M. *Productive thinking*. New York: Harper & Brothers, 1945.

Yontef, G. *A review of the practice of Gestalt therapy*. Los Angeles, Calif.: Trident Books, 1969. (Also in F. D. Stephenson (Ed.), *Gestalt therapy primer*. Springfield, Ill.: Charles C Thomas, 1975).

Yontef, G. Gestalt therapy: Clinical phenomenology. In V. Binder, A. Binder, & R. Rimland (Eds.), *Modern therapies*. New York: Prentice-Hall, 1976. (Also in *The Gestalt Journal*, 1979, *1*, 27-45.)

Yontef, G. The future of Gestalt therapy: A symposium with L. Perls, M. Polster, J. Zinker, & M. V. Miller. *The Gestalt Journal*, 1981, *4*, 7-11. (a)

Yontef, G. Gestalt therapy: A dialogic method. In K. Schneider (Ed.), *Gestalt Therapie und*

Neurose. München: Pfeiffer Verlag, 1981. (b)

Yontef, G. Mediocrity and excellence: An identity crisis in Gestalt therapy. *ERIC/ CAPS,* University of Michigan, 1981, 214, 062. (c)

Yontef, G. Gestalt therapy: Its inheritance from Gestalt psychology. *Gestalt Theory* 1982, *4,* 23-39.

Zinker, J. C. *Creative process in Gestalt therapy.* New York: Brunner/Mazel, 1977.

Zinker, J. D., & Fink, S. L. The possibility for psychological growth in a dying person. *Journal of General Psychology,* 1966, *74,* 185-189.

9

Reality Therapy

WILLIAM GLASSER

Reality therapy is a therapeutic system developed by a psychiatrist, William Glasser, in the 1950s and 60s. Originally it had no systematic theory, only the empirical idea that individuals are responsible for what they do. The therapist's task is to establish enough rapport so that clients gain the strength to accept this responsibility. This is accomplished by leading them to evaluate what they do and, if it isn't satisfactory for them and those they care for, to help them gain more responsible behaviors. A responsible behavior is defined as one that satisfies one's needs and does not prevent others from satisfying theirs.

Reality therapy is applicable to individuals with any sort of psychological problem, from mild emotional upset to complete psychotic withdrawal. It works well with behavior disorders of the aged and the young, and with drug-and alcohol-related problems. It has been applied widely in schools, corrections institutions, mental hospitals, general hospitals, and business management. It focuses on the present and upon getting people to understand that they choose essentially all their actions in an attempt to fulfill basic needs. When they are unable to do this they suffer, or cause others to suffer. The therapist's task is to lead them toward better or more responsible choices that are almost always available. In 1981 Glasser added

to the empirical beginning a complete theory based upon how the brain works as a control system.

Basic Concepts

In 1976, Glasser wrote *Positive Addiction*, depicting how powerful meditations can become both strengthening and addicting to the meditator, addicting because, when positive addicts attempt to give them up, they suffer the pains of withdrawal. After the book was written, so many confirmations of this observation poured in from all over the world that Glasser began actively to search for the reasons why these seemingly nonmental or passively mental activities such as running, Zen, bike riding, yoga, and other common meditations were so strengthening. He began to read as much as he could find on how our brain functions during meditation because, obviously, something happens inside the brain during these procedures that is extremely strengthening. While he could not find any book that explained why strength is gained through meditation, he ran across William Powers's *Behavior: The Control of Perception* (1973). Its description of how the brain works as a control system provided a theory for both reality therapy and positive addiction. With Powers's help Glasser moved these ideas far beyond pure theory and in his book, *Stations of the Mind* (1981), he related control theory to the clinical practice of reality therapy.

Present reality therapy theory is based on the concept that our brain works as a control system. While, in engineering, control theory has been in common use for 50 years, the idea that the brain works as a control system was first advanced by Norbert Weiner in 1948. Powers, picking up on Weiner's rather mechanistic cybernetics, expanded it into a biologic system which Glasser believes is the best explanation yet of how all living organisms behave. As Powers defines it, a control system acts upon the outside world, or upon itself as a part of the outside world, to fulfill some purpose intrinsic to the system. Therefore, if the brain is a control system, then all of our behavior is to fulfill needs built into the genetic structure of that system. This means that we, as well as all living organisms, spend our lives attempting to act upon, or more accurately, to control the world around us to fulfill powerful needs built into our structure. Therefore, we are not only completely internally motivated, in contrast to the concepts of most psychological systems which are some variation of externally motivated behaviorism, but all of our behavior is for the purpose of fulfilling needs built into the system.

It follows, therefore, that basic to reality therapy is the idea that people, who are suffering from any of the large variety of what are generally defined as psychological disorders, are failing in their attempt to act upon or to control the world around them to satisfy what they want right now. It makes no difference what the problem is, whether a simple behavioral disorder or a deep-seated psychosis, what reality therapy defines as the problem is how the individuals behave as they fail to control the world satisfactorily

enough to satisfy their needs. What are labeled pathological diagnoses are these same unsuccessful behaviors. Reality therapy attempts to help people control the world around them more effectively so that they are better able to satisfy their needs.

All living organisms from bacteria to human beings are driven by powerful needs built into their genetic structure. The lower the organism on the evolutionary scale the less complex are its needs. All existing organisms have succeeded in controlling the world around them to satisfy these needs, all others have become extinct.

To understand the brain as a control system, it is necessary to have some knowledge of the basic needs of humans. First, and most obvious, is the common need of all living organisms to stay alive and to reproduce. As organisms moved up the evolutionary scale, other needs evolved but only in humans have these needs become independent of survival. For example, humans experience the need to belong, to socialize, to cooperate, and to love as powerful, independent needs. While it likely evolved through the simple evolutionary process, that those who socialized and cooperated gained a survival advantage over those who did not, Glasser takes issue with many who claim that, even in humans, the need to survive is fundamental. He argues that if survival were the most basic human need, there would be no suicide. Certainly many people kill themselves because they are unable to satisfy their need to belong. Lonely and without love, they believe that the pain of their inability to satisfy this need can only be relieved through taking their own lives.

Glasser also believes that human beings have an independent need for power, for competition and the self-worth and recognition that can be gained through satisfying this need. At one time power was subordinate to survival, but as people became more gratified through its exercise, they gained a survival advantage over the less competitive. Certainly there is evidence that people resort to suicide or risk their life when they fear loss of power and, as in the need to belong, suicide, or risking death, is the acid test of whether or not a need is fundamental. Other fundamental needs that seem to drive humans are the need for fun and for freedom. People will risk their lives for both of these, even, at times, kill themselves when it seems hopeless to fulfill them. A human is like a building supported by these five essentials columns: the need for *survival, belonging, power, fun,* and *freedom.* When any column weakens we feel pain and immediately attend to the weakened column because all are needed for support. While some may be thicker than others, or the need they represent stronger, all are needed if the building is to stay erect and free from damage.

While reality therapy is not so naïve as to suggest that there are particular genes for these needs, it is believed that a complex set of genes causes our brain to recognize, consciously or unconsciously, that these needs do indeed exist. As people fail in the struggle to satisfy these genetic forces, it becomes the job of the reality therapist to help them to evaluate which need or needs is driving them as well as to help them to control the world to satisfy them all.

But to control the world, we must be able to sense it and particularly to sense what in it will satisfy our needs. To do this we have sensory receptors which can detect that we and the world exist. For example, if, based upon the survival need, the fluid level in our body drops below optimum, something in our hypothal-

amus detects this and transmits a message to our brain, thirst! To control the world—to satisfy this thirst—we have to perceive what thirst is and also how it can be satisfied. Therefore, when we are thirsty we become aware of an internal perception of ourselves drinking some fluid, such as water. Then, to satisfy our thirst we must act upon or control the world by looking for water. If we cannot find water, or some other potable fluid, we will die of thirst.

But it is not enough to find water. We must also be able to transfer it into our body only then can the need be satisfied. Therefore, all living organisms have only *two* fundamental ways to control the world: (1) to perceive what in the world can possibly satisfy their needs, input, and (2) to act upon or control what they perceive in the world will satisfy the needs, output.

Because this concept is so important, let's look at another example. You started to read this chapter because you are driven by the idea that this knowledge will add to your power. You then cast your perceptual system around until you find the book, *Current Psychotherapies,* you proceed to open it to this chapter, and then to read the chapter. Therefore, as William Powers emphasizes, all behavior is an attempt to control perception in a way that we perceive how one or more of the fundamental needs is to be satisfied. Our brain, therefore, acts as an input (or perceptual) control system to do this. Control theory is, at present, the only valid theory of reality therapy. Other theoretical material is valid only if it relates to control theory; if not, it is only of historical interest.

Other Systems

Reality therapy, as a control theory therapy, differs from other systems in one fundamental aspect. That is, most psychological systems, ranging from behaviorism to psychoanalysis, are based on the "commonsense" assumption that human behavior is primarily a reaction or response to events or forces in the outside world. These theories are all variations of what is best called stimulus-response psychology. Even though behaviorists now talk about reinforcement and analysts have always talked of id forces within the organism, they still operate as if the prime movers of behavior are events in the world around the organism. Reality therapy completely denies this theory and says that nothing that we do, feel, or think is a reaction to external events. All behavior is generated within ourselves for the purpose of satisfying one or more basic needs. And, for therapeutic purposes, all behavior is chosen, even though, at times, we often repress from conscious awareness the fact that we choose the current behavior. Keeping this fundamental difference in mind, reality therapy differs from conventional therapies, from analytic to behavioral, in the following ways.

1. Reality therapy rejects the orthodox concept of mental illness and all the conventional descriptions of mental illness such as psychosis, neurosis, schizophrenia, mania, or depression. All of these mental illness descriptions are based upon the notion that these illnesses are reactions to events in the outside world. A child is considered neurotic because his mother rejects him, or psychotic because he can't cope with harsh reality. The reality therapist would say that this conventional "reactive terminology" is an attempt to describe the behavior that we choose to control the world as we constantly attempt to satisfy our needs. Thus we choose "neurotic" behavior, such as anxiety, depression, compulsions or obsessions; "psychotic" behavior such as paranoia and

catatonia; "psychosomatic" behavior such as arthritis, or heart disease; and "addictive" behaviors such as alcoholism, heroin addiction, and gambling.

None of these happen to us. Painful and ineffective as they may be, all these strategies are our attempt to control the world to satisfy our needs and all these behaviors do control the world to some extent. If they did not work we would not use them, and some, such as depressing (depression must be called depressing, if it is a behavior), work well enough so that we may choose them for long periods. Most of these unsatisfactory behaviors we consciously choose, the others we choose without awareness because we block this choice from awareness to protect us from the fact that it would be painful to realize we choose misery. Therefore, there is no "stress" in the outside world, there are only situations we call stressful because we cannot control them satisfactorily with the behaviors we choose. But this "stress" is always unique to any one of us; in ordinary living there are few, if any, real stressful situations that no one can control.

2. Conventional psychotherapy places a great deal of emphasis on how the patient dealt with the outside world in the past. Reality therapy recognizes that in the past the patient attempted to control the world. But, if the attempt was unsuccessful, it is worthless to dwell on this failure in therapy. Reality therapists will look to the past for times when the patient successfully controlled the world and for behaviors that might again be effective. A reality therapist's constant attempt is to focus on the present because we must satisfy our needs right now. The past is at best a memory, often faulty, of what we did. It is often faulty because if we remembered accurately, it could be too painful. When we talk of the future what we are really saying is that this is our best attempt

to predict what may happen, at times reasonably good, but still, only a prediction. It is the present that is the cutting edge upon which we live our lives, and the reality therapist focuses upon how we could, more effectively, control the world right now through evaluating our behaviors and choosing better ones.

3. The reality therapist rejects the idea of transference seeing it as a false and misleading concept. People relate to the outside world as they perceive it. The reality therapist deals with this perception, whatever it may be, and doesn't attempt to teach patients that a perception is something other than what they may think it is. Traditional therapists attempt to put ideas into the patient's head when they impose the idea of transference upon the patient, or countertransference upon themselves. Reality therapists deal with themselves as part of the patient's control system. They realize that the patient is always trying to control the therapist to try to satisfy needs. They do not escape from this responsibility by saying to the client "you are transferring your perception of others to me." This may be so, but it's not relevant. Clients are still dealing with therapists and their perception is of them regardless of how this perception may also relate to others.

4. Conventional therapy deals largely with the unconscious and dreams. Reality therapy deals with what the patient is presently aware of and then works to make the patient aware of as much as possible. The reality therapist recognizes that patients tend to repress, or block from awareness the ineffective behaviors they are using to try to control the world. In working with the therapist, these repressions are easily removed and the patient becomes aware of choosing behaviors. As patients become aware that these are choices, they become more effective.

5. The reality therapist asks patients to take a hard look at their behavior and then, based on their own value system, to judge whether or not this behavior is effective in getting them what they desire. While this judgment is often difficult to make, especially when the patient's behavior affects others and their needs, or is torn by conflicting desires, it is still necessary that the patients make this judgment as best they can. The reality therapist does not shrink from pushing the patient to do this because it is only from coming to this judgment that the patient can be motivated to change.

Contrary to what is believed about reality therapy, however, and contrary to what O. Hobart Mowrer stated in the introduction to *Reality Therapy* (Glasser 1965), reality therapists do not take a moral position. The reality therapist is not an upholder of the standards of any social group or political system. The reality therapist's only interest is that patients recognize that each of us does have personal standards and every society also has standards. These must be considered when patients judge the effectiveness of their behavior to satisfy their needs. If they choose behaviors that differ from any of these standards, the reality therapist must make them aware that they risk serious problems when they attempt to behave contrary to their own or society's values.

6. Unlike conventional therapy, reality therapy spends a great deal of time attempting to teach people better ways or better behaviors to deal with the world. The reality therapist intends to help the patient control the world more effectively. This does not happen by wishing, hoping, or by gaining "insight." It happens only through examining what the patient is choosing, evaluating this choice and eventually helping him choose better behavior. Glasser believes all therapy is

teaching and to the extent that teaching leads to need fulfillment, it is therapeutic.

O. Hobart Mowrer broke with theories of behavior that pictured man as a helpless victim of heredity or environment. He developed a new method known as integrity therapy (Mowrer, 1961) for treating emotional problems. His philosophy is almost the opposite of Freudian theory. Mowrer stated that instead of mental problems resulting from the individual's attempts to live up to a naturally high moral code, they occur when people do not live up to their own moral convictions. Mowrer has stated that "the problem presented by psychopathology is one that is best conceptualized, not as illness, but rather as a kind of ignorance and moral failure and the strategy of choice of preventing and correcting these conditions is manifestly educational and ethical" (Mowrer, 1961).

Willard A. Mainord seems to agree with reality therapy concepts in many important respects. First, he is dissatisfied with orthodox therapy, especially psychoanalysis, as are Thomas Szasz, Albert Ellis, and many others. Second, he believes the mentally disturbed are not sick in the medical sense, but are irresponsible. Third, he believes the therapist must help the patient to discover that irresponsibility does not pay and responsibility does. Fourth, he thinks a good society is one where virtue is rewarded. "If the patient," says Dr. Mainord, "is held responsible for productivity and for accurate communication, the 'crazy' behavior will have no payoff value and will disappear, sometimes dramatically" (Mainord, 1973).

"The Third Force" psychology of Abraham Maslow (1954) is closely aligned to reality therapy. Maslow believed most individuals have a capacity for creativity, spontaneity, caring for others, curiosity, continual growth, the ability to love and be loved, characteristics found in self-actualized people. A person who is behaving badly is reacting to the deprivation of his basic needs. If his behavior improves, he begins to develop his true potential and move toward greater health and normalcy as a human. Maslow believed one of the great errors of the behavioral scientist is the belief that right and wrong behavior have no scientific basis. Maslow, like Glasser, thought that in the final analysis, irresponsibility was just as damaging to the individual as to his society.

HISTORY

Precursors

Glasser created reality therapy out of his own experience with clients. He does not deny that others before him may have come to similar conclusions, or that reality therapy seems closely related to the work of Alfred Adler and Albert Ellis. Almost all of his training, however, came from conventional psychoanalysts. As reality therapy concepts began to cross his mind he rebelled against his formal training and noticed that many of his teachers did not practice what they taught. As they demonstrated by their interactions with patients, he noticed that what seemed to work was not what they said worked. It was also apparent that what they did was different from what they professed, something that they either were not aware of, or would not admit. And what they did was often much closer to what later became reality therapy than what they taught.

One of his few nonanalytical teachers, G. L. Harrington, encouraged Glasser to put his ideas into practice and to discuss his thoughts. Harrington became his mentor and helped him to formalize reality therapy in the early 60s. Harrington was influenced by Helmuth Kaiser, a psychoanalyst who had worked with Harrington in the 1950s at the Menninger Clinic, and who, himself, had begun to turn away from conventional analysis. This is probably why Harrington was so encouraging to Glasser. Kaiser, however, had little direct effect upon Glasser.

Beginnings

Reality therapy began when Glasser became dissatisfied with psychoanalytic psychiatry as taught at the Veterans Administration Brentwood Hospital and at the University of California at Los Angeles. What disturbed him most was the endless ruminations about what went on in the patient "caused" by others in the patient's family or by a "harsh" world. The patient was generally seen as a victim of forces beyond his or her control and the analyst as the person to give the patient insight into his unconscious so he could regroup and cope. Only the analyst had the skills to help the patient gain access to his unconscious mind and, if this were shared under the right conditions, transference, the patient, with this miraculous insight, would free himself from malevolent forces inside himself. This made for interesting discussions but, in practice, Glasser saw no evidence at all that it worked. Patients were given insight after insight, transferences were worked through and through, but still the patient stayed the same or, even became worse, more locked into the problem because now, with the "aid" of therapy, patients took even less responsibility for what they did.

On his own, Glasser began to stay in the present and to try to get patients to realize that they were responsible for what they did, that they had to change themselves, and could not count on others to

change to help them no matter how much insight they gained. For example, one woman had been attending the clinic for three years and had spent most of that time blaming her nervousness and depression on her now dead grandfather. Glasser told her that he would see her only on the condition that she could never again mention her grandfather. She was shocked and responded, "If I don't talk about my grandfather, what will I talk about?" Glasser told her to talk about what she was doing now in her life to solve her problems, that her grandfather was dead and no longer had anything to do with her life. In a few short months, even with this early crude version of reality therapy, she stopped depressing and anxietying (control theory behavior terms) and started doing many things to fulfill her needs. She had taken control of her own life. For three years traditional therapy had deprived her of the chance to help herself.

Glasser timidly explained this unorthodox move to his residency consultant, G. L. Harrington. Instead of being reprimanded as he feared, Harrington shook his hand and said, "Join the club." This started a seven-year relationship during which Harrington continued to consult with Glasser and helped him formulate the ideas that became reality therapy. Harrington had been working along these lines for many years but he had not published or promoted his ideas even though he did teach them to those who showed interest.

In 1956 Glasser became consultant to the Ventura School, a California Youth Authority institution for delinquent girls. There also he found that the young women had all been told that they were emotionally disturbed and so were not responsible for their lawbreaking. The people who ran the school were upset at this irresponsible viewpoint and supported Glasser in his attempt to introduce the beginnings of reality therapy into this and other Youth Authority institutions. As interest in this approach grew, Glasser was invited to speak at the 1962 meeting of the National Association of Youth Training Schools and presented the new ideas that he called reality psychiatry. The response was phenomenal. Evidently many people doubted the effectiveness of any therapy that did not ask people to accept responsibility for what they chose to do with their lives. Several months later, while presenting these ideas to the British Columbia Correctional Association, he changed the name of the approach to reality therapy and this name has been used since. From this start reality therapy has grown to the point where it is now accepted as a major therapeutic approach.

Current Status

At present, reality therapy is recognized as an effective therapeutic medium. As of 1981, over 90 percent of the more than 200 armed forces clinics which treat drug and alcohol abusers use reality therapy as their preferred therapeutic approach as stated in a Department of Defense handout at the August 1981 Armed Forces Conference on Drug and Alcohol Abuse in Washington, D.C. The Institute for Reality Therapy was founded in 1968 and functions primarily to promote the teaching of these concepts and to hold courses through which candidates may become certified reality therapists. This teaching is accomplished primarily through three one-week courses. In the first week, reality therapy is introduced and taught through control theory lectures and roleplaying in small groups, under the guidance of an experienced reality therapy teacher. Small groups also participate in some experiential exercises to bring home the concepts of reality therapy, but most of the work is done through roleplays. After the first week, if candidates wish to become certified as reality therapists, they practice where they work for a minimum of six months and report what they do to a certified reality therapist in their community. When they reach a predetermined level of competence the therapist who follows them recommends that they are ready for the second of the three-week sequence. The second week is essentially a repeat of the first week at a higher level during which the candidate must demonstrate an understanding of control theory. At the end of the second week of training, the candidate is again followed in a practicum situation by a practicing reality therapist for at least 6 months with the proviso that both follow-up periods total 18 months and 60 hours of supervision. When this is done, if the trainees show sufficient understanding, they are recommended to come to Los Angeles for a certification week.

An important division of the Institute for Reality Therapy is the Educator Training Center. Here a staff of educators especially trained in the concepts of Schools without Failure, which is how reality therapy is applied to public and private schools, work with educators at all levels and with whole schools and school systems. Some of those who are taught go through the regular certification process, but most are taught in their schools and do not come for certification. The Educator Training Center was started because of Glasser's 1969 book, *Schools without Failure*. The fundamental idea in *Schools without Failure* is that when children are unable to control the world successfully, that is, succeed in school, it hurts so much that they often stop trying to learn. While Glasser was not aware of control theory when he wrote the book, control theory certainly confirmed the accuracy of the concepts of his educational approach. The purpose of a school without failure is to help children to gain adequate control over their education, something most cannot do if they fail in school. In the last quarter of this century it is almost impossible to satisfy our needs without, at the minimum, a high school education. Failure causes students to give up on education but since they can't give up on their needs they often turn to disruption or drugs for temporary satisfaction. Among the many tragedies of school failure is that to "succeed" many young people turn to delinquency. One study (Small, 1977) done in Canada shows that school failure, much more than a poor home, is the cause of young people entering prison. Over 250,000 teachers have been involved in the program of the Educator Training Center and all the schools involved report increased learning, 80-90 percent fewer discipline problems, and almost a total cessation of vandalism to school property.

In 1982 Glasser began teaching control theory to the general public. Glasser firmly believes that this is a true mental hygiene approach, that people who learn the control theory concepts will be able through this knowledge to take more effective control of their lives. In doing this they will be able to prevent many of the problems which eventually lead people to therapy. He also believes that if we do not, as a population, learn that biologically we operate as control systems and cannot be controlled by external forces, as the commonsense but incorrect S-R psychology maintains, we will not survive much longer in a nuclear age. If we assume that we can hold others in check with the threat of nuclear annihilation we will find out too late that this is impossible. The only way that the competing living control systems (i.e., our brains) can get along

with each other is through compromise and negotiation. Failure to learn how we are constructed can now be fatal.

PERSONALITY

Theory of Personality

The theory of personality revolves about how our brain operates as a control system. Although this was explained in a general way under the section, "Basic Concepts," it is now necessary to cover this theory in greater detail to show how our attempts to control the world mold our personality.

As already explained, we have a group of fundamental needs built into our genetic structure, which we must satisfy by acting upon or controlling the world. We develop an extremely detailed understanding of the world through our perceptual system which takes the energy which strikes our eyes, ears, and other sensory or perceptual receptors into our brain where it is translated into what we call the outside world or reality.

For example, to satisfy thirst, our sensory receptors, primarily located in our eyes, ears, nose, mouth, and skin, must find a potable fluid; for example, water. Unless we can learn what water is, we will die. Therefore, the light reflected from the water that strikes our eyes, the feel and the taste that is detected by our fingers and tongue is translated by the perceptual system of our brain into a perception, or simply stated, a picture of water as need satisfying. But this picture, which is our understanding of water, is created within our brain, or within the perceptual system of our brain.

Therefore, what we call the real world is actually almost completely created within our own brain. Although it is certain that there is a real world and we are a part of it, all that we can possibly know of it is what is detected by our sensory receptors. As they detect this energy they serve as the outpost or the first order of the 10-order perceptual system through which we perceive the world. Except for the sensory receptors this system exists within our brain, and within this system energy is acted upon order by order, each order adding a level of understanding, until it reaches an order high enough that it represents something in the real world which will satisfy our needs. In the thirst example we will understand it represents water.

A further example is that the energy that strikes the sensory receptors of our buttocks when we sit on a chair reading this book is simple first-order pressure energy. In this instance the first-order perception is usually raised to the second order (sensation) in our perceptual system because at this order it becomes understandable enough to help us to fulfill our need for comfort. Here, at the second order, we might say the chair is too hard and move to a softer one. There are, however, no absolutely hard or soft chairs or anything else hard or soft in the real world. The perception of hard or soft exists only in our head as a second-order perception. What is hard to me might be soft to you. Therefore, to repeat, because this point is so important, all that we know of the world beyond the simple energy that strikes our first-order receptors is subjective, in fact, objectivity, in the sense that people usually use the term, does not exist.

What we call objective is really a subjective perception that a lot of us agree upon, for example, that right now you are reading a book. Try to prove that you are holding a book in your hand to a man who has never seen a book and you will have a problem. Therefore, hard or soft, warm or cold, sweet or sour, only exist within each of our minds as what we individually define them to be to satisfy needs. They are examples of the second order, sensation, but to make sense of the world, we are capable of raising the orders up one at a time through at least 10 orders. How we understand the world through them is too complex to explain here but it is explained in great detail in Chapters 7 and 8 of *Stations of the Mind* (Glasser, 1981).

As we perceive the world and look for need-fulfilling perceptions, we store any and all perceptions that fulfill needs in an internal world, a hypothetical place that exists only within our mind. Because it contains only perceptions that fulfill one or more needs, such as cool water, soft chairs, and loving friends, our internal world can also be called our ideal world. These pictures of all we have discovered satisfy our needs and drive all of our behavior. For example, if you feel thirst right now, a "picture" of you drinking a glass of water will cause you to get up to obtain a glass of water. At any time we can call upon one or several of these need-fulfilling perceptions, or pictures of what we want, which we store by the millions in this ideal world. We satisfy general needs like love and fun by acting upon or controlling the outside world to try to get as close as we can to the picture from our internal world that we want. Simply stated when we want some fun we may go play tennis (*we are controlling for tennis* in control system terms) if we have a fun picture of ourselves playing tennis in our internal world.

Therefore, our personality is best described as the characteristic way in which we engage, act upon, or attempt to control the world to satisfy the pictures of what we desire. Some of us do it well and have a strong, responsible personality. By responsible we mean we are able to satisfy our many wants without interfering with the ability of others to satisfy theirs. You are responsible if we are both thirsty and you share the little water left in your canteen with me, when I have none. You might threaten your security by doing so, but you would increase your sense of belonging. And in my perceptual system, in which I perceive what is right or wrong, this is right, or moral, for me. Therefore, right and wrong, or morality, is one of the ways that any of us tries to resolve the constant potential conflict between needs, a conflict carried over into our internal worlds which has within it many conflicting wants. We can also have nonmoral conflicts like a picture of ourselves thin and a picture of a delicious chocolate sundae. Moral or not, however, we must learn to control the world to resolve these conflicts or feel as if we are being torn apart. How we do this is also a typical part of our personality and we can do it well or badly.

To control the world to get what we want we must develop behaviors which will effectively do this for us. This is done through a separate system which we call a behavioral system. To turn this system on, however, and start generating the behaviors that get us what we want, we need one more structure, a comparing station. Actually there are probably billions of these in our brain but since they all work the same way they can be described as one. Here, in these stations we compare what we want, which comes from our internal world, with what we perceive is available in the outside or real world. Simply stated it is a place or a station where we compare the picture of what we want from our internal world with the picture of whatever is now available from the external or real world.

For example, driven by thirst, we send a picture of a glass of water from our internal world to a comparing station. As soon as we do so we attempt to control the world to get water or, in control theory terms, we are now *controlling for* water. Then we must focus our perceptual system on the outside world to look for water. If we can't find water we will suffer a perceptual error which is the difference between the picture we want, a glass of water, and no water. This error will generate an error signal which we feel as an urge to behave because when this signal turns on our behavioral system we begin to look for water. We will then behave in every possible way; that is, do, think, feel, and even involve our body in the process until we find and drink water or we die trying.

As long as we want something, or *control* for it, we will behave in every possible way until we get it or, at least, convince ourselves that we are getting closer to it, or die in the attempt. We would not usually die for something simple and replaceable such as an ice cream cone, but we will risk our life for anything we believe we must have like water or love. In the case of ice cream, we will just take the picture out of the comparing stations and forget it, it is not that important. But, if we are rejected by a loved one, while it might be wise to remove his or her picture from our internal world, we may refuse to do so and go as far as to risk our lives in an attempt to overcome the rejection. This is because if we cannot replace the loved one with someone else, we will not be able to remove his or her picture as a need-filling perception because, driven by the need to love, we must always have the picture of someone who can fulfill that need in our internal world.

As previously explained, to control the world we must generate behaviors and these are all generated by a behavioral system. In this system there is no separation between feeling, thinking, doing, and even bodily activity. All behavior is made up of some mixture of these major components of behavior. If, for example, John loves Jane but she does not love him, John will generate doing behaviors, that is active, physical, acting upon the world, observable behaviors like sending her love letters. He will also think of what to write but when he writes he will describe his strong feelings because, if we want to control people, feelings are the strongest and most effective of the four behavioral components. Think of trying to persuade a resistant person to change without using persuasive feelings as part of your argument and it is apparent that we certainly are capable of generating these behaviors. Contrary to common sense, *feelings do not happen to us.* Therefore, one of the difficulties people have in understanding reality therapy is that we don't concentrate on feelings alone, but always on the total behavior of the person. In doing so, we always include the three psychological components of behavior which are what the client does, thinks, and *feels.*

All of these are chosen. We choose what we do, we choose what we think, and, hard as it may be to believe, we also choose what we feel because, like doing and thinking, our emotions are also generated by the behavioral system. Therefore, all of our common psychological disorders, such as depression, are behaviors of which feelings are the major component. These are best called *feeling behaviors,* which means that, in control theory, depression is depressing (a behavior), anxiety is "anxiety-ing," compulsions are "compulsing" and, even suicide attempts are "suiciding." Since these are all behaviors and are essentially chosen to control people, and since clients need to control to satisfy their needs, a major purpose of reality therapy is to help people to make better behavioral choices. Since reality therapists believe that none of these happen to us, we choose them all, better choices are certainly possible.

Variety of Concepts

While the human personality is best defined by the typical behaviors that we choose to control the world, there are a series of concepts associated with control theory and its application to reality therapy necessary to understand this method. First is the concept of perception itself. Difficult as this may be to grasp, all we know of anything inside or outside of ourselves is how we perceive it. Even when we talk of behavior what we are talking about is our perception of what we do; for example, when I walk across the room the only knowledge I have that I am actually walking is that I can perceive that this is what I am doing. And when I dream that I am walking the perception is just as real to me as if I were awake and perceiving the same activity. Therefore when we talk of what we do, think, or feel, we are actually talking about our perceptions of these activities. If you claim that you live in Chicago all you really know is that right now you perceive that you live in Chicago. We tend to live our lives as if what we perceive is real and that others who are sane perceive things the same way that we do. And because we are creatures of the same species, and have the same basic needs and must interact with each other to fulfill these needs, we do perceive the world in similar ways.

Difficulties arise when we fail to understand that even though we see things similarly we never can see anything exactly the same because no two people share exactly the same perceptual system. One of the main tasks of a reality therapist is to get clients to understand that the people around them do not necessarily perceive the world the same as they do. A parent may perceive smoking marijuana as the worst possible behavior, while his child perceives it as just a pleasant way to relax. Because they do not understand that they cannot possibly perceive this or anything else exactly the same, they spend a lot of time trying to force their perceptions on each other. As this cannot work, they find that instead of staying close to each other they are driving each other away. Part of the reality therapist's job is to teach clients simple control theory so they can understand that the way their brain is built to function no two humans can possibly perceive the world in the same way. If clients learn this they are much better able to negotiate the compromises necessary to fulfill their needs.

As we attempt to fulfill needs by attempting to control the world around us we must be aware that major problems arise when we try to control other people or even other living organisms. Controlling nonliving things, while it may be difficult, is never as hard as controlling people. Here the important concept is to learn that we can only control our own lives, we cannot control anyone else who does not want to be controlled by us. This means we cannot force anyone to do what he or she does not want to do. But this does not mean that we don't try. Almost every client we are asked to see for therapy is attempting to control someone and finding this to be frustrating. Wives and husbands try to make each other love them, parents try to make children study in school, managers try to make people work harder or more efficiently. Until they learn that this is not the way our brain is set up, that we are all internally, not externally motivated, many fail to get what they want and suffer increasing frustration. They

frequently turn to drink or drugs in a desperate effort to find something that feels good that they can control. Reality therapy teaches clients that they can only help others to fulfill their needs in a way that the client's needs are filled also, they can control no one. Living organisms that could be controlled by outside forces would have to depend upon these forces to act in their own interest, something patently impossible and totally against survival.

As we practice reality therapy we must also teach clients not to let others control them through painful feeling behaviors, but at the same time, if they care for the other person, not to run from them, fight them, reject them, or attempt to bribe them to stop using these uncomfortable, controlling behaviors. The major behaviors we tend to use in our attempt to control others, behaviors that do work for a while but never for very long, are painful feeling behaviors such as depressing, anxietying, guilting, headaching, backaching—to list a few. Painful as these may be to us, we are willing to suffer in our attempt to control those around us. A wife who uses "phobicking" to keep her husband home with her pays the price of not being able to leave the house. A husband who depresses and threatens suicide is often trying to get a wife who has left to come home. The reality therapist must teach many clients, who come because of the pain and suffering that they have chosen, that there are better choices, and other clients not to let themselves be controlled by these behaviors by those around them. We must also teach them that they must not reject the person trying to control them as they often do now, but rather to try to help themselves and the other person to fulfill their needs in better ways.

Finally, it is necessary to explain the control theory concept of conflict because few if any clients are free from this experience. In control theory terms, conflict is when we want two or more conflicting pictures (from our internal world) at the same time. We send these conflicting pictures to comparing stations; for example, a woman with children is in a loveless marriage but feels she cannot leave because of loyalty to her family, even to her husband. She finds a love interest outside the marriage and can't decide whether to leave or to stay. There is no single behavior that will resolve this common but serious conflict; that is, satisfy both pictures. No matter which way she contemplates going, she increases her error in respect to the other way. In this case two basic needs are in conflict, the need to love and the need for self-esteem or loyalty. She has her control system in an impossible situation and she may choose to depress or to drink in desperate effort to resolve the conflict but neither of these is good conflict resolving behavior. The truth is that there is no good conflict resolving behavior. It is only an illusion to think that there is.

Well-meaning friends and inexperienced therapists as well as general common sense will recommend that she choose one way or another. But if she continues to want both, no choice will work. She may shift her situation but the misery will remain in one form or another. Control theory, while it can offer no miracles here, at least points out what will not work which is to attempt to follow common sense. The reality therapist will treat this situation much differently than the woman expects by saying to her, "Don't choose." There is no therapeutic sense in suggesting that there is a choice when there is not. What will be suggested is that she do nothing relative to the conflict, just live with it and time may alter the situation, or her, so that it can be resolved. The

therapist will also suggest that she devote as much of her energy as possible to non-conflicted areas such as going out to work. Any energy that she devotes to need-fulfilling areas that are not a part of the conflict will leave less energy for the conflict causing her to feel as if it has been relieved to some extent.

Also, as she lives with the conflict the creative part of her behavioral system will come into play as it always does when there are no available behaviors to reduce the error. Creativity may point out a way, so waiting for the creative behaviors is sensible. As long as we are alive we are potentially creative. There is never any situation where only one behavior is possible short of running out of air. But before we are creative we may choose many painful behaviors as our best attempt to resolve the conflict. Living with these painful choices is hard but it is the best way. Try as we may we can never force ourselves to do happily what we don't want to do.

PSYCHOTHERAPY

Theory of Psychotherapy

The following eight steps describe the practice of reality therapy. The purpose of these steps is to help clients to take more effective control of their lives. As this occurs clients will also gain better control over the world around them but this therapy always focuses on the part of the world that is their own life.

Step 1: Make friends and ask clients what they want

In the first part the reality therapist attempts to get involved, establish rapport, or simply to make friends with the client. This is necessary because, in almost all instances, people who come for help are lonely. They are looking desperately for another human being to whom they can relate and from whom they can gain a sense of concern and a feeling of belonging. Partly to relieve loneliness, all clients attempt to control the world with inadequate behaviors such as depressing, guilting, and anxietying. The therapist must help clients to believe that they have a chance to control the world with more effective behaviors because there is now someone on their side.

The friendship between the client and the therapist is, however, a very specific kind of friendship; that is, the therapist makes himself available as a caring, belonging person, but not as someone that the client can control with her inadequate behaviors. Therapists should not allow clients to dominate or control them through depressing, angering, threatening, anxietying or paining. The therapist must avoid falling into the same trap with which the client has ensnared countless others in her desperate attempt to control the world with these behaviors.

In the second part of step 1 the therapist must find out what it is that the client wants, or in control theory language, what is the client *controlling for* at this time. Together the client and therapist must face what is in her internal world that she desperately wants and cannot satisfy. But even if clients express what they want, often it is impossible to achieve. For example, John, who has been rejected by Jane, when asked what he wants might say, "I want Jane to come back to me." A parent coming for help might say, "I want my son to stop smoking marijuana." An employee who has recently been let go might say, "I want my job back." These are legitimate wants, but fundamental to control theory is the axiom that we cannot control other people's lives, we can only control our own. Our behavioral system can only generate our behaviors, we

cannot cause another to behave. What we can do is to behave toward them in a way that helps them to satisfy both their needs and ours.

Therefore, the therapist, in asking "What do you want?" means, "What do you really want?" or "What do you want that is possible?" John may say, "Well, I guess what I really want is love." The parent, asked what he really wants might say, "I really want to get back the relationship that I had with my son before he started smoking marijuana." And the job loser might say, "I guess what I really want is another good job." When clients tell what they really want the therapist can move to step 2. As long as they want someone else or something else to change they will be frustrated because our behavioral system cannot control other people or impossible events. For example, I could say, I want to play tennis as well as Bjorn Borg, but what I really want is to play tennis well. To play as well as Bjorn Borg is beyond the capacity of my nervous system so the second part of step 1 is to focus as much as possible on what clients want that they can possibly achieve.

Step 2: Ask, what are you doing now?
This step is an attempt to get clients to focus on what they are doing, or in control theory terms, what they are choosing to do at this time. Here the therapist refers to step 1, and asks clients what they are doing now to get what they want. John might say, "I want love. I guess I can't have Jane, but I want love." The therapist then has to say, "All right, what are you doing now that will get you some love?" As this step unfolds, clients like John begin to understand that this is a fundamental step, that what they are choosing to do may not be gaining them love. The client may say, "Well, since Jane got married, I don't do anything. Socially I'm just a dud. I go to

work and then I go home and sit around and moan and groan. I'm just so depressed that I don't really do anything."

What the client does not realize is that he is choosing to sit home and choosing the behavior of depressing in a desperate attempt to control Jane and get her to come back, an attempt which has not worked. If he does not understand this, however, if he believes this happened to him, as all people who follow stimulus-response theory believe, it will be difficult, perhaps impossible, effectively and quickly, to help the client. The quickness and effectiveness of reality therapy is based upon getting the client to understand that he is choosing to sit home, he is choosing the miserable, defeatist thinking, and he is choosing the depressed feeling. He is choosing all three behavioral components that add up to the painful immobilization which we call *depressing*.

The therapist, however, focuses on the component of the behavior most amenable to change, therefore the therapist does not focus on the depression or the feeling component because this is the component that John will not admit he is choosing. But this is usually what John wants to focus upon because, to him, what he feels, which he believes has happened to him, is the most important part. It is what brought him to the office. The therapist points out the sitting home, the not socializing, and the thinking of defeatist thoughts by asking, "Aren't you choosing these?" The therapist, by focusing on the doing and thinking portion of the behavior, makes the client aware that sitting home every night has not happened to him, he is choosing to sit home. He will usually defend his sitting home on the basis that he is so depressed, but he cannot deny that he is choosing to sit home. The parent of the child who smokes marijuana, who is continually restricting,

browbeating, threatening, rejecting, bribing, and cajoling his child, will realize that this is what he is choosing to do. And sitting at home for the job seeker is not going to get work.

Step 3: Is what clients choose to do, getting them what they want?

Steps 2, 3, and 4 go so closely together it is hard to separate them, but Step 3 is to get clients to evaluate whether what they now realize they are choosing, is getting them what they claim they want. Is sitting home going to get John the love he wants? Is browbeating a child to stop smoking marijuana going to get the parent the good relationship he wants? For step 3 to be effective, step 1 must be accomplished. Here the therapist must get clients to judge their behavior and learn that their behavior is within their control.

A corollary to step 3 is to ask a student or probationer (or in any situation where a therapist acts as disciplinarian) is what they are doing against the rules? If you ask if it is getting them what they want, they will often come up with a smart aleck answer such as fighting is the only thing I want to do. To prevent this, after asking what are you doing, ask if it is against the rules. If the rules are reasonable, as most rules are today, this will work well. If they are not, the rules must be changed or discipline will not be possible.

Step 4: Make a plan to do better

Once clients judge that what they are doing is not working, then the next step is to help them work out a better way to get what they want or, in control theory, to take more effective control of their life. If Jane has left John for good, to help him to get out and socialize instead of sitting home depressing, and at the same time help him get Jane out of his life, means removing her from his internal world.

The therapist will guide the man whose child smokes marijuana to stop pushing his child away and start doing some enjoyable things with him. Once the man who has lost his job realizes that to sit around depressing is ineffective, then the therapist will talk about a plan to go out and find another job. Step 4 is planning, advising, helping, and encouraging.

While many therapies deny both the value and the need for the therapist to engage in planning and helping, these are important to reality therapy. The reason that advice and planning are not a part of most therapies is they are of no value if the client has not been through steps 1, 2, and 3. If clients have not focused on what they really want, have not been confronted with the behavior they choose, and have not evaluated the effectiveness of this behavior, then planning or advising is a waste of time. None of us will change until we realize that what we are doing is not working. If people ask for advice and don't use what is offered, it is plain that they have not made the decision that what they are doing is not working, so the advice is wasted. Therefore, even someone like "Dear Abby" serves a purpose because if her people have decided that what they are doing is not working, her advice can be quite helpful. It is our job as therapists to have some knowledge of how people might function more effectively and, when they admit that they are making bad choices, guide them toward better ones.

Step 5: Get a commitment to follow the plan worked out in step 4

Once a plan is worked out the therapist should ask for a commitment from the client to make an effort to follow through. Therapists can depend upon the first part of step 1, the strong relationship, to get clients to take the counselor into their internal world as a helping person. When they make the commitment it is firm because the counselor is now a need-fulfilling perception in the client's internal world. The commitment is strong because it is as much to themselves as to the therapist. Strong commitment means strong follow-through.

Step 6: No excuses

Reality therapy does not get involved with excuses, or reasons why plans are not carried through. Remember all behaviors work to some extent. Miserable as many of them are, they do give the client some control over his world, and clients are afraid to give up the little control they have achieved. Nevertheless, as we move toward step 6, and already exist in their head as a helping person, we should say, "I'm not interested in why you can't do it. I'm interested in when you can do it, and how you can do it." As we work this way, clients will focus more and more on the only thing they can do, which is choose better behaviors right now, and stop looking for reasons to be ineffective and miserable.

Reality therapy does not involve a detailed exploration of the client's past which, too often, in other therapies is used as a further excuse to avoid dealing with the present and to provide reasons based on past maltreatment, imagined or real, to allow clients to continue to give excuse after excuse for hanging on to inadequate behaviors such as depressing, anxietying, and guilting. Clients are looking for ways to change these ineffective behaviors and it is important that therapists do not encourage clients to continue to control their life (and their therapy) with endless excursions into the past because they are afraid new behaviors will not work or require too much effort.

Most therapies maintain that working in the past is important to understanding the present. This may, to some extent be true, but in practice, the traditional way of looking into the past, for past upset, maltreatment, or inadequacy is destructive to the goal of therapy which is to help the client function better now. There is little we can use now from past misery and much that is discouraging if dwelled upon too much. In reality therapy, beyond the necessary listening to the client's story that is a part of step 1, and should be limited to as little of the past as possible, all we look for from the past is when clients had been effective. Here we may find behaviors that they know and that may still work today. Therefore, when we look back into the past, we look for successes, for effectiveness, for behaviors that worked. We don't focus on past miseries, the present misery is enough to deal with.

Step 7: No punishment

In most counseling there is no cause for the counselor to worry about punishing wrongdoing, but in dealing with students in school and, perhaps, people on probation and parole, counselors must, at times, discipline. What we recommend is the imposition of reasonable consequences. We never try to impose pain for the sake of the (stimulus-response) effect of the pain alone. This means we do not hit, impose sentences, or permanently remove privileges; these are all punitive, not only because they cause error and pain, but because they leave no room for the wrongdoer to take control and decrease the error. For people with inadequate behaviors, any increase in error almost always makes their behavior worse, not better.

We have found that there are only two reasonable consequences: (1) to temporarily restrict freedom, or (2) temporarily to remove privileges. It is the *temporary* that is the key; that is, we only impose the restriction until the wrongdoer, with our help, can figure out a way to follow sensible rules. For example, tell a student, "You have to sit here until you can think of a better way," or tell an alcoholic prisoner that he can't gain his parole until he attends AA meetings. In what we do, miscreants have some control over when they get back freedom or privileges. And in getting them back, usually with reality therapy help, they learn effective behaviors that pay off in the future.

Punishment is the infliction of pain with no reasonable way to reduce or end the pain no matter what the wrongdoer does. The intent is that the punished person will remember the pain, or the sentence, and not break the rules again. There is no evidence that this ancient procedure, or anything else that does not help the wrongdoer gain control, is effective over any period of time.

Step 8: Never give up

It takes a long time for people to begin to realize they can gain effective control because they are so used to attempting to control the world with ineffective behavior. In many cases they have had therapists who gave up on them because they did not change. They are also resistant to change because they have controlled those around them with behaviors like depressing. And therapists who allow themselves to be controlled become uncomfortable and quit. We believe that the therapist must literally persevere with the patient long enough so that the patient begins to understand that therapists will neither give up nor let patients control them. In this slow and frustrating situation, the dogged therapist will become more and more a part of the patient's internal world, more and more seen as a helping, caring, concerned person, and more and more begin to accomplish the first part of step 1 which is to make friends. A good friend does not give up easily. When this is done, step 8 becomes the first part of step 1 and therapy begins to move.

These are the steps of reality therapy. They attempt to help patients use their brain as it is designed to function, to control the world around them through controlling their own lives more effectively. Any skillful reality therapist can practice these steps effectively. That these steps apply to a wide variety of clients is extremely well illustrated in *What Are You Doing?* (1980), edited by Naomi Glasser. People who are skeptical as to the effectiveness of this therapy can read successful case after case representing the most difficult clients that a therapist could conceivably encounter. Cases range from a patient on the back ward of a mental hospital eating his own feces to a totally out of control adolescent girl running around the world attempting to control it with sex and drugs. Reality therapy is not abstract, it is a therapy that works effectively and rather quickly once therapists learn to apply these eight principles and the control theory that is basic to them

Process of Psychotherapy

The reality therapist by overall general therapeutic standards can certainly be called verbally active. Viktor Frankl, the founder of logotherapy, when asked by one of his psychoanalytic colleagues to define *Logotherapy* in one sentence, reportedly asked his colleague first to define the essence of psychoanalysis in one sentence. The answer given to Frankl was "during psychoanalysis, the patient must lie down on a couch and tell you things that sometimes are very disagreeable to tell." Whereupon Frankl retorted, "Now, in Logotherapy the patient may remain sitting erect, but he must hear things that sometimes are very disagreeable to hear." Using this same model, we might define the essence of reality therapy as: "in reality therapy the patient and the therapist both

sit erect facing each other and the patient and the therapist hear things that are both very agreeable and very disagreeable." This is meant facetiously and certainly not meant as a true capsule version of reality therapy. Nonetheless, there is a conversational exchange between therapist and patient that encompasses both disagreeable as well as agreeable facets. However, the focus is on the individual's strengths, attributes, and potentials as related to his behavior and his experiences, particularly his current attempts to succeed in life.

Setting limits is an important part of the function of the reality therapist. The therapist assists the patient in understanding not only the limits of the therapeutic situation, although there may be an intense personal involvement, but also the limits as well as the nonlimits that life places upon the individual. For example, if a patient asks, "Can I call you after hours?" the reality therapist would, of course, respond with, "I certainly hope you would call if there is an urgent situation in which I can be of help." However, we believe that the therapist might also say, "I hope you would call if you have a significant success." Most patients are astounded and surprised when a therapist suggests he might be interested in good news as well as problems via telephone. However, the concept of emphasizing the positive is constantly in the reality therapist's mind. The contractual arrangement as discussed in the planning stage under the section "Theory of Psychotherapy" is a type of limit setting, since the plan may include the limits of the therapeutic involvement, and since, on occasion, it has been found helpful to set a specific time limit or duration for psychotherapy. At the end of this period, therapy is stopped at least for a time. Some people are able to work more effectively, more positively, when they know therapy will consist of a specific number of visits. This is particularly helpful in the area of marriage or family counseling.

A reality therapist focuses frequently on "pinning down the patient." This is also brought out in the planning phase of behavioral goals. Unfortunately, this is an area where many therapists of a variety of approaches do not follow through. For example, if a teenage girl who has never sought a job before says to the therapist, "Next week I am going to look for my first job," a reality therapist would not say, "Good, let me know how it works out," but might respond with a series of very precise questions such as:

Therapist: What day next week?

Girl: I don't know. I thought Monday or Tuesday.

Therapist: Which day? Monday or Tuesday?

Girl: Well, I guess Tuesday.

Therapist: You guess, or will it be Tuesday?

Girl: Tuesday.

Therapist: What time Tuesday?

Girl: Well, sometime in the morning.

Therapist: What time in the morning?

Girl: Oh, well, 9:30.

Therapist: Fine, that is a good time to begin looking for a job. What do you plan to wear?

Girl: Well, I never thought it would make a difference. What do you think I should wear?

Therapist: [Discusses several alternatives to grooming and dress relative to job hunting] How are you going to look up what jobs to apply for?

Girl: I thought I would look in the morning paper in the classified section.

Therapist: [The therapist might discuss the pros and cons of also looking in the Sunday paper as the girl may not be aware of the larger classified section on that day of the week. The therapist might even go through the classified section with her.]

The therapist might terminate the "pinning down" phase of dealing with the girl by saying, "What are you going to do if you are called in for an interview?" If the girl has difficulties and becomes uncomfortable explaining that she did not know it was a possibility, the therapist and the girl might even do some roleplaying with the therapist taking the position of a potential employer. Finally, the therapist might say to the girl, "What will you do if the first two or three, or four job interviews are unsuccessful?" The therapist would never say, "How would you feel?" That would be a totally fruitless question. Of course, the girl would feel badly, she might feel depressed. The therapist, by asking, "How would you feel?" is certainly not assisting the girl to deal with the potential failure in trying to obtain a position. Rather, the therapist might say, "If you are unsuccessful on the first day, what are your plans or what will you do?" That is a matter they can both deal with, by planning ahead. In general, the more specific the questions and the more a therapist "pins down" the patient with respect to the details of anticipated change in behavior, the more he is increasing the chances for the patient's successful handling of the situation.

Constructive arguing or intelligent heated discussions in some situations may be an integral part of the psychotherapeutic process. If the therapist asks the patient what the patient believes about something, and the patient answers and then asks the therapist his beliefs and disagrees with him, we do not believe there is always a hidden meaning behind the disagreement. Rather, the disagreement can be on a responsible and intellectual level. In fact, discussions of this sort can lend a great deal of support to the patient's self-concept as an individual who has something to offer, something of value to say and defend.

Humor is, and should be, a regular part of the whole therapeutic process. The ability to laugh freely is an integral part of a well-balanced self-concept and approach to life. In fact, the ability to laugh at one's own follies, one's own mistakes, and one's own accidental errors is one of the highest forms of a mentally healthy self-concept. When people become burdened and overwhelmed with emotional problems, it appears that this ability to laugh at themselves is the first facet of humorous expression that disappears. They may still retain the ability to laugh at others. Laughing and humor are related to joy and happiness. We are not suggesting this is all that joy and happiness are, but it is a part of a healthy life and a positive self-image.

Confrontations are used frequently, particularly when "no excuses" is the stance the therapist takes. This can be, and often is, one of the hardest positions for the therapist to assume. That is, to say to the individual who has failed, "You said you would do it, when will you do it?" The therapist will not accept excuses or rambling explanations for failure because this is how the patient attempted to control people in the past. The therapist may even forcefully intervene and tell the patient that he is full of bull or use some other strong "Wake up, you can't control me with your usual behavior" statement. This is not done frequently but does have a special place when timing, as well as degree of involvement, are taken into consideration. For example, a patient may say, "What do you think is wrong with me?" and the therapist might respond by saying, "I think you are crazy." After a pause and some reflections from the patient about that, the therapist should go on to explain that the word "crazy" as he meant it can be defined as someone who is acting in an irresponsible way, trying to fulfill his needs by hurting either himself or others.

Harrington was once asked by a patient, who was rambling on, why he (Harrington) was looking out of the window while the patient was talking, and Harrington retorted, "Anything is more interesting right now than what you are saying." This facetious kind of verbal shock confrontation or insult does have merit and value when used correctly and when the therapist has an understanding of the situation and of the patient. One is reminded of the definition that a gentleman never hurts anyone's feelings unintentionally!

Analysis of dreams is not part of the reality therapist's function. We believe there is virtually no evidence to indicate that analysis of dreams has any therapeutic value. That does not mean it does not have relevance or significance. The relating of dreams can even be used as a defense to avoid discussing one's current behavior. However, on occasion if a patient insists on relating a dream, most reality therapists would listen if the act of listening was felt to be meaningful to the patient.

Generally, however, we try to get involved with the patient in his real life. What he does, what he plans: we want to get him to evaluate this with us and remake plans and then carry them out. Ours is not a therapy where we do much speculation or listen to fantasy.

Mechanisms of Psychotherapy

What actually happens in psychotherapy that leads to improvement is difficult to pin down. Glasser, who has done much therapy as well as taught it for many years, thinks that no matter what the therapy, if the patient learns to function better, which means to use behaviors that are effective and feel good, what went on in therapy that caused this to happen is essentially the same thing. Therefore in a book filled with as many diverse therapies as this book he believes that when any one of them work, what made it work was essentially the same. He also believes that no matter how it occurs, whether in psychoanalysis or assertive therapy, that what clients learn is to take more effective control of their lives. It seems evident that all accepted therapies provide a structure for this to happen or they would not be effective enough to be known.

Therapy, however, is far from the only way this is achieved. All religions are based upon helping people to believe that with the help of a higher power the person can gain the control for which he is searching. Lawyers, general physicians, chiropractors, palm readers, and a variety of meditation practices and the yogis associated with them, all do the same if they are successful. So does joining cults like the Hare Krishna and other similar operations. We are all searching for control and we have no choice but to continue this search, it is the way all living organisms are constructed.

In reality therapy the patient begins to gain control first by being in a situation where he does not have to take control. This means that in the office with an accepting therapist he does not have to do anything difficult to fulfill his needs for the time of the session. He is accepted, listened to, supported, and encouraged that whatever he wants he has a reasonable chance to get. Here nothing specific is expected of him, he is in a situation where there is no attempt whatsoever to control him. Glasser often remarked when working in a good mental hospital that he wondered who were the best off, the

patients for whom everything was done, or the staff who were working hard to figure out and provide what the patients wanted. This may be an exaggeration, but it does show that for people who have lost effective control of their lives, being in an office or a hospital where there is no need for them to control, or worry about being controlled, must be an extremely refreshing experience. Harrington always stressed the value of rest, and a good therapy situation provides the most restful of all situations, a respite from the constant struggle to control. This may be the most important mechanism of good therapy and it is easily seen that this is common to many different situations besides therapy.

Within this respite, the reality therapist provides a framework for the patient to regain the control needed. To do this the therapist helps the patient learn that the world does not control him, that his misery is his unsuccessful attempt to control the world. Slowly the patient begins to learn the uncommon sense that he is in charge of his own life and he can exercise this well or badly. Mostly he learns this from a skilled therapist by the therapist resisting the patient's attempt to control the therapist. Most patients, when they gain a little strength in the respite of the office, resort to one of their many ineffective behaviors to try to control the therapist so that the therapist will do things for them or tell them what to do. When the patient learns that the therapist will not (he really cannot), the next move is to blame the therapist. When the therapist is not defensive to this blame and continues to be accepting, the patient begins to learn that the world is not at fault; what is at fault is his ineffective way of dealing with the world.

This is solidified by the therapist continually asking if what he is doing is helping him. In a sense, the therapist is saying over and over that you, the patient, are in control and you cannot control me or anyone else and get what you want if you choose ineffective behaviors. Not only won't they work, but instead of fighting you or rejecting you, as has happened in the past, I will stick by you and help you. Learning that they choose all they do, ineffective as well as effective, and that they can't control the therapist but the therapist will not reject them is the powerful mechanism of reality therapy. Once this lesson is learned in the therapy, then plans for what to do outside of the therapy, which seem the essence of the process but are really less important than learning this lesson, become easy. The patient gets the idea, "My God, it really is my life" and after this it just takes some time for the patient to expand his control and feel better. This is well illustrated in the "Case Example" later in this chapter.

APPLICATIONS

Problems

Since reality therapy is teaching people to control their lives effectively it can be applied, not only in psychotherapy, both group and individual, but also in all aspects of education. The only limit is the technical skill of the therapist. It is difficult to discuss its application to specific problems because the reality therapist does not look at people as objects to be classified according to diagnostic categories. Glasser, who is a physician, believes that the medical model of diagnosis is seriously flawed and applies almost as poorly to the complex diseases that face doctors today such as rheumatoid arthritis as it does to psychological conditions like depression. The mechanical idea that disease, whether physical or psychological in its obvious manifestation, can be ac-

curately diagnosed to a single cause and that cause remedied through specific treatment has stood up poorly to the test of time. Reality therapy is not involved in perpetuating this archaic misconception.

What Glasser and others in the holistic health movement believe is that most of the ailments, both physical and psychological, that people complain of, are manifestations of the way they have chosen to live their lives as they attempt to control the world around them to satisfy their needs. To help these people it is the function of the therapist, or teacher, to help them to understand that they are living their lives badly and to help them live more effectively. Whether the way they live their lives is with depressing to control people around them or with arthritis, as they ineffectively (for them) attempt to control the world and their immune system gets pathologically involved in the process and attacks their own joints to produce rheumatoid arthritis, what has to be done now is to help them to live more effectively. If they have a physical malfunction as a result of ineffective living this can be temporarily and usually only partly relieved by good medical care but they will not become well until they can control their world more effectively.

It makes little difference to a reality therapist what the presenting complaint of the client is; that complaint is a part of the way the client is choosing now to deal with the world. The therapist pays less attention to the complaint per se and more attention to what the client wants and how the client is now attempting to get what he or she wants. When the client begins to realize that instead of being the victim of some disease or diagnostic category he is a victim of his own ineffective behavior then therapy begins and diagnosis becomes irrelevant. Reality therapy is therefore an integral part of the holistic health movement even though it is little used at present because so few reality therapists are physicians.

Evaluation

The reality therapist evaluates clients by checking out three important facets of the client's functioning. First, the therapist attempts to find out how much the client is in touch with his or her internal world, or in simple terms, how willing is the client to come to grips with what he or she really wants. To do this, the therapist must try to get the client to describe accurately the pictures that are in his head of what it is he wants. It is not enough for the client to say I want to be happy or to feel better but to describe in some detail what it is he wants right now. This is not easy and many clients will refuse to do it because to come face to face with what they want is too painful. The therapist knows that the more a client is unwilling to do this the more difficult a problem the client will be.

The second thing the therapist looks for is what effective behaviors does the client still have. Even if a client is on the back ward of a mental hospital he does have some effective behaviors. The therapist looks for effective present behaviors and also asks about times in the past when clients functioned effectively. Any behavior which has been used in the past is probably still available or at least easier to relearn than to learn new behavior from scratch. The less effective behaviors the client has now and had in the past the more difficult the client will be to deal with.

Third, the therapist looks at how the patient views the world. The more aberrant his view of the world, the more difficult he will be to treat. For example, a patient that is rigidly moralistic and believes that this is the way the world should be will be more difficult to treat than a patient who is more flexible in his outlook. Part of therapy is to get patients to see that their view of the world is making it difficult for them to fulfill their needs and, if a person needs love but thinks sex is wrong, then this person is going to be frustrated because of his rigid views. Control theory teaches that we all view the world in our unique ways but it also teaches that we have to fulfill our need to belong with others around us. This means that unique as our way of perceiving is we must somehow find a way to accept the way others view the world also or we will not be able to satisfy our fundamental need to belong. The more a client has difficulty doing this the more difficult therapy will be.

Treatment

Reality therapy evolved in its initial phase in dealing with four different categories of problems: (1) Glasser's work with delinquent teenage girls (1956-67); (2) his work with private outpatients with a variety of problems (1956-82); (3) his work with the physically injured in a rehabilitation center (1957-66); and (4) the work of G. L. Harrington with severely psychotic individuals at a Veterans Administration Hospital (1955-62). It was found to be highly successful in these four disparate areas of application.

In Harrington's application of reality therapy in institutionalized psychotic patients, he found two additional modifications that enhanced his work with the patients. First was the initiation of a three-phase program within the single unit where he worked. That is, patients moved from phase I where they were essentially given custodial care to phase III when they were ready to seek outside employment and living situations. The system was geared so within the general milieu was a built-in motivation to progress from phase I to phase III and progression was based upon reduction of "crazy" talk and "crazy" behavior as well as increasing demonstration of responsible behavior and relevant conversation. This phase division has been used effectively by several other institutions practicing reality therapy, among them the William Roper Hull Progressive Education Center in Calgary, Alberta, Canada, whose director was Brian Sharpe (1972-75). This home and school for delinquent and disturbed boys and girls is run entirely on the principles of reality therapy and has four phases as developed by Sharpe. He found the principles of reality therapy as useful as Harrington did and was also able to enhance appropriate placement of staff according to their backgrounds, interests, and abilities in dealing with individuals in the specific phases.

One aspect of dealing with the so-called psychotic patient was spearheaded by Harrington when he did not allow the patient to talk "crazy." This technique has been used by others practicing reality therapy with similar success. Patients are told "I am not interested in hearing your crazy behavior, your delusions, and your hallucinations, but rather I am interested in what you want out of life, in your attempts to succeed in the world and in the healthy you. If you want to talk crazy, talk to someone else." Most reality therapists, therefore, rarely hear delusions or hallucinations since the client learns that these behaviors will not control the therapist. It has been long since known that in a situation where two individuals are meaningfully involved, each has strong desires to please the other. If one is involved with a "psychotic" individual having hallucinations and delusions, an interest in hallucinations and delusions

on the part of the therapist reinforces the patient's desirability to use them to control the therapist. When no interest or a negative interest is demonstrated, reality therapists find that hallucinations, delusions, and psychotic expressions begin to diminish rapidly. See Chapter 20 of *What Are You Doing?* (1980), for a dramatic description of this process working with a back ward mental patient.

If a therapist in the first visit asks a patient if he has any dreams and the patient responds by saying, "I do, but I never remember them," and the therapist continues to ask that question at each consecutive visit, usually at the end of five or six visits, the patient is enthusiastically and regularly remembering and reporting his dreams. In a meaningful and involved psychotherapeutic relationship, if the therapist asks often enough, he may get just what he wants, and if he asks about psychotic behavior continually he will likely get the patient to continue to be psychotic to continue to satisfy his need to belong with the therapist.

Reality therapy can be used in group as well as individual psychotherapy. The principles can easily and effectively be incorporated into the group process and the group is a very powerful instrument in which plan making and commitments can be put into practice. Consider, for example, an individual involved in a group situation making a plan and then a commitment, then writing the plan down and having each individual in the group read the plan and sign his or her name. The initial leverage to keep the commitment comes from involvement with meaningful others, which is reinforced when the individual is involved in a group setting. If she is involved with the group members and wants to retain this involvement, the motivation to keep the commitment is greatly enhanced every time she looks at the paper describing one of her plans signed by the group's members. Cotherapists are used regularly and found to be a useful adjunct in reality therapy groups.

Marriage therapy or conjoint marital counseling is often practiced by reality therapists. Usually this is a time-limited series of 2 to 10 visits. At the end of that period, if the couple has not made significant progress, a total reevaluation of the situation is in order or possibly a respite of several weeks or months in the continuation of therapy, after which another reevaluation would follow.

Initially in marriage counseling, it is important for the therapist to clarify the couple's goals by asking questions, such as "Are you here even though you have already made the decision to end the marriage, but want to be able to say 'we have tried everything'?" or "Are you here because you want to evaluate the pros and cons of continuing in this marriage?" or "Have you made the decision that you definitely want to preserve the marriage but are having difficulties that you have been unable to resolve effectively and want professional help?" If the patients and therapist are not first aware which of these reasons each of the partners has come to therapy for, he may be dealing with a couple who essentially want a divorce but do not say so while the therapist is actively seeking to improve the relationship. In marriage counseling, we recommend the therapist be quite active, asking a variety of questions in trying to understand the overall pattern of the marriage and of the interrelationship. What must be worked out is how the couple can live together without attempting to control each other in a way that one or both do not want to be controlled. If this cannot be worked out the marriage will usually fail. To do this, the therapist tries to get the couple to focus on: (1) their similarities and differences in taste and interests; (2) understanding how they go about seeking friends as a couple; and (3) understanding how much there usually is to know about each other, what each wants from the marriage, and how much of their "knowledge" is based upon assumption not on actually talking to each other about what each other wants. Familiarity is not intimacy. Just as many children, even as they grow to adults, know their parents only as "parents" and not as "people," the same is true frequently when a spouse is asked questions regarding the values and philosophies of their marriage partner.

In reality therapy, ancillary individuals are often asked to come into the office for a visit. They may be a friend, a spouse, a teacher, a child, or anyone else significant in the patient's life. This is done to help the therapist understand the patient and help the patient understand him/herself through the eyes of people he respects but is often trying to control or feels controlled by. These ancillary people are brought in not for the reality therapist to help them deal with their problems, but rather so that the therapist can ask them to help him to understand the patient better. They frequently benefit a great deal, however, from this brief exposure. It is our strong recommendation that except in highly unusual situations, these ancillary individuals in the person's life should always be seen in the session with the patient.

Reality therapy is a verbal therapy; it requires conversation and as such has some limitations. For example, it cannot be used by individuals who cannot talk. There have been several cases of people who were unable to speak and wrote their comments on a paper with a successful therapeutic conclusion; however, it requires an exchange of communication either by the spoken word or in unusual cases by the written word. Therefore, limitations include its inability to apply to autistic, nonverbal children and to severely mentally retarded individuals who cannot communicate adequately either verbally or through the written word. A skillful reality therapist will however devise ways to communicate where this seems impossible. See Chapter 6, "The Boy Who Wouldn't Talk," in N. Glasser's *What Are You Doing?* (1980), for a particularly skillful approach that got a mute 10-year-old boy to talk. Reality therapy has been used with moderately mentally retarded individuals quite successfully with little or no change from the standard approach. See Chapter 21, "When Are You Going to School?" in *What Are You Doing?* (1980), for a good description of how this process works with the mentally retarded.

As mentioned in previous sections of this chapter, there has been strong use of reality therapy principles with appropriate modifications in the school system and, as such, this use represents an important phase in the application of reality therapy to prevent mental illness. Reality therapy has been used in a significant way in race relations in that it was partly developed in the black community in Watts, California, and also was incorporated with success in schools facing problems with race relations. Multiple-family therapy has been used by at least one reality therapist to a limited degree with no difficulty in successfully applying these same principles.

In industry, reality therapy has been used to deal with organizational problems as well as to improve individuals' organizational effectiveness. Intensive two- or three-day group programs using reality therapy restricted to executives of specific firms, such as banks, have been found to be relevant and effective for improving organizational and individual functioning. See W. Glasser and C. Karrass, *Both-Win Management* (1980), for a description of this process.

Management

The reality therapist's goal during the first interview and perhaps the first several interviews is to establish an involvement with the patient that includes discussing his present attempts to succeed and, also, to help the individual see that he is responsible for his own behavior. We believe that no real therapeutic progress occurs unless and until an involvement between therapist and patient is established, as motivation and involvement are directly related. It is usually futile to attempt to direct patients in making plans and commitments to plans that would change their behavior unless there is a strong involvement. The commitment is as strong as the involvement. Further, until an individual acknowledges, accepts, and understands his responsibility for his own behavior, no truly constructive plan to change that behavior and hence therapeutic progress can occur.

Therapist and patient are seated comfortably in chairs positioned so the individuals can look at one another. No specific fee is recommended. Fees vary. Therapists from a variety of disciplines including psychiatry, psychology, and psychiatric social work practice reality therapy, and the average fees in these fields vary from city to city. Fees and plans for payment should be discussed openly, early in therapy.

Most reality therapists see their patients once weekly. We find it is rarely necessary to see a patient twice weekly but this may be done for a short time. Most reality therapists believe the duration of sessions should be flexible, but because of the practicality of maintaining schedules, most therapists see patients for 45 minutes to 1 hour per visit.

We do not believe any real significance should be attached to matching the patient and therapist. Certainly some personalities relate better to one another. However, of prime importance is the belief by the therapist that the patient can do better and/or be happier than he is right now. The therapist must also be willing to become meaningfully and responsibly involved with that patient.

Psychotropic medications are used conservatively by psychiatrists who practice reality therapy. In fact, control theory teaches that the effect of the medicine is a new way that the patient's brain now must function to control the world with the help or burden of the medication. Since the brain is millions of years old and capable of amazingly perfect functioning on its own it seems presumptuous to assume that a medicine which affects the brain in a powerful manner can be safe to use. Glasser uses no medication in his practice, but does accept the fact that used conservatively a little medication is sometimes helpful to get the patient to slow down his behaviors to the point where he may be reached by a therapeutic program. In the case of criminal offenders whose problems are acting out, Glasser holds that psychotropic medication tends to remove responsibility for behavior and justify irresponsible behavior. In his long and successful tenure as a psychiatrist for the California Youth Authority (1956-67), he used no medication at all.

Important to reality therapy is teaching the therapists that there are no rigid rules, no strict do's and don'ts. The therapist has a framework to follow which has been explained in this chapter but within that framework he or she should be as free as possible. Therapy is a creative art within a sensible parameter. Nothing is taught that would hamper that necessary creativity. If, for example, a patient states "I am a liar, I lie all the time and you can never believe anything I say," it would not be surprising for a reality therapist to say, "I believe you. Let's not waste our time by me trying to guess if you are telling the truth. I am going to believe everything you say and it is up to you whether you tell the truth." By using this creative technique, hostile patients are not rejected but they cannot control the therapy with their usual ineffective behaviors.

The so-called flight into health is a frequently discussed concept in therapeutic circles and seems to be variously defined but primarily indicates the unanticipated, rapid, positive recovery made by a patient after a short period of therapy. This is often doubted by the therapists and probably relates to a fear of "false recovery" and a probable return to previous irresponsible behavior. In reality therapy, this is something we generally do not find to be true and we accept any constructive, responsible changes in an individual as progress. Perhaps the single most useful and important test in ascertaining the depth and sincerity of a change to increasingly constructive behavior is a willingness to do something meaningful in an involved way for other people, in addition to doing something for oneself. In an institution, this is particularly a good test for an individual who is seemingly doing exceedingly well, yet may be acting in this manner as a so-called facade to "get out earlier." Of course, maintenance of this behavior even if it is initially started as a facade usually results in need fulfillment and a desire to continue to change. However, the additional desire to do something for another individual, another peer in the institution, is seen as a strong indication of the depth, the degree, and the quality of the change in behavior.

CASE EXAMPLE

This case was selected because it shows how the principles of control theory are integrated into reality therapy. The female client was a 24-year-old college graduate whose father and one sister had seen Dr. Glasser years ago for small situational problems. The father called and begged him to see her, saying that the family was at their wit's end. She had graduated from college with a bachelors in public health but had not been able to find a job in the field. She was living at home and working as a clerk, for minimum wage, at a department store. She was aggressively despondent and was constantly threatening the parents with suicide complaining that she had failed in everything. She kept them bound to the house evenings and Sundays with the threat that, if they left her home alone, she would kill herself. One or the other had to be with her except when she was at work. Her constant complaint was that she had no future, and no one would ever love her or employ her at a good job. She complained that she was fat and unattractive and that, since things would never change, she did not want to live.

Her only satisfaction was in compulsive eating, where during frequent binges she would not only eat all the sweets in the house but even go out to the garbage can and eat food that she had tried to throw away to keep from eating it. She was 20 to 30 pounds overweight, she had been as high as 50 pounds over and said that she was on her way back to this weight or more. She was trying to end a long-term

unsatisfactory love affair with a man whom she did not love but whom she continued to see because she was so desperately lonely. She also felt his interest was more for her family's money than for her. Her sexual relationship with him provided no satisfaction and she had never had a satisfactory sexual relationship even though she had intermittent involvements for the past six years.

Glasser felt from the first visit to his office that she was anxious to see him and motivated to change but that she had little confidence in therapy. She agreed to see him and for her father to pay the fee because her minimal salary barely covered car expenses and personal upkeep. What she wanted from therapy was to find a vocational goal worth working for, to control her overeating, to find someone whom she could love and eventually marry, and to stop being a burden to her parents. There was no difficulty making an initial relationship with her because she knew of Glasser and had heard good things about him from her father and sister.

The first hour was spent in getting to know her and trying to get some sort of a feeling for what she wanted most. It seemed to the therapist that most important was help toward deciding upon a professional career even if she had to go back to college. Her feelings of worthlessness here seemed to predominate, although she also felt worthless about the rest of her life, especially her binge eating and the unattractiveness it caused. The principal behaviors that she was choosing to control her life were complaining, depressing, threatening suicide, and overeating, the latter providing an almost orgasmic release. Everything she did was powerfully controlling of her parents, the only people she, and many like her, can control. It seemed to Glasser that the first thing he had to do was to help her to gain some sense of worth which would provide her with enough control over her own life so she would waste less energy with her infantile attempts to control her parents.

Because of the urgent suicide problem, Glasser decided not to see her in his office because it seemed to him she would be too comfortable. They would spend a great deal of time talking but this talk alone would not lead her quickly enough to the sense of control she needed to achieve. He offered to see her on a regular basis, twice a week, outside on a nearby street where they would run together and converse while running. Since this street is frequented by runners of all ages this was an appropriate setting. Their goal was to run for about 45 minutes, and she agreed to run alone for 45 minutes the other five days. In three months they had achieved this goal and after their four-to-five mile run they sat in a car and continued to talk for another 15-20 minutes.

When Glasser offered this approach she resisted but he said it was the only way he would see her because he thought that any other approach would take too long. She then quickly agreed. Glasser believed she understood that what he had in mind was to get her to do something which would give her the sense of worth that she badly needed. She viewed herself as athletically retarded, and the idea that she could learn to run appealed to her, although she expressed doubt that she could ever run five miles.

As they ran the five miles and conversed while running, she began to feel as if she had accomplished something and a glimmer of herself as a capable person started to emerge. Intermixed with the necessary friendly talk that led them into greater and greater rapport they continually went over what she was choosing to do with her life and whether this was leading to what she wanted. As they crystallized what she

wanted the possibility of doing something effective to get it now seemed possible. More and more she talked about caring for disturbed children but very soon this became more than talk. She found a rather menial job at a community agency that provided after-school care for difficult children. She soon saw that she could accomplish as much or more than the agency professionals and she came to the conclusion that with training she could excel at this work.

By doing such a good job she provoked rejection from the agency professionals, particularly when she created an art program that especially attracted the children. But, instead of being bothered, she was pleased, since no one had ever been jealous of her before. She enjoyed the work, did not bridle at the many menial assignments and began to think seriously of going back to college for professional training in dealing with problem children.

She continued working at the department store, ran each morning, and began to talk more of her accomplishments and less of her complaints. They did not discuss her overeating because Glasser had determined not to let her control him with this highly controlling behavior. He felt that she could solve it if she could break out of the conflict that was centered around her fear of growing up and becoming independent of her parents. She made much progress but her overeating and her threats of suicide, while abating, still continued, possibly because she was desperate to control her mother who denigrated her accomplishments at the child care job. Glasser felt the best way to resolve this conflict was to hold a family meeting. This was held at her house and was attended by her parents, sisters, and brother.

This meeting was a turning point. Glasser did very little except to focus the discussion on what they thought of her ability and it was dramatic that they all thought of her as a child who could do little except act childish. They were almost patronizing to Glasser, and to his therapeutic efforts, as someone who would keep her entertained for a while like an expensive paid companion. Her father did say that he was amazed at her persistent running, rain or shine, but the others thought that meant little because she still ate excessively. She was a child at the beginning of the meeting but as it continued, and the therapist did not step in to defend her, she changed. She got angry and said that she was not a child anymore and there was some heated defensive discussion on all sides. She held her own against the family and grew up significantly in front of Glasser's eyes.

Glasser has often experienced these dramatic turning points in therapy and believes they are integral to the process. Therapy is not gradual, it is a series of big hills that the clients suddenly decide to climb, sensing strength as they do so. The rest is to hold and solidify these accomplishments, but this was a real breakthrough. She never again was a child after this meeting and in steps 2 and 3, as she evaluated her behavior continually, she resisted the constant temptation to regress to childishness. Having experienced standing up as an adult to her whole family, she now was aware of the rewards of growing up and was determined not to regress.

As they had settled the question of what she wanted, the discussion now centered on how she could get there. She knew that she had to go back to college and become a serious student but she still lacked confidence in her ability. But, during this time about a year after she started therapy, an opening for a teacher's aide in the public schools developed. She applied and was accepted. She found this opening while investigating opportunities at a local college and also found out that she could enroll in the college and use this job as the required field placement. The pay was much more than the department store and she finally quit that security-blanket child job where, interestingly, she had worked in the baby's and children's department.

This was the turning point. From here on things really came together. She began to control all aspects of her life better. She not only did not depend upon her parents but she began to make plans to move out. Her mother, who had control over her while she was a failure, resisted this loss of control in many subtle and not too subtle ways. She dealt with this quite well because the child-adult conflict inside her no longer existed and she understood what her mother was doing and thought it was more funny than threatening. She also broke off the self-destructive relationship with her boyfriend and was able to maintain herself enough on her other adult accomplishments that she felt no urgent need to replace him. She reentered Weight Watchers® and they, recognizing she was serious and grown-up, offered her a job as monitor on the nights she attended. Here too, she felt more valuable, saved money, and began to lose weight steadily. This she did on her own, since Glasser never would discuss diet and weight control.

In the beginning of March, about 15 months after therapy started, the frequency of visits was reduced to once a week. Then in the beginning of April, Glasser told her that he was going away in May for about six weeks and he had confidence that she could continue to do well on her own. She was naturally nervous but they planned that her father would take about half the money that he no longer paid Glasser and subsidize her rent so she could move from home, something she now was desperate to do. She had completely changed from the frightened, dependent, controlling child to a capable young woman. Glasser heard from her after he returned but she never resumed therapy. She did stop by once and tell him how she was doing but this was a short, social visit between equals and it felt good for both of them.

About 18 months later Glasser saw her father who told him that she had finished her degree in Special Education and had a good job in the school system as a professional. He also said that she was to be married shortly and she sent Glasser a wedding announcement with a nice note. Through a good relationship, continual inquiry into what she wanted, and ongoing evaluation of the behaviors she was choosing to get it, she stopped attempting to control the world through the unsatisfactory feeling behaviors of complaining, depressing, threats of suicide, and overeating.

SUMMARY

The purpose of reality therapy is to help people take more effective control of their lives. Since our brain functions as a control system always acting upon the world to attempt to fulfill our needs we are all responsible for what we do. Unfortunately few people realize that this is the case because for too many years psychology has been dominated by stimulus-response theory which says we are controlled by the world and are not responsible for our behavior. Based on the theory of William Powers and described in detail in Glasser's *Stations of the Mind* (1981), reality therapy is an attempt to help people choose the effective, responsible behaviors necessary to fulfill the needs that drive us. Needs such as survival, belonging, power,

fun, and freedom are built into our genetic structure and all of our behavior is designed to control the world to satisfy these needs. We control the world; the world never controls us. Some of our behavior may be so weak and ineffective that it seems that we are controlled by the world but this is never the case. Weak, painful, and ineffective as it may be, it is always our best attempt to control the world around us and ourselves as part of the world.

Reality therapy is a series of therapeutic principles which are summarized in the following eight steps: (1) make friends and ask clients what they want; (2) ask clients what they are choosing to do to get what they want; (3) ask if their behavioral choice is working; (4) if it is not, as is almost always the case, help them to make better choices; (5) get a commitment to follow the better choices that have been worked out in the previous planning phase; (6) do not accept excuses for failure to carry out the plan. If it is impossible, replan; (7) do not punish, but ask clients to accept reasonable consequences for their behavior. Punishment does not work because it causes clients to lose even more control over their lives. A reasonable consequence is one where the client still maintains some control. In reality therapy this is called discipline; (8) do not give up. It takes some time to get this process started and to teach the client that it is possible to control his or her life more effectively.

ANNOTATED BIBLIOGRAPHY

Glasser, N. *What are you doing?* New York: Harper & Row, 1980.
Twenty-five successful cases of reality therapy are described in detail. Each case is selected to show a different facet of the therapy. All are by certified reality therapists and have been put together and edited by the author. Included in the

paperback edition (1982, Harper & Row) is a study guide in which the important features of each case are brought to the student's attention through a series of exercises that involve the student in the learning process of reality therapy.

Any of the 25 cases in this book of successful reality therapy cases would be good reading for a student of reality therapy. In the study guide appended to the book are a series of questions to aid the student in learning how reality therapy was applied to each case all of which are different and were selected by the editor to show the wide variety of problems that can be treated successfully. Included in a chapter is the 1980 update of reality therapy by William Glasser. Using this update and the study guide students and teachers can learn and teach reality therapy effectively. The cases range from a patient on the back ward of a mental hospital, drug and alcohol problems, rehabilitation of the physically handicapped, ambulatory psychotics, teenage delinquents, a wide variety of school problems including a child who would not talk in school, marital problems, problems of aging, and work with the mentally retarded.

Glasser, W. *Mental health or mental illness.* New York: Harper & Row, 1961.

In this, Dr. Glasser's first book, he describes in clear language how we function. He uses small, easily understood diagrams to show how neurotic, psychotic, and other behavior-disordered persons differ from people who function adequately.

Glasser, W. *Reality therapy.* New York: Harper & Row, 1965.

In this book, Dr. Glasser describes his concept of therapy. He postulates that because of loneliness and inadequacy, most people refuse to take the responsibility to fulfill their basic needs, which he claims are love and worth. He describes how the reality therapist gets personally involved with his client, and from the warm, friendly relationship, he teaches the client that

he is responsible for what he does and how to do it more responsibly. This book is a significant step in the change from psychoanalytic therapy to a therapy of personal involvement, with the emphasis on present behavior and the gaining of responsibility.

Glasser, W. *Schools without failure.* New York: Harper & Row, 1969.

In this book, Dr. Glasser applies the concepts of reality therapy to the schools. He shows how school failure causes a child to become discouraged, give up, and then begin irresponsible behavior. He describes many school practices that promote a sense of failure in the student and shows how these may be corrected through more teacher involvement, less failure, less rote instruction, more thinking, and more relevance.

Glasser, W. *The identity society.* New York: Harper & Row, 1972.

Here Glasser documents a shift in motivation that took place in the Western world shortly after World War II. Following the lead of Marshall McCluhan, he describes how people, rich and poor, shifted from goals such as security to roles such as personal identity and fulfillment. This shift has caused people to be much more demanding of what they want from life. He then discusses this motivation shift as it affects childrearing, the family, marriage and corrections. Throughout he shows how reality therapy works most effectively with this motivational shift.

Glasser, W. *Positive addiction.* New York: Harper & Row, 1976.

In this book, Dr. Glasser sets forth the thesis that addiction can be positive or strengthening as well as negative and weakening. He describes a variety of positive addictions such as running and meditation, explains how they are achieved, and sets forth a theory of how they may be strengthening. This is a true self-help book, because through positive addiction, anyone by himself or herself can grow stronger.

Glasser, W. *Stations of the mind.* New York: Harper & Row, 1981.

Glasser, in consultation with William Powers carries his control theory into its clinical applications and describes how our input and output systems apply to the way we lead our lives. In this book control theory is directly related to the concepts of reality therapy and positive addiction.

Glasser, W., & Karrass, C. *Both-win management.* New York: Lippincott, 1980.

Here Glasser outlines how reality therapy can be applied in business and management. Karrass, who teaches business people how to negotiate successfully in all business situations, outlines how his negotiation techniques can be applied to motivating workers at all levels. The two theories are complementary and the book is filled with many practical examples. (Note: this book is now only available through Karrass Seminars, 1625 Stanford Ave., Santa Monica, Calif. 90064.)

Powers, W. T. *Behavior: The control of perception.* Chicago: Aldine, 1973.

Powers explains how our brain works as an input control system by constructing a theoretical model that explains that our behavior is always our best attempt to control the way we perceive the world. He explains how we function as a feedback loop with input and output as all we can do. He theorizes as to the source of our creativity and how this can be both constructive and destructive. He carefully explains how this differs from the mechanistic concepts of traditional S-R (or S-O-R) psychology and why it is much more explanatory of all we do.

CASE READINGS

Glasser, W. The case of Aaron. In William Glasser, *Reality therapy.* New York: Harper & Row, 1965. Pp. 135-140. (Reprinted in D. Wedding & R. J. Corsini [Eds.], *Great Cases in Psychotherapy.* Itasca, Ill.: F. E. Peacock, 1979.)

This is one of the earlier cases reported by Glasser of an 11-year-old boy, the therapist's first child patient. A highly obnoxious person, Aaron had been treated very permissively by prior therapists, and Glasser tried without success using the same tactics. Finding no success in this procedure, Glasser shifted suddenly to being assertive and even aggressive, something new for this spoiled child. A firm, logical approach worked wonders. Part of the interest in this case is that at the time that Glasser reported his results he had not as yet formulated his reality approach, and this incident shows the growth of Glasser as a therapist and as a theorist.

REFERENCES

Glasser, N. (Ed.). *What are you doing?* New York: Harper & Row, 1980.

Glasser, W. *Reality therapy.* New York: Harper & Row, 1965.

Glasser, W. *Schools without failure.* New York: Harper & Row, 1969.

Glasser, W. *The identity society.* New York: Harper & Row, 1972.

Glasser, W. *Positive addiction.* New York: Harper & Row, 1976.

Glasser, W. *Stations of the mind.* New York: Harper & Row, 1981.

Glasser, W., & Karrass, C. *Both-win management.* New York: Lippincott and Crowell, 1980.

Mainord, W. A., "A therapy 52." In R. J. Ratiboray (Ed.), *Direct psychotherapies.* Coral Gables, Fla.: University of Miami Press, 1973.

Maslow, A. H. *Motivation and personality.* New York: Harper & Row, 1954.

Mowrer, O. H. *The crisis in psychiatry and religion.* New York: Van Nostrand, 1961.

Powers, W. T. *Behavior: The control of perception.* Chicago: Aldine, 1973.

Small, S. *Radius, a reality therapy school.* Masters thesis, University of Saskatchewan, 1977.

10

Existential Psychotherapy

ROLLO MAY and IRVIN YALOM

OVERVIEW

Existential psychotherapy was not founded by any single individual or group. It arose spontaneously in the minds and works of a number of psychologists and psychiatrists in Europe in the 1940s and 1950s, who were concerned with finding a way of understanding human beings that was more reliable and more basic than the then current psychotherapies. The "existential orientation in psychiatry," wrote Ludwig Binswanger, one of its spokesmen, "arose from dissatisfaction with the prevailing efforts to gain scientific understanding in psychiatry..." (1956, p. 144). These existential therapists believed drives in Freudian psychology, conditioning in behaviorism, archetypes in Jungianism, all had their own significance. But where was the actual, *immediate person* to whom these things were happening? How can we be sure that we are seeing the patient as he really *is*, or are we simply seeing a projection of our own theories *about* him?

These therapists were keenly aware that we are living in an age of transition, when almost every human being feels alienated from fellow humans, threatened by nuclear war and economic upset, perplexed by the radical changes in marriage and almost all other mores in our culture —in short, almost everyone is beset by anxiety. Hence our "age of angst." Thus

the writings of Jean-Paul Sartre (e.g. *Nausea*) and of Albert Camus (*The Stranger, The Plague*), and countless dramatists like Beckett (*Waiting for Godot*). Existential psychotherapy was born out of the urge to help people with the profound dilemmas of modern life.

Existential psychotherapy is essentially not a specific technical approach which presents a new set of rules for therapy. It asks deep questions about the nature of the human being, the nature of anxiety, despair, grief, loneliness, isolation, and anomie. It also deals centrally with the questions of creativity and love. Out of the understanding of the meaning of these human experiences, existential psychotherapists have devised methods of therapy which do not fall into the common error of distorting human beings in the very effort of trying to help them.

BASIC CONCEPTS

The I-AM experience
The realization of one's being—"I am now living and I could take my life"—can have a salutary effect on a patient. "The idea of suicide has saved many lives," said Nietzsche. The human being will be victimized by circumstances and other people until he is able to realize, "I am the one living, experiencing. I choose my own being."

It is not easy to define *being* because in

our society we subordinate the sense of being to one's economic status or the external type of life that somebody leads. A man is known (and knows himself) not as a being or a self, but as a ticket seller in the subway, a grocer, a professor, a vice president of AT&T, or as whatever his economic function may be. This loss of the sense of being is related to mass collectivist trends and widespread conformist tendencies in our culture. The French existentialist, Gabriel Marcel (May, Angel, & Ellenberger, 1958, p. 40), makes this trenchant challenge: "Indeed I wonder if a psychoanalytic method, deeper and more discerning than any that has been evolved until now, would not reveal the morbid effects of the repression of this sense [of being] and of the ignoring of this need."

Existential therapy endeavors to be this "deeper and more discerning" type of therapy.

A patient, the daughter of a prostitute, had been an illegitimate child and had been brought up by relatives.

I remember walking that day under the elevated tracks in a slum area, feeling the thought, *I am an illegitimate child.* I recall the sweat pouring forth in my anguish in trying to accept that fact. Then I understood what it must feel like to accept "I am a Negro in the midst of privileged white," or "I am blind in the midst of people who see." Later on that night I woke up and it came to me this way, "I accept the fact that I am an illegitimate child." But "I am not a child anymore." So it is "I am illegitimate." That is not so either: "I was born illegitimate." Then what is left? What is left is this, "I Am." This act of contact and acceptance with "I am," once gotten hold of, gave me (what I think was for me the first time) the experience "Since I Am, I have the right to be." (May et al., 1958)

This "I-Am" experience is not in itself a solution to an individual's problems. It is rather, the *precondition* for their solution. The patient above spent some two years

thereafter working through specific psychological problems, which she was now able to do on the basis of her experience of being.

This experience of being points also to the experience of *not being,* or nothingness. Nonbeing is illustrated in the threat of death, or destructive hostility, severe incapacitating anxiety, critical sickness, and so on. The threat of nonbeing is present in greater or lesser intensity, at all times. When we cross the street taking care to look both ways to guard against being struck by an automobile, when someone makes a remark that disparages us, or when we go into an examination ill-prepared—all of these represent the threat of nonbeing.

The "I-Am" experience, or the experience of being, is known in existential therapy as an "ontological" experience. This word comes from two Greek words, *ontos* meaning "to be" and *logical* meaning "the science of." Thus it is the "science of being." The term *ontological* is valuable in existential psychotherapy, as we shall see in the following discussion of anxiety.

Normal and neurotic anxiety

Existential therapists define anxiety more broadly than other psychotherapeutic groups. *Anxiety arises from our personal need to survive, to preserve our being, and to assert our being.* Anxiety shows itself physically in the faster beat of the heart, in the rising of blood pressure, the preparing of the skeletal muscles for fighting or fleeing, and most painful of all, the sense of apprehension within ourselves. Rollo May (1977) defines anxiety as, "the threat to our existence or to values we identify with our existence" (p. 205).

Anxiety is more basic than fear. In psychotherapy, one of our aims is to help the patient confront anxiety as fully as possible, thus reducing anxiety to fears, which are then objective and can be dealt with. But the main therapeutic function is to help the patient confront the normal anxiety which is an unavoidable part of the human condition.

Normal existential anxiety has three characteristics. First, it is proportionate to the situation confronted. Second, normal anxiety does not require repression: one can come to terms with it, such as in the fact that we all face eventual death. Third, such anxiety can be used creatively, for example as a stimulus to help identify and confront the dilemma out of which the anxiety arose.

Neurotic anxiety, on the other hand, is not appropriate to the situation. For example, parents may be so anxious that their child will be hit by a car that they never let the child go out of the house. Second, it is repressed, in the way most of us repress the fear of nuclear war. Third, neurotic anxiety is destructive, not constructive. Neurotic anxiety tends to paralyze the individual rather than stimulating creativity.

The function of therapy is *not* to do away with all anxiety. No person could survive completely without anxiety. The old cliché that mental health consists of living without anxiety is absurd. Mental health is living as much as possible without *neurotic* anxiety, but *with* the ability to tolerate the unavoidable existential anxiety of living.

Guilt and guilt feelings

The human experience of guilt has special meaning for the existential therapist. Guilt can, like anxiety, take both normal and neurotic forms. Neurotic guilt feelings (generally called guilt) often arise out of fantasized transgressions. Other forms of guilt, which we call normal guilt, sensitize us to the ethical aspects of our behavior.

Still another form of guilt is guilt toward one's self for failure to live up to our potentialities, for "forgetting being" as

Medard Boss puts it. The attitude toward such guilt in existential therapy is well illustrated in a case Medard Boss (1957b) cites of a severe obsessional-compulsive whom he treated. This patient, a physician suffering from hand washing compulsions, had gone through both Freudian and Jungian analyses. He had had for some time a recurrent dream involving church steeples, interpreted in the Freudian analysis in terms of phallic symbols and in the Jungian in terms of religious archetypal symbols. The patient could discuss these interpretations intelligently and at length, but his neurotic compulsive behavior, after temporary abeyance, continued as crippling as ever. During the first months of his analysis with Boss, the patient reported a recurrent dream in which he would approach a lavatory door which would always be locked. Boss confined himself only to asking each time why the door needed to be locked—to "rattling the doorknob," as Boss put it. Finally the patient had a dream in which he opened the door and found himself inside a church. He was waist deep in feces and was tugged by a rope wrapped around his waist leading up to the bell tower. The patient was suspended in such tension that he thought he would be pulled to pieces. He then went through a psychotic episode of four days during which Boss remained by his bedside, after which the analysis continued with an eventual successful outcome.

Boss (1957b) points out that the patient was guilty because he had locked up some essential potentialities in himself. *Therefore* he had guilt feelings. "If you lock up potentialities, you are guilty against (or indebted to, as the German word may be translated) what is given you in your origin, in your 'core.' In this existential condition of being indebted and being guilty, are founded all guilt feelings, in whatever thousand and one concrete forms and malformations they may appear in actuality." This is what had happened to the patient. He had locked up both the bodily and the spiritual possibilities of experience (what had been called the "drive" aspect and the "god" aspect, as Boss also phrases it). The patient had previously accepted the libido and archetype explanations and knew them all too well; but that is a good way, says Boss, to escape the whole thing. Because the patient did not accept and take into his existence these two aspects, he was guilty, indebted to himself. This was the origin of his neurosis and psychosis.

The three forms of world

Another basic concept in existential psychotherapy is what is called being-in-the-world. This is to say that we must understand the phenomenological world in which the patient now exists and participates.

A person's world cannot be comprehended by describing the environment, no matter how complex the description. The environment is only one mode of world. Even from a biological viewpoint, the biologist J. von Uexküll argues that one is justified in assuming as many environments as there are animals, depending on how the ant or the elephant or the fox participates in this environment. "There is not one space and time only," he goes on to say, "but as many spaces and times as there are subjects" (Von Uexküll, cited in May et al., 1958). How much more would it be true that the human being also has his own world? This confronts us with no easy problem: for we cannot describe world in purely objective terms, nor is world to be limited to our subjective, imaginative participation in the structure around us, although that too is part of being-in-the-world.

The human world is the structure of meaningful relationships in which a person exists and in the design of which, generally without realizing it, he participates. That is, the same past or present circumstances can mean very different things to different people. Thus, world includes the past events which condition each person's existence and all the vast variety of deterministic influences which operate upon one. But it is these *as one relates to them*, as one is aware of them, molds, constantly re-forms them. For to be aware of one's world means at the same time to be designing it, *constituting* one's world.

From the point of view of existential psychotherapy, there are three modes of world. The first is *Umwelt*, meaning "world around," the biological world, what is generally called the environment. The second is *Mitwelt*, literally the "with-world," the world of one's fellow men, one's community. The third is *Eigenwelt*, the "own-world," the mode of relationship to one's self.

The first, *Umwelt*, is the world of objects about us, the natural world. All organisms have an *Umwelt*. For animals and human beings the *Umwelt* includes biological needs, drives, instincts—the world we would exist in if, let us hypothesize, we had no self-awareness. It is the world of natural law and natural cycles, of sleep and awakeness, of being born and dying, desire and relief, the world of finiteness and biological determinism, to which each of us must in some way adjust. Existential analysts accept the reality of the natural world. "The natural law is as valid as ever," as Kierkegaard put it.

Strictly speaking, animals have an environment but human beings have a world. For world includes the structure of meaning designed by the interrelationship of the persons in it.

The *Eigenwelt*, or "own-world," is the mode which has been least adequately dealt with or understood in modern psychology and depth-psychology. Own-world presupposes self-awareness, self-relatedness, and is uniquely present in human beings. It is a grasping of what something in the world—this bouquet of flowers, this other person—means to me. D. T. Suzuki has remarked that in Eastern languages, such as Japanese, adjectives always include the implication of "for-me-ness." That is to say, "this flower is beautiful" means "for me this flower is beautiful."

One implication of this analysis of the modes of being in the world is that it gives us a basis for an understanding of love. The human experience of love obviously cannot be adequately described within the confines of *Umwelt*. One can never accurately speak of human beings as "sexual objects," as Alfred Kinsey, for one example, does; once a person is a sexual object, you are not talking about a person anymore. The interpersonal schools of personality theory, at home chiefly in *Mitwelt*, have dealt with love, as an interpersonal relationship, particularly in Harry Stack Sullivan's concept of the meaning of the word "chum," and in Erich Fromm's analysis of the difficulties of love in contemporary estranged society. But there is reason for doubting whether a theoretical foundation for going further is yet present in these or other schools. Without an adequate concept of *Umwelt*, love becomes empty of vitality, and without *Eigenwelt*, it lacks power and the capacity to fructify itself. The importance of *Eigenwelt* was stressed by Friedrich Nietzsche and Søren Kierkegaard, who continually insisted that to love presupposes that one must already have become the "true individual," the "Solitary One," the one who "has comprehended the deep secret that also in loving another person one must be sufficient unto oneself."

The significance of time

Existential psychotherapists are struck by the fact that the most profound human ex-

periences, such as anxiety, depression, and joy, occur more in the dimension of time than in space. Eugene Minkowski, a psychiatrist in Paris, has presented a case study which illustrates the time dimension. In his study of a depressed schizophrenic suffering under the delusion that he would be executed, Minkowski points out that the patient could not relate to time; that is, could not hope for the future, that every day was a separate island with no past and no future. The patient could not sense any continuity with tomorrow. Traditionally a psychiatrist would reason simply that the patient cannot relate to the future, cannot "temporize," *because* he has his delusion that he is going to be executed. Minkowski proposes the exact opposite. "Could we not," he asks, "on the contrary suppose *the more basic disorder is the distorted attitude toward the future*, while the delusion is only one of its manifestations?" (Minkowski cited in May et al., 1958, p. 66)

Minkowski goes on to consider this possibility in his case study. His original approach throws a beam of illumination on these dark, unexplored areas of time, and introduces a new freedom from the limits and shackles of clinical thought, in which time is bound only to the traditional conceptions. O. Hobart Mowrer (1950) held that "Time binding is the distinctive characteristic of human personality. That is, the capacity to bring the past into the present as part of the total causal nexus in which living organisms act and react, together with the capacity to act in the light of the long-term future—is 'the essence of mind and personality alike.' "

Existential therapists agree with Henri Bergson that "time is the heart of existence" and that our error in the modern day has been to think of ourselves primarily in terms of space, as though we were objects which could be located like substances at this spot or that. By this distortion we lose our genuine and real existential relation with ourselves, and indeed also with other persons around us. As a consequence of this overemphasis on spatialized thinking, says Bergson, "the moments when we grasp ourselves are rare, and consequently we are seldom free" (Bergson, cited in May et al., 1958, p. 56).

But in the with-world, the mode of personal relations and love, we can see particularly that quantitative time has much less to do with the significance of an occurrence. The nature or degree of one's love, for example, can never be measured by the number of years one has known the loved one. It is true, of course, that clock time has much to do with *Mitwelt*: many people sell their time on an hourly basis and daily life runs on schedules. We are referring rather to the inner meaning of the events. "No clock strikes for the happy one," says a German proverb. Indeed, the most significant events in a person's psychological existence are likely to be precisely the ones which are "immediate," breaking through the usual steady progression of time, like a sudden insight or a view of beauty that one sees in an instant, but which may remain in one's memory for days and months.

Finally, the *Eigenwelt*, the world of self-relatedness, self-awareness, and insight into the meaning of an event for one's self, has practically nothing whatever to do with clock time in which one hour routinely follows another. The essence of self-awareness and insight is that they are *there*—instantaneous and immediate—and the moment of awareness has its significance for all time. One can see this easily by noting what happens in one's self at the instant of an insight. The insight occurs with suddenness; it is born "whole," so to speak. One will discover that, though meditating on an insight for an hour or so

may reveal many of its further implications, the insight is not clearer—and disconcertingly enough, often not as clear—at the end of the hour as it was at the beginning.

Whether or not a patient can even recall the significant events of the past depends upon his decision with regard to the future. Every therapist knows that patients may bring up past memories *ad nauseam* without any memory ever moving them, the whole recital being flat, inconsequential, and tedious. From an existential point of view, the problem is not that these patients endured impoverished pasts; it is rather that they cannot or do not commit themselves to the present and future. Their past does not become alive because nothing matters enough to them in the future. Some hope and commitment to work toward changing something in the immediate future, be it overcoming anxiety or other painful symptoms or integrating one's self for further creativity, is necessary before any uncovering of his past by the patient will have reality.

Our human capacity to transcend the immediate situation

If we are to understand a given person as existing, dynamic, at every moment becoming, we cannot avoid the dimension of transcendence. Existing involves a continual emerging, in the sense of emergent evolution, a transcending of one's past and present in order to reach the future. Thus *transcendere*—literally "to climb over and beyond"—describes what every human being is engaged in doing every moment when not seriously ill or temporarily blocked by despair or anxiety. One can, of course, see emergent evolution in all life processes. Nietzsche has his old Zarathustra proclaim, "And this secret spake Life herself to me. 'Behold' said she, 'I am that which must ever surpass itself' " (cited in May et al., 1958, p. 72).

The neurobiological base for this capacity is classically described by Kurt Goldstein (cited in May et al., 1958, p. 72). He found that brain-injured patients—chiefly soldiers with portions of the frontal cortex shot away—had specifically lost the ability to abstract, to think in terms of "the possible." They were tied to any immediate concrete situation in which they happened to be. When their closets happened to be in disarray, they were thrown into profound anxiety and disordered behavior. They exhibited compulsive orderliness—which is a way of holding one's self at every moment rigidly to the concrete situation. When asked to write their names on a sheet of paper, they would typically write in the very corner, any venture out from the specific boundaries of the edges of the paper representing too great a threat. Goldstein held that the distinctive capacity of the normal human being is precisely this capacity to abstract, to use symbols, to orient one's self beyond the immediate limits of the given time and space, to think, in terms of "the possible." The injured, or "ill," patients were characterized by loss of range of possibility. Their world space was shrunk, their time curtailed, and they suffered a consequent radical loss of freedom.

We human beings possess the ability to transcend time and space by transporting ourselves back 2,000 years to ancient Greece, and we can watch the drama of Oedipus being performed in ancient Athens. We can instantaneously transport ourselves to the future, conceiving what life will be like in, say, the year 2500. These forms of transcendence are part and parcel of human consciousness. This capacity is exemplified in the human being's unique capacity to think and talk in symbols. Thus, to make promises presupposes conscious self-relatedness and is a very different thing from simple conditioned "social behavior," acting in terms

of the requirements of the group or herd or hive. Jean-Paul Sartre writes that dishonesty is a uniquely human form of behavior: "the lie is a behavior of transcendence," because to lie we must at the same moment *know* we are departing from the truth.

This capacity to transcend the immediate situation is not a "faculty" to be listed along with other faculties. It is rather given in the ontological nature of being human. To abstract, to objectivate, are evidences of it, but as Martin Heidegger puts it, "transcendence does not consist of objectivation, but objectivation presupposes transcendence" (cited in May et al., 1958, p. 75). The fact that the human being can be self-related gives him, as one manifestation, the capacity to objectify his world, to think and talk in symbols and so forth. This is Kierkegaard's point when he reminds us that to understand the self we must see clearly that "imagination is not one faculty on a par with others, but, if one would so speak, it is the faculty *instar omnium* (for all faculties). What feeling, knowledge, or will a man has depends in the last resort upon what imagination he has, that is to say, upon how these things are reflected. Imagination is the possibility of all reflection, and the intensity of this medium is the possibility of the intensity of the self" (Kierkegaard, 1954, p. 163).

Other Systems

First we shall consider the differences between existential theory and the theory of *behaviorism*. This radical distinction can be seen when we note the chasm between abstract truth and existential reality.

Kenneth W. Spence (1956) leader of one wing of behavior theory, wrote,

The question of whether any particular realm of behavior phenomena is more real or closer to real life and hence should be given priority in investigation does not, or at least should not, arise for the psychologist as scientist.

That is to say, it does not primarily matter whether what is being studied is real or not. What realms, then, should be selected for study? Spence gives priority to phenomena which lend themselves "to the degrees of control and analysis necessary for the formulation of abstract laws." Nowhere has this point been put more unabashedly and clearly than by Spence—what can be reduced to abstract laws is selected, and whether what is studied has *reality* or not is irrelevant to this goal. On the basis of this approach many an impressive system in psychology has been erected, with abstraction piled high upon abstraction—the authors succumbing, as we intellectuals are wont, to their "edifice complex" until an admirable and imposing structure is built. The only trouble is that the edifice has more often than not been separated from human reality in its very foundations.

The thinkers in the existential tradition held the exact opposite to Spence's view, and so do psychiatrists and psychologists in the existential psychotherapy movement. They insist that it is necessary and possible to have a science of man which studies human beings in their reality.

Orthodox Freudianism

Ludwig Binswanger and some other existential therapists came from training in Freudianism, but they differed from Freud in several important respects. One is the Freudian picture of the patient propelled by instincts and drives. As Sartre put it, Freudians, in their deterministic picture of mechanisms, have lost the man *to whom* these things happen.

The existentialists also question the Freudian view of the unconscious as a reservoir of tendencies, desires, and drives from which the motivation for behavior arises. This "cellar" view of the unconscious leads patients in therapy to avoid responsibility for their actions by such phrases as, "My unconscious did it, not I." Existentialists always insist that the patient in therapy accept responsibility for what he or she does, as put later in this chapter by asking such questions as, "Whose unconscious is it?"

The differences between existentialism and Freudianism are also seen in the modes of the world. The genius and the value of Freud's work lies in uncovering man in the mode of instincts, drives, contingency, and biological determinism. But traditional Freudianism has only a shadowy concept of the interrelation of persons as *subjects*.

The interpersonal school of psychotherapy

A consideration of the three modes of world discloses the differences between existential therapy and the interpersonal school, such as seen in the writings of Fromm and Sullivan. It is clear that the interpersonal schools do have a theoretical basis for dealing directly with *Mitwelt*. This is shown, to take only one example, in Sullivan's interpersonal theory. Though they should not be considered identical, *Mitwelt* and interpersonal theory have a great deal in common. The danger of this point, however, is that if *Eigenwelt*, one's "own-world," in turn is omitted, interpersonal relations tend to become hollow and sterile. Sullivan argued against the concept of individual personality and went to great efforts to define the self in terms of "reflected appraisal" and social categories; that is, the roles the person plays in the interpersonal world. Theoretically, this suffers from considerable logical inconsistency and indeed goes directly against other contributions of Sullivan. Practically, it tends to make the self a mirror of the group around one, to empty the self of vitality and originality, and to reduce the interpersonal world to mere "social relations." It opens the way to the tendency which is directly opposed to the goals of Sullivan and other interpersonal thinkers: namely, social conformity. At these points, existential therapy, with its emphasis on *Eigenwelt* differs from the interpersonal and cultural schools.

Jungian psychology

There are similarities between Jungianism and existential therapy. Medard Boss was a member for several years of the seminar which Jung called together in regular meetings at his house. But the main criticism existentialists make is that Jungianism too quickly avoids the immediate existential crises of the patients by leaping into theory. This is illustrated in Boss's case related in the section "Guilt and Guilt Feelings." Another patient who was afraid to go out of the house alone was analyzed by a Jungian therapist for half a dozen years, in the course of which the therapist interpreted several dreams as indicating, "God is speaking to you." The patient was flattered, but still couldn't go out of her house alone. She later was enabled to get over her crippling neurosis by an existential therapist who insisted that she could overcome her problem only if she actively *wanted* to, which was a way of insisting that she, not God, needed to take responsibility for her problem.

Client-centered approach

The difference between existentialism and Rogerian therapy is seen in some statements of Rollo May when he was acting as a judge of client-centered therapy in the client-centered experiment at the University of Wisconsin. Twelve outside experts were sent tapes of the therapy to listen to and to judge. Rollo May (1982) as one of the outside experts, reported that he often felt that there were not two distinct people in the room. When the therapist only reflects the patient's words, there transpires "only an amorphous kind of identity rather than two subjects interacting *in a world in which both participate, and in which love and hate, trust and doubt, conflicts and dependence, come out and can be understood and assimilated*" (p. 16). May was concerned that the therapist's over-identification with the patient could "take away the patient's opportunity to experience himself as a subject in his own right or to take a stand against the therapist, to experience being in an interpersonal world" (p. 16).

In spite of the fact that client-centered therapists, both individually and collectively, have advocated openness and freedom in the therapeutic relationship, the outside judges in the Wisconsin study concluded that "the therapist's rigid and controlling nature closed him off to many of his own as well as to the patient's experiences" (p. 16).

One of the Rogerian therapists, after experience as an independent therapist, wrote this criticism:

I used the early concept of the client-centered therapist to bolster the inhibition of my anger, my aggression, etc. I got some feedback at that time that it was difficult for people, because I was so nice, to tell me things that were *not* nice, and that it was hard for people to get angry at *me*. (Raskin, 1978, p. 367)

In other words, client-centered therapy is not fully existential in that it does not confront the patient directly and firmly.

HISTORY

Precursors

There are two streams in the history of human thought. One is of *essences*, seen most clearly in Plato's belief that there are in heaven perfect forms of everything, and the things on earth such as this chair or this pen are imperfect copies. These essences are clearest if we imagine mathematics: a perfect circle and a perfect square exist in heaven, of which our human circles and square are imperfect copies. This requires an abstraction which leaves the *existence* of the given individual thing out of the picture. For example, we can demonstrate simply that three apples added to three makes six. But this would be just as true if we substituted unicorns for apples. It makes no difference to the mathematical truth whether unicorns actually exist. That is to say, a proposition can be true without being real. Perhaps just because this approach has worked so magnificently in certain areas of science, we tend to forget that it necessarily involves a detached viewpoint and omits *the living individual.*

But there is another stream coming down through history: namely, *existence.* This viewpoint holds that truth depends upon the existing person, existing in a given situation (world) at that *time.* Hence the term *existential.* This is what Sartre meant in his famous statement, "Existence precedes essence." That is to say that the human being's awareness (i.e., his existence), precedes everything he has to say about the world around him.

Down through history, the existential tradition is exemplified in many thinkers. To mention only three: Augustine, who held that "Truth dwells in the inner man"; Duns Scotus who argued against Thomas Aquinas's rational essences, and insisted that human *will* must be taken as basic to any statement; and Blaise Pascal as in his famous statement, "the heart has its reasons which reason knows nothing of."

There remains in our day the chasm between truth and reality. And the crucial question which confronts us in psychology and other aspects of the science of man is precisely this chasm between what is abstractly true and what is existentially real for the given living person.

Beginnings

Kierkegaard, Nietzsche, and those who followed them accurately foresaw this growing split between truth and reality in Western culture, and they endeavored to call Western man back from the delusion that reality can be comprehended in an abstracted, detached way. Though they protested vehemently against arid intellectualism, they were by no means simple activists, nor were they antirational. Antiintellectualism and other movements in our day which make thinking subordinate to feeling must not be confused with existentialism. Either alternative—making man entirely subject or object—results *in losing the living, existing person.* Kierkegaard and the existential thinkers appealed to a reality underlying *both* subjectivity and objectivity. We must not only study a person's experience as such, they held, but even more we must study the man to whom the experience is happening, the one who is doing the experiencing.

It is by no means accidental that the greatest existentialists in the nineteenth century, Kierkegaard and Nietzsche, happen also to be among the most remarkable psychologists of all time. One of the contemporary leaders of existential philosophy, Karl Jaspers, was originally a psychiatrist and wrote a notable text on psychopathology. When one reads Kierkegaard's profound analyses of anxiety and despair or Nietzsche's amazingly acute insights into the dynamics of resentment and the guilt and hostility which accompany repressed emotional powers, one must pinch himself to realize that he is reading works written 75 and 100 years ago and not some new contemporary psychological analysis.

The existential therapists are centrally concerned with rediscovering the living person amid the compartmentalization and dehumanization of modern culture, and in order to do this they engage in depth psychological analysis. Their concern is not with isolated psychological reactions in themselves but rather with the psychological being of the living man who is doing the experiencing. That is to say, they use psychological terms with an ontological meaning.

The existential philosophers from whom the psychotherapists drew their principles included Martin Heidegger and Karl Jaspers in Germany; Jean-Paul Sartre and Gabriel Marcel in France, Nicolas Berdyaev, originally Russian but until his death a resident of Paris, and José Ortega y Gasset and Miguel de Unamuno y Jugo in Spain. Paul Tillich shows the existential approach in his work, and in many ways his book *The Courage to Be* (1952) is the best and most cogent presentation of existential philosophy as an approach to actual living available in English.

We have noted that existential therapy sprang up spontaneously in different parts of Europe and among different schools, and has a diverse body of researchers and creative thinkers.[1] There were psychiatrists

—Eugene Minkowski in Paris; Erwin Straus in Germany and then in America; V. E. von Gebsattel in Germany—who represent chiefly the first, or phenomenological, stage of this movement. There were Ludwig Binswanger, A. Storch, Medard Boss, G. Bally, and psychologists Roland Kuhn in Switzerland, J. H. Van Den Berg and F. J. Buytendijk in Holland, representing more specifically the second, or existential, stage. Von Gebsattel, Boss, and Bally are Freudian analysts; Binswanger, though in Switzerland, became a member of the Vienna Psychoanalytic Society at Freud's recommendation when the Zurich group split off from the International. Some of the existential therapists had also been under Jungian influence.

Current Status

Existential psychotherapy was introduced to the United States in 1958 with the publication of *Existence: A New Dimension in Psychiatry and Psychology*. This volume was edited by Rollo May, assisted by Ernest Angel and Henri Ellenberger. The main presentation and summary of existential therapy was in the first two chapters written by May "The Origins of the Existential Movement in Psychology," and the "Contributions of Existential Psychology." The remainder of the book is made up of essays and case studies by Henri Ellenberger, Eugene Minkowski, Erwin Straus, V. E. von Gebsattel, Ludwig Binswanger (two essays and a case study), and Ronald Kuhn. The first comprehensive textbook in existential psychiatry was by Irvin Yalom (1981) entitled *Existential Psychotherapy*.

The spirit of existential psychotherapy has never been for the formation of specific institutes because it deals with the *presuppositions underlying therapy of any kind*. Its concern was with the con-

---

1. In this orientation section we note the relation between existentialism and oriental thought as shown in the writings of Lao-tzu and Zen Buddhism. The similarities are striking. One sees this immediately in glancing at some quotations from Lao-tzu's *The Way of Life* (Bynner, 1946) "Existence is beyond the power of words to define: terms may be used but none of them is absolute." "Existence, by nothing bred, breeds everything, parent of the universe." "Existence is infinite, not to be defined; and though it seem but a bit of wood in your hand, to carve as you please, it is not to be lightly played with and laid down." "The way to do is to be." "Rather abide at the center of your being; for the more you leave it, the less you learn."

cepts about human beings and was not with specific techniques. This of course leads us to the dilemma in the situation that existential therapy has been quite influential but there are very few adequate training courses in this kind of therapy, simply because it is not a specific training in technique.

The founders of the existential movement believed and always stated that the specific training in techniques of therapy could be obtained at any number of schools of therapy, but the interested student was responsible to mold his or her own presuppositions in existential form.

Rollo May was an existentialist before he knew the word. That is, he found, growing up in the Middle West, that the existing person was the important consideration and not a theory *about* this person. He had argued, in his Ph.D. dissertation which was published under the title *The Meaning of Anxiety* in 1950, for a concept of normal anxiety as the basis for our theory of human beings. He had already, before his training in the William Alanson White Institute, experienced the futility of the orthodox practice of going to analysis five times a week for two years. He was trained as a psychoanalyst in the William Alanson White Institute, the Neo-Freudian Institute in New York, and was already a practicing analyst when he read in the early 50s about existential therapies in Europe. He felt these new concepts in existential psychology were the ones he needed but had, up till then, never been able to formulate.

The theme of the International Congress of Psychotherapy in 1958 in Barcelona, Spain, was "Existential Psychotherapy." Five hundred therapists, including such prominent psychiatrists as Medard Boss and Jacques Lacan, and a hundred therapists from the United States, attended this conference. Some present were trained in Freudianism, some Jungianism, some were from the William Alanson White Institute, but all paid tribute to the value of the insights and concepts of existential therapy.

The belief of the founders of existential psychotherapy is that its contributions will be absorbed into other schools of whatever persuasion. Fritz Perls, in the foreword of *Gestalt Therapy Verbatim* (1969), states quite accurately that Gestalt therapy is one form of existential psychotherapy. Therapists trained in different schools can legitimately call themselves existential if their assumptions are similar to those described in this chapter. Irvin Yalom was trained in the neo-Freudian tradition. Even such an erstwhile behavior therapist as Arnold Lazarus uses some existential presuppositions in his multimodal psychotherapy. All of this is possible because existential psychotherapy is a way of conceiving the human being. It goes deeper than the other forms of psychotherapy to emphasize the assumptions underlying all systems of psychotherapy.

Other related works are May's *The Meaning of Anxiety* (1977), *Man's Search for Himself* (1953) and *Existential Psychology*, (1961). Others are James Bugental's *The Search for Existential Identity* (1976); Medard Boss's, *The Analysis of Dreams* (1957a) and *Psychoanalysis and Daseinanalysis* (1982); and Viktor Frankl's, *Man's Search for Meaning* (1963). Helmut Kaiser has written valuably on existential therapy in his *Effective Psychotherapy* (1965). Leslie Farber (1966, 1976), Avery Weisman (1965), and Lester Havens (1974) have also contributed significantly to the existential literature.

PERSONALITY

Theory of Personality

Existential psychotherapy is a form of *dynamic psychotherapy*, which posits a dynamic model of personality structure. *Dynamic* is a commonly used term in psychology and psychotherapy. We often, for example, speak of the patient's "psychodynamics," or a "dynamic" approach to therapy. Dynamic has both lay and technical meanings and it is necessary to be precise about its meaning in the context of personality theory. In its lay meaning dynamic has the connotation of vitality; the word evokes such associations as dynamo, dynamite, a dynamic football player, or a dynamic political leader.

The technical meaning of dynamic relevant to personality theory refers to the concept of "force." Its use in personality theory was first invoked by Freud who viewed the personality as a system consisting of forces in conflict with one another. The resultant of this conflict is the constellation of emotions and behavior (both adaptive and pathological) that comprise personality. Furthermore (and this is an essential part of the definition), these forces in conflict *exist at different levels of awareness.* Indeed, some of the forces are entirely out of awareness and exist on an unconscious plane.

Thus, when we speak of the "psychodynamics" of an individual we refer to that individual's conflicting, conscious and unconscious forces, motives, and fears. "Dynamic psychotherapy" is psychotherapy based upon this dynamic model of personality structure.

There are many dynamic models of personality. To differentiate these various models and to define the existential model of personality structure we must ask: What is the *content* of the internal, conscious and unconscious struggle? Forces, motives, and fears conflict with one another within the personality. But which forces? Which motives? Which fears?

The existential view of the internal struggle can be made clearer by contrasting it with two other common dynamic views of personality: the Freudian model and the interpersonal (neo-Freudian) model.

The Freudian model of psychodynamics

The Freudian model posits that the individual is governed by innate instinctual forces which, like a fern frond, inexorably unfurl throughout the psychosexual developmental cycle. Freud postulated conflicts on several fronts: dual instincts collide with one another (ego instincts versus libido instincts in Freud's first theory or, in the second theory, Eros versus Thanatos); the instincts also collide with the demands of the environment and later the instincts collide with the superego (the internalized environment).

We can summarize the nature of the conflict in the Freudian dynamic model by stating that an instinctually driven being is at war with a world which prevents the satisfaction of these innate drives —primarily aggressive and sexual.

The interpersonal (neo-Freudian) model of psychodynamics

In the interpersonal model of personality (posited by theorists as Harry Stack Sullivan, Karen Horney, and Erich Fromm) the individual is not instinct guided and pre-programmed but is instead a being almost entirely shaped by the cultural and interpersonal environment. The child desperately requires acceptance and approval by the important survival figures surrounding him. But the child also has an inner press toward growth, mastery, and autonomy, and these tendencies are not always compatible with the demands of the major adults in the child's life. If the child is unlucky to have parents who are too caught up in their own neurotic struggles to be able to provide the child security *and* to encourage the child's autonomous development, then a conflict develops—a conflict between the need for security on the one hand and the child's natural growth inclinations on the other. In such a struggle growth is always compromised for the sake of security.

Existential psychodynamics

The existential model of personality rests on a different view of the content of the inner conflict. It postulates that the basic conflict is not with suppressed instinctual drives nor is it a conflict with the significant adults in the individual's early life; instead the conflict is between the individual and the "givens" of existence.

What are these "givens" of existence? The reflective individual can discover them without a great deal of effort. If we "bracket" the outside world, if we can put aside the busy, everyday concerns with which we ordinarily fill our lives and reflect deeply upon our situation in the world then we must confront certain "ultimate concerns" (to use Tillich's phrase) that are an inescapable part of the human being's existence in the world.

Yalom identifies four ultimate concerns that have considerable relevance for psychotherapy: *death, freedom, isolation,* and *meaninglessness* (1981). The individual's confrontation with each of these constitutes the content of the inner conflict from the existential frame of reference.

Death. Death is the most obvious, the most easily intuited ultimate concern. It is clearly apparent to all that we shall one day cease to be. Each individual learns that death will come and there is no escape. It is a terrible truth and at the deepest levels we respond to it with mortal terror. "Everything," as Spinoza (1954) states, "wishes to persist in its own being" (p. 6).

Thus from the existential point of view a core inner conflict is between the individual's awareness of inevitable death and the simultaneous wish to continue to live.

Death plays a major role in the individual's internal experience. It haunts the individual as nothing else. It rumples continuously under the membrane of life. The child at a much earlier age than is commonly thought is pervasively concerned with death and one of the child's major developmental tasks is to deal with the terror of obliteration.

To cope with this terror the individual erects defenses against death awareness. These defenses are denial based; they shape character structure and, if maladaptive, result in clinical syndromes. Psychopathology, to a very great extent, is the result of failed death transcendence; that is, symptoms and maladaptive character structure have their source in the individual terror of death.

Freedom. Ordinarily we do not think of freedom as a source of anxiety. Quite the contrary, freedom is generally viewed as an unequivocally positive concept. The history of Western civilization is punctuated by a yearning and striving toward freedom. Yet freedom in the existential frame of reference has a technical meaning—one which is riveted to dread.

In the existential frame of reference, freedom means that, contrary to everyday experience, the human being does not enter and ultimately exit from a structured universe with a coherent, grand design. Freedom refers to the fact that the human being is responsible for (i.e., is the author of) his own world, own life design, own choices and actions. The human being, as Sartre (1956) puts it, is "condemned to freedom" (p. 631). Rollo May (1981) holds that freedom, in order to be authentic, requires the individual to confront the limits of his destiny.

The existential position that the human being constitutes his own world has been percolating for a long time in philosophic thought. The heart of Kant's revolution in philosophy was his postulate that human consciousness, the nature of the human being's mental structures, provides the external form of reality. Kant (1967) stated that even space "is not something objective and real but something subjective and ideal; it is, as it were, a schema issuing by a constant law from the nature of the mind for the coordinating of all outer sensa" (p. 308).

This existential view of freedom has terrifying implications. If it is true, as philosophers such as Heidegger and Sartre argue, that we create our own selves and our own world then it also means that there is no ground beneath us: there is only an abyss, a void, nothingness.

An important internal dynamic conflict emanates from our confrontation with freedom: conflict issues from our awareness of freedom and of groundlessness on the one hand and, on the other hand, our deep need and wish for ground and structure.

The concept of freedom encompasses many themes which have profound implications for psychotherapy. The most apparent of these is *responsibility*. Individuals differ enormously in the degree of responsibility they are willing to accept for their life situation and differ in their modes of denying responsibility. For example, some individuals displace responsibility for their situation onto other people, onto life circumstances, onto bosses, spouses, and, when they enter treatment, transfer responsibility for their therapy to their psychotherapist. Other individuals deny responsibility by experiencing themselves as "innocent vic-

tims who suffer from a confluence of external events (and remain unaware that it is they themselves who have set these events into motion). Still others shuck responsibility by temporarily being "out of their minds"—they enter a temporary irrational state in which they are not accountable even to themselves for their behavior.

Another aspect of freedom is "willing." To be aware of responsibility for one's situation is to enter the vestibule of action or, in a therapy situation, of change. Willing represents the passage from responsibility to action. Willing, as May (1969) points out, consists first of wishing and then of deciding. Many individuals have enormous difficulties in experiencing or expressing a wish. Wishing is closely aligned to feeling and affect-blocked individuals cannot act spontaneously because they cannot feel and, thus, cannot wish. "Impulsivity" avoids wishing by failing to discriminate among wishes. Instead, individuals act impulsively and promptly on all wishes. "Compulsivity," another disorder of wishing, is characterized by individuals not pro-acting, but instead being driven by ego alien inner demands that often run counter to the individual's consciously held desires.

Once an individual fully experiences a wish, he or she is faced with decision. Many individuals can be extremely clear about what they wish but still not be able to decide or to choose. Often they experience a decisional panic; they may attempt to delegate the decision to someone else, or they act in such a way that the decision is made for them by circumstances which they, unconsciously, have brought to pass.

Isolation. A third ultimate concern is isolation. It is important to differentiate *existential* isolation from other types of isolation. *Interpersonal* isolation refers to the gulf that exists between oneself and other people—a gulf which results from deficient social skills and psychopathology in the sphere of intimacy. *Intrapersonal* isolation, a term first introduced by Freud, refers to the fact that we are isolated from parts of ourselves. Enclaves of self (of experience, affect, desire) are dissociated out of awareness and the goal of psychotherapy is to help the individual reclaim these split-off parts of self.

Existential isolation is a fundamental isolation from other individuals and from the world as well which cuts beneath other forms of isolation. No matter how closely we relate to another individual there remains a final unbridgeable gap. Each of us enters existence alone and must depart from it alone. Each individual in the dawn of consciousness, created a primary self ("transcendental ego") by permitting consciousness to curl back upon itself and to differentiate a self from the remainder of the world. Only after that does the individual, now "self-conscious," begin to constitute other selves. Beneath this act, as Mijuskovic (1979) notes, there is a fundamental loneliness; the individual cannot escape the knowledge that (1) he constitutes others and (2) he can never fully share his consciousness with others.

There is no stronger reminder of existential isolation than a confrontation with death. The individual who faces death invariably becomes acutely aware of isolation. Such a sequence is the theme of the medieval morality play, *Everyman.* Everyman is visited by the angel of death who informs him that he must take his final pilgrimage to God. Everyman pleads for more time but to no avail. Death informs him that he must make himself ready for the journey. Everyman then asks to be permitted to take companions on his trip. Death grants him that wish and the remainder of the play portrays Everyman's attempt to persuade others to accompany him on his journey. He appeals to a number of allegorical characters: fellowship, worldly goods, kindred, and knowledge. All refuse to accompany him and Everyman faces the terror of existential isolation. (Ultimately Everyman finds one companion, "good deeds," who is willing to take the journey with him. That is indeed the moral of the morality play: good works within the context of Christian faith provide a buttress against ultimate isolation.)

The third dynamic conflict, thus, is between the awareness of our fundamental isolation and the wish to be protected, to merge and to be part of a larger whole.

Fear of existential isolation (and the defenses against it) underlie a great deal of interpersonal psychopathology. This dynamic offers a powerful parsimonious explanatory system for the understanding of many miscarried interpersonal relationships—relationships in which one *uses* another for some function rather than *relates* to the other because he cares for the being of the other.

Although no relationship can eliminate isolation, it can be shared with another in such a way that the pain of isolation is assuaged. If one acknowledges one's isolated situation in existence and confronts it with resoluteness one will be able to turn lovingly toward others. If, on the other hand, the individual is overcome with dread in the face of isolation, he will not be able to turn toward others but instead will use others as a shield against isolation. In such instances relationships will not be true relationships at all but will be out of joint, miscarriages, distortions of what might have been an authentic relationship.

Some individuals (and this is particularly true of individuals with a borderline personality disturbance) experience panic when alone, emanating from a dissolution of one's ego boundaries. These individuals begin to doubt their own existence and believe that they exist only in the presence of another, that they exist only so long as they are responded to or are thought about by another individual.

Many attempt to deal with isolation through fusion: they soften their ego boundaries and become part of another individual. They avoid personal growth and the sense of isolation that accompanies growth. Fusion underlies the experience of being in love. The wonderful thing about romantic love is that the lonely "I" disappears into the "we." Others may fuse with a group, a cause, a country, a project. To be like everyone else—to conform in dress, speech, and customs, to have no thoughts or feelings that are different—saves one from the isolation of the lonely self.

Compulsive sexuality is also a common response to terrifying isolation. Promiscuous sexual "coupling" offers a powerful but temporary respite to the lonely individual. It is temporary because it is not relatedness but only a caricature of relationship. The sexually compulsive individual does not relate to the whole being of the other but relates only to the part of that individual which serves to meet his need. Sexually compulsive individuals do not know their partners; they show and see only those parts that facilitate seduction and the sexual act.

Meaninglessness. The fourth ultimate concern is meaninglessness. If each person must die, and each person constitutes his/her own world, and each is alone in an indifferent universe, then what possible meaning can life have? Why do we live? How shall we live? If there is no preordained design in life then each person must construct his own meaning in life. The fundamental question then becomes, "Is it possible that a self-created life meaning is sturdy enough to bear one's life?"

The human being appears to require meaning. Our perceptual neuropsychological organization is such that we instantaneously pattern random stimuli. We organize them automatically into figure and ground. When confronted with a broken circle we automatically perceive it as complete. When any situation or set of stimuli defies patterning we experience dysphoria which persists until we fit the situation into a recognizable pattern. In the same way the individual organizes random stimuli so too does he face his existential situation: in an unpatterned world the individual is acutely unsettled and searches for a pattern, an explanation, a meaning of existence.

A sense of life meaning is necessary for still another reason: from a meaning schema we generate a hierarchy of values. Values provide us with a blueprint for life conduct; values tell us not only *why* we live but *how* to live.

The fourth internal conflict stems from this dilemma: How does a being who requires meaning find meaning in a universe which has no meaning?

Variety of Concepts

The content of the internal conflict from the existential frame of reference consists of ultimate concerns and conscious and unconscious fears and motives spawned by them. The dynamic existential approach retains Freud's basic dynamic *structure* but has a radically different *content*. The old Freudian formula of:

DRIVE⟶ANXIETY⟶DEFENSE MECHANISM

is replaced in the existential system by:

**AWARENESS OF
ULTIMATE CONCERN⟶ANXIETY⟶DEFENSE MECHANISM**[2]

2. To Freud, anxiety is a signal of danger (i.e., if instinctual drives are permitted expression the organism becomes endangered; either the ego is overwhelmed or retaliation by the environment is inevitable). The defense mechanisms restrict direct expression of drives but provide indirect expression —that is, in displaced sublimated or symbolic form.

Both the Freudian system and the existential system place anxiety at the center of the dynamic structure. Anxiety fuels psychopathology: conscious and unconscious psychic operations (i.e., defense mechanisms) are generated to deal with anxiety; these psychic operations constitute psychopathology: though they provide safety they also restrict growth.

A very important difference between a Freudian and existential system is that Freud's sequence begins with "drive" whereas an existential framework begins with awareness. The existential frame of reference views the individual primarily as a fearful, suffering being rather than an instinctually driven one.

To an existential therapist anxiety springs from confrontation with death, groundlessness (freedom), isolation, and meaninglessness. The individual uses two types of defense mechanisms to cope with anxiety. The first, the conventional mechanisms of defense, thoroughly described by Sigmund Freud, Anna Freud, and Harry Stack Sullivan, defend the individual against anxiety regardless of source. The second are specific defenses which serve to cope with each of the specific primary existential fears.

For example, consider the individual's defense mechanisms for dealing with the anxiety emerging from death awareness.

Yalom (1981, p. 115) describes two major, specific intrapsychic defenses: an irrational belief in personal "specialness," and an irrational belief in the existence of an "ultimate rescuer." These defenses resemble delusions in that they are fixed, false beliefs. However they are not delusions in the pejorative sense, but are universally held irrational beliefs.

Specialness
The individual has a deep powerful belief in personal inviolability, invulnerability, and immortality. Although, at a rational level, he recognizes the foolishness of these beliefs, nonetheless, at a deeply unconscious level, the individual believes that the ordinary laws of biology do not apply to him.

No one has ever described this deep irrational belief in personal specialness more powerfully than Tolstoy who, through the lips of Ivan Ilych, says:

In the depth of his heart he knew he was dying, but not only was he not accustomed to the thought, he simply did not and could not grasp it.

The syllogism he had learnt from Kiezewetter's *Logic*: "Caius is a man, men are mortal, therefore Caius is mortal," had always seemed to him correct as applied to Caius, but certainly not as applied to himself. That Caius—man in the abstract—was mortal, was perfectly correct, but he was not Caius, not an abstract man, but a creature quite, quite separate from all others. He had been little Vanya, with a mamma and a papa, with Mitya and Volodya, with the toys, a coachman and a nurse, afterwards with Katenka and with all the joys, griefs, and delights of childhood, boyhood, and youth. What did Caius know of the smell of that striped leather ball Vanya had been so fond of? Had Caius kissed his mother's hand like that, and did the silk of her dress rustle so for Caius? Had he rioted like that at school when the pastry was bad? Had Caius been in love like that? Could Caius preside at a session as he did? "Caius really was mortal, and it was right for him to die; but for me, little Vanya, Ivan Ilych, with all my thoughts and emotions, it's altogether a different matter. It cannot be that I ought to die. That would be too terrible" (Tolstoy, 1960, p. 131).

If this defense is hypertrophied then the individual manifests one of a number of clinical syndromes: for example, the narcissistic character, the compulsive workaholic who is consumed by a search for glory, the self-aggrandizing, paranoid individual. The crisis in the lives of these individuals occurs when their belief system is shattered, and a sense of unprotected ordinariness intrudes. They frequently seek therapy when the defense of specialness no longer is able to ward off anxiety: for example, at times of severe illness or at the interruption of what had always appeared to be an eternal, upward spiral.

The belief in the existence of an ultimate rescuer

The other major mechanism of defense which serves to block death awareness is the individual's belief in a personal omnipotent servant which eternally guards him and protects his welfare, which may let him get to the edge of the abyss but will always bring him back. A hypertrophy of this particular mechanism of defense results in a characteristic clinical picture. A

character structure built around this motif displays passivity, dependency, and obsequiousness. Often such individuals dedicate their lives to locating and appeasing an ultimate rescuer. In Silvano Arieti's terms they live for the "dominant other" (1977, p. 864)—a life ideology that precedes and prepares the ground for clinical depression. These individuals may adapt well to life while basking in the presence of the dominant other but they decompensate and experience extraordinary distress at the loss of this dominant other.

Another major difference between the existential dynamic approach and other dynamic approaches lies in temporal orientation. The existential therapist works in the present tense. The individual is to be understood and to be helped to understand himself from the perspective of a here-and-now *cross section* not from the perspective of a historical *longitudinal section*. Consider the use of the word "deep." Freud always defined deep as "early" and so the deepest conflict meant the earliest conflict in the individual's life. Freud's psychodynamics are developmentally based. "Fundamental" or "primary" are to be grasped chronologically: each is synonymous with "first." Thus the "fundamental" sources of anxiety, for example, are considered to be the earliest calamities: separation and castration.

From the existential perspective, "deep" means the most fundamental concerns facing the individual at that moment. The past (i.e., one's memory of the past) is important only insofar as it is part of one's current existence and has contributed to one's current mode of facing ultimate concerns. The immediate, currently existing ground beneath all other ground is important from the existential perspective. Thus the existential conception of personality is in the awareness of the depths of one's immediate experiences. Existential therapy does not attempt to excavate and understand the past; instead it is directed toward the future becoming present and explores the past only as it throws light on the present. The therapist must continually keep in mind that we create our past, that our present mode of existence dictates what we choose to remember of the past.

PSYCHOTHERAPY

Theory of Psychotherapy

A substantial proportion of practicing psychotherapists consider themselves existentially (or "humanistically") oriented. Yet few, if any, have received any systematic training in existential therapy. One can be reasonably certain of this since there are few comprehensive training programs in existential therapy. Although many excellent books illuminate some aspect of the existential frame of reference (Becker, 1973; Bugental, 1965; May, 1953, 1977; May et al., 1958; Koestenbaum, 1978), Yalom's book (1981) is the first text which attempts to present a systematic, comprehensive view of the existential therapeutic approach.

When one asks existentially oriented therapists to describe their reasons for so labeling themselves, they describe not a system of psychotherapy but rather a mode of viewing the human being. Existential therapy is *not* a comprehensive psychotherapeutic system; it is a frame of reference—a paradigm in which one views and understands a patient's suffering in a particular manner.

The existential therapist begins with presuppositions about the sources of the patient's anguish and views the patient in human rather than behavioral or mechanistic terms. He may employ any of a large variety of techniques used in other approaches insofar as they are consistent with basic existential presuppositions and a human, authentic therapist-patient encounter.

The vast majority of experienced therapists, regardless of adherence to some particular ideological school, employ many existential insights and approaches. All competent therapists realize, for example, that an apprehension of one's finiteness can often catalyze a major inner shift of perspective, that it is the relationship that heals, that patients are tormented by choice, that a therapist must catalyze a patient's "will" to act, and that the majority of patients are bedeviled by a lack of meaning in their lives.

It is also true that the therapist's belief system determines the type of clinical data which he or she encounters. Therapists subtly or unconsciously cue patients to provide them with certain material. Jungian patients have Jungian dreams. Freudian patients discover themes of castration, anxiety, and penis envy. The therapist's perceptual system is affected by his ideological system. He "tunes in" to the material which he wishes to obtain. So too with the existential approach. If the therapist tunes his mental apparatus to the right channel it is astounding how frequently patients discuss concerns emanating from existential conflicts.

The basic approach in existential therapy is strategically similar to other dynamic therapies. The therapist assumes that the patient experiences anxiety which issues from some existential conflict which is at least partially unconscious. The patient handles anxiety by a number of ineffective, maladaptive defense mechanisms which may provide temporary respite from anxiety but ultimately so cripple the individual's ability to live fully and creatively that these defenses merely result in still further secondary anxiety.

The therapist assists the patient to embark on a course of self-investigation in which the goals are to understand the unconscious conflict, to identify the maladaptive defense mechanisms, to discover their destructive influence, to diminish secondary anxiety by correcting these heretofore restrictive modes of dealing with self and others, and to develop other ways of coping with primary anxiety.

Although the basic strategy in existential therapy is similar to other dynamic therapies, the content is radically different. In many respects, the process differs as well; the existential therapist's different mode of understanding the patient's basic dilemma results in many differences in the strategy of psychotherapy. For example, since the existential view of personality structure emphasizes the depth of experience at any given moment, the existential therapist does not spend a great deal of time in therapy helping the patient to recover a personal past. The existential therapist strives for understanding, but for an understanding of the patient's *current* life situation and *current* enveloping unconscious fears. The existential therapist believes, as do other dynamic therapists, that the nature of the therapist-client relationship is fundamental in good psychotherapeutic work. However the accent is not on transference; that is, on how the current relationship helps the patient to understand earlier relationships but instead upon the relationship as fundamentally important in itself.

Process of Psychotherapy

Each of these ultimate concerns (death, freedom, isolation, and meaninglessness) has its own implications for the process of therapy. Let us, for expository purposes, examine the practical, therapeutic impli-

cations of the ultimate concern of freedom. One of the major components of freedom is "responsibility"—a concept that deeply influences the existential therapist's therapeutic approach.

Sartre equates responsibility to authorship: to be responsible means to be the author of one's own life design. The existentially oriented therapist continually focuses upon each patient's responsibility for his or her own distress. It is not bad genes or bad luck that causes a patient to be lonely or chronically abused or neglected by others or an insomniac. Until the patient realizes that he is responsible for his own condition there is little motivation to change. If the patient continues to believe that distress is caused by others, by anything outside himself, why bother to invest energy in changing himself?

The therapist must be attentive to identify methods and instances of responsibility avoidance and then make these known to the patient. Therapists may use a wide variety of techniques to focus the patient's attention on responsibility. Many therapists interrupt the patient whenever they hear the patient avoiding responsibility. When patients say they "can't" do something the therapist immediately comments "you mean you 'won't' do it." As long as one believes in "can't," one remains unaware of one's active contribution to one's situation. Such therapists encourage patients to "own" their feelings and statements and actions. If a patient comments that he did something "unconsciously" the therapist might inquire "whose unconscious is it?" The general principle is obvious: whenever the patient laments about his or her life situation the therapist inquires how the patient created that situation.

Often it is helpful to keep the patient's initial complaint in mind and then, at appropriate points in therapy, juxtapose these initial complaints with the patient's in-therapy behavior. For example, consider a patient who sought therapy because of feelings of isolation and loneliness. During the course of therapy the patient expressed at great length his sense of superiority and his scorn and disdain of others. These attitudes were egosyntonic and rigidly maintained; the patient manifested great resistance to examining, much less changing these opinions. The therapist helped this patient to understand his responsibility for his personal predicament by reminding the patient, whenever he discussed his scorn of others, "and you are lonely."

Responsibility is one component of freedom. Earlier we described another, "willing," which, for expository purposes, may be further subdivided into "wishing" and "deciding." Consider the role in the process of therapy of "wishing." How often does the therapist participate with a patient in some such sequence as this:

"What shall I do? What shall I do?"

"What is it that stops you from doing what you want to do?"

"But I don't *know* what I want to do! If I knew that I wouldn't need to see you!"

These patients actually know what they should do, ought to do, or must do but do not experience what they *want* to do. Many therapists, in working with patients who have a profound incapacity to wish, have shared May's (1969) inclination to shout "Don't you ever *want* anything?" (p. 165). These patients have enormous social difficulties since they have no opinions, no inclinations, and no desires of their own.

Often the inability to wish is imbedded in a more global disorder—the inability to feel. For many patients the bulk of psychotherapy consists in helping to dissolve the patient's affect block. This therapy is slow and grinding: above all the therapist must persevere and time after time must continue to press the patient with "What do you feel?" "What do you want?" Repeatedly the therapist will need to explore the source and nature of the block and of the stifled feelings behind it.

Many therapists have attempted to dynamite the affect block with dramatic breakthrough efforts (for example, emotional flooding, primal scream, implosion therapy, intense feeling therapy, Gestalt therapy). The inability to feel and to wish is a pervasive characterological trait and considerable time and therapeutic perseverance are required to effect enduring change.

There are other modes of avoiding wishing in addition to blocking of affect. Some individuals avoid wishing by not discriminating among wishes, acting impulsively on all wishes. In such instances, the therapist must help the patient to make some internal discrimination among wishes and assign priorities to each. The patient must learn that two wishes which are mutually exclusive demand that one be relinquished. If, for example a meaningful, loving relationship is a wish, then a host of conflicting interpersonal wishes —such as the wish for conquest or power or seduction or subjugation—must be denied.

Decision is the bridge between wishing and action and some patients, even though they are able to wish, are still unable to act because they cannot *decide*. One of the more common reasons that deciding is difficult is that every "yes" involves a "no": renunciation invariably accompanies decision and a decis on requires a relinquishment of other options—often options that may never come again. There are other patients who cannot decide because a major decision makes them more aware of the degree to which they constitute their own lives. Thus a major irreversible decision is a boundary situation in the same way that awareness of death may be a boundary situation.

The therapist must help patients to begin to make choices. A useful strategy is to help patients consider the options available to them. The therapist must help patients recognize that they themselves, not the therapist, generate and choose from among options. In helping patients to communicate effectively, therapists teach that one must "own" one's feelings. It is equally important that one owns one's decisions. Some patients are panicked by the various implications of each decision. The "what ifs" torment them. *What if I leave my job and can't find another? What if I leave my children alone and they get hurt?* It is often useful to ask the patient to consider the entire scenario of each "what if" in turn, to fantasize it happening with all the possible ramifications and then to experience and analyze emerging feelings.

A general posture toward decision making is to assume that the therapist's task is not to *create* will but instead to *disencumber* it. The therapist cannot flick the decision switch or inspirit the patient with resoluteness. But the therapist can influence the factors that influence willing. After all, no one has a congenital inability to decide. Decision making is blocked by obstacles and it is the therapist's task to help remove obstacles. Once that is done the individual will naturally move into a more autonomous position just as Karen Horney (1950) put it, an acorn develops into an oak tree.

The therapist must help patients understand that decisions are unavoidable. One makes decisions all the time and often conceals from oneself that one is deciding. It is important to help patients understand the inevitability of decisions and to

identify how they make decisions. Many patients decide *passively* by, for example, letting another person decide for them. They may, for example, terminate an unsatisfactory relationship by unconsciously acting in such a way that the partner makes the decision to terminate the relationship. In such instances the final outcome (i.e., the dissolution of the relationship) is achieved, but the patient may be left with many negative repercussions. The patient's sense of powerlessness is merely reinforced and he continues to experience himself as one to whom things happen rather than being the author of his own life situation. The *way* one makes a decision is often as important as the content of the decision. An active decision reinforces the individual's active acceptance of his own power and resources.

Mechanisms of Psychotherapy

We can best understand the mechanisms of the existential approach by considering the therapeutic leverage inherent in some of the ultimate concerns.

Death and psychotherapy

There are two distinct ways in which the concept of death plays an important role in psychotherapy. First, an increased awareness of one's finiteness stemming from a personal confrontation with death may cause a radical shift in life perspective and lead to personal change. Second, the concept that death is a primary source of anxiety has many important implications for therapy.

Death as a boundary situation. A "boundary situation" is a type of urgent experience which propels the individual into a confrontation with an existential situation. The most powerful boundary situation is confrontation with one's personal death; such a confrontation has the power to provide a massive shift in the way that one lives in the world. There are innumerable examples both from great literature and from clinical work with dying patients which illustrate this principle (Yalom, 1981, p. 160).

Yalom (1981) reports a number of important personal changes that have occurred to cancer patients who confront their own deaths (p. 161). Some patients report that they learn simply that "existence cannot be postponed." They no longer postpone living until some time in the future; they realize that, in fact, one can really live only in the present. The neurotic individual rarely lives in the present: either continuously obsessed with events from the past or fearful of anticipated events in the future but never living fully in the immediate moment.

A confrontation with a boundary situation persuades individuals to count their blessings, to become aware of their natural surroundings: the elemental facts of life, changing seasons, seeing, listening, touching, and loving. Ordinarily what we *can* experience is diminished by petty concerns or by thoughts of what we cannot do or what we lack or by threats to our prestige.

Many terminally ill patients when reporting personal growth emanating from their confrontation with death have lamented, "what a tragedy that we had to wait till now, till our bodies were riddled with cancer to learn these truths." This is an exceedingly important message for therapists. The therapist can obtain considerable leverage to help "everyday" patients (i.e., patients who are not physically ill) increase their awareness of death earlier in their life cycle. With this aim in mind some therapists have employed structured exercises, that is, some artificial aid to confront the individual with personal death. There are many death awareness workshops reported in the literature (Yalom, 1981, p. 174). Some group leaders begin a brief group experience by asking members to write their own epitaph or obituary or they provide guided fantasies in which group members imagine their own death and funeral. The National Training Laboratory has offered a life cycle group experience in which participants spend time living, talking, and dressing like old people. They visit a local cemetery. They imagine their own dying, death, and funeral.

Many existential therapists do not believe that artificially introduced death confrontations are necessary or advisable. Instead they attempt to help the patient recognize the signs of mortality that are part of the fabric of everyday life. If the therapist, and consequently the patient, are "tuned-in," then there is considerable evidence of death anxiety in every course of psychotherapy. Every patient suffers losses through death of parents, friends, and associates. Dreams are haunted with death anxiety. Every nightmare is a dream of raw death anxiety. Everywhere around us there are reminders of aging: our bones begin to creak, senile plaques appear on our skin, we go to reunions and note with dismay how everyone *else* has aged. Our children grow up. The cycle of life envelops us.

An important opportunity for confrontation with death arises when the patients experience the death of someone close to them. The traditional literature on grief primarily focuses on two aspects of grief work: loss and the resolution of ambivalence which so strongly accentuates the dysphoria of grief. But a third dimension must be considered: the death of someone close to us confronts us with our own death. This is of course the point that John Donne made in the well-known lines: "and therefore never send to know for whom the bell tolls. It tolls for thee" (Donne, 1952, p. 332).

Often grief has a very different tone depending upon the individual's relationship with the person who has died. The loss of a parent confronts us with our vulnerability: if our parents could not save themselves, who will save us? When parents die, nothing remains between ourselves and the grave. At the moment of our parents' death, we ourselves constitute the barrier between our own children and their death.

The death of a spouse often evokes the fear of existential isolation. The loss of the significant other increases our awareness that, try as hard as we can to go through the world two by two, there is nonetheless a basic aloneness that we must bear. Yalom (1981) reports a patient's dream the night after learning that his wife had inoperable cancer:

I was living in my old house in _____ [a house that had been in the family for three generations]. A Frankenstein monster was chasing me through the house. I was terrified. The house was deteriorating, decaying. The tiles were crumbling and the roof leaking. Water leaked all over my mother. [His mother had died six months ago.] I fought with him. I had a choice of weapons. One had a curved blade with a handle, like a scythe. I slashed him and tossed him off the roof. He lay stretched out on the pavement below. But he got up and once again started chasing me through the house. (p. 168)

The patient's first association to this dream was "I know I've got a hundred thousand miles on me." Obviously his wife's impending death reminded him that his life and his body (symbolized in the dream by the deteriorating house) were also finite. As a child this patient was often haunted by the monster who returned in this nightmare.

Children try many methods of dealing with death anxiety. One of the most common is the personification of death—the imagining of death as some finite creature, a monster, a sandman, a boogey man, and so on. This is, of course, very frightening to a child but nonetheless far less frightening than the truth—that they carry the spores of their own death within them. If death is "out there" in some physical form then possibly it may be eluded, tricked, or pacified.

Another opportunity for the therapist to focus the patient on existential facts of life is the occurrence of milestones. Even simple milestones such as birthdays and anniversaries are useful levers. These signs of passage are often capable of eliciting pain (consequently for that reason we often deal with such milestones by reaction formation, in the form of a joyous celebration).

Major life events such as a threat to one's career, a severe illness, retirement, commitment to a relationship, and separation from a relationship are important boundary situations and offer opportunities for an increased awareness of death anxiety. Often these experiences are painful and the therapist feels compelled to focus entirely on pain alleviation. In so doing, however, one misses rich opportunities for deep therapeutic work which reveal themselves at those moments.

Death as a primary source of anxiety. The fear of death constitutes a primary fount of anxiety: it is present early in life, it is instrumental in shaping character structure, and it continues throughout life to generate anxiety that results in manifest distress and in the erection of psychological defenses. However, it is important to keep in mind that death anxiety, despite the fact that it is ubiquitous and has pervasive ramifications, exists at the very deepest levels of being, is heavily re-pressed, and is rarely experienced in its full sense. Often death anxiety per se is not easily visible in the clinical picture. It often does not become an explicit theme in therapy, especially in brief therapy. There are other patients, however, who are suffused with overt death anxiety at the very onset of therapy. There are often life situations in which the patient has such a rush of death anxiety that the therapist cannot evade the issue. In very long-term, intensive therapy explicit death anxiety is always to be found and must be con-sidered in the therapeutic work.

In the existential framework anxiety is so riveted to existence that it has a dif-ferent connotation from the way that "anxiety" is regarded in other therapeutic frames of reference. The existential thera-pist hopes to alleviate crippling levels of anxiety but not to eliminate it. Life cannot be lived (nor can death be faced) without anxiety. The therapist's task as May re-minds us (1977, p. 374) is to reduce anxiety to tolerable levels and then to use the anxiety constructively: as a guide and as a mode of increasing a patient's awareness and vitality.

It is important to keep in mind that, even though death anxiety may not ex-plicitly enter the therapeutic dialogue, a theory of anxiety based on death aware-ness may provide the therapist with a frame of reference, an explanatory system, that greatly enhances the therapist's effectiveness. Therapists, as well as patients, seek to order events into some type of coherent sequence. Once that is done the therapist begins to experience a sense of control and a sense of mastery which allows him to organize clinical material. The therapist's self-confidence and sense of mastery will help patients develop trust and confidence in the therapy process—an essential condition

of therapy. Furthermore, the therapist's belief system often serves to keep the patient and therapist cemented to one another while the real agent of change, the therapeutic relationship, germinates and matures.

The therapist's belief system provides a certain consistency. It permits the thera-pist to know what to explore so that the patient does not become confused. Al-though the therapist may not make full explicit interpretations about the un-conscious roots of a patient's problem the therapist may, with subtlety and good timing, make comments that at an un-spoken level "click" with the patient's un-conscious and allow the patient to feel understood.

Existential isolation and psychotherapy

Patients discover in therapy that though interpersonal relationships may temper isolation they cannot eliminate it. Patients who grow in psychotherapy learn not only the rewards of intimacy but also its limits: they learn what they *cannot* get from others. An important step in treatment consists of helping patients address existential isolation directly, to plunge into feelings of lostness and loneliness. Yet those who have lacked sufficient ex-periences of closeness and true relatedness in their lives are particularly incapable of tolerating isolation. Otto Will[3] made the point that adolescents from loving, sup-portive families are able to grow away from their families with relative ease and to tolerate the separation and loneliness of young adulthood. On the other hand those who grow up in tormented, highly conflicted families find it extremely dif-ficult to leave the family. One might expect

3. Oral communication. Child psychiatry Grand Rounds. Stanford University, Department of Psychiatry, 1978.

these individuals would kick up their heels with joy at the prospect of dancing away from such a family but the opposite occurs: the more disturbed the family the harder it is for progenies to leave—they are ill equipped to separate and therefore cling to the family for shelter against isolation and anxiety.

Many patients have enormous difficulty spending time alone. Consequently they construct their lives in such a way that they eliminate "alone" time. One of the major problems that ensues from this is the desperation with which they seek certain kinds of relationships. In one way or another they do not relate to or love another person but instead use another person to avoid some of the pain accompanying isolation. The therapist must find a way to help the patient confront isolation in a dosage and with a support system suited to that patient. Some therapists, at an advanced stage of therapy, advise or prescribe periods of self-enforced isolation during which the patient is asked to monitor and record thoughts and feelings.

Meaninglessness and psychotherapy

To deal effectively with meaninglessness, therapists must first increase their sensitivity to the topic, listen differently, and become aware of the importance of meaning in the lives of individuals. For some patients the issue is not crucial but for others the sense of meaninglessness is profound and pervasive. Carl Jung (1966) once estimated that over 30 percent of his patients seek therapy because of a sense of personal meaninglessness (p. 83).

The therapist must be attuned to the overall focus and direction of the patient's life. Is the patient reaching beyond himself or herself? Or is he or she entirely immersed in the daily routine of staying alive? Yalom (1981) reports that he has treated many young adults who are immersed in a California singles' lifestyle, characterized to a large extent by sensuality, sexual clamor and pursuit of prestige and materialistic goals. He noted that his therapy was rarely successful unless he was able to help patients focus on something beyond these pursuits (May, 1969, p. 165). Simply by increasing the sensitivity of patients to these issues the therapist can help them focus on values outside of themselves. Therapists, for example, can begin to wonder about the patient's belief systems, inquire deeply into the loving of another, ask about long-range hopes and goals, explore creative interests and pursuits.

Viktor Frankl (1969) who placed great emphasis on the importance of meaninglessness in contemporary psychopathology stated that "happiness cannot be pursued, it can only ensue" (p. 165).

The more we deliberately search for self-satisfaction the more it eludes us, whereas the more we fulfill some self-transcendent meaning the more happiness will ensue. Frankl suggested that this means that some patients must be helped to take their gaze off themselves; that is, some patients must be helped in the process of "dereflection."

Therapists must find a way to help such patients develop curiosity and concern for others. The therapy group is especially well suited for this endeavor: the pattern in which self-absorbed narcissistic patients "take without giving" often becomes highly evident in the therapy group. In such instances therapists may attempt to increase an individual's ability and inclination to empathize with others by requesting, periodically, that patients guess how others are feeling at various junctures of the group.

But the major solution to the problem of meaninglessness is engagement.

Wholehearted engagement in any of the infinite array of life's activities enhances the possibility of one's patterning the events of one's life in some coherent fashion. To find a home, to care about other individuals, about ideas or projects, to search, to create, to build—these and all other forms of engagement are twice rewarding: they are intrinsically enriching, and they alleviate the dysphoria that stems from being bombarded with the unassembled brute data of existence.

The therapist must approach engagement with the same attitudinal set that he approached wishing. The therapist cannot create engagement or inspirit the patient with engagement. That is not necessary: the desire to engage life is always there with the patient and therefore the therapist's activity should be directed toward the removal of obstacles in the patient's way. The therapist begins to explore what prevents the patient from loving another individual. Why does he obtain so little satisfaction from his relationship with others? Why is there so little satisfaction from work? What blocks the patient from finding work that is commensurate with his or her talents and interests or finding some pleasurable aspects of current work? Why has the patient neglected creative or religious or self-transcendent strivings?

APPLICATIONS

Problems

The clinical setting often determines the applicability of the existential approach. In each course of therapy the therapist must consider the goals appropriate to the clinical setting. To take one example, in an acute inpatient setting where the patient will be hospitalized for approximately one to two weeks the goal of therapy is crisis intervention. The therapist hopes to alleviate symptoms and to restore the patient to a precrisis level of functioning. Deeper, more ambitious goals (including the goal of increasing the patient's awareness of existential conflicts) are unrealistic and inappropriate to that situation.

In situations where patients desire not only symptomatic relief but also hope to attain greater personal growth, the existential approach is generally useful. A thorough existential approach with ambitious goals is most appropriate in long-term therapy but even in briefer approaches some aspect of the existential mode (e.g., an emphasis on responsibility assumption, deciding, an authentic therapist-patient encounter, grief work, and so on) is often incorporated into the therapy.

An existential approach to therapy is much more obviously appropriate with patients who confront some boundary situation, that is, a confrontation with death, the facing of some important irreversible decision, a sudden thrust into isolation, milestones which mark passages from one life era into another (e.g., as children leaving home and the empty nest feeling, retirement, career failure, marital separation and divorce, major physical illness). But therapy need not be limited to these more explicit existential crises. In every course of therapy, as we have indicated earlier, there is abundant evidence of patients' anguish stemming from existential conflicts. The availability of this data is entirely a function of the therapist's attitudinal set and perceptivity. The decision to work on these levels is one that should be a joint patient-therapist decision.

Evaluation

Psychotherapy evaluation is always a difficult task. As a general rule, the more focused and specific the approach and the goals, the easier is it to measure outcome. Symptomatic relief or behavioral change may be quantified with reasonable precision. But more ambitious therapies, such as the existential approach, which seek to affect deeper layers of the individual's mode of being in the world, defy quantification, and outcome assessment of these therapies must be based on a thorough self-report.

These problems of evaluation are illustrated by the following vignettes reported by Yalom (1981, p. 336).

A 46-year-old mother took the youngest of her four children to the airport where he departed for college. She had spent the last 26 years rearing her children and longing for this day. No more impositions, no more incessantly living for others, no more cooking dinners, and picking up clothes. Finally she was free.

Yet as she said goodbye she unexpectedly began sobbing loudly and on the way home from the airport a deep shudder passed through her body. "It is only natural," she thought. It was only the sadness of saying goodbye to someone she loved very much. But it was much more than that and the shudder soon turned into raw anxiety. The therapist whom she consulted identified it as a common problem: "the empty nest" syndrome. Of course she was anxious. How could it be otherwise? For years she had based her self-esteem on her performance as a mother and suddenly she found no way to validate herself. The whole routine and structure of her life had been altered. Gradually with the help of Valium, supportive psychotherapy, an assertiveness training group, several adult education courses, a lover or two, and a part-time volunteer job the shudder shrunk to a tremble and then vanished. She returned to her premorbid level of comfort and adaptation.

This patient happened to be part of a psychotherapy research project and there were outcome measures of her psychotherapy. Her treatment results could be described as excellent on each of the measures used—symptom checklists, target problem evaluation, self esteem. Obviously she had made considerable improvement. Yet, despite this, it is entirely possible to consider this case as one of missed therapeutic opportunities.

Consider another patient in almost precisely the same life situation. In the treatment of this second patient the therapist, who was existentially oriented, attempted to nurse the shudder rather than to anesthetize it. This patient experienced what Kierkegaard called "creative anxiety" and the therapist and the patient allowed the anxiety to lead them into important areas for investigation. True, this patient suffered from the "empty nest" syndrome; she had problems of self-esteem; she loved her child but also envied him for the chances in life she had never had (and, of course, she felt guilty because of these "ignoble" sentiments).

The therapist did not simply allow her to find ways to help her fill her time but plunged into an exploration of the *meaning* of the fear of the empty nest. She had always desired freedom but now seemed terrified of it. Why?

A dream illuminated the meaning of the shudder. The dream consisted simply of herself holding in her hand a 35-mm photographic slide of her son juggling and tumbling. The slide was peculiar, however, in that it showed movement; she saw her son in a multitude of positions all at the same time. In the analysis of the dream her associations revolved around the theme of time. The slide captured and framed time and movement. It kept everything alive but made everything stand still. It froze life. "Time moves on," she said, "and there's no way I can stop it. I didn't want John to grow up . . . whether I like it or not time moves on. It moves on for John and it moves on for me as well."

This dream brought her own finiteness into clear focus and, rather than rush to fill time in with various distractions, she learned to appreciate time in life in richer ways than previously. She moved into the realm that Heidegger described as authentic being: she wondered not so much at the *way* things are but *that* things are. Although one could argue that therapy helped the second patient more than the first it would not be possible to demonstrate this conclusion on any standard outcome measures. In fact, the second patient probably continued to experience more anxiety than the first did; but anxiety is a part of existence and no individual who continues to grow and create will ever be free of it.

Treatment

Existential therapy has its primary applications in an individual therapy setting. However, various existential themes and insights may be successfully applied in a variety of other settings including group therapy, family therapy, couples therapy, and so forth.

The concept of responsibility has particularly widespread applicability. It is a keystone of the group therapeutic process. Group therapy is primarily based on interpersonal therapy; the group therapeutic format is an ideal arena to examine and correct maladaptive interpersonal modes of behavior. However, the theme of responsibility underlies much of the interpersonal work. Consider, for example, the following sequence through which group therapists, explicitly or implicitly, attempt to guide their patients:

1. *Patients learn how their behavior is viewed by others.* (Through feedback from other group members patients learn to see themselves through others' eyes.)

2. *Patients learn how their behavior makes others feel.* (Through members' sharing their personal affective responses to one another.)

3. *Patients learn how their behavior creates the opinions others have of them.* (By sharing here and now feelings, members learn that, as a result of their behavior, others develop certain opinions and views of them.)

4. *Patients learn how their behavior influences their opinions of themselves.* (The information gathered in the first three steps leads to the patient formulating certain kinds of self-evaluations.)

Each of these four steps begins with the patient's own behavior which underscores the patient's own role in shaping his interpersonal relations; the end point of this sequence is that each group member begins to apprehend that he is himself responsible for how others treat him and that furthermore he is responsible for the way in which he begins to regard himself.

This is one of the most fascinating aspects of group therapy: all the members are "born" simultaneously. Each starts out in the group on an equal footing. Each gradually scoops out and shapes a particular life space in the group. Thus each person is responsible for the interpersonal position he scoops out for himself in the group (and, by analogy, in life as well). The therapeutic work in the group then not only allows individuals to change their way of relating to one another but also brings home to them in a powerful way the extent to which they have created their own life predicament—clearly an existential therapeutic mechanism.

Often the therapist uses his own feelings to identify the patient's contribution to his or her life predicament. For example, a depressed 48-year-old woman complained bitterly about the way her children treated her: they dismissed her opinions, were impatient with her, and, when some serious issue was at stake, addressed their comments to their father. When the therapist tuned in to his feelings about this patient he became aware of a whining quality in her voice which tempted *him* not to take her seriously and to regard her somewhat as a child. He shared his feelings with the patient and it proved enormously useful to her. She became aware of her childlike behavior in many areas and began to realize that her children treated her precisely as she "asked" to be treated (i.e., asked non-verbally through whining, through her excuses based on weakness, and through her depression and posture of help-lessness).

Not infrequently therapists must treat patients who are panicked by a decisional crisis. Yalom (1981) describes the thera-peutic approach in such a situation. The therapist's basic strategy consisted of help-ing the patient uncover and appreciate the existential, subterranean implications of the decision. The patient was a 66-year-old widow who sought therapy because of her anguish about a decision to sell a summer home (p. 336). The house (approximately 150 miles from her permanent residence) required constant attention to gardening, maintenance, protection, and seemed a considerable burden to a frail old woman in poor health. Finances affected the de-cision, as well and she asked many fi-nancial and realty consultants to assist her to make the decision.

The therapist and the patient explored many factors involved in the decision and then gradually began to explore more deeply. Soon a number of painful issues emerged. For example, her husband had died a year ago and she mourned him yet. The house was rich still with his presence, and drawers and closets brimmed with his personal effects. A decision to sell the house required also a decision to come to terms with the fact that her husband would never return. Another factor was the entertainment value of the home. She often referred to the house as her "hotel" since she had always entertained large numbers of people there. She considered her house as her "drawing card" and har-bored serious doubts whether anyone would pay a visit to her without the entice-ment of her lovely estate. Thus a decision to sell the house meant testing the loyalty of her friends and risking loneliness and isolation. Yet another reason centered on the great tragedy of her life—her child-lessness. She had always envisioned the estate passing on to her children and to her children's children. But she was the last leaf; the line ended with her. The de-cision to sell the house thus was a decision to acknowledge the failure of her major symbolic immortality project. The thera-pist used the house-selling decision as a springboard to these deeper issues and eventually helped the patient mourn her husband, herself, and her unborn children.

Once the deeper meanings of a decision are worked through the decision generally glides easily into place and after approxi-mately a dozen sessions the patient effort-lessly made the decision to sell the house.

Management

Existential psychotherapy is a para-digm, a frame of reference; it is not an organization with well-delineated rules. Hence everyday arrangements of practice cannot be satisfactorily described: they vary widely depending upon the thera-pist's organizational and ideological affiliation.

Existentially oriented therapists strive toward honest, mutually open relation-ships with their patients; consequently they arrange the therapeutic setting accordingly. No desks are placed between patient and therapist. No walls are covered with authority-inspiring diplomas. Therapist and patient address one another equally, generally both on a first name basis. The therapist strives toward demystification of the therapy process; answering questions openly and fully; not attempting to remain impassive in an effort to evoke transferential distortions.

The patient-therapist relationship serves many central functions in therapy. The patient-therapist relationship helps the patient clarify other relationships. Patients almost invariably distort some aspect of their relationship to the therapist and the therapist, drawing from self-knowledge and experience of how others view him or her, is able to help the patient distinguish distortion from reality.

But there is also potential benefit in the patient's developing a real (as opposed to a transferential) relationship to the therapist. Once a patient is able to relate deeply to a therapist then the patient has changed. He learns that the potential for love exists within himself and he experiences feelings that have lain dormant. No matter that the patient's relationship to the therapist is "temporary," the *experience* of intimacy is permanent and can never be taken away. It exists in the patient's inner world as a permanent reference point: a reminder of the patient's potential for intimacy.

It is obvious that the experience of an intimate encounter with a therapist has implications that extend beyond relationships with most other people. For one thing, the therapist is generally someone whom the patient particularly respects. But even more important, the therapist is someone, often the only one, who *really* knows the patient. To tell someone else all one's darkest secrets, all one's illicit thoughts, one's sorrows, one's vanities, one's passions, and still be fully accepted by that person is enormously affirmative.

There is much controversy over the nature of the ideal therapist-patient relationship. There is an inescapable dissonance in the world of the therapist: concepts like "50-minute sessions," "$X an hour," "third-party payments," do not fit comfortably with what we ordinarily think of as a genuine, caring relationship. Furthermore there is little or no reciprocity in the therapist-patient relationship. The patient comes to the therapist for help but the therapist does not come to the patient.

Existential thinkers such as Erich Fromm, Abraham Maslow, and Martin Buber all stress that true caring for another means to care about the other's growth and to want to bring something to life in the other. The therapist's raison d'être is to be midwife to the birth of the patient's yet unlived life. Buber uses the term *unfolding* which he suggests should be the way of the educator and the therapist. That means that one uncovers what was there all along. The term *unfolding* has rich connotations and stands in sharp contrast to the goals of the therapist in other therapeutic systems (for example, "reconstruction," "decondition," "behavioral shaping," "reparenting"). One helps the patient unfold by "meeting," by existential communication. The therapist is not a shaper or a director but is instead, in Sequin's (1965) terms, a "possibilitator" (p. 123).

Perhaps the most important concept of all in describing the patient-therapist relationship is what Rollo May et al. (1958) term *presence* (p. 80). The therapist must be present with the patient, must strive for an authentic encounter with the patient. Even though the therapist has spent only one hour a week with the patient it is of vital importance that the therapist *be there* with the patient for that hour, that the therapist be fully present and be intensely involved. If the therapist feels bored, irritated or removed from the patient, if the therapist is impatient for the end of the hour, then to that extent the therapist is failing to provide the relationship the patient so urgently requires.

CASE EXAMPLE

A Simple Case of Divorce

A 50-year-old scientist, whom we will call David, had been married for 27 years and had recently decided to separate from his wife. He applied for therapy because of the degree of anxiety he was experiencing in anticipation of confronting his wife with his decision.

The situation was in many ways a typical midlife scenario. The patient has two children; the youngest had just graduated from college. In David's mind the children had always been the main element binding him and his wife together. Now that the children were self-supporting and fully adult, David felt there was no reasonable point in continuing the marriage. He reported that he had been dissatisfied with his marriage for many years and on three previous occasions separated from his wife, but, after only a few days became anxious and returned, crestfallen, to his home. Bad as the marriage was, David concluded that it was less unsatisfactory than the loneliness of being single.

The reason for his dissatisfaction with his marriage? Primarily boredom! He met his wife when he was 17, a time when he had been extremely insecure, especially in his relationship with women. She was the first woman who had ever expressed interest in him and he hung on to her for dear life. David (as well as his wife) came from a blue-collar family. He was exceptionally intellectually gifted and was the first member of his family to attend college. He won a scholarship to an ivy league school, obtained two graduate degrees and embarked upon an outstanding academic research career. His wife was not gifted intellectually, chose not to go to college and during the early years of their marriage worked to support David in graduate school.

For most of their married life his wife immersed herself in the task of caring for the children while David ferociously pursued his professional career. He had always experienced his relationship to his wife as empty and had always felt bored with her company. In his view she had an extremely mediocre mind and was so restricted characterologically that he found it constraining to be alone with her and embarrassing to share her with friends. He experienced himself as continually changing and growing whereas his wife, in his opinion, had become increasingly rigid and unperceptive to new ideas.

The prototypic scenario of the male in midlife crisis seeking a divorce was made complete by the presence of the other woman—an intelligent, vivacious, attractive woman 15 years younger than himself.

David's therapy was long and complex. We shall examine some of the existential themes that emerged during the course of therapy. There are, however, a number of directions that therapy might have taken. Responsibility was an important issue in his decision to leave his wife. First, there is the moral sense of responsibility. After all, his wife gave birth to and raised his children and had supported him through graduate school. He and his wife were at an age where he was far more "marketable" than she; that is, he has significantly higher earning power and was biologically able to father children. What moral responsibility, then, did he have to his wife?

David had a high moral sense and would, for the rest of his life, torment himself with this question. It had to be explored in therapy and consequently, the therapist confronted him explicitly with the issue of moral responsibility during David's decision-making process. The most effective mode of dealing with this anticipatory dysphoria was to leave no stone unturned in his effort to improve and, thus, to save the marriage.

The existential concept of responsibility interdigitated with this process in close fashion. The therapist helped David begin to examine the question of his responsibility for the failure of the marriage. To what degree was he responsible for his wife's mode of being with him? For example, the therapist noted that in his interaction with David he felt somewhat intimidated by David's quick facile mind: the therapist also was aware of a concern about being criticized or judged by David. How judgmental was David? Was it not possible that he squelched his wife, that had he been a more generous person he might have helped his wife to have developed greater flexibility, spontaneity, and a greater sense of self-awareness?

The therapist also helped David explore another major issue. Was his marriage merely a symbol for another source of dysphoria in his life? Was he displacing onto the marriage dissatisfaction that belonged elsewhere in his life? An exploration of this issue soon led him into the middle of the typical dynamics of the mid-life crisis. A dream pointed the way toward some important dynamics:

I had a problem with liquefication of earth near my pool. John [a friend who was dying from cancer] sinks into the ground. It was like quicksand. I used a giant power auger to drill down into the quicksand. I expect to find some kind of void under the ground but instead I found a concrete slab five to six feet down. On the slab I found a receipt of money someone had paid me for $501. I was very anxious in the dream about that receipt since it was greater than it should have been.

One of the major themes of this dream had to do with death and aging. First, there was the theme of his friend who had cancer. David attempted to find his friend by using a giant auger. In the dream, David experienced a great sense of mastery and power during the drilling. The symbol of the auger seemed clearly phallic and initiated a profitable exploration of sexuality—David had always been sexually driven and the dream illuminated how he used sex (and especially sex with a young woman) as a mode of gaining mastery over aging and death. Finally, he is surprised to find a concrete slab (which elicited associations of morgues, tombs, and tombstones).

He was intrigued by the numerical figures in the dream (the slab was "five to six feet" down and the check was precisely $501). In his associations David made the interesting observation that he was 50-years-old and the night of the dream was his 51st birthday. Though he did not consciously dwell on his age the dream made it clear that at an unconscious level he had considerable concern about being over 50. Along with the slab which was "between five and six feet" deep and the receipt which was just over $500 there was his considerable concern in the dream about the amount cited in the receipt being too great. On a conscious level he used a lot of denial about his aging. His major attitude was that he was growing and expanding very rapidly. He was more physically fit than he had been for most of his life and recently had been running 10 miles a day. In his career, as well, he considered himself in a phase of rapid growth and considered himself on the verge of making an important scientific breakthrough.

If, in fact, David's major distress stemmed from his growing awareness of his aging and diminishment, then a precipitous separation from his wife might have represented an attempt to solve the wrong problem. Consequently, the therapist helped David plunge into a thorough exploration of his feelings about his aging and his mortality. The therapist's view was that only by fully dealing with these issues would he be more able to ascertain the true extent of the marital difficulties. The therapist and David explored these issues over several months. He attempted to deal more honestly with his wife than before and soon he and his wife made arrangements to see a marital therapist for several months.

After these steps were taken, David and his wife decided that there was nothing salvageable in the marriage and they separated. The months following his separation were exceedingly difficult. The therapist, of course, provided support during this time but did not try to help David eliminate his anxiety; instead he attempted to help David *use* his anxiety in a constructive fashion. David's inclination was to rush into an immediate second marriage whereas the therapist persistently urged him to look at his fear of isolation which had sent him on each previous separation back to his wife. It was important now to be certain that fear did not propel him into an immediate second marriage.

David found it difficult to heed this advice since he felt so much in love with the new woman in his life. The state of being "in love" is one of the great experiences in life; in therapy, however, being in love raises many problems; the pull of romantic love is so great that it engulfs even the most well-directed therapeutic endeavors. David found his new partner to be the ideal woman, no other woman existed for him, and he attempted to spend all of his time with her. When with her he experienced a state of continual bliss: all aspects of the lonely "I" vanished leaving only a very blissful state of "we-ness."

What finally made it possible for David to work in therapy was that his new friend became somewhat frightened by the power of his embrace. Only then was he willing to look at his extreme fear of being alone and his reflex desire to merge with a woman. Gradually he became desensitized to being alone. He observed his feelings, kept a journal of them and worked on them hard and well in therapy. He noted, for example, that Sundays were the very worst time. He had an extremely demanding professional schedule and had no difficulties during the week. Sundays were times of extreme anxiety. He became aware that part of that anxiety was that he had to take care of himself on Sunday. If he wanted to do something he himself had to schedule the activity. He could no longer rely on that being done for him by his wife. He discovered that an important function of ritual in culture and the heavy scheduling in his own life was to conceal the void, the total lack of structure beneath him.

These observations led him, in therapy, to face his need to be cared for and shielded. The fears of isolation and freedom buffeted him for several months but gradually he learned how to be alone in the world, and what it meant to be responsible for his own being. In short he learned how to be his own mother and father—always a major therapeutic objective of psychotherapy.

SUMMARY

Existential psychotherapy perceives the patient as an existing, immediate person, not as a composite of drives, archetypes, or conditioning. The instinctual drives and the history of the other person are obviously present, but they come into existential therapy only as parts of the living, struggling, feeling, thinking human being in unique conflicts and with hopes, fears, relationships. Existential therapy emphasizes that normal anxiety and guilt are present in all phenomena of life, and only the neurotic forms of these need to be changed in therapy. The person can be freed from neurotic anxiety and guilt only as he recognizes his normal anxiety and guilt at the same time.

The original criticism of existential therapy as "too philosophical" has lessened as people recognize that all effective psychotherapy has philosophical implications which must be dealt with.

Existential therapy is concerned with the "I Am" (being) experience, the culture (world) in which a patient lives, the significance of time, and the aspect of consciousness called transcendence.

The significance of the therapist's presence and encounter, both central existential emphases, are shown in a movie, *Ordinary People*. Here the therapist's chief characteristic was availability for an adolescent's aggression. Karl Jaspers, who was a psychiatrist and later became an existential philosopher, put his finger on this harmfulness of lack of presence and of its importance:

What we are missing! What opportunities of understanding we let pass by because at a single, decisive moment we were, with all our knowledge, lacking in the simple virtue of a *full human presence!*

It is this presence that existential therapy seeks to cultivate.

The central aim of the founders of existential psychotherapy is that its emphases would percolate into therapy of all schools. That this has been occurring is quite clear.

But that the influence of existential ideas goes deep is shown in what is called the existential neurosis. This refers to the condition of the person who feels life is meaningless. This neurosis is seen increasingly in patients in all schools. Freud in his formative years saw hysterical cases almost entirely. Nowadays, all schools of therapy report that their patients are rarely hysterics but are much more frequently afflicted with what are called "character neuroses," which is another description of existential neurosis.

Existential therapy always sees the patient in the center of his or her own culture. Most people's problems in our day are loneliness, isolation, and alienation.

Our present age is one of disintegration of cultural and historical mores of love and marriage, the family, the inherited religions, and so forth. This disintegration is the reason that psychotherapy of all sorts has burgeoned in the twentieth century; people cried for help for their multitudinous problems. Thus the existential emphasis on different aspects of the world (environment, social world, and subjective world) will, in all likelihood, become increasingly important. It is to be predicted that the existential approach in therapy will then become more widely used for modern men and women in their psychological trouble.

ANNOTATED BIBLIOGRAPHY

May, R. *The meaning of anxiety.* (rev. ed.). New York: Norton & Co., 1977. First edition published in 1950.

A discussion of the prevalence of anxiety in the twentieth century, and its roots in philosophy, biology, psychology, and modern culture. The first book written in America on the central theme of anxiety, and the third book in history on this topic, others having been written by Sigmund Freud and one by Søren Kierkegaard. *The Meaning of Anxiety* was the first firm presentation of anxiety as a normal as well as a neurotic condition, and it argues that normal anxiety has constructive uses in human survival and human creativity.

May, R. *Freedom and destiny*. New York: Norton, 1981.

This is a presentation of the basic existential concept that our human freedom is always in juxtaposition with destiny, the latter defined as the "givens" of life such as death, our biological inheritance, our culture, as well as the sheer circumstances of existence. We are free to the extent that we acknowledge, confront, and struggle with our destiny. Creativity is the outcome of this confrontation.

May, R., Angel, E., & Ellenberger, H. *Existence: A new dimension in psychology and psychiatry*. New York: Basic Books, 1958; paperback by Simon & Schuster.

This volume contains the two essays on existential psychotherapy: "The Origins of the Existential Movement in Psychology," and "Contributions of Existential Psychology" which introduced this form of therapy to America. The rest of the book consists of essays and case studies by Henri Ellenberger, originally from Germany, Eugene Minkowski from Paris, Erwin Straus from Germany but later a resident of America, V. E. von Gebsattel from Germany, Ludwig Binswanger from Switzerland, and Ronald Kuhn from Germany. Though these last articles may be difficult for the student, the first two essays are very readable. The book was described by Abraham Maslow as "Easily the best introduction available for Americans. . . . A strong antidote against triviality and superficiality in psychology."

Yalom, I. D. *Existential psychotherapy*. New York: Basic Books, 1980.

This volume offers a comprehensive clinical overview of the field of existential psychotherapy. A major task of the book is to build a bridge between theory and clinical application. It posits that psychopathology issues from the individual's confrontation with the ultimate concerns of death, freedom, isolation, and meaninglessness and explores the implications of each ultimate concern for the practice of psychotherapy.

CASE READINGS

Binswanger, L. The case of Ellen West. In Rollo May, Ernest Angel, & Henri Ellenberger (Eds.), *Existence: A new dimension in psychology and psychiatry*. New York: Basic Books, 1958.

Holt, H. The case of Father M—A segment of an existential analysis. *Journal of Existentialism*, 1966, *6*, 369-495. Also in D. Wedding and R. J. Corsini (Eds.), Great cases in psychotherapy. Itasca, Ill.: Peacock Publishers, 1979.

Jacobi, Y. A case of homosexuality. *Journal of Analytical Psychology*, 1969, *14*, 48-64.

REFERENCES

Arieti, S. Psychotherapy of severe depression. *American Journal of Psychiatry*. 1977, *134*, 864-868.

Becker, E. *Denial of death*. New York: Free Press, 1973.

Binswanger, L. Existential analysis and psychotherapy. In E. Fromm-Reichmann and J. L. Moreno (Eds.), *Progress in psychotherapy*. New York: Grune & Stratton, 1956.

Boss, M. *The analysis of dreams*. London: Rider & Co., 1957. (a)

Boss, M. *Psychoanalyse und Daseinsanalytik*. Bern and Stuttgart: Verlag Hans Huber, 1957. (b)

Boss, M. *Psychoanalysis and daseinanalysis*. New York: Simon & Schuster, 1982.

Bugental, J. *The search for existential identity*. San Francisco: Jossey-Bass, 1976.

Bugental, J. *The search for authenticity*. New York: Holt, Rinehart & Winston, 1965.

Bynner, W. (Ed.). *The way of life, according to Laotzu* (An American version). New York: John Day, 1946.

Donne, J. *Complete poetry and selected prose*. New York: Modern Library, 1952.

Farber, L. *The ways of the will: Essays toward a psychology and psychopathology of will*. New York: Basic Books, 1966.

Farber, L. *Lying, despair, jealousy, envy, sex, suicide, drugs, and the good life*. New York: Basic Books, 1976.

Frankl, V. *Man's search for meaning: An introduction to logotherapy*. New York: Pocket Books, 1963.

Frankl, V. *Will to meaning*. New York: World Publishing, 1969.

Havens, L. The existential use of the self. *American Journal of Psychiatry*, 1974, *131*.

Heidegger, M. *Being and time.* New York: Harper & Row, 1962.

Horney, K. *Neurosis and human growth.* New York: Norton, 1950.

Jung, C. G. *Collected works: The practice of psychotherapy* (Vol. 16). New York: Pantheon, Bollingen Series, 1966.

Kaiser, H. *Learning theory and personality dynamics.* New York: Ronald Press, 1950.

Kaiser, H. *Effective psychotherapy.* New York: Free Press, 1965.

Kant, I. In *The encyclopedia of philosophy,* P. Edwards (Ed.), vol. IV. New York: Macmillan and Free Press, 1954.

Kierkegaard, S. *Fear and trembling and the sickness unto death.* Garden City, N.Y.: Doubleday, 1954.

Koestenbaum, P. *The new image of man.* Westport, Conn.: Greenwood Press, 1978.

Lasch, C. *The culture of narcissism.* New York: Norton, 1979.

May, R. *Man's search for himself.* New York: Norton, 1953.

May, R. *Existential psychology.* New York: Random House, 1961.

May, R. *Love and will.* New York: Norton, 1969.

May, R. *The meaning of anxiety.* (rev. ed.) New York: Norton, 1977.

May, R. *Freedom and destiny.* New York: Norton, 1981.

May, R. The problem of evil: An open letter to Carl Rogers. *Journal of Humanistic Psychology,* 1982, *3*, 16.

May, R., Angel, E., & Ellenberger, H. (Eds.). *Existence: A new dimension in psychiatry and psychology.* New York: Basic Books, 1958.

Mijuskovic, B. *Loneliness in philosophy, psychology and literature.* The Netherlands: Van Gorcum, 1979.

Mowrer, O. H. Time as a determinant in integrative learning. In O. H. Mowrer (Ed.) *Learning theory and personality dynamics.* New York: Ronald Press, 1950.

Mowrer, O. H., & Ullman, A. D. Time as a determinant in integrative learning. *Psychological Review,* 1952, 61-90.

Perls, F. *Gestalt therapy verbatim.* Moab, Utah: Real People Press, 1969.

Raskin, N. Becoming—A therapist, a person, a partner, and a parent. *Psychotherapy: Theory, Research and Practice,* 1978, *4*, 15.

Sartre, J. P. *Being and nothingness.* New York: Philosophical Library, 1956.

Sequin, C. *Love and psychotherapy.* New York: Libra Publishers, 1965.

Spence, K. *Behavior theory and conditioning.* New Haven, Conn.: Yale University Press, 1956.

Spinoza, B. cited by M. de Unamuno, *The tragic sense of life,* trans. J. E. Flitch. New York: Dover, 1954.

Tillich, P. *The courage to be.* New Haven, Conn.: Yale University Press, 1952.

Tolstoy, L. *The death of Ivan Ilych and other stories.* New York: Signet Classics, 1960.

Van Kaam, A. *Existential foundations of psychology.* Pittsburgh: Duquesne University Press, 1966.

Weisman, A. *Existential core' of psychoanalysis: Reality sense and responsibility.* Boston: Little, Brown, 1965.

Yalom, I. *Existential psychotherapy.* New York: Basic Books, 1981.

11

Transactional Analysis

JOHN M. DUSAY and
KATHERINE MULHOLLAND DUSAY

OVERVIEW

Transactional analysis (TA), as originated by Dr. Eric Berne in the 1950s, is a
complete theory of personality; TA also
uses a wide variety of related treatment
techniques specifically designed to meet
the needs and goals of clients. TA adheres
to the presence of three active, dynamic,
and observable ego states labeled the
Parent, the Adult, and the Child, each of
which exists and operates in any individual. Each person has a basic innate need
for *strokes* (recognition) and will design a
life script (plan) formed during childhood,
based upon early beliefs about oneself
and others. These existential beliefs are
reinforced by the person engaging in
repetitive, stereotyped *games* (unstraight
social interactions) with others. The dynamic representation of any individual's
psychological energy forces (Critical
Parent, Nurturing Parent, Adult, Free
Child, and Adapted Child) may be
graphically portrayed on the person's
egogram (a bar graph of one's personality
portrait). One's egogram energy balance
will remain "fixed" unless one actively
decides to change one's behavior. An
effective TA therapist is a potent catalyst,
who facilitates change and growth in
clients.

Basic Concepts

TA therapists share certain challenges
and basic questions with all other psychotherapists: Why are people the way
they are? What are the basic human commonalities? How and why do individuals
differ from one another? Why do they develop and retain negative patterns of
thinking, feeling, and behaving even when
doing so hurts them? Why do people resist
changing, even when a therapist offers
them a vehicle for change? TA offers both
answers and effective directions to such
questions through its theoretical concepts and its systematic approach. TA's
simple vocabulary (Berne, 1964; Harris,
1969; James & Jongeward, 1971) is intentionally designed to enable clients
to demystify the esoteric jargon of traditional therapies. Some basic terms used
in TA are: Parent, Adult and Child *ego
states; transactions; games; strokes; scripts;*
and *egograms.* An important TA attitude
will be noted throughout this work: Concepts are not only expressed verbally, but
also have accompanying symbols—circles,
arrows, triangles, and bar graphs, which
increase clarity and understanding, as well
as represent a commitment by the therapist to explain his or her viewpoint. The
therapist and client both share these

mutual "tools" and simple vocabularies; and while this tends to eliminate some of the therapist's magic, the client is facilitated to "own" his appropriate share of responsibility for treatment.

Ego states

When Eric Berne discovered his client was sometimes thinking, feeling, and behaving like a child and at other times like a rational adult, he differentiated between two distinct ego states: the Child and the Adult. The *Child* ego state within each of us is sometimes creative, intuitive, and emotional; at other times, rebellious or conforming. Originally Berne labeled the Child ego state the *archaeopsyche*, which connoted the developmentally archaic, regressive ego state (Berne, 1961). The *Adult* ego state, which is the realistic, logical part of us, he termed the *neopsyche*, which referred to computing and data processing. Each ego state has its own observable mannerisms, special repertoire of words, thoughts, emotions, body postures, gestures, voice tones, and expressions. The Child ego state behaves, sounds, and "comes on" like an actual child, regardless of the person's biological age. The Adult ego state resembles a computer in that it takes in, stores, retrieves, and processes information about self and the environment. The Adult deals exclusively with facts and logical data in a nonemotional way.

Soon, another basic aspect of human behavior became evident—the *Parent* or *exteropsyche*, an introjection from and an identification with one's actual biological parents. The Parent ego state expresses one's value systems, morals, and beliefs. These attitudes may take the form of promoting growth in others as well as being critical and controlling. The Parent may portray traits and mannerisms of one's actual mother, father, and occasionally other parenting figures. The Parent in a person may be judgmental and opin-

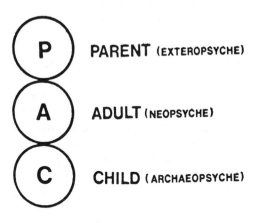

EGO STATE DIAGRAM

FIGURE 11.1

ionated, as well as nurturing and protective. One's Parent ego state is frequently familial and cultural in origin, often passed down from parents to their children, who in turn pass it down to their children. (The three ego states are capitalized as Parent, Adult, and Child to distinguish them from the biological entities of parents, adults, and children.)

The completed tripartite system of one's personality structure is symbolized by three connected, distinct circles to represent that they are unique, separate, and independent entities. Each ego state functions independently from the others and has separate boundaries, wherein it contains specific properties (see Figure 11.1). The three ego states are dynamic, unlike Freud's personality structure of id, ego, and superego which are hypothetical concepts and not observable phenomena.

Transactions

Social action begins when two (or more) people get together. Psychologically speaking, two people in a room means there are actually six structured ego states (three and three) present and these ego states may transact and communicate with one another. A transaction is a unit of human communication. *Transactions* are defined as a stimulus and a related response between two persons' ego states; the word *transaction* is preferred over the more general term *communication* for clarity and precision. There are two basic levels of transactions: the *social level*, which is overt or manifest, and the *psychological level*, which is covert or latent. These two levels of transactions are visually symbolized by arrows: the socially stated, overt transaction is represented by a solid-line arrow, and the psychologically stated, covert transaction is symbolized by a dotted-line arrow.

Games

When these two levels (psychological and social) are actively operating at the same time, a game is usually taking place. A *game* is defined as an orderly series of ulterior transactions (with both an overt and a covert level), which results in "payoffs" with specific bad feelings for both game players. The overt series of transactions is straightforward and in this particular example is an Adult-to-Adult transaction: The boss asks his secretary, "What time is it?" She answers, "3 o'clock." However, his covert nonverbal message (represented by the dotted lines of his Parent to her Child) is, "You're always late." Her hidden nonverbal response (dotted lines of her Child to his Parent) is, "You're always criticizing me." Even though neither the boss nor his secretary express these hidden sentiments out loud, each is fully aware of the hidden messages and each will receive a personal payoff of bad feelings. The boss is playing his part in the game colloquially known as *Now I Got You, You SOB* (NIGYYSOB), and he feels angry and powerful; his secretary is playing *Kick Me (KM)* and feels bad and picked on (see Figure 11.2). People transact in certain stereotyped ways that

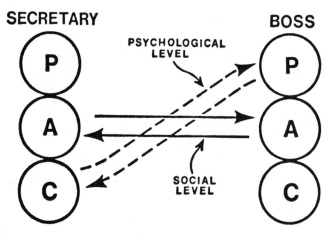

A GAME DIAGRAM

FIGURE 11.2

are predictable and unique for each person and these are called games; each of the players ends up with "bad feelings" called *rackets*. After several repeated episodes of these games with themselves and perhaps with other players, the secretary will entitle herself to a "free" depression while the boss will entitle himself to a "free" rampage and rage.

Strokes

The basic motivation for any human social interaction is based on one's ongoing needs for *strokes* (human recognition). When straightforward strokes are not available, that is, "I like you," people will employ ulterior methods and use games to receive strokes. Although positive strokes feel better than negative strokes, negative strokes are better than *no* strokes at all! Specific patterns of giving and receiving strokes are learned, and they are unique to each family. The ways that people give and get strokes serve to shape each individual's personality. During one's infancy and early childhood, "strokes" are hopefully given and received by actual touching, holding, and cuddling. This touching is necessary for the healthy survival of any newborn human infant (Spitz, 1945). Somewhere between the ages two and four, the stroking tends to become less physical and more verbal, although actual physical stroking remains important throughout life from infancy to old age. Stroking can be positive (caring and approving) or negative (damaging and disapproving). Because strokes are essential to each person's survival, negative strokes are sought if positive strokes are not available.

Script

Through one's early interactions with parents and others, a pattern of stroking develops, which may be either supportive or attacking (Berne, 1972). From this strok-

ing pattern, the child at some point early in life makes a basic existential decision about himself, essentially that he is either OK as a person or not OK. This basic decision is then reinforced by continuing messages, both verbal and nonverbal, the person receives throughout life. The developing child not only makes these crucial decisions about himself, but also develops a viewpoint about what other people are like. The child decides either that other people are OK and to be trusted or that they are not OK (Berne, 1964; Harris, 1969). This process of deciding about both oneself and others becomes one's basic belief system.

Through the script matrix (Steiner, 1971a), we can note the Parent ego states of both mother and father supply (1) their *values*, morals, opinions, and prejudices to the developing Parent ego state of their child. The Child ego states of both mother and father provide (2) the *injunctions* or the negative messages to the Child ego state of their child. On the basis of these early verbal (solid line) and nonverbal (dotted line) messages (which are frequently incongruent and incompatible), the Child ego state of the young child will *decide* what life will be like. The Adult ego states of usually the opposite-sex parent of the child usually provide (3) the "Here's How" message of how to make it through life (see Figure 11.3).

One's script or life course is based upon one's early existential decisions; scripts incorporate specific elements from myths, fairy tales, and theatrical dramas in that they include a wide variety of characters, along with the elements of suspense, surprise, triumph, tragedy, anger, scare, joy, and other emotions. One's life script may be either winning or losing, hamartic (tragic) or banal; and each script includes specific roles. Some people approach life as heroes and heroines (K. Dusay, 1975), and others operate as villains, rescuers,

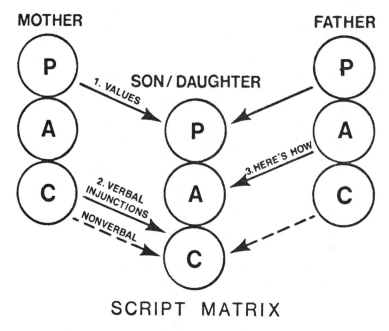

SCRIPT MATRIX

FIGURE 11.3

persecutors, victims (Karpman, 1968), or perhaps as innocent bystanders. After the child incorporates early messages from his parents, his script develops into a strong belief system, so when the client arrives at the psychotherapist's office some 20, 30, or more years later, his basic life script is both apparent and staunchly defended.

Egogram

Although TA's structure of personality is symbolized by the three circles of ego states, the function and amount of energy placed within these ego states is symbolized by the *egogram* (J. Dusay, 1972). The circles illustrate which ego states are involved in the transactions, and the egogram exemplifies, in bar graph form, *how much* energy exists in the five functional ego states of any person. The Parent is divided into its functional aspects of both

Critical Parent (CP) and Nurturing Parent (NP); the Adult (A) is not divided as it is unemotional and functions solely as a computer; and the Child is divided into its Free Child (FC) functions, which are natural and uninhibited, and its Adapted Child (AC) functions, which are compliant or rebellious. These basic psychological energies are present in each person in varying amounts.

Because each person has a distinct and unique personality, these five psychological forces are aligned in different amounts and balances in each individual. An egogram is constructed on a five-position bar graph that represents CP, NP, A, FC, and AC; the higher columns signify the greater amounts of time and energy expended in these ego states, and the smaller columns portray lesser degrees of time and energy. The egogram operates with a constancy hypothesis in that when one raises the time and energy in an ego state, another ego state will lose energy. This is a simple illustration of the growth model. A person's egogram will remain fixed and not change unless the person actively decides to change the energy balances in his ego states (see Figure 11.4). The *Critical Parent* is the part of one's personality that criticizes or finds fault; the CP is also assertive, directing, limiting, makes rules, enforces one's value system, and stands up for one's rights. (Too much CP is dictatorial.) The *Nurturing Parent* in a person is empathetic and promotes growth. (Too much NP is smothering.) The *Adult's* function is clear, rational thinking. The Adult is factual, precise, accurate, nonemotional, and nonjudgmental. (Too much Adult is boring.) The *Free Child* is spontaneous, curious, playful, fun, free, eager, and intuitive. (Too much FC is seen as out-of-control.) The *Adapted Child* is conforming, compromising, adapting, easy to get along with, and compliant. The Adapted Child may also manifest itself as a pseudorebel that does the opposite of everything that is expected. (A person with too much AC will manifest behavior in a myriad of ways; some of the most common ways are being guilty, depressed, or robotlike, or throwing temper tantrums reminiscent of small children.)

Since each person has a psychological energy portrait (or egogram) of his personality, the complexities and changes of the human personality can be described through this system. There are neither "good" nor "bad" egograms per se; but generalizations may be formed about certain egogram balances. A *bell-shaped egogram* implies that the personality has a well-balanced energy system with psychological energy fairly evenly distributed. A *Don Juan* will have a high Free Child (interested in fun and sexual trysts), a high Critical Parent (knows how to tell women to get lost), a low Nurturing Parent (does not care about their feelings), a medium high Adult (he logically knows how to find women), and a low Adapted Child (feels little guilt and will not compromise). A *Wallflower* by contrast is highest in Adapted Child (she is worried about what others will think about her), low in Free Child (is seldom playful or fun); her Critical Parent is low in that she will seldom assert herself or stand up for her rights. A depressed or suicidal person will be quite low on Nurturing Parent (both to oneself and others), and also low on Free Child (feels little zest for life and happiness).

Other Systems

TA differs from other systems of personality in that explanations about human behavior are viewed on the basis of Parent, Adult, and Child ego states. Human behavior not explained in terms of these ego states is not TA, although statements from other fields may sound similar to TA statements. Freud once remarked that it is one thing to flirt with an idea and another thing to be married to it. The transactional analyst is married to the concept of ego states.

A major difference between psychoanalysis and TA is that TA does not rely upon a theory of the unconscious. Although Berne himself never denied this theory, he and his followers find that the concept of a dynamic unconscious is unnecessary for the practice of TA. A basic difference between TA and Freudian theory is that while the Freudian structure of the id, ego, and superego are *hypothetical* constructs, the Parent, Adult, and Child ego states are *observable* phenomena. Ego-state recognition and the alignment of these states on an egogram enable one to

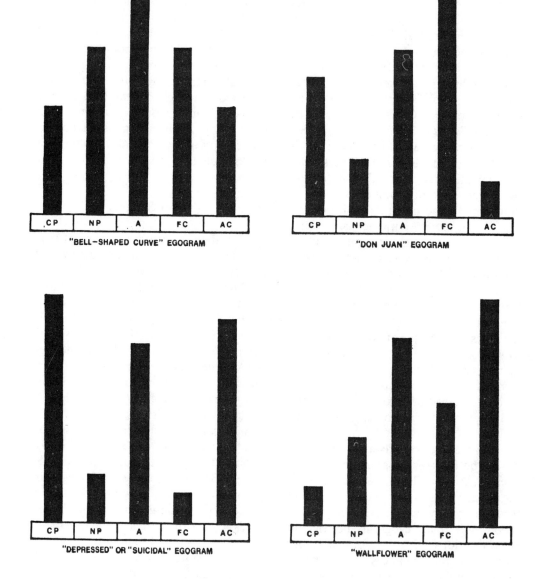

EXAMPLES OF EGOGRAMS

FIGURE 11.4

predict future behavior as well as make inferences of past history. A further difference is in methods of treatment. In classical psychoanalytical approaches, the therapist may attempt to remain anonymous or may welcome transferences. The TA therapist does not remain anonymous and will point out his or her transactions and, when applicable, his own game participations.

Myths, folk tales, and the occurrence of universal symbols are important to both the TA therapists as well as to Jungian analysts. TA-practitioners, however, emphasize the *direct* transactions that are passed down between the parents and their children, as well as other direct transactional influences such as the replaying of myths on television, radio, literature, movies, and other mass media. Jungian analysts adhere to a mystical transmission that occurs by way of archetypes or through the collective unconscious.

A TA practitioner will agree with Carl Rogers's person-centered approach in that one's growth potential may be released by a reality-based, nonjudgmental therapist. In addition to reflecting and validating the client's statements, the TA therapist will frequently stop, interrupt, confront, and point out inconsistencies to the client. Consequently, the TA therapist will be more overtly active than a Rogerian therapist.

Alfred Adler's individual psychology is compatible with TA, especially in script theory (Adler, 1963). Adler said, "If I know the goal of a person, I know in a general way what will happen ... psychic phenomenon ... can only be grasped and understood if regarded as a preparation for some goal ... an attempt at a planned final compensation and a (secret) life plan." Berne (1972) said, "The only exceptions which a script analyst would take to these [Adler's] statements are (1) that

the life plan is not unconscious; (2) that the person is by no means solely responsible for it; and (3) that the goal and the manner of reaching it (the actual transactions, word for word), can be predicted much more precisely than even Adler claimed" (p. 59).

TA differs from Albert Ellis's rational-emotive therapy (RET) in that the TA therapist places the burden of explanation and interpretation mainly upon the client rather than the therapist. In TA the client is provided specific tools for growth, yet is ultimately encouraged to make his own explanations and interpretations. As compared to RET, TA has more recently placed less emphasis on rational explanations; rather, TA emphasizes that a client should directly replay early emotions and feelings about the problem rather than talk about emotions, and then go through a redecision process (Goulding, 1974).

Both TA and behavior modification have as their goals manifest changes in the clients' behavior. Where these two systems differ is in the TA focus on the redecision process. TA emphasizes that when a person is young, he reacts to environmental stresses, receives injunctions, and then makes basic decisions about himself and others. These early decisions become manifest in here-and-now thinking, feeling, and behaving. TA analysts encourage clients to trace these stereotyped, learned, not-OK experiences back to their prototype, earlier childhood origins. When this episode is reestablished, the client is then encouraged to maintain a self-conversation between the scripted Child part and a positive "growth" ego state that is represented on his egogram. Although Skinner's behavior modification theory views a person more as a helpless victim who reacts to external stimuli, TA, by contrast, sees each person as autonomous, responsible, and able to restructure his behavior by making *new* decisions about self and life.

Many TA therapists incorporate versions of Gestalt techniques that were practiced by Fritz Perls (1969). Although TA emphasizes a person's intellectual cognition (which was discounted by Perls), TA also supports a client's emotional expressions (which was favored by Perls). TA's use of cognitive models is evident in its clearly stated theory of personality; by comparison, Perls left little in the way of a clear record or system for his later theories and techniques. The major difference between TA and Gestalt is TA's use of a therapeutic treatment contract. TA therapists and their clients use specific, oral, measurable goals by which both the therapist and the client are mutually involved and directed.

Although TA compatibly shares the basic focus on personal responsibility for one's own behavior with reality therapy, as developed by William Glasser, the TA therapist places greater importance on history and antecedent behavior. Although working in the present, and considering that the future is important, the TA therapist views present behavior patterns that lead to problems as *rackets*—repetitive behavior with corresponding emotions—originating in early script messages. The reality therapist says, "We must face reality and admit that we cannot rewrite history"; the TA therapist begins with the here-and-now expression of "bad" feelings and encourages the client to trace these back to the early decisive moments and redecide.

As far as actual living in the world is concerned, TA shares with existential analysis a high esteem for personal qualities of honesty, integrity, autonomy, and authenticity—and the most important social manifestation of intimacy. However, TA places importance on personality structure and views the problem of "self"

to be a balance of ego state structure and function. The internal dialogue between Parent, Adult, Child, and the social expression of criticism, nurturing, logic, creativity, and adaptation (compliance or rebellion) have a stereotyped habitual pattern in those who lack autonomy. Pathology exists and follows rules, and recognizing what is, is a step in the direction of autonomy, and freedom from old habits.

Similarities exist between Encounter and TA in that both are practiced in groups, workshops, and marathons. Many techniques used by encounter leaders are also used by TA therapists; however, TA therapists use specific techniques tailor-made for each individual to raise low energies in an individual's deficient ego states. No particular type of encounter maneuver is thought by the TA analyst to be appropriate for everyone. Rather, each technique is geared and designed for each individual's unique personality egogram. Pillow pounding, rage, and anger expressions are beneficial only for those people who have a poorly developed Critical Parent; they are *not* indicated for those who already have too much anger! Likewise, exercises in expressing feelings are necessary only for those who have too much Adult and have limited their emotional and social responses; these techniques are not as beneficial for those who are already uninhibited and open with their feelings.

A comparison of TA with eclectic systems is difficult since each eclectic psychotherapist will operate idiosyncratically. TA therapists use their mutual, firm, solid, consistent theory; this foundation is liberating for both the therapist and the client. Therapists who call themselves eclectic may or may not use certain ideas in common with TA. Eclectics frequently mix bits and pieces from other theoretical approaches; they may also jump back and forth from one framework to another in theory, and thereby may confuse structures, function, behavior, phenomenology, history, and social systems with one another. This resembles mixing apples with oranges, and frequently, a clear path or a defined strategy may be missing.

HISTORY

TA was evolved by Eric Berne in the mid-1950s, at a time when psychoanalysis was the primary psychotherapy; communication theory was being applied to emotional problems; and group therapy was emerging as an important modality. The literature and impact of these three influences were especially important to the development of TA.

Precursors

Ego-state precursors
Wilder Penfield's research (1952) at McGill Medical School, where Berne was a medical student, deserves special mention. Penfield reported that the memories of epileptics are retained and replayed in their natural form.

The subject feels again the emotions which the situation originally produced in him, and he is aware of the same interpretation, true or false, which he himself gave to the experience in the first place. This evoked recollection is not the exact photographic reproduction of past scenes and events. It is a reproduction of what the patient saw and heard and felt and understood (p. 178).

Penfield's remarkable neurosurgical experiments demonstrated that different ego states (Penfield did not use the term *ego state*) are reexperienced under direct electrical stimulation of the brain and that one experiences a complete revival in the present of both the experience and the memories along with the corresponding feelings of a past situation (Penfield & Roberts, 1959). Berne, a psychiatrist, was especially interested in ego psychology,

then an important topic in the New York Psychoanalytic Institute circles because of the influence of Heinz Hartmann, Ernst Kris, and others. Berne was impressed with the apparent intact structure of the past states of the ego.

Pharmacological studies in the early work with LSD-25 by Chandler and Hartman (1960) describe the reactivation of the archaic states, and they discuss the employing of two simultaneous states: one oriented to current external and psychological reality; and the other reliving (not merely recalling) scenes dating back to the first year of life. These scenes are accompanied by vivid color, detail, and a feeling of actual experience with all of the original intensity.

Paul Federn (1952), Berne's analyst, first expressed in the psychiatric field what Penfield and the drug experimenters later proved: The complete states of the ego are permanently retained and may be reactivated. Federn used the term *ego state* and this met resistance from those more accustomed to thinking in orthodox conceptual terms, rather than shift to a phenomenological approach. Eduardo Weiss (1950), Federn's exponent, described ego states as one's actually experienced reality, with the complete contents that one relived from a past period. Weiss reiterated what Penfield proved: The ego states of former age levels are maintained in a potential existence within the personality, and they may be evoked under special conditions: hypnosis, dreams, and psychosis.

Before Berne's elucidation of the structure of the three basic ego states, ego psychologists described, and anatomists and pharmacologists proved, the general existence of intact ego states.

Games and transactions precursors
Although many general communication theorists such as Alfred Korzybski and

Norbert Wiener were studied by Berne and other early TA theorists, the application of the communication-system theory to the psychological issues by Gregory Bateson and Jurgen Ruesch (1951) and their Palo Alto associates in the Bay Area of San Francisco where TA was concomitantly developing, became a direct influence. Bateson (Bateson, Jackson, Haley, & Weakland, 1956) espoused the double-bind theory of schizophrenia, a communication model that essentially postulates there are two different and incompatible levels of communication between a schizophrenogenic mother and her child. As each level is incompatible with the other, the dependent child has no easy escape except for psychosis. Berne independently specified these two types of levels (overt and covert), and from this he developed rules for games (the corresponding game for a double bind is *Corner*).

Years before, Karl Abraham (1948) had described various character types, and he related these personality characteristics and behaviors to specific fixations that occurred at various stages of psychosexual development. He labeled these according to specific orifices: oral, anal, urethral, and genital; he described their patterns of interaction with other people. Berne later compared Abraham's analyses of character types with specific game patterns: Oral types play *Do Me Something*; anal types play *Schlemiel* or *Now I Got You, You SOB*; urethral types play *Kick Me*; and genital types may play *Rapo*. Berne was quite impressed by Abraham's work, and he presented a panel entitled "Character Types and Game Analysis" at the American Psychiatric Association meeting in 1969.

René Spitz's work (1945) emphasized the importance of both the quantity and quality of early mother-to-child transactions; this research is frequently quoted by TA writers and became the inspiration for the term *strokes* (see page 395).

Script precursors

The notion of *scripts* is not new; many allusions in classical and modern literature are made to the fact that the world is a stage and all the people on it are players. Joseph Campbell (1949), the mythologist, takes the view that human lives follow the similar patterns of myths; his works are influential to TA script theorists; Berne once remarked that Campbell's *The Hero with a Thousand Faces* is the best textbook for script analysts. Much of Campbell's thinking is based on Jung's and Freud's ideas. Jung's notion of *archetypes* (which correspond to Berne's "magic figure" in a script) and the *persona* (the style in which a script is played) were useful to Berne, who, although he admired Jung's focus of attention on myths and fairy tales, found that mystical discussions were difficult to understand and relate to real people without elaborate training. Freud directly related many aspects of human living to a single drama: Oedipus. Berne, a serious student of psychoanalysis for three decades, initially accepted and later rejected the notion that each patient is an Oedipus who exhibits the same reactions and drama within his head. Instead, Berne viewed Oedipus as a single possibility of the many that may take place in a patient's life.

Adler (1963) was interested in an individual's goal, which he likened to a secret life plan. Goals, types of scripts, and therapeutic contracts became an important influence to Berne.

Action and energy precursors

Abraham Maslow (self-actualization), Will Schutz (encounter), Fritz Perls (Gestalt transfer of energy), and other growth therapists had a profound precursory effect upon the present practice of TA. More direct theoretical applications have been employed by his followers since Berne's death in 1970. Berne occasionally went to Esalen Institute, the influential growth center on the Big Sur Coast of California, and met with Fritz Perls (Gestalt), Will Schutz (encounter), Virginia Satir (family dynamics), Michael Murphy (human growth), and others involved in the human-potential movement. Robert Goulding, John Dusay, and other TA teachers conducted Esalen workshops; and Berne's followers became directly exposed to growth psychologies that appeared simultaneously with TA's development in northern California. Indeed, many encounter, marathon, and Gestalt leaders embraced TA's theories, as they would enrich TA with their human experiential techniques.

Beginnings

Like many psychiatric innovators, Eric Berne was formally trained in classical psychoanalysis. However, in the mid-1950s, he amiably parted from the psychoanalytical school of thought in favor of employing more rapidly effective techniques to cure patients. TA's history until Berne's death in 1970 is the history of his theory and techniques (J. Dusay, 1975). Berne began doing group therapy when he was an army major in World War II; following his discharge, he began unique experiments on the nature of intuition; he published six articles on intuition between 1949 and 1962 summarized by J. Dusay (1971), and published posthumously in 1977 (Berne, 1949, 1977). The intuition articles reflect the evolution of TA, and they trace development as the leader of an innovative approach.

The most important discovery for TA was the dynamic nature of three distinct ego states, which occurred in 1955 when Berne worked in a group with Belle, a 40-year-old disturbed housewife who was discharged from a state hospital, and behaved in two distinct ways toward the men in her life:

Belle would subtly mock and jeer at men whom she considered weak and tease and torment those men whom she felt were strong. She was continually intrigued and confused as to whether the therapist was weak or strong, and she confessed her fantasy that she could see the conformation of his genitals and then attempted to determine if his penis were flabby or erect. She remembered doing the same with her father. Her husband reminded her of a strong man implacable as stone, whose tremendous erections frightened her. . . . She became . . . nauseated when her husband had an erection and could not bear to fantasize about it . . . . She became . . . indisposed when her husband told her a graphic joke about an erection. . . . She could intellectually discuss the vagina but could not bear thinking of it as actually pictured, "a raw, red slimy gash." The image terrified her and she desperately avoided it . . . . Smells also played a significant part in this type of imagery with her (Berne, 1955, pp. 634-58).

Berne called these images Belle experienced *primal images*. They gave rise to the primal judgments she made about men in her life: "This man is flaccid," and "This man is virile." Berne observed these same types of primal judgments occurring in everyday life: "He's an asshole (prick, stinker, jerk, pushover, fart, bleeding heart)." Primal judgments were also seen to be zonal and connected to oral, gastrointestinal, anal, genital, and excretory function. People relate to others according to their primal images and judgments. Berne noted that the "bleeding heart" and the "jerk" were prone to find each other.

The first phase of TA began with Berne's discovery and delineation of ego states (J. Dusay, 1977a), which are a coherent system of thinking, feeling, and behaving. Berne elucidated his discovery of ego states:

An 8-year-old boy vacationing at a dude ranch in his cowboy suit helped the hired man unsaddle a horse. When they were finished, the hired man said, "Thanks, Cowpoke." The "assistant" replied, "I'm not really a cowpoke. I'm just a little boy." The patient went on to remark, "That's just the way I feel. Sometimes I feel that I'm not really a lawyer. I'm just a little boy."

This story illustrates the separation of two ways of feeling, thinking, and behaving in this particular patient; everything that was said was heard by two different people, one an adult lawyer and the other an inner little boy. This particular patient was in treatment for a compulsive gambling habit. Sometimes he used a rational, logical gambling system, which was occasionally successful, but more often he governed his behavior with superstitious and little-boy ways of explaining his losses. . . . It became apparent that there were two types of arithmetic employed (Berne, 1957, p. 611).

Both systems were conscious, deliberate, visible, and active parts of the patient's ego system.

Berne emphasized that the archaic intuitive faculty of the Child could be cultivated by the therapist. Dynamically, intuition works best when the Child predominates, the Adult monitors, and the Parent reduces its influence. To Berne, creativity was the Child knowing and the Adult confirming.

TA moved into its second phase (1958-65) with Berne's attention to the *transaction*, which is a stimulus from one person's ego state and the corresponding response from another person's ego state. Berne's interest in communications theory enabled him to recognize that there were often two different types of messages emanating from one source. For instance, a radio would emit a meaningful message, "It's raining in California," and another simultaneous type of communication would be pops, whirrs, and radio static. With these two types of communication in mind, Berne observed what happens when people get together, and he formulated a specific, concise definition of communication, along with the corresponding three rules (see p. 411). By observing both the overt and covert levels of transacting individuals, Berne began to classify games.

Human behavior that involves two levels of communication, with predictable, stereotyped, and destructive actions that are motivated by hidden desires and lead to specific *payoffs* (bad feelings), were labeled games. The first game Berne analyzed was *Why Don't You . . .? Yes, But . . .*, which occurred during one of his therapy groups:

Patient S: I wish we could fix the leak in our roof.

Respondent 1: Why don't you ask your husband to do it?

Patient S: That's a good idea, but he has to work this weekend.

Respondent 2: Why don't you do it yourself?

Patient S: I would but I don't have any tools.

Respondent 3: Why don't you get some tools?

Patient S: Yes, but we overspent our budget this month.

Respondent 4: Why don't you . . .?

Patient S: Yes, but . . . yes, but . .

On the overt social level, Patient S provides an Adult stimulus by requesting help for her specific problem; the respondents reciprocate with straightforward Adult advice. On her covert psychological level, she is transacting on a Child-Parent level and secretly implying, "Just you try to suggest something I haven't already thought of, hee-hee." The group members try and try with the result that they become frustrated and S maintains a triumphant, coy smile on her face.

An entire classification of psychological games has been elucidated (Berne, 1964) in *Games People Play*. People are inclined to have a specific repertoire of favorite games they play; they base their entire social relationships upon finding suitable partners to play the corresponding opposite roles. Berne and members of the original San Francisco TA seminar were pursuing the question, "Why do different people play the same games over and over?" Freud's repetition compulsion was an appealing, yet obscure, notion that did not satisfactorily answer this question. Because plausible explanations were sought, TA historically moved into its third phase (1960-70), which resulted in script theory. A *script* is "a life plan based on a decision made in childhood, reinforced by the parents, justified by subsequent events, and culminating in a chosen alternative" (Berne, 1972). The direct script message transmissions from parents to their children became symbolized by Claude Steiner (1971a) with the script matrix (see Figure 11.3).

As TA theorists began to delve into folk and fairy tales, they found various lifestyles were based on specific characters with whom patients and their relatives identified. These could be traced back to ancient myths, with their victims, persecutors and rescuers (Karpman, 1968), and the more popular heroines and heroes who starred in popular folk tales, dramas, movies, novels, and television shows (K. Dusay, 1976). One's script became written and fixed in the Child (p. 39) and reinforced through fantasies, dreams, and, later, "reality."

Berne was a prolific writer who published 64 articles and 8 books. He originated the TA Bulletin, which later emerged as a quarterly, *Transactional Analysis Journal*. Berne was at the height of his creativity, insight, and power when he died of a coronary infarction in the summer of 1970.

Current Status

Since Berne's death, a fourth phase of TA has emerged: energy transfers, distribution, and action. The *egogram* (J. Dusay, 1972) symbolizes the amount of time and energy any person exudes in one's ego states. The energy system of an egogram remains constant, unless a person actively changes his balance and relationship to others through direct energy transfers (raising weak, underused ego states). Since 1970, TA practitioners have developed many suitable techniques for raising energy levels in the various ego states.

The clinical use of TA will relate to one of the four phases of TA's development: (1) ego states, (2) transactions and games, (3) script analysis and redecision, and (4) egogram energy shift.

The San Francisco TA Seminar was formerly called the San Francisco Social Psychiatry Seminar (founded by Berne in 1958) and is now known as the Eric Berne Seminar of San Francisco. This is the world's longest ongoing weekly seminar for group therapy. From the original eight members who met in Berne's office in the 1950s, the *International Transactional Analysis Association* (ITAA) presently includes over 10,000 members in the United States and throughout the world. The ITAA is experiencing rapid growth in Europe, Japan, South America, and India.

Berne maintained that trying to "look" professional was not as important as curing patients. He willingly taught his system to all interested persons in the helping professions. Through the ITAA, an advanced, rigorous training program is available for members to train formally for a period of two to five years to attain clinical competency and certification as TA therapists and teachers. Two distinct lines of advance training have evolved and presently exist: advanced clinical training (for mental-health professionals) and special fields training (for teachers and business-oriented persons).

In 1971, the Editorial Board of the *Transactional Analysis Journal* instituted the Eric Berne Memorial Scientific Awards for outstanding contributions to TA theory and practice. Each year, TA persons are nominated who have devised original and applicable concepts to Berne's goal of "curing patients faster"; the winner is chosen by the advanced members' votes of the ITAA. In 1971, Claude Steiner (1971) received the award for his development of the *Script Matrix*; in 1972 Stephen Karpman (1968) received the second award for the *Drama Triangle*; in 1973 John Dusay (1972) received the third award for his development of the *Egogram and the Constancy Hypothesis*; in 1974 Jacqui and Aaron Schiff (1969, 1971) jointly received the award for their development of the *Reparenting Techniques and Passivity Confrontation* they employ in their residential treatment centers for schizophrenics; in 1975 Robert and Mary Goulding (1976) won the award for *Childhood Decisions and Redecisions*; in 1976 Patricia Crossman (1966) won it for recognizing the importance of *Permission, Protection and Potency*; and in 1977 Taibi Kahler (1975) received it for the *Miniscript*. In 1978, Fanita English (1972) won the award for her delineation of the distinction between authentic feelings and learned pathological rackets. In 1979, the award went to Stephen Karpman for his development of transactional options (1971). Claude Steiner received the award in 1980 for his further elaboration on the necessity of strokes (1971b) and Ken Mellor (1975a, 1975b) and Eric Sigmend's (1975) work on discounting and redefining. In 1981, Frank Ernst's elaboration of the existential posi-

tions of childhood decisions was cited (1971). Richard G. Erskine and Marilyn J. Zalcman won the award in 1982 for their analysis of the racket system (1979). Muriel James received the 1983 award for self reporting (1974). The Eric Berne Scientific Award winners' theories are viewed as part of TA theory and practices.

PERSONALITY

Theory of Personality

The basic motivating factor for all human social behavior is a lifelong need for human recognition, which TA therapists term *strokes*. Strokes may be either physical (a hug) or verbal ("you're nice"). René Spitz (1945), a child psychoanalyst, studied the mortality rate of infants in two types of orphanages in England; he found that the extent to which the children were physically stroked and handled had a profound effect upon their survival.

TA analysts maintain that continual strokes are necessary throughout one's life; a lack of strokes has a deleterious and long-lasting effect, both physically and emotionally.

Habitual criminals with high recidivism rates illustrate that negative strokes are better than no strokes at all. The primate studies of Harry Harlow (1958) demonstrate that isolated baby monkeys reared either without mother monkeys or those "fed" by surrogate wire monkeys become emotionally disturbed and exhibit abnormal behaviors. Sensory-deprivation experiments with normal adults at Harvard (Vernon, 1961) illustrate that both cognitive and motor functioning will rapidly deteriorate and deficits will persist for days, even after the persons go back into a normal environment. Illusions and hallucinations can be produced by a temporary lack of sensory stimuli. More than 700 TA articles and descriptions of strokes have appeared in scientific journals and related literature since 1957 (Blair & McGahey, 1974, 1975).

Human children growing up begin to look for ways to get both verbal and symbolic strokes from others when physical strokes are not forthcoming. Although spoken words may become the major sources of strokes for people in later life, it is doubtful whether words alone can ever completely replace actual physical touching. In *Having a baby*, K. Dusay states that many mothers actually stroke their bellies throughout pregnancy which becomes the infants' earliest strokes (Bert, D., et al, 1984).

As specific stroking patterns develop, they may be more clearly understood by attention to both the structural and functional analyses of ego states, transactions, psychological games, and scripts.

Structural analysis

Ego states are defined as a consistent pattern of feeling and experiences directly related to a corresponding consistent pattern of behavior. A distinct tripartite system of Parent, Adult, and Child, which are

separate entities, has been described and is the subject of structural analysis proper. Although most of the salient features of ego states have been presented in the History section, it is important to re-emphasize that ego states are a phenomenological system based upon here-and-now observable data, in contrast to psychoanalytic concepts that primarily emphasize developmental stages and view pathology as resulting from fixations in development.

One's ego states are not related to chronological age, except developmentally during early childhood when one's Adult and Parent are not yet fully developed. A teenager may have a staunch moral and value system (P); an 8-year-old boy may look to the right and left for oncoming cars before crossing the street (A); a 65-year-old chairman of the board will gleefully chase his young, sexy secretary around the conference table (C).

Certain pathologies in personalities can be structurally understood with the three ego states (see Figures 11.5, 11.6, and 11.7). Figure 11.5 illustrates a normal personal-

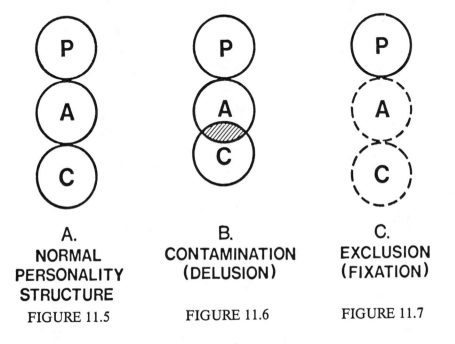

A.	B.	C.
NORMAL PERSONALITY STRUCTURE	CONTAMINATION (DELUSION)	EXCLUSION (FIXATION)
FIGURE 11.5	FIGURE 11.6	FIGURE 11.7

ity structure, whereby each ego state has a distinct and separate boundary. Figure 11.6 is the structure of a delusion. In this instance, there is a Child-Adult delusion in that the separating boundaries have broken down. The Child's fantasies and dreams are inappropriately mixed in with Adult reality and logic testing. This person might say, "The TV is giving me special instructions." His Adult is accurate that there is a TV transmitting information. The Child ego has regarded itself as the center of the TV's attention, thereby causing a break in the boundaries between the Adult and the Child. Figure 11.7 illustrates the structure of an exclusion. The Parent is represented by a heavy, dark, solid circle; the Adult and the Child have only dotted lines. This strong boundary insures that the Parent is in charge, and the Adult and Child are excluded. A fundamentalist country preacher who obsesses himself with finding sins is operating from an excluding Parent ego state.

The functional aspects of personality

The structural description of ego states with their circles and boundaries indicates the "what and where" of the personality; the concept of "how much energy" of the five ego state forces (Critical Parent-CP; Nurturing Parent-NP; Adult-A; Free Child-FC; and Adapted Child-AC) is answered by the functional approach of the egogram.

Any group of trained ego-state observers

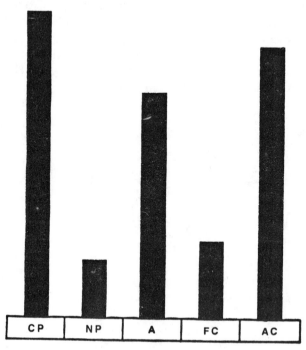

SELF DESTRUCTIVE EGOGRAM

FIGURE 11.8

can readily identify these five basic forces within people, and each will construct similar egograms of the same person. They will consensually agree on the personality-force balance, or imbalance, as depicted on the subject's egogram. These same egograms can be drawn accurately week after week by different trained observers. The ego states will line up differently on each person's egogram, and correspond directly to the specific complaints and problems these people express. An egogram with an excessively high CP, a high A, a high AC, a low NP, and a low FC is characteristically associated with a person who is self-destructive (see Figure 11.8). Other consistent findings reveal that when a very high AC is combined with a very low NP, the common complaint will be of loneliness and lack of friends (see Figure 11.9). A certain type of obesity, colloquially labeled "Big Mama," is correlated with a very high NP, a high AC, a low CP, and a very low FC. This Big Mama egogram is common among overweight persons in the helping professions: social workers, nurses, dieticians, and those who live with demanding spouses and children who seem to require an abundance of nurturing and strokes. These persons spend most of their energies giving to others and unfortunately get very little back for their FC in the way of strokes. People who are too low in CP get taken advantage of and pushed around. Persons who are quite low in NP are lonely, depressed, and ungiving;

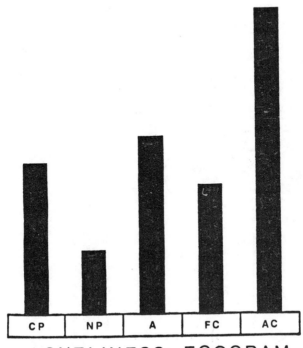

CP NP A FC AC

LONELINESS EGOGRAM

FIGURE 11.9

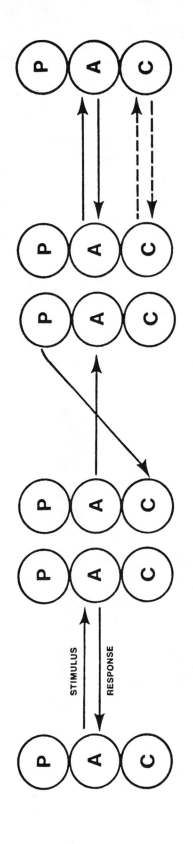

A.
COMPLEMENTARY

STIMULUS

RESPONSE

S. BOSS : "WHAT TIME IS IT?"
R. SECRETARY : "THREE O'CLOCK"

FIGURE 11.10

B.
CROSSED

S. BOSS : "WHAT TIME IS IT?"
R. SECRETARY : "LOOK AT YOUR
OWN WATCH—STUPID!"

FIGURE 11.11

C.
ULTERIOR

S. BOSS : "WHAT TIME IS IT?"
R. SECRETARY "WOULDN'T YOU
LIKE TO KNOW"

S. BOSS : "LET'S PLAY"
R. SECRETARY : "HEE HEE"

FIGURE 11.12

TRANSACTIONS

those low in A have difficulty concentrating and problem solving; those low in FC have lost their creativity, intuition, and the zest of life. Persons who are low in AC do not compromise or conform, and are difficult to get along with.

A person's egogram reflects the type of person one is, the probable types of problems, and the strengths and weaknesses within one's personality. The egogram also provides a personal map for growth and change. Although there is no ideal egogram, people experience difficulties when one ego state is extremely low and another is disproportionately high. Relative to that, a harmonious egogram becomes a matter of balance in the relationship between the ego states. A creative artist needs a high FC; a successful district attorney needs a high CP; an accountant needs a strong A; a diplomat needs lots of AC; and a therapist needs a well-developed NP.

Transactions and the three rules of communication

TA focuses keen attention upon how different individuals tend to communicate with one another. A *transaction* is defined as a stimulus and a related response between various ego states of two or more people, and, graphically, they are symbolized by arrows. The two primary types of transactions are the *social* overt and easily observed level, represented by a solid arrow; and the *psychological* covert, body-language level, represented by a dotted arrow.

The three specific types of transactions, with their three corresponding rules of communication, have been delineated (see Figures 11.10, 11.11, 11.12). In Figure 11.10, entitled Complementary Transaction, the arrows are parallel. The boss (A) asks the secretary (A), "What time is it?" He gets a complementary straightforward,

overt response (A to A), "It's 3 o'clock." The first rule of communication involves a complementary transaction: *Whenever the arrows are parallel, communication can proceed indefinitely.* Communication does not have to be A-A; it can be P-P, C-C, P-C, C-P, C-A, A-P, P-A, or the reverse. In Figure 11.11 there is a crossed transaction and the arrows are crossed. The boss asks (A-A), "What time is it?" and the secretary angrily answers (P-C), "Look at your own watch!" This crossed transaction effectively stops the communication about "time" between them. Therefore, the corresponding second rule of communication is: *Whenever the arrows cross, communication on the specific subject ceases immediately.* This second rule of communication clarifies the phenomena of *transference* as described in psychoanalytic literature. The therapist says, "You seem to be late for your Friday appointment" (A-A), and the client reports, "You're always criticizing me for being late—just like my father" (C-P). A *countertransference* is when a therapist crosses a complementary transaction; that is, the client says, "How long do you think my treatment will be?" (A-A). The therapist replies, "You shouldn't ask questions like that" (P-C). Figure 11.12 illustrates an ulterior transaction with dual levels (the social and the psychological) occurring simultaneously. The boss again asks the secretary the time (A-A social level and C-C hidden psychological level). She gives him the time (A-A social level and C-C playful psychological level). A dual-level transaction with an ulterior message is necessary for a psychological game. This leads to the third rule of communication: *Behavior cannot be predicted by attention to the social level alone; the psychological message is the key to predicting behavior and understanding the meaning.* The first game ever discovered (p. 404), *WHY DON'T YOU . . . YES, BUT*

..., is one in which the client enticed the group to "try" to help her solve her problem. After continuing to try, they became frustrated and finally gave up, while the client coyly smiled and triumphantly exulted that no one could solve her problem (ha-ha). Analyzing and identifying the ulterior transactions are necessary to understanding psychological games.

Psychological games

A *game* is played between two or more people, and each game has certain traits in common. The players transact on an *open* (overt) level, and at the same time transmit a *hidden* agenda (covert level). Consider Fanny the secretary, who complained that she was unable to hold a job, having been fired 20 times in 10 years. She stated she wanted a solid, long-term working relationship with an employer (she also wanted a long-term, social relationship in her life). Her therapist agreed with her goal and contracted to work with her to achieve it. During their initial interview, Fanny started by criticizing the therapist's necktie; then she began to rearrange her chair and the rest of the office furniture; and finally, she "accidentally" knocked over the therapist's favorite lamp. As Fanny was apologizing and bending over to reposition the lamp, she placed the distinctive target of her posterior near the therapist's foot, which he instantly considered kicking. Suddenly, with an intuitive laugh, he checked his anger and his foot. Fanny turned to face him with a knowing look, and she, too, began to laugh

as they both became aware that she was playing a physical version of her favorite *Kick Me* game (see Figure 11.2).

On the obvious social level (solid lines), Fanny said to the therapist (A-A), "Please help me with my problem." The therapist responded (A-A), "Your problem seems psychological. Let's work it out." On the surface, their conversation sounded A-A; however, on the hidden psychological level (broken lines), Fanny's C was inviting the therapist's P to kick her as she insulted his clothing, rearranged his furniture, and knocked over his favorite lamp. This same pattern of interaction, occurring in the therapist's office, directly corresponded with her past history of repeated rejections and was reflected in her chief complaint. In Fanny's case, an unknowing therapist may have actually responded by playing her game, by kicking her out of treatment as an inappropriate candidate for psychotherapy, and by thinking, "Some patients just mess up the office and don't get any better, no matter what you do." Fanny's payoff could have been, "Why do rejections always happen to me?"

A TA analyst understands a personality by first observing the "here-and-now" transactional sequences between himself and the client. Games conform to a general yet specific game formula (Figure 11.13): $C + G = R \rightarrow S \rightarrow X \rightarrow P$. The initial Con (C) is the "bait" in which the client (Fanny) transacts on an ulterior level from her C to the therapist's P. On the surface, her transaction looks like a straight-

$$C + G = R \dashrightarrow S \dashrightarrow X \dashrightarrow P$$

GAME FORMULA

FIGURE 11.13

forward request for help; yet underneath, she is secretly asking for a rejection as she "hooks" the therapist's feeling of omnipotence, which is seen as the Gimmick (G). His response (R) is initially accepting and forgiving, as he continues to overlook her critique of his necktie and her rearrangement of his furniture. Fanny continued to annoy him; yet the therapist remained composed until the final Switch (S) of feelings. The therapist and client both felt a Cross-up (X), which quickly led to the final Payoff (P) for both. Had the therapist not stopped the game, his Payoff would have entitled him to feel angry at his ungrateful client; and Fanny's Payoff would have entitled her to another desired rejection as well as a potential banishment. Certain symptoms and syndromes of psychopathology can be understood by analyzing the final payoffs of games. By playing their favorite games, people will repetitively collect payoff *trading stamps*, which are those specific treasured feelings about themselves and others; Fanny received "black and blue" trading stamps each time she was kicked out and fired. After she collected enough stamps, she would entitle herself to a "free depression" and perhaps end up in the hospital. Although some psychotherapists will observe the precipitating event, the TA analyst will look at the entire system of events for each interactional pattern. These continuing repetitive patterns of payoffs and their corresponding negative feelings are seen as *racket feelings*. These are common feelings that persons have chosen to use, since a young age, whenever they are in stressful situations. Persons will commonly choose racket feelings of being sad, scared, or angry. A racket feeling is the same feeling used over and over, regardless of whether it is appropriate. Game sequences and rackets are important to the therapist in understanding a client's present behavior and personality, as well as being indicators for probable future behavior. A person who commits suicide has a long history of collecting rejections and playing self-negating games. Therefore, by correctly diagnosing and interrupting games, rather than unknowingly entering into them, the therapist can thwart a client's entire payoff system.

Berne referred to the first-, the second-, and the third-degree states of games (1964). A *first-degree game* is considered socially acceptable in that no one gets physically hurt, although one may be admonished or yelled at. A *second-degree game* is more serious, in that there is frequently a punch in the nose or face slap. A *third-degree game* is deadly serious and may be "played for keeps." The payoffs are frequently ostracism, a messy divorce, a trip to the court room, or to the morgue. Game switches are characteristically sudden, abrupt, and dramatic—particularly in second- and third-degree games.

Game players operate from three distinct roles—the victim, the persecutor, and the rescuer—and they make switches between these roles. The role switches are illustrated on a drama triangle (Karpman, 1968). Each role is interchangeable and persons frequently switch back and forth during the course of the game (see Figure 11.14). Fanny entered treatment as a *victim*, complaining of being fired and of having a miserable childhood. The unwitting therapist commenced as a *rescuer*. Fanny then switched into a *persecutor* by criticizing the therapist's necktie, rearranging his furniture, and knocking over his lamp, while the therapist became a victim of her persecutions. Quickly, he switched into a persecutor as his anger mounted, while Fanny quickly switched back into her familiar victim role and positioned her bottom by his foot. Role switches occur quickly and dramatically; they have been

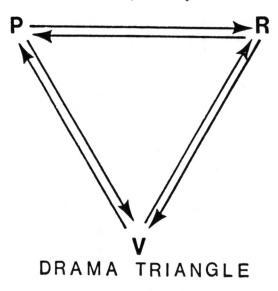

DRAMA TRIANGLE

FIGURE 11.14

the backbone of drama and theater throughout the centuries. Role switches occur throughout mythology, fairy tales, all successful literature, and even in everyday TV soap operas (K. Dusay, 1976).

Authentic behavior is differentiated from game behavior, although it may have some similarities. The client enters the therapist's office, and straightforwardly says, "Help, I need some support." The therapist offers support, and the client says, "Thank you," smiles and leaves. No dramatic switch has occurred; this exchange remains a straightforward simple set of complementary transactions.

Scripts

The important question for understanding personality is: why do different individuals choose specific games? The answer is found by analyzing the crucial transactions between parents and their children during the early development years; this system is illustrated on a script matrix (Steiner, 1971a; Fig. 11.3). Fanny

was given a typical Standard Success Story (SSS) by her parents: "Go to college, make money, get married, and have children." These *values* (Arrow 1) were introjected from the P ego states of her parents to her developing P ego state. Fanny accepted her parents' values and eventually made them her own. The *injunctions* (Arrow 2) are usually unspoken and delivered as a "curse" from a parent's C to the child's C (technically the Adapted Child—not the autonomous Free Child). Injunctions are usually delivered from the parent of the opposite sex and they are frequently symbolized by a dotted line, in that they are seldom discussed or stated out loud. Fanny's father had difficulty in being close and intimate, and he would insinuate "get lost" messages. Because he nonverbally ignored her with his scowl and frowns, Fanny began to decide she was not a worthwhile person and could not make it ("don't be" and "don't make it"). The *values* from her father ("be a success") directly contradicted his injunctions ("don't be" and "don't make it"). Confronted with the dilemma of these incongruent messages, Fanny looked to her mother for an answer of how to get along in a family like this. As a child, Fanny noted that her mother pestered and irritated her father for attention—her *technique* (Arrow 3). After her father mentally and physically assaulted her mother, the mother would sulk into her separate bedroom. Fanny's mother thus "showed" Fanny specific techniques how to be a pest and get rejected, the *here's how* (Arrow 3), which was her personal version of the *Kick Me* game. Values, injunctions, and techniques comprise the elements of one's script. The values are also called the *counterscript* or *counterinjunction*. When Fanny was not getting "kicked," she was being a success-oriented, well-behaved person.

Scripts have been written and theorized about by TA analysts throughout the last decade. Berne's views about script formation are found in *What Do You Say after You Say Hello?* (1972). Berne classified specific types of scripts: an *over and over* script corresponds to the myth of Sisyphus; an *always* script relates to persons who perpetually suffer; an *until* script insures that the individual will be unhappy until a significant event happens; a *never* script forbids happiness and love; an *after* script requires that the person complete many things first, and then enjoy himself after; *open-ended* scripts insure that persons will lose their vitality and enthusiasm as they drift into old age. To Berne the five requirements of a script are (1) directives from parents, (2) a corresponding personality development, (3) a confirming childhood decision about oneself and life, (4) a penchant for either success or failure, and (5) a convincing way of behaving.

Berne viewed how the contents of one's script and their corresponding myths and fairy tales would occur in the therapist's office. As was Berne's style, he would begin with the presenting problem, and then he would take it back into the past. A client wearing a bright red, hooded cape came into his office complaining that her wolfish boyfriend had just jilted her, and she sighed, "Why does this always happen to me? Wolves seem to prey on me." Not surprisingly, her favorite fairy tale was Little Red Riding Hood, frequently told to her by her mother when she went to bed at night. The Child part of her mother would emphasize that wolves prey on helpless victims. Berne traced the genesis of this human script back to the tale of Europa who was kidnapped by Zeus disguised as a bull. Berne's impression was that the mythologies in the fairy tales show up in modern living. Steiner's book *Scripts People Live* (1971) distinguishes between banal scripts and *hamartic* (tragic) scripts. K. Dusay (1975) has made an analysis of the recurrence of fairy tales and myths in the therapist's office by analyzing the scripts and egograms of classical heroes and heroines throughout history.

Variety of Concepts

Varieties within the TA family

Although all TA therapists work with the psychology of ego states, there are divergencies and different focuses, depending upon the various types of problems encountered.

Robert and Mary Goulding work mainly with therapists and mental health professionals in a marathon or retreat setting. Jacqui and Aaron Schiff work basically with schizophrenics who are either unable or unwilling to be responsible for themselves at the onset of treatment. Claude Steiner works with counter-culture radicals, students, and alternate life-style individuals. Martin Groeder set up the Aescalapian program in prison systems. Dru Scott, Dorothy Jongeward, Muriel

James, and others problem solve in nonclinical settings with business and industry. The uses and ramifications of TA continue to be widespread and diverse, as the refinement in personality theory inevitably develops.

Decision-redecision methods

Robert and Mary Goulding are the co-directors of the Western Institute for Group and Family Therapy and they provided an important redecision model used by many TA therapists, especially in the treatment of nonpsychotic individuals. They emphasize early childhood decisions wherein a young child decides to be an "OK" or "not-OK" person, based upon the injunctions he received. The Gouldings have identified and classified the types of childhood decisions that result from injunctions such as "don't be you," "don't think," "don't feel," "don't be a child," "don't grow up," and "don't be." Because one's basic life decision had survival value in early childhood, the individual develops racket feelings that are the same habitual, stereotyped, emotional responses to each situation. Early decisions and racket feelings are carried throughout life, and a client will protect them in therapy through impasses (Goulding & Goulding, 1976).

In redecision work, a milieu for change is created, the individual reexperiences decision moments and then chooses to redecide about himself by self-confrontation.

Reparenting

The Cathexis approach to TA (or Schiff family method) was founded by Jacqui Lee Schiff. Both her theoretical model and treatment are focused upon seriously disturbed persons who have generally been diagnosed as schizophrenic. Although the common end point of therapy is autonomy, initially the client is passive, dependent, and accepts no responsibility for his behavior. Four passivity behaviors have been identified by Jacqui and Aaron Schiff (1971): (1) doing nothing; (2) overadaptation; (3) agitation; and (4) incapacitation or violence. These behaviors are attempts to reestablish or maintain a symbiotic relationship (see Figure 11.15).

In a *symbiotic* relationship, a mother and her child become intimately linked in a mutually dependent way, and they behave as a *single* individual; usually the mother functions as the operating Parent and Adult, and her offspring maintains only the Child ego state. In other words, two persons are operating as one complete individual in a symbiotic relationship. Symbiosis is normal during early infancy; later it is seen as pathological. A discount is an internal mechanism whereby a person will deny oneself and others as responsible or capable. Jacqui and Aaron Schiff have identified the four principal discounts that maintain a symbiosis and "entitle" the person to remain passive. One can discount: (1) the existence of a problem ("The fire in the house is not a problem"); (2) the significance of the problem ("Well, the house is on fire but it isn't important"); (3) the solution to the problem ("Well, the house is on fire, but there's nothing that can be done about it"); and (4) discounting oneself and others ("yes, the house is on fire, and it possibly could be changed, but I cannot do anything about it and neither can you"). By employing these discounts, a person effectively removes his responsibility to solve problems. *Grandiosity* is another mechanism defined by the Schiffs that involves either a maximized or minimized exaggeration about a person, problem, or event, in which a person entitles himself to stay the same and thus justify the symbiosis ("I am too scared to think").

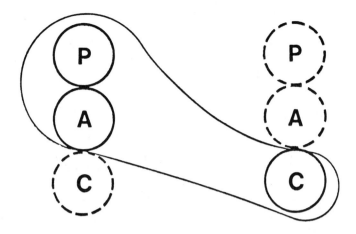

SYMBIOSIS

FIGURE 11.15

The Schiffs employ unique, and frequently controversial, treatment methods (J. Schiff et al., 1975).

TA and variations from other theories

Comparisons among TA and some other important therapies were made in the Overview section. TA theory is based upon the "here-and-now" social interactions, and does not adhere to a theory of the dynamic unconscious. The "unconscious" mind is not focused upon by TA analysis; instead, actual stroking patterns are. One's drives are viewed as being script determined and programmed by early parental messages, rather than being seen as drives and instincts. Transference and countertransference phenomena are seen as two specific types of transactions. *Homeostasis* is considered from an energy system on the egogram. *Resistances* to one's growth and change in psychotherapy are viewed functionally as a stronger ego state force holding down a lower force. A highly critical individual (high CP, low FC, and low NP) was being seen in a TA group because he had few friends. His case illustrates the principles of resistance. When the TA therapist asked the group members to take off their shoes and sit on the floor, this "true grit" person stood up, banged his fist, and roared, "I won't take off my shoes—that's stupid! I came here to get friends—not to take off my shoes!" His resistance was seen as protecting the homeostasis of his personality (his CP holding down his FC).

Rebellion to a TA analyst is a type of conformity to a script injunction and is seen as a pseudorebellion. Taking exotic pills is following an early message of "You're crazy." Authentic rebellion is breaking away from the script.

A final note to consider when comparing conceptual variations among different psychotherapies was made by Eric Berne (1963) when he noted that a great fallacy, to either affirm or negate a particular argument, is to employ different viewpoints. Any finding may be described functionally, structurally, phenomenologically, clinically, chemically, molecularly, and so on. Many times theorists will mix up these systems and will thus negate a finding in one modality by using a frame of reference from another mode, which gives an end result of mixing apples and oranges.

PSYCHOTHERAPY

Theory of Psychotherapy

Transactional analysts focus upon three primary areas for psychotherapy: egogram balances, game interruptions, and script redecisions. A client's change in one area will facilitate a corresponding change in his other areas. *Balance* is a key word in personality change; and although a TA therapist does not expect clients to be *homogenized* (all with the same egogram), efforts are made to insure that no one ego-state force is gravely underenergized. One's awareness of specific games one plays will lead to a position of choice for interrupting these stereotyped, habitual patterns. A game-free individual is frequently rewarded both with interpersonal and social intimacy, which is not possible through game playing. A person's script redecision will facilitate the individual in living an autonomous life, free from the influences of parental injunctions.

Although a TA therapist becomes a catalyzer of change, there is a basic underlying TA assumption that the client alone is responsible for his life, choices, and basic survival in the unique family environment. A person's negative existential life decisions (I'm not OK, or you're not OK) about himself and others do not need to be dragged around throughout life like a bag of dirty laundry. Instead, people have the ability to review their negative childhood decisions and thereby change their minds, personalities, and life-styles. Unfortunately, many people give up their recognition of personal power and active-

ly deny and defend their lack of responsibility.

A few TA approaches have unique views concerning the individual's responsibility. Steiner's "radical" therapy focuses upon oppressive social institutions, and emphasizes positive social action in addition to personal psychotherapy. The Schiff family techniques are designed for psychotic clients who may initially regress to a dependent child state and are then reparented and reraised with new OK messages. Eventually these clients establish a personal responsibility for their lives.

Process of Psychotherapy

To facilitate a client's personal responsibility, a TA therapist will use a simple, common vocabulary; will enter into a contractual treatment goal; and will then use specific techniques designed to enhance each individual's own power and responsibility. These three areas are generally used by all TA therapists and are seen and heard in TA treatment settings.

Simple language

The simple vocabulary of TA, ego states (Parent, Adult and Child), games (colloquially expressed, for example, *Now I Got You, You SOB*), scripts, and strokes are easily learned and have also been successfully taught to mentally retarded people who can understand these concepts. Family members (parents and their children) are on an equal vocabulary footing, and even well-educated professionals are encouraged to talk straight and not hide behind big words and complex jargon. The time and energy a client spends in treatment is directed toward getting better—not in defining and redefining.

Unfortunately, naive critics of TA sometimes focus exclusively upon the colloquial words they have heard about so they can quickly discount the scientific profundity of the theory. A popular joke in TA circles concerns a TA therapist who sat next to an astronomer on an airplane flight. The astronomer asked what he did for a living and the TA therapist replied that he did TA. The astronomer then exclaimed, "Oh, I know all about that—'I'm OK, You're OK!' " The TA therapist politely smiled, then asked, "What do you do for a living?" and the response was "I'm an astronomer." The TA therapist smiled, and quipped back, "Oh, I know all about that—'Twinkle, Twinkle, Little Star!' "

Contractual therapy

A key question in contractual therapy is, "How will both you and I know when you get what you came for?" This statement immediately clarifies that the client and therapist are mutual allies working to accomplish a mutual goal. Throughout the therapy contract, each will be defining their mutual responsibilities in achieving the goal; the therapist will not enter in a passive spectator position and the client will not sit back waiting for the therapist to perform a miracle (seen as the game of *Do Me Something*). A TA treatment contract has the four major components of a legal contract:

1. Mutual assent. A simply stated contract *goal* between the Adult ego states of both the therapist and the client is made; both persons become Adult ego state allies. "I will have sex again," from an impotent man; "I will hold a job for at least one year," from an habitually fired person; "I will not kill myself accidentally, or on purpose," from a suicidal person, are all examples of contracts. Contracts are also stated by specific egogram changes, "I'll be satisfied when the group constructs my egogram with my Free Child to be greater than my Adapted Child." Therapy contracts are frequently reviewed, updated, and changed. Mini or weekly contracts may also lead to a more profound change —"I will speak to three people this week" —as a step' toward a long-term goal of having an intimate social relationship.

Initial difficulties in making contracts may take the form of games that a TA therapist will need to be aware of. A client may take two hours off from work and risk being fired, or he may pay a substantial fee to the therapist and continue to say that he does not know what he wants to change about himself. A TA therapist may then ask, "What does your Parent say you *should* get out of treatment? What *fantasies* does your Child have? What will your Adult decide to be a worthwhile goal?" Unless a therapist and client have mutual assent about a common goal, the therapist may become a nontherapeutic, rescuing, advice giver, and not a catalytic mutual ally of the client.

2. Competency. The TA therapist will agree to provide only those services he can *competently* deliver in the area of his expertise. The therapist will also actively confront the client's misperceptions and fantasies about the assumed "magical" powers of the therapist. A competent therapist would not contract with a 55-year-old man to become the world's champion 100-yard-dash runner. However, the therapist may contract with him to exercise and become healthy. A client also needs to be competent in achieving his goals of the contract. If the client is still legally or financially dependent upon parents, they need to be included in the treatment contract. Occasionally social agencies and legal guardians need be a part of a treatment-contract planning session. Therapists will attest to this when working with families that quickly pull the client out of therapy when he begins to change.

3. Legal object. The contract must have a *legal* aim or objective. "Provide me with mind altering drugs, Doctor, so I can become more aware of myself," is not a legal contract. "I want to graduate from college with a B-average," may be an acceptable contract.

4. Consideration. Usually the *consideration* is the therapist's fee the client agrees to pay. The therapist will provide his expertise and the therapeutic time. TA therapists who treat clients either in social agencies or under circumstances where the client is not expected personally to pay for therapy will encourage the client to offer a type of consideration, perhaps in the form of a service, a painting, a poem, or some other product which represents the client's commitment to therapy.

Specific techniques to enhance personal responsibility

People who experience themselves as powerless to change continue to reinforce this position by habitually broadcasting their plight. The TA therapist will confront this observation to create an awareness of self-power in the individual. When a client says, "I *can't* think," the TA therapist will confront with, "I *won't* think!" When a client says, "*She makes* me feel bad," the therapist will correct with, "*I choose to feel* bad—in response to her." Persons who continually say, "You know," and other cliches, are confronted and shown why others do not take them seriously. *Gallows humor* is inappropriate smiling, laughing, and inviting others to laugh at one's tragic situation. A client with a serious drinking problem who says, "I just had one little drink . . . hee-hee," is confronted with the fact that drinking himself to death is not funny. J. McNeel (1975) has elaborated specific, commonly used TA techniques and attitudes

that clients use to rob themselves of power, based on observations of a three-day TA treatment marathon led by Robert and Mary Goulding (see "Applications" section). Blackboards are commonplace in TA groups so clients can visually represent their explanations in clear ways to commit their ideas. Chalk is frequently handed to clients who play the game of *Stupid*, to provide them with permission to problem-solve. TA emphasizes symbols and simple diagrams so both the therapist and the client can clearly delineate their ideas.

Although TA therapists use simple vocabularies, treatment contracts, and specific pertinent techniques to restore the client's power, the types of therapy may differ widely. Originally, Berne designed TA as an adjunct to psychoanalysis, to be practiced in small groups with seven or eight clients that meet for two hours weekly. Now people are seen individually, in families, as couples, in marathons, in inpatient and outpatient wards, in prisons, and in business and industry settings. Each modality has certain advantages and disadvantages. What can be typically seen and heard by TA practitioners varies widely beyond the above general processes, depending upon the types of problems, the treatment settings, and the styles of the therapists. Therapists are encouraged to use their personal attributes and not fit into a TA mold. Some common processes are discussed below, and although attention to games, scripts, and ego-state structure and function does not follow a particular order in treatment, the descriptions provide the historical development of these processes.

Game analysis by confrontation

During the initial interview, the therapist observes the usual social amenities, like saying "Hello," and neither uses gimmicks to increase stress, nor leans over backward to provide comfort. The business of establishing a treatment contract, deciding on whether the therapist and client are able to work together, and choosing a proper treatment setting (individual, group, family, etc.) are the usual topics.

Because games are habitual, stereotyped patterns of transacting, they will usually begin to manifest in the initial interview and the therapist is keenly interested in picking up game clues, such as a person telling a sad history of failure and then subtly smiling. This tips off the therapist that two levels of transactions are occurring, and as soon as the therapist is aware of a game occurring, the decision to intervene is made (see "Applications," pages 427-430, for a description of intervention).

In addition to observing the client's dual levels of transacting, the communication pattern between therapist and client is also observed. Eric Berne called himself a "martian" in therapy and indeed called all TAers "martians." This implied that the therapist transcended the setting and observed how he and the client transacted with each other; that is, "When the therapist offers a suggestion the client says, 'Yes...but...,' and the therapist looks disgruntled." The therapist therefore observes the process and himself as well as observing the client; this is reminiscent of Theodore Reik's (1948) "Listening with the Third Ear" and Harry Stack Sullivan's concept of observing the interpersonal processes.

More important than the therapist's knowing what is happening is the awareness of the client and *interruption* of the patterns. Groups are often useful because of the increased transactional possibilities, and other clients may pick up blind spots of the therapist. Verbal interruptions are extremely important for counteracting games; that is, the therapist quickly says, "But . . . ," just before the client says it himself; or when a young female *Rapo* player is complaining that men are just interested in her body, as her skirt slips slowly up her thighs, the therapist acknowledges the seductive moves, and says, "I think I know why!"

In addition to verbal interruption, the therapist may stand up and ask the client to do likewise; they then both comment on what is going on between the two of them; like Berne's "martian" observers, they have an Adult to Adult ego-state conversation. Occasionally an empty chair is offered and the client is asked to sit in it and describe the ongoing interaction.

Game interruption by psychodrama

When a client enters into a game with either the therapist or another group member, or even when the client talks about a game he played with someone outside of the group ("My wife and I had another *Uproar*"), the TA therapist may structure a psychodrama. The client becomes the director and is asked to stand up (a client-empowering technique) and then choose two people in the group to play his and his wife's roles in the game in the identical ways they play "*Uproar*."

The therapist encourages the client-director to think, direct, and plot out the important game moves that will lead to the usual conclusion or the negative payoff feelings that both players received. The client-director may actually reexperience his own feelings while directing the psychodrama which will provide clarity and even release of affect. By using this type of psychodrama, the client is able to step outside of his own game system; in this way he can view, think, and direct his own part in the game. This client-director role is seen as the "martian" position in that the client can be an interested observer, rather than a habitual participant in his own behavior. Through these maneuvers, the client will gain a new awareness and experiment with corrective procedures.

Script treatment

An individual will gain social control by an intact, aware Adult; yet many individuals need also to direct their energies into reversing their basic life scripts.

Fanny, the woman who was repeatedly fired from her jobs, was able to catch herself and stop playing *Kick Me* when she used her Adult. She also decided to continue her therapy to make a script change. Fanny remembered being kicked out of many groups while she was growing up: the Brownies' summer camp, various grade school classes, high school classes, a social club, her college sorority, and finally being fired from each job she held. Her earliest memories included banishment and punishments for her behavior by her impatient parents. She developed negative stroking patterns that became the foundation of her script. Her early injunctions were "Get lost, you bother me." After receiving a bombardment of these injunctions, Fanny decided to live her life getting put down and kicked as this was how she got "strokes" and survived in her family. Through therapy and script redecisions, Fanny was able to change her script and stop her negative patterns.

Script reversal

Berne devised the original script-change technique in the 1960s; he believed in a mutual, trusting relationship between the client and the therapist, which would facilitate the client receiving a potent *counterinjunction* (the opposite of what mother or father said to the client), thereby removing the negative influences. Berne, after attaining a suicidal client's trust, would state decisively, "*Do not kill yourself.*" Many suicidal clients responded to him that *no one* ever said that to them before.

Eric Berne, Claude Steiner, Stephen Karpman, Patricia Crossman, John Dusay and other participants of the early San Francisco seminars considered the script injunction to be like an electrode lodged in the Child. The term *electrode* is appropriate because scripted individuals habitually and automatically react in predictable, destructive manners under a wide variety of circumstances. Therefore, Berne's powerfully potent, curative, counterscript message, delivered at the proper time, enabled persons to revise their scripts.

Reparenting

Another form of script intervention is the *reparenting* technique developed by Jacqui Schiff and others. Reparenting was developed for severely disturbed and psychotic patients. Severely disturbed individuals have a natural tendency to regress and relive early childhood experiences. Reparenting is done in a therapeutic, residential treatment center, and the clients are reared by positive parenting. This treatment may take many years and there is a direct, active commitment by the therapist who performs the functions of the new parents; although reparenting is viewed as controversial, it has been found to be effective in work with "untreatable" schizophrenics (J. Schiff, 1970; J. Schiff et al., 1975).

Redecision

A popular and effective technique to bring about script change is *redecision therapy* in a TA framework using Gestalt techniques, formulated by Fritz Perls. By the use of double chairs, Perls had the client separate the negative and the positive parts of self to oppose one another.

Robert and Mary Goulding took this further by combining Perls's techniques and Berne's theories to create an environment for a client's growth and change (Goulding, 1972, 1974). They are chiefly credited for the development of redecision work. Berne once said that anything that has been learned can be unlearned. This is also valid for redecision, and a detailed description is included in the "Applications" section (pages 427-430).

Ego-state oppositions

Persons can change their weaknesses into their strengths and redecide about their life scripts by transferring their ego-state energies to lesser used ego states (J. Dusay, 1972). (See Figure 11.16.)

Script decisions commonly take three general forms: (1) "I'm sad," a person who has decided he is not OK in relation to others; (2) "I'm mad," a person who decided to be OK at the expense that other people are considered to be not OK; and

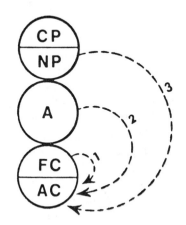

EGO STATE OPPOSITION

FIGURE 11.16

(3) "I'm scared," a person who has decided he is not OK and neither are the other people. Individuals coming into treatment will, during times of stress, revert into their habitual stereotyped patterns of thinking, feeling and behaving. A person who has decided to be not OK will look, think, feel and behave depressed. The same will occur with a person who has decided to be scared or one who has decided to become mad. A trained TA therapist will watch for these habitual script patterns to occur and then will move into an ego-state opposition process and employ the techniques described by John Dusay in his TA *Treatment-Training Manual* (1978). The process goes this way:

1. The client is encouraged to enhance the here-and-now expression of the "racket" feelings. The therapist may recognize telltale signs and symptoms of the client's racket behavior, such as tense muscles, and will instruct the client to become temporarily more tense. This facilitates the client's reexperiencing of negative feelings so that he can move from the here-and-now back to earlier decisive moments of childhood.

2. The individual is asked via a regressive technique, such as hypnosis or guided fantasy, to close his eyes and trace the same feeling back to the earliest recollection. Breuer and Freud (1893/1962) termed these early feelings *hyperesthetic memories*.

3. When a person has gone back to an early moment of making a script decision, the therapist encourages the client to *oppose* that decision with another growth ego state. For instance, depressed persons will oppose their scripted Adapted Child ego states with their underused Free Child states by being directed to switch between them using empty double chairs (Arrow 1). A "mad" person who is frequently para-

noid will be encouraged to oppose the Adapted Child with the Adult to distinguish clearly which persons are friends and which are not (Arrow 2). A scared person will be encouraged to oppose that part with the Nurturing Parent for reassurance (Arrow 3). This process hastens the transfer of psychological energy and begins the road toward a script redecision. The client, not the therapist, uses and summons his own psychological strengths to oppose these stubbornly held viewpoints of himself.

4. Resistances commonly arise when the client slips out of the "curative" ego state and back into the "stuck" scripted state. An adroit TA therapist will quickly confront this behavior so the resistant person will not reinforce the stuck pathology.

There are several advantages to doing script redecision work in a group setting. Other members are inspired and can reflect on their own situation; the therapist is aided as other members confront resistances; other group members can correct blind spots that occasionally occur in one-to-one therapy; and the client himself or herself is both congratulated and happily stroked for positive work.

When redecision work is not successful, the usual reason occurs when the client is opposing the negative, adapted self with a non-growth force. Sometimes the growth force (nurturing, logic, or creativity) is overwhelmed by the strength (stubbornness) of the scripted part. This is where attention to transfer of energy seen on the egogram is important.

Egogram transfer of energy

When one shifts energies from an overused ego state to a low-power ego state, the experience is exhilarating and becomes self-reinforcing. Fanny usually behaved as a "naughty little pest" intent on provoking negative responses from others.

The initial scripting she accepted dictated that this behavior was her most profitable method of getting strokes. Her *Kick Me* game behavior was functionally part of her Adapted Child ego state, and it was this part of her personality that overwhelmed other people (see Figure 11.17).

The delightful and creative side of Fanny's Child ego state, her Free Child, was barely functioning as she experienced little fun, creativity, or sexual enjoyment. It was as if her annoying "pesty" part, the Adapted Child, had most of the power and drained it away from the fresh and creative side. Her Adult was solid; she was bright and a good thinker. However, she seldom had any spare energy to help or console others, and this was reflected in her relatively low-functioning Nurturing Parent. Fanny copied her father's temper and judgmental nature when she criticized and found fault with others. This was reflected in the high amount of energy in her Critical Parent.

For Fanny functionally to approach the world in a different and more constructive way, a shift is necessary (Figure 11.17). Her Free Child and her Nurturing Parent need enhancement and greater energy investment, and this is one of the reasons the group-therapy milieu may be superior to individual psychotherapy. In a group, exercises can be repeated and practiced with others to raise a low-energy ego state; for example, nurturing can be developed by hugging, or the exercise of giving authentic positive comments to other people can be practiced. She at first resisted doing this, but she started out slowly and persisted until she raised and became conditioned in her low ego states. After nurturing others, she was better able to nurture herself. Many encounter-group techniques are useful in raising low-energy ego states in people. Free Child, important for Fanny, is elicited by humor.

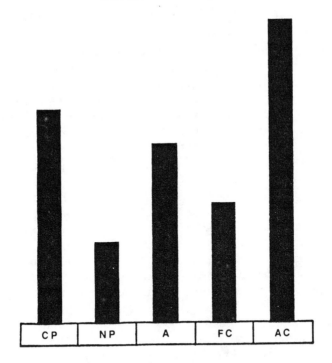

FANNY'S EGOGRAM

FIGURE 11.17

Creativity exercises are encouraged in the group-therapy setting, such as looking for nonverbal clues.

Each person has different ego-state imbalances and needs to raise, energize, and strengthen lower, weaker ego states. Briefly, those who are low in the Critical Parent aspect are encouraged to use assertiveness techniques; those low in Nurturing Parent will need empathy and caring-for-others techniques; persons low in Adult are given thinking exercises; those who do not have enough Free Child are invited to be spontaneous and participate in creative, intuitive activities; and those low in Adapted Child are encouraged to practice the art of compromise and getting-along-with-others exercises. An important concern in

shifting psychological energies is that individuals practice *raising what is low for them* and that they do not take what is a useful technique for others and indiscriminately apply it to themselves.

To facilitate a script redecision, a client is encouraged to go back in time to an early feeling and decisive moment; he is then directed to oppose a well-established ego-state force, which becomes a major problem for the client in that his personality is already low in the very force that is needed to bring about a cure. For example, Fanny was depressed, and to overcome depression, she needed to oppose and raise her Free Child in relation to her Adapted Child. Her greatest problem was that her Free Child was low and her

Adapted Child was high (see Figure 11.17). It took many weeks of Free Child raising techniques for her to be able to confront her own Adapted Child self to a significant degree. A person's weak ego states need strengthening as they are the very personality forces needed to make a redecision and change the balance of one's egogram. Lonely persons, chronically anxious people, and those with severe dependency needs who fear abandonment need to nurture themselves and others; however, the Nurturing Parent is the lowest force on their egograms. By analyzing someone's egogram, one can predict the curative oppositional force for that particular individual. Likewise, a low Adult force is prevalent for distrustful paranoid problems (a low Nurturing Parent and a low Adult are evident in severe examples). Suicidal, depressed, and lethargic persons manifest a low Free Child.

A growth-oriented opposing force needs to be sufficiently developed to reverse a lifelong (early childhood decision) pattern that shows up in one's "here-and-now" manifestation of personality.

Various settings provide an effective milieu for change. These retreats come in various forms such as Esalen Institute, the Western Institute for Group and Family Therapy, and other therapeutic centers where persons may reside for several weeks and months in a strong Nurturing Parent, Adult, and Free Child atmosphere to undergo personal, lasting changes. TA groups provide a similar safe atmosphere where both growth and change are stroked and reinforced.

In summary, the major ways that people change are through their own efforts by stopping games, redeciding scripts, and redistributing the energy balances on their egograms.

Mechanisms of Psychotherapy

Many clients enter treatment because they are in pain, meaning they receive their strokes in negative self-destructive ways. A few are in a crisis situation. Some enter because they are bored or lonely, or just not receiving enough strokes. Some are so unaware of their own social difficulties that others bring them to treatment. Some enter out of curiosity or for a growth experience; many trainees pursue this course. Whatever leads a client to a therapist's door, if change is to occur, there will be a difference in stroke receiving.

Thinking, feeling, and behaving are important in change, and are all included in the basic definitions of ego states. TA is an ego psychology.

Mechanisms underlying the psychotherapy triad of game interruption, script redecision, and ego-state energy shift cause the difference. A game is a habit, with a stereotyped social set of behavior, thinking (from Parent or Child ego state) that justifies the behavior; for example, "I'm just a loser," he says, as he belts down another drink. Even the accompanying affect is habitual. When asked, "Have you ever felt this way before?" the answer is usually, "Always." The mechanism of game interruption is the bringing to awareness the client's involvement with different ego states and establishing the Adult as the executive. With the Adult in control and monitoring, usually brought about by the therapeutic operation (sometimes by the receiving of information alone), the client can choose. Berne said that treatment was at a terminal phase when choice was available (1966, p. 245): "At this juncture, transactional analysis has completed its task with or without interpretation in the area under consideration. TA does not try to 'make the patient better' but to bring him into a position where he can exercise an Adult option to get better." The therapist is, in an existential sense at least, indifferent as to which choice the patient makes. All he can do is make it possible for the patient to choose. There is, however, no use in trying to conceal from the patient the fact that the therapist is biased by his own prejudices in favor of health and sanity.

When games are successfully interrupted, the client has social control. Although clients may substitute other games, equally destructive, they also have an excellent chance of developing positive new ways of relating.

The underlying mechanism of script redecision is usually accomplished concomitantly with game therapy, by overcoming early childhood decisions and by applying an opposing force against stubbornly held decisions. A chief reason for using a psychoregressive technique is to lay bare the earlier moments before the client added years of justification (by game playing) and reinforced his script decision. Although the TA therapist may use double chairs to separate ego states and allow for their external replay, the same forces are occurring in the client's head. Although one's feelings and affect are primary in script redecision work, they are usually followed by one's Adult, cognitive confirmation and discussion.

The mechanism of ego-state energy shift is mainly behavioral. It is necessary to build up weak areas on an egogram to oppose the adapted script-bearing part. Most TA groups use humor and encourage the airing of hunches and intuition to develop the Free Child. Nurturing behavior such as touching, hugging, and giving authentic positive strokes is encouraged; and away from the treatment setting, the client prescribes corrective nurturing behavior for himself, for example, taking an orphan to the zoo, and so on.

Just when a person actually strengthens a weaker ego-state force is difficult to ascertain, but an analogy with the physical conditioning of a jogger seems appropriate. The unconditioned runner does not "feel" like jogging; to him it is a burden; however, if he persists and overcomes the "this just isn't the real me" resistance and keeps on practicing, he changes. The first time his change is noticeable is when he cannot run on a given day and he feels uncomfortable and sluggish because he cannot run! He is now a conditioned runner and he feels different. People become psychologically conditioned by exercising previously weak areas.

APPLICATIONS

Problems

Because TA begins with the observation of what goes on between human beings, theoretically, all problems can be analyzed. Being a contractual treatment, TA requires the cooperation and willingness of the client to seek and participate in treatment. A distinction is made between what is primarily a "caring" relationship between therapist and client as compared to actual "curing" TA treatment. In "caring" the client receives support and nurturing from the therapist as *the* major activity. The therapist is a primary source of strokes and the relationship is not working toward the attainment of an ultimate goal, or as time goes by, the early goals are forgotten or neglected. This is labeled *care* and not TA psychotherapy. (Certainly care is often an important and desirable activity.)

In contrast, TA treatment, although

emphasizing the importance of the nurturing and caring personality of the therapist, primarily focuses on change as defined by the treatment contract based on an Adult to Adult agreement between the therapist and the client about what will be the process and the desired goal. Rather than being a primary source of strokes, except temporarily, the TA therapist is a catalyst for the client's own efforts.

TA is devised for those who will exert enough responsibility to undertake a contract. However, TA has been applied to severely disturbed individuals who are not able to make an Adult contract at the time of onset of treatment. Jacqui and Aaron Schiff (J. Schiff, 1969) represent a special group of TA therapists who have developed an alternative, yet compatible, theory with specific techniques that encourage clients to regress to earlier infantlike states, which may be preverbal. Although the client is expected to be as responsible as possible, the expectation during this phase of treatment is different from expectation of chronologically mature, nonregressed individuals. The approach is controversial, not accepted by all TA therapists, and is considered an offshoot of TA.

TA is effectively used with both couples and family relationships in that TA's game theory focuses on the common, predictable, destructive game patterns of behavior that occur among individuals. These patterns can be easily recognized, dealt with, and ultimately changed to strengthen the relationship. Berne chose the game *If It Weren't For You* to illustrate game principles in his work, *Games People Play* (1964), and stated that this is the most commonly occurring game among married couples. By the maneuvers in the game, the wife complains that, "If it weren't for my husband, then I would be a princess . . ." and so on. In his initial uncovering of this game, Berne discovered that the wife was actually struggling from fears of being active in public life, but justified her position by choosing a controlling man as a mate, who expected her to stay in the home. Thus, she was protected from her fear and habitually justified her position by claiming that it was her husband's fault. She was only one half of the game. Her husband chose a "stay-at-home wife" and was tyrannical in his part of the game system, thus protecting himself from his deep fear of abandonment. TA is especially useful in relationship problems as games are interrupted; thus basic fears are bared and script redecision can be approached. The tendency for different people to polarize and lock themselves into positions in relationships is explained by egograms, that is, husband (Critical Parent) overbalance; wife (Adapted Child) overbalance. Unfortunately, in both the home as well as on the job, people will maintain the same balances on their egograms; therefore, people will be continually reacted to in predictable ways based upon their egograms. Persons frequently are given nicknames that represent their particular egograms: "pushover," "dictator," "snob," "crazy," "dumb," and "sulky" are a few examples of the large assortment of nicknames.

Difficulties with authority figures are special applications of TA in human relationships. Most frequent is the *Kick Me* player, who at an early age decides he is not OK and then develops a personality with a high Adapted Child and routinely gets kicked. Fanny, previously mentioned, is a classical example of a person with authority conflicts. Also noted is that the same patterns that occur with the boss, school authorities, and others also tend to occur with the therapist or other group members.

The problem of self-concept has two special considerations. First, the client may not actually see himself the way others do, being psychologically blind. When an entire TA group constructs an egogram and they agree, this is potent feedback about how one appears to others. By increasing perception and sharpening intuition about others, self-perception tends to become more acute. The second problem of self-concept is resistance to change even if someone does not like what they see in themselves. Basic script redecisions to review early decisions of not being OK and game interruption that halts the process of reinforcement of basic script acceptance of what has become a self-belief, are employed.

Fears of a crippling or phobic nature may be treated at the level of personality identity as portrayed by the egogram by exercising and strengthening underdeveloped ego states. People who fear abandonment cling to others and even to the therapist by playing *Do Me Something* (a game by which the client offers the therapist some bait in the nature of a potentially resolvable problem such as insomnia, then says, "That's not good enough," after the therapist tries drugs, interpretations, or other maneuvers). By structuring time and performing exercises such as nurturing or assertive exercises, the client takes on more Parent energy and is therefore not as frightened.

The client fearing abandonment is asked to join a TA group, not to talk about himself, but to focus on the needs of others, encouraging nurturing. When this force develops, it is easier to nurture oneself and decrease the fear. Script redecision may also be used in overcoming fears, for instance, when the client decided at an early age that life is scary.

Maladjustments occur as a result of psychological blindness. For example, a high Free Child, low Adapted Child person may, in good spirits, take a job as an accountant, which requires lower Free Child (unless the corporation wants a creative accountant) and high Adapted Child, which encourages conformity. Recognizing strengths and weaknesses of personality forces allows one to choose jobs and relationships that are most compatible.

So-called *perversions* can best be understood at the script level. An individual may be told to be "normal" on the value level, but at the injunction (Child of mother or father to the Child of the biological child) level, the message is, "You are different." Even though this message may be nonverbal and hidden, if the child accepts this injunction, *perverse* behavior later in life is seen as conformity not to values, but to injunctions. Social difficulties such as teenage drug problems, and what is commonly called rebellious behavior, which may best be called pseudorebellion, is actually viewed as conformity to script (J. Dusay, 1977a).

Personality trait problems are best understood by considering the egogram. Assertiveness is too much Critical Parent, while too little Critical Parent corresponds with the passive acceptance of oppression —getting psychologically pushed around by others. Too much Nurturing Parent is overbearing and actually inhibits the independent growth of children; too little Nurturing Parent makes one inconsiderate, and a low Nurturing Parent corresponds with loneliness. High Adult is technical but perhaps boring; with a low Adult, one lacks logic and orderly causal thinking and problem solving is difficult. Someone with too high a Free Child, although creative and zesty, may fail to pay the rent. Low Free Child is associated with depression. People who are too high in the Adapted Child trait overconform and are too accepting or compromising, but with too little, the problem is the opposite—too little compromise in human relationships. Personality trait disturbances are seen by looking not at one specific trait on the egogram but by looking at the balance or imbalance of the total mosaic. One's specific problems, trait disturbances, and specific egogram imbalances are directly related to one's early script decisions as well as the specific games the person developed to reinforce this script.

Delusions are structurally seen as a contaminated ego state where the boundaries between Parent, Adult, and Child are broken down (Figure 11.6). The subject of psychosis is quite involved and the controversy that rages between different academicians and therapists of many persuasions also occurs within the TA family. Some mention that the basic lesion is genetic or biochemical and that psychotherapy should be directed toward better social adjustment. Others vigorously pursue the developmental motive of psychosis, structure a long-term (years) live-in environment, encourage regression in severe psychosis, and basically start over. This approach is naturally limited by the sheer amount of energy investment needed on the part of the therapist, but seems to have been effective in some cases. Basic expansion in TA theory has been necessitated by exploration in this area (Schiff, 1971).

Most of what was previously called neurosis is redefined by TA practitioners into more useful theory-related terms. The depressive neurotic, for example, would be seen as a person who made an existential life decision of I'm Not OK—You Are OK, in response to an injunction script message of "Get Lost" (or some specific variation). Then, after this, he played a long string of decision-justifying and reinforcing games such as *Kick Me* or *Reject Me* by gathering put-downs from others. His personality developed as a high Adapted Child and a low Free Child. A TA diagnosis will commonly state that the client has too much AC, too little A, too much CP, too little NP, and so on. This is more effective terminology than diagnosing

"neurosis" or "psychosis" because the TA diagnosis immediately suggests the curative ways to proceed for treatment of the person's problems. Cures are accomplished when the clients strengthen and build up their underdeveloped ego states to achieve harmonious balances on their egograms. Criminal behavior traditionally labeled psychopathic or sociopathic may also be better understood by attention to the clients' long rap sheets that frequently elucidate their common games of either *Kick Me* (for those who set it up continually to get both hurt and caught) or *NIGYYSOB* (for those who are intent on not getting caught as they hurt others).

Evaluation

TA, like most psychotherapies, was developed outside of the university setting and early in its history reported mainly anecdotal individual case histories. Although these early reports were enthusiastic, they lacked controls or comparison to other methods, a basic problem in most psychotherapy outcome research. The culmination of this type of reporting occurred in 1968, when Berne, Dusay, and Ray Poindexter reviewed their TA case loads and presented the results to the San Francisco TA Seminar of how many clients achieved their goals as stated in the TA treatment contract. The results were that 80 percent of the clients stated they got what they came for and their therapists agreed.

Following the first decade of TA, independent investigators began to review the outcome of TA treatment. One of the most important outcome studies ever made was a comparison of TA and behavior modification (McCormick, 1973). Behavior modification is generally also a contractual therapy based on research data. The project studied the effects of treatment on hard data changes in a population of 904 young men aged 15, 16 and 17 who were in two schools of the California Youth Authority. Almost all of the subjects had serious arrest records, most failed as probationers in the home community, and all had serious emotional or behavioral problems. More than 60 percent had used drugs (a third were heroin or LSD users). The average reading level was seventh grade; arithmetic level, sixth grade. There was random assignment to TA methods (460) and behavior modification (444). Both populations improved more than was expected in outcome; in math grade-equivalent scores, the TA group gained 0.91 and behavior modification 0.62. In reading, the average improvement was 1.48 in behavior modification and 1.16 in TA, far above ordinarily expected gains. Although both TA and behavior modification showed significant improvement over controls, the TA population was treated for 7.6 months at which time the TA program was completed (as defined by the goals of the therapists). To achieve similar improvement, the behavior modification subjects were treated for 8.7 months. TA achieved similar results in significantly less time, an early claim of TA enthusiasts.

Another hard data gain was in the area of parole success. Before the treatment project, parole revocation within a year was at the rate of 43 percent. After the project, the return rate had dropped to 33 percent for both TA and BM groups, but this decrease did not occur for two youth authority groups that served as controls.

Although both methods achieved significant positive results, the TA program took less time than the behavior modification program and the therapists, youth authority employees, and the subjects claimed that TA was more fun and enjoyable (McCormick, 1973).

The greatest research interest has been in the evaluation of the basic concepts of TA. The foundation of TA, the ego state, has been subjected to several investigations. Very important is the research project of George Thomson (1972), which established that ego states are observable, that trained TA experts have a high inter-rater agreement about which ego state is in operation in a given subject, and that naive observers can be trained to correctly (in agreement with experts) identify ego states. Thomson used a tape recorder to preserve nine hours of group-therapy sessions. From these tapes, he extracted a research tape whereby each participant was heard to say a couple of words or phrases for a few seconds. When played back, there were varied words, tones, and inflections on each segment. These were presented to a panel of TA experts who were asked to judge between Parent, Adult, and Child. The experts had a 95 percent consensual agreement about the ego state classification. Naive listeners from various backgrounds were then presented the research tape and were found to do poorly; after a week's training, their proficiency at identifying ego states improved markedly. Thomson proved what Berne and early transactional analysts claimed: that ego states are observable and that people can spot ego states, classify them, mimic them, and actually improve upon their ability to do so by study and observation.

Thomson went further by hypothesizing that certain clinical problems would impair ego-state identification; that is, that "schizophrenics" and "depressives" would have more difficulty in identifying Parent ego states than normals. This seems to be the case on his research tape, but those people being diagnosed as psychopaths had a better than average ability (for normals) to identify Parent. This also seemed to be the case and Thompson hypothesized that psychopaths need to be keenly aware of Parent-type people to be successful.

John Hurley and Howard Porter (1967) categorized 194 college students enrolled in a study-methods course, notable for immature academic behavior, into Adapted Child (AC) types and Natural Child (NC) types (this corresponds with FC) and found they were able to distinguish 47 as belonging in one or the other category during 20 twice-a-week, 50-minute class periods. AC is characterized by a general inhibition of impulse expression grounded on the fear of disturbing others; NC functioning is directed against external restraints and is expressed in openly self-indulgent or assertive acts. The construct validity of the AC versus NC distinction was tested by comparing the two groups to their performance on certain standard psychological tests. All completed the MMPI Psychopathic deviate (Pd) and the Marlowe-Crowne Social Desirability (SD) scales. A true-false version of the LaForge Interpersonal Checklist (ICL) provided scores on the orthogonal factors, LOV (love-hate continuum), and DOM (dominance-submissiveness continuum).

It was hypothesized that the AC functioning group would correspond with lower Pd and DOM scales (rebellious and dominating tendencies) and with higher SD and LOV scores (conforming and acceptant tendencies) than characterized by the NC functioning group. Confirmation was found for both sexes except on the SD measure, which failed to differentiate between the AC and NC categories. However, all group differences were in the hypothesized direction except for an insignificant Pd reversal among females. These findings not only support the construct validity of certain ego-state formulations, but indicated that relatively untrained raters (the observers) can effectively distinguish subgroups in the college classroom.

Five advanced members of the weekly San Francisco TA Seminars (now known as the Eric Berne Seminar of San Francisco) volunteered themselves as egogram subjects in 1971. Their egograms were drawn by 15 other seminar members who had known them for varying lengths of time. While the 15 persons drew each subject's personality profile privately, the subjects also drew their own. The result was 100 percent agreement on both the high and low columns of the five ego-state graph. This finding led to further formal and informal investigation.

John Kendra (1977) viewed a sample of Rorschach reports of various psychiatric patients. He constructed egograms from these projective tests and was able to distinguish a group of egograms different from the others that were characteristically low in Nurturing Parent and Free Child, while the Critical Parent, Adult, and Adapted Child were markedly high (the Adult slightly lower). These turned out to correspond with the successful suiciders (Figure 11.8).

While Kendra used intuition to construct his suicide egogram, Robert Heyer (1979) began to develop a concept-oriented written test. Heyer's ego-state profile questionnaire is still undergoing modification; at present (1983) it consists of 49 researched items which the subject rank orders himself. Heyer's dissertation data was presented to the 2,000-subject sample of the California Poll (Field Poll) two weeks before the presidential election in 1976. The subjects were asked to rate themselves as the item statements consciously applied to them, and then they were asked to construct a profile for the two presidential candidates, Jimmy Carter and Gerald Ford. The responses were not random and produced a distinct and significant difference between the two candidates (as they appeared to the voter through the media). There are some indications that the voters' self-perceived egogram has a correlation with candidate choice (they were also asked who they were voting for). Egogram profiles have now been constructed for various populations such as San Quentin prisoners, outpatient clinics, alcoholics, attendees at weekend growth-encounter groups, students, and government employees.

Ego states and egograms especially lend themselves to research. With the development of a standard hard data test research possibilities are expanding.

Treatment

TA historically and traditionally has been practiced in groups, although through the years, since its beginnings in the late 1950s, TA has been diversely applied by therapists from different backgrounds with varying levels of professional education and training, who have approached the entire gamut of psychological problems and challenges. Therefore, TA has been successfully practiced in almost all settings. The earlier observations in groups tend to hold up in dyadic, family, marathon, and other settings.

Berne (1966) distinguished between six possible ways that people spend their time with each other, in ascending order of stroke potential. They will be defined as they relate to therapy:

Withdrawal
Occasionally, people *withdraw* in the presence of others, either by fantasy or by delusion. The therapist discourages withdrawal by stroking and encouraging conversation.

Ritual
There are formal and informal *rituals.* Formal rituals are culturally determined

and of little concern for psychotherapy; however, informal rituals are encouraged as a warmup. The greeting ritual of saying hello followed by a hello response is an example. This gives a stroke and also illustrates the almost syllable-for-syllable nature (stroke-for-stroke) quality. If one person says, "Hello, how are you? Haven't seen you in weeks," and gets a simple "Hello" in response a game is developing. Overresponding likewise becomes a game; for example, one person says, "How are you?" The respondent replies, "I'm glad you asked. My hemorrhoids ache. I can't sleep," and so on. Again a game is started. Informal rituals are mainly social courtesies, not encouraged beyond a warmup and good-bye; however, the breaking of a mundane ritual is seen as a takeoff for possible game behavior.

Pastimes
These are an orderly series of transactions designed simply to while away the time in a socially acceptable, but nonmeaningful, manner. Unlike games, there is no distinct payoff of negative feelings. A popular *pastime* is called *General Motors* whereby one player says, "I like Chevy, Plymouth, Ford (choose one), better than Chevy, Plymouth, Ford because . . . (fill in with 25 words or less)." There is a tendency for therapy groups to play pastimes, sometimes for an entire session, to avoid more meaningful activity. This is called playing *Psychiatry.* The therapist breaks up pastimes to get to more meaningful work.

Work
This is goal-directed activity to solve problems or expand potentials. Much TA is at this level.

Games
Clients frequently slip into *games* to reinforce their basic script decisions and, by

doing so, avoid work and prevent intimacy. This is counteracted by the TA therapist.

Intimacy

This is a straightforward human interaction, and is none of the above. Intimacy is a desired goal in human relationships and is encouraged in TA treatment.

TA therapists as group leaders pay attention to the above possibilities, encouraging work and intimacy, interrupting games, and avoiding meaningless pastimes. Beyond attention to group functioning, Berne in observing himself and his trainees delineated eight specific therapeutic interventions (1966):

Interrogation

A TA therapist *interrogates* to document specific points that may be clinically useful in the future. "Did you actually hit her?" is directed to the client's Adult. Over-interrogation is to be avoided or the client will be prone to play *Psychiatric History*.

Specification

This is a declaration on the part of the therapist that categorizes certain information. "So you have always viewed yourself as having an excessive temper" is intended to fix *specifically* certain information about the client so it can be referred to later in therapy.

Confrontation

A TA therapist will use information previously elicited to disconcert the patient's Parent, Child or contaminated Adult, by pointing out incongruencies. The client: "I can't stop smoking." The therapist: "Will you say, 'I *won't* stop smoking'?" This *confrontation* is intended to disturb one's egogram energy balance and hopefully cause a redistribution of energies. The client may insightfully say, "There I

go giving away my power again," which indicates a switch from his Child to Adult.

Explanation

The therapist will encourage clear *explanations* to strengthen the client's Adult. The therapist may say, "Sometimes your Child becomes overactive and that's when your Adult fades out. Quite possibly you reach for a cigarette without thinking."

Interrogation, specification, confrontation and explanation are *interventions*. The next operations are more than that. They are *interpositions* that are an attempt by the therapist to interpose something between the patient's Adult and his other ego states to stabilize his Adult and make it more difficult for him to slide into Parent or Child activity.

Illustration

This becomes an anecdote or comparison that follows a successful confrontation; the purpose is to reinforce the confrontation and avoid possibly undesirable effects. The therapist may interpose by saying, "You are saying *can't* just like Gladys does," as Gladys is listening. Some illustrations are remote, yet provide humor or meaning to the Child. "Your going to the party is similar to Little Red Riding Hood going to the woods—they both have a lot of wolves there."

Illustration is an artful form of psychotherapy that may be effectively used when both the client's Adult is listening and the Free Child is finding it humorous. When working with a self-righteous, literal Parent (as with many paranoids), the therapist may be chided for "making fun of me" if an illustration is attempted.

Confirmation

The interposition of a *confirmation* by the therapist is to stabilize the patient's Adult. The therapist encourages the client to offer further material to confirm the confrontation and this will reinforce the ego boundaries and the Adult functioning. If the client says, "I just can't do this—Oops, I mean, I *won't* do it," the therapist will immediately confirm and acknowledge the client's awareness.

Each of these operations has a primary objective to activate the client's functional Adult. The client will then possess a clear, defined, competent, uncontaminated Adult. When the client's Adult is in control, he is filled with positive choices and options for growth.

Interpretation

A psychodynamic *interpretation* may go into the realm of, "You have given away your power. Your Child has decided to remain powerless and helpless because your mother would say, 'Don't leave me.'" Interpretations are not necessary for treatment to be successful; in fact, occasionally the reverse is true. Overzealous therapists may interpret the games and symbols to their clients and receive a passive acceptance, with the message frequently forgotten. Each of the operations before this is employed to strengthen the client's Adult so a clear interpretation will be assimilated by an informed Adult. Little benefit accrues just by telling a person what is going on.

Crystallization

TA's technical aim is to facilitate the client to accept an effective crystallization statement from the therapist. This takes the form of an Adult-to-Adult statement: "So now you're in a position to stop playing that game if you choose."

Often the client will incorporate the statement, which may represent his readiness to terminate and begin an autonomous, choice-making existence. Berne himself would emphasize the importance of strengthening the client's Adult, which would enable the person to make better choices. Berne would interrupt the client's usual habitual patterns by directly confronting and intervening; rather than remaining passive and anonymous, and he became an active therapist. Berne's active techniques of the mid-1960s are still used today; however, TA has developed into an even more active and dynamic system of psychotherapy since Berne's time. McNeel (1975) studied what was actually done in a weekend TA session conducted by Robert and Mary Goulding. The following techniques and attitudes are commonly employed by many TA therapists:

Emphasis on the client's personal power and responsibility

Each individual is *responsible* for his life and has adequate *power* to be in charge of his life. Clients may feel they are victims of events or circumstances, and confrontations will reinforce their feelings of responsibility. A client who says, "You make me feel . . ." will be confronted since this is a common ploy to deny one's responsibility for his own feelings. A person who habitually says "I can't" will be confronted and encouraged to substitute "I won't," which illustrates that the person is making a choice not to do something.

Developing a nurturing environment

Nonjudgmental *nurturing* is an effective milieu, and persons are warmly stroked for taking personal responsibility for their actions and feelings. Likewise, the use of humor is prevalent, although there is an avoidance of laughing at gallows humor, which is encouraging others to laugh at pathological behavior (drinking, overeating, etc.).

Separating myth from reality

Many clients cherish myths about themselves; and the effective confrontation is,

"Do you really believe that?" Clients then receive permission to question and discard their myths.

Confrontation of incongruity

When a client offers two *incongruent* communications at the same time (verbal and nonverbal), the therapist needs to recognize that both forms of communication are important. A "no" head shake that accompanies a "yes" verbal response and a smile that grins during a tragic story are examples of the incongruous behaviors that therapists will interrupt.

Specific techniques

Analysis is used to raise a deficient Adult. Double-chair techniques aid a participant to "own" all of his psychological parts and reach the emotions of the Child ego state. Verbally saying good-bye to the past is also important in that people will drag their negative past experiences around with them, like a ball and chain. Techniques may involve roleplaying a deceased parent and then saying good-bye. Fantasy techniques are used to raise the Free Child. Parent ego-state interviews in which the therapist interviews the client's Parent projections are also useful.

Procedural rules

During therapy, there is no small talk or gossip. An actual time limit is put on each client's work so it will not go on indefinitely. In effective therapy, there are specific rules such as no violence or threats of violence; sex only with attending partners in weekend functions; no alcohol or mind-altering drugs to be used. Persons also make a commitment to remain in therapy for a specific period.

The above observations already indicate what is done by leading TA therapists to create a milieu conducive to redecision and change.

Management

The setting

TA therapy may effectively take place in a wide variety of settings. Certain TA therapists prefer a home-like atmosphere, comparable to a living room with the accompanying furniture, books, plants and artwork; some like a more traditional office setting; while others enjoy conducting therapy outdoors in retreat settings and at resorts. While some therapists utilize traditional couches and chairs, others prefer conducting therapy on the floor or cushions. An important commonality with TA therapists is that no tables or desks are used which could block the participants' full view of one another. Because body language, postures and other non-verbal clues to personality are important in doing TA therapy, there must be good lighting as well as non-obstructive seating arrangements.

The majority of TA treatment environments utilize the customary blackboards and giant paper pads that can be used by both the therapists and their clients to draw pictures, elucidate games and transactions, construct egograms, and also to engage in Adult ego-state clarifications. (At this writing, not a single transference to a blackboard has been reported.) Some therapists may employ audio-visual aids which may facilitate client feedback, awareness and understanding. Because of the wide and diverse backgrounds of professionally trained TA therapists (from office-practicing psychiatrists to inmates working within the confines of a prison), it becomes impossible to generalize about a typical TA therapeutic setting.

Relationships

A prevailing attitude exists among TA therapists with their clients—they provide a supportive, nurturing environment conducive for growth and change. An agreement of confidentiality is respected by both the therapist and the clients. The therapist provides permission for the client to maintain an active role in change and therapy process. The client is also given protection and encouragement from the therapist as he begins to change and validate a new way of thinking, feeling and behaving. For the therapist's permission and protection to be effective, the therapist must be potent, well-trained and competent to be in this role. Authentic TA therapists undergo years of required training, schooling and clinical experience under authorized clinical teaching members of the ITAA before they are endorsed as certified TA therapists by the ITAA. TA therapists may work independently or in co-therapy teams. They conduct therapy with individuals, couples, families, and group members according to the specific needs of the client.

The simple vocabulary of TA and commonly understood words, are used in therapeutic sessions so that time isn't wasted with unclear verbiage or confusing concepts. The client is viewed as an equal partner in the therapeutic process. The common goal of each TA therapist is to catalyze a cure—defined as reaching therapy goals—and to do so as quickly as possible. A TA therapist is generally an active participant in the client's process and will frequently operate on intuitive perceptions and will invite clients to be open and intuitive as well.

Client problems

Whenever there is a break from the agreed-upon course of action, for instance, non-payment of the therapist's fee or missing scheduled appointments, the therapist will view these transactions as psychological games and will provide therapy from this standpoint. The simplest to the most severe human psychological problems have been successfully resolved through TA therapy.

CASE EXAMPLE

Judd was diagnosed as a hypochondriac by many physicians who had treated him. He complained about being weak, weary, headachey, and jittery as he displayed his collection of pills and remedies. Judd's belief that he was sick was seen to reach far back into his past as he nostalgically reminisced about his family's medicine cabinet and remembered his mother taking his temperature, giving him pills, and stroking him for being a weak, sickly child. He was able to repeat his early life-style with his wife, whose attitude toward Judd was similar to his mother's. Both wife and mother had high Nurturing Parents and high Adapted Childs on their own egograms.

At his first TA group session, the other members drew his egogram (Figure 11.18) and he established a treatment contract: to experience a full month without having a noticeable headache.

In a subsequent session, Judd was habitually complaining of feeling "sick" and another group member, Wayne, who in contrast to Judd had a critical personality (high CP), told him to "stand up for yourself." Judd appeared especially frightened and the therapist, noticing this, asked him if he wanted to work on his feelings. Judd nodded affirmatively.

Knowing that this "feeling" was a repetitive racket, the therapist did not comfort Judd; rather, the negative feelings were enhanced by instructing Judd to exaggerate his tight jaw and tense wrinkled brow. When Judd was in obvious pain, the therapist asked him to close his eyes to enable him to leave the here-and-now of the group setting and begin to trace his racket

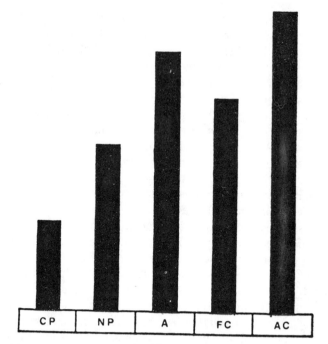

JUDD'S EGOGRAM (BEFORE TA)

FIGURE 11.18

feeling back to a childhood prototype episode of his script decision.

After pausing briefly at the reexperience of his wedding ceremony, then at school episodes, Judd began to quiver, and said, "I'm five years old, and I want my Mommie to come to nursery school with me, but she won't. Please, Mommie, I'm not big enough. I'm scared... I'm sick!" Beads of perspiration formed on his forehead and he rubbed his stomach. He was instructed to place his fantasized "Mommie" in the empty chair and tell her what he was feeling. The roleplaying served to enhance his emotional state.

Judd [age five]: I'm scared. My tummy aches and my head aches, and I want to stay home with you.

Mommie [played by Judd]: I know you don't feel very good, so let me give you some pills for your head and tummy and then you can go to school.

Judd: I feel so sick. I don't think the medicine will help.

Mommie: Well, then, I'll put you back to bed now, and I'll give you some pills, and by tomorrow you'll feel good enough to go to school.

Judd [very relieved]: Okay. If I'm sick and stay home, at least I won't be so scared.

"What are you deciding about yourself now?" the therapist asked.

"I'm scared of people," Judd replied. "I'm scared of going to school and being with the other little boys. If I stay sick, I won't have to face them."

Judd's real mother, for her own psychological reasons, probably was nervous about having a healthy child who could someday leave her. She passed her anxiety and scared feelings on to Judd by the usual scripting process (see Figure 11.19). From her Parent, she sent him the life value,

"Go to school." (Later in life, this expressed itself as "Be a man," and so on.) But her Child ego state sent him the incompatible injunction, "Don't leave me!" Eventually Judd's Adapted Child made his decision, "I'm scared and sick. I won't leave you." This basic childhood decision

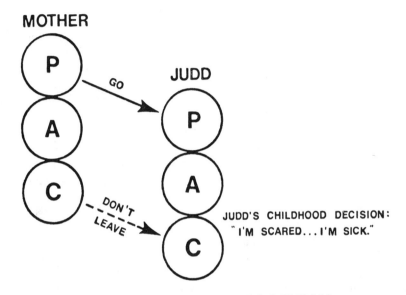

JUDD'S SCRIPT MATRIX

FIGURE 11.19

carried through his life. In treatment Judd was encouraged to reexperience his "little boy" ego state feeling and express it fully. By surfacing his early feelings and thoughts, he was able to view the original scene that set the tone for his life.

To change, one must redecide. Judd was soon reintroduced to his other powers by focusing on the other forces in his egogram. His Adult was chosen to oppose his scripted Adapted Child because this logical force was quite strong in him, and although his Nurturing Parent force would also be helpful, a conversation between his weak, conforming Adapted Child and his

scientific, rational Adult was structured. As before, he switched chairs as he switched ego states:

Judd (AC): I feel sick and I'm scared to go to school by myself.

Judd (A): Why are you scared?

Judd (AC): Because I'm afraid I'll get lost and I can't take care of myself.

Judd (A): Little five-year-olds can't take care of themselves!

Judd (AC): I know! I'm so scared and I think my stomach hurts.

Judd (A): You said you *think* your stomach hurts?

Judd (AC): Well, it kind of hurts, and my

mother thinks it hurts.

Judd (A): Do you think you might have talked yourself into this?

Judd (AC): Yes, I think so. My stomach doesn't hurt me any more than anyone else's stomach hurts, but it helps me forget about my scare.

Judd (A): How long do you want to keep scaring youself and have stomach aches?

Judd (AC): No longer. I don't have anything to be scared of. I can take care of myself now. I'm not so little anymore.

The conversation was stopped and Judd said he felt great, as if he were healthy for the first time in his life. He no longer was dominated by the little boy in his head. Others in the group were happy for him and freely gave him hugs and congratulations. Judd, with tears in his eyes, spontaneously said, "There is one more thing I'm going to say to that little boy in me." He then went to another chair and said in a nurturing voice, "You're really an OK person."

Judd decided he would be OK, not scared, and thought that getting into good physical shape would be helpful in reinforcing outside of the group what he had redecided in therapy. He committed himself to jogging even though it did not feel right at first. He soon worked up to running at least two miles a day and exercised at the local gym. His legs and lungs felt better and he soon lost his craving for cigarettes. He chose a new set of friends at the office who shared his new interest in exercise and nourishing foods. The structures in his life supported his new healthy view of himself.

Unfortunately, when the redecision process is not successful, it is due to a resistance. The intrapsychic resistance occurs, in Judd's case, when he slips from his Adult or Nurturing Parent, into his Adapted Child. In this instance, he would be switching back and forth, from chair to chair commiserating with his Adapted Child. This occurs as follows in the example:

Judd (AC): I feel bad.

Judd (A becoming AC): Gulp! I feel bad, too.

When this occurs, the therapist quickly introduces a third observer chair, to combat the slippage. The chair is placed perpendicular to the ongoing dialogue chair and Judd is asked to switch and describe what he is observing. Usually this successfully allows Judd to confront his own resistance. If not, he is probably not ready for redecision and needs to have more group experience to strengthen his Adult and/or other curative ego state forces that are low on his egogram. Then he will reapproach the problem with increased strength.

In addition to his own internal resistance, Judd challenged the subtle resistances from outside himself: socially at home, institutionally at work, and even culturally in the rest of his environment. When Judd announced to his wife he was going to start jogging and was not going to have headaches anymore, she was outwardly full of joy, but somehow did not seem to know what to do with herself. She was used to the old Judd, whom she greeted every day with, "How are you feeling today?" His typical response had been, "Not so good." When he overcame his script injunction, his answer became, "Oh, I feel fine." This was met by a sickening smile from his wife and she would plead, "Are you sure?" The first few times this happened, Judd replied, "Well, now that you mention it, I think I do have a little ache in my neck." Temporarily he succumbed to this volley of social resistances from his wife. Soon he increased his awareness of these day-to-day hindrances and gathered support from those who had no vested interest in his being sick (the group members). As he insisted on being treated as a healthy person, his wife became more and more frantic. "It's about time to go to the doctor and get your prescription filled," she said. Judd's response was, "I don't need medicine anymore." It can be predicted in advance that close social contacts will resist the change at least as hard as the person undergoing it. Game analysis and group support were aids at this level.

Institutional resistances also confront the individual and usually involve economics. In Judd's case, the drug industry was involved. When Judd walked into the doctor's office, he was walking into an institution that, like his wife, did not give up easily. After multiple complaints, the frustrated doctor, hoping to do something beneficial, would reach for his prescription pad and give him one of the newer pills that had been advertised heavily in the medical journals.

Cultural resistances to personal change are subtle, ever present, and strongly influential. One of the Western civilization's "cultural truths" is that if you are feeling bad, the remedy is to open your mouth and put in some magic elixir, as did the Greek deity Bacchus. Television advertising abounds with graphically suffering men and women who are dramatically "cured" by ingesting the right product. Fairy tales passed from generation to generation reinforce the belief in the power of magic potions to influence life. Just as Ponce de León wandered in search of the fountain of youth, Judd sought the elixir for "relief from his chronic pain and discomfort" and for everlasting health and vigor. Judd's mother also bought this mythology, as evidenced by her intriguing medicine cabinet. The commonly shared myths made it easy and culturally acceptable for Judd to avoid facing his real problems.

Judd's egogram, constructed again after more than a year of rigorous attention to change via diagnosis of weak areas, surfacing inner conflicts, confronting resistance, redeciding, practicing, exercising both psychologically and physically, overcoming resistances, showed his Critical Parent gained power as he was able to say "NO" to harmful outside influences and stop being a social patsy (see Figure 11.20). His Adult gained particularly in his ability to see himself more accurately. Also, he laughed more as his Free Child grew. The most dramatic change was the decrease in his Adapted Child as he lived his life with personal strength and freedom from psychological slavery.

SUMMARY

Historically, transactional analysis developed in an exciting era for psychotherapies, between the mid-1950s when classical psychoanalysis, with its emphasis on therapist anonymity and client insight, was supreme, through the early 1970s in which the "psychological revolution" erupted with the emphasis on emotional expression and experience. TA went through several phases and continues to evolve at the present. The first phase, ego states (1955-62), focused upon Eric Berne's discovery that the dynamic personality can be observed by paying attention to "here-and-now" phenomena. The therapist and client are able to predict future as well as infer past history by attention to things such as present attitude, gestures, voice, vocabulary, social response, and other observable criteria. Eric Berne at that time used these findings about ego states in group psychotherapy as an adjunct for his psychoanalytic approach but

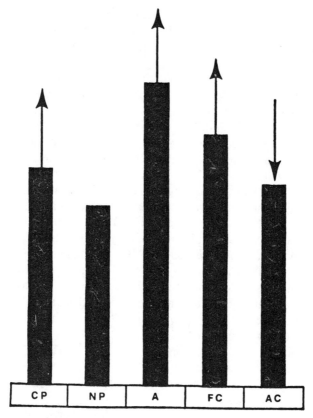

JUDD'S "AFTER" EGOGRAM

FIGURE 11.20

it soon became clear that the concept of the dynamic unconscious was not necessary for clients to gain insight and social control.

The second phase of transactional analysis focused on transactions and games (1962-66). This was when a totally fresh view of human interaction was made possible by the delineation of "games." Transactional analysis during this period was basically an intellectual approach, still imbued with the idea that insight or "catching onto" what is happening would be curative. This, of course, was true for many individuals, but certainly not for the majority. It was during this phase that TA became popular, because of its forthright and simple vocabulary and because people could readily identify their game patterns. The third phase, script analysis (1966-70), encouraged strong emotional reexperience in the practice of transactional analysis. Clients not only analyzed but relived those decisive moments in their lives with the emotions that accompanied childhood decisions. Transactional analysts began to incorporate other systems, especially Robert Goulding's combination of Gestalt techniques with TA. The fourth phase, action (1970 onward), was stimulated by the action techniques of the human-potential movement, Gestalt, psychodrama, encounter, and many of the other explosive energy-liberating systems. The new model, the egogram, was developed to bridge the gap between the more structural definitions and theories of early transactional analysis and provide a model for the otherwise haphazard explosive action techniques.

TA has had a rather full history in a short time and has a remarkable amount of clinical and theoretical research for such a young psychotherapy movement (Blair & McGahey, 1974, 1975). Because of its easily understood vocabulary and because of the willingness of therapists to share ideas with clients, TA became a rapidly popular psychotherapy. As such TA has been used not only by psychiatrists, psychologists, social workers, and other traditional therapists, but also by paraprofessionals who found the theoretical aspects of TA were easy to learn and had direct applicability to their concerns. Indeed, street workers and prison inmates have become outstanding TA therapists. Effort for the TA therapist is in practical applications rather than in decoding mystical jargon.

The future of TA seems to be moving in the direction of action, emotive, and energy models to correct overconcentration upon "understanding," resulting in a balance between affect and cognition. The history of TA is a history of rapid change to new and more effective techniques rather than adherence to earlier models. The structural concepts of ego states, the transaction (the unit of social action), and

the script or games theory will not be discarded; however, the techniques employed to bring about change have and will be distinctly shifted from the major reliance upon understanding and insight (which is still thought to be important) to an approach that is more experiential and emotive.

From eight early members in 1958, there are in 1983 over 10,000 members in the worldwide TA organization. Transactional analysis, unlike many of the "new psychologies," is amassing a large written literature. Like most of the newer approaches, TA has been applied gradually to a wider array of psychological and social problems, even to the analysis of destructive and oppressive social institutions.

ANNOTATED BIBLIOGRAPHY

Berne, E. *Games people play.* New York: Grove Press, 1964.

Written as a handbook for transactional group therapists, this book, because of its readability and forthright vocabulary, became a best seller in 1965. This book summarizes the early phases of TA: ego states, transactions, and games. The theory of games opened an entirely new psychology of human relationships.

Berne, E. *Principles of group treatment.* New York: Oxford University Press, 1966.

This is a widely used textbook for those interested in the broad field of group interaction and treatment of individuals in a group setting. Although written from a TA standpoint, Berne provides an excellent comparative approach and a workable model for group structure and process.

Berne, E. *What do you say after you say hello?* New York: Grove Press, 1972.

This is Berne's final statement, published posthumously, and outlines the total theory of personality that evolved after 15 years of TA. The occurrence of *scripts* is the major focus.

Dusay, J. *Egograms: How I see you and you see me.* New York: Harper & Row, 1977.

An expansion of TA via a functional and energy model is presented for the first time. Egograms represent a growth model which is specific and departs from a theory of a dynamic unconscious.

Steiner, C. *Scripts people live.* New York: Grove Press, 1974.

A comprehensive discussion of script theory by the creator of the script matrix. There is a special focus on political and social institutions; abuses of psychiatry and overcoming oppression are well described, and an era of social action is opened.

CASE READINGS

Berne, E. Case example. In *Sex in human loving.* New York: Simon & Schuster, 1970.

Dusay, J. Case example. In B. Ard, Jr. (Ed.), *Counseling and psychotherapy.* Palo Alto, Calif.: Science and Behavior Books, 1975.

Dusay, J., & Steiner, C. Case example. In H. Kaplan & B. Sadock (Eds.), *Comprehensive group psychotherapy.* Baltimore: The Williams and Wilkins Company, 1971.

Holland, G. Case example. In R. J. Corsini (Ed.), *Current psychotherapies.* Itasca, Ill.: F. E. Peacock Publishers, 1973.

Jongeward, D., & Scott, D. Case example. In *Affirmative action for women.* Reading, Mass.: Addison-Wesley, 1973.

REFERENCES

Abraham, K. *Selected papers.* London: Hogarth Press, 1948.

Adler, A. Individual psychology. In G. B. Levitas (Ed.), *The world of psychology.* New York: Braziller, 1963.

Bateson, G., & Ruesch, J. *Communication.* New York: Norton, 1951.

Bateson, G., Jackson, D., Haley, J., & Weakland, J. Toward a communication theory

of schizophrenia. *Behavior Science,* 1956, 1. Reprinted in D. Jackson (Ed.), *Communication, family and marriage.* Vol. 1. Palo Alto, Calif.: Science & Behavior Books, 1968.

Berne, E. The nature of intuition. *Psychiatric Quarterly,* 1949, *23,* 203-26.

Berne, E. Intuition IV. Primal images and primal judgment. *Psychiatric Quarterly,* 1955, *29,* 634.

Berne, E. Intuition v. the ego image. *Psychiatric Quarterly,* 1957, *31,* 611-27.

Berne, E. *Transactional analysis in psychotherapy.* New York: Grove Press, 1961.

Berne, E. *Structure and dynamics of groups and organizations.* Philadelphia: Lippincott, 1963.

Berne, E. *Games people play.* New York: Grove Press, 1964.

Berne, E. *Principles of group treatment.* New York: Oxford University Press, 1966.

Berne, E. *What do you say after you say hello?* New York: Grove Press, 1972.

Berne, E. *Intuition and ego states.* San Francisco: Harper & Row, 1977.

Bert, D., Dusay, K., Haydock, A., Keel, S., Oei, M., Steel-Traina, D., Yanehiro, J. *Having a baby.* New York: Delacourt, 1984.

Blair, M., & McGahey, C. *Transactional analysis research index, volumes I and II.* Tallahassee: Florida Institute for Transactional Analysis, 1974, 1975.

Breuer, J., & Freud, S. On the physical mechanism of hysterical phenomena. In J. Strachey (Ed.), *Standard edition of the complete psychological works of Sigmund Freud, vol. III.* London: Hogarth Press, 1962 (originally published 1893).

Campbell, J. *The hero with a thousand faces.* New York: Pantheon Books, 1949.

Chandler, A., & Hartman, M. Lysergic acid diethylamid (LSD-25) as a facilitating agent in psychotherapy. *Archives of General Psychiatry,* 1960, *2,* 286-299.

Crossman, P. Permission, protection and potency. *Transactional Analysis Bulletin,* 1966, *5,* 152-53.

Dusay, J. Eric Berne's studies of intuition, 1949-1962. *Transactional Analysis Journal,* 1971, *1,* 34-44.

Dusay, J. Egograms and the constancy hypothesis. *Transactional Analysis Journal,* 1972, *2,* 37-41.

Dusay, J. Eric Berne. In A. Freedman, H. Kaplan, & B. Sadock (Eds.), *Comprehensive textbook of psychiatry/II.* Baltimore: Williams & Wilkins, 1975.

Dusay, J. Four phases of TA. In G. Barnes (Ed.), *Transactional analysis after Eric Berne.* New York: Harper's College Press, 1977. (a)

Dusay, J. *Egograms: How I see you and you see me.* New York: Harper & Row, 1977. (b)

Dusay, J. *TA treatment-training manual,* 1978.

Dusay, K. The hero in your head (an analysis of the hero). Master's thesis in psychology. San Francisco: Lone Mountain College, 1975.

Dusay, K. Recurring themes throughout world literature: Persecutors, rescuers and victims. Master's thesis in English. San Francisco: San Francisco State University, 1976.

English, F. Episcript and the hot potato game. *Transactional Analysis Bulletin,* 1962, *8,* 77-82.

English, F. The substitution factor: Rackets and real feelings. Part I. *Transactional Analysis Bulletin,* 1971, *1.*

English, F. The substitution factor: Rackets and real feelings. Part II. *Transactional Analysis Bulletin,* 1972, *2.*

Ernst, F. The OK Corral: The grid for get-on-with-it. *Transactional Analysis Bulletin,* 1971, *1.*

Erskine, R., & Zalcman, M. The racket system: A model for racket analysis. *Transactional Analysis Bulletin,* 1979, *9,* 1.

Federn, P. *Ego psychology and the psychoses.* New York: Basic Books, 1952.

Glasser, W., & Zunin, L. Reality therapy In R. J. Corsini (Ed.), *Current psychotherapies.* Itasca, Ill.: F. E. Peacock Publishers, 1973.

Goulding, R. New directions in transactional analysis: Creating an environment for redecision and change. In C. Sager and H. Kaplan (Eds.), *Progress in group and family therapy.* New York: Brunner-Mazel, 1972.

Goulding, R. Thinking and feeling in psychotherapy (three impasses). *Voices,* 1974, *10,* 11-13.

Goulding, R., & Goulding, M. Injunctions, decisions, and redecisions. *Transactional Analysis Journal,* 1976, *6,* 41-48.

Harlow, H. The nature of love. *American Psychologist,* 1958, *13,* 673-685.

Harris, T. *I'm OK, you're OK.* New York: Harper & Row, 1969.

Heyer, R. Development of questionnaire to measure ego states with some applications to social and comparative psychiatry. *Transactional Analysis Journal,* 1979, *9.*

Hurley, J., & Porter, H. Child ego state in the college classroom. *Transactional Analysis Bulletin,* 1967, *6,* 28.

James, M., & Jongeward, D. *Born to win.* Reading, Mass.: Addison-Wesley, 1971.

James, M. Self-reparenting. *Transactional Analysis Journal,* 1974, *4,* 3.

Kahler, T. Scripts: Process and content. *Transactional Analysis Journal,* 1975, *5,* 277-279.

Karpman, S. Script drama analysis. *Transactional Analysis Bulletin,* 1968, *26.*

Karpman, S. Options. *Transactional Analysis Journal,* 1971, *1,* 1.

Kendra, J. Research presentation at ITAA Conference 1973. In J. Dusay, *Egograms: How I see you and you see me.* San Francisco: Harper & Row, 1977.

McCormick, P. TA and behavior modification: A comparison study. *Transactional Analysis Journal,* 1973, *3,* 10-14.

McNeel, J. Redecisions in psychotherapy: A study of the effects of an intensive weekend group workshop. Ph.D. dissertation. San Francisco: California School of Professional Psychology, 1975.

Mellor, K., & Sigmend, E. (née Schiff). Discounting. *Transactional Analysis Journal,* 1973, *5,* 3. (a)

Mellor, K., & Sigmend, E. (née Schiff). Redefining. *Transactional Analysis Journal,* 1975, *5,* 3. (b)

Penfield, W. Memory mechanisms. *Archives of Neurology and Psychiatry,* 1952, *67,* 178-198.

Penfield, W., & Roberts, L. *Speech and brain mechanisms.* Princeton: Princeton University Press, 1959.

Perls, F. *Gestalt therapy verbatim.* Lafayette, Calif.: Real People Press, 1969.

Reik, T. *Listening with the third ear.* New York: Farrar, Strauss, 1948.

Schiff, E., & Mellor, K. Discounting. *Transactional Analysis Journal,* 1975, *5,* 303-311.

Schiff, J. Reparenting schizophrenics. *Transactional Analysis Bulletin,* 1969, *8,* 47-62.

Schiff, J. *All my children.* New York: Evans, 1970.

Schiff, J., et al. *The cathexis reader.* New York: Harper & Row, 1975.

Schiff, J., & Schiff, A. Passivity. *Transactional Analysis Journal,* 1971, *1,* 71-78.

Spitz, R. Hospitalism: Genesis of psychiatric conditions in early childhood. *Psychoanalytic Study of the Child,* 1945, *1,* 53.

Steiner, C. A script checklist. *Transactional Analysis Bulletin,* 1964, *6,* 38-39.

Steiner, C. *Games alcoholics play.* New York: Grove Press, 1970.

Steiner, C. *Scripts people live.* New York: Grove Press, 1971. (a)

Steiner, C. The stroke economy. *Transactional Analysis Journal,* 1971, *1,* 3. (b)

Thomson, G. The identification of ego states. *Transactional Analysis Journal,* 1972, *2,* 196-211.

Vernon, J., et al. The effect of human isolation upon some perceptual and motor skills. In Solomon, et al. (Ed.), *Sensory deprivation.* Cambridge, Mass.: Harvard University Press, 1961.

Weiss, E. *Principles of psychodynamics.* New York: Grune & Stratton, 1950.

12

Family Therapy

VINCENT D. FOLEY

OVERVIEW

Family therapy, as the name clearly states, is the theory of families. The focus is not on an individual, identified patient, but rather is on the family as a whole. The basic concept of this form of treatment is that it is more logical, faster, more satisfactory and more economical to treat all members of a system of relationships—in this case, the primary nuclear family— than to concentrate on the person who is supposed to be in need of treatment. The task of the family therapist is to change relationships between members of the troubled family, so that symptomatic behavior disappears. To accomplish this, family therapists have developed a variety of different strategies and techniques, based on somewhat different theories, for the ultimate goals of realigning relationships in the family to achieve better adjustment of all individuals in the family, including the so-called identified patient.

Basic Concepts

Family therapy may be defined broadly as the attempt to modify the relationships in a family to achieve harmony. A family is seen as an open system, created by interlocking triangles, maintained or changed by means of feedback. Therefore, there are three basic concepts in family therapy: *system, triangles,* and *feedback.*

According to Thomas Kuhn (1962), a *paradigm* is a way of looking at scientific data and is the critical dimension in how one goes about investigating evidence. Family therapy offers a new paradigm that brings with it new concepts and new ways of making interventions (Haley & Hoffman, 1967; Levenson, 1972). Family therapy is a quantum leap from (*a*) the prior paradigm of viewing people as individuals apart from one another to (*b*) seeing them strictly in their relationships with others. As a result, the locus of pathology is shifted from the *individual* to the *system*. The attention of the therapist shifts from the "disturbed" individual to the dysfunctional system. In family therapy, the "identified patient" is seen as but a symptom, and the system itself (the family) is viewed as the client.

Concept of system

A *system* (Buckley, 1967) is made up of sets of different parts with two things in common: (1) the parts are interconnected and interdependent with mutual causality each affecting the other, and (2) each part is related to the other in a stable manner over time. A heating unit in a house is a system, whereas people traveling to work on a bus are not. If a system has a continuous flow of elements entering and leaving, it is an *open* system. If it lacks such a flow, as in the case of a heating system, it is a closed system (Von Bertalanffy, 1974). An open system, such as a family, has three important properties: wholeness, relationship, and equifinality.

Wholeness means the system is not just the sum of its parts taken separately, but also includes their interaction. It follows from this that one cannot understand a given part unless one understands its connection to the other parts. Therapeutically, this means a client must be seen in the context of his life, especially his relationship to his family. Wholeness, therefore, refers to the interdependence between the parts of the system. This wholeness represents a Gestalt conception since the whole is more than and different from the sum of its parts. So the family consists of the people in it *and* also the relationships between the individuals.

Relationship refers to the property of a system that considers what is happening between the parts and examines interactions. It puts an emphasis on *what* is happening rather than *why* it is happening. This shift results from the use of a paradigm based on the system concept rather than a paradigm based on a collection of separated and separable individuals. *What* becomes more important than *why*. The family therapist asks, "*What* is the family doing?" rather than, "*Why* is the family doing this?" If the ongoing patterns of interaction can be seen and understood, the therapist believes an ameliorative change can be made in the system without uncovering the *why* of the pattern. We shift our attention from what is going on *inside* family members to what is going on *between* them.

Equifinality, or the self-perpetuation of structures, means that if interventions are made here and now, changes can be produced since open systems are not governed by their initial conditions. A system has no "memory." This concept has enormous importance for family therapy because it justifies concentrating on the here-and-now. Regardless of the origin of a problem, any difficulty can be removed if a change is made at any point in time in the system. Silvano Arieti (1969) suggests that avoiding getting involved in the past, what he calls the "genetic fallacy," might be the most important contribution system thinking has made to therapy. Almost all other therapeutic systems, especially psychodynamically oriented ones, concentrate on the past, seeking for underlying causes, making interpretations about past events, implying that the "real problem" is in the past. The family therapist does not deny the importance of the past, but emphasizes that what perpetuates the problem is the current interaction within the system. For example, say that a man began heavy drinking 20 years ago because he had unresolved problems with his mother, but if he drinks now it may be because of the present relationships with his wife. If the interaction between husband and wife can be altered, the drinking may be changed without ever getting involved in the why or in the past. Equifinality has many practical ramifications in the way in which a therapist will make interventions into a family system.

Interlocking triangles

A series of *interlocking triangles* are the basic building blocks of the family relationship system (Bowen, 1971). An emotional network such as a family is composed of a series of interlocking triangles that lend stability to the system. They are a means of reducing or increasing the emotional intensity of a system. One can formulate an axiom as follows: *Whenever the emotional balance between two people becomes too intense or too distant, a third person or thing can be introduced to restore equilibrium to the system and give it stability.* This is why frequently marriages in trouble have presenting problems such as husbands having affairs or becoming "workaholics" or alcoholics and wives becoming overinvolved with children, clubs, or family. These troubling behaviors can be viewed either (*a*) as the result of problems of the individuals or (*b*) as tactics for gaining closeness or distance within the context of the marriage or the family. Family therapy takes this latter view. To repeat the basic point of view: family therapy is therapy of the family and not of the individuals.

Analyzing the various triangles in a system and making interventions to change the system are the primary tasks of the family therapist. Murray Bowen and his associates of the *family systems theory* school of thought (see Liebman et al., 1976) are particularly concerned with triangles over three generations involving grandparents, parents, and children. Salvador Minuchin (1974) and *structuralists* in general are more concerned with triangles in the nuclear family of father, mother, and child. Both, however, work on the triangles as a way of producing change and not with individuals in the system.

Feedback

In system theory, *feedback* refers to the process whereby a system adjusts itself. *Negative feedback* is the process by which the deviation in a system is corrected and previous equilibrium is restored. *Positive feedback* destroys a system by forcing it to change, not allowing it to return to its former state.

A frequently observed clinical pattern illustrating the concept of negative feedback would be the following. John's parents ask for help with their son who is labeled "school phobic." The therapist views John's problem as a response to the family system; he is overclose with his mother and too distant from his father. He sees John, the identified patient, as a "coverup" for parental problems. The counselor works with the parents and their marriage. John is thereby relieved and begins to go to school. The marriage, however, worsens as more and more problems between husband and wife are uncovered. John senses their worsening relationship and begins to become phobic again. The parents now unite and stay together "for the sake of the child." John's school phobia can be labeled as "negative feedback" needed to maintain the old system.

Positive feedback has been aptly described by Carl Whitaker (1975) as the "leaning tower of Pisa" approach. A therapist instead of correcting a symptom pushes the problem in the other direction so the system falls of its own weight. This approach uses the absurdity of a symptom, and instead of restoring balance, moves it into further chaos to its ultimate destruction. The most recent and creative use of positive feedback can be found in the writings of Mara Palazzoli and her associates in Milan, Italy (1978). Originally trained as a child analyst she came under the influence of Gregory Bateson by way of the Palo Alto group (Mental Research Institute) and incorporated their ideas into her work with anorectic children, adapting them for use with Italian cultural norms.

Other Systems

Many early pioneers in family therapy such as Murray Bowen and Nathan Ackerman were trained as psychoanalysts and, consequently, there are similarities between their ideas and those of psychoanalysis. There are many interfaces between family therapy and psychoanalytic thinking, and some family therapists, such as Ivan Boszormenyi-Nagy and Geraldine Spark (1973), and Helm Stierlin (1974) in particular, work on these. A major difference between psychoanalysis and family therapy is that in psychoanalysis, parental involvement is excluded as a hindrance to the development of the transference neurosis, which is seen as necessary to successful therapy; whereas, in family therapy all members of the family are brought into the therapy sessions.

Adlerian psychotherapeutic theory shares much with family therapy. Its emphasis on family constellation is a major concept borrowed by family therapists. Adler's approach was holistic and so is family therapy. The use of paradox, a major weapon in family therapy, has its roots in Alfred Adler (Mozdzierz, Macchitelli, & Lisiecki, 1976). Likewise, an emphasis on the conscious and the present are Adlerian concepts. The freedom to improvise is a feature of family therapy and it, too, has its roots in Adler. Adler died in 1937 before the full impact of system thinking so, although he took the family system into account in therapy, he did not give it the same importance as do family therapists. The basic concepts of family therapy are found in a latent state in Adler's thinking (Christensen, 1971).

Client-centered therapy, similarly to family therapy, stresses the here-and-now, puts responsibility for behavior on the person, and views man holistically. However, client-centered therapy is totally individual and does not use system thinking. Its basic model is alien to the family therapist.

Rational-emotive. therapy (RET), too, uses a different model. The similarities between it and family therapy are superficial: sharing here-and-now emphasis and taking responsibility. Its differences are major. RET stresses rugged individualism and overemphasizes the cognitive; whereas family therapy strives to strike a balance between being an independent self and relating to others in the family.

Behavior therapy has been used by several family therapists (Liberman, Wheeler, De Visser, Kuehnel, & Kuehnel, 1980; Lieberman, 1976; Engeln, Knutson, Laughy, & Garlington, 1976). The frequently used technique known as "prescribing the symptom" has aspects of behavior modification. However, there is a critical difference between behavior therapy and family therapy. Behavior therapy regards the "problem" as the symptomatic client; family therapy sees the "problem" as a response to a system, as a notice that something is wrong in the system. Behavior therapy puts the burden of change on the individual, family therapy on the system.

Gestalt therapy clearly shares a common base with family therapy. Its concern for the present and its emphasis on behavior and active participation by the therapist are common to both approaches. However, with families, Gestalt gives more importance to feelings and confrontation than do most family therapists (Kempler, 1974).

Reality therapy, likewise, stresses responsibility and the present, but places more of a burden on the individual than does family therapy. Reality therapy is too individualistic and does not take into account the influence of the family system. Family members, especially children, are not totally aware of the system in which they live. Escaping from one's family of origin is not easily done and physical distance does not necessarily bring emotional peace. Reality therapy grants too much freedom to the individual and fails to take into account the power of the family system. In addition, it is too cognitive. Family systems are powerful precisely because they "hook" an individual in his "guts" more than in his head.

Transactional analysis (TA) uses an interpersonal model and tends to emphasize the "why" rather than the "what" as in family therapy. TA recognizes the importance of triangles in its concept of games (Berne, 1964) and shares the belief that symptoms are strategies to control the behavior of others, especially in alcoholics (Steiner, 1971). Nevertheless, TA rarely uses the family as the unit of treatment, preferring to deal with the individuals either alone or in therapeutic groups.

Psychodrama is the basis for a technique known as *family sculpting*, widely used in family therapy, in which a family member recreates his family of origin in space and position. For example, does Mr. Jones place his mother next to his father or at his feet looking up at him? Does he put his sister equidistant between them or close to his father? Where does John himself fit in the family? Sculpting is a way of visualizing the closeness or distance experienced in a family. The difference between sculpting and psychodrama, however, is that the latter is used to relive and resolve a traumatic event, whereas sculpting is more concerned with closeness and space as a means of understanding emotional involvement (see Papp, Silverstein, & Carter, 1973).

Group therapy bears some resemblance to family therapy in that it takes into account the importance of others, but there are two major differences. First, the group does not have a history. It has no past and no future. The family has both. Second, the agent of the change is the group with the therapist in the role of facilitator (Yalom, 1975). The family therapist, on the other hand, serves more as a model or teacher than facilitator.

In summary, family therapy has simi-larities to most active therapies and borrows techniques liberally from many. The critical difference between family therapy and other approaches is the role given to the family system. Other therapies deal either with the individual, the dyadic unit, or the group, but only family therapy sees the family system as the "client." The family is treated, not the individuals. Family therapy is concerned with *how* family members interact and not with *why* they so act. It is a therapy of the family as a system of relationships and not the treatment of maladjusted persons as individuals. We may even say it is concerned with the "spaces" between people—their relationships—rather than the individual processes. As such, it has much in common with Asian personality theory (Pedersen, 1977).

HISTORY

Precursors

A humanistic approach to the alleviation of suffering due to relationship problems began with the psychological discoveries of Freud. In addition, with reference to the precursors of family therapy as we know it today, two other therapists were important: Alfred Adler and Harry Stack Sullivan.

Sigmund Freud

There are two discernible threads in the thinking of Freud. The first, coming from his early training in the physical sciences, is his theory of instincts. The second, going beyond instinct to a more psychological explanation, culminated in the theory of the Oedipus complex. Most of Freud's life was spent in examining instincts; and it was left to others, especially Sullivan and other object relational thinkers or ego analysts such as Melanie Klein, Ronald

Fairbairn, and Heinz Hartmann, to elaborate on the more purely psychological aspects (Guntrip, 1971).

As early as 1909, Freud (1964) saw the connection between a young boy's phobic symptoms and his relationship with his father. Nevertheless, Freud chose to treat young Hans independently of the father, and this choice was to influence therapists in that direction. Freud was probably bound to the mechanical model he had inherited from his early teachers.

Alfred Adler

Adler has had an important but indirect influence on family therapy in a number of ways. The most influential of the so-called social thinkers in therapy, Adler saw context and environment as essential. Man was not primarily an instinctual being but rather a social, purposeful being motivated not by drives but by goals. He was, in brief, a responsible agent able to make choices. Change in the here-and-now, despite one's past, was not only possible but attainable. Virginia Satir (1972) says it simply, "All of the ingredients in a family that count are changeable and correctable" (p. XI).

Second, Adler stressed the importance of the family constellation. It was not just a case of looking at the interaction of child and parent—the concept had to be widened to include siblings and their relationships. Adler's emphasis on sibling position has become one of the essential concepts in the thinking of a school of family therapy associated with Murray Bowen (1971).

Adler emphasized the conscious, the positive, and one's ability to change. This typifies family therapy. The family therapist is less concerned with the past than with the present. He looks at the positive in family relations, its communication, and at the "growing edge" of the family, as well as its dysfunction. Oscar Christensen (1971), an Adlerian family therapist, says, "Adler would view behavior as movement, communication, movement toward others, and the desire to belong—the desire to be part of" (p. 19). This is a description of family therapy.

Harry Stack Sullivan

Sullivan's contribution to family therapy lies in his investigation of schizophrenia. His interpersonal theory is a development of that psychological thread mentioned above in Freud. Sullivan moved away from a biological answer and toward a psychological one, sensing that the primitive relationship between mother and child was critical in schizophrenia. Sullivan's thinking shifted the focus of therapy from purely intrapsychic to the interpersonal. Therapy was moving toward a system concept.

Sullivan's thinking entered family therapy through Don Jackson who, while a resident at Chestnut Lodge in Maryland, was under the influence of Sullivan's disciple, Frieda Fromm-Reichmann. Jackson later moved to the West Coast and began a school of family therapy at Palo Alto that stressed the importance of communication, and the use of paradox.

Beginnings

The beginnings of the modern family-therapy movement started in the mid-1950s and focused largely on research in schizophrenia. This produced a series of concepts known under various labels that became the core ideas in family therapy. The following are some major concepts.

The double bind

In 1956 a paper on communication, "Toward a Theory of Schizophrenia," combined the thinking of Gregory Bateson, Don Jackson, Jay Haley, and John

Weakland. They discovered that in schizophrenic families, a process known as *double binding* occurred regularly. This means a person is put into a situation in which he cannot make a correct choice, because whatever choice he makes, it is unacceptable. "He is damned if he does and damned if he doesn't." No real choice can be made because, in fact, no good choice is possible. The "victim" in a double bind, however, is not aware of his dilemma. A child, for example, is told, "Mommy loves you." On the verbal level, such a message shows love and concern. However, in a double-bind situation, the message is delivered in a cold, distant manner. Consequently, he is told (verbally), "I love you," and is informed (non-verbally), "I don't love you." If the child cannot deal with the two contradictory messages, he cannot deal effectively with this problem. The authors of the paper suggested that such double binding is frequently found in the communication of schizophrenic families. Repeated episodes of double binding produce bewilderment and ultimately withdrawal. Such behavior is then labeled "abnormal" and the person in question is "put away."

Fusion

Bowen (1971) used this term to describe a process he observed in schizophrenic families. By this he meant that various family members are related to each other in such a way that none of them has a true sense of self as an independent individual. The boundaries between the family members tend to be blurred, and the family forms into an amorphous mass without distinguishing characteristics. Family members can neither gain true intimacy, nor can they separate and become persons. They have a quality of *fusion* that gives them no freedom or option to move closer or to get away.

Schism and skew

Theodore Lidz, Alice Cornelison, Stephen Fleck, and Dorothy Terry (1957) at Yale observed two processes in particular in families. One pattern involved a dominant spouse who took control of the relationship. This pattern was labeled *marital skew*, meaning the marital relationship was not an equal partnership. Another pattern involved a marriage in which the husband and wife could not attain role reciprocity or in which there was an overattachment to the parental home of one of the spouses. This pattern called *marital schism* was particularly evident in marriages in which there was a schizophrenic member. The primary alliance that should exist between a husband and wife in their role as parents was noticeably absent and in its place was a violation of the boundaries between husband and wife brought about by an alliance between one parent and that parent's parent.

Pseudomutuality

Lyman Wynne, Irving Ryckoff, Juliana Day and Stanley Hirsch (1958) coined the phrase *pseudomutuality* to describe a false kind of closeness they observed in schizophrenic families. This they defined as "a predominant absorption in fitting together at the expense of the differentiation of the identities of the persons in the relations" (p. 207). To be in such a family is to lose one's boundaries, to become disoriented. The consequence of this process of confusion is to lead one into a state of dependency on the family. Family members are caught and cannot leave. There is no true intimacy or closeness, only a pseudo-love or caring. The family becomes all not by choice but by necessity.

Mystification

R. D. Laing in England, in doing research with the families of hospitalized schizophrenic teenage girls, noted a process of confusion and obfuscation that he called *mystification*, defined as, "One person (p) seeks to induce in the other some change necessary for his (p's) security" (1965, p. 349). He found this process to be rampant in these families, what in popular language might be called "double talk," a blatant form of manipulation. Laing came to the conclusion that frequently such girls identified as patients by their parents and others were, in fact, often the healthiest members of the family.

Interlocking pathologies

Nathan Ackerman began his career as an orthodox child psychiatrist who did not see parents of patients. In time, however, he realized it was impossible to understand children without getting some idea of the family environment and dynamics. His book *The Psychodynamics of Family Life* (1958) was the first major work in the field in which the relationships between an individual and his family were investigated. Ackerman (1956) referred to the difficulties in a family as *interlocking pathologies*, in that the problems of one member could not be understood apart from those of other family members.

His contribution to family therapy is special for two reasons. First, he did not work with schizophrenic families exclusively and thus considered relationship processes in less disturbed families. Second, he brought family therapy to the attention of a largely hostile community of psychodynamically oriented therapists and acted as a go-between for many years between the more traditional approach and that of family therapy.

These various ideas and concepts began to jell into a more coherent form when in 1962 Ackerman and Don Jackson united to found *Family Process*, a journal dedicated to examining family research and

treatment. The family-therapy movement now had a vehicle through which ideas could be filtered and concepts developed.

Current Status

Since its beginning with Freud, psychotherapy has moved through a series of paradigms from the individual to the interpersonal to the system. Although family therapy began with an interpersonal model, it has now moved to a system concept. Some family therapists, although using systems thinking, spend much time on past relationships and so can be distinguished from those who deal more with the here-and-now presenting problems and current system functioning. We can identify four schools of family therapy in terms of the emphasis given to various aspects of the treatment process (Foley 1974)

Object relations

This viewpoint has close connections with the traditional one of ego psychology and in particular with the theory of *object relations* as articulated by Ronald Fairbairn (Guntrip, 1971). Whereas Freud maintained that instinctual gratification was the fundamental need, others, such as Melanie Klein and Ronald Fairbairn, opted for a satisfying object relationship as more basic. The word *object* in this connection refers to "people." The inability of a person to work out such a relationship with the family of origin carries over and "contaminates" the new family system in relation to one's mate and the children. Boszormenyi-Nagy (1965) states that family pathology is "... a specialized multiperson organization of shared fantasies and complementary need gratification patterns, maintained for the purpose of handling past object loss experience" (p. 310). Others who use this kind of framework include James Framo (1970, 1982), Gerald Zuk (1975), and Norman and Betty Paul (1975). In an object relations approach, the identified patient is often seen as the carrier of the split-off and unacceptable impulses of other family members (Steward, Peters, Marsh, & Peters, 1975). In therapy much time will be spent on working with these prior relationships for those who use an object relations theoretical viewpoint. The main center for this approach is the Eastern Pennsylvania Psychiatric Institute in Philadelphia.

Family systems

This school is largely the work of Murray Bowen and his associates (Bowen, 1978; Kerr, 1981).

Bowen began his work in family therapy in the 1950s when he first developed the idea of the triangle as a way people handled conflict. Since that time he has elaborated on this basic notion and evolved a theory made up of eight concepts (Bowen, 1978). They are as follows:

1. Triangles.
2. Differentiation of self (which measures the amount of fusion between people).
3. The nuclear family emotional system (how a given generation patterns itself).
4. Family projection process (how a family selects a member to be the identified patient).
5. Emotional cut-off (the extent to which a family member relates to a member of his family of origin).
6. Multigenerational transmission (how pathology is passed from one generation to another).
7. Sibling position (this determines one's existential view of the world).
8. Societal regression (patterns found in a family occur in a similar fashion in society) (Kerr, 1981, pp. 241-252).

Bowen maintains that people are born into complex family systems and destined for certain roles in the system. Fusion is a common problem in families and the goal of family therapy is to teach people to *respond* and not to *react* to their system. Reacting means to act on the basis of feeling alone not taking into account what the individual wants. Responding, on the other hand, means taking into account the needs of others but still making a rational choice rather than an emotional one.

It should be noted that in the Bowen system one does not make an either/or choice of self or the system. The goal is to stay in touch with the system while, at the same time, maintaining an "I" position. An individual has to learn to be both a self and also a member of a system as both are necessary to healthy functioning.

At present the Bowen system has two centers: Family Studies in the Department of Psychiatry at Georgetown University in Washington, D.C., where Bowen teaches, and at the Center for Family Learning in New Rochelle, New York.

Learning to become a self is a process developed over a period of time and is ongoing. The struggle for balance is always an issue and can never be regarded as over. In the course of therapy one learns to become less reactive and eventually to develop a solid self, that is, one is able to take "I" positions.

Structural family therapy

Salvador Minuchin (et al., 1967; Minuchin, 1974) has taken the concepts of "alignments" and "splits" of Lyman Wynne (1961) and developed a theory of family process which sees pathology as being either "enmeshed" or "disengaged." The structural family therapist works on either loosening the boundaries or establishing them depending on the amount of closeness or distance in the family structure. Here, as in Bowen theory, triangles are important. Minuchin, however, focuses attention on the parent-child relationship rather than the three-generational analysis of Bowen (1976).

The most recent work by Minuchin and his associates has been in the area of psychosomatic medicine (1978, 1981). The relationship of the symptom to the family system is most clearly set forth in an interview with an anorectic girl (Aponte & Hoffman, 1973). In the article the process of realignment is made clear as the therapist restructures the family system without getting into family history.

The main center for structural family therapy is the Philadelphia Child Guidance Clinic.

Strategic intervention

This school grows out of the ideas generated by Don Jackson and Jay Haley, two of the pioneers in the family therapy field. It is perhaps the most exciting approach in family therapy currently in vogue and has established centers in Palo Alto, Milan, and New York City.

The term *strategic intervention* comes from Jay Haley (1973). Haley sees therapy as a power struggle between client and therapist. The critical issue is one of control. In a family system the identified patient is in control making others feel helpless. It is the role of the therapist to reestablish family boundaries and to restructure the system (Haley, 1980). To do so the therapist must devise strategies or ways of changing the power balance (Haley, 1977), hence the term *strategic intervention.*

Haley is interested in structures and power but the therapists at the Mental Research Institute are almost exclusively concerned with the "symptom" as the problem and not the structure of the family. Briefly stated the MRI approach involves: (*a*) the symptom *is* the problem; (*b*) these problems arise because the system cannot handle change, for example, birth, death, and adolescence; (*c*) attempted solutions fail because "they are more of the same"; (*d*) intensifying the problem (i.e., by prescribing the symptom) is often the solution (Weakland, Fisch, Watzlawick, & Bodin, 1974).

A group of therapists based in Milan, Italy, has taken the basic thinking of Jackson and the MRI and developed it into a theoretical approach called the *systemic model* (Palazzoli, Boscolo, Cecchin, & Prata, 1978). The theory states that the problem in families is *hubris,* the Greek word for "overweening pride." In their view everyone wants to control the family without openly declaring this. In fact, however, all members are involved in the process since family causality is *circular* and not *linear.* This notion goes back to Bateson et al. who first stated the concept in 1956. What the Milan group has added to the notion is the need to devise strategies that involve all the family members and give each person's motivation a positive connotation. They emphasize the need, therefore, to find tasks for the family which will force it into change. The book *Paradox and Counterparadox* by Palazzoli, Boscolo, Cecchin, & Prata (1978) is a clear statement both of theory and practice.

A third center using this approach is the Nathan W. Ackerman Institute in New York. Their thinking has been greatly influenced by the Milan group and it is described by Lynn Hoffman (1981).

It should be noted that the strategic approach, especially in the Milan model, is not just a technique of change but a method tied intimately to a theory of family process.

The issue in family therapy for the coming decade is the relationship of epistemology or theory to its art and practice.

The interface between the two is the growing edge of family therapy (Keeney & Sprinkle, 1982).

Summary. The four schools mentioned share things in common; yet each has different approaches to time, level, and intensity of treatment. All agree that troubling, symptomatic behavior is the result of dysfunctional interaction in the family system. Schools 1 and 2 believe that more time and energy have to be spent on clarifying relationships from the past, and schools 3 and 4 (see Figure 12.1) take more literally the concept of equifinality and stress that if the present system can be changed, the past need not be an issue. The schools presented have the same basic concept of the family: a commonality of thought and approach that unites them, but at the same time, each school differentiates itself from the others in terms of its special viewpoints.

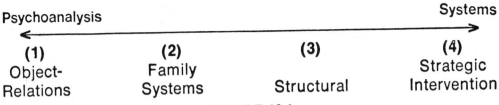

FIGURE 12.1

Four Schools of Family Therapy Schematized in Terms of Continuum Ranging from "Ego Psychology" of Psychoanalysis to the Objective Theory of Strategic Intervention.

PERSONALITY

Family therapy is essentially an approach to psychotherapy that sees the family as the primary unit of treatment. It is not a personality theory in the traditional understanding of that term, but it implies essentially a unique theory of personality. This is true of any approach to therapy because underlying any treatment approach is a concept of what is human nature, what is health, what is sickness, and what can a therapist do to intervene.

Theory of Personality

Family personality theory states that the psychological development of any person results from his family system. The family is the basic source of health or sickness. Family theory focuses on the family system more than other psychotherapeutic systems, because all things being equal, the major force in the development of an individual is his family. In terms of time and emotional force, the family is dominant. Other social systems compete with it but neither the school nor the church nor any other group has as much effect on a young person as does one's primary family.

Murray Bowen noted that an identified patient who functioned adequately in the hospital would often regress when sent back into his family. Bowen discovered that family forces often opposed the interventions of the therapist. The emotional pull of forces exerted by the family was extremely powerful and potent.

There can be little argument with the notion of the family as the most critical factor in the determination of personality. What we are genetically and how we look, think, feel, and act are all influenced by the family into which we are born.

Family therapy views man in a holistic manner considered not only in himself but in relation to his environment. Although it affirms the importance of heredity, it stresses more the importance of environment. A person is the net result of his interactions, and foremost among these is his family of origin. Therefore, the explanation of the development of an individual's personality, its growth, and its decline will be found by examining the family. From this arises the notion that making interventions that restructure the system is the method of choice in the therapy of people in families.

In family therapy, when one talks about personality theory, one is talking about the family nexus. Three issues must be discussed: (1) What is a family? (2) What is a "dysfunctional" family? (3) Why must a family change?

What is a family?
Each individual has basic needs: some physical, some emotional. The physical ones are easily recognized; the emotional ones are less obvious. Emotional needs can be reduced to three dimensions: *intimacy, power,* and *meaning*. People need to be close to others, to belong. They also need to express themselves, to be unique. Finally, there must be some meaning or purpose in their lives. For most people, the first dimension involves a heterosexual relationship; the second involves work; the third involves having children.

Although it can be argued that the family unit is not necessary to fulfill these goals, nevertheless, in very few instances is it possible to achieve these three needs without a family. A family is the social unit in which people by mutual choice attempt to attain their needs for these three dimensions.

People usually marry each other because they find that choice is the most satisfactory way of getting the things they need emotionally. The way in which they negotiate differences determines the success or failure of the marriage. *Can I be close to you and still remain myself? Can I avoid being swallowed up by you? Does our relationship make sense in my life?* The process of marriage answers these questions.

What is a "dysfunctional family"?
Family therapists prefer talking about *dysfunction* rather than sickness because this states more clearly what they see as the fundamental problem—the inability of family members to attain the desired goals of closeness, self-expression, and meaning. When these goals cannot be attained, symptomatic behavior takes place. For example, the husband gets involved in an affair; the wife becomes depressed; a child becomes school phobic.

The difference between seeing symptoms as system oriented or as the property of an individual is not merely semantic. Working from a theoretical model of a system, the therapist believes the other members of the system are critically important if change is to be made in the identified patient. In the more traditional approach, family members are likely to be seen as obstacles to treatment who interfere with the transference process. In a family system concept, however, the other members are an essential part of the therapeutic process.

A *functional family* is one in which the needs of various family members are met. In a *dysfunctional family*, such needs are not being met and therefore symptomatic behavior occurs. The important difference between a functional family system and a dysfunctional one is not the presence or absence of conflict, but rather the attainment of need satisfaction. In either case, there will be *conflict* in the family. Such conflict should be expected because the goals of various people or subsystems in the family rarely coincide.

For example, the father of a family may want his children at home on Christmas Eve with his wife and himself, feeling this will foster his goal of closeness for the family. His son John, however, wants to be with his friends at a basketball game. Mary and Jane, John's sisters, who form a family subsystem based on a common interest in ice skating, want to practice. The mother sides with the girls, pointing out that they have spent the day decorating the tree and deserve some time to themselves. Clearly the goals of the father, mother, son, and daughters are in conflict. Their ability to solve such differences will answer the question regarding the functioning of the family. A functioning family will make compromises; a dysfunctional one will not.

It should be noted in the example given that the issues that ultimately are critical are those of closeness, self-expression, and meaning, especially meaning.

Why must a family change?

Just as an individual passes through a series of stages, so does the family. In the beginning of the family, the husband and wife need to unite into a functional system. They must form a functional "we" in addition to their own personalities.

The next step is opening the system, allowing others to enter: the children (Entwistle & Doering, 1981). This critical step presents the couple with a crisis situation. The presence of a third party means the possibility of alignments and splits. Husband and wife must assume a new role, that of parents. This is a much different role from that of spouse. The anxiety level of many people is aroused by be-

coming a parent, but society tends to emphasize the positive aspect of parenthood, playing down the doubt and anxiety of the new parent.

System thinking explains the difference and the difficulty in parenthood by the concept of feedback. If a husband displeases his wife, feedback can be instant and immediate correction can be made. This is not true in the role of parent. The parent must wonder about what he or she is doing. *Am I too strict? Am I too easy?* The answer will not be known for many years. Feedback is not immediate.

The birth of subsequent children likewise creates a change in the family system. A second child is not simply an addition but rather is a change in the family system. As noted earlier, in a system concept, one plus one does not equal two. An additional family member means the system is restructured.

A new stage in family process is introduced by children going to school. The family system must again open, this time to outsiders. This may prove traumatic in many instances. The phenomenon of school phobia is seen as the inability of the system to make a proper adjustment, to widen its boundaries, and not just as the inability of a child to leave his mother. It can be seen how a new paradigm leads to a new way of conceptualizing a problem and a new way of approaching treatment. The family therapist asks, "What is going on in the *family* that produces school phobia in this child?"

Adolescence brings a need for further freedom for children. Overcloseness between a parent and a child may result in symptomatic behavior in one of the family members. A mother, for example, may not be able to allow a child freedom because it means a loss of meaning in her life.

The separation of children and parents through marriage creates a crisis situation for the parents. It means, frequently, a loss of meaning in life, the so-called empty-nest syndrome. The unresolved problems of the beginning of marriage may now surface as children move away, creating the possibility of marital difficulties.

The stages of the family and their relationship to therapy are described at length in Carter & McGoldrick (1981). The changes brought about by developmental issues are also central to Palazzoli (1978) and Haley (1977, 1980). See also Palazzoli, Boscolo, Cecchin & Prata (1978).

Variety of Concepts

In family therapy, an individual personality—how one thinks, feels, and acts —is seen as the result of myriad, complex relationships that go on in the family. What has been traditionally called *intrapsychic*, the depth dimension of personality, is the result of the process of the family system. Harry Stack Sullivan recognized this by emphasizing the importance of others, especially the mother, in personality development. Alfred Adler, likewise, gave the family constellation an important place in his thinking. He thought one's personality is affected by one's ordinal position in the family. Thus, older children tend to be more responsible as adults, more traditionally minded; middle children are more likely to be difficult and moody; while younger children, who came into the family systems late, tend to be spoiled and remain relatively incapable as adults (Adler, 1949). Family therapy has taken these insights and emphasized three dimensions: (*a*) the marital subsystem, (*b*) the sibling subsystem, and (*c*) homeostasis.

Marital subsystem
Family therapists vary widely in their approach to both theory and practice, but all are agreed on the above three dimensions.

The beginning of a family system whether functional or dysfunctional starts with the couple. They must form a "oneness" that places them squarely on one side of the fence, apart from others. The violation of generational boundaries in particular is the beginning of family dysfunction. The process of differentiation is one that must be made both by an individual and a couple. "Fusion," or "enmeshment," is the result of an inability to separate from a family or origin with a concomitant over-closeness to a parent, spouse, or child. The boundaries are violated to the detriment of all.

Symbolically, the ability to "close a door," to shut out others, is vital for a healthy marriage in the thinking of family therapists. Husband and wife ought to have secrets from their parents and children. There should be an intimacy between them that maintains their privacy. Early researchers in schizophrenia noted the obtrusiveness of parents into their children's lives and vice versa.

Another way of saying this is that in a good marriage the spouse is first and any others are second. Children-oriented marriages are always dysfunctional. Children ought to add meaning to a marriage and express the creativity and warmth of the parents, but they must always be subservient to the marital relationship. A man should always be a husband first and then a father, and a woman a wife first and then a mother.

Perhaps, paradoxically, the most successful parents are those in which each partner is spouse first and parent second. The reason seems to be that a normal married person does not need the child for fulfillment or to give life or the marriage meaning. Being satisfied in himself or herself and with the marriage, the spouse can give children freedom of choice. The child is not caught in the bind of conforming to the parent and being angry—or of "doing his own thing" and feeling guilty.

The triangle that exists among husband, wife, and child is kept less activated when the spouses are united. If they have a coalition, this prevents the child from forming a permanent alliance with one of the parents. It requires the child to seek a relationship with others of his own generation, especially with brothers and sisters.

Sibling subsystem

A natural consequence of the parental coalition is the formation of a sibling subsystem that affords each child a chance to build a closeness with his brothers and sisters. Family therapists insist that children should have secrets from parents: matters that pertain to their private lives. Each subsystem, like each person, should have appropriate boundaries. A rule for determining dysfunction in families is to look at the presence or absence of discernible boundaries. Are parents clearly separated from children? Are children differentiated among themselves? Older children should be treated differently from younger children. If given more responsibility, they should be given more privileges.

As children grow, individual differences should be respected. Privacy is important for the development of personality. Reading mail addressed to others and not knocking before entering another's room are not merely signs of discourtesy but represent essential issues in a family. How much freedom will be given to children in a family is determined by two factors: maturity and culture.

Children do not grow at the same speed physically or intellectually or emotionally. The pace will be unique in each case. Consequently, one cannot say that because A was given a privilege, B should get the same privilege at the same time. Obviously, this can become an area of difficulty. It certainly will be one of conflict. The willingness to discuss differences and to compromise are signs of a functional family system. The issue is one of negotiation and the ability to bring harmony among conflicting goals in the family.

Closely allied with the above are the norms of a given culture or subculture, such as a neighborhood. Perhaps the most neglected area in family therapy is the impact of culture. The concepts of the spouse subsystem and the sibling subsystem find general agreement among family therapists. How they will be worked out concretely, however, will differ from culture to culture. How affection is expressed, money used, time spent with others, and so on are issues that vary greatly (Papajohn & Spiegel, 1975).

The relationship of cultural norms to family therapy is found in *Ethnicity and Family Therapy* (McGoldrick, Pearce, & Giordano, 1982) examining all the major ethnic groups in the United States. Some family therapists have suggested that a particular approach to a family may be more effective by reason of cultural dimension. For example, a Bowenian approach emphasizing the individual seems best suited to Irish families whereas a paradoxical one might be more effective with an Italian one because of its attitude toward authority (McGoldrick & Pearce, 1981). The relationship between the two is just in its beginning phase.

Culture determines the kind of relationship the nuclear family has with the extended family. In traditional rural settings, this has been very close; in modern, urban ones, it is more diffuse. Which is more effective is open to dispute. How spouses should relate to each other is similarly a cultural issue. Until recently, the man has been considered to be the instrumental leader, and the woman the affectional-expressive one. Social changes currently in progress seem to be destructive to this way of thinking. Although there may be a greater exchange of roles between husband and wife in the future, it seems safe to say that in any case, there will be no exchange of basic dependency between parent and child. The generational boundaries will probably remain intact.

Homeostasis

How the marital and the sibling subsystems interact results in what family therapists call the *homeostasis*, or balance, in a family. Any system operates within given limits, and when these are transgressed, the system experiences difficulty. If that difficulty cannot be corrected, the system will eventually disintegrate.

The family system operates within limits determined in part by its members and in part by its culture. Families coming to a new culture frequently encounter "cultural shock," which destroys the family balance if the changes dictated by the new culture cannot be absorbed into the old system.

In family therapy, one looks at the behavior patterns in the family as balance mechanisms of the system more than as individual properties of family members. An alcoholic, for example, in a family concept is seen differently than in other approaches. Traditionally, therapists have regarded such behavior as bad or destructive and have attempted to deal with the alcoholic and his drinking in that light. In family therapy, however, the therapist regards alcoholism as a property of the system that performs a *positive* role in the family by maintaining its homeostasis. Rather than deal with the alcoholic as an individual, the family therapist prefers looking at the system to understand better its need for this behavior.

The goal of family therapy is change in the system: the creation of a new homeo-stasis, a new way of relating. If *therapy* is defined as the process of working through resistance, *family therapy* means working through the resistance to creating new ways of interacting. The key issue in the conflict is homeostasis, with the family fighting to hold on to its old way of relating and the therapist trying to produce a new one. Sometimes the battle is overt, but more often it will be covert. In either case, there will be a conflict if the therapy is to be effective. Conflict cannot be avoided because the family will define the issue as this or that member's bad behavior, and the therapist will see it as involving the entire family. The ability to move the family from its prior point of view to the new one—the view of the therapist—is the measure of his skill and the success of the therapeutic process.

Several family therapists believe that the concept of homeostasis fails to account adequately for all the data (Dell, 1982; Hoffman, 1981). Paul Dell (1982) states that the term *homeostasis* is superfluous because an interactional system is a result of the individuals who compose it and not because of any "homeostatic mechanism" or "family rules" (p. 37). He suggests the term *coherence* as a more accurate one.

A family therapist is most concerned with the process by which the family system operates: How does a family maintain itself? Specifically, this is done by examining the marital subsystem and the sibling subsystem within the context of a given culture. How one will go about this, the process itself, will vary among therapists depending on the weight given to issues of power, communication, and meaning.

PSYCHOTHERAPY

Family therapy is essentially a unique way of viewing pathology that sees problems within the context of the family system. Historically, it is a development of a process that began with concentration on an individual, emphasizing intrapsychic aspects, and then moved to individuals as family members emphasizing interpersonal relationships and communication modalities. Family therapy focuses on the way a system is organized and structured. Pathology is viewed as the result of the incorrect way in which the system is organized. The system of relationships is to be changed to achieve desirable changes in individuals, and not the intrapersonal aspects of the identified client. Or more exactly, it is the person who is to be changed—but indirectly through changing the structure and texture of family relationships.

Theory of Psychotherapy

The heart of therapy is change in behavior. Philosophers have broken down human behavior into three areas: the emotional, the cognitive, and the volitional. Therapists, following this pattern, talk about feeling, thinking, and action. These divisions are arbitrary because a human being cannot be divided into sections but must be regarded as an indivisible entity. Nevertheless, in individuals or groups, one of these modes tends to dominate. Change in family therapy is ultimately change in behavior, change in interaction. What one feels and how one thinks are important, but unless these get put into action, nothing really changes. A primary goal in family therapy therefore is producing overt behavior change, even if the family members are unaware of what is happening. Therapists who use paradox, in particular, are concerned mostly with altering the family behavioral system. If this can best be done apart from the family's awareness of the process, that goal takes precedence.

Insight is not important in family therapy. Getting the family to see what it is doing and why members are acting as they do is not a goal for most family therapists. Insight is considered an intellectual game that prevents real change from taking place or an epiphenomenon. It is not important for the family to understand the way it is structured; this is only important for the therapist. Jay Haley (1963) represents a large number of family therapists in maintaining that getting the family aware of its interaction is actually antitherapeutic since real change is one of behavior and not just of thinking.

Family therapists see different dimensions of therapy as having varying degrees of importance.

History

How important for the therapist is a knowledge of the past to change the present? This is the question raised by the issue of the role of *history* in therapy.

Object relations theory and family systems theory regard a knowledge of the family's history as important for understanding the present structure of the family. The present family system is seen as a reflection of past structures and a transference-like process operates in the here-and-now. For family systems therapists, the triangles that constitute the system extend over several generations and must be examined. Structural family and strategic intervention therapists are less interested in family history since they believe the important dimension is the current structure, and this can be changed without an involved analysis of the family history. How things got the way they are is relatively unimportant. What to do about things the way they are now is what is important. The analogy is of a broken leg. Does it really matter to the doctor how it snapped? It is broken—and the issue is how to fix it. Setting the bone will be the same whether the bone was broken from a fall or a kick or from a blow.

Diagnosis

Traditional therapy pays much attention to getting a correct *diagnosis*. It is considered important to know if a client is neurotic, has a character disorder, or is psychotic. In family therapy, there is less concern for diagnosis. In part, this is due to a paucity of ways of measuring family dysfunction as it pertains to a system. One can talk about the specific feelings of a family member or the role one plays in the pathology of another, but an adequate nomenclature or classification system has not yet been developed. Some work has been done on how people solve problems in families or how they cooperate in performing a task. There has been a general resistance to diagnosis because many feel it better serves the needs of the therapist than it does the client or family.

Diagnosis, in a wide sense, as a way of evaluating the current functioning is used, but it is used more for clinical convenience than for research purposes. Diagnosis in family therapy does not have the same value as in more traditional approaches.

Affect

Feelings are thought by family therapists to be the result of behavior and therefore not given a primary position. Apart from Virginia Satir, and to a lesser degree Salvador Minuchin, most family therapists would not use family feelings to any great extent. This is one of the neglected aspects in family therapy due to an overwhelming emphasis on the concept of system, which tends to minimize the role and importance of emotion. This lack will probably change as more work is done with cultural dimensions.

Minuchin (1974; Minuchin & Fishman, 1981) uses feelings but more as a technique to change the family interaction than by addressing himself to the feelings themselves. For example, he will become angry with a father who allows his son to make fun of him to get the father to make some changes in his relationship to the son. He will not concentrate on the lack of feeling that the father is experiencing as such, but rather on the way in which that lack can be used to move the system in another direction.

The role of learning

To some extent, all therapies use *learning*. The issue usually is how to make the client or family aware of the learning process. Object relations therapists spend time analyzing past relationships and discussing how they influence the present. Teaching the family members new ways of relating will be a goal for object relations therapists. The learning process, furthermore, tends to be conscious and deliberate. Likewise, family systems therapists who regard themselves as teachers of self-differentiation underline the importance of learning new and effective ways of interacting. The other family therapists tend to play down the conscious aspect of learning, believing that an emphasis on this cognitive process slows the rate of change.

Transference and the unconscious

In the psychodynamic model, the locus of pathology is thought to be deep in the client. The process of cure is said to depend on the development of a *transference* neurosis, which most analysts maintain is the critical step in therapy (Greenson, 1967). In family therapy, however, the locus of the pathology is the very structure itself and the critical step is restructuring the system. Transferencelike phenomena do occur between the therapist and the family, but no true transference is developed because the medium of therapy is not their relationship but the impact of the therapist's interventions, the force of the feedback into the system. Murray Bowen (1971) and Don Jackson and Jay Haley (1968) insisted that transference was not a necessary part of family therapy. This might be of some concern for those therapists in the object relations group because they are generally concerned with the role of the *unconscious* on family process. Transference and countertransference have a unique role in the thinking of Carl Whitaker (Whitaker & Keith, 1981). Whitaker uses his own feelings and reactions to help move the family system seeing therapy as a growth process both for himself and the family. This is why he calls his approach an experiential one. This issue of transference is not one of great importance for other family therapists.

Therapist as teacher and model
Family therapists generally agree that the medium of change is the therapist not as an object of transference but as a model or teacher. He is either the model of communication or the teacher of individuation. The family learns new ways of solving problems and of avoiding dead-end discussions. Behavior is analyzed and relabeled and seen in a new light. For example, a mother complains that her son is "impossible," by which she means that he has some problem inside of him that causes him to act in a certain manner. The therapist listens to her and patiently examines her interaction with the boy. In the light of this, he is able to relabel the behavior from another point of view such as the mother's inability to communicate with the child.

In the practice of family therapy, despite differences in approach, all therapists are active and not passive. They are not nondirective, reflecting feelings, but rather make interventions according to certain guidelines. In no way are they

blank screens upon which projections are made. There is an attempt to be themselves and not to assume a role. This accounts for the wide divergence observed among family therapists as to therapeutic styles. Beneath these differences, however, is the striving to teach or to model behavior for the family.

Process of Psychotherapy

The course of family therapy varies widely with the goals of the therapist. It can range from several sessions to several years depending on a number of interconnected issues.

Families being treated by object relations and family systems therapists will tend to be seen over a longer period than those by structural or strategic intervention therapists. This is due to a difference in goals. In the first group, deep changes in interactional patterns will be the goals; in the latter, the problem is more symptom oriented and treatment time will be shorter. This illustrates how the way a problem is posed influences the treatment process.

Initial interview
This is a most important session because it sets the tone for the therapy. Specifically, it will determine who will control the process. There are two goals in this interview: first, to relabel the presenting problem; second, to engage the family.

Phases
The therapist, let us presume, has gathered all the family members for the initial session. He proceeds in a series of phases or stages in the treatment process.

Warm-up
The therapist generally allows the family members who enter the room to sit where they choose. He should have more chairs

present than people, giving them a freedom of placement. This is the first live contact with the family and how they arrange themselves tells much about how they relate to one another, how they feel about the therapist in relation to the family, and how successful therapy will be.

How does the family distribute itself? Do the parents sit next to each other? Does a child sit between them? Does a family member pull his chair back from the others? Do the girls sit close to each other? Do the boys sit far apart? Frequently, the way such sitting occurs gives the family therapist a clue to the underlying problems and to the alliances and splits in the family.

Typically, one of the children will be presented by a parent as the "problem." He is therefore the identified patient. It is best for the therapist to begin the session by saying something like, "Before we talk about some of the problems in the family, I'd like to say 'hello' to each of you and to find out something about you." He should then address the parent who made the initial contact saying something like, "It's nice to meet you in person, Mrs. Jones." He should then address himself to the other parent. In this way, he is recognizing the existence and importance of the marital subsystem. He can then turn to the other members of the family. It is helpful to follow some sequence based on age. In this way, the sibling subsystem is acknowledged and the fact that there are differences among the children. This first meeting is a *warm-up* phase. It is important for two reasons: First, it shows the family the therapist's personality, which is something each of them has only been able to fantasize, and diminishes the "therapeutic mystique" by mitigating the transference phenomenon; second, it says indirectly that the "family problem" is not the only issue or fact of life in the family.

This simple first phase is important because the therapist is an outsider and he is being judged by the family as to his worthiness to be allowed inside the family boundaries. Accommodating himself to the family enables him to join the system, and anything he can do to accomplish this is important. He is showing himself to the family before he asks them to expose themselves.

Relabeling the "problem"

Phase two begins after all the family members have been met. The therapist initiates it by saying to the parent who made the contact, "I'm wondering, Mrs. Jones, if you would tell me what brings you to see me." Or "Could you tell me in what way you think I can help you?"

These simple statements communicate to the family certain important attitudes of the therapist. Asking Mrs. Jones to state her reason for seeking help makes her put her request into the specific form of defining a person or a feeling or a behavior as the family problem. For example, it is certain that other family members will not agree with the mother's formulation of the problem. Instead of making this obvious comment, the therapist can conclude this phase of the process by noting, "It seems that some of you have different ideas on what the problem is in this family." This second phase relabels or redefines the problem. By proceeding in this way, the therapist avoids painful hassles with family members about the "real" problem.

Spreading the problem

Phase three heightens the conflict in the family by pointing out the different ways how the problem may be defined. The therapist, having listened to the parents or their formulation of the problem and perhaps also listened to the children's comments or objections, may simply reformulate the problem quite differently as a kind of hypothesis, getting all to think differently about the "real" issues. This is also a way of pointing out the family's need for outside help. It tends to reduce guilt and to enhance hope. Comments on the pain in the family, its frustration, unhappiness, and so on are useful in emphasizing the impotence of the family system to solve its own problems.

Need for change

Phase four begins when the therapist asks the family what solutions have been tried in the past in dealing with its pain. The issue is getting the family to focus on change. The therapist may ask: "What have you done about this problem?" and "Have you done anything about this problem?" These statements are made to reinforce awareness of the inability of the family either (1) to find successful techniques for dealing with the problem, or (2) to point out that nothing constructive has been done about the problem so far. It stresses the need for new attempts to solve the problem or develop new techniques. In either case, the emphasis is on *change* among all the family members. The therapist focuses on behavioral change and the inability up to this point of family members to make those changes. This narrows down the problem to behavior and keeps it within the boundaries of the family.

Changing pathways

Phase five begins when the therapist begins to make his interventions into the family by means of suggestions. In more technical terms, he begins to try to change the pathways of communication by making interventions. To illustrate: he may request that an uninvolved parent take charge of a child's behavior, thus building an alliance between that parent and the child while putting some distance between the child and the overinvolved parent. He may ask the uninvolved parent to plan a day of fun with the child he cannot talk to and not to tell the other parent about it. Or he may ask the mother to teach the child how to light matches with the help of a child who plays mother's helper (Minuchin, 1974). The possibilities are endless.

These suggestions for how the initial interview should go follow most closely the procedures of the structural school but are similar for the other family approaches as well. More family background information, or more concentration on family of origin, or more use of specific tactics such as paradoxical injunctions might be featured by other schools of family therapy. However, in all schools, the therapist informs the family that each member is part of the process and that any problem is never to be seen as the personal property of that person, but always involves two or more family members, and that the behavior of the family in the here-and-now is either creating or perpetuating the problem.

The first interview is important in family therapy as in other approaches because it concerns the issue of the therapeutic contract. It should state in a clear manner what family therapy is. In addition to these theoretical goals, it should begin the process, if possible, in the session itself by not only talking about the process but reenacting it.

Use of techniques

Some techniques employed by family therapists include the following:

Reenactment

If a presenting problem is the inability of a father and son to talk to each other, instead of asking for an example, the therapist might request that the two talk to each other in the session. If the father complains that when he tries to talk to his son, his wife interferes, the therapist might ask them to begin talking and then have her intrude into their conversation. If a problem can be reenacted in the therapy session, this is frequently done. The obvious advantage of this approach is that the therapist can see for himself what is happening in the family and he does not have to rely on reports. This is an effective technique, what Moreno called "psychodrama *in situ*," because so many complaints relate to the inability of two people to talk with each other. Communication problems can become the major substance of the sessions.

Homework

As the name indicates, this refers to actions the therapist asks family members to perform between sessions. It has the value of making the therapy sessions places where solutions to problems are found and not just where talking takes place. In addition, it accustoms family members to understand that if they change their behavior, they can change how they feel and think as well. The homework assignments restructure family pathways by building coalitions and changing the intimacy-distance lines between members.

Family sculpting

As mentioned previously (page 451), this is the name given to a process by which the dimensions of closeness and power within the family are examined in a nonverbal manner. For example, a father is asked to describe his parents and his place in the family not by words but by using space. Family sculpting has the advantage of making visible feelings about family structures. It also explains to current family members reasons why their parents may act in a certain way, as one of the con-

cepts underlying family sculpting is that people tend to repeat earlier patterns (Papp, Silverstein & Carter, 1973).

Genogram

Family system theorists, in particular, are interested in the emotional climate of a family and how this exerts influence on the relationships within the family system. Boundaries within the family, between the family and the outside world, and membership within the family are some of the more pertinent issues that some believe can best be handled by using this approach. A *genogram* is "a structural diagram of a family's three-generational relationship system. This diagram is a road map of the family relationship system" (Guerin & Pendagast, 1976, p. 452). It is a means of getting at significant issues in a more graphic manner than by simply talking about them. It is widely used by followers of Bowen's system although other schools of thought employ genograms also (see Figure 12.2).

Behavior modification techniques

This area of rapid growth in the field is closely tied to research. The underlying concepts are derived from social psychology (Thibaut & Kelly, 1959) in which reward is maximized and cost is minimized. Complete studies of this approach can be found in Liberman, Wheeler, De Visser, Kuehnel & Kuehnel (1980) and Jacobson and Margolin (1979). Another brief but clear treatment of behavioral marital therapy (BMT) is also by Jacobson (1981).

There are similarities between the techniques of BMT and the strategic approach but the former derives its epistemology from behavior modification and the latter from Gregory Bateson. Although there is some question of its effectiveness with more serious problems (Gurman & Kniskern, 1981a), nevertheless, it is an

Genogram

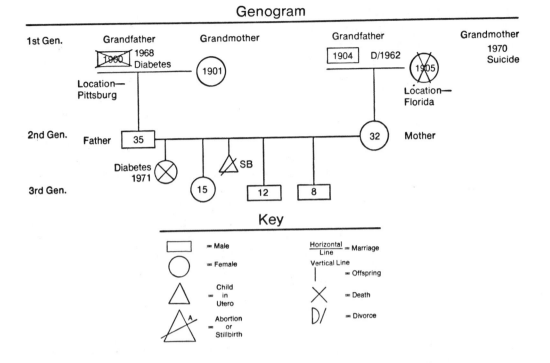

FIGURE 12.2

approach that is of wide interest and whose results are well researched (Jacobson & Weiss, 1978).

Multiple family therapy

This technique involves seeing several families at the same time. It has a long history in the field of family therapy (Laqueur, 1973). It has two advantages. First, it offers family members a glimpse of other families and allows them to see firsthand that there are similarities in problems, enabling family members to identify with others; second, by permitting others to participate in a quasi-therapist role, it tends to lessen the authority of the therapist, which at times may be most advantageous. Vincent Foley (1975), for example, has found that with black, disadvantaged families, multiple-family therapy helps hasten the therapeutic alliance by breaking down hostile feelings of the family for a white therapist.

The techniques of modifications mentioned above are only illustrative. Since family therapy is based on a model that sees pathology as the result of dysfunctional relationships, it is freer than other approaches in adopting techniques to help change the interactional system. Family therapy is open to any number of techniques as long as they serve to change family process.

Length of treatment

Family therapy treatment can last from a few sessions to a period of years. Structural and strategic interventionists tend to be briefer than object relationists and family system therapists. Gerald Zuk (1975) sees the length of treatment as dependent on the goals presented by the family. If its main goal is to reduce tension, sessions tend to be one to six interviews. If symptom reduction is the aim, it more likely will be 10 to 15 sessions. If better communication is sought, 25 to 30 sessions over a 6- to 8-month period are called for. If a restructuring of the family with better differentiation of family members is considered, the length will tend to be 40 more sessions over an extended period. James Trotzer (1982) has elaborated on Zuk's categories as an indication of the outcome of therapy and suggests the longer the better. In contrast, Richard Wells (1982) points out that engagement is perhaps a more sophisticated process.

Indications and contraindications

Lyman Wynne (1965) suggested that problems such as adolescent separation and interlocking problems, those one family member believes cannot be solved without the cooperation of another, were good indicators of the need for family therapy. In general, problems of paranoia and sexual acting out in the family are considered poor indicators for this kind of treatment.

It is difficult to make absolute statements about the issue of what problems are suitable for family therapy other than to say that therapists who incline more toward a system concept would tend to see most psychological adjustment problems as amenable to family therapy, and those coming from a more traditional psychoanalytic background are inclined to be less certain.

Mechanisms of Psychotherapy

Despite all the theoretical concepts any system uses to justify its existence, ultimately one question matters, "How does change take place?" Within that question, one finds related ones such as: Can the process that one describes be analyzed into its component parts? Is it measurable? Is it teachable? In the final analysis, is it beyond articulation? Is it an art or a science?

At this point in family therapy, there is more speculation than hard data. Most therapists do not take pretests and posttests either in individual or family therapy. Most of the data gathered are self-reports of the families. Unfortunately, self-reports can be unreliable. With these observations in mind, let us now proceed with some tentative answers.

Family therapists concentrate on changes in behavior as evidence of progress. Changes in feelings and thinking are considered less important. How is behavior change accomplished? There is a growing belief among family therapists that therapy is a power struggle between the therapist and the client. It is a battle of wills in which the stronger one prevails.

Jay Haley (1963) drew an analogy between the therapist and the hypnotist in that both seem to ask for change while at the same time denying it. Haley took the position that the therapist has the responsibility for change and that failure is always his failure. It is his responsibility to analyze problems correctly and to devise tactics that lead people into change. Feelings do not produce change nor does thinking. Empathy, although important for engaging the family, is not corrective. Insight is even less helpful because it can provide a convenient way of avoiding change, giving the family intellectual games to play. The name of the game is power. The therapist must create situations that force the family into a bind. Either it continues its behavior, but does so under the command of the therapist, or it rebels, thus producing the desired change. In either case, the family system is under assault.

Most family therapists, although perhaps not taking as extreme a position as Haley, would tend to accept his thinking, seeing all family therapy as a power struggle. Family therapists tend to be more open about the power element in therapy. Giving directives or telling people what to do can be either overt or covert. In either case, it is at the heart of therapy. The nondirective therapist, for example, is covertly giving directives by picking up on the client's comments about feelings. He is teaching him that a response is given when he approaches things in that manner. The cues are reinforced by other nonverbal comments, such as nods of the head and smiles.

Some family therapists might object to the emphasis Haley gives to the power struggle, but at some level, all will likely agree with the notion of relabeling as a critical step in the change process. To accept this concept is to agree with the idea of power as the main ingredient in change. To illustrate: a family comes for help with a child who will not go to school. A long story of the family's failure to be effective in dealing with this problem is recounted. Kindness has been tried and found wanting, punishment has followed and has not worked, and now the child is labeled as "sick." He is labeled a problem to the family and has become an outcast or pariah. The therapist, however, may see the school phobia as the child's response to difficulties between husband and wife. This becomes clearer as the parents talk about the problem, the mother being overinvolved with the child and the father underinvolved. The therapist may suggest that the father spend more time with the child and that he should take command of the problem.

The therapist may have in his own mind relabeled the problem as a conflict between husband and wife, which is not being dealt with overtly in their roles as father and mother. Instead of bringing this redefinition or relabeling into the open where it can be denied, the therapist may shift the family balance about, in effect neutralizing the mother's power. This can be made even more effective if he then instructs the wife that she is to keep after the husband to make sure he carries out his job of being a good father.

Once the child's behavior has calmed down as a result of this power change, the covert conflict of husband and wife will surface as that of husband-and-wife rather than father-and-mother. At this point, the child might be dismissed from the sessions and work might be done with just the couple. Changes have been accomplished not by interpretation or insight or by improving communication but by making structural variations in the way in which the family operates. Thus, the therapist who covertly reinterprets the family's problem relabels the pathology and suggests changes without giving explanations, leading to new behaviors and affecting family relationships by his intervention.

At this point, a therapist might want to work with issues of closeness or meaning with the couple or investigate areas of differentiation of self.

This example of a school-phobia problem taken from a structural family model illustrates the process of relabeling, but similar examples could be given from any of the other schools as well. Change in family therapy begins with a shift from the way the family sees the problem to the way the therapist sees it. This is best done by maneuvers that realign the family rather than cognitive measures—by action, not talk.

Change in family therapy is accomplished by modifying the structures of the system. This means working on the triangles that compose it and producing new alignments. This in turn produces changes in behavior that influence feelings. Devising techniques that change existing structures is the major goal of psychotherapy for family therapy. Change in how the system operates produces change in individual members of the system.

APPLICATIONS

Problems

Family problems
Problems labeled "family ones" by the family itself are most amenable to treatment. However, such presenting problems are rarely encountered. People with a disturbed member in their family rarely think the essential cause is that the family itself is in need of treatment. This should not be surprising since the idea of thinking in terms of systems—field psychology—has not filtered down to the public, and indeed the concept of restructuring the field is still a minority concept with psychotherapists. The general tendency in families and also among therapists is to locate and deal with the so-called identified patient who from the point of view of a family therapist is in reality the scapegoat for the family. However, from time to time, referring people, such as principals of schools or medical doctors, do realize that the symptomatic person is a function of a disordered family.

Marital problems—both partners
Frequently family problems are labeled "marital problems" rather than "family problems." Marriage counseling is well known to most people, and columns on such problems are a staple in most magazines. Newspapers, too, carry columns such as *Ann Landers* and *Dear Abby*, and a large percent of their questions concern marriage. However, even though a client may call and state, "We are having some problems with our marriage," it is soon evident that one of the partners to the marriage believes the problem is the exclusive domain of the other. In an initial interview of a couple, the caller will often begin with, "My husband drinks too much," or "My wife is depressed," or "I know I'm not perfect, but my wife/husband *really* has problems." The clear implication is that the other one is the so-called identified patient.

Individual problems
At times one encounters the isolated individual who is truly alone, not part of any family system. This, however, is rare. Most people in our society are married and have families. A spouse, children, parents, and siblings are relationships that are deepest and most lasting. Literally, we never get over them. They should be the context within which therapy takes place. Individual problems can be seen as the exclusive property of a person or as a response to the context of a family. Family therapy clearly opts for the latter.

Other relationships
It should be clear that system thinking applies to any system, not just the family. This means that difficulties in meetings, PTA groups, and other social systems can be analyzed as individual problems or system difficulties. When seen in the former way, one concludes that some people are "difficult" or "destructive." If seen in the latter way, one looks at the process of the system as the cause of the behavior. The staff member who "messes up" and forgets can be considered as "dumb" or as responding to the system in a hostile, non-verbal manner.

Family therapists state that all systems are built of interlocking triangles, not just family systems. Analyzing the structure of such triangles and learning how to deal with them by responding instead of reacting is a possibility open to all. Family therapy is system thinking and it involves a search to find ways to change the system. The first step is to analyze the structure of the system; the second, to see one's role in it; the third, to change one's behavior in that system. These concepts can be applied to any human relations system whether it be a club, a factory, a team, a military unit, a congregation, a union, a partnership, and so on.

Evaluation

Evaluation can be divided into two sections: (1) *process*, and (2) *outcome* research. The former refers to the interaction between the family and therapist and the latter refers to the results obtained after treatment. An excellent summary of process research is given by Pinsof (1981) and a definitive chapter by Gurman and Kniskern (1981a) summarizes outcome research.

1. Process research

Self-report and direct observation have been the usual means of doing process research. Under the heading of self-report the studies of Hollis (1967a, 1967b, 1968a, 1968b), Shapiro and Budman (1973), and Rice (Rice, Fey, & Kepecs, 1972; Rice, Gurman, & Razin, 1974; Rice, Razin, & Gurman, 1976) are noteworthy.

Hollis developed her research originally in individual casework but later (1968b) applied it to marital counseling comparing individual sessions with conjoint ones, using the process notes of the therapist. The weakness in her study is the fact that process notes do not necessarily reflect what occurs in the sessions.

The Shapiro and Budman study (1973) shifts the emphasis from the therapist to the family and indicates that the activity of the therapist is critical in determining the continuation or termination of the family's treatment. The research finding matches the theoretical constructs of many theorists in the field (Haley, 1980; Minuchin, 1974).

The Rice et al. studies (1972, 1974, 1976) have produced a valuable questionnaire on the behavior of the therapist. Despite overlapping samples and some lack of specificity (i.e., it is not aimed exclusively at family therapists), it is labeled by Pinsof (1981) as research which "... generates reliable, accurate and valid data" (p. 705).

Direct observation has been more widely used in process research. Direct observation of the therapist was used twice by Sigal et al. (Sigal, Lasry, Guttman, Chagoya & Pilon, 1977; Sigal, Presser, Woodward, Santa-Barbara, Epstein, & Levin, 1979). In the 1977 study Sigal et al. compared simulated and real responses in therapy and in 1979 examined the relationship between the responses of family therapy trainees and the outcome of therapy for families they had treated. The results were mixed. However, out of these studies done at the Jewish General Hospital in Montreal has come a research tool called the Family Therapy Intervention Scale (FTIS-1) that has been used in several other studies (Sigal et al., 1979). Its weakness is its reliance on the response of the therapist.

Pinsof (1979a) at Northwestern University developed the Family Therapist Behavior Scale (FTBS) that differentiates 19 specific kinds of verbal intervention. Pinsof (1979b) also developed another coding system known as the family therapist coding system (FTCS), a more sophisticated tool aimed at identifying and differentiating the verbal behaviors of therapists with differing orientations. This instrument is currently being tested for reliability and validity (Pinsof, 1981) and is clearly the most developed research instrument in this area.

Coming from an Adlerian framework, Allred and Kersey (1977) have developed a system for analyzing the verbal behavior of counselors and clients in marriage and family sessions called the Allred Interaction Analysis for Counselors (AIAC). This system shows considerable promise. Emilia Dowling (1979) in Wales has also developed a family therapist coding device of interest because of its cross-cultural dimension. In particular, she notes that self-report measures are of doubtful use because in her findings even experienced therapists are poor evaluators of their own behavior.

Direct observation of the family has a long and significant history in family therapy. In an early study Zuk et al. (Zuk, Boszormenyi-Nagy, & Heiman, 1963) postulated that laughter during sessions disguised anxiety. Although there are flaws in the study it indicated the potential for direct observation.

Lyman Wynne and Margaret Singer (1963) did research on the role of the identified patient in a schizophrenic family demonstrating that his behavior was merely a reflection of a larger disturbance in the family unit.

Another study was done in Montreal as a complement to the therapist coding system in which Guttman et al. (Guttman, Spector, Sigal, Epstein, & Rakoff, 1972) measured the underlying affective content of the family as expressed verbally. Allred and Kersey (1977) also devised two categories in their instrument (AIAC) assessing the verbal behavior of clients, but further testing is needed to establish its usefulness.

De Chenne (1973) used the widely recognized Experiencing Scale (EXP) in conjoint marital therapy. The instrument has been shown to have predictive and discriminant validity (Kiesler, 1973) and De Chenne demonstrated that the EXP scale was valid for measuring client progress in therapy.

Winer (1971) attempted to measure Murray Bowen's basic concept "differentiation of self," by developing the Change (c) Ratio which purported to measure the number of "I" statements made during therapy. Her study is indicative of the attempt in the field to operationalize basic concepts as a way of giving some support to theoretical concepts.

Summary

The area of process research is just beginning. Pinsof (1981) says it exactly: "The field of family process research has just been born" (p. 700). There are numerous reasons for this. Foremost among them is the inherent difficulty in developing an instrument. Family therapy involves a number of people and thereby increases the variables to be controlled. A second factor is the lack of replication. At this point there is more need for work on the various instruments that have been used. Finally, there is a great need to make constructs more precise and distinctive so that categories do not overlap.

2. Outcome research

This area is more developed than that of process research due largely to the work of Alan Gurman (1973, 1975, 1978) in collaboration with David Kniskern (Gurman & Kniskern, 1978, 1981a, 1981b).

Wells et al. (Wells, Dilkes, & Trivelli, 1972) identified only 13 studies they felt were relevant to outcome in family therapy. Six years later Gurman and Kniskern (1978) found a total of 200 relevant outcome studies. An extensive review of the field can be found in Gurman (1978) and Gurman and Kniskern (1981a). A summary of their findings in a brief form also is available (1981b).

The value in the work of Gurman and Kniskern is that outcomes from all perspectives have been studied and evaluated with reasonable objectivity but with some disagreement (Jacobson & Weiss, 1978). This lends added importance to their conclusions. Gurman and Kniskern (1981b) reach 19 conclusions vis-à-vis family therapy. Among the more significant ones are : (*a*) nonbehavioral marital therapies are of benefit in about two thirds of the cases; (*b*) therapy with both spouses is more effective than therapy with only one; (*c*) length of treatment does not correlate with effectiveness; (*d*) at times family therapy makes relationships worse; (*e*) this seems related to the inactivity of the therapist; (*f*) individual therapy is ineffective with marital problems; (*g*) conjoint therapy is most effective; (*h*) behavioral family therapy seems more effective with less distressed families; (*i*) co-therapy does not enhance effectiveness; and (*j*) the severity of a problem is not a determining factor in outcome.

Gurman and Kniskern (1981a) elaborate on those family therapies which are most effective. They cite Minuchin's work with psychosomatic families (structural family therapy), Stanton and Todd's (1979) work with drug-addicted families (structural family therapy), operantly oriented behavioral family therapy in changing intrafamilial childhood behaviors (Patterson, 1971), and the functional family therapy of Alexander (Barton & Alexander, 1981) combining social learning and family systems with adolescents. These systems have received the most support in outcome research. This is not to say that other approaches are not effective

but only that they have not been researched as well. It should be clear that this area is a sensitive one in which the adherents of one school sometimes suggest their approach is more effective than another. In the absence of further research such claims are invalid.

Summary

The infancy stage of outcome research is over. If the field is to continue to be fruitful and grow it needs to pay attention to several issues regarding the family and the therapist. In regard to the family, focus must be given to such factors as what constitutes change, for example, is it the identified patient, a dyad or the family; duration of "cure"; number of family members present; or the effectiveness of various methods with specific disorders, e.g., anorexia.

In regard to the therapist, focus must be given to such factors as: the need to know (or not to know) individual dynamics; the need for the therapist to have undergone personal therapy; and the relevance of a cotherapist or cotherapists because of the growing importance of the Milan model.

In brief, it is clear that family therapy has demonstrated its power to produce change but it is not clear *how* that is accomplished or *why* one approach seems more effective with a given population. It is the task of the researcher in this decade to devise studies making both the process and the outcome of family therapy more specific.

Treatment

In family therapy, the mode, or the way treatment is carried on, will vary among therapists following their theoretical orientations and/or differences in personality. Therapy is always a blend of three factors that interact: (1) the theoretical stance of the therapist; (2) his personal style of relating; (3) the type of family he faces, its current state of functioning, and where it is developmentally.

Theoretical stance

Therapists of the object relations and family system schools are concerned with issues that deal with generational conflict, intimacy or distance, and unresolved problems of the past, in particular, grief. Therapists who are more system oriented, those of the structural and the strategic intervention schools, will be more symptom oriented and concerned with how the system boundaries are structured and what techniques may prove helpful in getting change to occur. If a therapist believes issues of the past are important, the therapy will tend to resemble a more traditional approach and be of a longer duration. If he is governed more by the notion of equifinality, his therapy will tend to be more situational and of shorter duration.

Personal style

Personal style varies widely among family therapists. There are some basic concepts that one must accept to be classified as a family therapist, but the manner in which one works will be highly individualized. Unlike other training approaches, such as psychoanalysis, family therapy is not rigidly structured. Some therapists are warm and empathic; others tend to be more distant and cognitive; still others use a virtually idiosyncratic approach. What binds them together as family therapists is the way in which they conceptualize family interaction, not the way in which they operationalize it. Family therapy has long regarded this as its strength because it allows for the personality of the therapist to shine through so he can be himself and not play a role called "therapist." This

is also why family therapy has not been controlled by any single group in the field of mental health but has been open to people from varied backgrounds.

Type of family

The family the therapist meets also can be classified according to its (a) closeness or distance, (b) current state of functioning, and (c) where it is developmentally.

Whether a family can be classified as enmeshed-disengaged or open-closed will be important to the therapist in his evaluation. These classifications enable him to know how much the family will open up to admit an outsider or close to keep him out. More importantly, it will give him a good idea of the flexibility of the system and how much stress it can handle. This in turn will govern the tactics used to change the structure.

Current state of functioning refers to the amount of stress that presently exists. Is this a family under unusual pressure and about to "fall apart," or is it reporting minor chronic problems? The therapist is interested in finding out what therapeutic leverage he will have. Families in crisis are generally more open to outside inputs than those that are not in crisis. There is less resistance to the therapist. Some family therapists, such as Minuchin and Barcai (1969), argue for the necessity sometimes of creating a disturbance in the system if one is not present. The issue is one of homeostasis. The family frequently wants to maintain or reestablish the old balance and cannot accomplish this. They then call in a professional, one with expertise, to produce calm once again. This is often found in rigid families facing the problem of adolescence.

Developmental issues, too, cause constant family tensions (Carter & McGoldrick, 1980). People are always undergoing change because of the need to adapt to ever-changing circumstances. Intimacy wanes between a husband and wife, economic changes affect the marriage, and above all, children grow into adolescents. Parents who tend to be over-protective and all-knowing often have problems with their growing children. The need of the family to open and allow the children to move out is absent and conflict follows between the generations. The behavior of such children is labeled as "bad" or "sick," and finally a therapist is summoned. The therapist must decide what are the developmental issues in the family. Some recent research indicates that such families are intrusive, overresponsive to each other, intolerant of change, and tend to produce family members who suffer psychosomatic symptoms, especially abdominal pain (Liebman et al., 1976). The therapist will seek to alleviate the presenting problems but more importantly will strive to restructure the system to eliminate the need for such behavior.

Family therapy then is a blend of theory, style, and family structure. Theory will conceptualize the presenting problem as one of the system. It will be attacked in line with the style of the therapist using a variety of tactics. The depth of the problems will be determined in part by the factors mentioned: closeness or distance, crisis state or chronic state, and stage of development of the family, that is, a new family, school problems, adolescent problems, transition to marriage of the children, and so on.

Taking into account the three factors of therapy, the therapist then makes a choice of how to proceed. He is like a director of a drama. One might well liken family therapy to the theatre, in particular Brechtian theatre, with its use of paradox as a means of dramatizing family issues. The comparison is not bizarre but in line with what family therapists would consider the relationship of the therapist to the client-family.

Therapy is a drama—a tension-filled process that takes place between a therapist and traditionally one person or, more recently, with a couple or a family. The focus may be on the past, present, or future, but in any event, the process of change, whether of feeling, thinking, or doing, is always in the present. Therapy means a change of one or all of these ways of speaking about human beings. How is it accomplished?

Family therapists in general would say that therapy begins by the therapist informing the client or clients that things are not what they seem to be. Psychoanalysts will interpret seemingly harmless dreams or actions into complex entities that are largely unconscious. Other therapies use similar ways of confounding clients. It is evident that therapy is a power struggle. Family therapists explain the struggle in terms of communication theory, which says that every communication is both a report and a command that attempts to define the relationship. To illustrate: if I talk about trivia, I am telling the other person I am not interested in getting serious about our relationship. If, however, he asks, "Why don't you ever say anything about how you feel?" he is attempting to change the relationship and move it to a more intense level.

This shift can be overt or covert. It is overt when the other says so in words; covert, when it is more subtle, when done behaviorally. This method, in fact, is a very powerful one because usually it is followed by the comment, "I can't help it." The person is saying that such behavior is involuntary. The child who "throws up," the wife who has "blinding headaches," the husband who "forgets," can be viewed as having problems in themselves but also as covertly commenting on the relationships within their family system. These behaviors or symptoms can be considered as tactics in the struggle to deal with the relationship.

In family therapy, the therapist sees symptoms as control tactics, but instead of pointing to them and analyzing their purpose, he will often say, "Of course you can't help it," and then tell the person to continue doing voluntarily what he claims is involuntary. He thereby creates a *benign* "double bind," in which the person is faced with either (*a*) stopping the behavior, or (*b*) continuing the behavior but now doing it under control of the therapist. In either case, he is showing that it is voluntary. Frankl (1960) calls this process *paradoxical intention.*

The family therapist may attempt to change the *context* of the system so the previous undesired behavior is no longer possible. The literature abounds with examples of how this can be done (Bowen, 1971; Haley, 1963; Minuchin, 1974; Watzlawick, Weakland, & Fisch, 1974). In more technical terms, changing the context means producing not just a substitution of one thing for another (first-order change) but a change of the structure (second-order change) (Watzlawick, Weakland, & Fisch, 1974). One effective way of doing this is the aforementioned "prescribing the symptom," telling the person to continue doing what he has been doing. For example, a therapist may demand that an overinvolved woman become even more concerned about her children and even to set aside a special hour each day for "worrying." This use of paradox is an example of how one might prescribe a symptom to produce a second-order change (Palazzoli, 1978).

Management

The setting

Family therapists function in all traditional settings and add the possibility of working in the home and the probability of at least making one home visit during treatment. This, of course, is understandable in light of the emphasis given to the context in which treatment takes place. Some would go so far as to say, "The beginning family therapist should require this (home visits) of himself routinely, and *without exception*" (Bloch, 1973, p. 44).

Seeing people in their ordinary home conditions has two distinct advantages: (1) People tend to be more relaxed and open on their own turf; and (2) the important issue of nurturance is more easily observed in the home. *To whom does a child go for attention? How is the request handled? What kinds of interaction go on between the parents in relation to the children's immediate needs? With what warmth or lack of it are they nurtured?* Observing these things in an office or clinic setting is sometimes impossible and usually unsatisfactory. The therapist gets a better idea of what is going on by visiting the family.

How patients come

Most referrals for family therapy come from mothers looking for help in dealing with either (*a*) adjustment problems in school for children making the transition from home to school or (*b*) adolescent conflicts centering about how much freedom to give the growing child or parents' inability to maintain control. Experience has shown that the most effective way of dealing with such referrals is to ask the whole family to come in initially for three sessions as a way of getting to know each other. This is normally sufficient time to redefine the problem in terms of other family members as well as working on the present problem. Objections to bringing in other family members can be handled by saying, "Of course he's got a problem, but I can't do much about it without your help." Since most people like to think of themselves as being helpful, this usually will bring them into a session. If the therapist can get them physically present, he should be able to involve them in treatment.

Confidentiality

Murray Bowen (1975) believes the issue of confidentiality must be reevaluated in the light of family therapy. This does not mean the family therapist becomes an indiscriminate gossip, but that he uses his knowledge for the good of the system. The shift in perspective from seeing the individual as the client to seeing the family as the client necessitates a shift from viewing the relationship of an individual to a therapist to one in which the family is the center. How a therapist accomplishes his role in regard to confidentiality takes much sophistication and clinical skill. The family members are trying to set up an alliance between themselves and the therapist by triangling him into their relationships. This he must avoid or he will be pulled into the system. He must create a new context in which behavior will change, and he cannot do this if he gets pulled into the ways in which the family normally interacts.

There are several ways of handling confidentiality. One is to announce at the first session that the therapist is relating to the family as a whole and therefore will not see individuals alone, and any attempts at violating this rule, such as a telephone call, will be reported to the rest of the family. If it becomes necessary to see parts of the family alone, say, the parents alone or only the children, the therapist should inform all concerned that he or she will make the choice of sharing or not sharing what he finds out with other family members.

A second way of handling requests for secrets is to ask how others feel about the alliance between the therapist and a family member who asks for a private interview. For example, a husband asks to see the therapist alone. Before granting the request, the therapist inquires about how other family members feel. "Mrs. Jones, your husband wants to tell me something that he doesn't want you to know. Do you think that's helpful to you or to the family?" Such a question focuses on the value of secrets to the family process.

In family therapy, raising the question of confidentiality is a ploy to control the system. It is a way of tying the hands of the therapist and setting up an alliance between himself and another family member. These "secret" sessions are to be discouraged. This does not mean that each and every issue in a family should be talked about in front of all other members. Family therapy is particularly concerned about boundaries between the generations. The sexual life of the husband and wife is a private matter and need not be discussed in the presence of the children. Similarly, the privacy of a child must be preserved in enmeshed and intrusive families.

Family structure can be destroyed by collusion between a member of one generation and another. Here the legitimate boundaries are not observed, to the detriment of all. The family therapist must not become part of the destructive process by entering into separate secret pacts with some family members in the name of confidentiality. The most effective way for a therapist to avoid the problem is to make clear from the beginning that he will not tolerate such alliances. If that is clear, the problem will rarely arise.

Recording.

Family therapists have pioneered in the area of showing others what they do. Most therapies are arcane; the outsider has little knowledge of how sessions are conducted. This is not true in family therapy. Recordings, both video and audio, are common. The use of one-way mirrors is increasing. Live supervision, where the supervisor watches the session in progress and calls in his observations on a phone or even enters the therapy session, is also used. Of course, for all of these observations, permission must be given by the family.

Recordings are invaluable for family therapy. They serve a double purpose; First, they preserve the process of the family therapy sessions and can be used for teaching purposes; second, the material used with one family can be shared with another. For example, the Browns may have a problem similar to that of the Smiths. Showing them a videotape of the Smiths may provide the kind of feedback necessary for them to change. Showing the family themselves at earlier points can also be an enlightening experience. In particular, videotape is invaluable for getting at nonverbal communications that take place among the family members (Alger, 1973).

Family therapy has the most complete collection of films and videotapes of any therapeutic approach. Those offering material include:

Eastern Pennsylvania Psychiatric
   Institute
Family Psychiatry Department
   Philadelphia, Pennsylvania
Mental Research Institute
   Palo Alto, California

Nathan W. Ackerman Family Institute
   New York, New York
Philadelphia Child Guidance Clinic
   Philadelphia, Pennsylvania

CASE EXAMPLE

Background

Mr. Jones had been referred by a local minister who had seen him previously for a problem with drinking. The man subsequently quit drinking and joined AA. Shortly thereafter his wife went into a depression, and following that his son was arrested for stealing. The man called the minister, saying, "My son is in trouble." Sensing that the issue involved all the family members, the minister referred the man to a therapist who dealt with "family problems."

The family therapist on the telephone asked Mr. Jones to bring his wife and son to the initial session. After a brief introduction, Mr. Jones began by saying that about a year ago he decided, at the urging of his boss, to give up drinking and he also stated that he began drinking 19 years previously, shortly after the birth of his son. As a first corrective step, he had gone to his minister who had urged him to join AA and become active in the church. He continued seeing the minister for about three months. About that time, his wife complained of feeling "down." She went to a family doctor and was given medication. She became worse and was sent to a psychiatrist who suggested that at age 45 she was beginning to experience a change of life and a loss of feeling sexually attractive to her husband. She began seeing the psychiatrist weekly for private sessions. During this period, their son, who had been considered by all as a "model child," became more overtly hostile in his comments, careless about his appearance, and indifferent in his school work. Finally, he was arrested for stealing an automobile but was told he would not be charged with the crime if he got "help." The father sent him to the psychiatrist who referred him to a psychologist whose field of expertise was adolescent problems. The psychologist agreed to see the boy privately on a weekly basis.

The father stated he did not see any change in either his wife or son and was becoming more upset himself. The wife said she was not being helped but would continue in treatment; the son said his sessions were a waste of time and he wanted to quit. The father said he was tempted to return to drinking, and this fear finally drove him again to call his minister.

In retelling the story, the father mentioned his fear of "falling off the wagon," and the son, quiet until then, commented, "At least then we'd know what to do with you." The therapist asked the son to elaborate on the comment, and he said that since sobriety his father had become a "pompous ass." The mother smiled at this comment as she looked at the son approvingly.

The therapist then asked the wife to "tell me something about youself." She began by mentioning the difference between life before and after her husband's drinking. It was clear that she had more roles while her husband was drinking and also more gratification. When the father was drinking, the son acted in the role of surrogate husband and had a closeness with the mother, which was inappropriate —a violation of the generational boundary.

The therapist began his first intervention by asking the son John to change places with him so the son could sit next to his father. The therapist then sat between the father and mother so the boundary between them might be visibly established. In moving his position, he commented to the mother, "As a good mother, Mrs. Jones, I'm sure you'd like to see your husband and son get along better." "Of course," she responded, although her face indicated otherwise. The therapist then asked the father and son to talk about interests they had in common.

Problem

The case is typical of many in that a number of different analyses of it can be given. For example, the father can be considered an orally dependent man as evidenced by his drinking. He could be seen alone in treatment. The drinking of the father and the depression of the mother can be viewed from a communication point of view as signs of their inability to express themselves in words. If this is the formulation of the problem, the therapist can work on their communication. Or the therapist can see the behavior of all three as related to each other and more importantly as contributing to the dysfunction in the here-and-now. From this viewpoint, one would want to work with all three members of the system. This last viewpoint is known as *field thinking* and represents family therapy concepts in that each person is viewed in the context of the system.

Two observations may be made about the minister's role in Mr. Jones's sobriety. First, he failed to take into account the positive role of alcohol in the family system. Simply put: the drinking served a homeostatic function in the family. Mr. Jones was taken care of; Mrs. Jones had a meaning and purpose in doing this; John received special attention from his mother. When Mr. Jones stopped drinking, the position of everyone changed. Second, the initiative for change came less from Mr. Jones than from his boss who had promised him a substantial raise. The minister reinforced the passivity by being so active in moving Mr. Jones toward involvement in AA and the church. Mr. Jones went from a dependency on his wife to a dependency on the minister and then on AA.

The problem in this case is to understand how each of the family members is entangled in the system and to observe the ongoing patterns of interaction that keep the system dysfunctional. It is the role of the family therapist to see this interaction and to make interventions that will restructure the system.

One could analyze the family in terms of dysfunctional triangles. The wife by her overcloseness to the son prevented her husband from getting close. He in turn triangled in a "bottle." Having gotten rid of the bottle, he then triangled in work and the church. The son's growing up and wanting more distance from the mother, combined with the husband's distancing, produced depression in the wife as she was still isolated from her husband even when he was sober. She got depressed as a way of gaining recognition. This produced some sign of caring by the husband and guilt-induced caring by the son. However, the constant demands of his mother made the son angry, and he expressed this in his sullenness and eventually by stealing. The symptomatic response of all the family members can be regarded as tactics for survival and control of the system as well as properties of each person within it.

The therapist made the choice of intervening between father and son because he thought the best way of changing the system would be to get an alliance between them. At the same time, he put the mother in a bind by saying she should support such an alliance. Had he attacked the overcloseness by suggesting that the mother-son coalition was unhealthy, he probably would have met massive resistance. Rather than attacking, he felt a more effective strategy would be to create more closeness between father and son. This alliance, it is true, would produce more isolation for the mother, but instead of leading into a further depression, she could now bring this to the therapist who in turn could reintroduce it into the system.

At the initial session, father and son had agreed to go fishing, an activity they both enjoyed. It also gave them a time and place for talking. Predictably, such activity caused the wife to become upset. After several fishing weekends, the wife called the therapist saying she was very happy about how things were going between her husband and son, but she now felt isolated. The therapist commented that he chose this alliance knowing it might cause her problems but did so because he knew she had great strength. He agreed, however, that it might be best to bring this problem up in the next session and further suggested that they leave John out of that session.

Mr. and Mrs. Jones came alone to the next session. Instead of dealing symptomatically with her isolation, she was able to verbalize it in the session. Mr. Jones at first was angry at his wife when she told him of her isolation. She responded to his anger by crying, and saying, "It's no use." The therapist commended Mr. Jones for his anger, interpreting it as a way of showing concern, but an ineffective way, because it turned off his wife. He then asked him if he wanted to take responsibility for moving toward his wife. The therapist continued probing the husband trying to find out how much commitment he wanted to make to the relationship and how much energy he wanted to invest. The delicate and tedious task of rebuilding their relationship was under way.

Treatment

In family therapy, as in other therapeutic approaches, one can discern various phases or stages. Three phases can be distinguished: (1) observation, (2) intervention, and (3) consolidation.

The initial interviews focus on observing patterns of interaction. What kinds of information are exchanged? By whom? And how? Can certain sequences be observed: What are the alliances and splits?

Although one can make interventions from the beginning, as noted in the case given, most family therapists tend to try out hypotheses before making interventions. These would be done to change the interaction of the system and constitute a second phase of treatment. Controlling the presence and absence of members at sessions, requesting people to dialogue with each other, and finding issues around which to build closeness, for example, fishing, are ways of intervening.

Consolidation is the last phase of treatment and most important. The presence of the therapist creates a new system; his absence may allow the old one to return. It is necessary, therefore, that he be sure his interventions are of such magnitude that they last after his removal from the system. The question to ask is, "Can the system function in my absence or will it again become dysfunctional?" Termination must be a process and not a sudden withdrawal from the family. The possibilities for growth and decline must be discussed and examined.

In the case of the Jones family, it was decided that the husband and wife would be seen twice a month, Mr. Jones and his son once a month, and the three together once a month. In this way, the marital subsystem, the father-son subsystem, and the family system itself would receive attention. The husband's tentative moves toward his wife diminished her feelings of isolation and, at the same time, made her less demanding of her son's attention. This removal of pressure enabled John to feel better toward his mother, which showed itself in his willingness to drive her

to the store and to give other assistance. His father's attempts at moving closer made him feel more confidence in the father and his ability to take care of the needs of the mother. John then was able to move outside appropriately toward peers without either anger or guilt. Mr. Jones began to spend more time with his wife because she was more responsive. His involvement in outside activities continued but in a more controlled way.

Resolution

In any family, there are individual problems usually seen in symptomatic ways, for example, feelings of depression; interpersonal problems seen in behavioral ways, such as husband overinvolved at work; family problems seen in the inability of family members to solve problems or to get closure on important issues.

The resolution of the Jones family meant restructuring the system so each member would have options other than the stereotyped ones they had shown. This was accomplished over a period of 24 sessions without getting involved in issues of why and when and staying with those of what and how.

Follow-up

After 24 sessions, the family was seen twice a month for a period of three months and then once a month for six months, at which time, on the basis of mutual consent, therapy was discontinued. In all, 36 sessions were held over a period of one and one-half years. Since that time (1972), no further help has been requested, and no symptomatic expressions of depression, drinking, or antisocial behavior have been reported.

Each family case is unique and has its own specifics. Treatment will be governed in part by the theories of the therapists and in part by the family. Some would work more on intergenerational issues and some more on symptoms. Some would hold fewer sessions, and some would hold more. In all cases, however, the focus would be on the system as the client and not on any single member in it.

SUMMARY

Family therapy started about the middle 1950s. The question must be asked about its future. Will it grow or will it decline? Its future looks bright for several reasons. First, the whole movement in therapy is away from a focus on the individual and toward the context in which one lives. Man is a social creature, and the more he is isolated from others, the less social and the more like animals he becomes. Second, there is growing interest in family, in one's "roots." Interest in communal living is further evidence that if one cannot relate in the context into which one is born, one seeks a substitute family. These reasons give support to the feeling that family therapy will continue to grow in importance.

Family therapy is concerned with the most basic relationships in life, those of the family. Instead of dealing with the ghosts from the past, it brings them into the session itself. It teaches a person to be a self while remaining in touch with others. It attempts to hold on to both because each of them is of value. It strikes a balance between the self and the family because mental health requires a development of the self together with a meaningful relationship with others.

George Mora (1974), a historian of psychiatry, notes, "Within the limits of psychiatry proper, there is no question that the field of family psychiatry will continue to develop, at the expense not only of individual psychotherapy but also of child and adolescent psychotherapy" (p. 71).

This is due to the introduction of context into the process of therapy. No longer can the therapist lock himself into a room and shut out the world. If he is to produce change, it must begin by bringing significant others into the therapy.

The history of therapy in the movement from Freud to the present has gone from the individual to the interpersonal to the system. If therapy is to be viable in the future, it must become ecological since ecology studies organisms in relation to their environment, and family therapy is the most ecological of all therapies because it always looks at a person in his context, in relation to his environment. Health and sickness are not attributes of an individual alone but are produced by the world in which he lives. Change is contained within the system in which an individual lives. This power has only begun to be tapped, and those therapies that hope to survive must soon learn either to use the context of a client's life or cease to be effective.

ANNOTATED BIBLIOGRAPHY

Bowen, M. *Family therapy in clinical practice.* New York: Jason Aronson, 1978.

The definitive statement of *family systems theory* (School 2) by its founder and major theorist. The articles represent a lifetime of thought and although at times repetitious, they also document the genesis of a major theory in the field. Of special value is the article "Towards a Differentiation of Self in One's Own Family," which is a step-by-step process of how Bowen became differentiated in his family of origin.

Foley, D. *An introduction to family therapy.* New York: Grune and Stratton, 1974.

This book is a primer meant for the beginning student in the field at a master's level. It is designed to be used for a one-semester course in family therapy. It is divided into four sections. Part one deals with the seminal ideas in the field: the double bind, pseudomutuality, schism and skew, mystification, and general system theory. Part two treats the major historical figures: Nathan Ackerman, Virginia Satir, Don Jackson, Jay Haley, and Murray Bowen. Part three notes the similarities and differences in their concepts. Part four looks at the current state in the field and makes suggestions about the future.

This book provides the reader with a structure within which he can understand the evolution of thinking in family therapy from its beginnings to the present. In the light of it, he can read the works below with more understanding.

Framo, J. *Exploration in marital and family therapy: Selected papers of James L. Framo.* New York: Springer, 1982.

A good explanation of the *object relations* approach to family therapy (School 1). Framo writes clearly about the relationship between the intrapsychic and the interpersonal and represents the best model of one who is an integrationist working at the interface between the two. The evolution of his thought can be found in these papers.

Gurman, A., & Kniskern, D. *Handbook of family therapy.* New York: Brunner/Mazel, 1981.

Nearly 800 pages of double columns, this book has everything in it: Theory, practice and research. All the major thinkers are here following a general outline of the editors which makes comparison easier. At times it is overpowering and is best used with a knowledgeable guide.

Hoffman, L. *Foundations of family therapy.* New York: Basic Books, 1981.

This is a book that begins with Gregory Bateson and ends with a discussion of epistemology and its role in family therapy. It is both a history of family therapy and an elaboration of a theory based on an evolutionary paradigm, elaborating on the seminal thinking of Bateson. Although free of jargon and tersely written, it requires a sophisticated knowledge of the field to be fully appreciated.

Minuchin, S. *Families and family therapy.* Cambridge: Harvard University Press, 1974.

This is the best explanation of the theory of the structural position by its major exponent. Most of the book is taken up with examples of how the *structural approach* (School 3) is used with functional and dysfunctional families at various points in the developmental process.

Watzlawick, P., Weakland, J., & Fisch, R. *Change: Principles of problem formation and problem resolution.* New York: Norton, 1974.

This book contains a complete explanation of the *strategic intervention approach* (School 4) to therapy. It gives philosophical concepts upon which it is based together with excellent and detailed examples of how these concepts are applied. It explains the difference between first- and second-order change and the function of paradox in reframing messages.

CASE READINGS

Family therapy has an extensive amount of material on videotape, audiotape, and case studies. Two works in particular are devoted to cases. *Techniques of Family Therapy* (J. Haley & L. Hoffman [Eds.] New York: Basic Books, 1967) gives the transcripts of initial interviews with 5 family therapists and their comments. *Family Therapy: Full Length Case Studies* (P. Papp [Ed.] New York: Gardner Press, 1977) presents 12 therapists with varying approaches and their work with families in treatment. Of special interest are two cases by Nathan Ackerman and Don Jackson since many of the current techniques in family therapy have their roots in their work.

Ackerman, N. Rescuing the scapegoat. In N. Ackerman (Ed.), *Treating the troubled family.* New York: Basic Books, 1966, pp. 210-36.

A good example of Ackerman's style, which

he called "tickling the defenses." Ackerman redefines the family conflict, thus shifting the focus from Henry, 14, the identified patient, to the family system itself. This shift enables him to unearth the reason for his father's role as family martyr, namely, his way of dealing with the memory of his father who was an irresponsible gambler. The roots of the current object relations approach can be seen in this case.

Aponte, H., & Hoffman, L. The open door: A structural approach to a family with an anorectic child. *Family Process*, 1973, 12, 1-44.

This article is a commentary on a videotape of an initial family interview, conducted by Drs. Salvador Minuchin and Marriano Barragan with a family whose presenting problem is a 14-year-old girl diagnosed as anorectic. It is of special value because it can be read in conjunction with viewing the tape so one can get a clearer notion of the relationship of theory and practice in structural family therapy.

Fisch, R. Sometimes it's better for the right hand not to know what the left hand is doing. In P. Papp (Ed.), *Family therapy: Full length case studies*. New York: Gardner Press, 1977, pp. 199-210.

This case study is a good example of the brief therapy practiced by the Palo Alto school. It is an extension and development of the ideas of Don Jackson. The therapist defines an issue as *the problem* as a first, critical step. He then uses paradox, prescribing the symptom, and therapeutic double binding as means of resolving the problem in a time limited setting.

Foley, V. Alcoholism and couple counseling. In R. Stahmann & W. Hiebert (Eds.), *Counseling in marital and sexual problems*. Baltimore: Williams & Wilkins, 1977, pp. 146-59.

An analysis of a case in which a system approach to the role of alcohol in the family is examined. Drinking is seen as a homeostatic balance in the family and not just as a dysfunction of the identified client. In addition, the manipulation of the therapist by the client is analyzed. Finally, three stages of treatment —observation, intervention, and consolidation —are suggested. The case illustrates a structural approach with emphasis on what is happening in the system rather than why it is happening.

Framo, J. In-laws and out-laws. A marital case of kinship confusion. In P. Papp (Ed.), *Family therapy: Full length case studies*. New York: Gardner Press, 1977, pp. 167-81.

A good example of an object relations approach to family therapy. Framo gives a clear demonstration of the connection between current family difficulties and unresolved issues of the past. He shows how a skilled clinician can use history in a way that makes it relevant in defining current family problems and more importantly in finding solutions for them.

Guerin, P. The use of the arts in family therapy: I never sang for my father. In P. Guerin (Ed.), *Family therapy: Theory and practice*. New York: Gardner Press, 1976, pp. 480-500.

This brief article examines the well-known play and movie, *I Never Sang for My Father*, by Robert Anderson, from the point of view of a therapist trained by Murray Bowen. The Garrison family becomes a case study for the therapist who examines the script in terms of interlocking triangles, the possibility of relationships, the conflictual issues in the system, and the critical incidents that might have moved the system in a more healthy and differentiated direction.

Jackson, D. The eternal triangle. In J. Haley & L. Hoffman (Eds.), *Techniques of family therapy*. New York: Basic Books, 1967, pp. 176-264.

This is a classic case in which Jackson demonstrates his ability to relabel a problem in terms of the family interaction rather than as that of the identified patient. He accomplishes this by "prescribing the symptom" rather than by working toward insight.

REFERENCES

Ackerman, N. Interlocking pathologies in family relationships. In S. Rado & G. Daniels (Eds.), *Changing concepts in psychoanalytic medicine*. New York: Grune & Stratton, 1956.

Ackerman, N. *The psychodynamics of family life*. New York: Basic Books, 1958.

Ackerman, N. *Treating the troubled family*. New York: Basic Books, 1966.

Adler, A. *Understanding human nature*. New York: Permabooks, 1949. (Originally published, 1918.)

Alger, I. Audio-visual techniques in family therapy. In D. Bloch (Ed.), *Techniques of family psychotherapy.* New York: Grune & Stratton, 1973.

Allred, G., & Kersey, F. The AIAC, a design for systematically analyzing marriage and family counseling: A progress report. *Journal of Marriage and Family Counseling,* 1977, *3,* 17-25.

Aponte, H., & Hoffman, L. The open door: A structural approach to a family with an anorectic child. *Family Process,* 1973, *12,* 1-44.

Arieti, S. General systems theory and psychiatry—An overview. In W. Gray, F. Duhl, & N. Rizzo (Eds.), *General systems theory and psychiatry.* Boston: Little Brown, 1969.

Barton, C., & Alexander, J. Functional family therapy. In A. Gurman & D. Kniskern (Eds.), *Handbook of family therapy.* New York: Brunner/Mazel, 1981.

Bateson, G., Jackson, D., Haley, J., & Weakland, J. Towards a theory of schizophrenia. *Behavioral Science,* 1956, *1,* 251-264.

Berne, E. *Games people play.* New York: Grove Press, 1964.

Bloch, D. The clinical home visit. In D. Bloch (Ed.), *Techniques of family psychotherapy.* New York: Grune & Stratton, 1973.

Boszormenyi-Nagy, I. The concept of change in conjoint family therapy. In A. Friedman (Ed.), *Psychotherapy for the whole family.* New York: Springer, 1965.

Boszormenyi-Nagy, I., & Spark, G. *Invisible loyalties.* New York: Harper & Row, 1973.

Bowen, M. The use of family theory in clinical practice. In J. Haley (Ed.), *Changing families.* New York: Grune & Stratton, 1971.

Bowen, M. Family therapy after twenty years. In D. Friedman & K. Juzrud (Eds.), *American handbook of psychiatry* (Vol. 5). New York: Basic Books, 1975.

Bowen, M. Theory in the practice of psychotherapy. In P. Guerin (Ed.), *Family therapy.* New York: Gardner Press, 1976.

Bowen, M. *Family therapy in clinical practice.* New York: Jason Aronson, 1978.

Buckley, W. *Sociology and modern systems theory.* Englewood Cliffs, N.J.: Prentice-Hall, 1967.

Carter, E., & McGoldrick, M. (Eds.). *The family life cycle: A framework for family therapy.* New York: Gardner Press, 1980.

Christensen, O. Family counseling: An Adlerian orientation. In G. Gazda (Ed.), *Proceedings of a symposium of family counseling and therapy.* Athens, Ga.: University of Georgia Press, 1971.

De Chenne, T. Experiential facilitation in conjoint-marriage counseling. *Psychotherapy: Theory, research and practice,* 1973, *10,* 212-214.

Dell, P. Beyond homeostasis: Toward a concept of coherence. *Family process,* 1982, *21,* 21-41.

Dowling, E. Co-therapy: A clinical researcher's view. In S. Walrond-Skinner (Ed.), *Family and marital therapy.* London: Routledge & Kegan Paul, 1979.

Engeln, R., Knutson, J., Laughy, L., & Garlington, W. Behavior modification techniques applied to a family unit—A case study. In G. Erickson & T. Hogan (Eds.), *Family therapy: An introduction to theory and technique.* New York: Jason Aronson, 1976.

Entwistle, D., & Doering, S. *The first birth: A family turning point.* Baltimore: Johns Hopkins Press, 1981.

Foley, V. *An introduction to family therapy.* New York: Grune & Stratton, 1974.

Foley, V. Family therapy with black, disadvantaged families: Some observations on roles, communication and techniques. *Journal of Marriage and Family Counseling,* 1975, *1,* 29-38.

Framo, J. Symptoms from a family transactional viewpoint. In N. Ackerman, J. Lieb, & J. Pearce (Eds.), *Family therapy in transition.* Boston: Little Brown, 1970.

Framo, J. *Family interaction: A dialogue between family therapists and family researchers.* New York: Springer, 1982.

Frankl, V. Paradoxical intention: A logotherapeutic technique. *American Journal of Psychotherapy,* 1960, *14,* 520-535.

Freud, S. Analysis of phobia in a five-year-old boy. In J. Strachey (Ed.), *The complete works of Sigmund Freud.* London: Hogarth Press, 1964.

Greenson, R. *The technique and practice of psychoanalysis.* New York: International University Press, 1967.

Guerin, P. (Ed.). *Family therapy.* New York: Gardner Press, 1976.

Guerin, P., & Pendagast, E. Evaluation of family system and genogram. In P. Guerin (Ed.), *Family therapy.* New York: Gardner Press, 1976.

Guntrip, H. *Psychoanalytic theory, therapy and the self.* New York: Basic Books, 1971.

Gurman, A. The effects and the effectiveness of marital therapy: A review of outcome research. *Family Process,* 1973, *12,* 145-170.

Gurman, A. Couples' facilitative communication skill as a dimension of marital therapy outcome. *Journal of Marriage and Family Counseling,* 1975, *1,* 163-174.

Gurman, A. Contemporary marital therapies: A critique and comparative analysis of psychoanalytic, behavioral and systems theory approaches. In T. Paolino & B. McCrady (Eds.), *Marriage and marital therapy.* New York: Brunner/Mazel, 1978.

Gurman, A., & Kniskern, D. Research on marital and family therapy: Progress, perspective and prospect. In S. Garfield & A. Bergin (Eds.), *Handbook of psychotherapy and behavior change* (2d ed.). New York: Wiley, 1978.

Gurman, A., & Kniskern, D. Family therapy outcome research: Knowns and unknowns. *Handbook of family therapy.* New York: Brunner/Mazel, 1981. (a)

Gurman, A., & Kniskern, D. The outcomes of family therapy: Implications for practice and training. In G. Berenson & H. White (Eds.), *Annual review of family therapy* (Vol. I). New York: Human Sciences Press, 1981. (b)

Guttman, H., Spector, R., Sigal, J., Epstein, N.; & Rakoff, V. Coding of affective expression in conjoint family therapy. *American Journal of Psychotherapy,* 1972, *26,* 185-194.

Haley, J. *Strategies of psychotherapy.* New York: Grune & Stratton, 1963.

Haley, J. *Uncommon therapy: The psychiatric techniques of Milton Erickson, M.D.* New York: Norton, 1973.

Haley, J. *Problem-solving therapy.* San Francisco: Jossey-Bass, 1977.

Haley, J. *Leaving home.* New York: McGraw-Hill, 1980.

Haley, J., & Hoffman, L. *Techniques of family therapy.* New York: Basic Books, 1967.

Hoffman, L. *Foundations of family therapy.* New York: Basic Books, 1981.

Hollis, F. Explorations in the development of a typology of casework treatment. *Social Casework,* 1967, *48,* 335-341. (a)

Hollis, F. The coding and application of a typology of casework treatment. *Social Casework,* 1967, *48,* 489-497. (b)

Hollis, F. A profile of early interviews in marital counseling. *Social Casework,* 1968, *49,* 35-43. (a)

Hollis, F. Continuance and discontinuance in marital counseling and some observations on joint interviews. *Social Casework,* 1968, *49,* 167-174. (b)

Jackson, D., & Haley, J. Transference revisited. In D. Jackson (Ed.), *Therapy, communication and change.* Palo Alto: Science and Behavior Books, 1968.

Jacobson, N. Behavioral marital therapy. In A. Gurman & D. Kniskern (Eds.), *Handbook of family therapy.* New York: Brunner/Mazel, 1981.

Jacobson, N., & Margolin, G. *Marital therapy: Strategies based on social learning and behavior exchange principles.* New York: Brunner/Mazel, 1979.

Jacobson, N., & Weiss, R. Behavioral marriage therapy: III. The contents of Gurman et al. may be hazardous to our health. *Family Process,* 1978, *17,* 149-164.

Keeney, B., & Sprenkle, D. Ecosystemic epistemology: Critical implications for the aesthetics and pragmatics of family therapy. *Family Process,* 1982, *21,* 1-19.

Kempler, W. *Principles of Gestalt family therapy.* Salt Lake City: Deseret Press, 1974.

Kerr, M. Family systems theory and therapy. In A. Gurman & D. Kniskern (Eds.), *Handbook of family therapy.* New York: Brunner/Mazel, 1981.

Kiesler, D. *The process of psychotherapy: Empirical foundations and systems of analysis.* Chicago: Aldine, 1973.

Kuhn, T. *The structure of scientific revolutions.* Chicago: University of Chicago Press, 1962.

Laing, R. D. Mystification, confusion and conflict. In I. Boszormenyi-Nagy & J. Framo (Eds.), *Intensive family therapy.* New York: Harper & Row, 1965.

Laqueur, P. Multiple family therapy: Questions and answers. In D. Bloch (Ed.), *Techniques of family psychotherapy.* New York: Grune & Stratton, 1973.

Levenson, E. *The fallacy of understanding.* New York: Basic Books, 1972.

Liberman, R.; Wheeler, E.; De Visser, L.; Kuehnel, J; & Kuehnel, T. *Handbook of marital therapy: A positive approach to helping troubled relationships.* New York: Plenum Publishing, 1980.

Liberman, R. Behavioral approaches to family and couple therapy. In G. Erickson & T. Hogan (Eds.), *Family therapy, an introduction to theory and technique.* New York:

Jason Aronson, 1976.

Liebman, R., et al. An integrated treatment program for psychogenic pain. *Family Process*, 1976, *15*, 397-405.

Lidz, T., Cornelison, A., Fleck, S., & Terry, D. The intrafamilial environment of schizophrenic patients: II, Marital schism and marital skew. *American Journal of Psychiatry*, 1957, *114*, 241-248.

McGoldrick, M., & Pearce, J. Family therapy with Irish-Americans. *Family Process*, 1981, *20*, 233-241.

McGoldrick, M., Pearce, J., & Giordano, J. *Ethnicity and family therapy*. New York: Guilford Press, 1982.

Minuchin, S. *Families and family therapy*. Cambridge, Mass.: Harvard University Press, 1974.

Minuchin, S., & Barcai, A. Therapeutically induced family crisis. In J. Masserman (Ed.), *Science and psychoanalysis, Vol. 14*. New York: Grune & Stratton, 1969.

Minuchin, S., & Fishman, H. *Family therapy techniques*. Cambridge, Mass.: Harvard University Press, 1981.

Minuchin, S., Rosman, B., & Baker, L. *Psychosomatic families anorexia nervosa in context*. Cambridge, Mass.: Harvard University Press, 1978.

Minuchin, S., et al. *Families of the slum*. New York: Basic Books, 1967.

Mora, G. Recent psychiatric developments (since 1939). In S. Arieti (Ed.), *American handbook of psychiatry, Vol. 1*. New York: Basic Books, 1974.

Mozdzierz, G. J., Macchitelli, F. J., & Lisiecki, J. The paradox in psychotherapy: An Adlerian perspective. *Journal of Individual Psychology*, 1976, *32*, 169-184.

Olson, D., & Dahl, N. *Inventory of marriage and family literature, Vol. 3, 1973-1974*. Minneapolis: University of Minnesota Press, 1975.

Palazzoli, M. *Self-starvation*. New York: Jason Aronson, 1978.

Palazzoli, M., Boscolo, L., Cecchin, G., & Prata, G. *Paradox and counterparadox*. New York: Jason Aronson, 1978.

Papajohn, J., & Spiegel, J. *Transactions in families*. San Francisco: Jossey-Bass, 1975.

Papp, P., Silverstein, O., & Carter, E. Family sculpting in preventive work with "well families." *Family Process*, 1973, *12*, 197-212.

Patterson, G. Behavioral interventions procedures in the classroom and in the home. In A. Bergin & S. Garfield (Eds.), *Handbook of psychotherapy and behavior change*. Chicago: Aldine, 1971.

Paul, N., & Paul, B. *A marital puzzle*. New York: Norton, 1975.

Pedersen, P. B. Asian personality theories. In R. J. Corsini (Ed.), *Current personality theories*. Itasca, Ill.: F. E. Peacock Publishers, Inc., 1977.

Pinsof, W. The family therapist behavior scale (FTBS): Development and evaluation of a coding system. *Family Process*, 1979, *18*, 451-461. (a)

Pinsof, W. The family therapist coding system (FTCS) coding manual. *Center for Family Studies*, Department of Psychiatry, Northwestern University Medical School, Chicago, 1979. (b)

Pinsof, W. Family therapy process research. In A. Gurman & D. Kniskern (Eds.), *Handbook of family therapy*. New York: Brunner/ Mazel, 1981.

Rice, D., Fey, W., & Kepecs, J. Therapist experience and "style" in co-therapy. *Family Process*, 1972, *11*, 1-12.

Rice, D., Gurman, A., & Razin, A. Therapist sex, style and theoretical orientation. *Journal of Nervous and Mental Diseases*, 1974, *159*, 413-421.

Rice, D., Razin, A., & Gurman, A. Spouses as co-therapists: Variables and implications for patient-therapist matching. *Journal of Marriage and Family Counseling*, 1976, *2*, 55-62.

Satir, V. *Peoplemaking*. Palo Alto: Science and Behavior Books, 1972.

Shapiro, R., & Budman, S. Defection, continuation and termination in family and individual therapy. *Family Process*, 1973, *12*, 55-67.

Sigal, J., Lasry, J., Guttman, H., Chagoya, L.; & Pilon, R. Some stable characteristics of family therapists' interventions in real and simulated therapy sessions. *Journal of Consulting and Clinical Psychology*, 1977, *45*, 23-26.

Sigal, J., Presser, B., Woodward, C., Santa-Barbara, J., Epstein, N., & Levin, S. Therapists' interventions in a simulated family as predictors in outcome in family therapy. Unpublished Manuscript. *Institute of Community and Family Psychiatry*, Jewish General Hospital, Montreal, 1979.

Stanton, M. & Todd, T. Structural family therapy with drug addicts. In E. Kaufman

& P. Kaufmann (Eds.), *Family therapy of drug and alcohol abuse.* New York: Gardner Press, 1979.

Steiner, C. *Games alcoholics play.* New York: Ballantine Books, 1971.

Stewart, R., Peters, T., Marsh, S., & Peters, M. An object-relations approach to psychotherapy with marital couples, families and children. *Family Process,* 1975, *14,* 161-177.

Stierlin, H. *Separating parents and adolescents.* New York: Quadrangle, 1974.

Thibaut, J., & Kelly, H. *The social psychology of groups.* New York: Wiley, 1959.

Trotzer, J. Engaging families in therapy: A pilot study. *International Journal of Family Therapy,* 1982, *4,* 4-19.

Von Bertalanffy, L. General system theory and psychiatry. In S. Arieti (Ed.), *American handbook of psychiatry* (Vol. 1). New York: Basic Books, 1974.

Watzlawick, P., Weakland, J., & Fisch, R. *Change: Principles of problem formation and problem resolution.* New York: Norton, 1974.

Weakland, J., Fisch, R., Watzlawick, P., & Bodin, A. Brief therapy: Focused problem resolution. *Family Process,* 1974, *13,* 141-168.

Wells, R. Discussion: Engaging families in therapy: A pilot study. *International Journal of Family Therapy,* 1982, *4,* 20-22.

Wells, R., Dilkes, T., & Trivelli, N. The results of family therapy: A critical review of the literature. *Family Process,* 1972, *7,* 189-207.

Whitaker, C. Psychotherapy of the absurd: With a special emphasis on the psycho-therapy of aggression. *Family Process,* 1975, *14,* 1-16.

Whitaker, C., & Keith, D. Symbolic-experiential therapy. In A. Gurman & D. Kniskern (Eds.), *Handbook of family therapy.* New York: Brunner/ Mazel, 1981.

Winer, L. The qualified pronoun count as a measure of change in family psychotherapy. *Family Process,* 1971, *10,* 243-248.

Wynne, L. The study of intrafamilial alignments and splits in exploratory family therapy. In N. Ackerman, F. Beatman, & S. Sherman (Eds.), *Exploring the base for family therapy.* New York: Family Service Association, 1961.

Wynne, L. Some indications and contraindications for exploratory family therapy. In I. Boszormenyi-Nagy & J. Framo (Eds.), *Intensive family therapy.* New York: Harper & Row, 1965.

Wynne, L., Ryckoff, I., Day, J., & Hirsch, S. Pseudomutuality in the family relations of schizophrenics. *Psychiatry,* 1958, *21,* 205-220.

Wynne, L., & Singer, M. Thought disorder and family relations of schizophrenics I: Research strategy. *Archives of General Psychiatry,* 1963, *9,* 191-198.

Yalom, I. *The theory and practice of group psychotherapy* (2nd ed.). New York: Basic Books, 1975.

Zuk, G. *Process and practice in family therapy.* Haverford, Pa.: Psychiatry and Behavioral Science Books, 1975.

Zuk, G., Boszormenyi-Nagy, I., & Heiman, E. Some dynamics of laughter during family therapy. *Family Process,* 1963, *2,* 302-314.

13

Multimodal Therapy

ARNOLD A. LAZARUS

OVERVIEW

Multimodal therapy is a systematic and comprehensive psychotherapeutic approach developed by Arnold Lazarus, a clinical psychologist. While respecting the assumption that, whenever possible, clinical practice should adhere firmly to the principles, procedures, and findings of psychology as an experimental science, the multimodal orientation transcends the behavioral tradition by adding unique assessment procedures, and by dealing in great depth and detail with sensory, imagery, cognitive, and interpersonal factors and their interactive effects. A basic premise is that patients (or clients) are usually troubled by a multitude of specific problems that should be dealt with by a similar multitude of specific treatments. A multimodal assessment examines each area of a person's BASIC I.D. (B = Behavior, A = Affect, S = Sensation, I = Imagery, C = Cognition, I = Interpersonal relationships, D = Drugs/Biology.) It provides an operational way of answering the question—What works, for whom, and under which conditions?

Basic Concepts

Multimodal therapy is personalistic and individualistic. A diligent scrutiny for individual exceptions to general rules and principles characterizes the approach; the search is for appropriate interventions for each person. Clinical effectiveness is predicated on the therapist's flexibility, versatility, and *technical* eclecticism. The *theoretical* eclectic tends to draw from diverse systems that may be epistemologically incompatible, whereas the technical eclectic uses procedures drawn from different sources without necessarily subscribing to the theories or disciplines that spawned them. The upshot is a consistent, systematic, and testable set of beliefs and assumptions about human beings and their problems, and an armamentarium of effective therapeutic strategies for remedying their afflictions.

While remaining technically eclectic, multimodal therapy rests primarily on the theoretical base of *social learning theory* (Bandura, 1969, 1977) while also drawing from *general system theory* (Bertalanffy, 1974; Buckley, 1967) and *group and communications theory* (Watzlawick, Weakland, & Fisch, 1974). There seem to be no postulates or paradigms in these theoretical systems that are mutually contradictory or incompatible—they blend harmoniously into a congruent framework.

Most of our experiences comprise moving, feeling, sensing, imagining, thinking, and relating to one another. In the final analysis, we are biochemical/neurophysiological entities. Human life and conduct is a product of ongoing *b*ehaviors, *a*ffective processes, *s*ensations, *i*mages, *c*ognitions, *i*nterpersonal relationships, and *b*iological functions. BASIC IB is derived from the first letters of each of these modalities, but by referring to the biological modality as "Drugs/Biology" (since one of the most common biological interventions is the use of psychotropic medication), we have the more compelling acronym BASIC ID, or the preferred BASIC I.D. (I.D. as in "identity"). It is crucial to remember that "D" stands not only for drugs, medication, or pharmacological intervention, but also includes nutrition, hygiene, exercise, and all basic physiological and pathological inputs.

The BASIC I.D. is presumed to comprise human "temperament and personality," and it is assumed that everything from anger, disappointment, disgust, greed, fear, grief, awe, contempt, and boredom, to love, hope, faith, ecstasy, optimism, and joy, can be accounted for by examining components and interactions within a person's BASIC I.D. It is also essential to recognize and include factors that fall outside the BASIC I.D. such as sociocultural, political, and other macroenvironmental events. While external realities are not part of "temperament and personality," "psychopathology and society are inextricably bound together" (Nathan & Harris, 1980, p. xvii). There are obviously crucial differences in adaptive interpersonal styles between people raised and living in New York and New Guinea, but regardless of an individual's background, detailed descriptions of salient behaviors, affective responses, sensory reactions, images, cognitions, interpersonal dealings, and biological propensities, will provide the principal ingredients of one's psychological makeup. To appreciate further the interactions among the various modalities—for ex-

ample, how certain behaviors influence and are influenced by affects, sensations, images, cognitions, and significant relationships—is to know a great deal about individuals and their social networks.

The term *bespoke therapy* has been used to describe the multimodal orientation (see Zilbergeld, 1982) and aptly conveys the custom-made, personalistic emphasis. The form, style, and cadence of therapy are fitted, whenever possible, to each client's perceived requirements. The basic question is: *Who or what is best for this particular individual?* Some clients respond best to therapists who are warm and empathic; others are apt to progress by more distant and formal relationships. Quiet, passive, reflective listeners are especially suited to some clients; others want therapists who are active, directive, and bluntly outspoken. The same client may respond favorably to various therapeutic styles at different times. How is the therapist to gauge whether pensive reflection is more likely to be the correct intervention rather than direct disputation? Largely by noting the client's implicit and explicit expectations, and by observing the impact of applying various tactics. Even effective therapists will make mistakes relative to gauging clients' expectations and relative to tactics applied, but capable therapists, on noticing these errors, will usually make adjustments to change the course of therapy. The choice of a particular therapeutic style and the selection of techniques are not capricious affairs. After drawing up a detailed Modality Profile (a chart depicting excesses and deficits across the client's BASIC I.D.), the multimodal therapist resorts to two main procedures—bridging and tracking.

Bridging refers to a procedure in which the therapist deliberately tunes into the client's preferred modality before branching off into other dimensions that seem likely to be more productive. For example, instead of challenging a client or even pointing out that he or she tends to eschew the expression of feelings by erecting intellectual barriers, we find it better first to enter into the client's domain and then gently lead him or her into other (potentially more meaningful) channels. Here is an example:

Client: I think that Molly resorts to what I call a "three-down" maneuver when we disagree about virtually anything. In other words, I am not placed in a one-down position, but I am seen as the lowest man on the totem pole.

Therapist: How does that make you feel?

Client: I realize why she does it. It is exactly what her mother does to her father, and Molly is very much like her mother in many ways.

Therapist: [Going along with client's cognitive leanings.] So Molly has imitated her mother and uses her tactics. What are some of the other things she does that remind you of her mother?

Client: Well, there are a couple of things that come to mind immediately. First . . . [Client intellectualizes about the alleged similarities between Molly and her mother.]

Therapist: [Bridging] When you think about all these ties that Molly has to her mother, and the way she puts you down, are you aware of any feelings or sensations in your body?

Client: Right now I've got a knot in my stomach.

Therapist: Can you concentrate fully on that stomach tension? Can you focus on that knot?

Client: It feels like a vise is gripping it.

Therapist: Do you feel tension anywhere else in your body?

Client: My jaws feel tight.

Therapist: Will you concentrate on the tension in your jaws and your stomach and tell me what feelings or mental pictures come to mind?

Client: I feel sad. I think it gets down to the fact that I am afraid that my relationship with Molly will be a carbon copy of her parents' marriage.

Therapist: Let's hear more about your fears and your feelings of sadness.

The therapist wanted to move into affective areas right from the start but instead went along with the client's apparent desire to dwell on cognitive components. Shortly thereafter, when the therapist again inquired about affective and sensory responses, the client was willing to reveal his sensations and then to verbalize his feelings. Failure to tune into the client's presenting modality often leads to feelings of alienation—the client feels misunderstood, or may conclude that the therapist does not speak his or her language. Thus, multimodal therapists *start where the client is* and then bridge into more productive areas of discourse.

Tracking refers to a careful examination of the "firing order" of the different modalities. For example, some clients tend to generate negative emotions by dwelling first on sensations (S) (e.g., a slight dizziness accompanied by mild heart palpitations), to which they attach negative cognitions (C) (e.g., ideas of illness and death), immediately followed by aversive images (I) (e.g., pictures of hospitals and catastrophic disease), culminating in maladaptive behavior (B) (e.g., unnecessary avoidance or extreme withdrawal). Other people tend to experience a different firing order. Rather than a sensory-cognitive-imagery-behavioral sequence as outlined above, they may display a CISB pattern (Cognitive-Imagery-Sensory-Behavior), an

I.BSCA order (Interpersonal-Behavior-Sensory-Cognitive-Affective), or any other combination. Here is an example of an I.BSCA firing order.

At a social gathering, a man insults one of his friends (I) and walks out of the room (B). He starts feeling hot and shaky, and develops a severe tension headache (S). He then regrets having acted aggressively and impulsively, but starts rationalizing his conduct (C). Nonetheless, he concludes that he is a stupid and unbalanced person. Soon he begins to feel depressed (A).

Firing orders are not fixed tendencies. A person may generate negative affect through a particular sequence on some occasions, and follow a different pattern at other times. Different emotions may follow distinct firing orders. Thus, a client when anxious, found that a CISB sequence was operative, but when depressed, an I.BI.S order was established. Most people, however, report a reasonably stable proclivity toward a particular firing order much of the time. By tracking the precise sequence of events that results in the affective disturbance, the therapist enables the client to gain insight into the antecedent events, and also enables him/her to intercede appropriately. The therapist may elect to track the I.BSCA order more closely. Thus, questions might be asked to determine what thoughts or feelings had led the client to insult his friend in the first place, thereby uncovering additional antecedent factors. Such precise information permits intervention at any of several entry points in the sequence.

Tracking also enables one to select the most appropriate intervention techniques. An agoraphobic woman complained of panic and anxiety. Medication helped to control her outbreaks of panic, but when exposing herself to feared situations (such as shopping in a supermarket) she never-theless experienced considerable anxiety. When asked to take particular note of how these anxious feelings arose, she observed a cognitive-imagery-sensory-affective sequence (CISA). First, she tended to *think* about the probability of becoming anxious, and this, in turn, led to other negative self-statements such as, "What if I pass out?" "What if I start feeling weak and dizzy?" Soon, she formed mental *images* of these unpleasant events—in her mind's eye she would see herself hyperventilating and fainting. As these thoughts and images grew stronger, she would notice a *sensation* of lightheadedness and her palms would become sweaty. She would immediately feel tense and anxious. Following her firing order, she was first given *self-instructional training* (Meichenbaum, 1977) in which her irrational, self-defeating thoughts were replaced with self-statements that tend to mitigate anxiety. ("I will handle the situation." "I will remain in control." "I will stay cool, calm, and collected.") Next, she was taught *coping imagery* (Lazarus, 1978, 1982), which involves picturing oneself coping, vividly imagining oneself remaining calm and in control. In the sensory modality, she was taught slow abdominal breathing and differential muscle relaxation. While shopping in the supermarket, she was to follow a specified sequence—first to use positive self-instructions, then to add positive mental imagery, and then to employ breathing while deliberately relaxing those muscles she was not using at the time.

If the client had reported a different firing order, say sensory-imagery-cognitive-affect (SICA) she would have been advised to commence with slow abdominal breathing and differential relaxation, followed by coping images. The positive self-statements would have been her third line of defense. Our clinical observations suggest that when one selects techniques that follow the client's habitual sequence, the positive impact is greater. While this finding awaits experimental verification or disproof, clinically, it appears that if a client has, for example, a CIS sequence and is treated first with sensory procedures, followed by imagery techniques, and then with cognitive methods (i.e., an SIC treatment order) the results are less impressive than outcomes that adhere to the client's firing order.

Other Systems

It has often been pointed out that most approaches to psychotherapy share common features. A bond or a therapeutic relationship usually develops in psychotherapy, and most systems advocate a stance of mutual respect and regard for the other person(s). Therapists generally serve as facilitators who provide direct or indirect guidance with the intention of helping their clients. It is widely agreed that it is often necessary to alter clients' self-perceptions, as well as the ways in which they perceive the world. These and many other commonalities can be delineated, but upon close scrutiny, these similarities are more specious than real.

For example, both multimodal therapy and psychoanalysis regard "conflict resolution" as necessary for successful treatment outcomes. Upon closer scrutiny, these phenotypical similarities reflect vast genotypical differences. The meaning of "conflict," its origins, functions, effects, and its overall impact, as well as the best ways of dealing with or resolving conflicts are all quite different according to psychoanalytic and multimodal tenets (Lazarus, 1981). It is a serious error to emphasize insignificant similarities at the expense of significant differences.

There are literally hundreds of different schools of psychological thought and practice (e.g., Corsini, 1981; Herink, 1980). When examining the claims and counterclaims of their proponents, one discerns a number of trends or clusters. There are those who advocate particular techniques or procedures and tout them as virtual panaceas. Thus, one finds relaxation pundits, meditation gurus, scream advocates, and promulgators of megavitamins, hypnosis, psychodrama, rebirthing, or some other unimodal intervention. These one-track procedures are the antithesis of multimodal therapy, which views human disquietude as multilayered and multileveled, and calls for the correction of deviant behaviors, unpleasant feelings, negative sensations, intrusive images, irrational beliefs, stressful relationships, and physiological difficulties. Yet multimodal therapy is equally opposed to those theoretical eclectics who endeavor to unite the morass of competing systems, models, vocabularies, and personal idiosyncrasies into a unified whole, thus ending up with an agglomerate of incompatible and contradictory notions (which may be called *multimuddle therapy*).

Each system can be evaluated as to the extent to which it assesses and treats, or ignores, each modality of the BASIC I.D. For example, it is evident that Gestalt therapy tends to neglect the cognitive domain in favor of "gut reactions," and lacks precise and disciplined behavioral retraining procedures. Cognitive-behavior therapy does not delve as thoroughly into sensory and imagery modalities as we advocate; nor are behavior therapists sufficiently sensitive to systems networks (interpersonal factors) or to certain unexpressed emotions (affective reactions). The best known clinician whose orientation is perhaps the polar opposite of the multimodal approach is Carl Rogers. His "person-centered" approach offers the therapist's genuineness, empathy, and unpossessive caring to all clients, and regards these "facilitative conditions" as necessary and sufficient for therapeutic growth and change. The multimodal position emphasizes that people have diverse needs and expectancies, come from very different molds, and require a wide range of stylistic, tactical, and strategic maneuvers from the therapist. Furthermore, no amount of empathy, genuineness, or unpossessive caring is likely to fill the gaps left by impoverished learning histories (behavioral and attitudinal deficits). These require teaching, coaching, training, modeling, shaping, and directing.

Nevertheless, when a multimodal therapist is consulted by a client who requires no more (and no less) than a genuine, empathic, and unpossessive listener, there is nothing to prevent the multimodalist from adopting a Rogerian stance (or referring the client to a "person-centered" colleague if he or she is unable or unwilling to adopt this therapeutic posture). Multimodal therapists constantly ask: What works, for whom, and under which particular circumstances? Thus, they take care *not* to attempt to fit the client to a predetermined treatment. With most practitioners, the client seems to get only what the therapist practices—which may not necessarily be what is best for the client. In multimodal therapy, there is a deliberate attempt to determine precisely what type of relationship, what type of interactive posture, each particular client will respond to. The multimodal orientation emphasizes therapeutic flexibility and versatility above all else. There is no unitary way to approach peoples' problems. To exude empathy and warmth to a client who prefers distant, formal people's businesslike interactions is likely to impede treatment. In some cases, instead of attempting to match the client to the ther-

apy and therapist, the multimodal therapist may prescribe *no therapy*. For example, we were consulted by a middleaged woman who had been seeing therapists on and off for years. She complained of vague anxiety, depression, tension, and general dissatisfaction with her life. After conducting a BASIC I.D. assessment we gave the following advice: "Use that money that you would spend on therapy to have someone clean your house once a week, to visit the beauty parlor once a week, and have a tennis lesson once a week. You will still have some change left over to meet a friend for coffee or a snack. Be sure to engage in these activities on four different days each week, and after doing this for two months, please call and let us know if you are enjoying life more, if you feel less tense, less anxious and less depressed." This no-treatment-prescription appeared to result in a distinct amelioration of her problems.

Many therapists express the need for flexibility. Thus, Haley (1976) stated: "A skillful therapist will approach each new person with the idea that a unique procedure might be necessary for this particular person and social situation" (p. 10). Nevertheless, he then goes on to say: "Today it is assumed that to begin therapy by interviewing one person is to begin with a handicap" (p. 10). Haley then stresses that "at every stage of the interview *all* family members should be involved in the action, and particularly during the greeting stage" (p. 15). We have seen several cases at the various Multimodal Therapy Institutes who were greatly put off by various family therapists' insistence that significant others had to be present at initial meetings. After working with these individuals and gaining their trust and confidence, we were then able to get them to bring family members into the treatment (if and when indicated). The multimodal therapist will shift the focus of attention back and forth from the individual and his or her parts, to the individual in his or her social setting.

Were an observer able to watch a multimodal therapist in action, he or she might see this therapist acting rather cold and austere with one client on a particular day, but being warm and effusive with the same client (or with someone else) at a different time. Yet another client might be exposed to a question-and-answer session. The next one might be treated in a directive, demanding manner, whereas a different client would receive a very soft, warm, and accepting mode. Multimodal therapists constantly adjust to the client in terms of that mode of interaction most likely to achieve the desired aims of the therapy.

Zilbergeld (1982) summarized the multimodal position succinctly and accurately:

The aim of MMT is to come up with the best methods for each client rather than force all clients to fit the same therapy. . . . Three depressed clients might be given very different treatments depending on their therapists' assessments and the methods they prefer. . . . The only goal is helping clients make desired changes as rapidly as possible; everything else, even MMT, can be sacrificed. (p. 85)

Since the BASIC I.D. is presumed to represent the pillars of human temperament and personality, any system that glosses over one or more of these seven dimensions during assessment or therapy is bound to be incomplete. The reader should have no difficulty, when reading the other chapters in this book, in determining .which systems deal *explicitly* with maladaptive behaviors + affective disorders + negative sensations + intrusive images + faulty cognitions + interpersonal difficulties + biological factors. It seems to us that most systems are based

on unimodal, bimodal, or at best, trimodal conceptions of human functioning—affect, behavior, and cognition.

HISTORY

Precursors

How far back in time should one go to find the precursors of multimodal therapy? Should one reach into antiquity and show that Hippocrates (*c.* 400 B.C.) was aware that human personality is multilayered, that he underscored the need for eliciting a complete life history of all patients, and that he recognized the importance of relationship factors in therapy? Shall we acknowledge our debt to Galen, in the second century, and to the 19th-century Swiss psychiatrist, Paul Dubois? Certainly, W. H. Burnham's *The Normal Mind* (1924) foreshadowed many of the best tactics advocated by multimodal therapists. One may traverse the course of history and note many similarities between present-day multimodal conceptions and early or more recent writings. Thus, in 1874, Franz Brentano's *Psychologie vom Empirischen Standpunkte* underscored the importance of acts (including ideation), together with feeling states, and "sensory judgments." There is considerable overlap between multimodal eclecticism and the theory of functionalism put forth by William James (1890).

The direct precursors date back to the 1950s when Lazarus was a student at the University of the Witwatersrand in Johannesburg, South Africa. The psychotherapeutic climate was predominantly Freudian and Rogerian. There were some followers of Melanie Klein, Harry Stack Sullivan, and Carl Jung. Two behavioristic faculty members—C. A. L. Warffemius and Alma Hannon—underscored the internal inconsistencies in psychoanalytic theory and emphasized the untestable nature of most Freudian postulates. The contributions of the late James Taylor of the University of Cape Town, and visiting lectures by Joseph Wolpe, a general medical practitioner, who was applying "conditioning methods" to his patients, led to a coterie of "neobehaviorists." The members of this group embraced animal analogues, extrapolated from infrahuman to human levels of functioning, and focused heavily on classical conditioning paradigms.

Clinically, it became apparent that performance-based methods were usually better than purely verbal and cognitive approaches at effecting change. Whereas the psychotherapeutic establishment viewed behavior as the outward manifestation of more fundamental psychic processes, the neobehaviorists stressed that behavior per se is often clinically significant. It became clear that people could acquire insight or alter significant beliefs, and still engage in self-destructive behavior. Yet, after behaving differently, it was evident that people were inclined to feel and think differently. Nevertheless, most professionals still viewed overt behavior as "the tip of the iceberg," as symptomatic of an underlying disease, as symbolic of unconscious complexes. To legitimize behavioral intervention as an essential part of effective clinical practice, Lazarus (1958) introduced the terms *behavior therapy* and *behavior therapist* into the scientific and professional literature. The observation and quantification of significant actions became firmly established as a crucial starting point for effective clinical interventions. Coupled with the search for relevant antecedents as well as maintaining variables, the focus on maladaptive behaviors and their remediation resulted in positive outcomes. But when follow-up studies revealed a disappointingly high relapse rate for people who were exposed

to behavioral methods alone, it became necessary to employ techniques that were considered outside the boundaries of traditional behavior therapy.

Beginnings

Lazarus (1965) wrote a paper on the need to treat alcoholism from a multidimensional perspective. The main components involved:

1. Medical care to return the patient to physical well-being.
2. Aversion therapy and anxiety-relief conditioning to mitigate the patient's uncontrolled drinking.
3. A thorough assessment to identify "specific stimulus antecedents of anxiety" in the patient's environment.
4. The use of additional techniques including systematic desensitization, assertiveness training, behavior rehearsal, and hypnosis.
5. The development of a cooperative relationship with the patient's spouse.

This was foreshadowed by Lazarus's (1956) statement that "the emphasis in psychological rehabilitation must be on a *synthesis* which would embrace a diverse range of effective therapeutic techniques, as well as innumerable adjunctive measures, to form part of a wide and all-embracing re-educative programme."

These earlier publications reveal a definite penchant for broad-based, or comprehensive psychotherapeutic procedures. By 1966 Lazarus had become suspicious of what he subsequently termed *narrow band behavior therapy* and published "Broad-Spectrum Behavior Therapy and the Treatment of Agoraphobia" (Lazarus, 1966). This article not only challenged narrow stimulus-response formulations, but also elaborated on the notion that dyadic transactions, or interpersonal systems, are an integral part of the genesis and maintenance of agoraphobia. The durability of narrow-band behavior therapy was seriously questioned, and in *Behavior Therapy and Beyond* (Lazarus, 1971), a "broad-spectrum" approach was advocated. The work of Salter (1949) and Ellis (1962) had an enduring impact on underscoring the crucial significance of "emotional freedom" and "rational thinking" as integral elements of the broad-spectrum therapy.

While A. A. Lazarus was gathering outcome and follow-up data, a number of questions arose repeatedly. When do behavior therapy techniques suffice? What sorts of people with what types of problems seem to require more than behavior therapy? When the clinician steps outside the bounds of behavior therapy, which effective "nonbehavioral" methods are best incorporated into what types of specific treatment programs for which particular problems, under what set of circumstances, and with which individuals (cf., Paul, 1967)? The careful scrutiny of case notes revealed that positive results were made by individuals with situational crises, circumscribed phobias, specific adjustment problems, transient or relatively mild sexual inadequacies, stress and tension-related difficulties, and some psychobiological disorders. Enduring benefits seemed to accrue to those who needed support over a trying period, or reassurance about difficult life decisions, and to those who lacked assertion and other social skills. Less impressive results were obtained with obsessive-compulsive individuals (despite the use of flooding and response prevention procedures), in cases with self-destructive tendencies, with addicts (be the addiction drugs, food, or alcohol), and with highly anxious individuals who were prone to panic attacks.

The search for additional systematic interventions led to an awareness that cognitive restructuring often called for more than the correction of misconceptions or the straightforward alteration of negative self-talk. For example, when intrusive images conjure up a gloomy and troubled future, no amount of rational self-talk seems to alter the depressive affect—it is necessary to change the negative imagery itself. Thus, a wide range of specific imagery techniques was added to the clinical armamentarium—goal rehearsal, time projection, coping imagery, and many others (see Lazarus, 1978, 1982). Similarly, people with sensory complaints (e.g., tension headaches, muscle spasms, bruxism) required specific sensory techniques (e.g., deep muscle relaxation, biofeedback, muscle toning exercises) in addition to behavioral change, cognitive shifts, affective expression, and attention to other aspects of functioning. It seemed important to separate "affect" from "sensation" as well as "imagery" from "cognition." The importance of overt behavior was well documented in the writings and practices of behavior therapists, but they seemed to gloss over crucial interpersonal factors. A comprehensive appraisal of human interactions called for an examination of Behavior, Affect, Sensation, Imagery, Cognition, and Interpersonal relationships. (The first letters form the acronym BASIC I.) To ignore the physical/medical aspects would obviously bypass the fundamental realities of the neurophysiological/biochemical elements that contribute to human personality and temperament. Hence the "D" modality was added to the BASIC I. (It should be emphasized again that the "D" stands for "Drugs/Biology" and represents far more than an awareness that some people require medication—it deals with all aspects of physical well-being—diet, exercise, sleep habits, and all aspects of psychophysiology such as CNS pathology, endocrinopathy, metabolic disorders, and recreational and therapeutic drugs that impinge on psychological processes.)

Initially (Lazarus, 1973, 1976) the term *multimodal behavior therapy* was used to describe BASIC I.D. assessment and treatment, but since emphasis is on comprehensive coverage of *all* the modalities, it was misleading to single out one particular dimension (the approach could just as well be regarded as "multimodal cognitive therapy," or "multimodal affective therapy," or "multimodal interpersonal therapy"). While multimodal therapy is essentially "behavioral" (i.e., it places great value on meticulous observation, careful testing of hypotheses, and continual self-correction on the basis of empirically derived data), it has evolved into an approach that employs additional (extrabehavioral) assessment and treatment procedures and strategies. Kwee (1981), in a critical review of multimodal therapy, underscores its historical development from narrow-band via broad-spectrum behavior therapy, and concludes that "whether or not multimodal therapy can be classified as behavior therapy is less important than the method itself" (p. 65).

Current Status

Since the appearance of the first presentation of multimodal therapy as a distinctive orientation (Lazarus, 1973), a considerable number of clinicians have been using the BASIC I.D. framework in assessment and therapy. The first book on multimodal procedures had 11 contributors (Lazarus, 1976). Two entire issues of *Elementary School Guidance and Counseling* (Volume 13, 1978 and Volume 16, 1982) were devoted to multimodal approaches. Nieves (1978a) has provided a multimodal self-assessment procedure in a manual dealing with self-control

systems for minority college students, and in a related publication (Nieves, 1978b) has described a multimodal self-help program for college achievement. Several textbooks on abnormal psychology have outlined the multimodal orientation (Davison & Neale, 1982; Gallatin, 1982; Nathan & Harris, 1980) and numerous articles in professional journals have focused on the BASIC I.D. format. Books, articles, and chapters on multimodal therapy have been written or translated into several languages—German, Italian, Portuguese, Spanish, and Dutch. In the latter regard, Kwee (1978, 1979, 1981) has published papers in Dutch journals, and in the new British journal, *Current Psychological Reviews*. He has a wide-ranging exposition and critique of multimodal therapy. There are, at present, four books on multimodal therapy (Brunell & Young, 1982; Keat, 1979; Lazarus, 1976, 1981).

Training in multimodal therapy has been a formal aspect of the clinical doctoral program at Rutgers University, New Jersey, since 1972, and a number of former students now teach multimodal therapy at various universities and centers throughout the United States. Several unpublished doctoral dissertations have focused on specific aspects of the approach. There are several additional doctoral dissertations in progress.

There are, as of 1984, eight Multimodal Therapy Institutes in the United States.

PERSONALITY

Theory of Personality

We are products of the interplay among our genetic endowment, our physical environment, and our social learning history. American psychologists have tended to be "environmentalists," but as geneticists have shed more light on the impact of DNA on various behaviors, the crucial relevance of our genetic heritage has grudgingly been brought back into the picture. It seems foolhardy to deny the biological substrate, or the physiological basis of temperament and personality.

At the physiological level, the concept of *thresholds* is most compelling. People have different pain-tolerance thresholds, different frustration-tolerance thresholds, different stress-tolerance thresholds. The foregoing are largely innate, as are the wide range of capacities for withstanding anything from environmental pollution to the rigors of direct sunlight. While psychological interventions can undoubtedly modify various thresholds, the genetic diathesis will usually prevail in the final analysis. Thus, a person with extremely low pain-tolerance thresholds may, through hypnosis and other psychological means, be brought to a level of withstanding pain at somewhat higher intensities, but a penchant for overreacting to pain stimuli will nevertheless remain omnipresent. Expressed somewhat differently, individuals are inclined to react to a variety of arousing stimuli with a distinctive pattern of autonomic nervous system activity. The person whose autonomic nervous system is *stable* will have a different "personality" from someone with *labile* autonomic reactions. The latter are "anxiety prone" and are apt to become pathologically anxious under stressful conditions (Tyrer, 1982).

While the importance of relatively fixed thresholds over a wide variety of reactions is noted, the concept of traits is not held in high esteem. The specificity of behavior is emphasized, so that exposure to different people and different situations at various times, evinces varied reactions, rather than fixed, predictable global dispositions. Nonetheless, people tend to favor some BASIC I.D. modalities more than others. Thus, we may speak of a "sensory reactor," or an "imagery reactor," or a "cognitive reactor." This does not imply that a person will always favor or react in a given modality, but over time, a tendency to value certain response patterns can be noted. Thus, when a person's most highly valued representational system is visual, he or she is inclined to respond to the world and organize it in terms of mental images. As Bandler and Grinder (1976) point out, visualizers tend to "make pictures" out of what they hear. In terms of split-brain research (Galin, 1974; Kimura, 1973; Sperry, Gazzaniga, & Bogen, 1969) "imagery reactors" are probably right-hemispheric dominant, whereas "cognitive reactors" are perhaps left-hemispheric dominant. Then there are "sensory reactors" who may be further subdivided into each of the five basic senses. "Imagery reactors" tend to be predominately *auditory* or *visual*. These proclivities appear to be evident within the first decade of life.

A person with a high frustration tolerance, but a low pain tolerance, someone who is extremely active and whose mental imagery is penetratingly clear, is bound to have a very different "personality" from someone who succumbs easily to frustration, who is at best moderately active, deeply analytical (cognitive), and incapable of forming more than fleeting visual images. *Structural profiles*[1] may readily be drawn up from the following instructions: "Here are seven rating scales that pertain to various tendencies that people have. Using a scale of 0 to 6 (6 is high—it characterizes you, or you rely on it greatly; 0 means that it does not describe you, or you rarely rely on it) please rate yourself in each of the seven areas."

---

1. These differ from "modality profiles" that list problems and proposed treatments across the BASIC I.D.

1. *Behavior:* How active are you: How much of a "doer" are you? Do you like to keep busy?

Rating: 6 5 4 3 2 1 0

2. *Affect:* How emotional are you? How deeply do you feel things? Are you inclined to impassioned, or soul-stirring inner reactions?

Rating: 6 5 4 3 2 1 0

3. *Sensation:* How much do you focus on the pleasures and pains derived from your senses? How "tuned in" are you to your bodily sensations — to sex, food, music, art?

Rating: 6 5 4 3 2 1 0

4. *Imagery:* Do you have a vivid imagination? Do you engage in fantasy and day-dreaming? Do you "think in pictures?"

Rating 6 5 4 3 2 1 0

5. *Cognition:* How much of a "thinker" are you? Do you like to analyze things, make plans, reason things through?

Rating 6 5 4 3 2 1 0

6. *Interpersonal:* How much a "social being" are you? How important are other people to you? Do you gravitate to people? Do you desire intimacy with others?

Rating: 6 5 4 3 2 1 0

7. *Drugs Biology:* Are you healthy and health conscious: Do you take good care of your body and physical health? Do you avoid overeating, ingestion of unnecessary drugs, excessive amounts of alcohol, and exposure to other substances that may be harmful?

Rating: 6 5 4 3 2 1 0

These subjective ratings are easily depicted on a graph. Consider the structural profiles in Figure 13.1.

Person A, essentially a "doer" and a "thinker," would have a very different makeup or disposition from Person B, a deeply feeling, imaginative, social, and sensitive being. In couples' therapy, it can prove illuminating for partners to compare their structural profiles, and also to anticipate what ratings their mates will give them in each modality (see Lazarus, 1981). Despite the arbitrary and subjective nature of these ratings, useful clinical information is often derived. When the therapist asks the client about the meaning and relevance of each rating, important insights are often gained. In addition to global self-ratings, structural profiles may be obtained for specific areas of functioning. For example, in the realm of *sexuality*, the degree of activity, emotional-

ity, sensuality, imagery, or fantasy may be rated on separate scales, together with questions about how highly valued sexual participation is (cognition), its specific interpersonal importance, and the rater's overall biological adequacy.

Having described the importance of thresholds and specific BASIC I.D. tendencies in determining the tone and quality of "personality functioning," let us now address the main factors responsible for the content of personality. How, when, where, and why are certain behaviors, outlooks, ideas, fantasies, and interpersonal patterns acquired?

It is well documented that *association* plays a key role in all learning processes. Events that occur simultaneously or in close succession are more likely to be connected. Two stimuli that occur frequently in close temporal proximity are likely to become associated. An association may be

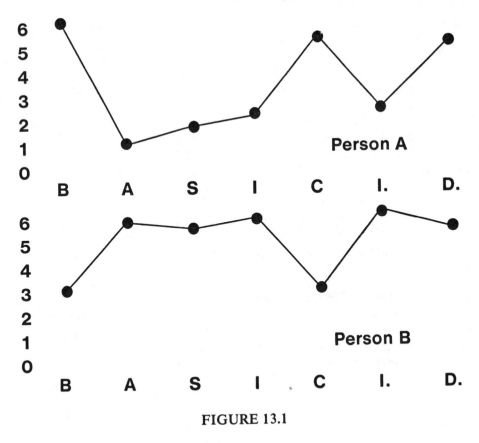

FIGURE 13.1

said to exist when responses evoked by one stimulus are predictably and reliably similar to those provoked by another stimulus. Without becoming embroiled in the controversies and intricacies of "learning theory" in general, or "classical and operant conditioning" in particular, it may be emphasized that a good deal of human thoughts, feelings, and behaviors are due to conditioning. Many aversions appear to result from *classical conditioning*. A client stated: "After undergoing surgery a few years ago, I experienced post-operative nausea for two days during which time the man in the next bed kept playing a cassette recording of Beethoven's *Moonlight Sonata*. Now every time I hear any part of that composition, I feel sick to my stomach!"

Operant conditioning is based on the observation that behavior is frequently a function of its consequences. Another client stated: "I now realize that my headaches were in large part due to the fact that the only time my husband showed me any real caring was when I was in pain." In therapy, one endeavors to overcome "classically conditioned" problems by the deliberate introduction of new associations (as in desensitization techniques that help the client insert coping images and feelings of serenity in place of anxiety). Difficulties engendered by "operant conditioning" call for a reorganization of consequential behaviors.

Besides association or conditioning, how else do we acquire the totality of habits that make up our "personalities"? If we had to rely solely on conditioning for all our learned responses, errors made during the acquisition phase of various skills would prove hazardous. It would probably prove fatal to rely on trial and error or successive approximation methods when learning to swim or to drive a car. In mastering these tasks and many complex occupational and social requirements, success often depends on imitation, observational learning, and identification, which Bandura (1969, 1977) subsumes under *modeling and vicarious processes*. Human personality (if not survival) is strongly determined by our ability to acquire new responses by watching someone else performing an activity and then doing it ourselves. We tend to learn what to do and what not to do by observing positive and negative consequences experienced by others.

To reiterate

Our personalities stem from the interplay among our genetic endowment, our physical environment, and our social learning history. The basic social learning triad—classical (respondent) conditioning; operant (instrumental) conditioning; modeling and vicarious processes—does not account for the fact that people are capable of overriding the best-laid plans of contiguity, reinforcements, and example by their idiosyncratic perceptions. People do not respond to some *real* environment but rather to their *perceived* environment. This includes the personalistic use of language, semantics, expectancies, encoding and selective atten-

tion, problem-solving competencies, goals, and performance standards, and the impact of numerous values, attitudes, and beliefs. As Bandura's (1978) principle of "reciprocal determinism" underscores, people do not react automatically to external stimuli. Their *thoughts* about those stimuli will determine which stimuli are noticed, how they are noticed, how much they are valued, and how long they are remembered.

This brief outline of the structure and content of "personality" from the multimodal perspective has not addressed the specific ways in which mental and emotional disorders arise. The role of genetics in the schizophrenic disorders and major affective disorders is more than suggestive. The median risk of developing schizophrenia where both parents are schizophrenic is about 40 percent (Rosenthal, 1974). In bipolar depressive disorders, a review of six twin studies indicated a concordance rate of 74 percent for monozygotic twins, and a 19 percent rate for dizygotic twins, even when the monozygotic twins were reared apart (Mendels, 1974). These are only the more striking and better documented examples of the importance of biological determinants in mental and emotional disorders; but the role of *learning* may be no less compelling.

As we have emphasized, the main learning factors are our conditioned associations (respondent and operant responses) and the models with whom we identified and whom we imitated—deliberately or inadvertently. During the course of exposure to these inputs, we may have acquired conflicting information, faulty cognitions, and a variety of inhibitions and needless defenses. The way in which this would undermine our prosocial, adaptive life-styles may be as depicted in Figure 13.2.

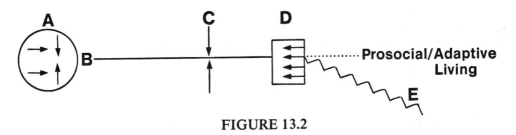

FIGURE 13.2

A. The person at birth is a product of a genetic endowment and the impact of intrauterine and other environmental influences.
B. The life trajectory proceeds toward "prosocial/adaptive living."
C. Various conflicts, the acquisition of faulty information, and/or traumatic events are encountered.
D. A barrier is erected.
E. The person moves off the adaptive pathway and may be characterized by several self-defeating and maladaptive responses.

Figure 13.3 addresses the fact that emotional problems and disorders also arise from inadequate or insufficient (as opposed to faulty) learning. Here the problems do *not* arise from conflicts, traumatic events, impositions from significant others, or false ideas. Rather, gaps in the person's repertoire—they were never given necessary information and essential coping processes—render them ill-equipped to deal with societal demands.

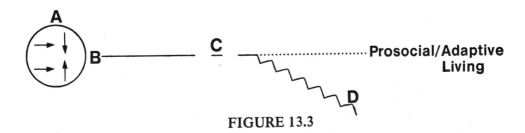

FIGURE 13.3

A. The person at birth is a product of a genetic endowment and the impact of intrauterine and other environmental influences.
B. The life trajectory proceeds toward "prosocial/adaptive living."
C. Gaps or deficits in experience and social learning (due to inadequate role models or the happenstance of missed opportunities for acquiring necessary information and skills) create lacunae.
D. Due to these response deficits the person moves off the adaptive pathway and displays incongruence, distortion, and self-defeating and maladaptive responses.

The multimodal view of problem formation emphasizes that most clients suffer from conflicts, and aftermath of unfortunate experiences, *and* various deficits in their social and personal repertoires. Hence unimodal remedies are bound to leave significant areas untouched.

Variety of Concepts

What concepts are necessary for the full understanding of human personality? Can we do without instincts, racial unconscious, Oedipal desires, archetypes, organ inferiority, psychic energy, the soul, and scores of other notions that are employed to account for the intricacies of human interaction? Psychotherapists could communicate their ideas with greater precision if they used everyday language instead of esoteric jargon. It could be argued that certain technical terms are useful for rapid and shorthand communication, but couldn't we keep these to the bare minimum? Moreover, if we heed Occam's razor (which holds that explanatory principles should not be needlessly multiplied) we can avoid much of the "psychobabble" that has arisen (Rosen, 1977).

In accounting for the structure and content of human personality, the previous section underscored the role of the biological substrate and the impact of learning (classical and operant conditioning, modeling, vicarious processes, and private events—thoughts, feelings, images, and sensations). Since much of our learning is neither conscious nor deliberate (Shevrin & Dickman, 1980), is it not essential to include "the unconscious" in our compendium of basic concepts? Unfortunately, "the unconscious" has become a reified entity, and we prefer the term *nonconscious processes*. This merely acknowledges (1) that people have different degrees and levels of self-awareness, and (2) that despite a lack of awareness or conscious comprehension, unrecognized (sublim-

inal) stimuli can nevertheless influence one's conscious thoughts, feelings, and behaviors. This completely bypasses the psychoanalytic notions of "the unconscious" with its topographical boundaries, putative complexes, and intrapsychic functions, all tied into the intricate mosaic of elaborate inferences about state, stage, and trait theories of personality development.

Similarly, psychodynamic theory views the "defense mechanisms" as perceptual, attitudinal, or attentional shifts that aid the ego in neutralizing overbearing id impulses. In the multimodal orientation these convoluted theories are not necessary to account for the fact that people are capable of truncating their awareness, of beguiling themselves, of mislabeling their feelings, and of losing touch with themselves (and others) in various ways. We are apt to defend against or avoid pain, discomfort, or negative emotions such as anxiety, depression, guilt, and shame. The term *defensive reactions* avoids the surplus meanings that psychodynamic theory attaches to the mechanisms of defense. Empirically, it is clear that one may overintellectualize and rationalize. While attempting to reduce dissonance, we may deny the obvious or falsely attribute our own feelings to others (projection). We can readily displace our aggressions onto other people, animals, or things.

The addition of *nonconscious processes* and *defensive reactions* to our assemblage of basic concepts should not be misconstrued as falling into the quagmire of Freudian constructs. But it is not possible to have a comprehensive understanding of human personality without addressing the fact that people are capable of disowning, denying, displacing, and projecting numerous thoughts, feelings, wishes, and impulses. Furthermore, it has been demonstrated time and again that during altered states of consciousness one may have access to memories and skills that are not amenable to conscious recall. Nevertheless, when acknowledging and accounting for these important reactions, it is not necessary to resort to psychoanalytic hypotheses. It cannot be overstated that multimodal therapy is not a conglomeration of psychoanalysis, behavior therapy, and many other systems. While effective techniques may be drawn from many available sources, one need not subscribe to any of their underlying theories. The differences between technical eclecticism and theoretical eclecticism have already been stated.

As we enter the interpersonal modality and examine various dyadic and more complex interactions, communication breaks down (literally and figuratively) unless we add another explanatory concept. People not only communicate; they also *metacommunicate* (i.e., communicate about their communications). The use of *paradox* in therapy draws its impetus from the process of metacommunication (e.g., Fay, 1978; Frankl, 1960, 1978; Haley, 1973; Rabkin, 1977; Watzlawick, Weakland, & Fisch, 1974; Weeks & L'Abate, 1982; Zeig, 1982). Effective communication requires one to step back, as it were, and examine the content and process of patterns of communication in ongoing relationships.

PSYCHOTHERAPY

Theory of Psychotherapy

A fundamental premise of the multimodal approach is that clients are usually troubled by a multitude of specific problems that should be dealt with by a similar multitude of specific treatments. Multimodal therapy is very different from those systems that cluster presenting problems

into ill-defined constructs and then direct one or two treatment procedures at these constructs. The basic assumption of the multimodal approach is that durability of results is a function of the amount of effort expended by client and therapist across the seven dimensions of personality (BASIC I.D.). The more adaptive and coping responses clients learn in therapy, the less likely they are to relapse afterward. Lasting change at the very least seems to depend upon combinations of techniques, strategies, and modalities. This outlook vitiates the search for a panacea, or a single therapeutic modality.

Multimodal therapy (MMT) overlaps cognitive behavior therapy (CBT) and rational emotive therapy (RET) in many important respects. Some of the major points MMT, CBT, and RET have in common are:

1. Most problems are presumed to arise from deficient or faulty social learning processes.
2. The therapist-client relationship is more that of a trainer and trainee than that of a doctor treating a sick patient.
3. Transfer of learning (generalization) from therapy to the client's everyday environment is not considered automatic but is deliberately fostered by means of homework and other in vivo assignments.
4. Labels, fixed diagnostic categories, traits, and global descriptions are avoided in favor of behavioral and operational definitions.

There are also important differences between MMT and other cognitive and behavioral orientations. The personalistic emphasis of MMT goes beyond the lip service often paid to tailoring treatment procedures to different problems in different people. The *goodness of fit* in terms of client's expectancies, therapist-client compatibility, matching, and the selection of techniques is examined in great detail by multimodal therapists. Moreover, the scope of assessment and specific information obtained when examining sensory, imagery, cognitive, interpersonal factors, and their interactive effects, goes beyond the confines of the usual stimulus and functional analyses conducted by behavior therapists. As will be *italicized* in subsequent sections of this chapter, significant *procedural* differences set MMT apart from CBT and RET.

Another fundamental assumption is that without "new experiences" there can be no change. In multimodal therapy clients are inspired and encouraged to do different things and to do things differently. Therapeutic change usually follows methods that are *performance based*; purely cognitive or verbal methods are often less effective. Yet before certain clients can take effective action, they require help in eliminating barriers in their interpersonal domain, in their sensory reactions, mental images, and cognitive processing. Indeed, from the multimodal perspective, some of the most important *insights* are gained when clients develop an awareness and understanding of content areas and interactive relationships within their BASIC I.D. patterns. As one client put it,

I never realized what an impact my mother and her older sister had on my life—how I let them shape my attitudes, how I treated my husband and children the way they treated my father, my uncle, my cousins, and me. Now I see that I even copied *their* aches and pains. ... When I get a mental image I see their faces and hear their words. ... Now I'm rewriting my BASIC I.D. the way *I* want to be. I'm tuning into *my* thoughts, *my* feelings, *my* images. ... I've also learned to change my CISB pattern. If I catch myself thinking the way they think, I crowd out their ideas with my ideas, and then I picture myself coping, I see myself succeeding.

This has ended my tensions, my headaches, and all the neurotic cop-outs.

MMT strongly differs with those who believe that as long as the client-therapist relationship is good, techniques are of little concern. Certainly, it is necessary for the therapist to be respected by clients, and to establish sufficient trust for them to confide personal and emotionally significant material. Without the attainment of rapport, there will be little inclination for people to disclose distressing, embarrassing, and anxiety-provoking information. Woody (1971, p. 8) stressed that an effective therapist "must be more than a 'nice guy' who can exude prescribed interpersonal conditions—he must have an armamentarium of scientifically derived skills and techniques to supplement his effective interpersonal relations." In keeping with the pluralistic philosophy of the multimodal tradition, we see the client-therapist relationship on a continuum extending from a rather formal, businesslike investment at the one end, to a very close-knit, dependent bonding at the other. In multimodal therapy, the client-therapist relationship is examined or discussed only when there is reason to suspect that it is impeding therapeutic progress. When therapy is proceeding well, why waste time analyzing the feelings vis-à-vis client and therapist? (See Lazarus, 1981.)

Multimodal therapy is predicated on the assumption that the more disturbed the client, the greater will be the specific excesses and deficits throughout the person's BASIC I.D. The model employed may be viewed as "actualization" and "self-determination" rather than as based on pathology. Everyone can benefit from a change in behavior that eliminates unwanted or surplus reactions while increasing the frequency, intensity, and duration of creative, fulfilling responses. Likewise, the control or elimination of unpleasant emotions and the augmentation of positive feelings is a worthy goal. In the sensory modality, it is eminently worthwhile to extinguish negative sensations, coupled with the benefits of deriving more pleasure and meaning from each of our five basic senses. Our mental imagery—those "mental pictures" that ultimately coalesce in a series of "self-images"—has a direct impact on the tone and cadence of our actions and feelings. Thus, we would do well to focus heavily on various coping images and try to keep them overridingly positive. Faulty assumptions, misconceptions, and irrational cognitions clearly undermine effective living. They are best replaced with as many reality-oriented, factual, and rational assumptions as can be mustered. Everyone would do well to cultivate the specific skills and prosocial interactions that produce good, close, and rewarding interpersonal relationships.

Process of Psychotherapy

Multimodal therapy places primary emphasis on the uniqueness of each and every person. Hence, there is no typical treatment format. When tuning into the expectancies and demand characteristics of one client, the therapist may adopt a passive-reflective stance. At other times, or with someone else, the same therapist may be extremely active, directive, and confrontative. Bearing in mind that fundamental question—who or what is best for this individual—the first issue is whether or not the therapist will work with the client or refer him/her to someone else. If the client displays grossly bizarre or inappropriate behaviors, delusions, thought disorders, and other signs of "psychosis," nonmedical therapists would effect referral to a psychiatrist or a psychiatric facility. Similarly, evidence of strong homicidal or suicidal tendencies often requires medical and custodial intervention.

In general, the initial interview focuses on presenting complaints and their main precipitants. Antecedent events are carefully assessed, as are those factors that appear to be maintaining the client's maladaptive behaviors. One endeavors to ascertain what the client wishes to derive from therapy. It is also useful to elucidate the client's strengths and positive attributes. Overriding each of these specific details is the question of adequate client-therapist compatibility. The therapist also tries to determine whether there are any clear indications or contraindications for the adoption of particular therapeutic styles (e.g., directive or nondirective postures).

The initial meeting may be with an individual, a couple, or a family. To put the client(s) at ease, therapists may begin the first session with small talk, followed by the noting down of formal details such as name, address, phone numbers, marital status, and occupation. This gives the client an opportunity to adjust to the environment of the consulting room, to experience a verbal interchange, and to be primed for the detailed inquiry that soon follows. After taking down formal details, the therapist may simply say, "Over to you;" or "Will you please put me into the picture?" or "What seems to be troubling you?" As various complaints are mentioned, the therapist pays particular attention to which modality of the BASIC I.D. they apply, and two additional interlocking factors are carefully noted: (1) What has led to the current situation? and (2) Who or what is maintaining it?

In multimodal therapy, it is not uncommon for specific interventions to be made during the initial interview. One does not wait until the full assessment procedures are completed before commencing to alleviate distress, or to correct misconceptions, or to redefine the presenting complaint. Here is an example from the initial interview with a 38-year-old man.

Therapist: What seems to be troubling you?

Client: Well, according to my wife, I'm a premature ejaculator.

Therapist: Exactly what does that mean?

Client: I was married before for 10 years. I got married because she was pregnant, but we really never should have gotten together because we just were too different and never got along. I met my present wife about a year ago, and we've been married almost three months. She's a psychiatric social worker.

Therapist: Just how rapidly do you ejaculate? Do you last 2 seconds, 30 seconds, 60 seconds?

Client: Well, I can go for about, um, 10 vigorous thrusts. If I go slower, I can last longer. I've tried adding numbers in my head, pinching my thigh, thinking of work, wearing two condoms . . .

Therapist: Do these things help?

Client: To some extent, but it sure takes most of the pleasure away.

Therapist: Have you ever ejaculated before entering your wife, or immediately after penetration?

Client: No. Like I said, if I do it vigorously, I come on the stroke of 10 [Laughs]

Therapist: At which point you turn into a pumpkin.

Client: I become a jerk. My wife says I need help, so here I am!

Therapist: Is your pattern the same with other women? For example, were you the same with your first wife?

Client: Pretty much, but it never seemed to bother her or any of the others.

If I wait 15-20 minutes and do it a second time, I can last almost indefinitely.

Therapist: Even with vigorous movements?

Client: That's right. If I feel myself getting too excited I just stop for a few moments and then I can keep going.

Therapist: Well, from what you've told me, you are not a "premature ejaculator." You come fairly rapidly the first time, but after a rest pause you have excellent control. Do you usually want intercourse a second time, or after the first orgasm are you fully satisfied and maybe drop off to sleep?

Client: Let's put it this way. If the woman remains interested I'm always willing and ready to give it a second go round. But I'm really happy to hear you say that I'm not a sexual cripple.

Therapist: Have you ever masturbated before having sex with your wife so that you will last longer right from the start of intercourse?

Client: Yes, but my wife says I shouldn't have to resort to that.

Therapist: If I may put it bluntly, I think your wife has several false ideas and you are a victim of her irrational shoulds.

Client: Her what?

Therapist: *Shoulds.* That you should do this and shouldn't do that. That this is a must. That everything is black or white.

Client: That's her alright! You've hit the nail on the head.

Therapist: I have the feeling that you take all this crap, that you allow yourself to be labeled, put-down, and led by the nose. And my guess is that you endured a different type of abuse from your first wife until you reached a breaking point and got a divorce.

Client: I've always put women on a pedestal.

Therapist: What does that imply? That you treat women as your superiors, that you look up to them, that you do not see men and women as equal but different?

Client: [±30 second silence] I can't really say for sure. I know this sounds awfully Freudian, but my mother has always been sort of scary. [He appears to be deep in thought.]

Therapist: Well, if I can sum up my impressions, it seems to me that your problem is not premature ejaculation but a general male-female assertiveness or lack of assertiveness, plus some subtle attitudes and values that are tied into this whole perception. What do you think?

Client: I think you're right. I know you're right. A long time ago one of my buddies—he's a psychologist with Bell Labs—said I seem to be attracted to castrating bitches. You seem to be saying the same thing.

Therapist: Well, I wouldn't put it that way. Frankly, my guess is that you bring out the worst in women by the way you react to them. At any rate, I feel you and I have a few things to sort out, and maybe, a bit later, you and your wife might meet with me so that we can perhaps establish better communication and upgrade your marriage.

[The course of treatment was neither simple nor straightforward. As the multimodal assessment continued, several additional inadequacies were brought to light that called for extensive attention to his behavioral, cognitive, imagery, and interpersonal domains. The wife, a woman apparently riddled with many problems of her own, elected to see a female therapist and refused marital therapy. After about 15 months the couple met with the therapist for an "evaluation session" and both claimed that individually and maritally, things were decidedly better.]

At the end of the initial interview, the usual adult outpatient is given a Multi-modal Life History Questionnaire, a 12-page printed booklet that asks a myriad of crucial questions about antecedent events, ongoing problems, and maintaining factors (Lazarus, 1981, appendix 1). The answers are divided into BASIC I.D. categories. The client is asked to bring the completed questionnaire to the second session. (Obviously, young children and many mental hospital patients are incapable of filling out questionnaires. Keat (1979) has addressed the multimodal treatment of children, and Brunell and Young (1982) have provided a multimodal handbook for mental hospitals.)

By the start of the third session, the therapist usually has gleaned sufficient information from the first two meetings and the Life History Questionnaire to construct a preliminary Modality Profile (i.e., a list of specific problems in each area of the client's BASIC I.D.). Typically, the client is invited to scrutinize the profile and to comment upon or modify specific items. Client and therapist then discuss the particular strategies and techniques that may be applied, and a general treatment plan is instituted.

A 33-year-old client with the presenting complaint of "depression" agreed that the following Modality Profile summed up her main problems:

Behavior:	Withdrawal, avoidance, inactivity.
Affect:	Depression, guilt, self-recrimination.
Sensation:	Heavy, sluggish, enervated.
Imagery:	Death images, visions of family rejection.
Cognition:	Monologue about past failures, self-statements about personal worthlessness.
Interpersonal:	Unassertive, passive.
Drugs/ Biologicals	After being on a tricyclic antidepressant for three months, the medication was changed to an MAO inhibitor ± four weeks ago.

MULTIMODAL LIFE HISTORY QUESTIONNAIRE

Purpose of This Questionnaire:

The purpose of this questionnaire is to obtain a comprehensive picture of your background. In psychotherapy, records are necessary, since they permit a more thorough dealing with one's problems. By completing these questions as fully and accurately as you can, you will facilitate your therapeutic program. You are requested to answer these routine questions in your own time instead of using up your actual consulting time.

It is understandable that you might be concerned about what happens to the information about you because much or all of this information is highly personal. Case records are strictly confidential.

NO OUTSIDER IS PERMITTED TO SEE YOUR CASE RECORD WITHOUT YOUR PERMISSION.

If you do not desire to answer any questions, merely write "Do Not Care to Answer."

* *

1. General Information: Date: _____

Name: _____

Address: _____

_____

Telephone Numbers: (days) _____ (evenings) _____

Age: _____ Occupation _____ Sex _____

By whom were you referred: _____

Marital Status (circle one):   Single   Engaged   Married   Separated   Divorced   Widowed

Remarried (how many times? _____)   Living with someone

Do you live in: house, hotel, room, apartment _____

2. Description of Presenting Problems:

State in your own words the nature of your main problems: _____

_____

_____

_____

_____

_____

On the scale below please estimate the severity of your problem(s):

Mildly   Moderately   Very   Extremely   Totally

Upsetting_____Upsetting_____Severe_____Severe_____Incapacitating____

When did your problems begin (give dates): _____

_____

_____

_____

Published by:
Multimodal Therapy Institute
28 Main Street
Kingston New Jersey 08528

The interview with the client went as follows:

Therapist: Is there anything else we should add to the list?

Client: I don't know. The medicine helps me sleep better and I'm eating more, but I still don't *feel* any better.

Therapist: Well three things stand out for me. First, regardless of how you feel, we've got to get you to *do* more things, to get out, to stop hiding from the world.

Client: [Shakes her head negatively.]

Therapist: It's tough but necessary. The two other things are your negative images and all that nonsense you tell yourself about being utterly worthless. That needs to be changed.

Client: [On the verge of tears] My brother was right. He said to me, "You're nothing!" God how that hurt. I always heard that from my father. Us girls were nothing. But I looked up to my brother, and coming from him . . . [Cries].

Therapist: It seems that you desperately want approval from your father, your brother, perhaps all the men in the world before you will feel adequate. Can you close your eyes and picture saying to your father and to your brother, "I don't need your approval!"

Client: I wish I could say that and mean it.

Therapist: Shall we try some roleplaying? I'll be your brother. "You're nothing! You are just a complete zero!" Now will you challenge that?
[Roleplaying, with considerable role reversal, in which the therapist modeled assertive answers, ensued for ±20 minutes.]

Client: I can say the right words but the wrong feelings are still there.

Therapist: As long as you start with the right words and use them in the right places and to the relevant people, the feelings will soon start to change.

* * * * *

Client: I just have these awful ideas about death. I dream about being at funerals, or getting lost in a cemetery. . . . And my mind often goes back to my cousin's death, and how my brother cried for him, all these horrible thoughts.

Therapist: Let's deal with that, but first, I'd like to review the treatment plan. First, I want to be sure that you will increase your activity level, go out and do things. I want you to keep notes of the things you do, of the activities you wanted to avoid but did not avoid. Second, I want to be sure that you will express your feelings and not be passive, especially with your husband and your brother. No matter how miserable you feel, can you promise me that you will do these two things this week?

Client: I'll try.

Therapist: Promise me you'll do it.

Client: [Cries]

Therapist: If I'm coming on too strong, tell me to back off.

Client: I realize it's for my own good.

Therapist: So can I count on you?

Client: I'll do my best.

Therapist: Good. Now let's delve into those death images. Why don't we start with your dream about being lost in the cemetery. Close your eyes. Settle back and relax. You're in your dream, lost in the cemetery. Tell me what happens.

Client: [±30-second pause] I feel awfully afraid. The ground is soggy as if it just rained. I see the tombstones but I can't make out the names. . . . There's someone else there [pause] I'm frightened. [pause] I've seen him before, but his features are indistinct, he's too far for me to make out who it is.

Therapist: You have binoculars or a zoom lens. Look through the eyepiece. Who is it?

Client: It's . . . no it's not. It looked like

my cousin for a moment. He went away.

Therapist: Let's bring your cousin into the dream so that he can talk to you. Can you bring him into the picture?

Client: [Pause] Peculiar! He s dressed like a funeral director in a black suit.

[Over several sessions, guided imagery was used to conjure up encounters with several of her deceased relatives—her cousin, maternal grandmother, and several paternal aunts and uncles. A theme emerged. She had been close to all of her deceased relatives for the first 12-20 years of her life and had, what Gestalt therapists call "unfinished business" with each of them. Imaginary dialogues with every one in turn, with the therapist encouraging her to assume an assertive position throughout, seemed to serve an important function. The problems in the other BASIC I.D. areas received equal attention. She was constantly encouraged to increase her activity level, to express her feelings, and her cognitive errors were corrected by emphasizing their irrational underpinnings.]

When treatment impasses arise, it is often helpful to introduce a *Second-Order BASIC I.D.* assessment. This consists of subjecting a problematic item on the initial Modality Profile to more detailed inquiry in terms of behavior, affect, sensation, imagery, cognition, interpersonal factors, and drugs or biological considerations. For example, the forementioned woman remained extremely resistant to implementing assertive behaviors. While she acknowledged feeling less depressed, and stated that her images and cognitions were more positive and rational, she remained interpersonally passive and unassertive. When asked for her BASIC I.D. associations to the concept of "assertiveness," the following emerged:

Behavior:	Attacking
Affect:	Angry.
Sensation:	Tension.
Imagery:	Bombs bursting.
Cognition:	Get even.
Interpersonal:	Hurting.
Drugs/ Biologicals:	High blood pressure.

She had been told, and paid lip service to understanding, the essential differences between "assertion" and "aggression." Nevertheless, the Second-Order BASIC I.D. indicated that in her mind, an assertive response was tantamount to a vicious attack. This alerted the therapist to model, explain, rehearse, and define "assertive behaviors" in much greater detail.

Again, it must be understood that what has been outlined is by no means a 'typical" multimodal treatment of depression. With a different depressed individual, the treatment, while addressing all BASIC I.D. problem areas, might be quite dissimilar (Fay & Lazarus, 1981).

Mechanisms of Psychotherapy

Consonant with the pluralistic outlook of the multimodal tradition, different mechanisms are responsible for positive change in different people. Thus, for some, the mere nonjudgmental acceptance of a highly respected outsider is sufficient to offset faulty attitudes and behaviors. For others, the main mechanism is largely didactic—they have learned more effective ways of processing information, of responding to significant others, of coping with the exigencies of life. The primary factors responsible for therapeutic change may be outlined by reference to the BASIC I.D.

Some of the main mechanisms and ingredients of psychotherapeutic change

Behavior

Extinction (e.g., when applying methods such as massed practice, response prevention, and flooding). *Counterconditioning* (e.g., when using incompatible response techniques such as graded exposure and desensitization). *Positive reinforcement, negative reinforcement, and punishment* (e.g., when using operant procedures such as token economies, contingent praise, time-out, and aversion therapy).

Affect

Abreaction (e.g., when reliving and recounting painful emotions in the presence of a supportive, trusted ally). *Owning and accepting feelings* (e.g., when therapy permits the client to acknowledge affect-laden materials that were nonconscious).

Sensation

Tension release (e.g., through biofeedback, relaxation, or physical exercise). *Sensory pleasuring* (e.g., the acquisition of positive tactile sensations during sexual retraining).

Imagery

Changes in self-image (e.g., when success in any modality is sustained). *Coping images* (e.g., when able to picture self-control, or self-achievement in situations where these images had been impossible to evoke).

Cognition

Cognitive restructuring (e.g., changes in dichotomous reasoning, self-downing, overgeneralization, categorical imperatives, non sequiturs, and excessive desires for approval). *Awareness* (e.g., awareness of antecedents and their relation to ongoing behaviors; appreciation of how specific "firing orders" culminate in various affective reactions).

Interpersonal

Modeling (e.g., the therapist as role-model through selective self-disclosure, and deliberate modeling as during role reversal exercises). *Dispersing unhealthy collusions* (e.g., when treating a family and changing counterproductive alliances). *Paradoxical maneuvers* (e.g., when countering double-binding responses with meta-communications). *Nonjudgmental acceptance* (e.g., when clients realize that in therapy they are offered desiderata not usually available in most social relationships).

Drugs/Biologicals

In addition to medical examinations and interventions when warranted, the implementation of better exercise, and nutrition, substance abuse cessation, the use of psychotropic medication is sometimes essential—particularly in the treatment of schizophrenia, affective disorders, and some anxiety states.

In the broadest terms, psychological problems may be due to *learning* and/or *lesions*. The latter falls into the "D" modality; learning is exemplified by the BASIC I. Full understanding of the exact mechanisms of change in any modality is yet to be achieved. Indeed, even in the "D" modality, while new knowledge about receptor sites, neurotransmitters, biological markers, and other biochemical parameters have emerged, much remains unknown. Perusal of the psychotropic drugs listed in the *Physicians' Desk Reference* reveals that most of the descriptions under "Clinical Pharmacology" state that "The mechanism of action of... is not definitely known." In the psychological sphere, the exact and precise "mechanisms of action" are even less well elucidated.

APPLICATIONS

Problems

The multimodal orientation has implications both for prevention and treatment. Its purview extends from individuals, couples, families, and groups, to broader community and organizational settings. Thus, some multimodal therapists have special expertise in dealing with children (Keat, 1979), applying multimodal methods in classroom settings (Gerler, 1979), in a child care agency (O'Keefe & Castaldo, 1980), in multimodal parent training (Judah, 1978), mental retardation (Pearl & Guarnaccia, 1976), management (O'Keefe & Castaldo, 1981), and applying multimodal methods in an institutional setting (Roberts, Jackson, & Phelps, 1980). Brunell and Young's (1982) edited volume *Multimodal Handbook for a Mental Hospital* shows the versatility of the multimodal framework to a variety of inpatient problem areas. The multimodal framework was even shown to have relevance when dealing with a community disaster (Sank, 1979).

Two distinct questions may be posed regarding the types of individuals and the variety of problems that may be dealt with multimodally: (1) Who can be helped by a multimodal practitioner? (2) Who can be helped by multimodal therapy?

Multimodal therapists are drawn from the full range of "health service providers." Psychiatrists, psychologists, social workers, psychiatric nurses, pastoral counselors, and other "mental health workers" each have members within their disciplines who are well versed in, and employ, multimodal methods. The therapist's professional background and personal qualities will equip him or her with special skills, talents, and knowledge to handle certain problems, particular individuals, and to function in specific settings. Thus, some multimodal therapists are highly skilled at using biofeedback, others have a strong background in behavioral medicine, and there are those who are especially gifted and clinically adept with sub-

stance abuse disorders, or sexual offenders, or school-related problems, and so forth. A multimodal psychiatrist, when prescribing medication to control psychotic behaviors (addressing the "D" modality) is not practicing multimodal therapy. However, when the psychotic symptoms are in remission, the multimodal psychiatrist will systematically deal with the other six modalities (the BASIC I). When specific clients require services that lie outside the realm of the given multimodal therapist's compass of skills, referral to an individual or agency better equipped to deal with the situation is a standard procedure. Surely this is true for every responsible clinician? Unfortunately not. While nearly everyone agrees, in principle, that it is undesirable to fit the client into one's system, and widespread lip service is paid to avoiding procrustean maneuvers by carefully tailoring treatment to the needs of the consumer, in practice the client is apt to receive what the therapist employs, whether or not this is what he or she needs (see Lazarus, 1981, pp. 1-5).

Multimodal practitioners constantly inquire *who or what is best for this individual (or couple, or family, or group)*. Referral to appropriate personnel is considered a most important "technique." Thus, if the therapist is not equipped herself or himself to manage the client's problems, the multimodal practitioner, if true to the canons of this tradition, will not continue seeing the client (even if he or she is attractive, pleasant to be with, and affluent). Nor is it sufficient for a multimodal therapist simply to inform the client that his or her clinical problems call for skills that the therapist does not possess—it is the clinician's duty to try and effect a judicious referral.

All therapists encounter clients who are so marginally adjusted that they require long-term supportive therapy—the development of a stable relationship with a caring person. A well-trained multimodal therapist is oriented and equipped to do more than offer concern and empathy. Within the context of a supportive therapeutic relationship, specific attention to critical BASIC I.D. excesses and deficits can transform a "holding pattern" into one where constructive learning takes place. Thus, when the mesh and artistry between client and therapist was such that thorough coverage of the BASIC I.D. was accomplished, successful outcomes were obtained even with floridly psychotic individuals, repeated substance abusers, and vegetatively depressed persons who had failed to respond to years of chemotherapy and other psychiatric interventions. Nevertheless, it is obviously easier to achieve noteworthy gains with clients whose excesses and deficits across the BASIC I.D. are not especially rigid, encrusted, or pervasive.

Discussions with colleagues at the various Multimodal Therapy Institutes reveal consistent positive outcomes and follow-ups with the following problem areas: marriage and family problems; sexual difficulties; childhood disorders; inadequate social skills; smoking; fears and phobias; anxiety states; obesity; psychosomatic complaints; and depression. Some of our colleague also report impressive results with certain obsessive-compulsive problems.

Evaluation

In multimodal therapy, the evaluation of treatment outcomes is usually straightforward. Since Modality Profiles are routinely constructed (i.e., lists of specific excesses and deficits throughout the client's BASIC I.D.), ongoing treatment evaluations are an integral part of the client-therapist interaction. Thus, instead of assuming that some ill-defined entity such as "emotional maturity" has evolved, the multimodal therapist specifies particular gains and achievements in each modality:

Behavior:	Less withdrawn. Less compulsive. More outspoken.
Affect:	More warm, less hostile. Less depressed.
Sensation:	Enjoys more pleasures. Less tense, more relaxed.
Imagery:	Fewer nightmares. Better self-image.
Cognition:	Less self-downing. More positive self-statements.
Interpersonal:	Goes out on dates. Expresses wishes and desires.
Drugs/Biologicals:	Stopped smoking. Sleeps well. Exercises regularly.

Structural Profiles, before and after multimodal therapy, tend to reflect only minor changes in most instances; that is, doers are still doers and thinkers are still thinkers. People who are active, tuned into sensory pleasures, imaginative and social before therapy will usually show the same tendencies after therapy. If a high score on the Interpersonal Scale reflected an overly dependent penchant, this may decrease a few points after therapy. Conversely, if a low score on the Interpersonal Scale before treatment was a function of shyness and withdrawal, the posttherapeutic score will usually show an increase of several points. Depressed people are inclined to show the greatest pre- and posttreatment differences. While depressed, they usually show a low activity level, few or no feelings apart from sadness, a conspicuous absence of sensory pleasures, and decreased social participation. They may rate themselves fairly high on "imagery" and "cognition" because of visions of doom, loneliness, illness, and failure, and because of high self-blame and pervasive ideas of self-worthlessness (Fay & Lazarus, 1981). When therapy is successful, Structural Profiles do tend to depict significant changes in terms of greater activity, positive affect, sensory joys, and social participation.

In evaluating marital therapy, the use of a 12-term marital satisfaction questionnaire (Lazarus, 1981) has been useful. The questionnaire pinpoints the most important areas of personal and familial distress, and quantitative changes in this pencil-and-paper test usually reflect significant improvements in marital happiness.

A three-year follow-up evaluation of 20 "complex cases" who had completed a course of multimodal therapy (e.g., people suffering from obsessive-compulsive rituals, extreme agoraphobia, pervasive anxiety and panic, depression, alcohol addiction, or enmeshed family and marital problems) showed that 14 maintained their gains or had made additional progress without further therapy; 2 felt the need for medication from time to time, for which they had consulted their family physicians (1 person had suffered from extreme panic attacks; the other was prone to bouts of recurring depression), 1 man considered himself "pretty good," although his wife revealed that he was still "too compulsive"; and 3 other cases (an anorectic woman and 2 patients with chronic alcohol abuse) had failed to maintain their initial gains. A 70 percent successful follow-up with a sample of complex and difficult cases, some of whom were seemingly intractable, is most encouraging. In terms of some overall statistics, over the past seven years we have consistently found that treatment goals were achieved with more than 75 percent of the people who consulted us. Follow-

ups reveal a relapse rate of less than 5 percent.

Treatment

The mean duration of a "complete" course of multimodal therapy is approximately 50 hours (i.e., about a year of therapy at weekly intervals). Acutely disturbed people or those with special problems (e.g., work or family crises) may require more frequent sessions, but once a week is often the best frequency in order to give people sufficient time to do the recommended "homework." Fewer than 30 percent of the clients seen at the various Multimodal Therapy Institutes seem to require, or are willing to undergo, as much as 50 hours of therapy. While some clients may require extended support and trust building and therefore remain in therapy for several years, the majority favor short-term therapy (15-20 sessions). Multimodal therapy also lends itself extremely well to crisis intervention. Moreover, when clients learn to monitor each area of the BASIC I.D., self-management seems to be greatly enhanced.

Various treatment formats have been applied. Outpatient individual psychotherapy is perhaps the most frequent, although when the interpersonal modality becomes the focus of attention, spouses and other family members are usually seen as well. Thus, what often starts out as one-to-one psychotherapy, may immediately shift to couples therapy, or family therapy, or the client may be invited to join a group. These decisions are based entirely on the therapist's assessment of who or what appears most likely to benefit the client, and their implementation depends on the concurrence of the client and the willingness of significant others to participate. Thus, the well-trained multimodal therapist is capable of treating individuals, couples, families, and groups. On some occasions, as many as 20 multimodal therapists have formed a *multiple psychotherapy* format to treat one client, or one couple, in several "brainstorming" sessions. When a staff member at one of the Multimodal Therapy Institutes encounters a particularly difficult or challenging case, the therapist is encouraged to invite the client to a multiple therapy meeting. On the age-old principle that if 2 heads are better than 1, 10 or 20 heads may be 5 or 10 times better than 2, most of these "brainstorming" sessions have been constructive. Of course, some clients are terrified at the prospect of being seen by so many therapists at one time and reject the idea of multiple therapy. (The obviously poor cost-effectiveness ratio is offset by the fact that this is an excellent training opportunity.)

Regardless of the specific treatment format, multimodal therapy encompasses: (*a*) specification of goals and problems; (*b*) specification of treatment techniques to achieve these goals and remedy these problems; and (*c*) systematic measurement of the relative success of these techniques. In essence, this boils down to eliminating distressing and unwanted responses throughout the BASIC I.D., and also overcoming deficits that exist in any of these modalities.

It is worth reiterating the main procedural sequences followed in multimodal therapy.

1. Information from the initial interviews and the Life History Questionnaire result in a Modality Profile (i.e., a systematic list of problems in each area of the client's BASIC I.D.).

2. The therapist, usually in concert with the client, selects specific strategies to deal with each problem area. If treatment impasses arise, a Second-Order BASIC I.D. is carried out (i.e., the unresponsive problem is reexamined in each of the seven modalities).

3. Generalized complaints such as "anxiety and panic attacks" are usually dissected into Modality Firing Orders. Thus, some clients create anxiety by dwelling on negative sensations which lead to catastrophic thoughts, followed by terrifying images (an S-C-I sequence), whereas others may commence with negative self-statements, followed by distressing images, which result in unpleasant sensations (a C-I-S pattern). Appropriate techniques are selected to deal with each distressing element in turn.

It is worth repeating that in multimodal therapy, attention to what is traditionally called "transference" and "countertransference" phenomena—what we simply regard as the examination of client-therapist relationship variables—takes place only when there is reason to suspect that therapeutic progress will ensue. Sometimes, treatment impasses are due to specific client-therapist interactions that need to be addressed, but when therapy is proceeding well, why bother to examine the therapeutic relationship?

In multimodal marriage therapy, the couple is usually seen together for the initial interview, and the main presenting complaints are discussed. Each partner is given the Life History Questionnaire to take home and fill out independently. An individual session is then arranged with each one for the purpose of examining the completed questionnaire and constructing an initial Modality Profile. Thereafter, the treatment processes are tailored to the individuals and their unique dyadic requirements (see Lazarus, 1981, pp. 165-186).

Participants in multimodal groups construct their own Modality Profiles which serve as a "blueprint" for the specific gains they wish to derive. Groups can be particularly helpful in dispelling various myths (consensual validation tends to carry more weight than the views of one person, even if that person is a highly respected authority). When interpersonal deficiencies are present, group therapy can provide a more veridical training milieu. Groups lend the opportunity for vicarious or observational learning and offer a rich variety of modeling opportunities. Roleplaying, behavior-rehearsal and other enactments are enhanced by the psychodramatic nuances that groups provide. Lonely and isolated individuals particularly tend to benefit from group therapy, especially when the group provides a springboard for the development of friendships. Extremely hostile, paranoid, deluded, or severely depressed individuals are excluded from multimodal groups because they are usually too disruptive. Similarly, people who are locked into pervasive obsessive-compulsive rituals have responded poorly in multimodal groups. These people are better treated individually or, preferably, in marital or family contexts.

The use of standardized tests is not a usual procedure but certain problems may necessitate their application. Intelligence tests (especially with children) may augment the appreciation of specific cognitive abilities and deficits. Neuropsychological assessment may shed light on matters of "organicity," and tests of aptitude and special abilities may also be used to good effect with certain clients. The "test" that is most frequently used is a structured, interactive, projective procedure called the *deserted island fantasy technique* (Lazarus, 1971, 1981). In essence, the client is asked to describe what he or she imagines might transpire if on a deserted island for six months in the company of a companion (a congenial person unknown

to the client). As clients describe their fantasies about their island sojourn, the therapist is usually able to discern several important facets. The presence or absence of the ordinary give-and-take of personal interaction emerges quite clearly. Some clients are unable to picture themselves suspending their hostility, aggression, or depression. One easily detects those instances where people are especially afraid of close contact. Evidence of autistic thinking may emerge. Direct questions concerning the evolution of friendship on the island can provide important clues about the way in which the therapeutic relationship should be structured. Many additional insights tend to be gained. An entire chapter has been devoted elsewhere (Lazarus, 1981) to this technique.

The application of multimodal therapy to inpatient settings is beyond the scope of this chapter. The interested reader is referred to the book edited by Brunell and Young (1982) which contains a wealth of information about designing, planning, and implementing multimodal treatment programs with hospitalized psychiatric patients.

Management

Setting
Tastefully and comfortably furnished waiting rooms and offices tend to have a positive "placebo effect." Some of the Multimodal Therapy Institutes provide soft background music from FM radio stations or cassette tapes in the waiting and reception areas. It is impressed upon the receptionists that they play a crucial role in setting the emotional tone and interpersonal ambience of the institute. They are schooled in putting clients at ease, allowing them to feel comfortable, and they are told to offer tea or other beverages if clients are early or if the therapist is running overtime. Similarly, their

telephone manner is required to be tolerant, polite, and patient.

The consulting rooms are carpeted, are relatively soundproof, and are furnished with armchairs, and usually have books, plants, and artwork to create a homelike atmosphere. Most of the therapists seem to prefer no desk between the therapist and the client. There is usually a couch or a recliner (for the practice of relaxation, biofeedback, imagery exercises, or hypnosis). Many of the offices have blackboards, or flip charts which multimodal therapists often use in underscoring a point. The foregoing reflects the educational emphasis that underlies the orientation. Clients are encouraged to have notepads and writing materials at hand. Following Albert Ellis's example, many clients are encouraged to tape-record each session and to study the recordings as a homework assignment between meetings.

Most clients are referred by friends and relatives who had benefited from multimodal therapy. Physicians, attorneys, and other professionals are also important referral sources. Advertisements and public lectures are somewhat unpredictable in terms of referrals. In this regard, weight-reduction groups have been the most cost effective.

While the majority of sessions are held in the therapist's office, the flexibility of multimodal procedures leaves open a variety of other settings. In dealing with certain clients who do not show some improvement in a short period of time, Fay and Lazarus (1982) emphasized that it may be helpful to shift the locus of therapy outside of the office, such as outdoor walking sessions or a session in the park, or, under certain circumstances, a home visit by the therapist. The use of ancillary personnel is also often found to facilitate extensive in vivo work. Thus, nurses, psychiatric aides, teachers, parents, and other paraprofessional volunteers may expedite desensitization, provide reinforcement of adaptive responses, and offer helpful modeling experiences.

Relationships

It is worth reemphasizing that, in keeping with individuals' needs and expectancies, multimodal therapists see relationships with clients on a continuum. Some clients thrive when the relationship is formal, rather distant, and businesslike. At the other extreme some clients require close, warm, and empathic bonding. The multimodal therapist is not likely to foster dependent, romantic, or other deep attachments since much of the therapy remains task oriented. Of course, some people are bound to develop elaborate fantasies and project upon the therapist strong feelings of love and/or hate, but we find this the exception rather than the rule. When it does occur it has to be dealt with and may well become an important therapeutic focus.

It is widely held that people enter therapy with implicit (if not explicit) expectations and that the effectiveness of therapy is often linked with these expectations. If the therapist's personality and approach are very much at variance with the client's image of an effective practitioner, a therapeutic impasse is likely to result. This, however, should not be construed as a passive and inevitable process. Clients' expectations can be modified by the therapist. Many clients, for instance, expect the therapist to "cure them" and seem unprepared to take responsibiity for the treatment process and outcome. In these instances considerable therapeutic skill and artistry may be required to elicit the client's active cooperation. The most elegant outcomes often depend on a reasonable degree of congruence between the client's BASIC I.D. and the therapist's BASIC I.D. When inappropriate matching results in an absence of rapport, it is often advisable to effect referral to a more compatible resource instead of insisting that the client-therapist difficulties can or should be "worked through."

Multimodal therapists make extensive use of "bibliotherapy." If a picture can be worth a thousand words, a well-chosen book can be worth more than a dozen sessions. When a book is recommended to a client, he/she is asked to read it carefully, to underline points that seem important, and perhaps even summarize it in a notebook that can be kept for ready reference. The readings are discussed during the session so that the therapist can ascertain what impact the book has had, and any ambiguities can be clarified. Similarly, audiotherapy (the use of cassette recordings) is also a most useful therapeutic adjunct.

Fees are on a sliding scale depending on income and third-party coverage, among other considerations. Trainees may see clients for no fee in order to obtain supervision from experienced therapists. All in all, we try to avoid incurring economic hardships for our clients in exchange for "mental health"!

CASE EXAMPLE

Background

A 33-year-old woman presented with a fear of becoming pregnant, hypochondriasis, and several somatic symptoms—headaches, chest pains, and gastrointestinal distress. A complete medical evaluation disclosed no organic pathology. She also suffered from severe premenstrual tension—becoming irritable, bloated, anxious, and dysphoric a few days before menstruating, and experiencing almost incapacitating dysmenorrhea. Her gynecologist had prescribed analgesics, but she was "frightened of taking pills."

She had majored in mathematics at college and was working as a computer programmer. Her husband, a successful company president, had expressed a strong desire for children over the previous three years. "For the first five or six years of our marriage, neither of us wanted to have kids, but when Bill became very successful at work, he seemed to look for other outlets. That's when I realized that pregnancy, childbirth, and that whole scene terrifies me."

For the past two and a half years she had been in therapy with a psychologist. The client was most articulate about the treatment areas they traversed. "We explored my relationship with my mother, my father, my brother, and we also looked into my general home atmosphere. . . . We spoke a lot about attachment and separation. . . . It was very interesting." The client realized that what was "interesting" was not necessarily "effective," and after reading a newspaper article, she consulted a "behavior therapist" who attempted (unsuccessfully) to desensitize her to her fears of pregnancy. "I think he hypnotized me and I was to see myself going through the whole pregnancy, including the labor and delivery." She acknowledged having fewer negative anticipations, but her overall clinical status remained essentially unchanged. Her brother (a 28-year-old architect, married, with one child) advised her to try multimodal therapy. His senior partner's wife had mentioned that their son and daughter had both benefited from multimodal therapy after failing with other treatment approaches.

Main problem areas

The foregoing information was obtained during the initial interview. The Life History Questionnaire (Lazarus, 1981), was completed and returned before her second visit. The following *Modality Profile* was drawn up:

Behavior:	Excessive cigarette smoking; insufficient exercise.
Affect:	Anger/resentment/hostility (seldom directly expressed). Fear (of pregnancy).
Sensation:	Headaches. Palpitations. Stomach pains. Tremors. Chest pains. Menstrual pain.
Imagery:	Death images. Not coping. Failing.
Cognition:	Perfectionistic. False romantic ideas. Overconcerned about parental approval.
Interpersonal:	Resorts to passive-aggressive tactics (spiteful), especially with husband.
Drugs/ Biologicals:	May require medical intervention for menstrual dysfunction.

During the second session, the Modality Profile was discussed and the client indicated that her most distressing problems were numerous sensory discomforts which she feared were symptoms of organic disease (despite reassurances from physicians). Exploration of her "death images" resulted in graphic pictures of her succumbing to a heart attack. Thus, "fears heart attack" was added to her profile under *Affect*.

Treatment

It became clear immediately, that the client's modality "firing order" almost invariably followed an S-I-C-A sequence (Sensation - Imagery - Cognition - Affect). First, she would observe sensory discomforts whereupon she would dwell on them, thereby intensifying untoward pains and bodily tensions. Unpleasant and frightening images would then become intrusive. For example, she would recall vivid scenes of her maternal grandmother suffering a fatal heart attack when the client was 15 years old. Her negative imagery would lead her to label herself organically ill. "Instead of ignoring it and going about my business, I start thinking of all the things that could be wrong with me." Her unpleasant images and negative cognitions culminated in severe bouts of anxiety. In keeping with her modality firing order, the following treatments were applied:

1. Biofeedback was administered by means of an EMG apparatus attached to her frontalis muscles. She was given relaxation training cassettes for home use.

2. Associated imagery was employed. She was asked to relax, close her eyes, and picture her grandmother's heart attack. When the image was vivid and clear, she was asked to focus on any other images that emerged. As each image was attended to, a pattern began to take shape. She appeared to have overidentified with her grandmother, but on an accelerated time frame. Thus, many of her physical complaints and infirmities paralleled those that her grandmother had suffered and finally succumbed to in her late 70s. Time projection was employed wherein she imagined herself going forward in time, remaining free from organic disease until she reached her late 70s. She was advised to practice the time projection exercise at least twice daily for 5-10 minutes each time.

3. Positive self-statements were implemented. "If I do take after my granny, I too will enjoy good health until I'm about 75. So I'll start worrying 40 years from now." These positive self-statements were to be practiced in conjunction with the time projection images.

The foregoing procedures were administered in two sessions. She arrived for her next session feeling "weepy and depressed" although she was not premenstrual. Exploration of her feelings was unproductive and it seemed appropriate to carry out the Deserted Island Fantasy. Five distinct themes emerged:

1. She would inevitably be disappointed with her island companion. "I just know that I will feel let-down."
2. She felt that someone would have to be in charge. (Strong, overcompetitive tendencies became evident.)
3. Boredom would lead her to engage in compulsive projects.
4. She would withhold information from her island companion—she would not disclose all relevant aspects of her life. (This led the therapist to speculate about important matters that were being kept from him.)
5. She would never initiate any acts of affection but would always wait for the companion to do so. (She attributed her inhibitions in this area to her father who showed affection "only when he was good and ready." She claimed that, as a young child, she learned that spontaneous acts of affection had punitive consequences when her father happened to be in a bad mood.)

The relevance of her island fantasies to ongoing life situations were clearcut. She felt let down by her husband who was less affectionate, less nurturing, than she desired. She was inclined to compete with him and tried, unsuccessfully, to take charge of his life. She never initiated sex or engaged in acts of spontaneous affection, although she craved for greater warmth and caring. She frequently felt a childlike rage toward her husband, much of which was expressed in passive-aggressive and essentially indirect ways. Yet she felt a desire to achieve a close and loving relationship with him. Further clarification of her wishes indicated that her reluctance to have children was not due to phobic anxiety of the childbirth process.

"I think my real hangup is that kids will take Bill away from me even further than he is already." She had come to realize that before feeling able to make an emotional investment in a child, she would have to feel more secure within herself and in the marriage.

Therapy then focused on assertiveness training with special attention to: (*a*) the direct expression of anger and resentment (instead of her indirect, spiteful, manipulative responses), and (*b*) making requests, particularly asking for attention and affection. Roleplaying and coping imagery (in which she pictured herself withstanding rejection and behaving rationally) were helpful facilitators of overt action.

Approximately two and a half months after her initial consultation (eight sessions), some progress was evident. Her gains across the BASIC I.D.* were as follows:

B She had stopped smoking.

A Feelings were expressed more openly and more frequently.

S She reported feeling more relaxed and was less bothered with physical discomforts.

I She was obtaining clear coping images of herself living a long and healthy life.

C She was somewhat less perfectionistic.

I. She was taking emotional risks with her husband (e.g., asking for his affection).

D. She had seen her physician again, and this time had agreed to take medication for her menstrual difficulties.

A week later, the client mentioned that

---
*BASIC I.D. is summary of seven modalities: Behavior, Affect, Sensation, Imagery, Cognition, Interpersonal relationships, and Drugs/biological factors.

the physician had prescribed a diuretic to be taken five-six days prior to menstruation together with oxazepam (15mg b.i.d.). On the first day of menstruation she was to take zomepirac sodium tablets for pain, as needed. (This combination of drugs proved highly effective.)

At the start of the ninth session she suggested going for a walk instead of meeting inside the office. "I feel like talking today," she said, "I'm not in the mood for hypnosis, or imagery, or stuff like that. The Herrontown Woods are less than five minutes away. Can we spend about half-an-hour on one of the trails?" Whereas traditional therapists would probably be disinclined to leave the professional confines of their offices, multimodal therapists tend to be more flexible in such matters. Initially, client and therapist admired the scenery, and then the client asked the therapist for his views on extramarital relationships. Was this a proposition? The therapist very much doubted it. He explained that he had no fixed rules, that he was neither blindly for, nor universally opposed to extramarital sex. The client then revealed that she had been having an affair for the past year-and-a-half. She had taken courses in computer science and had become sexually involved with her instructor with whom she enjoyed "coffee and sex" once a week. She derived a good deal of flattery and attention from this clandestine relationship. The therapist inquired if this was having an adverse impact on her marriage, whereupon she insisted that one had nothing to do with the other. The therapist's insinuation that her affair was perhaps partly based on her wish to "get even" with her husband for his lack of emotional support and nurturance met with denial. She appeared eager to drop the subject. The topic switched to her use of coping imagery. Additional material from the Deserted

Island Fantasy test was also discussed.

At this juncture, therapy sessions were scheduled every two weeks, so that she had time to practice her imagery exercises and other homework assignments. She continued to make progress for a month and then began having palpitations, chest pains, and tension headaches. After some evasive comments she admitted having stopped using the relaxation cassettes, the time projection images, and the cognitive self-statements, and she had also reverted to her unassertive (but aggressive) stance vis-à-vis her husband. The following dialogue ensued:

Client: If you're mad at me and want to yell at me I won't blame you. Go ahead.

Therapist: It's your life. You've got the tools to make it better. I can't force you to use them. Do you want me to yell at you? What good will that do?

Client: You're angry with me. I can tell.

Therapist: It sounds like you want me to get angry with you. What's happening? Did you decide to have a relapse in order to spite me? Is this some kind of test to see if I care? Or are you annoyed with me and you don't want to give me the satisfaction of having helped you?

Client: I've never seen you like this. You sound like Bill.

Therapist: That's a good observation. I feel you set me up the way you tend to set him up. It seems like some kind of a test. But whatever is going on it is not direct, honest, frank, or positive.

Client: Okay. I'll do the relaxation and all the rest of it.

Therapist: Not for my sake I hope. Stop looking for my approval, or your father's approval, or anybody's approval. Do what's best for *you*.

Client: Arguing with you is like arguing with Bill. I can't win. You're both too smart, too well educated. You both think very fast on your feet.

Therapist: It's interesting that you feel we are arguing, and I am intrigued by the way you have bracketed me with your husband.

Client: I think I've always felt that Bill is too good for me. He is intellectually superior, his earning power is astronomical compared to mine.

Therapist: This brings us back to your overcompetitive feelings and it also shows me something else that was not apparent —you have a terrible self-concept.

Client: It took you this long to realize that?

Therapist: I never appreciated its full extent. We really need to do something to raise your self-esteem. [Pause] I wonder if it would be a good idea one of these days for me to meet with you and Bill.

Client: What for?

Therapist: To upgrade the marriage.

Client: I would prefer you to meet with Bill alone so that you can get to know him first before seeing us together.

There were no further setbacks. In each dimension of her BASIC I.D. the client diligently addressed the relevant issues and carried out the prescribed exercises. We reverted to weekly sessions, and dwelled heavily on the false cognitions that led to her self-abnegation. The husband was seen only once. The therapist impressed upon him that the client desired a much more intense level of intimacy and emotional support and reassurance. The husband was under the false impression that his wife's disinclination to have children was due to her own career aspirations. A brief discussion cleared up this misconception. The therapist explained the client's competitive reactions as a cover-up for her feelings of insecurity and advised the husband to perceive them as cries for love and support from him.

Eight months after the initial interview, therapy was discontinued by mutual consent. The client casually mentioned that she had terminated her affair.

Resolution and follow-up

About four weeks after therapy had ended, the client called to say that she was pregnant and felt "very pleased" about it. During the brief telephone conversation the client added that she felt "infinitely more relaxed and self-confident" and said: "I'm so assertive these days that I even put my father in his place."

Approximately a year later she called for an appointment. Her baby boy was about four months old and she was delighted with motherhood. She had maintained all of her gains and added that since the birth of her son, her menstrual pains had cleared up, although she still took oxazepam a few days before her period. The reason she had made the appointment was to discuss the pros and cons of returning to work. As a result of the session, she decided to take a year's leave of absence and to take evening courses to maintain viability in the job market and ward off boredom.

SUMMARY

Multimodal therapy is a comprehensive, systematic, and holistic approach to psychotherapy that seeks to effect durable change in an efficient and humane way. It is an open system in which the principle of technical eclecticism encourages the constant introduction of new techniques and the refinement or elimination of existing ones, but never in a random or "shotgun" manner. The major emphasis is on flexibility. There are virtues not only in using a variety of techniques but even a variety of therapists. The client always comes first, even if it means referring him or her to someone else. Multimodal therapists subscribe to no dogma other than the principles of theoretical parsimony and therapeutic effectiveness.

Assessments and interventions are structured around seven modalities summarized by the acronym BASIC I.D. (*be*havior, *affect*, *sensation*, *imagery*, *cogni*tion, *interpersonal* relationships, and *drugs*/biological factors). This framework allows the therapist to take into account the uniqueness of each individual and to tailor treatment accordingly. The emphasis is constantly on who or what is best for this individual (couple, family, or group)? By assessing significant deficits and excesses across the client's BASIC I.D., thorough coverage of diverse interactive problems is facilitated.

The therapist's role and the cadence of client-therapist interaction differs from person to person and even from session to session. Some clients respond best to somewhat austere, formal, businesslike transactions; others require gentle, tender, supportive encouragement. Two specific procedures that seem to enhance treatment effects are *bridging* and *tracking*. (Bridging refers to a procedure in which the therapist deliberately tunes into the client's preferred modality before branching off into other dimensions that seem likely to be more productive. Tracking refers to a careful examination of the "firing order" of the different modalities.)

The BASIC I.D. framework facilitates the roles of artistry and science in clinical intervention. For example, a recursive application of the BASIC I.D. to itself (a "second-order" assessment) often helps to shed new diagnostic light and helps to overcome some seemingly recalcitrant

problems. A graphic representation of the BASIC I.D. in terms of a *Structural Profile* is most illuminating in couples therapy. Examination of each specific modality and its interactive effect on the other six, readily enables the therapist to shift the focus of attention between the individual and his or her parts, to the person in his or her social setting.

In general, the trend in current psychotherapy is toward multidimensional, multidisciplinary, and multifaceted interventions. Rigid adherents to particular schools seem to be receding into a minority. Multiform and multifactorial assessment and treatment procedures have become widespread. We believe that the multimodal (BASIC I.D.) framework permits the clinician to identify idiosyncratic variables and thereby *not* fit clients to preconceived treatments. It also offers an operational means for "talking the client's language." Apart from its heuristic virtues, the multimodal structure readily permits an examination of its own efficacy. It needs to be understood that while all multimodal therapists are eclectic, all eclectic therapists are not multimodal therapists.

ANNOTATED BIBLIOGRAPHY

Brunell, L. F., & Young, W. T. (Eds.). *Multimodal handbook for a mental hospital.* New York: Springer, 1981.

This book is a practical guide to the use of multimodal therapy in mental hospitals, residential facilities, day hospitals, and other complete care centers. The book includes comprehensive details on goals and procedures for various treatment modules from art and occupational therapy to social and problem skills training. Discussions focus on essential phases of patient assessment, program design, treatment, and evaluation of both patient progress and the hospital system. Specific chapters transcend clinical, case-oriented considerations and address large-scale applications of multimodal procedures. The eight authors have pointed the way to more efficient and effective therapeutic interventions with people who are often given little more than custodial care.

Keat, D. B. *Multimodal therapy with children.* New York: Pergamon Press, 1979.

The artistry and technical repertoire of an effective child-therapist involves specific skills that are not required by a clinician who is gifted with young or elderly adults. To reach certain children, the therapist must be equipped with numerous techniques, including games, stories, and songs, and have a flair for communicating in special ways. This book shows how an imaginative clinician applies the BASIC I.D. to many problems and disorders of children.

Lazarus, A. A. (Ed.) *Multimodal behavior therapy.* New York: Springer, 1976.

This is the first book in which the BASIC I.D. is explicitly employed in the assessment and therapy of clinical cases. The 17 chapters are divided into two parts. The first 7 chapters deal with theoretical and clinical foundations, and the remaining 10 chapters consist of clinical reports and case studies. The 12 authors show how the multimodal format is applied by therapists of different personalities and backgrounds. Specific problem areas are delineated—depression, anxiety, obesity, sexual inadequacy, mental retardation, and other disturbances in children and adults. Specific techniques are incorporated into the multimodal framework (e.g., paradoxical therapy and the use of hypnosis). As Cyril Franks mentions in the foreword, "it can be used wisely as a basis for further research and controlled clinical investigation."

Lazarus, A. A. *The practice of multimodal therapy.* New York: McGraw-Hill, 1981.

This book is pragmatic and focuses on the common clinical situations confronting most psychotherapists. It spells out

exactly how to conduct a thorough and comprehensive assessment. An attempt is made to integrate knowledge from diverse orientations into a coherent approach. The book is essentially a condensation of the author's own experience, the recorded experience of others, and scientific data. Transcripts from actual sessions and vignettes of typical transactions provide rich clinical material. The book also contains a glossary of 37 separate therapeutic techniques.

CASE READINGS

Breunlin, D. C. Multimodal behavioral treatment of a child's eliminative disturbance. *Psychotherapy: Theory, Research and Practice,* 1980, *17,* 17-23.

Briddell, D. W., & Leiblum, S. R. The multimodal treatment of spastic colitis and incapacitating anxiety: A case study. In A. A. Lazarus (Ed.), *Multimodal behavior therapy.* New York: Springer, 1976.

Keat, D. B. Multimodal therapy with children: Two case histories. In A. A. Lazarus (Ed.), *Multimodal behavior therapy.* New York: Springer, 1976.

Popler, K. Agoraphobia: Indications for the application of the multimodal conceptualization. *The Journal of Nervous and Mental Disease,* 1977, *164,* 97-101.

REFERENCES

Bandler, R., & Grinder, J. *The structure of magic: A book about communication and change.* Vol. II. Palo Alto, Cal.: Science and Behavior Books, 1976.

Bandura, A. *Principles of behavior modification.* New York: Holt, Rinehart & Winston, 1969.

Bandura, A. *Social learning theory.* Englewood Cliffs, N.J.: Prentice-Hall, 1977.

Bandura, A. The self-system in reciprocal determinism. *American Psychologist,* 1978, *33,* 344-358.

Bertalanffy, L. von. General system theory and psychiatry. In S. Arieti (Ed.), *American handbook of psychiatry,* Vol. 1. New York: Basic Books, 1974, pp. 1095-1117.

Brentano, F. *Psychology from an empirical standpoint.* New York: Humanities Press

1972. (Originally published in 1874.)

Brunell, L. F., & Young, W. T. (Eds.). *Multimodal handbook for a mental hospital.* New York: Springer, 1982.

Buckley, W. *Modern systems research for the behavioral scientist.* Chicago: Aldine, 1967.

Burnham, W. H. *The normal mind.* New York: Appleton, 1924.

Corsini, R. J. (Ed.). *Handbook of innovative psychotherapies.* New York: Wiley, 1981.

Davison, G. C., & Neale, J. M. *Abnormal psychology* (3d ed.). New York: Wiley, 1982.

Ellis, A. *Reason and emotion in psychotherapy.* New York: Lyle Stuart, 1962.

Fay, A. *Making things better by making them worse.* New York: Hawthorn, 1978.

Fay, A., & Lazarus, A. A. Multimodal therapy and the problems of depression. In J. F. Clarkin & H. Glazer (Eds.), *Depression: Behavioral and directive treatment strategies.* New York: Garland Press, 1981.

Fay, A., & Lazarus, A. A. Psychoanalytic resistance and behavioral nonresponsiveness: A dialectical impasse. In P. L. Wachtel (Ed.), *Resistance: Psychodynamic and behavioral approaches.* New York: Plenum, 1982.

Frankl, V. E. Paradoxical intention: A logotherapeutic technique. *American Journal of Psychotherapy,* 1960, *14,* 520-535.

Frankl, V. E. *The unheard cry for meaning.* New York: Simon & Schuster, 1978.

Galin, D. Implications for psychiatry of left and right cerebral specialization. *Archives of General Psychiatry,* 1974, *31,* 572-583.

Gallatin, J. *Abnormal psychology.* New York: Macmillan, 1982.

Gerler, E. R. Preventing the delusion of uniqueness: Multimodal education in mainstreamed classrooms. *The Elementary School Journal,* 1979, *80,* 35-40.

Haley, J. *Uncommon therapy.* New York: Norton, 1973.

Haley, J. *Problem solving therapy.* San Francisco: Jossey-Bass, 1976.

Herink, R. *The psychotherapy handbook.* New York: Meridian, 1980.

James, W. *Principles of psychology.* New York: Macmillan, 1890.

Judah, R. D. Multimodal parent training. *Elementary School Guidance and Counseling,* 1978, *13,* 46-54.

Keat, D. B. *Multimodal therapy with chil-dren.* New York: Pergamon Press, 1979.

Kimura, D. The asymmetry of the human brain. *Scientific American,* 1979, *228,* 70-78.

Kwee, M. G. T. Gedragstherapie en neurotische depressie. In J. W. Orlemans, W. Brinkman, W. P. Haaijam, & E. J. Zwaan (Eds.), *Handboek voor gedragstherapie.* Deventer: Van Loghum, 1978.

Kwee, M. G. T. Over de ontwikkeling van een multimodale strategie van assessment en therapie. *Tijdschrift voor Psychotherapie,* 1979, *5,* 172-188.

Kwee, M. G. T. Towards the clinical art and science of multimodal psychotherapy. *Current Psychological Reviews,* 1981, *1,* 55-68.

Lazarus, A. A. A psychological approach to alcoholism. *South African Medical Journal,* 1956, *30,* 707-710.

Lazarus, A. A. New methods in psychotherapy: A case study. *South African Medical Journal,* 1958, *32,* 660-664.

Lazarus, A. A. Towards the understanding and effective treatment of alcoholism. *South African Medical Journal,* 1965, *39,* 736-741.

Lazarus, A. A. Broad spectrum behavior therapy and the treatment of agoraphobia. *Behavior Research and Therapy,* 1966, *4,* 95-97.

Lazarus, A. A. *Behavior therapy and beyond.* New York: McGraw-Hill, 1971.

Lazarus, A. A. Multimodal behavior therapy: Treating the BASIC I.D. *Journal of Nervous and Mental Disease,* 1973, *156,* 404-411.

Lazarus, A. A. *Multimodal behavior therapy.* New York: Springer, 1976.

Lazarus, A. A. *In the mind's eye: The power of imagery for personal enrichment.* New York: Rawson, 1978.

Lazarus, A. A. *The practice of multimodal therapy.* New York: McGraw-Hill, 1981.

Lazarus, A. A. *Personal enrichment through imagery.* New York: BMA Audiocassettes, 1982.

Meichenbaum, D. *Cognitive behavior modification.* New York: Plenum, 1977.

Mendels, J. Biological aspects of affective illness. In S. Arieti & E. B. Brody (Eds.), *American handbook of psychiatry* (Vol. 3). New York: Basic Books, 1974.

Nathan, P. E., & Harris, S. L. *Psychopathology and society* (2nd ed.). New York: McGraw-Hill, 1980.

Nieves, L. *The minority college student ex-*

perience: A case for the use of self-control. Princeton, N.J.: Educational Testing Service, 1978. (a)

Nieves, L. *College achievement through self-help.* Princeton, N.J.: Educational Testing Service, 1978. (b)

O'Keefe, E. J., & Castaldo, C. A multimodal approach to treatment in a child care agency. *Psychological Reports,* 1980, *47,* 250.

O'Keefe, E. J., & Castaldo, C. Multimodal management: A systematic and holistic approach for the 80s. *Proceedings of the Marist College Symposium on Local Government Productivity.* June 1981.

Paul, G. L. Strategy of outcome research in psychotherapy. *Journal of Consulting Psychology,* 1967, *31,* 109-118.

Pearl, C., & Guarnaccia, V. Multimodal therapy and mental retardation. In A. A. Lazarus (Ed.), *Multimodal behavior therapy.* New York: Springer, 1976.

Rabkin, R. *Strategic psychotherapy.* New York: Basic Books, 1977.

Roberts, T. K., Jackson, L. J., & Phelps, R. Lazarus' multimodal therapy model applied in an institutional setting. *Professional Psychology,* 1980, 150-156.

Rosen, R. D. *Psychobabble.* New York: Atheneum, 1977.

Rosenthal, D. The genetics of schizophrenia. In S. Arieti & E. B. Brody (Eds.), *American handbook of psychiatry* (Vol. 3). New York: Basic Books, 1974.

Salter, A. *Conditioned reflex therapy.* New York: Farrar, Strauss, 1949.

Sank, L. I. Community disasters: Primary prevention and treatment in a health maintenance organization. *American Psychologist,* 1979, *34,* 334-338.

Shevrin, H., & Dickman, S. The psychological unconscious: A necessary assumption for all psychological theory? *American Psychologist,* 1980, *35,* 421-434.

Sperry, R. W., Gazzaniga, M. S., & Bogen, J. E. Interhemispheric relationships: The neocortical commissures; syndromes of hemisphere disconnection. In P. J. Vinken & G. W. Bruyn (Eds.), *Handbook of clinical neurology* (Vol. 4). Amsterdam: North-Holland, 1969.

Tyrer, P. J. Anxiety states. In E. S. Paykel (Ed.), *Handbook of affective disorders.* New York: Guilford Press, 1982.

Watzlawick, P., Weakland, J., & Fisch, R. *Change: Principles of problem formation and problem resolution.* New York: Norton, 1974.

Weeks, G. R., & L'Abate, L. *Paradoxical psychotherapy.* New York: Brunner/Mazel, 1982.

Woody, R. H. *Psychobehavioral counseling and therapy: Integrating behavioral and insight techniques.* New York: Appleton-Century-Crofts, 1971.

Zeig, J. K. (Ed.). *Ericksonian approaches to hypnosis and psychotherapy.* New York: Brunner/ Mazel, 1982.

Zilbergeld, B. Bespoke therapy. *Psychology Today,* 1982, *16,* 85-86.

14

Innovative Psychotherapies

RAYMOND J. CORSINI

The term *innovative* as used here does not necessarily mean some system of psychotherapy which has been recently developed (even though most of the innovative ones are usually also relatively new), but rather the term is used to imply that the system is unusual, having a unique or idiosyncratic point of view or methodology.

For the reader to have a comprehensive view of all of psychotherapy, some knowledge of unusual methods is important. The *Handbook of Innovative Psychotherapies* (Corsini, 1981) includes some 66 innovative methods of psychotherapy and lists a total of 250 innovative methods. I shall summarize in this chapter a dozen methods all of which are basically sensible in their theories with methodologies related to their theories, and each of which, in my judgment, is quite different not only from each other, but also from the standard 12 major systems which take up the major part of this book.

WHY SO MANY THERAPIES?

Why should there be so many different systems of psychotherapy? The reason is simple: therapists, dissatisfied with the method or technique or system that they had been operating with, got an idea for a new way of operating, tried it, found it good, and explored it more fully. Having much better success with the new method, it was used extensively until the developers were certain that it was good, and then they began to explain their ideas to others, mainly through the various professional journals.

Having had close personal contact with many prime initiators of innovative psychotherapies I can say with some degree of authority that each is a passionate believer in the essential and unique value of his or her system, and most are eager to explain their thinking and methodologies to others. Among theorists those I have known are George Bach (creative aggression), Paul Bindrim (aqua-energetics), Albert Ellis (rational-emotive therapy), Werner Erhard (Erhard seminar training), Viktor Frankl (logotherapy), Eugene Gendlin (focusing), Harold Greenwald (decision therapy), Werner Karle (functional psychotherapy), Nira Kefir (impasse/priority therapy), Eugene Landy (twenty-four hour therapy), Arnold Lazarus (multimodal therapy), Arthur Lerner (poetry therapy), Lew Losoncy (encouragement therapy), J. L. Moreno (psychodrama), O. H. Mowrer (integrity therapy), Walter O'Connell (natural high therapy), Leonard Orr (rebirthing), Robert Postel (primary relationship therapy), Carl Rogers (person-centered therapy),

Will Schutz (holistic education), John and Helen Watkins (ego-state therapy), Joseph Wolpe (reciprocal inhibition), and Robert Zaslow (Z-process attachment therapy).

I shall now proceed, giving the various systems equal space, to attempt to provide an understanding of a dozen current innovative systems of psychotherapy.

BODY THERAPIES

Précis

It is generally accepted that there is some kind of relationship between the body and the "mind": thus if the body is abused, say by ingestion of noxious substances, the mind will be affected. It is evident that traumatic physical events, such as a blow to the head, high fever, and lack of sleep, can affect a person's mind as shown by defects in judgment, misperceptions, and so on.

Consequently, one can assume that there is an interaction between body and mind, and that the total person can be treated in two ways: through reaching the mind (as in verbal therapy) and through operating through the body (as by exercise).

There are a number of so-called body therapies in existence which operate fundamentally on the premise that total personality modifications can be made by dealing primarily with the body. Such methodologies have a long history and are best exemplified by some Eastern practices such as Yoga in which practitioners contort their bodies into various peculiar postures, such as wrapping their legs in a particular manner to aid in achieving a desired state of mind. Such thinking is foreign to Westerners and may appear to be rather peculiar. However, students of

psychology would do well to understand the long traditions of the Orient relative to these matters.

Theory

We shall not attempt here to discuss Eastern theories which call for a total reorientation of conceptualizations relative to personality. Many excellent accounts are available, however, for those interested in such matters (e.g., Pedersen, 1983). Even within the Western tradition there are a plethora of different body therapy theories. Perhaps the best known is one developed by Wilhelm Reich who observed that his patients appeared to have problems with their postures. This led to his theory of Vegetotherapy and the concept of body armor. He conceptualized seven horizontal planes down from the head to the pelvis. If any of these areas was frozen or hardened then there would be a blocking of vital energy. The task of the therapist was to loosen the patient's body area so that a free flow of energy (which he called Orgone) could occur.

Many other theoreticians followed Reich's lead, or developed independent but similar systems. Alexander Lowen who developed bioenergetics is perhaps best known. Moishe Feldenkrais and Ida Rolf are two others who have established their own ways of operating relative to the body. We can attempt to classify the various body therapies into two categories: *active* (in which the patient is called to do something, such as move differently) or *passive* (in which the therapist does something to another's body). According to Green (1981), body therapies can be classified in four categories: (*a*) manipulation of deep tissue (such as Rolf massage); (*b*) deep tissue release systems (such as Arica Chua K'); (*c*) emotional release systems (such as primal therapy); and (*d*) movement awareness systems (such as Feldenkrais movement).

Summary

Two main routes of psychotherapy are through cognition (verbal-symbolic therapies) and through body work. Possibly the final cause of any final successful change is through new concepts of self (cognition) but the route in some cases is through body work of various kinds.

Therapy

We shall describe briefly two systems, a passive one and an active one. In Ida Rolf's deep massage treatment, the patient is kneaded, often in a painful way, in an attempt to change the structure of the connective tissues of the body. A simple example might be a person who tends to stoop with shoulders hunched. The practitioner may then work on attempting to get the client to stand straight and tall with shoulders back through working with fingers, knuckles, elbows, and so on to break down the old muscle groupings to achieve a better posture.

Another example of body therapy is movement therapy and possibly the best example is dance therapy which is a use of movement to further emotional and physical integration of the individual. According to Duggan (1981), it is "a holistic approach that in recognition of complex body/mind interaction deals with disturbances of emotional, cognitive and physical origin through intervention on a body movement level" (p. 229).

Having myself participated in a dance therapy session, I can attest that under the guidance of a competent dance therapist that people do find that directed movements in rhythm have psychological ef-

fects, with people sometimes changing dramatically from being stiff and awkward to being free-flowing and relaxed. Dance therapists will ordinarily have interspersed sessions of verbal communications during which time the members of the groups interact symbolically. This is a feature not found in pure dance classes and which may be an important classification difference between dance per se and dance therapy.

EGO-STATE THERAPY

Précis

The premise of ego-state therapy is that all of us have multiple personalities. What we call the "self" according to this point of view consists of a number of discrete elements, such as perceptions and emotions, a kind of confederacy of states. These elements are organized into groupings or enclaves having a functional unity with each state having a distinct personality. The concept of a self divisible into parts is found also in psychoanalysis and in transactional analysis, but in ego-state therapy the personality is not divided into logical aspects such as parent/child/adult but rather in distinct complete subpersonalities. This method of therapy according to John and Helen Watkins (1979a, 1979b) is specifically designed for the resolution of conflicts between the different ego states— that is to say between the different personalities within us. While some unusual cases of multiple personalities have been identified (Prince, 1906; Thigpen & Cleckley, 1957), according to the Watkins we all have multiple personalities.

Theory

The theory of ego-state therapy depends on the concept of dissociation: certain parts of the personality are submerged or unknown to the person normally. When an entire segment of a personality is no longer sensed as part of the self, then that personality is disowned, even though it is still in existence. This "rejected" personality may sometimes take over and become "activated" and when this happens the new personality will be frequently quite different from the normal or usual personality. For many people, these part personalities are unknown, there being no permeability between the normal state and these other states; but for some people a certain amount of awareness of other selves exists. Normal individuals when hypnotized can have their inner states activated, and each personality that emerges is distinct.

According to the Watkins, neuroses are frequently due to conflicts between the underlying ego-states and therapy represents a kind of family council in which the various elements of the mind recognize and deal with each other.

Therapy

The methodology of treatment calls for activating these disparate personalities. Hypnosis is the method of choice, but a nonhypnotic method using chairs to represent the different ego-states can be used. The exact methodology is quite complex (H. Watkins, 1978) calling for the therapist to be persistent in eliciting these various personalities to emerge and to communicate with the therapist and through the therapist with each other. Here is an example of a hypothetical interview: T is the therapist, Lu is the normal state, Ann is another state.

T: Tell me about yourself?
Lu: I am scared.
T: What are you scared of?

Lu: I don't know.
T: What can I call you?
Lu: [In tears, does not answer.]
T: Is there someone who can help you?
Lu: Ann can but she is always too busy.
T: Step aside Lu, let me talk to Ann. Ann, when you are here, say so.
Ann: I'm here.
T: Are you busy?
Ann: No. Lu does not want me around.
T: Are you willing to help Lu?
Ann: Sure.
T: Does Lu know you exist? Talk to her. She thinks you are too busy.
Ann: Lu, I am never too busy. I want to help you.

Summary

Ego-state therapy is possibly one of the most controversial of the psychotherapies since it depends on accepting the notion not only of an unconscious but also of discrete independent personalities. The notion of multiple personalities is a hotly debated one, having been advanced in a number of criminal cases as an explanation for aberrant behavior. A good deal of research is being done by Hilgard (1977) and by John and Helen Watkins (1979a, 1979b) in this area of divided consciousness.

The interested reader should examine the literature cited in this account for a more complete account of multiple personalities and ego-state therapy.

IMPASSE/PRIORITY THERAPY

Précis

The client who starts in impasse/priority therapy will be entering a structured situation which has four parts. First, individual meetings are held with a therapist who will first operate to obtain a diagnosis and come to a decision about an overall treatment plan. Next, the client participates in an intensive marathon which will run for five consecutive days, eight hours a day with about 20 people. The third stage will run over 40 sessions, take a year and is called *the workshop.* There are six types of workshops, for example, one for married couples and another for teenagers, and so on. Every second week, all current workshop members attend a five-hour session and every other week, the various members will be at each other's homes—so there are 20 large group five-hour meetings and 20 smaller group meetings, alternating. The final stage is called advanced study and community work. Now, the members are expected to begin to study psychology in greater depth and to get involved in doing community work.

This method is included for several reasons in this book: first, it is a method developed in Israel and to my knowledge only used there even though its developer, Nira Kefir, an Israeli psychologist, has presented a number of workshops, primarily in the Washington, D.C., area. Second, it is the most complex and long-lasting of any therapy that I know with its different stages and preplanned elements. Third, it uses an interesting development from the client being with a single therapist, moving through an intensive marathon and then to two different kinds of group meetings, and finally evolves into a process in which the person becomes increasingly socially oriented.

Theory

Kefir's theory has ethical-social implications. She illustrates her theory with concentric circles, in the manner of a target. These are called circles of belong-ing. The person who is maladjusted is within the smallest circle, bound up with self, disregarding, to some extent, others. The next larger circle would include concern for family members. Each circle expands the relationship with a larger number of people. The last circle would in theory encompass all people on earth. A person who has love and concern for all is the essence of the ultimately perfect person—and Kefir's system is intended to help the individual move out from the small circle to a larger one.

What keeps people from moving outward are *impasses* that result from negative learning: fears established early in life. To avoid impasses, people develop patterns of behavior which Kefir calls priorities. She classifies all people in terms of four major priorities or personality clusters. The impasses are fear of: (1) appearing ridiculous, (2) being insignificant, (3) being rejected, and (4) having stress. The concomitant priorities or personality correlates are: (1) controller (to avoid ridicule), (2) superior (to avoid being insignificant), (3) pleaser (to avoid being rejected), and (4) avoider (to avoid tension).

In the first stage, the therapist seeks to discover the person's priority, and to clarify it, and throughout the therapy, the client is made aware of the impasses and priorities and steps taken to give the client an opportunity to make fundamental changes which occur concomitantly with the broadening of the circles of belongingness.

Therapy

This kind of therapy depends strongly on the concept that people can improve themselves and others. The therapist is a diagnostician and also an arranger. Interpretation, advice, secrecy, and depth discussions are avoided, or at least not emphasized. Through interaction with others and with periodic evaluations of one's life-style in terms of impasses and priorities, one acquires a bigger picture of life and of others and develops a greater interest and concern for others.

Summary

Impasse/priority therapy has only had one publication thus far (Kefir, 1981) but is likely to have far-reaching implications as a relatively efficient type of therapy which should also be relatively inexpensive. Its structured stages leading to the person becoming a helper of others in social interest work or in going into in-depth study of psychology and allied areas is something brilliantly different from other systems of psychotherapy. It appears from this point of view ideal for the lonely, the discouraged, the fearful.

MORITA PSYCHOTHERAPY

Précis

Over the centuries it has appeared to many people that troubled people simply need rest—to "get away from it all"—a change of environment, relief from stress, and indeed this is what many people do. Generally, such behavior is called taking a vacation.

Historically, in the treatment of nervous and mental diseases, one went to a healing spa. One such spa existed in Epidaurus, Greece, for well over 1,000 years. People went there to drink the waters, to rest, to be massaged, to lie in the sun, to listen to music—changing from one's normal life of tension to one of relaxation. In Europe many physicians recommend spas for a variety of human problems, physical and mental.

An American physician and author, S. Wier Mitchell (1829-1914), developed a procedure for so-called nervous patients which included complete and absolute bed rest. The patient was to do practically nothing in this mode of treatment but to stay in bed. Essentially the same concept was developed by a Japanese psychiatrist, Kengi Morita, known as Morita therapy.

Theory

The theory of Morita therapy is that people with emotional problems are exhausted and they need complete rest. Consequently, in terms of the three major modalities of psychotherapy behaviorally they are to remain in bed and do as little activity as possible; in terms of feelings they are to let them flow and not try to control them; relative to cognition they are to understand that all behavior is manageable and that one must learn to have trust in one's ability to cope. The excuse of "nervous exhaustion" is over-ambition and a selfish desire to be superior to others (Reynolds, 1976).

Therapy

Morita treatment is highly directive: the ideal therapist, operating in a warm and concerned manner, nevertheless controls the situation: he is a guide and a teacher and also a protective parent-surrogate.

The patient is put to bed for a week of complete rest: no TV, radio, or reading is permitted. Isolation is almost absolute. Three simple meals daily and going to the bathroom are all that are permitted that first week. The therapist visits daily to help direct the patient to better thinking, to learn to flow with his feelings, to learn to relax and to accept fewer responsibilities and to realize that one cannot control everything.

After this first week if the treatment is done in an institution, the patient is put to simple repetitive work such as weaving or knitting. There are daily interviews intended to generate greater self-recognition and a more philosophical attitude toward life. Readings may be assigned and other activities suggested depending on the judgment of the therapist.

Summary

This method, employed in Japan and developed by S. Morita, a psychiatrist, has been used with limited success in the United States, and in a sense is a good example of the statement that there is nothing new under the sun since variations of this procedure have been used for centuries in less formal manners. Morita takes the term *nervous exhaustion* almost literally, and calls first for complete bed rest and then guided discussions leading to greater self-awareness and philosophical acceptance.

This system is included here to show a method of psychotherapy compatible with Eastern and Western thinking which may appeal to some people due to its simplicity, common sense, and absence of complex theory. It can be considered a type of regressive treatment, with the patient being kept in a safe bed, and watched over carefully by a loving and powerful parent figure who will control the patient.

NEUROLINGUISTIC PSYCHOTHERAPY

A young college student has broken up with her boyfriend and believes she cannot find another. Her therapist asks if this was her first boyfriend. The answer is no. The therapist now asks her how she recovered from this first loss. The client searches her memory for the strategy that "worked" to achieve recovery in the past. The therapist notes that her client's eyes move from upper left to center left, then to lower right and then to lower left. While this is observed, the client is accessing the picture of remembered events.

When the therapist asks the client what she is saying to herself she replies, "It's OK. I will get over it. There will be someone else." The therapist asks her to look down to the lower right and check on her feelings as she makes that statement. She now reports feeling calmer and more sure of herself. The therapist now asks her to imagine a movie with sound effects of the recent loss of her boyfriend, to describe her feelings, and then directs her to look down to the left. Together they decide on an appropriate self-message for the situation.

In summarizing the session the therapist teaches this woman the steps of her own successful coping strategies, encouraging her to follow this procedure whenever needed, adding that she should be careful not to give herself negative messages, but instead should have positive auditory self-messages.

Theory

Neurolinguistic psychotherapy is based on cognitive-behavioral theories of personality and studies of linguistics.

Neurolinguistics is a theory of the relationship between the brain and language, concerned with the processing of information through the senses, proceeding through the neurons and neural pathways of the brain, expressed in language and behavior. Basic research in brain functioning related to neurolinguistic psychotherapy are brain hemisphere specializations relating to analytic and synthetic functions, including contralateral eye movements that reflect activation of the right or left hemispheres of the brain, the processing of internal and external cues, visual and auditory experiences of dissociation, and the use of sensory words as language representations of primary sensory information.

These basic relationships are tailored in therapy for each individual's presenting problems for maximum use of total resources available to the individual for accessing problem solutions.

Therapy

The therapist initially attempts to determine the information processing strategies that have worked for the client in the past. The Sensory Modality Checklist (Haynie, 1982) is a quick and general assessment of an individual's preferred sensory modality for learning and self-expression.

The therapist will then teach the client to increase and broaden her sensory awareness for optimal balance of understanding of self as well as appropriate behavior to overcome deficits. Deficits may include being unable to visualize, insensitivity to spoken words, inappropriately strong emotional reactions to stimuli, or self-defeating messages to one's inner self. The key question asked of the client is *How?*: "How do you know when to feel angry? How do you solve this kind of problem? How do you make right choices for yourself?" This model depends on conceptions of visual, auditory, and kinesthetic modalities of processing of information (Dilts, Grinder, Bandler, Cameron-Bandler & DeLozier, 1980).

Summary

The basic concept of neurolinguistic psychotherapy is that even though all humans are endowed with essentially equivalent sensory organs and brain structures, nevertheless no two humans understand a particular event in the same way. Each individual learns to depend primarily on only one sensory system to perceive and understand the world. This idiosyncratic characteristic of humans generates patterns that differ between individuals. The therapist is interested in discovering the client's preferred sensory system and related learning strategy as the primary tool for effective therapeutic improvement and then instructing the client in how to use these modalities for effective functioning.

PRIMAL THERAPY

Précis

Imagine being in a large soundproofed room in which several dozen people are on the floor, some of them screaming in apparent agony. The therapist comes over to one, holds the person and encourages him to scream even louder. The client goes into convulsions and in a rage pounds the floor, writhing and shouting imprecations. Meanwhile others who have been in apparent states of inaction start off screaming and pounding also, with the therapist urging them on to give everything in a paroxysm of energy.

This sort of behavior which can occur occasionally in other methods of psychotherapy, especially psychodrama, is the very essence of primal therapy.

Theory

Primal therapy has a number of basic theoretical assumptions, most of them generated by Arthur Janov (1970), who originally developed this procedure, to which a number of others have added contributions. According to Schaef, Kirkman and Ungashick (1981), there are 11 basic assumptions of primal therapy, four of which will be reported here.

Experiences are stored in the organism from conception on.

Early traumatic experiences have profound effects and are blocked from awareness.

Fragments of these experiences persist and can be retrieved and can be jettisoned.

The experiencing and integrating of these blocked feelings is of therapeutic benefit.

Therapy

This system of psychotherapy has a variety of methodologies all leading to the release of feelings in a dramatic manner. Generally, the whole program will take several weeks of intensive treatment, and due to the dramatic nature of the process, careful screening is done ordinarily to make certain that the participants can stand the strain of the procedures and to determine whether the individuals involved will be likely to benefit from this particular procedure.

The therapy will consist of diagnostic sessions, individual interviews, and group sessions. The group sessions ordinarily occur in a padded room, with no furniture or other means of getting hurt. The therapist(s) attempt to get the participants to open up, reporting all feelings, including guilts, hates, and other emotionally laden elements, attempting to lead to a cathartic expression.

Summary

During the course of the usual verbal interactive psychotherapies, people will occasionally cry or express verbal violence. The typical therapist will attempt to calm the client, or reason with the troubled person. In some modes of therapy, especially psychodrama, the person may go into fits of rage and anger. This "blowing off of steam" is seen as cathartic. In primal therapy the intent of the therapist is to get the person to be cleared of repressed angers and other stored-up emotions through generating feelings of safety and trust so that one will be free to express all feelings verbally and behaviorally.

A very similar type of situation is found in aqua-energetics (Bindrim, 1981) in which clients are induced to go into temper tantrum-type rages in a pool, while being held by the therapist and others.

The reasons for the apparent value of primary therapy are not too clear: however, as in the case of psychodrama and aqua-energetics, there is a total participation of the three modalities of therapy: cognitive (through expressing verbally and being aware of past hurts), emotional (through allowing one's feelings to surface), and behavioral (through physical efforts).

This system of therapy is complex and calls for very careful selection of clients who should be under close supervision by highly qualified personnel.

PROVOCATIVE PSYCHOTHERAPY

Précis

What would you as a client think were a therapist to say to you:

... you talk like a slut; you dress like a slut; you walk like a slut and you look like a slut ...

or suppose you heard a bit of conversation between a patient and the therapist that went like this:

I am going to teach you how to be joyfully sadistic.

What's that?

How to inflict pain on others and get to love it.

These are quotes from a book by Farrelly & Brandsma (1974) relative to a system of psychotherapy known as provocative psychotherapy, a method which uses a variety of procedures including exaggerations, criticisms, insults, and other "shock tactics" in an effort to change the thinking, feeling, and behavior of clients. This method of psychotherapy depends on humor as the major therapeutic modality, attempting to make the client see the ridiculousness of his thinking and acting, to "spit in his soup" as an Adlerian might say, so that once the client sees the stupidity of his thinking he will no longer be able to enjoy the nonsensical behavior of the past.

Theory

There are 10 assumptions relative to the theory of provocative therapy. I restate them in an altered and shortened form from Farrelly & Matthews (1981, pp. 682, 683):

1. People change in response to a challenge.
2. They can change if they want to.
3. They have more potential for change than generally assumed.
4. Psychological fragility of clients is generally overrated.
5. All maladaptive attitudes and behavior can be drastically altered.
6. Current experiences are as important as childhood ones.
7. A client's interaction with the therapist reveals his dynamics.
8. People are relatively easy to understand.

9. Judicious expressions of "therapeutic hate and joyful sadism" can be paradoxically beneficial.
10. Nonverbal messages are more important than verbal ones; how something is said is more important than what is said.

There are also two hypotheses:

1. If a client is provoked by a therapist, the client will move in a direction opposite to the therapist's definition of the client.
2. If a client is urged (humorously) to continue in self-defeating behavior, the client will instead engage in self- and other-enhancing behavior.

Therapy

What distinguishes this form of psychotherapy from other verbal therapies is the use of confrontation, the eschewing of "professionalism" and the use of mordant humor with the intention of getting down quickly to the heart of the problem. The client is provoked by the therapist: (*a*) to affirm his self-worth (often in defense against the therapist's "attacks"), (*b*) to assert himself, (*c*) to defend himself, (*d*) to test reality in terms of the therapist's challenges, and (*e*) to take chances in the real world.

In short, the therapist operates in ways to provoke the client to do what is necessary to change self-defeating behavior and rather than using a process of acceptance uses instead a rejection of the client's position, constantly challenging, demanding, criticizing, and ridiculing the client. So, when the therapist says, after sighing, "Give me three good reasons, Sweetheart, why anyone would want to go out with you?" (Farrelly & Matthews, 1981, p. 686) the intent is to help by mobilizing the client's defenses through this sarcasm.

Summary

Provocative psychotherapy depends strongly on the concept of reactance theory (Brehm & Brehm, 1981) and on the theory of paradoxical intention (Frankl, 1965). It is a procedure that apparently deviates from the usual friendly and accepting role expected of therapists and attempts to deal directly and firmly with clients. In addition, provocative psychotherapy reflects the influence of Albert Ellis's rational-emotive therapy.

PSYCHOIMAGINATION THERAPY

Précis

Many methods of psychotherapy employ visualization of images as the major method of personality change including: autogenic training (Luthe, 1969); cognitive behavior therapy (Meichenbaum, 1977); covert conditioning (Cautela, 1981); eidetic psychotherapy (Ahsen, 1965), implosive therapy (Stampfl & Levis, 1967); psychoimagination therapy (Shorr, 1974); radix neo-Reichian therapy (Kelley, 1974); reciprocal inhibition (Wolpe, 1958); and relaxation therapy (Jacobson, 1938).

Rather than select one of these for special attention, an attempt will be made to give the essence of the general procedure. The various methods differ somewhat in their theories and procedures, but they have more commonalities than differences.

Theory

Essentially, these methods are concerned with covert and overt behavior, or, using more common terminology, thinking and action. The two are considered equivalent states, balanced and interactive. Changing one can affect the other.

It is the intent of the therapist to attempt to change overt behavior through changing covert behavior. This means usually attempting to get the person who is being treated to visualize something in a direction believed to generate overt behavioral changes. The visualization can be a rehearsal, as in planning some overt behavior; or it can be a retrospective analysis, such as reevaluating some prior behavior; or it can be a kind of covert conditioning, associating two or more conditions, and so on.

Therapy

A client is grossly overweight and has tried "everything" to reduce weight, but nothing works. He now comes to a therapist who uses psychoimagination. The therapist might now ask the client to relax and to visualize the following:

You will start a regimen designed to help you lose weight. You step on the scale and you note that you weigh 240 pounds, when you know you should weigh 150 pounds. You are therefore 90 pounds overweight. Imagine being on a scale with a huge dial, and as you step on it, the needle begins to move up and around, going past 100, past 125, past 150 where you should be and keeps on moving and moving and moving until it stops at 240 pounds. You step off, discouraged.

It is now one year later. You again step on the scale and now you weigh only 150 pounds. You have done it, you have lost 90 pounds in one year through self-control. You look in a mirror, and you are slim and fit. You did it on your own: no pills, no inducements, no artificial aids. All on your own.

Still another type of visualization is a kind of counterconditioning, getting the person to avoid certain behaviors. In the implosive technique, the therapist may continue such visualizations for several hours. For example, if a client abuses chocolates, the visualization might go as follows:

Imagine a garbage can. It is filled with vomit and feces. Someone reaches in and pulls out a chocolate bar, and it is covered with horrid matter. This person brings the chocolate towards you and forces it in your mouth. You want to gag and throw up, but you are forced to swallow, and then another piece is pulled out of the garbage can and . . .

Summary

Essentially, the use of imagination and of visualization may be considered the obverse of body therapy: by generating images which may relate to successful behavior or by attempting to condition the individual through associating either pleasant or unpleasant imaginings, behavior is changed.

There appears to be considerable evidence that this general procedure of psychoimagination therapy can be quite effective in dealing with a variety of behavioral changes (Brunn & Hedberg, 1974; Mahoney, 1974; Wolpe, 1958).

PSYCHODRAMA

Précis

Psychodrama consists of a variety of action techniques of the action-fantasy type on which a person acts out a situation with the assistance of others who play roles also. During the process of the action, the client-patient is simultaneously thinking, feeling and acting. Later, through discussions, the former actor gains new understanding, new feelings and new skills.

A person from a group volunteers to be the client and comes on the psychodrama "stage," which may be the center of a circle. The therapist begins questioning the client, and learns that she and her husband are having problems. He asks for a recent problem and she tells him that

only that day her husband informed her that he had made arrangements for the car to be serviced and so she could not have it. She reports that her reaction to this news for some unknown-to-her reason made him angry.

The therapist asks for someone in the audience to play the role of her husband. The therapist asks where the incident occurred, the kind of car, why she needed the car, how she reacted, what kind of a person the husband was, and what bothered her most—and to this last question she said how he turned his back and went away from her angry—something she just couldn't understand.

The volunteer who is to play the "husband" is asked if he understands the situation, and he replies affirmatively. The wife is asked to react precisely as she did in the morning and so the situation unfolds. When she is told the car is not available, she has the equivalent of a temper tantrum, screams, stamps her foot in great anger—and the "husband" moves away from her.

It is obvious to all why the real husband reacted as he did but she has no insight at all about the violence of her behavior. Another woman in the group volunteers to reenact the wife's behavior. After seeing herself as if in a mirror the wife cannot believe that she acted in such a manner—but everyone in the audience assures her that this was a rather exact duplicate of her behavior.

The therapist now interviews her and asks her if things went that way, and she replies in the affirmative, and when asked if she can guess why he walked away in anger she says she has no idea.

The same situation is replayed with her in the audience. The same man plays the role of husband. The actress imitating the client goes through the same scene and acts just as the client did.

The client returns to the stage and on being questioned denies acting the same as the person who substituted for her. The therapist now asks the group to react to everything and there is universal agreement that she had a miniature temper tantrum and that the actress who imitated her did a good job.

Theory

Essentially the theory of psychodrama is an attempt to get a person to act in an interactive situation so that the person is simultaneously thinking, feeling, and acting in a spontaneous manner for the purpose of learning more about himself or herself either through self-perception of personal behavior or through (as in the example just given) the comments and observations of others. (Corsini, 1966)

Therapy

The varieties of psychodrama are considerable, but essentially the procedures are simple: the therapist deals ordinarily with one person, called the hero and gets that person to interact with a number of others called assistants, who play various roles in that person's "social atom." In the incident described, the woman first participated in a repetition of an earlier situation which she did in a realistic manner, and then she observed someone else acting in her place. When the group insisted that the person who imitated her did so accurately, she then had an opportunity for insight about her behavior at that time and possibly in general.

Summary

Psychodrama is essentially a technique, and as such can be used by therapists of any persuasion. Its theory is quite limited.

It is an extremely powerful technique, which only few people can handle well. Every therapist should attempt to gain proficiency in this procedure which has considerable generality. (Some suggested readings are Blatner, 1973; Corsini, 1966; Fine, 1979; Moreno, 1946; Starr, 1977.)

STRATEGIC THERAPY

Précis

Let us suppose that you were seated next to the driver of an old-fashioned stagecoach pulled by six huge horses, each weighing at least a ton. The horses suddenly become frightened and begin galloping madly straight ahead, heading directly towards a canyon. You are positive that they cannot be stopped and you are about to jump off, when the driver, to your surprise, picks up his whip and begins lashing the horses, yelling at them to go faster.

If you can understand the reason for the driver's 'paradoxical' behavior (this is a real example of how these stagecoach drivers acted in such emergencies) you will be able to understand the heart of strategic therapy (also known as Systems Therapy and Brief Therapy). Note that the driver was not concerned with the causation of the behavior. (A systems therapist does not care about origins of problems.) Note also that he did not try what common sense might dictate (pull on the reins and yell "Whoa") but instead did what appeared to be exactly the wrong thing: he shouted at them to go even faster and whipped them to greater speed. (Systems therapists generally operate in terms of paradoxical behaviors.)

Now, why this behavior? The stage driver would probably tell you that that was the way to operate but he may have no understanding of why this is the thing to do. We can explain the procedure by saying that the horses were in a panic and any attempts to control them by going counter to their intention to run as fast as they could would be useless. What one had to do was to go along with them—or appear to go along. So, when the driver beat the horses and urged them to go even faster, he was on their side, and they (in a real sense) listened to him, and then once he had them doing what he (and they wanted) then he could disclose his real intention—which was to get them to stop. And now, having obeyed him in running they were in a mood to obey him in stopping.

Systems therapists use this almost exact procedure in what they call the Leaning Tower of Pisa technique, advising exactly the opposite to a logical process. For example, I personally have often advised parents who worry about their children not getting enough sleep, because they are disinterested in sleeping, to keep them up night after night hours after their bedtime, and then waking them up at the usual hour in the morning. Within a week, to the parents' surprise, children now want to go to bed on time.

Also, to continue the analogy, the problem was real and immediate. The person mostly concerned was the stage driver who had a clear-cut objective: to save his own life and that of his passengers as well as the horses. He then applied his remedy which was opposed to common sense. As a result he succeeded in his goals while a less experienced driver who would have used common sense would have sent everything and everyone over the cliff to death and destruction.

Theory

In the theory of systems therapy, still in the process of development, there are a number of basic principles. Below are some of them:

1. Concern is with the interrelationships between the various individuals in a social system, such as a 'family' rather than with any individual identified as the "problem" in the system.

2. There is no concern with history or causation. Systems therapy is concerned with here-and-now and is ahistorical.

3. Maladjustment is seen as a dynamic process, maintained by the reinforcing behavior of people within the system to keep the maladjusted behavior from changing. It is accepted that people within the system will resist change.

4. The treatment procedure generally has commonsense and paradoxical elements. For example, as a commonsense element, the therapist seeks the one person in the system most likely to follow orders, and will work with that one person. As a paradoxical element, a member of the system may be asked to deliberately try to make the situation worse—as evidence that change can occur. Another example would be for the therapist to suggest to make changes slowly of what may appear to be relatively unimportant elements.

5. The treatment process generally involves careful examination of the whole system (such as the family relationships), determining a clear-cut goal and making specific suggestions with the entire therapy to take place within a relatively brief period, usually from five to ten sessions.

Therapy

The general treatment procedure, after the usual investigation, calls for *reframing* the problem. This refers to getting one or more of the people in the system to see the problem in a different way. For example, if a parent is told that punishing a child is actually helping the child to continue in his bad behavior, since this will justify the child misbehaving, the parent sees that present attempts at correction are doing exactly the opposite of what is intended, and so 'sees' the situation differently.

A second important element is the *prescription*. For example, consider the case of a family in which a child was overweight. The parents had literally put locks on food cabinets and the refrigerator and had asked friends and neighbors to not give the child food (none of which helped for the child then stole food from grocery stores and was found rummaging in garbage cans, etc.). The parents were told to buy chocolates and to ask, and even try to force, the child to eat chocolates—a procedure which the parents thought 'insane' at the time, but which demonstrated to them clearly the folly of their previous position, for then the child refused to eat the candy.

In systems therapy, termination takes place as soon as possible when there is evidence of a small but durable change and the 'patient' believes that he or she can continue. The word 'patient' is put in quotes to indicate that the so-called 'identified patient' (the one with the evident problem) is usually not the one that the system therapist works with. Indeed, that person may not even know that the true patient (who may be the parent) has gone to therapy.

Summary

Systems therapy is an uncommonsense method of operating which has no concern for history, diagnoses, causation, etc., but sees maladjustment as a dynamic process in which the 'identified patient' may be the victim of the thinking and acting of others, who in an attempt to improve things may actually be the cause. The treatment process calls for a clarification of the dynamics of behavior, locating someone who really wants to see a change, and giving that person a new view of the problem (*reframing*) and suggestions, usually paradoxical in nature (*prescriptions*) for changing, with injunctions to 'go slow' and to try to make 'least important changes' with credit being given to the 'patient' and discontinuing the therapy as soon as it seems that the proper direction will continue.

Major references are Bateson, Jackson, Haley and Weakland (1956), Haley (1963), and Watzlawick, Weakland and Fisch (1974).

TWENTY-FOUR HOUR THERAPY

Précis

This particular method calls for the therapist to have complete control of a client 24 hours a day. A team of people, under the direction of the therapist, maintains surveillance over the patient, controlling his or her physical, social, financial, and sexual environments. The purpose of this highly radical procedure is to confront patients with reality leading them to develop self-sufficiency and control over their lives. Among those who have publicly acknowledged the value of this procedure are a number of well-known actors and other entertainers (Landy & Dahlke, 1981).

Theory

The central concept in the use of twenty-four hour therapy is the notion of *adequacy*. This is more psychological than actual, more personal than social. For example, an individual may be viewed by others in terms of the impression that he makes as quite adequate. One's history may also show that one is adequate. However, these are outside views: the person may perceive himself or herself inadequate despite all evidence to the contrary. Many reported instances of people going deeply into alcoholism, drug abuse, and suicide are linked to these feelings of inadequacy or of inferiority.

An important notion in twenty-four hour therapy is the idea that people who may appear to some as inadequate may feel adequate while some quite adequate people (in the eyes of others) may feel inadequate. And some, of course, are inadequate both from an external and an internal point of view.

Let us consider the situation from the point of view only of a person who is truly (or has been) adequate but who believes himself or herself so inadequate that he will go to bed and refuse to leave—perhaps even for months or years. How can such a person be treated with this stubborn insistence on inadequacy, with a refusal to even get out of bed?

Therapy

The therapy begins with getting legal and moral control over the client; approval of the use of the 24-hour technique by family members, a lawyer, a physician, and any others who may in any way be considered within the client's social atom. An individually designed program is orchestrated by the therapist which may last from as short as one week to one year, intended to achieve eight stages: (1) initiation, (2) discovery, (3) inadequacy, (4) preadequacy, (5) self-adequacy, (6) self-functioning, (7) adequacy, and (8) termination.

Normally, the client is treated in his normal environment, but at times the person may be moved out of the environment. His home may be sold by the therapist. He may have a good deal of money but may not be allowed any money at all, since the therapist has control. The client is accompanied 24 hours a day by the therapist's associates, who report to him by telephone what is going on, and who follow directions. In the case of Robert (Landy & Dahlke, 1981), during phase 3 (inadequacy) at one point because 27-year-old Robert did not get a job, he was evicted from his apartment and lost his car. Landy placed Robert in a board and care home, and after a while he was given a job at $5 a day. Robert was the son of a wealthy man who had been maintained by his father on an allowance of $35,000 a year prior to going into 24-hour therapy. He had already been divorced twice, and had in a variety of ways shown his inadequacy.

Summary

Twenty-four hour therapy is an extreme example of a paradoxical treatment: attempting to help a person to become adequate through taking complete charge of the person. Essentially, it is an example of natural and logical consequences and of re-parenting. Landy, who has developed this system of therapy, believes that most traditional therapies which have the client seeing the therapist for one out of the 168 hours in a week are ineffective for many cases, and heroic methods are called in some cases.

Naturally, this method has all kinds of legal-ethical implications. It is indeed strong medicine, and seems called for when all other methods either have not worked or cannot work for people who really have the potential for adequacy. We can see this as a logical extension of reality therapy, and an important development in psychotherapeutic theory and practice.

Z-PROCESS ATTACHMENT THERAPY

Précis

The client comes into a room, and seated at two facing benches are eight people, four on a side. The client is induced to lie down on his or her back on the laps of the eight people who now hold the client firmly by the arms, legs, and body. The person at the top left is the therapist, who wraps his left arm around the client's head, and during the interview may tickle the patient's rib cage in an attempt to infuriate the client so that the client will go into a rage. Meanwhile, the client is helpless to move being held down firmly by the therapist and the other seven people, who usually are friends and family members.

This bizarre procedure represents a real innovation in psychotherapy and may be one of the most important breakthroughs in the treatment of autistic children and adult schizophrenics. Developed by Robert W. Zaslow, a psychologist in California, it is currently being tested with a variety of people with serious attachment problems.

Theory

Autistic children and schizophrenic adults have been a great puzzle in terms of both etiology and treatment. Throughout the history of psychiatry, a considerable number of theories have been suggested and a wide variety of treatments for these conditions have been employed. The earliest theory was that such individuals were possessed by the devil and accordingly the treatment was to torture the

person to drive out the devil, and if this failed, to burn the person alive. A slightly more humane early method of treatment was to frighten these people into normality. At one time schizophrenics were literally lowered into a snake pit for this purpose. Another mode of treatment has been to mistreat the insane by such techniques as spraying them with high-powered hoses of cold water. Another method has been to give them electric shocks. Still another method has been to give them injections of substances that would be painful or frightening such as metrazol or insulin. Still another mode of treatment has been to put a probe into the brain to destroy part of it, the method of lobotomy. Most of these modes had no logical theory except perhaps the notion that such people, if faced with real pain or fright, might improve. Still another mode of treatment, which also has not had much success, has been to talk with patients in the hope that they would change their mind about being insane. This was the technique used by Paul Dubois who called his system of therapy medical moralizations. A more recent procedure has been to treat these schizophrenics with various drugs with considerable success in some cases.

However, no purely psychological method has worked well. Zaslow's theory can be visualized somewhat as follows: imagine a triangle with the top corner representing psychological normality. The lower left-hand corner represents aggressiveness—hostility—anger. The lower right-hand corner represents apathy—rejection—escape—avoidance. Autistics and schizophrenics are in the right-hand corner, avoiding people, ignoring them, having no reality orientation, separated. The problem is to get them up from the right-hand corner to the top corner. We may conceive attempts at kind treatment as moving symbolically along the right edge of the triangle—which has not worked well. We may conceive as attempts at harsh treatment as moving them toward the left corner of aggressiveness—which has not worked well either. Zaslow's genius has been to combine both at the same time—to show love and concern (and this is why the person is held down by people who care and want to help) and to enrage the person (which is why the person is induced to get into a state of rage). Now, this apparently brutal procedure is under the control of the client who will find that if he or she cooperates by acting normal, such as replying to questions, release will follow.

The basic theory may be conceived as follows: the schizophrenic rejects everything, and is firmly committed to a course of avoidance. Through this holding down procedure, rage is engendered, and in the course of the rage, the person finally looks the therapist in the eye with pure anger, knowing that the therapist is the cause of the restrictions. *This is a contact!* With the contact made, a relationship can begin. And now, the normal process of psychotherapy can proceed.

Therapy

An autistic child is observed in his normal unusual behavior: he runs about aimlessly, does not respond to questions, cries without reason, and shows other evidence of childhood schizophrenia. Such a child is put on the therapist's lap, and the child tries to squirm out. The therapist wraps his arms and legs about the child who goes into a panic state and tries to escape. The therapist states to the child that he will only let the child go if the child will tell his name. The child (who has never answered this question to anyone) eventually gives up his struggles,

looks the therapist in the eye and gives his name. He is then released and shows immediate desired alteration of behavior.

Follow up sessions continue with the holding becoming less frequent and moving to discussions.

Summary

Z-process attachment therapy is something new under the sun, based on a novel theory and an unusual procedure. This account is very skimpy and the reader is advised to read Zaslow's own accounts of this interesting and potentially valuable system of psychotherapy (Zaslow, 1970, 1981; Zaslow & Menta, 1976, 1977).

REFERENCES

Ahsen, A. *Eidetic psychotherapy: A short introduction.* Lahore, Pakistan: Nai Mat Booat, 1965.

Bateson, G., Jackson, D., Haley, J., & Weakland, J. Toward a theory of schizophrenia. *Behavioral Science,* 1956, *1,* 251-264.

Blatner, H. *Acting in: Practical applications of psychodramatic methods.* New York: Springer, 1973.

Brehm, S. S., & Brehm, J. W. *Psychological reactance: A theory of freedom and control.* New York: Academic Press, 1981.

Brunn, A. C., & Hedberg, A. G. Covert positive reinforcement as a treatment procedure for obesity. *Journal of Consulting Psychology,* 1974, *2,* 117-119.

Cautela, J. R. Covert conditioning. In R. J. Corsini (Ed.), *Handbook of innovative psychotherapies.* New York: Wiley, 1981.

Corsini, R. J. *Roleplaying in psychotherapy.* New York: Free Press, 1966.

Corsini, R. J. (Ed.), *Handbook of innovative psychotherapies.* New York: Wiley, 1981.

Corsini, R. J. (Ed.), *Encyclopedia of psychology.* New York: Wiley, 1984.

Dilts, R. B., Grinder, J., Bandler, R., Cameron-Bandler, L., & DeLozier, J. *Neurolinguistic programming. I.* Cupertino, Calif.: Meta Publications, 1980.

Duggan, D. Dance therapy. In R. J. Corsini (Ed.), *Handbook of innovative psychotherapies.*

New York: Wiley, 1981.

Farrelly, F., & Brandsma, J. *Provocative therapy*. Cupertino, Calif.: Meta Publications, 1974.

Farrelly, F., & Matthews, S. Provocative therapy. In R. J. Corsini (Ed.), *Handbook of innovative psychotherapies*. New York: Wiley, 1981.

Fine, L. Psychodrama. In R. J. Corsini (Ed.), *Current psychotherapies, 2nd ed.* Itasca, Ill.: F. E. Peacock Publishers, Inc., 1979.

Frankl, V. *Doctor and the soul*. New York: Knopf, 1965.

Green, B. Body therapies. In R. J. Corsini (Ed.), *Handbook of innovative psychotherapies*. New York: Wiley, 1981.

Haley, J. *Strategies of psychotherapy*. New York: Grune & Stratton, 1963.

Haynie, N. Sensory modality checklist. In G. M. Gazda, W. Childers, and R. Walters (Eds.), *Interpersonal communication: A handbook for health professionals*. Rockville, Md.: Aspen Publications, 1982.

Hilgard, E. R. *Divided consciousness*. New York: Wiley, 1977.

Jacobson, E. *Progressive relaxation*. Chicago: University of Chicago Press, 1938.

Janov, A. *The primal scream*. New York: Vintage Books, 1970.

Kefir, N. Impasse/priority therapy. In R. J. Corsini (Ed.), *Handbook of innovative psychotherapies*. New York: Wiley, 1981.

Kelley, C. R. *Education in feeling and purpose*. Ojai, Calif.: The Radix Institute, 1974.

Landy, E. E., & Dahlke, A. E. Twenty-four hour therapy. In R. J. Corsini (Ed.), *Handbook of innovative psychotherapies*. New York: Wiley, 1981.

Luthe, W. *Autogenic therapy*. New York: Grune & Stratton, 1969.

Mahoney, M. J. *Cognition and behavior modification*. Morristown, N.J.: General Learning Press, 1974.

Meichenbaum, D. *Cognitive behavior modification*. Morristown, N.J.: General Learning Press, 1974.

Meichenbaum, D. *Cognitive-behavior modification: An integrative approach*. New York: Plenum, 1977.

Moreno, J. L. *Psychodrama: Volume 1.* New York: Beacon House, 1946.

Painter, G., & Vernon, S. Primary relationship therapy. In R. J. Corsini (Ed.),

Handbook of innovative psychotherapies. New York: Wiley, 1981.

Pederson, P. B. Asian personality theory. In R. J. Corsini & A. J. Marsella (Eds.), *Personality theories, research, & assessment*. Itasca, Ill.: F. E. Peacock, 1983.

Prince, M. *The disassociation of a personality*. New York: Longmans-Green, 1906.

Reynolds, D. K. *Morita therapy*. Berkeley, Calif.: University of California Press, 1976.

Schaef, R. F. A., Kirkman, D. O., & Ungashick, B. Primal therapy. In R. J. Corsini (Ed.), *Handbook of innovative psychotherapies*. New York: Wiley, 1981.

Schiff, J. L. *All my children*. New York: Evans, 1970.

Shorr, J. E. *Psychotherapy through imagery*. New York: Intercontinental Medical Book Corp., 1974.

Stampfl, T. G., & Levis, D. J. Essentials of implosive therapy: A learning theory based on psychodynamic behavioral therapy. *Journal of Abnormal Psychology*, 1967, *23*, 375-412.

Starr, A. *Psychodrama: Rehearsal for living*. Chicago: Nelson-Hall, 1977.

Thigpen, C. H., & Cleckley, H. M. *Three faces of Eve*. New York: McGraw-Hill, 1957.

Watkins, H. H. Ego-state therapy. In J. G. Watkins (Ed.), *The therapeutic self.* New York: Human Sciences Press, 1978.

Watkins, J. G., & Watkins, H. H. Theory and practice of ego-state therapy. In H. Grayson (Ed.), *Short-term approaches to psychotherapy*. New York: Human Sciences Press, 1979. (a)

Watkins, J. G., & Watkins, H. H. Ego states and hidden observers. *Journal of Altered States of Consciousness*, 1979, *5*, 3-18. (b)

Watzlawick, P., Weakland, J., & Fisch, R. *Change: Principles of problem formation and problem resolution*. New York: Norton, 1974.

Wolpe, J. *Psychotherapy by reciprocal inhibition*. Stanford, Calif.: Stanford University Press, 1958.

Zaslow, R. W. *Resistances to growth and attachment*. San Jose, Calif.: San Jose State University Press, 1970.

Zaslow, R. W. Z-process attachment therapy. In R. J. Corsini (Ed.), *Handbook of innovative psychotherapies*. New York: Wiley, 1981.

Glossary*

Abreaction (PA). The reliving of painful emotional experiences in psychotherapy, usually involving conscious awareness of previously repressed material. See also *catharsis*.

Adapted child (TA). A personality ego-state that has two functions, either conforming or rebelling to what another person wants. One's *adapted child* is a highly complex ego-state and contains one's script.

Adult (TA). An ego state that is analytical, rational, and nonjudgmental. The objective part of the personality. The *adult* problem solves and obtains information.

Aggression (G). For Fritz Perls, aggression was the basic biological energy underlying personality (similar to Freud's use of the term *libido*).

Agoraphobia. An excessive fear of open spaces and/or leaving one's own home.

Aha! (G). Awareness of a situational Gestalt in which a number of disparate elements come together to form a meaningful whole; sudden insight into the solution to a problem or the structure of a situation.

Anal stage (PA). Freud's second phase of psychosexual development, extending roughly from 18 months to three years, in which most libidinal pleasure is derived from retaining and expelling feces.

Anima (J). The feminine component of the male personality.

Animus (J). The masculine component of the female personality.

*The following abbreviations are used: (PA) Psychoanalysis; (A) Adlerian psychotherapy; (J) Analytical psychotherapy; (PC) Person-centered therapy; (RET) Rational-emotive therapy; (BT) Behavior therapy; (G) Gestalt therapy; (R) Reality therapy; (E) Existential therapy; (TA) Transactional analysis; (MMT) Multimodal therapy; (FT) Family therapy.

Antisuggestion (A). See *paradoxical intention.*

Applied behavior analysis (BT). A form of behavior therapy, which is closely tied to Skinner's philosophy of radical behaviorism. Applied behavior analysis stresses observable behavior rather than private events and uses single-subject experimental design to determine the relationship between behavior and its antecedents and consequences.

Archetypes (J). Primordial images which serve as the building blocks of the *collective unconscious*. Examples include the Wise Old Man, the Earth Mother, the *Anima*, the *Animus*, and the *Shadow*.

Assertion training (BT). A treatment procedure designed to teach clients to openly and effectively express both positive and negative feelings.

Basic I.D. (MMT). An acronym which groups together the fundamental concerns of the multimodal therapist: *Behaviors, Affective* processes, *Sensations, Images, Cognitions, Interpersonal* relations, and *Drugs* (i.e., biological functions).

Basic mistakes (A). Myths used to organize and shape one's life. Examples include overgeneralizations, a desperate need for security, misperceptions of life's demands, denial of one's worth, and faulty values.

Bridging (MMT). A procedure in which the therapist deliberately tunes into the client's preferred modality before branching off into other dimensions that seem likely to be more productive.

Broad-spectrum behavior therapy (MMT). The treatment approach advocated by Arnold Lazarus, prior to development of multimodal therapy.

Catharsis (PA). The expression and discharge of repressed emotions. Sometimes used synonymously with *abreaction*.

Child (TA). A basic ego state which consists of feelings, impulses, and spontaneous acts. As a function of learning history, this ego state can take the form of the *adapted child* or the *natural child.*

Classical conditioning (BT). A form of learning in which existing responses are attached to new stimuli by pairing those stimuli with those that naturally elicit the response. Also referred to as *respondent conditioning.*

Cognitive behavior modification (BT). A recent extension of behavior therapy which treats thoughts and cognition as behaviors amendable to behavioral procedures. Cognitive behavior modification is perhaps most closely associated with the work of Aaron Beck, Albert Ellis, and Donald Meichenbaum.

Cognitive restructuring (BT & RET). An active attempt to alter maladaptive thought patterns and to replace them with more adaptive cognitions.

Collective unconscious (J). That part of unconscious material which is phylogenetically determined, in contrast to the *personal unconscious* which is determined by individual personal experience. The *collective unconscious* contains symbolic access to archetypal reality.

Confluence (G). A boundary disturbance in which the distinction between self and environment is lost. In *confluence,* one does not experience self as distinct and merges self into the beliefs, attitudes, and feelings of others.

Congruence (PC). Agreement between the feelings and attitudes a therapist is experiencing and his or her professional demeanor. One of the necessary conditions for therapeutic change.

Coping imagery (MMT). A technique which pairs relaxation with images of successful self-control in previously anxiety-eliciting situations.

Counterconditioning (BT). Replacing a particular behavior by conditioning a response antithetical to the maladaptive behavior.

Countertransference (PA). The activation of unconscious wishes and fantasies on the part of the therapist toward the patient; the tendency to respond to patients as though they were significant others in the life or history or fantasy of the therapist.

Critical parent (TA). An ego state which is critical and fault finding. The *critical parent* may also be assertive and self-sufficient. Contrast with *nurturing parent.*

Defense mechanisms (PA). Methods used by the ego to fight off instinctual outbursts of the *id* and *superego.* Examples include *repression, projection,* and *reaction formation.*

Deflection (G). A means of avoiding contact and awareness by failure to give or receive feelings directly. Vagueness, verbosity, and understatement are forms of deflection.

Dementia praecox. An antiquated term for schizophrenia.

Determinism (PA). The assumption that every mental event is causally tied to earlier psychological experience.

Dichotomy (G). A *split* in which a field is experienced as comprised of competing and unrelated forces which are not meaningfully integrated into a Gestalt.

Discriminative stimulus (BT). A stimulus or set of stimuli that signify that reinforcement will (or will not) occur.

Double bind (FT). A situation in which a person receives simultaneous contradictory requests or demands. Any action taken leads to at least partial failure. Gregory Bateson theorized that double binding played an important role in the etiology of schizophrenia.

Early recollections (A). Salient memories of single incidents from childhood used as a projective technique by Adlerian therapists.

Eclecticism. The practice of drawing from multiple and diverse sources in formulating client problems and devising treatment plans. Multimodal therapists are technical eclectics (e.g., they employ multiple methods without necessarily endorsing the theoretical positions from which they were derived).

Ego (PA). That part of the mind that mediates between external reality and inner wishes and impulses. The Ego is the executant for all the agencies of the mind.

Ego states (TA). There are three structural ego states which represent distinct and independent levels of psychological functioning. These ego states are the *Parent, Adult,* and *Child.* They are capitalized to distinguish them from parents, adults, and children.

Egogram (TA). A visual representation of

one's personality using a bargraph to display the amount of energy emanating from the five functional ego states: *Critical Parent, Nurturing Parent, Adult, Free Child,* and *Adapted Child.*

Eigenwelt (E). One level of the way each individual relates to the world. *Eigenwelt* literally means "own world" and refers to the way each of us relates to self.

Electra complex (PA). Erotic attraction of the female child for her father with accompanying hostility for her mother. The female equivalent of the *Oedipus complex.* In Greek mythology, Electra persuaded her brother to kill their mother to avenge their father's murder. The term is rarely used in contemporary psychoanalysis.

Empathic understanding (PC). The ability to appreciate a client's phenomenological position and to accompany the client as he or she progresses in therapy. One of the necessary conditions for therapeutic change.

Eros (PA). The life instinct, fueled by libidinal energy and opposed by *Thanatos,* the death instinct.

Existential neurosis (E). Feelings of emptiness, worthlessness, despair, and anxiety resulting from inauthenticity, abdication of responsibility, failure to make choices, and a lack of direction or purpose in life.

Existentialism (E). A philosophical movement associated with Soren Kierkegaard, Martin Heidegger, Jean-Paul Sartre, Karl Jaspers, Martin Buber, and others. Existentialists stress the importance of actual existence, the fact that existence precedes essence, one's responsibility for and determination of one's own psychological existence, the centrality of authenticity in human relations, the primacy of the here and now, and the use of people's actual experience in the search for knowledge.

Extinction (BT). In *classical conditioning* extinction refers to repeated presentation of the conditioned stimulus without the unconditioned stimulus, and the resulting gradual diminution of the conditioned response. In *operant conditioning* extinction occurs when reinforcement is withheld following performance of a previously reinforced response.

Family constellation (A). The number, sequencing, and characteristics of the members of a family. The *family constellation* is an important determinant of *lifestyle.*

Free association (PA). A basic technique of psychoanalysis in which patients are asked to report, without structure or censure, whatever thoughts come to mind.

Free child (TA). That part of the personality which is spontaneous, eager, and playful. People who possess too much *free child* lack self-control.

Games (TA). Stereotyped and predictable patterns of behavior based on transactions which are partially ulterior and which result in negative payoffs for the players. They have names like "Kick Me," "Rapo," and so on, and are classified as first, second, or third degree, depending on the seriousness of their consequences.

Gemeinschaftsgefühl (A). A combination of concern for others and appreciation of one's role in a larger social order; usually translated as *social interest.*

Generalization (BT). The occurrence of behavior in situations that resemble but are different from the stimulus environment in which the behavior was learned.

Genital stage (PA). The final stage of psychosexual development, usually attained in late adolescence, in which sexual gratification occurs through intercourse and is not limited to specific body areas.

Genogram (FT). A three-generation structural diagram of a family system.

Genuineness (PC). See *congruence.*

Hysteria (PA). An early term for conversion reaction, a disorder in which psychological disturbance takes a somatic form (e.g., paralysis in the absence of organic disturbance). Many of Freud's theories grew out of his experience in treating hysterical patients.

Id (PA). The sum total of biological instincts including sexual and aggressive impulses. At birth, the *id* represents the total personality.

Imagery reactor (MMT). An individual who responds to the environment predominately in terms of images, usually auditory or visual.

Inferiority complex (A). An exaggeration of feelings of inadequacy and insecurity resulting in defensiveness and neurotic behavior. It is usually, but not always, abnormal.

Latency stage (PA). A quiescent period of psychosexual development that follows the *phallic stage* and lasts till puberty.

Leaning Tower of Pisa approach (FT). A variation of paradoxical intention in which a therapist exacerbates a problem until it falls of its own weight and is thereby resolved.

Libido (PA). The basic driving force of personality in Freud's system. It includes sexual energy but is not restricted to it.

Life tasks (A). The basic challenges and obligations of life: society, work, and sex. The tasks of spiritual growth and self-identity are included by Rudolf Dreikurs and Harold Mosak.

Life-style (A). One's characteristic way of living and pursuing long-term goals.

Logotherapy (E). A therapeutic approach developed by Viktor Frankl emphasizing value and meaning as prerequisites for mental health and personal growth.

Marital schism (FT). A situation in a marriage which results in poor relationships and psychological separation usually as a result of the inability of one of the marriage partners to break a tie with the parental home.

Marital skew (FT). A marital relationship characterized by one spouse's excessive dominance.

Mitwelt (E). One way in which each individual relates to the world, socially and through being with others. The age we live in, our age, our own times, the present generation, our contemporaries.

Modality profile (MMT). A specific list of problems and proposed treatments across the client's *BASIC I.D.*

Multiple psychotherapy (A). A technique in which several therapists simultaneously treat a single patient.

Musturbation (RET). A term coined by Albert Ellis to characterize the behavior of clients who are absolutistic and inflexible in their thinking, maintaining that they *must* not fail, *must* be exceptional, *must* be successful, etc.

Natural child (TA). A form of the *child* ego state which is impulsive, spontaneous, and creative. Contrast with the *adapted child.*

Negative reinforcement (BT). Any behavior which increases the probability of a response by terminating or withdrawing an unpleasant stimulus. *Negative reinforcement* always increases the likelihood of the future occurrence of the behavior it follows.

Neurosis. A dated but common term which refers to a variety of relatively mild disorders in which the patient distorts (but does not deny) reality.

Nurturing parent (TA). A personality ego state that is warm, supportive, and caring. Contrast with the *critical parent.*

Oedipus complex (PA). Erotic attraction of the male child for his mother. Freud borrowed the term from the Greek myth of Oedipus, who unwittingly killed his father, king of Thebes, and married his mother, Jocasta. See also *Electra complex.*

Operant conditioning (BT). A type of learning in which responses are modified by their consequences. *Reinforcement* increases the likelihood of future occurrences of the reinforced response; *punishment* and *extinction* decrease the likelihood of future occurrences of the responses they follow.

Oral stage (PA). The earliest phase of psychosexual development, extending from birth to approximately 18 months, in which most libidinal gratification occurs through biting, sucking, and oral contact.

Organ inferiority (A). Perceived or actual congenital defects in organ systems which were believed by Adler to result in compensatory striving to overcome these deficits.

Paradoxical intention. A therapeutic strategy in which the client is instructed to engage in and magnify the very behaviors of concern. See also *antisuggestion.*

Persona (J). That presented aspect of self which mediates between the *unconscious* and external adaptive experience. A disguised or masked attitude useful in interacting with one's environment but frequently at variance with true identity. Carl Jung borrowed the term from the Latin word for the masks worn by actors of antiquity.

Personal unconscious (J). The surface layer of the *unconscious*, consisting largely of subliminal perceptions and repressed experiences. Contrast with the *collective unconscious.*

Phallic stage (PA). The third stage of psychosexual development in which libidinal gratification occurs through direct experience with the genitals. This phase occurs between the age of three and seven and involves a desire to possess the parent of the opposite sex and to replace the parent of the same sex. See also *Oedipus complex* and *Electra complex.*

Phenomenology (G&E). A method of exploration that primarily uses human experience as the source of data and attempts to include all human experience without bias (external observation, emotions, thoughts, and so on). Subjects are taught to distinguish between current experience and the biases brought to the situation. *Phenomenology* is the basic method of most existentialists.

Pleasure principle (PA). The basic human tendency to avoid pain and seek pleasure, especially salient in the first years of life. Contrast with the *reality principle.*

Positive reinforcer (BT). Any stimulus which follows a behavior and increases the likelihood of the occurrence of the behavior which it follows.

Projection (P&G). Attributing to others unacceptable personal thoughts, feelings, or behaviors.

Pseudomutuality (FT). An artificial closeness in some families which fosters dependency and a loss of self-identity.

Psychoanalysis (PA). A system of psychotherapy closely tied to the work of Sigmund Freud and his followers. The techniques of psychoanalysis include *free association,* dream analysis, and working through *transference* issues.

Punishment (BT). An aversive event likely to terminate any behavior followed by this event.

Racket feelings (TA). Habitual patterns of emotion (e.g., sadness, fear, or anger) that a person engages in over and over throughout their lives. Games are played to emphasize racket feelings (mad, sad, scared, confused, and so forth).

Reaction formation (PA). A defense mechanism through which an individual replaces an anxiety-eliciting impulse with behavior that is the exact opposite of the initially desired behavior.

Reality principle (PA). The guiding principle of the *ego,* the *reality principle* permits postponement of gratification in order to meet the demands of the environment or to secure greater pleasure at a later time. Contrast with the *pleasure principle.*

Reinforcement (BT). The presentation of a reward or the removal of an aversive stimulus following a response. *Reinforcement* always increases the future probability of the reinforced response.

Repression (PA). A major defense mechanism in which distressing thoughts are barred from conscious expression.

Respondent conditioning (BT). See *classical conditioning.*

Retroflection (G). A contact boundary disturbance in which a person substitutes himself for the environment and does to himself what he originally did or tried to do to others. *Retroflection* is the chief mechanism of isolation.

Scripts (TA). Basic existential decisions about one's life plan made at an early age regarding one's self and others. *Script* positions relate to I'm OK, You're OK; I'm not OK, You're not OK, and so on. *Scripts* incorporate early parental messages, *games,* and *racket feelings.*

Second Order BASIC I.D. (MMT). A recursive application of the *BASIC I.D.* to itself which often helps to shed new diagnostic light.

Self-actualization (PC). A basic human drive toward growth, completeness, and fulfillment.

Self-instructional training (BT). A technique, described by Donald Meichenbaum, for replacing self-defeating thoughts with self-enhancing cognitions.

Sensate focus (BT). A series of exercises used in sex therapy and designed to reintroduce clients to receiving and giving sensual pleasure.

Sensory-reactor (MMT). An individual who interacts with the world primarily in terms of the five basic senses.

Shadow (J). A term used to refer to that aspect of the *unconscious* to which the *ego* does not have a conscious relational access. The *shadow* is that part of ourselves to which we are not sufficiently well related.

Social learning theory (BT). A theoretical system developed primarily by Albert Bandura. It combines operant and classical conditioning with cognitive mediational processes (e.g., vicarious learning and symbolic activity) to account for the development, maintenance, and modification of behavior.

Splitting (G). A situation in which a person splits off part of self as a polar opposite. When aware of one pole, the person is oblivious to the other. For example, an individual may split into competent and incompetent selves and vacillate between these roles. A *split* is one form of a *dichotomy*.

Stimulus control (BT). Arranging the environment in such a way that a given response is either more likely or less likely to occur (e.g., buying only one pack of cigarettes per day in order to decrease the likelihood of smoking).

Strategic intervention therapy (FT). An approach to family therapy, associated with Don Jackson, which employs specific strategies such as paradox in order to force changes in behavior.

Strokes (TA). Recognition from others. *Strokes* can be positive ("warm fuzzies") or negative ("cold prickles").

Structural profiles (MMT). A graphical display of the relative involvement of each of the elements of the *BASIC I.D.*

Structuralism (FT). An approach to family therapy, associated with Salvador Minuchin, which emphasizes the importance of the nuclear family and seeks to change pathological alliances and splits in the family.

Stuck-togetherness (FT). A situation observed in schizophrenic families in which roles and boundaries are blurred and no family member has an identity distinct from the family.

Superego (PA). A portion of the personality structure that grows out of the *ego* and reflects early moral training and the parental injunctions.

Thanatos (PA). An instinct toward death and self-destruction, posited by Freud to oppose and balance *Eros*, the life-instinct.

Tracking (MMT). A careful examination of the "firing order" of the *BASIC I.D.* modalities to facilitate more effective sequencing of the treatment procedures.

Trait theory. The belief in stable and enduring personality characteristics which can be measured by psychological tests. *Trait theory* is rejected by most behavior therapists.

Transactions (TA). The basic unit of human communication; any exchange between the various *ego states* of two or more individuals. *Transactions* may have an overt social level and a covert psychological level.

Transference (PA). The therapy situation in which the patient responds to the therapist as though he or she were a significant figure in the patient's past, usually a parent.

Umwelt (E). A way of relating to the world through its biological and physical aspects; one's relationship with nature; world around us, (social) surroundings, milieu, environment.

Unconditional positive regard (PC). A nonpossessive caring and acceptance of the client as a human being, irrespective of how heinous the client's behavior might be. One of the necessary conditions for therapeutic change.

Unconscious. A division of the psyche; the repository of psychological material of which the individual is unaware.

Vicarious learning (BT). Learning through observation and imitation. Important in Albert Bandura's thought. *Syn.:* modeling.

Will to power (A). Individual striving for superiority and dominance in order to overcome feelings of inadequacy and inferiority. Alfred Adler borrowed the term from Friedrich Nietzsche but used it in a very different sense and eventually came to equate the term with the striving for competence.

Zeitgeist. The spirit of the times; the prevailing cultural climate.

Name Index

Subject Index

Abreaction, 203, 515, 550
Acceptance, in analytical therapy, 129
Acting "as if," 82
Actualizing tendency, 156
Adapted child, 550
Adlerian modality, in other psychotherapies, 6
Adlerian psychotherapy, 16, 57–107; action techniques, 81–82; "as if," 82; basic mistakes, 78–79; catching oneself, 83–84; child and family applications, 85; compared to Freudian, 60–61; compared to others, 63; compared to RET, 62, 199; compared to Rogerian, 62; creating images, 83; dreams, 79–80; evaluation of, 85–86; faith, 73–74; hope, 74; insight, 80; interpretation, 80–81; life-style conviction groups, 69; life-style investigation, 77–79; love, 74–75; other verbal techniques, 81; pushbutton technique, 84; Question, 58–59; reorientation, 80; schools, 67; setting, 88–90; task setting, 82–83; tests, 90; therapeutic relationship, 75–77; therapist, 82, 90–92
Adolescence, RET in, 224
Adult ego state, in TA, 392–93, 395–97, 550
Advances in Behavior Research and Therapy, 247
Aescalapian prison program, 415
Affect, in family therapy, 474
Affection, 6–7
Age of angst, 354
Aggression, 550
Aggression instinct, 65
Aggressive drive, 24
Agoraphobia, 35, 550; behavior therapy of, 243, 259, 261, 267–69; multimodal therapy of, 498–99
Aha!, 84, 303, 550
Alcoholism, multimodal therapy of, 498
Alfred Adler: His Influence on Psychology Today, 100
Allred Interaction Analysis for Counselors (AIAC), 474

American Academy of Psychoanalysis, 23
American Psychoanalytic Association, 22–23, 37
American Psychoanalytic Association Journal, 23
American Society of Adlerian Psychology, 66
The Analysis of Dreams, 365
Anal stage, 25, 550
Analytical psychotherapy, 108–41; acceptance, 129; applications of, 130–35; collective unconscious, 110–11, 114–15, 121; compared with existential, 362; compared with Freudian, 126; compared with other systems, 111–13; compared with TA, 399; complex, 114; dreams, 108–10, 112, 117–20, 123–28; personal/nonpersonal unconscious, 116–20; relationship to inner world, 129; relationship of therapist/client, 134–35; setting, 134; transference, 129–30
Anima/animus, 118–20, 139
Annual Review of Behavior Therapy: Theory and Practice, 247, 274
Antisuggestion, 83, 550
Anxiety, existential definition of, 355–56, 371; in person-centered therapy, 159
Applied behavior analysis, 550
Aqua-energetics, 531, 539
Archetypes, 110–11, 139, 550; and magic figure, 402
Arica Chua K', 532
The Art and Science of Love, 227
Assertion training, 550; in RET, 224
Assertiveness, 258
Assessment, behavioral, 255–56
Association, in multimodal therapy, 502
Association for the Advancement of Behavior Therapy (AABT), 246
Association test, 114
Autistic children, z-process therapy for, 547
An Autobiographical Study (Freud), 19
Autoeroticism, 26
Autogenic training, 541

BOOK MANUFACTURE

Current Psychotherapies, Third Edition was typeset at Printech, Schaumburg, Illinois. Printing and binding was by Kingsport Press, Kingsport, Tennessee. F. E. Peacock Publishers art department designed the text. The typeface is Times Roman.